Economic Dynamics in Discrete Time

Economic Dynamics in Discrete Time

Jianjun Miao

The MIT Press
Cambridge, Massachusetts
London, England

MIT Press books may be purchased at special quantity discounts for business or sales promotional use. For information, please email special_sales@mitpress.mit.edu.

This book was set in Palatino by diacriTech, Chennai. Printed and bound in the United States of America.

Library of Congress Cataloging-in-Publication Data
Miao, Jianjun, 1969-
Economic dynamics in discrete time / Jianjun Miao.
    pages cm
Includes bibliographical references and index.
ISBN 978-0-262-02761-8 (hardcover : alk. paper) 1. Econometric models. 2. Economics—Mathematical models. 3. Statics and dynamics (Social sciences) 4. Discrete-time systems. I. Title.
HB141.M53 2014
330.01′5195—dc23

2014003867

to Angela and Michael

Contents

Preface

This book is about the analytical and numerical tools used for solving dynamic economic problems. My main intention is to introduce recursive methods that should be in every economist's toolbox. Basically recursive methods are used to characterize economic dynamics by a set of state variables and a pair of functions. One function, called the state transition function, maps the state and the control (or action) of the model today into the state tomorrow. The other function, called the policy function, maps the state into the control of the model. Economic data may come from either a dynamic optimization problem or a market equilibrium. The data may be extremely complicated, and hard to analyze, but by using a finite number of state variables and a pair of functions to summarize economic data, we can simplify the analysis considerably.

This book shows the reader how to apply recursive methods to a variety of dynamic economic problems. The book starts by introducing the theory and numerical methods of solving linear and nonlinear systems of deterministic and stochastic difference equations. These systems can be derived from dynamic optimization or equilibrium conditions. The discussion includes the theory and numerical methods of solving dynamic optimization problems. One powerful tool is dynamic programming; another powerful tool is the maximum principle or the Lagrange method. Though this book focuses on the former tool, the connection between these two tools is discussed, and the latter tool is used whenever it is more convenient.

An important feature of this book is that it combines theoretical foundations with numerical methods. For each topic the theoretical foundations and explicit definitions are provided along with rigorous proofs and then the numerical methods and computer codes used to implement them. In earlier years it was quite cumbersome to numerically solve dynamic stochastic general equilibrium (DSGE) models. Students and researchers found it hard to replicate numerical results in published papers. This changed in the 1990s. Researchers finally developed efficient numerical methods to solve medium- to large-scale DSGE models and to perform Bayesian estimations of these models. These methods were made popular with the launch of Dynare in the late 1990s. Dynare is a software platform for handling a wide class of economic models, and in particular, DSGE models and overlapping generations (OLG) models. It is available for Windows, Mac, and Linux systems and can be run on both the commercial software Matlab and the free software Octave. A large part of this book is designed to introduce the reader to Dynare. Many examples are provided that demonstrate how to use Dynare to numerically solve DSGE models and to perform Bayesian estimations of DSGE models.

The book consists of four parts. Part I presents the theory of dynamical systems and numerical methods of solving dynamical systems. This part lays the foundation for other parts of the book. Chapters 1 and 2 introduce the analytical and numerical tools of solving deterministic and stochastic linear and nonlinear systems of difference equations. These two chapters also show how to use Dynare to implement these numerical methods. Chapter 3 introduces the theory of Markov processes and their convergence. This theory is important for setting up dynamic optimization problems. Chapter 4 presents ergodic theory and stationary processes. Ergodic theory is important for understanding long-run properties of stochastic processes, and it has many applications in econometrics.

Part II presents the theory and applications of dynamic optimization. Chapter 5 shows how to set up a dynamic optimization problem in terms of the Markov decision process model. Chapters 6 and 7 introduce finite- and infinite-horizon dynamic programming, respectively. These two chapters show how to analyze the Bellman equation and properties of the value function and of the policy function. The maximum principle and its relation to dynamic programming are also discussed. Chapter 8 provides a variety of applications of dynamic programming, including discrete choice, consumption/saving, portfolio choice, inventory, and investment. Chapter 9 introduces linear-quadratic models and robust control. Applications to policy analysis are discussed, including notions of commitment and time inconsistency. Chapter 10 presents filtering and control under partial information. In particular, this chapter introduces the Kalman filter, which is important for the Bayesian estimation studied in chapter 15. Chapter 11 presents numerical methods for solving dynamic programming problems. Projection methods, perturbation methods, and value function iteration methods are emphasized. Chapter 12 introduces methods of structural estimation of dynamic programming problems. It covers the generalized method of moments, the maximum likelihood method, and the simulated method of moments.

Part III presents equilibrium analyses of a variety of core models in macroeconomics. For each model the basic structure is described and then its various extensions. Chapter 13 describes models of complete markets' pure exchange economies. These models are useful for understanding consumption insurance and asset pricing. Chapter 14 introduces neoclassical growth models. These models are the cornerstone of modern macroeconomics. Chapter 15 demonstrates how to use Dynare to implement Bayesian estimation of DSGE models. Chapter 16 presents overlapping generations models. These models are fundamental in public finance and can also generate asset price bubbles. Chapter 17 introduces a particular type of incomplete markets model, the Bewley–Aiyagari–Huggett model. In this model, market incompleteness comes from missing markets. Chapter 18 introduces search and matching models. These models are useful for understanding unemployment. Chapter 19 presents the dynamic New Keynesian models. These models are useful for understanding inflation and monetary policy.

Part IV presents three additional topics. Chapter 20 describes recursive utility. Recursive utility has become increasingly popular in finance and macroeconomics. Recursive methods, by way of dynamic programming, can be tractably applied to models with recursive utility. Also in this chapter are embedded a variety of static utility models from decision theory in the dynamic framework of recursive utility. These static models typically depart from the rational expectations hypothesis and are motivated by experimental evidence such as the Allais paradox and the Ellsberg paradox. Embedding them in the framework of recursive utility allows these models to be used to address many dynamic asset-pricing puzzles.

Chapter 21 presents dynamic games and credible government policies. The main tool of the analysis is that developed by Abreu, Pearce, and Stacchetti (1990; henceforth, APS). With this tool came a significant breakthrough in the application of recursive methods. Unlike the traditional method of dynamic programming based on the Bellman equation, the object of the APS method is sets rather than functions. The key idea is to use the continuation value as a state variable to make the problem recursive. Chapter 22 introduces recursive contracts. Models with incentive problems are hard to analyze because of the history dependence of contract terms. Spear and Srivastava (1987), Thomas and Worrall (1988), and APS (1990), all make a significant breakthrough by incorporating the continuation value promised by the principal to the agent as a state variable in order to make the problem recursive.

Four mathematical appendixes are included to refresh the reader's memory of basic concepts and results from linear algebra, real and functional analysis, convex analysis, and measure and probability theory. Therefore this book is self-contained inasmuch as all the necessary mathematical concepts and results beyond the undergraduate analysis, linear algebra, and probability theory are collected in the appendixes.

This book uses Matlab programs to solve various examples and exercises. These programs are referred to in a special index at the end of the book. They can be downloaded from the website, https://sites.google.com/site/jianjunmiaobook/home/matlab-codes.

Other books whose treatments overlap some of the topics covered here include Sargent (1987), Blanchard and Fischer (1989), Stokey, Lucas, and Prescott (1989), Cooley (1995), Farmer (1993), Azariadis (1993), Chow (1997), Judd (1998), Miranda and Fackler (2002), Adda and Cooper (2003), Woodford (2003), Hansen and Sargent (2008), Acemoglu (2008), Walsh (2010), DeJong and Dave (2007), Romer (2012), and Ljungqvist and Sargent (2004, 2012).

Each of the books mentioned has its own aims and themes. What is new about the present book is the emphasis on the balance between analytical and numerical methods and the up-to-date treatment of the recent developments in economic dynamics. Theoretical results are stated as propositions or theorems and proved rigorously. Numerical methods are presented with theoretical foundations and their computer implementations are provided whenever possible. Because since the late 1990s the field of economic dynamics has developed rapidly, this book further incorporates such recent developments as numerical methods for solving linear and nonlinear rational expectations models, robust control, Bayesian estimation of DSGE models, perturbation methods, projection methods, asset price bubbles, recursive models of ambiguity and robustness, recursive utility, and recursive contracts.

This book focuses exclusively on discrete-time models and on the analytical and numerical tools rather than empirical applications. The book does not present data analysis nor discuss how to tie the theory to the data. Many basic ideas for discrete-time models can nevertheless be applied to continuous time. Continuous-time models typically admit closed-form solutions and are analytically convenient in many contexts, especially in the theory of finance and economic growth. In order to keep the text to a manageable length, I have decided to treat continuous-time problems in another book, in which I will also cover some important topics left out of this book such as endogenous growth, fiscal policy, and optimal taxation.

While most applications in the present book focus on macroeconomics, the theory and methods should be valuable in other fields of economics. For example, the theory and numerical methods of dynamic programming can be applied to analyze any dynamic optimization problems in any field of economics. The treatment of dynamic games and recursive contracts in chapters 21 and 22 should be of interest to game theorists. The introduction of recursive utility in chapter 20 should be valuable in decision theory. The discussion of asset pricing in chapters 13 and 20 is useful in finance.

This book can be used for many different courses. Here are some examples:

- A one-semester first-year graduate macroeconomics course: chapters 1–3, 5–7, and 13–16.

- A second-semester first-year graduate macroeconomics course: chapters 8–9, 11, 17–19, and any chapter from chapters 20–22.

- A graduate course on economic dynamics: The core materials are in parts I and II. Instructors can select any chapters from the remaining parts depending on the students' interest.

- A second-year graduate course on topics in macroeconomics or financial economics: Any chapters from parts III and IV.

Solutions to odd-numbered end-of-chapter exercises are available in an accompanying Student Solutions Manual.

Acknowledgments

I have benefited from research collaboration over the years with many coauthors, including Rui Albuquerque, Jess Benhabib, Dan Bernhardt, Hui Chen, Larry Epstein, Zhigang Feng, François Gourio, Xin Guo, Dirk Hackbarth, Takashi Hayashi, Nengjiu Ju, Larry Kotlikoff, Hening Liu, Zheng Liu, Erwan Morellec, Adrian Peralta-Alva, Manuel Santos, Neng Wang, Pengfei Wang, Bin Wei, Danyang Xie, Lifang Xu, Zhiwei Xu, Tao Zha, and Hao Zhou.

This book is based on my lecture notes for the graduate course, Economic Dynamics, that I have taught at Boston University for about nine years. I thank Bob King for suggesting and encouraging me to create this course. I also thank many students at Boston University and Central University of Finance and Economics for comments on the book. I would especially like to thank Brittany Baumann, Chenyu Hui, Yue Jiang, Hyosung Kwon, Xiao Yang, and Fan Zhuo. Albert Zevele also gave me useful feedback. I appreciate the comments of outside reviewers and Dana Andrus who edited the book at the MIT Press. Finally, I deeply appreciate the support from my wife, Qian Jiang, during my writing of this book. Without her support, the book could not have been completed.

I Dynamical Systems

The dynamics of economic variables are typically described by the following system of p-order difference equations:

$$x_{t+p} = f\left(x_t, x_{t+1}, ..., x_{t+p-1}, z_t, z_{t+1}, ..., z_{t+p-1}\right),$$

where $f : \mathbb{R}^{np} \times \mathbb{R}^{n_z p} \to \mathbb{R}^n$, $x_t \in \mathbb{R}^n$, $z_t \in \mathbb{R}^{n_z}$ for all $t = 0, 1, ...$, and n, n_z, and p are natural numbers. The vector z_t consists of exogenously given forcing variables. We need to impose certain initial or terminal conditions to solve these equations. The conditions typically depend on the economic problems at hand. By an appropriate change of variables, we can often transform the expression above into a system of first-order difference equations. If the sequence $\{z_t\}$ is deterministic, then the equations constitute a deterministic system. In chapter 1 we study this case. If $\{z_t\}$ is a stochastic process, then the system of equations is a stochastic system. In this case we introduce an information structure and require f to satisfy certain measurability condition. In a dynamic economy, economic agents must form expectations about future variables. If system of equations given above characterizes a rational expectations equilibrium, we must introduce conditional expectations into this system. We study the stochastic case in chapter 2. Researchers typically use a recursive approach to study dynamic equilibria. Under this approach, equilibrium variables typically satisfy certain Markov properties. In chapter 3 we study Markov processes and their convergence. A central issue is the existence and uniqueness of a stationary distribution. In chapter 4 we discuss ergodic theory and its applications to stationary processes. We establish several strong laws of large numbers for stationary processes and for Markov processes in particular.

1   Deterministic Difference Equations

In this chapter we focus on deterministic dynamics characterized by systems of first-order linear difference equations. We distinguish between singular and non-singular systems because different solution methods are applied to these two cases. We also introduce lag operators and apply them to solve second-order linear difference equations. Finally, we provide a brief introduction to nonlinear dynamics.

1.1   Scalar First-Order Linear Equations

Consider the following scalar first-order linear difference equation:

$$x_{t+1} = bx_t + cz_t, \quad t \geq 0, \tag{1.1}$$

where x_t, b, c, and z_t are all real numbers. Assume that $\{z_t\}$ is an exogenously given bounded sequence. If z_t is constant for each t, then (1.1) is **autonomous**. When $cz_t = 0$ for all t, we call (1.1) a **homogeneous** difference equation. These concepts can be generalized to systems of higher order difference equations introduced later.

In the autonomous case, we can suppose that $z_t = 1$ for all t in (1.1) without loss of generality. We then obtain

$$x_{t+1} = bx_t + c. \tag{1.2}$$

A particular solution to this difference equation is a constant solution $x_t = \bar{x}$ for all t, where

$$\bar{x} = \frac{c}{1-b} \quad \text{for } b \neq 1.$$

This solution is called a **stationary point** or **steady state**. The general solution to (1.2) is given by

$$x_t = (x_0 - \bar{x})\, b^t + \bar{x}. \tag{1.3}$$

Table 1.1
Solution to the difference equation (1.2)

	x_0 given	x_0 unknown
$|b| > 1$	Exploding unless $x_0 = \bar{x}$	$x_t = \bar{x}$ all $t \geq 0$
$|b| < 1$	Globally asympototically stable	Indeterminancy

We are interested in the long-run behavior of solution in (1.3):

- If $|b| < 1$, then the solution in (1.3) converges asymptotically to the steady state $\bar{x}$ for any initial value x_0. In this case we call $\bar{x}$ a **globally asymptotically stable** steady state. If x_0 is not exogenously given, then the solution is **indeterminate**. Starting from any initial value x_0, equation (1.3) gives a solution to (1.2).

- If $|b| > 1$, then the solution in (1.3) explodes or is unstable for any given initial value $x_0 \neq \bar{x}$, unless $x_0 = \bar{x}$. In this case we often assume that x_0 is unknown and solve for the entire path of x_t. The only stable solution is $x_t = \bar{x}$ for all $t \geq 0$.

Table 1.1 summarizes the solution to the difference equation (1.2).

In the nonautonomous case, we may solve for $\{x_t\}$ in two ways depending on whether the initial value x_0 is exogenously given. First, consider the case where x_0 is exogenously given. Then we solve for x_t backward by repeated substitution to obtain the backward-looking solution:

$$x_t = c \sum_{j=0}^{t-1} b^j z_{t-1-j} + b^t x_0. \tag{1.4}$$

If $|b| < 1$, then

$$\lim_{t \to \infty} x_t = \lim_{t \to \infty} c \sum_{j=0}^{t-1} b^j z_{t-1-j}, \tag{1.5}$$

where a finite limit exists because we assume that $\{z_t\}$ is a bounded sequence. Thus, for any given initial value x_0, the difference equation in (1.1) has a solution for $\{x_t\}$, which converges to a finite limit in (1.5). We call this limit a **generalized steady state**. It is globally asymptotically stable. If $|b| > 1$, then (1.4) shows that $\{x_t\}$ diverges. If $|b| = 1$, then the solution does not converge to a finite limit unless $\sum_{j=0}^{\infty} z_j$ is finite. Even if a finite limit exists, it depends on the initial condition x_0, so the solution is not globally stable.

Second, suppose that x_0 is not exogenously given. For example, x_t represents an asset's price. Let b be the gross return and $-cz_t > 0$ be the asset's dividends. Then equation (1.1) is an asset-pricing equation. We can solve for x_t forward by repeated substitution:

$$x_t = \left(\frac{1}{b}\right)^T x_{t+T} - \frac{c}{b} \sum_{j=0}^{T-1} \left(\frac{1}{b}\right)^j z_{t+j} \tag{1.6}$$

for any $T \geq 1$. Taking $T \to \infty$ and assuming the **transversality condition** (or **no-bubble condition**),

$$\lim_{T \to \infty} \left(\frac{1}{b}\right)^T x_{t+T} = 0, \tag{1.7}$$

we obtain the forward-looking solution:

$$x_t = -\frac{c}{b} \sum_{j=0}^{\infty} \left(\frac{1}{b}\right)^j z_{t+j}. \tag{1.8}$$

If $|b| > 1$, then the infinite sum above is finite since $\{z_t\}$ is a bounded sequence. Clearly, the solution in (1.8) also satisfies the transversality condition (1.7). This solution is **stable** in the sense that x_t is bounded for all $t \geq 0$.

If we remove the transversality condition (1.7), then (1.1) admits many unstable solutions. Let x_t^* denote the solution given by (1.8). Thus, for any B_t satisfying

$$B_{t+1} = bB_t, \tag{1.9}$$

the expression $x_t = x_t^* + B_t$ is a solution to (1.1). We often call x_t^* the **fundamental value** and B_t a **bubble**. The bubble grows at the gross rate b.

If $|b| < 1$, then the infinite sum in (1.8) is unlikely to converge in general. There is an infinity of bubble solutions that are globally stable rather than exploding. For example, let $z_t = 1$ for all t, then the expression below is a solution to (1.1):

$$x_t = \frac{c}{1-b} + B_t,$$

where B_t satisfies (1.9) and B_0 is any given value. This is related to indeterminacy discussed earlier for the autonomous system. Theorem 1.4.3, studied later, will consider more general cases.

Example 1.1.1   (Asset prices under adapted versus rational expectations) *Consider the following asset-pricing equation:*

$$p_t = \frac{{}_t p_{t+1}^e + d}{R}, \tag{1.10}$$

where d represents constant dividends, R is the gross return on the asset, p_t is the asset price in period t, and ${}_t p_{t+1}^e$ is investors' period-t forecast of the price in *period $t + 1$. An important question is how to form this forecast. According to the adapted expectations hypothesis, the forecast satisfies*

$$_t p^e_{t+1} = (1 - \lambda)\, _{t-1} p^e_t + \lambda p_t, \tag{1.11}$$

where $\lambda \in (0, 1)$. This means that investors' current forecast of the next-period price is equal to a weighted average of the current price and the previous-period forecast of the current price. Using equation (1.10) to substitute for $_t p^e_{t+1}$ and $_{t-1} p^e_t$ into equation (1.11), we obtain

$$Rp_t - d = (1 - \lambda)(Rp_{t-1} - d) + \lambda p_t.$$

Simplifying yields

$$(R - \lambda)\, p_t = (1 - \lambda)\, Rp_{t-1} + \lambda d.$$

Solving this equation backward until time 0, we obtain the backward-looking solution:

$$p_t = a^t p_0 + \frac{(1 - a^t)\, d}{R - 1},$$

where $a = \frac{R(1-\lambda)}{(R-\lambda)}$. We need to assign an exogenously given initial value p_0. For this solution to be stable, we must assume that $|a| < 1$. In this case, p_t converges to its steady state value $\bar{p} = d/(R - 1)$, starting at any initial value p_0.

We next turn to the case under rational expectations. In a deterministic model, rational expectations mean perfect foresight in the sense that $_t p^e_{t+1} = p_{t+1}$. That is, investors' rational forecast of the future price is identical to its true value. In this case we rewrite (1.10) as

$$p_t = \frac{p_{t+1} + d}{R}. \tag{1.12}$$

Solving this equation forward, we obtain

$$p_t = \frac{d}{R - 1} + \lim_{T \to \infty} \frac{p_{t+T}}{R^T}.$$

Ruling out bubbles, we obtain the forward-looking solution $p_t = d/(R - 1)$, $t \geq 0$. This means that the stock price in each period is always equal to the constant fundamental value.

Example 1.1.2 (Dividend taxes) *Suppose that dividends are taxed at the constant rate τ_1 from time 0 to time T. From time $T + 1$ on, the dividend tax rate is increased to τ_2 forever. Suppose that this policy is publicly announced at time 0. What will happen to* *the stock price at time 0? Given the rational expectations hypothesis, we solve the price at time T:*

$$p_T = \frac{(1 - \tau_2)d}{R - 1}.$$

At time 0, we use equation (1.6) to derive the forward-looking solution:

$$p_0 = \frac{1}{R^T}p_T + \frac{1}{R}\sum_{j=0}^{T-1}\frac{(1 - \tau_1)d}{R^j}$$

$$= \frac{(1 - \tau_1)d}{R - 1} + \frac{1}{R^T}\left(\frac{(1 - \tau_2)d}{R - 1} - \frac{(1 - \tau_1)d}{R - 1}\right).$$

Thus the stock price drops immediately at time 0 and then continuously declines until it reaches the new fundamental value. Figure 1.1 shows a numerical example. The dashed and solid lines represent the price path without and with tax changes, respectively.

In this section we have seen that two conditions are important for solving a linear difference equation: (1) whether the initial value is given and (2) whether the coefficient b is smaller than one in absolute value. We will show below that similar conditions apply to general multivariate linear systems. In particular, the first condition determines whether the variable x_t is **predetermined**, and the second condition corresponds to whether the eigenvalue is stable.

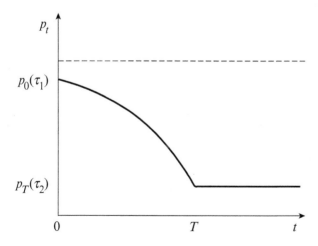

Figure 1.1
Impact of dividend taxes on the stock price

1.2   Lag Operators

Lag operators provide a powerful tool for solving difference equations. They are also useful for analyzing economic dynamics and time series econometrics. We now introduce these operators.[1]

Consider a sequence $\{X_t\}_{t=-\infty}^{\infty}$. The lag operator $\mathbf{L}$ on this sequence is defined by

$$\mathbf{L}X_t = X_{t-1}, \quad \mathbf{L}^n X_t = X_{t-n}, \quad \text{for all } n = \dots, -2, -1, 0, 1, 2, \dots.$$

Moreover $\mathbf{L}^n c = c$ for any constant c that is independent of time. The following formulas are useful in applications:

$$\frac{1}{1 - \lambda \mathbf{L}^n} = \sum_{j=0}^{\infty} \lambda^j \mathbf{L}^{nj},$$

$$\frac{1}{\left(1 - \lambda \mathbf{L}^n\right)^2} = \sum_{j=0}^{\infty} (j+1) \lambda^j \mathbf{L}^{nj},$$

for $|\lambda| < 1$, and

$$\left(I - A\mathbf{L}^n\right)^{-1} = \sum_{j=0}^{\infty} A^j \mathbf{L}^{nj},$$

if all of the eigenvalues of the matrix A are inside the unit circle. Here n is any integer.

1.3   Scalar Second-Order Linear Equations

Consider the following scalar second-order linear difference equation:

$$x_{t+2} = ax_{t+1} + bx_t + cz_t, \tag{1.13}$$

where $x_0 \in \mathbb{R}$ is given, a, b, and c are real-valued constants, and $\{z_t\}_{t \geq 0}$ is an exogenously given bounded sequence of real numbers. We will use the lag operator introduced in the previous section to solve (1.13). We write this equation as

$$\left(\mathbf{L}^{-2} - a\mathbf{L}^{-1} - b\right) x_t = cz_t. \tag{1.14}$$

We define the characteristic equation as

$$\lambda^2 - a\lambda - b = 0.$$

---

1. The reader is referred to Sargent (1987) and Hamilton (1994) for a more detailed introduction.

This equation has two (possibly complex) characteristic roots λ_1 and λ_2, satisfying $\lambda_1 + \lambda_2 = a$ and $\lambda_1 \lambda_2 = -b$. As will be clear later, these roots correspond to eigenvalues of a linear system. We then factorize the left-hand side of (1.14) to derive

$$\left(\mathbf{L}^{-1} - \lambda_1\right)\left(\mathbf{L}^{-1} - \lambda_2\right) x_t = c z_t. \tag{1.15}$$

The solution method below relies on this factorization. For this reason it is often called the method of factorization (Sargent 1987). A particular solution is given by

$$x_t^p = \frac{c z_t}{\left(\mathbf{L}^{-1} - \lambda_1\right)\left(\mathbf{L}^{-1} - \lambda_2\right)}.$$

If we can find a solution x_t^h to the homogeneous equation

$$x_{t+2} = a x_{t+1} + b x_t, \tag{1.16}$$

then the solution to the nonhomogeneous equation (1.13) is given by $x_t = x_t^h + x_t^p$. Thus we focus on the homogeneous case below. There are three cases to consider.

Case 1   The two roots λ_1 and λ_2 are real and distinct. The general solution to (1.16) is given by

$$x_t^h = c_1 \lambda_1^t + c_2 \lambda_2^t, \tag{1.17}$$

where c_1 and c_2 are constants to be determined by the initial value condition and an additional boundary condition. If $|\lambda_1| > 1$ and $|\lambda_2| > 1$, then this solution explodes as time proceeds. The steady state is called a **source**. If $|\lambda_1| < 1$ and $|\lambda_2| < 1$, then for any initial value, the solution converges to the steady state. This steady state is called a **sink**. Without imposing an additional boundary condition at a finite time, the two constants c_1 and c_2 cannot be uniquely determined. Thus the solution is indeterminate. The interesting case is when one characteristic root is bigger than 1 and the other is less than 1 in absolute value. The solution for this case is often called the **saddle path** solution. The associated steady state is called a **saddle point**.

Without loss of generality, we assume that $|\lambda_1| < 1$ and $|\lambda_2| > 1$. It follows from (1.15) that

$$\left(\mathbf{L}^{-1} - \lambda_1\right) x_t = \frac{c z_t}{\mathbf{L}^{-1} - \lambda_2} = \frac{-c z_t}{\lambda_2 \left(1 - \lambda_2^{-1} \mathbf{L}^{-1}\right)}. \tag{1.18}$$

We then obtain

$$x_{t+1} = \lambda_1 x_t - \frac{c}{\lambda_2} \sum_{j=0}^{\infty} \lambda_2^{-j} \mathbf{L}^{-j} z_t$$

$$= \lambda_1 x_t - \frac{c}{\lambda_2} \sum_{j=0}^{\infty} \lambda_2^{-j} z_{t+j}.$$

Given an initial value x_0, this equation shows the solution to (1.13). Note that we have assumed that $\{z_t\}$ is a bounded sequence for the infinite sum above to converge.

Case 2   The two roots λ_1 and λ_2 are identical. The general solution to the homogeneous equation (1.16) is given by

$$x_t^h = (c_1 + tc_2)\,\lambda_1^t,$$

where c_1 and c_2 are two constants to be determined by two boundary conditions. For stability, we need the two roots to be less than 1. Again, without imposing a boundary condition at a finite time, the solution is indeterminate since c_1 and c_2 cannot be uniquely determined. To verify the solution above, we perform the following computation:

$$
\begin{aligned}
x_{t+2} - ax_{t+1} - bx_t &= \left(\mathbf{L}^{-1} - \lambda_1\right)^2 x_t = \left(\mathbf{L}^{-1} - \lambda_1\right)^2 (c_1 + tc_2)\,\lambda_1^t \\
&= \left(\mathbf{L}^{-1} - \lambda_1\right)\left[(c_1 + (t+1)\,c_2)\,\lambda_1^{t+1} - \lambda_1\,(c_1 + tc_2)\,\lambda_1^t\right] \\
&= \left(\mathbf{L}^{-1} - \lambda_1\right)c_2\lambda_1^{t+1} = 0.
\end{aligned}
$$

Case 3   The two roots are complex. Suppose that $\lambda_1 = re^{i\theta}$ and $\lambda_2 = re^{-i\theta}$, where $i = \sqrt{-1}$. The general solution to (1.16) is given by

$$x_t^h = c_1\lambda_1^t + c_2\lambda_2^t = r^t\left(c_1 e^{i\theta t} + c_2 e^{-i\theta t}\right),$$

where c_1 and c_2 are two constants to be determined. If boundary conditions involve real numbers only, then the solution must be real. Thus we need some restriction on c_1 and c_2. We can show that

$$
\begin{aligned}
x_t^h &= r^t\left(c_1 e^{i\theta t} + c_2 e^{-i\theta t}\right) \\
&= r^t c_1\left[\cos(\theta t) + \sin(\theta t)\,i\right] + r^t c_2\left[\cos(\theta t) - \sin(\theta t)\,i\right] \\
&= r^t\,(c_1 + c_2)\cos(\theta t) + r^t\,(c_1 - c_2)\sin(\theta t)\,i.
\end{aligned}
$$

Thus, if c_1 and c_2 are conjugate complex numbers, then both $c_1 + c_2$ and $(c_1 - c_2)\,i$ are real numbers. Consequently we can write the solution as

$$x_t^h = r^t\left[A\,\cos(\theta t) + B\,\sin(\theta t)\right],$$

where A and B are two real numbers to be determined by two boundary conditions. This solution oscillates and $\theta/2\pi$ is the frequency of the oscillations. If $r < 1$, then the oscillations are damped; if $r > 1$, then they are explosive.

1.4   First-Order Linear Systems

An alternative way to solve the second-order linear difference equation (1.13) is to transform it into a system of linear difference equations:

$$\begin{bmatrix} x_{t+1} \\ x_{t+2} \end{bmatrix} = \begin{bmatrix} 0 & 1 \\ b & a \end{bmatrix} \begin{bmatrix} x_t \\ x_{t+1} \end{bmatrix} + \begin{bmatrix} 0 \\ c \end{bmatrix} z_t. \tag{1.19}$$

In this case, x_t is predetermined, but x_{t+1} is non-predetermined. In a similar way, we can transform any higher order linear difference equation into a system of linear difference equations. In this section we turn to the study of linear systems. Consider a general system of the following form:

$$Ax_{t+1} = Bx_t + Cz_t, \quad t = 0, 1, 2, ..., \tag{1.20}$$

where $x_t \in \mathbb{R}^n$ is endogenous, $z_t \in \mathbb{R}^{n_z}$ is a vector of exogenous forcing variables, and A, B, C are conformable matrices. As we will show later, many economic problems can be described by this form.

Following King and Watson (1998), we make the following regularity assumption:

Assumption 1.4.1   (Regularity) $\det(A\alpha - B) \neq 0$ *identically in* α.

When the pair (A, B) satisfies this assumption, we say it is regular. This assumption is essentially a solvability condition. If this assumption is violated, then (1.20) may not have a solution for generic exogenous sequences $\{z_t\}$. To see this, we rewrite (1.20) as

$$\left(A\mathbf{L}^{-1} - B\right) x_t = Cz_t.$$

If $A\alpha - B$ is singular identically in α, then its rows are linearly dependent, and hence there exists a row vector polynomial $\psi(\alpha)$ such that $\psi(\alpha)(A\alpha - B) = 0$ identically in α. Thus we have $\psi\left(\mathbf{L}^{-1}\right) Cz_t = 0$. This equation cannot hold for all sequences $\{z_t\}$. As a simple example, consider the scalar difference equation: $ax_{t+1} = bx_t + cz_t$. If $a = b = 0$, then there is no α such that $\det(A\alpha - B) \neq 0$. Thus assumption 1.4.1 is violated and there is no solution to the difference equation for $cz_t \neq 0$.

Sometimes we make the following assumption:

Assumption 1.4.2   *There exists* $T > 0$ *such that* $z_t = \bar{z}$ *for all* $t \geq T$.
Under this assumption, it is possible for system (1.20) to have a steady state.

Definition 1.4.1   *A **steady state** or **stationary point** of a sequence* $\{X_t\}$ *is a point* $\bar{X}$ *such that if* $X_t = \bar{X}$, *then* $X_s = \bar{X}$ *for all* $s > t$.

In words, if a sequence arrives at a steady state, then it always stays at this state. Let assumption 1.4.2 hold. If $A - B$ is invertible, then the solution to (1.20) has a unique steady state $\bar{x}$ given by

$$\bar{x} = (A - B)^{-1} C\bar{z}. \tag{1.21}$$

We introduce the following definitions for sequences in an arbitrary finite-dimensional Euclidean space:

Definition 1.4.2   *A sequence $\{X_t\}$ is **stable** if there exists $M > 0$ such that $\|x_t\|_{\max} < M$ for all t, where $\|X\|_{\max} = \max_j |X_j|$ for any $X \in \mathbb{R}^n$.*

This definition rules out growth in the sequence in order to derive nonexploding solutions. In principle, we can relax this definition to allow for growth. Whenever there is growth in a sequence, we can normalize it by the growth factor to obtain a stable sequence.

Definition 1.4.3   *A point $\bar{X}$ is **asymptotically stable** for the sequence $\{X_t\}$ if $\lim_{t \to \infty} X_t = \bar{X}$ for some X_0. The **basin** (or **attraction**) of an asymptotically stable steady state $\bar{X}$ is the set of all points X_0 such that $\lim_{t \to \infty} X_t = \bar{X}$.*

Definition 1.4.4   *A point $\bar{X}$ is **globally (asymptotically) stable** for the sequence $\{X_t\}$ if $\lim_{t \to \infty} X_t = \bar{X}$ for any initial value X_0.*

We make the following assumption throughout this section:

Assumption 1.4.3   *$\{z_t\}$ is a stable sequence.*

Our goal is to find a stable solution to (1.20). Given assumption 1.4.2, we will also discuss the issue of asymptotic stability.

1.4.1   Nonsingular System

The solution to (1.20) for the case of nonsingular A is first studied by Blanchard and Kahn (1980). In this case we rewrite (1.20) as

$$x_{t+1} = A^{-1} B x_t + A^{-1} C z_t. \tag{1.22}$$

The regularity assumption (1.4.1) is always satisfied.[2] Define $W = A^{-1}B$. By the Jordan form (appendix A), there exists a nonsingular matrix P (left eigenvectors

---

2. If z is not an eigenvalue of $A^{-1}B$, then $\det(Az - B) = \det(A)\det(Iz - A^{-1}B) \neq 0$.

of W) such that $W = P^{-1}JP$, where J is a Jordan matrix:

$$J = \begin{bmatrix} J_1 & & & \\ & J_2 & & \\ & & \ddots & \\ & & & J_l \end{bmatrix}, \quad \text{with } J_i = \begin{bmatrix} \lambda_i & 1 & & \\ & \lambda_i & 1 & \\ & & \ddots & 1 \\ & & & \lambda_i \end{bmatrix}_{m_i \times m_i},$$

where $\lambda_1, ..., \lambda_l$ are the eigenvalues of W satisfying $\det(W - \lambda I) = 0$. Some of these eigenvalues may be repeated.

Definition 1.4.5   *An eigenvalue of some matrix is **stable** if it has modulus less than 1. It is **unstable** if it has modulus greater than 1. A matrix is **stable** if all its eigenvalues have modulus less than 1.*

Define

$$x_t^* = Px_t \quad \text{and} \quad C^* = PA^{-1}C. \tag{1.23}$$

It follows from (1.22) that

$$x_{t+1}^* = Jx_t^* + C^*z_t. \tag{1.24}$$

Solving this equation backward, we obtain the backward-looking solution:

$$x_t^* = J^t x_0^* + \sum_{j=0}^{t-1} J^j C^* z_{t-1-j}, \quad t \geq 1, \tag{1.25}$$

where

$$J^t = \begin{bmatrix} J_1^t & & & \\ & J_2^t & & \\ & & \ddots & \\ & & & J_l^t \end{bmatrix}, \quad \text{with } J_i^t = \begin{bmatrix} \lambda_i^t & t\lambda_i^{t-1} & \frac{t(t-1)}{2}\lambda_i^{t-2} & \cdots \\ & \lambda_i^t & t\lambda_i^{t-1} & \cdots \\ & & \ddots & \\ & & & \lambda_i^t \end{bmatrix}.$$

If the initial value x_0 is exogenously given, then $x_0^* = Px_0$ is determined. By (1.25), we can then solve for $\{x_t^*\}$. Transforming back, we obtain the solution to (1.22): $x_t = P^{-1}x_t^*$. We next study the stability issue:

Theorem 1.4.1   *Suppose that A and $I - W$ are nonsingular and assumption 1.4.2 is satisfied. Let $\bar{x}$ be given by (1.21). Then there is a solution $\{x_t\}$ such that $\lim_{t \to \infty} x_t = \bar{x}$ for any given x_0 if and only if all eigenvalues of W are stable.*

Proof   We have constructed a solution previously. Suppose that $z_t = \bar{z}$ for $t \geq T$. As in (1.25), we can derive

$$x_{t+1}^* = J^{t-T+1} x_T^* + \sum_{j=0}^{t-T} J^j C^* z_{t-j}$$

$$= J^{t-T+1} x_T^* + \sum_{j=0}^{t-T} J^j C^* \bar{z}.$$

If all eigenvalues of W are stable, we obtain

$$\lim_{t \to \infty} x_{t+1}^* = \lim_{t \to \infty} \sum_{j=0}^{t-T} J^j C^* \bar{z} = (I - J)^{-1} C^* \bar{z}.$$

Thus, by definition (1.23),

$$\lim_{t \to \infty} x_{t+1} = \lim_{t \to \infty} P^{-1} x_{t+1}^* = P^{-1} (I - J)^{-1} C^* \bar{z} = (I - W)^{-1} A^{-1} C \bar{z} = \bar{x}.$$

The converse is also true.   ∎

If the condition in this theorem is satisfied, the steady state is called a **sink**. If all eigenvalues of W lie outside of the unit circle, then the steady state is called a **source**. What if some components of the initial value x_0 are not given? For the deterministic case we call a variable **predetermined** if its initial value is exogenously given. Otherwise, it is a **non-predetermined** or **jump variable**. In the presence of non-predetermined variables, we cannot use the backward-looking solution (1.25) and hence theorem 1.4.1 does not apply.

Next we turn to this case. We order components of x_t as $x_t = [k_t', y_t']'$, where the vector y_t contains n_y non-predetermined variables and the vector k_t contains $n_k = n - n_y$ predetermined variables. Suppose that W has n_u unstable eigenvalues and $n_s = n - n_u$ stable eigenvalues. We rule out the case where some eigenvalues are on the unit circle. We partition its Jordan matrix J as

$$J = \begin{bmatrix} J_s & \\ & J_u \end{bmatrix},$$

where all eigenvalues of the $n_s \times n_s$ matrix J_s are stable and all eigenvalues of the $n_u \times n_u$ matrix J_u are unstable. We partition x_t^* and C^* as

$$x_t^* = \begin{bmatrix} s_t \\ u_t \end{bmatrix}, \quad C^* = \begin{bmatrix} C_s^* \\ C_u^* \end{bmatrix},$$

so that they are conformable with the partition of J. We then rewrite (1.24) as

$$\begin{bmatrix} s_{t+1} \\ u_{t+1} \end{bmatrix} = \begin{bmatrix} J_s & \\ & J_u \end{bmatrix} \begin{bmatrix} s_t \\ u_t \end{bmatrix} + \begin{bmatrix} C_s^* \\ C_u^* \end{bmatrix} z_t. \tag{1.26}$$

By (1.23), we write

$$\begin{bmatrix} s_t \\ u_t \end{bmatrix} = P \begin{bmatrix} k_t \\ y_t \end{bmatrix} = \begin{bmatrix} P_{sk} & P_{sy} \\ P_{uk} & P_{uy} \end{bmatrix} \begin{bmatrix} k_t \\ y_t \end{bmatrix}, \tag{1.27}$$

where we partition P conformably. For example, P_{uy} is an $n_u \times n_y$ matrix. Let $R = P^{-1}$. By definition,

$$\begin{bmatrix} k_t \\ y_t \end{bmatrix} = R \begin{bmatrix} s_t \\ u_t \end{bmatrix} = \begin{bmatrix} R_{ks} & R_{ku} \\ R_{ys} & R_{yu} \end{bmatrix} \begin{bmatrix} s_t \\ u_t \end{bmatrix}, \tag{1.28}$$

where we have partitioned R conformably.

Now we are ready to prove the following theorem from Blanchard and Kahn (1980).

Theorem 1.4.2 *Suppose that the following three conditions hold: (a) the number of unstable eigenvalues of $W = A^{-1}B$ is equal to the number of non-predetermined variables, $n_u = n_y$; (b) P_{uy} is nonsingular; and (c) W has no eigenvalues on the unit circle. Then the system (1.22) has a unique stable solution for any given k_0 and any stable sequence $\{z_t\}$.*

Proof   We first solve for u_t. We use the lag operator $\mathbf{L}$ to rewrite equation (1.26) as

$$\mathbf{L}^{-1} u_t = J_u u_t + C_u^* z_t,$$

where J_u contains all unstable eigenvalues. Solving forward yields the forward-looking solution:

$$\begin{aligned}
u_t &= \left(\mathbf{L}^{-1} - J_u \right)^{-1} C_u^* z_t \\
&= -J_u^{-1} \left(I - \mathbf{L}^{-1} J_u^{-1} \right)^{-1} C_u^* z_t \\
&= -\sum_{j=0}^{\infty} J_u^{-j-1} C_u^* z_{t+j},
\end{aligned} \tag{1.29}$$

where we need $\{z_t\}$ to be stable for the series to converge.

By equation (1.27), we obtain

$$s_t = P_{sy} y_t + P_{sk} k_t, \tag{1.30}$$

$$u_t = P_{uy} y_t + P_{uk} k_t. \tag{1.31}$$

When P_{uy} is nonsingular, we can solve for y_t as

$$y_t = P_{uy}^{-1} u_t - P_{uy}^{-1} P_{uk} k_t. \tag{1.32}$$

To solve for k_t, we use (1.28) to derive

$$k_{t+1} = R_{ku} u_{t+1} + R_{ks} s_{t+1}.$$

Substituting (1.26) into this equation yields

$$
\begin{aligned}
k_{t+1} &= R_{ku}\left(J_u u_t + C_u^* z_t\right) + R_{ks}\left(J_s s_t + C_s^* z_t\right) \\
&= R_{ku}\left(J_u u_t + C_u^* z_t\right) + R_{ks}\left[J_s\left(P_{sy} y_t + P_{sk} k_t\right) + C_s^* z_t\right] \\
&= R_{ku}\left(J_u u_t + C_u^* z_t\right) + R_{ks}J_s P_{sy}\left(P_{uy}^{-1} u_t - P_{uy}^{-1} P_{uk} k_t\right) \\
&\quad + R_{ks}J_s P_{sk} k_t + R_{ks}C_s^* z_t,
\end{aligned}
$$

where we have substituted (1.30) for s_t in the second equality and have used (1.32) to substitute for y_t in the third equality. Simplifying the equation yields

$$
\begin{aligned}
k_{t+1} &= R_{ks}J_s R_{ks}^{-1} k_t + \left(R_{ku}C_u^* + R_{ks}C_s^*\right) z_t \\
&\quad + \left(R_{ku}J_u P_{uy} + R_{ks}J_s P_{sy}\right)P_{uy}^{-1} u_t,
\end{aligned}
\tag{1.33}
$$

where, by the partition of R and the assumption that P_{uy} is nonsingular, we deduce that R_{ks} is also nonsingular and

$$
R_{ks} = \left[P_{sk} - P_{sy}P_{uy}^{-1}P_{uk}\right]^{-1}.
$$

Finally, (1.29) and (1.32) give the solution for y_t. Note that because J_s contains all stable eigenvalues, (1.33) implies that $\{k_t\}$ is stable.   ∎

The first two conditions in theorem 1.4.2 are often called the Blanchard–Kahn conditions in the literature. They are equivalent to the conditions that (a) $n_s = n_k$ (order condition) and (b) R_{ks} or P_{uy} is invertible (rank condition), given that we rule out eigenvalues on the unit circle. The intuition behind the proof is the following. We first use a forward-looking solution to determine the transformed variables related to unstable eigenvalues. The number of these transformed variables is equal to the number of unstable eigenvalues. Next, to transform these variables back to the original non-predetermined variables, we need a certain matrix to be invertible and also the number of non-predetermined variables to be equal to the number of unstable eigenvalues. Finally, we use a backward-looking solution to determine the predetermined variables. The proof of the theorem given above is constructive and gives a solution algorithm to derive the stable solution of the linear system (1.22).

An immediate corollary of the theorem above is the following:

Corollary 1.4.1 *If the conditions in theorem 1.4.2 and assumption 1.4.2 are satisfied, then the solution to (1.22) satisfies* $\lim_{t \to \infty} x_t = \bar{x}$, *where* $\bar{x}$ *is the steady state defined in (1.21).*

In this case the steady state $\bar{x}$ is called a **saddle**. By (1.32), the initial value (k_0, y_0) satisfies

$$y_0 = P_{uy}^{-1} u_0 - P_{uy}^{-1} P_{uk} k_0. \tag{1.34}$$

All points (k_0, y_0) satisfying the equation above form an n_k-dimensional subspace of $\mathbb{R}^n$; this space is called the **stable manifold** or **stable arm** of (1.22).

What happens if some eigenvalues of W are on the unit circle? We note that the solution constructed in the proof of the previous theorem still applies to this case. However, the solution may not be stable. For example, suppose that $n_k = 1$. Then (1.33) shows that k_t behaves like a random walk, which is not stable in general. Condition (c) in theorem 1.4.2 is often called a **hyperbolic condition**.

What happens if the Blanchard–Kahn conditions are violated?

Theorem 1.4.3 *If $n_u > n_y$, then there is no solution to (1.22). If $n_u < n_y$, then there are infinitely many solutions to (1.22).*

Proof From equation (1.31) we obtain

$$u_0 = P_{uy} y_0 + P_{uk} k_0, \tag{1.35}$$

where k_0 is given, u_0 is derived from (1.29) and P_{uy} is an $n_u \times n_y$ matrix. If $n_u > n_y$, there is no solution for y_0. If $n_u < n_y$, there are infinitely many solutions for y_0. ∎

Intuitively, if the number of unstable eigenvalues is greater than the number of non-predetermined variables, then we have too many restrictions on the initial values of the non-predetermined variables. Therefore these initial values cannot be determined. If the number of unstable eigenvalues is less than the number of non-predetermined variables, then there are too few restrictions on these initial values so that infinitely many solutions may satisfy those restrictions. In this case the solution is **indeterminate**.

1.4.2 Singular System

In many economic problems the assumption of nonsingular A is violated. To illustrate this point, consider a simple version of the Cagan (1956) model. Let R_t be the nominal interest rate, p_t be the logarithm of the price level, and m_t be the logarithm of the money stock. The model consists of a Fisher equation, $R_t = p_{t+1} - p_t$, and a monetary equilibrium condition, $m_t - p_t = -\alpha R_t$. Writing these equation in a linear system gives

$$\begin{bmatrix} 0 & 1 \\ 0 & 0 \end{bmatrix} \begin{bmatrix} R_{t+1} \\ p_{t+1} \end{bmatrix} = \begin{bmatrix} 1 & 1 \\ \alpha & -1 \end{bmatrix} \begin{bmatrix} R_t \\ p_t \end{bmatrix} + \begin{bmatrix} 0 \\ 1 \end{bmatrix} m_t.$$

In this system A is singular. This example shows that whenever there are some intratemporal relations, A will be singular.

King and Watson (1998, 2002), Sims (2000), and Klein (2000) provide algorithms to solve the case of singular A. We follow the approach of Klein (2000). We first introduce some definitions:

Definition 1.4.6 *A scalar $\lambda \in \mathbb{C}$ is a **generalized eigenvalue** of the matrices (A, B) if there is a nonzero vector $x \in \mathbb{C}^n$ such that $Bx = \lambda Ax$.[3] We call x the corresponding **right generalized eigenvector**.*

Let $\lambda(A, B)$ denote the set of all generalized eigenvalues of (A, B). Let d_{ij} denote the element in the ith row and the jth column of any matrix D.

Theorem 1.4.4 (**Complex generalized Schur form**) *Let the $n \times n$ matrices A and B be regular; that, is assumption 1.4.1 holds. Then there exist $n \times n$ **unitary matrices**[4] of complex numbers Q and Z such that*

a. $QAZ = S$ is upper triangular;

b. $QBZ = T$ is upper triangular;

c. for each i, s_{ii} and t_{ii} are not both zero;

d. $\lambda(A, B) = \{t_{ii}/s_{ii} : s_{ii} \neq 0\}$;

e. the pairs (s_{ii}, t_{ii}), $i = 1, ..., n$, can be arranged in any order.

The proof can be found in Golub and van Loan (1996) and is omitted here. The generalized Schur form is also called **QZ decomposition**. Note that the possibility that $s_{ii} = t_{ii} = 0$ for some i is ruled out by assumption 1.4.1. Note that $\lambda(A, B)$ may contain elements less than n, since, if A is singular, then we could have $s_{ii} = 0$. Since s_{ii} and t_{ii} cannot be both equal to zero, we interpret an eigenvalue corresponding to $s_{ii} = 0$ as infinity. So it is unstable. Let S and T be arranged in such a way that the n_s stable generalized eigenvalues come first. The remaining n_u generalized eigenvalues are unstable. Define $x_t^* = Z^H x_t$, where $Z^H = Z^{-1}$ denotes the conjugate transpose of Z. As in the previous subsection, we use the partition

$$x_t = \begin{bmatrix} k_t \\ y_t \end{bmatrix} \begin{matrix} n_k \times 1, \\ n_y \times 1, \end{matrix} \qquad x_t^* = \begin{bmatrix} s_t \\ u_t \end{bmatrix} \begin{matrix} n_s \times 1, \\ n_u \times 1. \end{matrix}$$

We also partition Z conformably with the partition above:

$$Z = \begin{bmatrix} Z_{11} & Z_{12} \\ Z_{21} & Z_{22} \end{bmatrix},$$

where, for example, Z_{11} is $n_s \times n_k$.

---

3. $\mathbb{C}$ is the space of complex numbers.
4. See appendix A for the definition of unitary matrix.

Theorem 1.4.5 *Suppose that the following conditions hold: (a) $n_s = n_k$; (b) Z_{11} is invertible; and (c) (A, B) has no generalized eigenvalue on the unit circle. Then system (1.20) has a unique stable solution for any given k_0 and any stable sequence $\{z_t\}$.*

Proof We apply theorem 1.4.4 and rewrite (1.20) as

$$Sx_{t+1}^* = Tx_t^* + QCz_t.$$

We partition matrices conformably so that

$$
\begin{bmatrix} S_{11} & S_{12} \\ 0 & S_{22} \end{bmatrix}
\begin{bmatrix} s_{t+1} \\ u_{t+1} \end{bmatrix}
=
\begin{bmatrix} T_{11} & T_{12} \\ 0 & T_{22} \end{bmatrix}
\begin{bmatrix} s_t \\ u_t \end{bmatrix}
+
\begin{bmatrix} Q_1 \\ Q_2 \end{bmatrix}
Cz_t.
\tag{1.36}
$$

By the ordering of stable generalized eigenvalues, S_{11} is invertible because all diagonal elements s_{ii} of S_{11} cannot be zero. T_{22} is also invertible because all diagonal elements t_{ii} of T_{22} cannot be zero. Similar to the proof of theorem 1.4.2, we use the following steps:

Step 1. Solve for $\{u_t\}$. By construction, all generalized eigenvalues of (S_{22}, T_{22}) are unstable. We can then derive the forward-looking solution:

$$u_t = -T_{22}^{-1} \sum_{j=0}^{\infty} \left[T_{22}^{-1} S_{22} \right]^j Q_2 Cz_{t+j}. \tag{1.37}$$

Step 2. Solve for $\{s_t\}$. By the first block of (1.36),

$$S_{11}s_{t+1} + S_{12}u_{t+1} = T_{11}s_t + T_{12}u_t + Q_1 Cz_t.$$

Manipulating it yields the backward-looking solution:

$$s_{t+1} = S_{11}^{-1}T_{11}s_t + S_{11}^{-1}T_{12}u_t - S_{11}^{-1}S_{12}u_{t+1} + S_{11}^{-1}Q_1 Cz_t. \tag{1.38}$$

We need to determine s_0. By definition, $x_t = Zx_t^*$, so we obtain

$$k_t = Z_{11}s_t + Z_{12}u_t, \tag{1.39}$$

$$y_t = Z_{21}s_t + Z_{22}u_t. \tag{1.40}$$

Since Z_{11} is invertible by assumption, we obtain

$$s_0 = Z_{11}^{-1}(k_0 - Z_{12}u_0).$$

Step 3. Solve for $\{k_t\}$ and $\{y_t\}$. Equations (1.39) and (1.40) give the solutions for $\{k_t\}$ and $\{y_t\}$ given that $\{s_t\}$ and $\{u_t\}$ are obtained in steps 1 and 2. ∎

To apply the preceding theorem to solve the system (1.20), one has to specify the exogenous forcing sequence $\{z_t\}$. A typical specification is given by $z_{t+1} = \Phi z_t$, where Φ is an $n_z \times n_z$ stable matrix. In this case we can simplify the computation of u_t in (1.37). Another way is to rewrite the system (1.20) as

$$\begin{bmatrix} I_{n_z} & 0 \\ 0 & A \end{bmatrix} \begin{bmatrix} z_{t+1} \\ x_{t+1} \end{bmatrix} = \begin{bmatrix} \Phi & 0 \\ C & B \end{bmatrix} \begin{bmatrix} z_t \\ x_t \end{bmatrix}.$$

As a result we need to solve a linear system for $(z_t', x_t')'$ without a forcing variable. We can simplify some formulas in the proof of theorem 1.4.5. For example, on the one hand, we have $u_t = 0$. On the other hand, the transformed matrices A and B are larger. We have to manipulate these larger matrices, which may be computationally costly.

We can state a corollary similar to corollary 1.4.1 if assumption 1.4.2 and the conditions in theorem 1.4.5 are satisfied. We will not repeat it here.

1.5   Phase Diagrams

Phase diagrams are intuitive graphical devices showing the orbits of a two-dimensional dynamic system. They are useful for analyzing both linear and non-linear systems. Here we use a linear system to illustrate their usefulness.

Consider the following linear system:

$$x_{t+1} = \tilde{a}x_t + by_t - e,$$
$$y_{t+1} = cx_t - \tilde{d}y_t + f,$$

where x_0 is given. Define $\Delta x_t = x_{t+1} - x_t$, $\Delta y_t = y_{t+1} - y_t$. We then have

$$\Delta x_t = ax_t + by_t - e,$$
$$\Delta y_t = cx_t - dy_t + f,$$

where $a = \tilde{a} - 1$ and $d = \tilde{d} + 1$. We assume that a, b, c, d, e, and f are positive. In the plane (x_t, y_t), we draw isoclines $\Delta x_t = 0$ and $\Delta y_t = 0$ and the arrows indicating directions of changes in x_t and y_t. These arrows are called **vector fields**.

Because

$$\Delta x_t \geq 0 \iff y_t \geq -\frac{a}{b}x_t + \frac{e}{b},$$
$$\Delta y_t \geq 0 \iff y_t \leq \frac{c}{d}x_t + \frac{f}{d},$$

we deduce that x_t increases if and only if it is above the isocline $\Delta x_t = 0$, and y_t increases if and only if it is below the isocline $\Delta y_t = 0$. Figure 1.2 illustrates the isoclines and vector fields.

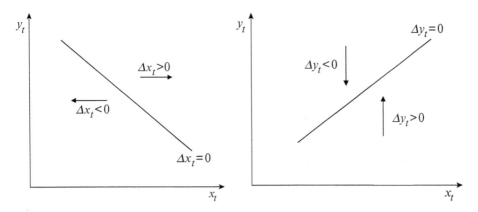

Figure 1.2
Isoclines. Left- and right-panels plot the isoclines $\Delta x_t = 0$ and $\Delta y_t = 0$, respectively

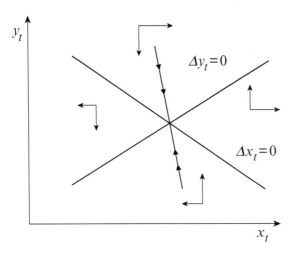

Figure 1.3
Phase diagram

Combining the two panels in figure 1.2, we obtain a phase diagram in figure 1.3. This diagram suggests that the existence of a convergent saddle path through the upper and lower quadrants and that all other paths diverge.

1.6 Nonlinear Systems

Consider the following first-order nonlinear system:

$$f(x_{t+1}, x_t, z_t) = 0, \tag{1.41}$$

where $x_t \in \mathbb{R}^n$ is endogenous, $z_t \in \mathbb{R}^{n_z}$ is a vector of exogenous forcing variables, and $f : \mathbb{R}^{2n} \times \mathbb{R}^{n_z} \to \mathbb{R}^n$. Many high-order nonlinear systems can be transformed to a first-order system by a suitable change of variables as we have done previously. In order to study the steady state of this nonlinear system, we assume that there exits $T > 0$ such that $z_t = \bar{z}$ for all $t \geq T$. Then the steady state of $\{x_{t+1}\}$ defined in (1.41) is the point $\bar{x}$ such that $f(\bar{x}, \bar{x}, \bar{z}) = 0$. We now take a first-order Taylor approximation to (1.41) about $\bar{x}$:

$$0 = f_{x'} \, dx_{t+1} + f_x \, dx_t + f_z \, dz_t, \tag{1.42}$$

where $f_{x'}$, f_x, and f_z are the partial derivatives of f with respect to x_{t+1}, x_t, and z_t, respectively, evaluated at the steady state. We can interpret dX_t for any variable X_t as the level deviation from the steady state, namely $dX_t = X_t - \bar{X}$. Sometimes we also consider a variable's log deviation from its steady state. We adopt the following notation:

$$\hat{X}_t = \frac{dX_t}{\bar{X}} = \frac{X_t - \bar{X}}{\bar{X}} \simeq \ln\left(\frac{X_t}{\bar{X}}\right).$$

Since equation (1.42) is a linear system of the form in (1.20), we may apply the method discussed before to analyze this system. The critical conditions for stability are based on the properties of the generalized eigenvalues of the pair of Jacobian matrices $(f_{x'}, -f_x)$ evaluated at the steady state.

Example 1.6.1 (Optimal growth) *Consider a social planner's problem:*

$$\max_{\{C_t, K_{t+1}\}} \sum_{t=0}^{\infty} \beta^t u(C_t)$$

subject to the resource constraint

$$C_t + K_{t+1} - (1 - \delta) K_t = f(K_t), \quad K_0 \text{ given}, \tag{1.43}$$

where $\beta, \delta \in (0,1)$. Assume that u and f are increasing, concave, and twice continuously differentiable and satisfy the usual Inada condition. The optimal allocation satisfies the system of difference equations, (1.43), and

$$u'(C_t) = \beta u'(C_{t+1}) \left(f'(K_{t+1}) + 1 - \delta\right).$$

The steady state $(\bar{K}, \bar{C})$ satisfies the system of equations:

$$C = f(K) - \delta K,$$
$$1 = \beta \left(f'(K) + 1 - \delta\right).$$

To analyze the stability of this steady state, we linearize the dynamical system around the steady state:

$$u''dC_t = \beta u'' (f' + 1 - \delta) dC_{t+1} + \beta u' f'' dK_{t+1},$$

$$dC_t + dK_{t+1} - (1 - \delta) dK_t = f' dK_t.$$

Simplifying yields

$$\begin{bmatrix} \frac{\beta u' f''}{u''} & 1 \\ 1 & 0 \end{bmatrix} \begin{bmatrix} dK_{t+1} \\ dC_{t+1} \end{bmatrix} = \begin{bmatrix} 0 & 1 \\ f' + 1 - \delta & -1 \end{bmatrix} \begin{bmatrix} dK_t \\ dC_t \end{bmatrix}.$$

This is a nonsingular linear system, which is equivalent to

$$\begin{bmatrix} dK_{t+1} \\ dC_{t+1} \end{bmatrix} = \begin{bmatrix} 1/\beta & -1 \\ \frac{f''(\bar{K})}{A(\bar{C})} & 1 - \frac{\beta f''(\bar{K})}{A(\bar{C})} \end{bmatrix} \begin{bmatrix} dK_t \\ dC_t \end{bmatrix},$$

where $A(\bar{C}) = -u''(\bar{C})/u'(\bar{C})$. The coefficient matrix above has trace

$$T = 1 + \frac{1}{\beta} - \frac{\beta f''(\bar{K})}{A(\bar{C})} > 1 + \frac{1}{\beta} > 2,$$

and determinant $D = 1/\beta > 1$. Thus the characteristic equation $\lambda^2 - T\lambda + D = 0$ has two positive real roots satisfying $0 < \lambda_1 < 1 < \lambda_2$. As a result the steady state is a saddle point.

Nonlinear systems can generate complicated dynamics.

Definition 1.6.1 *A point x^* is called a **periodic point of period** p for the dynamical system $x_{t+1} = f(x_t)$ if it is a fixed point for the pth iterate of f, namely if $f^p(x^*) = x^*$ and p is the smallest integer for which this is true. The set of all iterates of a periodic point*

$$\left\{ x_1^* = x^*, x_2^* = f(x^*), ..., x_p^* = f^{p-1}(x^*) \right\}$$

*is called a **periodic orbit of period** p or a **p-cycle**.*

Here we will not study the general conditions for the existence of a periodic cycle.[5] Instead, we give a simple example taken from Stokey, Lucas, and Prescott (1989):

$$x_{t+1} = f(x_t) = 4x_t - 4x_t^2.$$

---

5. See Azariadis (1993) for a good introduction of nonlinear dynamics.

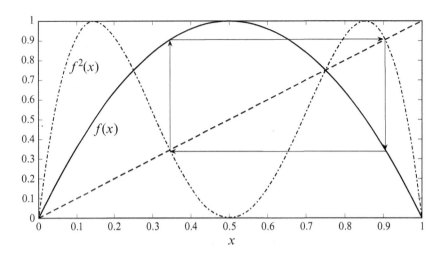

Figure 1.4
Two-cycle. Here $f(x) = 4x - 4x^2$ and f^2 is the second iterate of f. Points on the 45-degree line are fixed points.

We can compute the second iterate of f and obtain

$$x_{t+2} = f^2(x_t) = 4\left(4x_t - 4x_t^2\right) - 4\left(4x_t - 4x_t^2\right)^2$$
$$= 16x_t - 80x_t^2 + 128x_t^3 - 64x_t^4.$$

Figure 1.4 plots $f(x)$ and $f^2(x)$. It is straightforward to verify that f has two fixed points, 0 and 0.75, and that f^2 has four fixed points, 0, 0.3455, 0.75, and 0.9045. The two points 0.3455 and 0.9045 constitute a two-cycle.

1.7 Numerical Solutions Using Dynare

There are several Matlab codes publicly available on the World Wide Web that implement the algorithm discussed earlier. Here we provide a brief introduction of a powerful and convenient software: Dynare.[6] Dynare is a software platform for solving and estimating dynamic stochastic general equilibrium (DSGE) and overlapping generations (OLG) models. It can also solve deterministic linear or nonlinear systems of difference equations. Dynare typically handles models based on the rational expectations hypothesis. But it can also handle models where expectations are formed differently: on one extreme, models where agents perfectly

---

6. See Adjemian et al. (2011) for the reference manual. Dynare can be freely downloaded from the website: http://www.dynare.org/.

anticipate the future; on the other extreme, models where agents have limited rationality or imperfect knowledge of the state of the economy and, hence, form their expectations through a learning process. Dynare can solve complicated models that include consumers, productive firms, governments, monetary authorities, investors, and financial intermediaries. Dynare can also handle heterogeneous-agent models by including several distinct classes of agents in each of the aforementioned agent categories.

A Dynare program is named as a filename.mod file. To run a Dynare program, in the Matlab command line simply type: dynare 'filename.mod'. Dynare has its own timing convention. In particular, the timing of each variable reflects when that variable is decided. A variable x_t chosen at time t is written as x in Dynare. Similarly x_{t-j} is written as $x(-j)$ and x_{t+j} is written as $x(+j)$. A variable that was chosen at time $t - 1$ and is known at time t, such as the capital stock, is often denoted as k_t at time t but is written as $k(-1)$ in Dynare. This convention applies to any predetermined variable and is important for Dynare to identify which variable is predetermined. A (+1) next to a variable tells Dynare to count the occurrence of that variable as a jumper, forward-looking, or non-predetermined variable. For other particulars of Dynare, the reader is referred to the *Reference Manual* by Adjemian et al. (2011) and the *User Guide* by Griffoli (2010).

In this section we explain how to use Dynare to solve deterministic models. In section 2.5 and chapter 15, we will explain how to use Dynare to solve stochastic models and to estimate these models, respectively.

Dynare solves the nonlinear system (1.41) using a Newton-type algorithm (see Juillard 1996). It is much more accurate than the linear approximation method described in the previous section. To explain the basic idea, we let $x_t = (k_t', y_t')'$, where k_t is $n_k \times 1$ vector of predetermined variables and y_t is an $n_y \times 1$ vector of non-predetermined variables. The initial value $k_0 = k_0^*$ is given. Suppose that the terminal value $y_{T+1} = y_{T+1}^*$ is known at time $T + 1$. Our objective is to solve for the $(T + 1) \times (n_k + n_y)$ unknowns, $\{k_1, k_2, ..., k_{T+1}; y_0, y_1, ..., y_T\}$. We derive a system of $(T + 1) \times (n_k + n_y)$ nonlinear equations using (1.41):

$$F(k_t, y_t, k_{t+1}, y_{t+1}, z_t) \equiv f(x_t, x_{t+1}, z_t) = 0, \quad t = 0, 1, ..., T.$$

We can then use a Newton-type root-finding method to solve this system. For an infinite-horizon problem the terminal condition is often expressed in terms of transversality conditions. We then solve for a stable solution. We use a shooting algorithm by specifying a time $T + 1$ at which the system has reached a steady state, such that $F(\bar{k}, \bar{y}, \bar{k}, \bar{y}, \bar{z}) = 0$. We then set $y_{T+1} = \bar{y}$ and use the algorithm above. Finally, we adjust T until the solution for k_{T+1} is sufficiently close to $\bar{k}$. The Blanchard–Kahn condition must be satisfied for this algorithm to find a stable solution.

Using Dynare timing conventions, Dynare solves any deterministic model of the following form:

$$F\left(y_{t-1}^-, y_t, y_{t+1}^+, e_t\right) = 0, \tag{1.44}$$

where y_t is a vector that contains endogenous variables, y_{t-1}^- is a subset of predetermined variables or variables with a lag, y_{t+1}^+ is a subset of variables with a lead, and e_t is a vector of exogenous forcing variables. Note that this form is more general than (1.41) in that a variable with both one-period lag and one-period lead can enter the system. The initial value for y_{-1}^- is given.

We use a simple example to illustrate how to use Dynare:[7]

$$\max_{\{C_t, N_t, K_{t+1}\}} \sum_{t=0}^{\infty} \beta^t \left\{\ln\left(C_t\right) + \chi \ln\left(1 - N_t\right)\right\},$$

subject to

$$C_t + K_{t+1} - (1 - \delta) K_t = z_t K_t^\alpha N_t^{1-\alpha}, \quad K_0 \text{ given}, \tag{1.45}$$

$$\ln z_t = \rho \ln z_{t-1} + \sigma e_t, \quad z_0 \text{ given}, \tag{1.46}$$

where the deterministic sequence $\{e_t\}$ is exogenously given. The equilibrium consists of a system of three equations:

$$\frac{1}{C_t} = \frac{\beta}{C_{t+1}} \left(z_{t+1} \alpha K_{t+1}^{\alpha-1} N_{t+1}^{1-\alpha} + 1 - \delta\right),$$

$$\frac{\chi C_t}{1 - N_t} = (1 - \alpha) z_t K_t^\alpha N_t^{-\alpha},$$

and (1.45) with three unknowns C_t, N_t, and K_{t+1}. Note that z_t is often treated as an "endogenous" variable and equation (1.46) is used to solve this variable. In this case, z_{t-1}, z_t, and z_{t+1} enter the equilibrium system in the form of (1.44).

A Dynare program consists of the following blocks:

Preamble   The preamble generally involves three commands that tell Dynare what are the model's variables, which variables are endogenous, and what are the parameters. The commands are as follows:

- `var` starts the list of endogenous variables, to be separated by commas.
- `varexo` starts the list of exogenous variables that will be shocked.
- `parameters` starts the list of parameters and assigns values to each.

---

7. The Dynare code is deterministicgrowth.mod.

For our example, the preamble block may be written as

```
var c k n z;
varexo e;
parameters beta chi delta alpha rho;
alpha = 0.33;
beta = 0.99;
delta = 0.023;
chi = 1.75;
rho = 0.95;
```

Model One of the beauties of Dynare is that we can input our model's equations naturally using Dynare conventions. The following is a list of these conventions:

- The model block of the .mod file begins with the command `model` and ends with the command `end`.

- There must be as many equations as we declared endogenous variables using `var` (this is actually one of the first things that Dynare checks; it will immediately let us know if there are any problems).

- As in the preamble and everywhere along the .mod file, each line of instruction ends with a semicolon (except when a line is too long and we want to break it across two lines. This is unlike Matlab where if we break a line, we need to add "...").

- Equations are entered one after the other; no matrix representation is necessary. Note that variable and parameter names used in the model block must be the same as those declared in the preamble, and variable and parameter names are case sensitive.

For our example, the model block reads:

```
model;
  (1/c) = beta*(1/c(+1))*(1+alpha*(k^(alpha-1))*exp(z(+1))*
(n(+1))^(1-alpha)-delta);
  chi*c/(1-n) = (1-alpha)*(k(-1)^alpha)*exp(z)*(n^(-alpha));
  c+ k-(1-delta)*k(-1) = (k(-1)^alpha)*exp(z)*n^(1-alpha);
  z = rho*z(-1)+e;
end;
```

Note that both $z(-1)$ and $z(+1)$ appear in the model block. Dynare treats it as both a predetermined variable and a non-predetermined variable. Thus there are three non-predetermined variables, C, N, z, and two predetermined variables, K, z.

Steady State and Initial Values   The Dynare commands in this block consist of `initval`, `endval`, `steady`, and `check`. Deterministic models do not need to be linearized in order to be solved. Thus technically we do not need to provide a steady state for these models. But in applications, researchers typically study how the economy responds to a shock starting from an initial steady state and ending up in a new steady state. If we wanted to shock our model starting from a steady-state value, we would enter approximate (or exact) steady-state values in the `initval` block, followed by the command `steady`, which computes the initial steady state. Otherwise, if we want to begin our solution path from an arbitrary point, we would enter those values in our `initval` block and not use the `steady` command.

Solving a steady state is typically the most difficult part. For complicated models, the Dynare command `steady` may not be able to find a steady state because one has to start with a good initial guess to get convergence. In this case one could write a separate Matlab file to compute the steady state using a reverse engineering strategy. By this strategy, one would solve for some parameter values such that some steady-state values are prespecified using moments from the data.

Following `steady`, one would use the command `check` to display the generalized eigenvalues to check the Blanchard–Kahn condition. For our example, we need three generalized eigenvalues larger than two in modulus for the Blanchard–Kahn condition to hold.

If the shock is temporary, then the new steady state is identical to the initial steady state. The `endval block` is not needed. For our example, if we consider the impact of a temporary technology shock, then we would write the block for the steady-state or initial values as

```
initval;
  k = 9;
  c = 0.76;
  n = 0.3;
  z = 0;
  e = 0;
end;
steady;
```

If the shock is permanent, then we would have to use the command `endval` following the `initval` and `steady` block. The `endval` block gives the terminal condition after a permanent shock. This terminal condition is often the new steady state. Thus the command `steady` is often used after the `endval` block.

For our example, if we consider the impact of a permanent technology shock when e_t changes from 0 to 0.01 permanently, then we would write

```
endval;
  k = 9;
  c = 0.76;
  n = 0.3;
  z = 0;
  e = 0.01;
end;
steady;
```

The output of steady is saved in the vector oo_.steady_state. Each element corresponds to a variable defined in var, arranged in the same order.

Shocks To study the impact of a temporary shock, the duration and the level of the shock must be specified. To specify a shock that lasts ten periods on e_t, for instance, we would write

```
shocks;
var e; periods 1:10;
values 0.01;
end;
```

Given these codes, Dynare would replace the value of e_t specified in the initval block with the value of 0.01 for periods 1 to 10. Note that we could have entered future periods in the shocks block, such as periods 5:10, in order to study the impact of an anticipated temporary shock.

If the shock is permanent and starts immediately in period 1, then the shock block is not needed. But if the shock is permanent but starts in the future, then we have to add a shocks block after the endval block to "undo" the first several periods of the permanent shock. For instance, suppose that the technology shock e_t moves to 0.01 permanently starting in period 10. Then we would follow the endval block above with

```
shocks;
var e; periods 1:9;
values 0;
end;
```

Computation The Dynare command for this block is simul. The input is periods, which specifies the number of simulation periods. In applications, one may choose an arbitrary large number of period and then adjust this number until the solution does not change within an error bound. The output is stored in the matrix oo_.endo_simul. The variables are arranged row by row, in order of declaration in the command var. Note that oo_.endo_simul also contains initial and terminal conditions, so it has two more columns than the value of `periods` option. For our example, we would write

```
simul(periods=200);
```

Results   The final block presents the results of the computation in terms of graphs and tables. The results can also be stored in some variables. This block is not needed in Dynare and is user defined. In our example, to plot the solutions for the impact of the temporary shocks, we write

```
tt=0:201;
figure
subplot(2,2,1);
plot(tt, oo_.endo_simul(1,:), width,tt,
oo_.steady_state(1)*ones(1,202));
title('C')
subplot(2,2,2);
plot(tt, oo_.endo_simul(2,:), tt,
oo_.steady_state(2)*ones(1,202));
title('K')
subplot(2,2,3);
plot(tt, oo_.endo_simul(3,:), tt,
oo_.steady_state(3)*ones(1,202));
title('N');
subplot(2,2,4);
plot(tt,oo_.endo_simul(4,:));
title('z');
```

We present the results in figure 1.5. Note that according to the Dynare convention, the first columns in the output `oo_.endo_simul` give the initial value before the shock. This corresponds to period 0. Endogenous variables respond to shocks starting in period 1 in the horizontal axis.

1.8   Exercises

1. Consider the deterministic Cagan (1956) model:

$$m_t - p_t = -\alpha \left(p_{t+1}^e - p_t \right), \quad \alpha > 0,$$

where m_t is the log of the nominal money supply and p_t is the log of the price level. Under rational expectations, $p_{t+1}^e = p_{t+1}$. Suppose that money supply satisfies

$$m_{t+1} = \rho m_t + \mu, \ \rho \in [0,1], \quad m_0 \text{ given.}$$

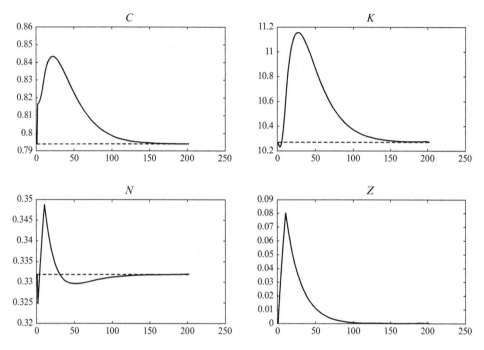

Figure 1.5
Transitional dynamics in response to a temporary technology shock

a. Give conditions on the parameters such that there exists a unique stable solution for p_t. Derive this solution.

b. Suppose there is a public announcement that the money supply will increase on a future date T. In particular, the money supply $m_t = \bar{m}$ for $t < T$, and $m_t = \bar{m}' > \bar{m}$ for $t \geq T$. Derive the path for $\{p_t\}$.

2. Consider the following version of the Dornbusch (1976) model:

$$y_t^d = \delta\left(e_t + p^* - p_t\right) - \gamma r_t + \phi y + g,$$
$$p_{t+1} - p_t = \theta\left(y_t^d - y\right),$$
$$m_t - p_t = \alpha y - \beta r_t,$$
$$r_t = r^* + e_{t+1} - e_t,$$

where y_t^d is the domestic aggregate demand, e_t is the nominal exchange rate, m_t is the exogenous domestic money supply, p_t is the price level, y is the constant domestic output supply, g is the constant domestic government spending, r_t is the domestic nominal interest rate, and an asterisk denotes the corresponding foreign variable. All these variables are in terms of the logarithm. Assume that all parameters are positive. In addition, p_t is sluggish to adjust so that it is predetermined.

  a. Derive the steady state of this model.

  b. Give conditions on parameter values such that there is a unique stable solution.

  c. Draw the phase diagram.

  d. Assume $m_t = \bar{m}$ for all t. Analyze the effect of an unexpected permanent increase in the money supply from $\bar{m}$ to $\bar{m}'$ at date zero, assuming that the economy is in the steady state initially.

  e. In the previous question, say there is a public announcement that the money supply will increase to $\bar{m}'$ on a future date T, meaning $m_t = \bar{m}$ for $t < T$, and $m_t = \bar{m}' > \bar{m}$ for $t \geq T$. Analyze the equilibrium dynamics.

3. Consider the example studied in section 1.7. What will happen if you set `periods = 50` option in `simul`? Experiment with other specifications and discuss how to choose this option.

4. Consider the example studied in section 1.7. Use Dynare to solve for output Y_t, investment I_t, the wage rate w_t, and the rental rate R_t. Plot transitional dynamics for these variables in response to

  a. a temporary shock such that e_t is equal to 0.015 from periods 5 to 10;

  b. a permanent shock such that $e_t = 0.015$ starting from period 1 on.

2   Stochastic Difference Equations

In this chapter we introduce stochastic shocks into the deterministic systems studied in chapter 1. We focus on solution methods for linear rational expectations models. We fix a probability space $(\Omega, \mathcal{F}, \Pr)$ and a filtration $\{\mathcal{F}_t\}_{t \geq 0}$ throughout this chapter.[1] A **stochastic process** $\{X_t\}_{t \geq 0}$ with state space $\mathbb{X}$ is a sequence of random variables valued in $\mathbb{X}$. We say that $\{X_t\}$ is **adapted to** $\{\mathcal{F}_t\}$ if X_t is measurable with respect to $\mathcal{F}_t$ for each $t = 0, 1, 2 \ldots$. In this case we also call $\{X_t\}$ an **adapted process**. Unless we make it explicit, all stochastic processes in this chapter are assumed to be adapted to $\{\mathcal{F}_t\}$ and valued in some finite-dimensional Euclidean space. We use E_t to denote the conditional expectation operator given information $\mathcal{F}_t$.

2.1   First-Order Linear Systems

We often assume that exogenous shocks $\{z_t\}$ are governed by the following first-order linear difference equation:

$$z_{t+1} = \Phi z_t + \Sigma \varepsilon_{t+1}, \quad z_0 \text{ given,} \tag{2.1}$$

where $\{z_t\}$ is an $\mathbb{R}^{n_z}$-valued stochastic process, Φ is an $n_z \times n_z$ matrix, Σ is an $n_z \times n_\varepsilon$ matrix, and $\{\varepsilon_{t+1}\}$ is a stochastic process satisfying

$$E_t \varepsilon_{t+1} = 0 \quad \text{and} \quad E_t \varepsilon_{t+1} \varepsilon_{t+1}' = I, \tag{2.2}$$

with I as an identity matrix. Many stochastic processes can be written as in (2.1).

Example 2.1.1 (Scalar first-order autoregression with nonzero mean) *Let*

$$y_{t+1} = b y_t + d + \sigma \varepsilon_{t+1},$$

---

1. Formally, $\{\mathcal{F}_t\}_{t \geq 0}$ is an increasing sequence of σ-algebras $\mathcal{F}_0 \subset \mathcal{F}_1 \subset \mathcal{F}_2 \subset \ldots \subset \mathcal{F}$.

where b, d, and σ are constants satisfying $1 - b \neq 0$. Define $z_t = y_t - d / (1 - b)$. We obtain

$$z_{t+1} = b z_t + \sigma \varepsilon_{t+1}.$$

Example 2.1.2   (First-order scalar mixed moving average and autoregression) *Let*

$$y_{t+1} = b y_t + \varepsilon_{t+1} + c \varepsilon_t,$$

where b and c are constants. Rewrite the preceding equation as

$$\begin{bmatrix} y_{t+1} \\ \varepsilon_{t+1} \end{bmatrix} = \begin{bmatrix} b & c \\ 0 & 0 \end{bmatrix} \begin{bmatrix} y_t \\ \varepsilon_t \end{bmatrix} + \begin{bmatrix} 1 \\ 1 \end{bmatrix} \varepsilon_{t+1}.$$

Example 2.1.3   (Vector autoregression) *Let*

$$y_{t+1} = A_1 y_t + A_2 y_{t-1} + C \varepsilon_{t+1},$$

where $\{y_t\}$ is $\mathbb{R}^n$-valued stochastic process. We rewrite the equation as

$$\begin{bmatrix} y_{t+1} \\ y_t \end{bmatrix} = \begin{bmatrix} A_1 & A_2 \\ I & 0 \end{bmatrix} \begin{bmatrix} y_t \\ y_{t-1} \end{bmatrix} + \begin{bmatrix} C \\ 0 \end{bmatrix} \varepsilon_{t+1}.$$

We are interested in characterizing the first and second moments of $\{z_t\}$ defined in (2.1).

Definition 2.1.1   *A stochastic process $\{X_t\}$ is **covariance stationary** if it has a constant mean $m = E X_t$, finite second moments, $E X_t^2 < \infty$, and a covariance matrix $E\left[(X_t - m)(X_s - m)' \right]$ that depends only on the time difference $|t - s|$.*

Assume that all eigenvalues of the matrix Φ are inside the unit circle. Then $\{z_t\}$ has a unique stationary distribution. Assume that z_0 is drawn from the stationary distribution with mean $\mu_0 = E z_0$ and covariance matrix $E (z_0 - \mu_0)(z_0 - \mu_0)'$. We will compute these moments and all the autocovariance matrices as well. Taking mathematical expectations on both sides of equation (2.1), we obtain $\mu_{t+1} = \Phi \mu_t$, where $\mu_t = E z_t$. If all eigenvalues of the matrix Φ are inside the unit circle, then $\mu_t \to 0$ as $t \to \infty$. Thus, when we set $\mu_0 = 0$, we have $\mu_t = 0$ for all t.

Next we compute the stationary covariance matrices:

$$C_z(0) \equiv E\left[z_t z_t' \right] = \Phi C_z(0) \Phi' + \Sigma \Sigma'.$$

This equation is a discrete **Lyapunov equation** in the $n_z \times n_z$ matrix $C_z(0)$. It can be solved numerically by successive iteration. To compute the autocovariance matrix, we note that

$$z_{t+j} = \Phi^j z_t + \Sigma \varepsilon_{t+j} + \Phi \Sigma \varepsilon_{t+j-1} + \dots + \Phi^{j-1} \Sigma \varepsilon_{t+1}.$$

Postmultiplying both sides by z_t' and taking expectations, we can show that the autocovariance matrix satisfies

$$C_z(j) \equiv E\left(z_{t+j}z_t'\right) = \Phi^j C_z(0).$$

After we solve for $C_z(0)$, the equation above gives the whole sequence of autocovariance matrices. We call it the **autocovariogram**.

Now we turn to the impulse response function. We still assume that all eigenvalues of the matrix Φ are inside the unit circle. Using the lag operator $\mathbf{L}$, we obtain

$$(I - \Phi\mathbf{L})z_{t+1} = \Sigma\varepsilon_{t+1}.$$

Thus

$$z_{t+1} = \Sigma\varepsilon_{t+1} + \Phi\Sigma\varepsilon_t + \Phi^2\Sigma\varepsilon_{t-1} + ... + \Phi^j\Sigma\varepsilon_{t+1-j} + ...$$

Viewed as a function of the lag j, $\Phi^j\Sigma$ is called the **impulse response function**. It gives the impact of ε_{t+1} on future values of z_{t+1+j} for all j. Or it gives the impact of all past ε_{t+1-j} on z_{t+1}.

2.2   Scalar Linear Rational Expectations Models

Scalar linear rational expectations models can typically be solved analytically. Here we introduce two widely adopted methods: the lag operator method and the method of undetermined coefficients.

2.2.1   Lag Operators

We adopt the following rule for the lag operator $\mathbf{L}$ on any stochastic process $\{X_t\}$:

$$\mathbf{L}^j X_t = X_{t-j}, \ \mathbf{L}^j E_t X_{t+i} = E_t X_{t+i-j},$$
$$\mathbf{L}^{-j} X_t = E_t X_{t+j}, \quad i \geq 0, j \geq 0.$$

According to this rule, the lag operator shifts the date of the variable X_{t+i}, but not the date of the conditional expectation E_t. In addition, because $\mathbf{L}^j E_t X_{t+j} = E_t X_t = X_t$, we define the inverse lag operator $\mathbf{L}^{-j}$ in the same way as above.

To illustrate the usefulness of lag operators, we first consider the following scalar first-order difference equation:

$$E_t x_{t+1} = bx_t + cz_t,$$

where b, c are constants, and $\{z_t\}$ is a bounded stochastic process. Suppose that $|b| > 1$. Using the inverse lag operator, we rewrite the preceding equation as

$$\left(\mathbf{L}^{-1} - b\right) x_t = cz_t.$$

Thus we obtain the forward-looking solution or the fundamental solution:

$$x_t = \frac{cz_t}{\mathbf{L}^{-1} - b} = \frac{-cz_t}{b(1 - b^{-1}\mathbf{L}^{-1})}$$

$$= -c\sum_{j=0}^{\infty} b^{-j-1}\mathbf{L}^{-j}z_t = -c\sum_{j=0}^{\infty} b^{-j-1}E_t z_{t+j}. \tag{2.3}$$

In general, there is a solution with bubbles:

$$x_t = x_t^* + B_t,$$

where x_t^* denotes the fundamental solution given in (2.3) and B_t is the bubble solution satisfying

$$E_t B_{t+1} = bB_t. \tag{2.4}$$

If we impose a transversality (or no-bubble) condition

$$\lim_{T\to\infty} b^{-T}E_t x_{t+T} = 0, \tag{2.5}$$

then bubbles cannot exist.

Example 2.2.1   (Asset price bubbles; Blanchard and Watson 1982) *Suppose that the stock price satisfies the asset-pricing equation*

$$p_t = \frac{E_t p_{t+1} + d_t}{R},$$

where $R > 1$ and d_t satisfies

$$d_t = \rho d_{t-1} + \varepsilon_t, \qquad |\rho| < 1.$$

Assume that ε_t is independently and identically distributed (IID) with mean zero. The general solution for the stock price is given by

$$p_t = \frac{d_t}{R - \rho} + B_t,$$

where the bubble $\{B_t\}$ satisfies

$$B_{t+1} = \begin{cases} \frac{RB_t}{q + e_{t+1}} & \text{with probability } q, \\ e_{t+1} & \text{with probability } 1 - q, \end{cases}$$

$$E_t e_{t+1} = 0.$$

This process satisfies (2.4). The bubble bursts with probability $1 - q$ each period and continues with probability q. If it bursts, it returns to zero in expected value. Imposing a transversality condition like (2.5) will rule out bubbles.

Next we apply lag operators to solve the following stochastic second-order difference equation:

$$E_t x_{t+1} = a x_t + b x_{t-1} + c z_t,$$ (2.6)

where $x_0 \in \mathbb{R}$ is given, a, b, and c are real-valued constants, and $\{z_t\}_{t \geq 0}$ is an exogenously given bounded stochastic process. We rewrite the preceding equation as

$$\left(\mathbf{L}^{-1} - a - b\mathbf{L} \right) x_t = c z_t.$$ (2.7)

Let λ_1 and λ_2 are the two characteristic roots defined in section 1.3. Assume that $|\lambda_1| < 1$ and $|\lambda_2| > 1$. We rewrite (2.7) as

$$\left(\mathbf{L}^{-1} - \lambda_1 \right) \left(\mathbf{L}^{-1} - \lambda_2 \right) \mathbf{L} x_t = c z_t.$$ (2.8)

It follows from (1.15) that

$$\left(\mathbf{L}^{-1} - \lambda_1 \right) \mathbf{L} x_t = \frac{c z_t}{\mathbf{L}^{-1} - \lambda_2} = \frac{-c z_t}{\lambda_2 \left(1 - \lambda_2^{-1} \mathbf{L}^{-1} \right)}.$$ (2.9)

We then obtain the solution:

$$x_t = \lambda_1 x_{t-1} - \frac{c}{\lambda_2} \sum_{j=0}^{\infty} \lambda_2^{-j} \mathbf{L}^{-j} z_t$$

$$= \lambda_1 x_{t-1} - \frac{c}{\lambda_2} \sum_{j=0}^{\infty} \lambda_2^{-j} E_t z_{t+j}.$$

Finally, we consider the following stochastic second-order difference equation:

$$E_t x_{t+1} = a_0 x_t + a_1 E_{t-1} x_t + a_2 x_{t-1} + c z_t,$$ (2.10)

where a_0, a_1, a_2, and c are constants, and $\{z_t\}$ is a bounded stochastic process. A special feature of this equation is that it involves a conditional expectation at date $t - 1$. To solve this equation, we first take conditional expectations given information at $t - 1$ to derive

$$E_{t-1} x_{t+1} = a_0 E_{t-1} x_t + a_1 E_{t-1} x_t + a_2 x_{t-1} + c E_{t-1} z_t.$$

Next we apply lag operators and rewrite the equation above as

$$(\mathbf{L}^{-1} - (a_0 + a_1) - a_2 \mathbf{L}) E_{t-1} x_t = c E_{t-1} z_t.$$

This equation is similar to (2.7) and can be solved in the same way. After we solve for $E_{t-1} x_t$, we can obtain the solution for $E_t x_{t+1}$ by shifting one period forward. Finally, substituting the solutions for $E_{t-1} x_t$ and $E_t x_{t+1}$ into (2.10), we obtain the solution for x_t.

2.2.2   Method of Undetermined Coefficients

The method of undetermined coefficients is extremely useful for solving linear models. To apply this method, we first guess the form of the solution; then we verify the guess and solve the undetermined coefficients. We use the stochastic second-order difference equation (2.6) to illustrate this method. We assume that $\{z_t\}$ satisfies

$$z_t = \rho z_{t-1} + \varepsilon_t,$$

where $|\rho| < 1$ and ε_t is IID with mean zero.

We also guess the solution is linear:

$$x_t = G x_{t-1} + H z_t,$$

where G and H are coefficients to be determined. We substitute this guess into (2.6) to derive

$$E_t \left(G x_t + H z_{t+1} \right) = a \left(G x_{t-1} + H z_t \right) + b x_{t-1} + c z_t$$
$$= G^2 x_{t-1} + G H z_t + \rho H z_t.$$

Matching coefficients on x_{t-1} and z_t gives

$$G^2 = aG + b,$$

$$GH + \rho H = aH + c.$$

The first equation is quadratic, which has two roots. Assume that one root has modulus less than 1 and the other has modulus greater than 1. To have a stable and nonexploding solution, we pick the solution with modulus less than 1. Once we obtain G, the second equation gives the solution for H. Uhlig (1999) provides a tool kit for solving linear and nonlinear systems using the method of undetermined coefficients.

2.3   Multivariate Linear Rational Expectations Models

Multivariate linear rational expectations models can be typically characterized by the following first-order system:

$$A E_t x_{t+1} = B x_t + C z_t, \tag{2.11}$$

where x_t is an $n \times 1$ random vector, A and B are $n \times n$ matrices, C is an $n \times n_z$ matrix, and z_t is an n_z-dimensional exogenously given stochastic process. We maintain the regularity assumption 1.4.1 for the same reason as discussed in section 1.4.

Definition 2.3.1 *A stochastic process* $\{X_t\}$ *is* **stable** *if there exists* $M > 0$ *such that* $\|X_t\|_{\max} < M$ *for all* t, *where* $\|x\|_{\max} = \max_j E |x_j|$ *for any* $\mathbb{R}^n$-*valued random variable* x.[2]

We assume that $\{z_t\}$ is a stable stochastic process. In applications we typically assume that $\{z_t\}$ takes the form as in (2.1). We intend to solve for a stable solution to (2.11).

Two issues are important for solving (2.11): (1) The matrix A may not be singular. (2) Some components of x_t are predetermined and others are non-predetermined. The three methods discussed below deal with these two issues in different ways.

2.3.1 Blanchard–Kahn Method

We first introduce the Blanchard and Kahn (1980) method. As in the deterministic case discussed in section 1.4.1, Blanchard and Kahn (1980) assume that A is nonsingular. Hence we define $W = A^{-1}B$ and apply the Jordan decomposition to W. We can then apply a similar method in the deterministic case studied in section 1.4.1. However, we have to redefine the notion of predetermined variables. According to Blanchard and Kahn (1980), a stochastic process $\{X_t\}_{t\geq 0}$ is **predetermined** if X_0 is exogenously given and if X_{t+1} is measurable with respect to $\mathcal{F}_t$, that is, $E[X_{t+1}|\mathcal{F}_t] = X_{t+1}$.

As in the deterministic case, let $x_t = [k_t', y_t']'$, where the vector y_t contains n_y non-predetermined variables and the vector k_t contains $n_k = n - n_y$ predetermined variables. Suppose that W has n_u unstable eigenvalues and $n_s = n - n_u$ stable eigenvalues. Then theorem 1.4.2 and corollary 1.4.1 still apply with small changes. In particular, the forward-looking solution for the transformed variables corresponding to the unstable eigenvalues is given by

$$u_t = -J_u^{-1}\left(I - \mathbf{L}^{-1}J_u^{-1}\right)^{-1} C_u^* z_t = -\sum_{j=0}^{\infty} J_u^{-j-1} C_u^* E_t z_{t+j}. \tag{2.12}$$

The rest of the formulas in the proof of theorem 1.4.2 still apply. As a result we obtain the certainty equivalence principle for linear rational expectations models: the solution for x_t in the stochastic case is identical to that in the deterministic case except that the conditional expectation operator E_t is applied to all terms related to $\{z_t\}$ in the stochastic case. In particular, if $\{z_t\}$ is given by (2.1) and $\Sigma = 0$ in the deterministic case, then the two solutions give identical expressions. In addition theorem 1.4.3 in the deterministic case also applies here.

---

2. Following Blanchard and Kahn (1980) and Sims (2000), we can generalize the notion of stability to include growth. In applications, one often uses detrended variables.

Example 2.3.1 (Interest rate rule in a New Keynesian model) *We consider a simple log-linearized New Keynesian model:*

$$\pi_t = \kappa x_t + \beta E_t \pi_{t+1}, \tag{2.13}$$

$$x_t = E_t x_{t+1} - \frac{1}{\gamma}(i_t - E_t \pi_{t+1}) + \varepsilon_t^x, \tag{2.14}$$

where π_t is the log inflation rate, x_t is the output gap, i_t is the log gross nominal interest rate, and e_t represents exogenous IID shocks, and $\kappa, \beta,$ and γ are positive constants. Equation (2.13) represents the short-run aggregate supply relation or the Phillips curve. Equation (2.14) represents the aggregate demand relation or the IS curve. An equilibrium is obtained once we specify the central bank's policy rule. Here we suppose that monetary policy is represented by the following rule for interest rate:

$$i_t = \rho_r i_{t-1} + \varepsilon_t, \tag{2.15}$$

where $|\rho_r| < 1$ and ε_t is IID. Combining (2.13), (2.14), and (2.15) gives the following system:

$$\begin{bmatrix} 1 & 0 & 0 \\ -1/\gamma & 1 & 1/\gamma \\ 0 & 0 & \beta \end{bmatrix} \begin{bmatrix} i_t \\ E_t x_{t+1} \\ E_t \pi_{t+1} \end{bmatrix} = \begin{bmatrix} \rho_r & 0 & 0 \\ 0 & 1 & 0 \\ 0 & -\kappa & 1 \end{bmatrix} \begin{bmatrix} i_{t-1} \\ x_t \\ \pi_t \end{bmatrix} + \begin{bmatrix} \varepsilon_t \\ -\varepsilon_t^x \\ 0 \end{bmatrix}. \tag{2.16}$$

Premultiplying both sides by the inverse of the matrix on the left gives

$$\begin{bmatrix} i_t \\ E_t x_{t+1} \\ E_t \pi_{t+1} \end{bmatrix} = W \begin{bmatrix} i_{t-1} \\ x_t \\ \pi_t \end{bmatrix} + \begin{bmatrix} 1 & 0 & 0 \\ -\gamma^{-1} & 1 & \gamma^{-1} \\ 0 & 0 & \beta \end{bmatrix}^{-1} \begin{bmatrix} \varepsilon_t \\ -\varepsilon_t^x \\ 0 \end{bmatrix},$$

where

$$W = \begin{bmatrix} \rho_r & 0 & 0 \\ \frac{\rho_r}{\gamma} & 1 + \frac{\kappa}{\beta\gamma} & -\frac{1}{\beta\gamma} \\ 0 & -\frac{\kappa}{\beta} & \frac{1}{\beta} \end{bmatrix}.$$

The preceding system has a unique stable solution if and only if the number of eigenvalues of W outside the unit circle is equal to the number of non-predetermined variables, in this case, two. Since $|\rho_r| < 1$ by assumption, we can show that only one eigenvalue of W is outside the unit circle. Thus the equilibrium is indeterminate.

This example illustrates that an exogenous policy rule that does not respond to endogenous variables can cause indeterminacy. In exercise 2 below, the reader is asked to give conditions for the existence of a unique equilibrium when the interest rate responds to inflation or the output gap.

2.3.2   Klein Method

Klein (2000) allows A to be singular. In addition Klein (2000) generalizes the definition of predetermined variables given by Blanchard and Kahn (1980). To introduce this definition, we define the following concepts.

Definition 2.3.2   *A stochastic process $\{X_t\}$ is a* **martingale** *if $E_t X_{t+1} = X_t$ for all $t \geq 0$. It is a* **martingale difference process** *if $E_t X_{t+1} = 0$.*

Definition 2.3.3   *A stochastic process $\{X_t\}$ is a* **white noise** *if $E[X_t] = 0$ and*

$$E[X_t X_s'] = \begin{cases} 0 & \text{if } s \neq t, \\ \Sigma & \text{if } s = t, \end{cases}$$

where Σ is a matrix.

A martingale process may not be stable. It is stable if it is uniformly bounded. A white noise process is stable. The process $\{\varepsilon_{t+1}\}$ satisfying (2.2) is a white noise. However, a white noise may not satisfy (2.2).

Definition 2.3.4   *A process $\{X_t\}$ is* **predetermined** *or* **backward-looking** *if (a) the prediction error $\{\xi_t\}$ defined by $\xi_{t+1} = X_{t+1} - E_t X_{t+1}$ is an exogenously given martingale difference process and (b) the initial value X_0 is measurable with respect to $\mathcal{F}_0$ and exogenously given.*

When $\xi_{t+1} = 0$, we obtain the Blanchard and Kahn (1980) definition. We assume that k_t is predetermined in the sense of definition 2.3.4 with exogenously given prediction error $\{\xi_t\}$. We also make the same assumptions as in theorem 1.4.5.

We now use the generalized Schur decomposition theorem and similar steps in the proof of theorem 1.4.5. In step 1 we modify equation (1.37):

$$u_t = -T_{22}^{-1} \sum_{j=0}^{\infty} \left[T_{22}^{-1} S_{22} \right]^j Q_2 C E_t z_{t+j}. \tag{2.17}$$

We modify step 2 as follows. We replace equation (1.38) with

$$E_t s_{t+1} = S_{11}^{-1} T_{11} s_t + S_{11}^{-1} T_{12} u_t - S_{11}^{-1} S_{12} E_t u_{t+1} + S_{11}^{-1} Q_1 C z_t.$$

We also have

$$k_{t+1} = Z_{11} s_{t+1} + Z_{12} u_{t+1}.$$

Since $\{k_t\}$ is predetermined with exogenously given prediction error $\{\xi_t\}$, we derive

$$\xi_{t+1} = k_{t+1} - E_t k_{t+1} = Z_{11} (s_{t+1} - E_t s_{t+1}) + Z_{12} (u_{t+1} - E_t u_{t+1}).$$

Since Z_{11} is invertible, we plug in the preceding expressions for $E_t s_{t+1}$ and u_t to derive

$$s_{t+1} = S_{11}^{-1} T_{11} s_t + S_{11}^{-1} T_{12} u_t - S_{11}^{-1} S_{12} E_t u_{t+1} + S_{11}^{-1} Q_1 C z_t$$
$$- Z_{11}^{-1} Z_{12} (u_{t+1} - E_t u_{t+1}) + Z_{11}^{-1} \xi_{t+1}.$$

The rest of the steps are identical to those in the proof of theorem 1.4.5. Unlike in the Blanchard and Kahn method, $\{\xi_t\}$ enters the expressions of the solution because of the new definition of predetermined variables. We can simplify the solution if we assume that $\{z_t\}$ satisfies (2.1). In this case the solution will be of the following form:

$$y_t = A_{yk} k_t + A_{yz} z_t,$$
$$k_{t+1} = A_{kk} k_t + A_{kz} z_t + \xi_{t+1},$$

where k_0 and z_0 are given. We refer readers to Klein (2000) for details.

To illustrate the usefulness of the previous generalized notion of predetermined variables, we consider the following linear-quadratic control problem:

$$\max_{\{u_t\}} \quad -\frac{1}{2} E \sum_{t=0}^{\infty} \beta^t [x_t', u_t'] \begin{bmatrix} Q & S \\ S' & R \end{bmatrix} \begin{bmatrix} x_t \\ u_t \end{bmatrix}$$

subject to

$$x_{t+1} = A x_t + B u_t + C \xi_{t+1}, \quad x_0 \text{ given,} \tag{2.18}$$

where $\{\xi_t\}$ is an exogenously given white noise process. Let $\mathcal{F}_t$ be the σ-algebra generated by $\{x_0, \xi_1, \xi_2, ..., \xi_t\}$. Assume that $\{x_t\}$ and $\{u_t\}$ are adapted to $\{\mathcal{F}_t\}$. Then $\{x_t\}$ is predetermined with the prediction error $\{\xi_t\}$. Suppose that the matrix

$$\begin{bmatrix} Q & S \\ S' & R \end{bmatrix}$$

is symmetric and positive semidefinite so that the first-order conditions, together with the transversality condition, are necessary and sufficient for optimality.

Let $\beta^{t+1}\lambda_{t+1}$ be the Lagrange multiplier associated with (2.18). We obtain the linear system as in (2.11):

$$
\begin{bmatrix} I & 0 & 0 \\ 0 & 0 & -\beta B' \\ 0 & 0 & \beta A' \end{bmatrix} \begin{bmatrix} E_t x_{t+1} \\ E_t u_{t+1} \\ E_t \lambda_{t+1} \end{bmatrix} = \begin{bmatrix} A & B & 0 \\ S' & R & 0 \\ -Q & -S & I \end{bmatrix} \begin{bmatrix} x_t \\ u_t \\ \lambda_t \end{bmatrix}.
$$

In this system u_t and λ_t are forward-looking or non-predetermined variables. We can then apply the Klein method to solve the system. This method does not require the matrix R to be invertible and is more general than many other methods discussed in Anderson et al. (1996). See chapter 9 for linear-quadratic models.

2.3.3 Sims Method

Sims (2000) proposes a different method. He represents the rational expectations model in the following form:

$$
\Gamma_0 y_t = \Gamma_1 y_{t-1} + C + \Psi z_t + \Pi \eta_t, \tag{2.19}
$$

where y_t is an $n \times 1$ random vector, z_t is an exogenously given $n_z \times 1$ random vector, η_t is endogenously determined $m \times 1$ vector of prediction errors satisfying $E_t \eta_{t+1} = 0$. Additionally Γ_0 and Γ_1 are $n \times n$ matrices, C is an $n \times 1$ constant vector, Ψ is an $n \times n_z$ matrix, and Π is an $n \times m$ matrix. Without loss of generality, we can assume that $C = 0$ by appropriate change of variables as in example 2.1.1. We can also assume that $\{z_t\}$ is serially uncorrelated with mean zero if it is a process given by (2.1), since we can append z_t to y_t and replace z_t in (2.19) with ε_t. For these reasons we consider the following system:

$$
\Gamma_0 y_t = \Gamma_1 y_{t-1} + \Psi \varepsilon_t + \Pi \eta_t, \tag{2.20}
$$

where $E_t \varepsilon_{t+1} = 0$.

As in the Klein method, Γ_0 can be singular. We assume that the pair (Γ_0, Γ_1) is regular in that it satisfies assumption 1.4.1. Unlike the methods of Blanchard and Kahn (1980) and Klein (2000), the Sims method does not need to define what variables are predetermined and non-predetermined in the first place. This method determines endogenously a linear combination of variables that are predetermined. Moreover the Sims method adopts the convention that all variables dated t are observable at t, meaning all variables are adapted to $\{\mathcal{F}_t\}$.

We apply the generalized Schur decomposition to (Γ_0, Γ_1). There exist unitary complex matrices Q and Z, and upper triangular matrices S and T such that $Q\Gamma_0 Z = S$ and $Q\Gamma_1 Z = T$. Let S and T be ordered in such a way that the first n_s

generalized eigenvalues are stable and the remaining n_u generalized eigenvalues are unstable. Define $y_t^* = Z^H y_t$. We partition y_t^* as

$$
y_t^* = \begin{bmatrix} s_t \\ u_t \end{bmatrix} \begin{matrix} n_s \times 1, \\ n_u \times 1. \end{matrix}
$$

Premultiplying by Q on the two sides of equation (2.19) yields

$$
S y_t^* = T y_{t-1}^* + Q \left(\Psi \varepsilon_t + \Pi \eta_t \right).
$$

We partition matrices conformably so that

$$
\begin{bmatrix} S_{11} & S_{12} \\ 0 & S_{22} \end{bmatrix} \begin{bmatrix} s_t \\ u_t \end{bmatrix} = \begin{bmatrix} T_{11} & T_{12} \\ 0 & T_{22} \end{bmatrix} \begin{bmatrix} s_{t-1} \\ u_{t-1} \end{bmatrix} + \begin{bmatrix} Q_{1\cdot} \\ Q_{2\cdot} \end{bmatrix} \left(\Psi \varepsilon_t + \Pi \eta_t \right), \tag{2.21}
$$

where $Q_{1\cdot}$ is the first n_s rows of Q and $Q_{2\cdot}$ is the last n_u rows of Q.

Because u_t corresponds to unstable generalized eigenvalues, we solve it forward to obtain

$$
u_t = -T_{22}^{-1} \sum_{j=1}^{\infty} \left[T_{22}^{-1} S_{22} \right]^j Q_{2\cdot} \left(\Psi \varepsilon_{t+j} + \Pi \eta_{t+j} \right). \tag{2.22}
$$

Taking expectations E_t gives

$$
E_t u_t = u_t = 0 \quad \text{for all } t,
$$

where we have used the convention that u_t is $\mathcal{F}_t$ measurable. We partition $y_t^* = Z^H y_t$ as

$$
y_t^* = \begin{bmatrix} s_t \\ u_t \end{bmatrix} = \begin{bmatrix} Z_1^H \\ Z_2^H \end{bmatrix} y_t.
$$

It follows that

$$
Z_2^H y_t = 0, \quad t \geq 0.
$$

This equation gives the condition for the initial value of y_t to satisfy.

From equation (2.21) and $u_t = 0$ for all t, we obtain

$$
\underbrace{Q_{2\cdot}}_{n_u \times n} \left(\Psi \varepsilon_t + \Pi \eta_t \right) = 0. \tag{2.23}
$$

Our goal is to solve for η_t in terms of exogenous shocks ε_t.

Lemma 2.3.1 *For every ε_t, there exists $\eta_t \in \mathbb{R}^m$ satisfying equation (2.23) if and only if there exists an $m \times n_z$ matrix Λ such that $Q_{2.}\Psi = Q_{2.}\Pi\Lambda$.*

Proof For the "if" part, we obtain (2.23) by setting $\eta_t = -\Lambda\varepsilon_t$. For the "only if" part, let the jth column of Λ be an η_t that solves (2.23) for $\varepsilon_t = I_j$, where I_j is the jth column of the $n_z \times n_z$ identity matrix, $j = 1, ..., n_z$.   ∎

Thus, for a solution to (2.20) to exist, we must impose the following:

Assumption 2.3.1 *The column space of $Q_{2.}\Psi$ is contained in that of $Q_{2.}\Pi$; that is, there exists an $m \times n_z$ matrix Λ such that $Q_{2.}\Psi = Q_{2.}\Pi\Lambda$.*

This assumption generalizes the usual existence condition $n_u \leq m$. The generalization allows for the possibility of linearly dependent rows in $Q_{2.}\Pi$. In other words, we could have existence even if $n_u > m$. In addition we need the following assumption for uniqueness:

Assumption 2.3.2 *There exists an $n_s \times n_u$ matrix Ξ such that*

$$Q_{1.}\Pi = \Xi Q_{2.}\Pi.$$

Given this assumption, we premultiply (2.21) by $\begin{bmatrix} I & -\Xi \end{bmatrix}$ to derive

$$\begin{bmatrix} S_{11} & S_{12} - \Xi S_{22} \\ 0 & I \end{bmatrix} \begin{bmatrix} s_t \\ u_t \end{bmatrix} = \begin{bmatrix} T_{11} & T_{12} - \Xi T_{22} \\ 0 & 0 \end{bmatrix} \begin{bmatrix} s_{t-1} \\ u_{t-1} \end{bmatrix} + \begin{bmatrix} Q_{1.} - \Xi Q_{2.} \\ 0 \end{bmatrix} (\Psi\varepsilon_t + \Pi\eta_t), \tag{2.24}$$

where we append the lower block to incorporate $u_t = 0$. Using assumption 2.3.2, we derive

$$\begin{bmatrix} S_{11} & S_{12} - \Xi S_{22} \\ 0 & I \end{bmatrix} \begin{bmatrix} s_t \\ u_t \end{bmatrix} = \begin{bmatrix} T_{11} & T_{12} - \Xi T_{22} \\ 0 & 0 \end{bmatrix} \begin{bmatrix} s_{t-1} \\ u_{t-1} \end{bmatrix} + \begin{bmatrix} Q_{1.} - \Xi Q_{2.} \\ 0 \end{bmatrix} \Psi\varepsilon_t.$$

Using $y_t = Z y_t^*$ and the equation above, we obtain the solution to (2.20):

$$y_t = \Theta_1 y_{t-1} + \Theta_2 \varepsilon_t,$$

where

$$\Theta_1 = Z \begin{bmatrix} S_{11} & S_{12} - \Xi S_{22} \\ 0 & I \end{bmatrix}^{-1} \begin{bmatrix} T_{11} & T_{12} - \Xi T_{22} \\ 0 & 0 \end{bmatrix} Z^H,$$

$$\Theta_2 = Z \begin{bmatrix} S_{11} & S_{12} - \Xi S_{22} \\ 0 & I \end{bmatrix}^{-1} \begin{bmatrix} Q_{1.} - \Xi Q_{2.} \\ 0 \end{bmatrix} \Psi.$$

The following theorem summarizes our analysis.

Theorem 2.3.1 *The necessary and sufficient conditions for the existence of a unique stable solution to (2.20) are assumptions 2.3.1 and 2.3.2.*

The conditions in this theorem are different from the Blanchard and Kahn conditions, which check a rank condition and also check whether the number of unstable eigenvalues n_u is equal to the number of non-predetermined variables (possibly m). To practically apply the conditions in theorem 2.19 and to implement the previous algorithm, we use the **singular value decomposition (SVD)** of the $n_u \times m$ matrix $Q_2.\Pi$ (appendix A). Since its rows are potentially linearly dependent, it is convenient to work with its SVD:

$$Q_2.\Pi = \underbrace{U}_{n_u \times n_u} \underbrace{D}_{n_u \times m} \underbrace{V^H}_{m \times m}$$

$$= \begin{bmatrix} U_{.1} & U_{.2} \end{bmatrix} \begin{bmatrix} D_{11} & 0 \\ 0 & 0 \end{bmatrix} \begin{bmatrix} V_{.1}^H \\ V_{.2}^H \end{bmatrix}$$

$$= \underbrace{U_{.1} \ D_{11} \ V_{.1}^H}_{n_u \times r \ \ r \times r \ \ r \times m}, \tag{2.25}$$

where D_{11} is a nonsingular $r \times r$ diagonal matrix and U and V are unitary matrices satisfying $U^H U = UU^H = I$ and $V^H V = VV^H = I$. We use the notation $U_{.1}$ to denote the first r columns of U and $U_{.2}$ to denote the remaining columns. Then $V_{.1}V_{.1}^H + V_{.2}V_{.2}^H = I$, $V_{.1}^H V_{.1} = I$, and $V_{.1}^H V_{.2} = 0$. Similar equations hold for U.

If $m = r$, then $V_{.2} = 0$. In this case we obtain

$$\Lambda = V_{.1}D_{11}^{-1}U_{.1}^H (Q_2.\Psi) \quad \text{and} \quad \Xi = (Q_1.\Pi) V_{.1}D_{11}^{-1}U_{.1}^H.$$

We thus have proved the following result:

Corollary 2.3.1 *Given assumption 2.3.1, a necessary and sufficient condition for the uniqueness of a stable solution to (2.20) is $m = r$.*

Lubik and Schorfheide (2003) generalize this result and show that if $m > r$, there are infinitely many stable solutions. They also provide a computation algorithm to solve this case. Qu and Tkachenko (2012) refine and implement this algorithm. This algorithm applies (2.25) to (2.23), yielding

$$\left(U_{.1} D_{11} V_{.1}^H \right) \eta_t = -Q_{2.} \Psi \varepsilon_t.$$

This is a system of n_u linear equations for m unknown variables η_t. The general solution is given by

$$\eta_t = -V_{.1} D_{11}^{-1} U_{.1}^H Q_{2.} \Psi \varepsilon_t + V_{.2} e_t, \tag{2.26}$$

where e_t is an arbitrary vector conformable with $V_{.2}$ and satisfying $E_{t-1} e_t = 0$. Note that $V_{.2} e_t$ is a solution to the homogeneous equation, since V is a unitary matrix. We may interpret e_t as a sunspot shock.

If assumption 2.3.2 is not satisfied, we take

$$\Xi = Q_{1.} \Pi V_{.1} D_{11}^{-1} U_{.1}^H.$$

Then

$$Q_{1.} \Pi - \Xi Q_{2.} \Pi = Q_{1.} \Pi \left(I - V_{.1} V_{.1}^H \right),$$

which is not equal to zero in general.

As in the determinate case, we can derive (2.24). But we have to solve

$$
\begin{aligned}
(Q_{1.} - \Xi Q_{2.}) \Pi \eta_t &= (Q_{1.} - \Xi Q_{2.}) \Pi \left(-V_{.1} D_{11}^{-1} U_{.1}^H Q_{2.} \Psi \varepsilon_t + V_{.2} e_t \right) \\
&= -Q_{1.} \Pi \left(I - V_{.1} V_{.1}^H \right) V_{.1} D_{11}^{-1} U_{.1}^H Q_{2.} \Psi \varepsilon_t \\
&\quad + Q_{1.} \Pi \left(I - V_{.1} V_{.1}^H \right) V_{.2} e_t \\
&= Q_{1.} \Pi \left(I - V_{.1} V_{.1}^H \right) V_{.2} e_t,
\end{aligned}
$$

where we have used (2.26) in the first equality.

We can now use (2.24) to derive

$$
\begin{bmatrix} S_{11} & S_{12} - \Xi S_{22} \\ 0 & I \end{bmatrix} \begin{bmatrix} s_t \\ u_t \end{bmatrix} = \begin{bmatrix} T_{11} & T_{12} - \Xi T_{22} \\ 0 & 0 \end{bmatrix} \begin{bmatrix} s_{t-1} \\ u_{t-1} \end{bmatrix}
$$
$$
+ \begin{bmatrix} Q_{1.} - \Xi Q_{2.} \\ 0 \end{bmatrix} \Psi \varepsilon_t + \begin{bmatrix} Q_{1.} \Pi \left(I - V_{.1} V_{.1}^H \right) \\ 0 \end{bmatrix} V_{.2} e_t.
$$

Using $y_t = Zy_t^*$ and the equation above, we obtain the solution to (2.20):

$$y_t = \Theta_1 y_{t-1} + \Theta_2 \varepsilon_t + \Theta_3 e_t,$$

where Θ_1 and Θ_2 are the same as before and

$$\Theta_3 = Z \begin{bmatrix} S_{11} & S_{12} - \Xi S_{22} \\ 0 & I \end{bmatrix}^{-1} \begin{bmatrix} Q_{1.} \Pi \left(I - V_{.1} V_{.1}' \right) \\ 0 \end{bmatrix} V_{.2}.$$

This solution shows that sunspot shocks can influence the equilibrium allocations and prices in the economy.

Example 2.3.2 *We use the model in example 2.3.1 to illustrate how to apply the Sims method. Let $E_t \pi_{t+1} = \xi_t^\pi$, $E_t x_{t+1} = \xi_t^x$, $\eta_t^\pi = \pi_t - \xi_{t-1}^\pi$, and $\eta_t^x = x_t - \xi_{t-1}^x$. We rewrite system (2.16) in terms of the Sims form (2.20):*

$$\begin{bmatrix} 1 & 0 & 0 & 0 & 0 \\ -\gamma^{-1} & 1 & \gamma^{-1} & 0 & 0 \\ 0 & 0 & \beta & 0 & 0 \\ 0 & 0 & 0 & 1 & 0 \\ 0 & 0 & 0 & 0 & 1 \end{bmatrix} \begin{bmatrix} i_t \\ \xi_t^x \\ \xi_t^\pi \\ x_t \\ \pi_t \end{bmatrix} = \begin{bmatrix} \rho_r & 0 & 0 & 0 & 0 \\ 0 & 1 & 0 & 0 & 0 \\ 0 & -\kappa & 1 & 0 & 0 \\ 0 & 1 & 0 & 0 & 0 \\ 0 & 0 & 1 & 0 & 0 \end{bmatrix} \begin{bmatrix} i_{t-1} \\ \xi_{t-1}^x \\ \xi_{t-1}^\pi \\ x_{t-1} \\ \pi_{t-1} \end{bmatrix}$$

$$+ \begin{bmatrix} 1 & 0 \\ 0 & -1 \\ 0 & 0 \\ 0 & 0 \\ 0 & 0 \end{bmatrix} \begin{bmatrix} \varepsilon_t \\ \varepsilon_t^x \end{bmatrix} + \begin{bmatrix} 0 & 0 \\ 1 & 0 \\ -\kappa & 1 \\ 1 & 0 \\ 0 & 1 \end{bmatrix} \begin{bmatrix} \eta_t^x \\ \eta_t^\pi \end{bmatrix}.$$

To derive decision rules for x_t and π_t directly, we have appended x_t and π_t and two identity equations $\eta_t^\pi = \pi_t - \xi_{t-1}^\pi$ and $\eta_t^x = x_t - \xi_{t-1}^x$ to the system.

2.4   Nonlinear Rational Expectations Models

Many nonlinear rational expectations models can be represented by the following system:

$$E_t \left[f \left(y_{t+1}, y_t, x_{t+1}, x_t \right) \right] = 0, \tag{2.27}$$

where x_t is an $(n_k + n_z) \times 1$ vector of predetermined variables and y_t is an $n_y \times 1$ vector of non-predetermined variables in the sense of Blanchard and Kahn (1980). Let $n = n_k + n_z + n_y$ and assume that the function $f : \mathbb{R}^{2n} \to \mathbb{R}^n$. The vector

x_t consists of n_k endogenous variables and n_z exogenous shocks: $x_t = [k_t', z_t']'$. Besides the initial values for k_0 and z_0, there is a terminal condition in the form of transversality conditions. Rather than specifying transversality conditions explicitly, we will focus on a stable solution (see definition 2.3.1) that satisfies these conditions trivially.

Assume that z_t satisfies (2.1), where all eigenvalues of Φ are inside the unit circle. Suppose that the system (2.27) has a deterministic steady state $(\bar{x}, \bar{y})$ such that $f(\bar{y}, \bar{y}, \bar{x}, \bar{x}) = 0$. We intend to find a linearized solution locally around the deterministic steady state. We totally differentiate (2.27) to obtain the linearized system:

$$f_{y'} \, E_t dy_{t+1} + f_y \, dy_t + f_{x'} \, E_t dx_{t+1} + f_x \, dx_t = 0,$$

where the Jacobian matrix of f is evaluated at the steady state. Adopting the notation introduced in section 1.6, we can also derive a log-linearized system. Both systems are in the form of (2.11):

$$\begin{bmatrix} f_{x'} \ f_{y'} \end{bmatrix} \begin{bmatrix} E_t dx_{t+1} \\ E_t dy_{t+1} \end{bmatrix} = - \begin{bmatrix} f_x \ f_y \end{bmatrix} \begin{bmatrix} dx_t \\ dy_t \end{bmatrix}. \tag{2.28}$$

We can thus apply previous methods to solve these systems. The stable solution will be of the following form:

$$dy_t = A_{yk} \, dk_t + A_{yz} \, dz_t,$$

$$dk_{t+1} = A_{kk} \, dk_t + A_{kz} \, dz_t,$$

$$dz_{t+1} = \Phi \, dz_t + \Sigma \varepsilon_{t+1},$$

where dk_0 and dz_0 are given.

Linearly approximated solutions are inaccurate to compute the risk premium and welfare. Higher order approximations are needed to compute such objects. We now introduce the second-order approximation method studied by Schmitt-Grohé and Uribe (2004). This method is actually an application of the more general perturbation method that will be introduced in section 11.3. To apply this method, we introduce a perturbation scalar $\sigma \in \mathbb{R}$ in (2.1):

$$z_{t+1} = \Phi z_t + \sigma \Sigma \varepsilon_{t+1},$$

where $\{\varepsilon_t\}$ is an IID process with bounded support.

Suppose that the solution to (2.27) takes the following form:

$$y_t = g(x_t, \sigma), \quad x_{t+1} = h(x_t, \sigma) + \eta \sigma \varepsilon_{t+1}, \tag{2.29}$$

where g and h are functions to be determined and η is an $n_x \times n_\varepsilon$ matrix defined by

$$\eta = \begin{bmatrix} 0 \\ \Sigma \end{bmatrix}.$$

Our goal is to find an approximate solution for g and h. We will consider local approximation around a particular point $(\bar{x}, \bar{\sigma})$. In applications a convenient point to take is the nonstochastic steady state $(\bar{x}, 0)$. At this point $f(\bar{y}, \bar{y}, \bar{x}, \bar{x}) = 0$. We then write the Taylor approximation up to the second order:

$$g(x, \sigma) = g(\bar{x}, 0) + g_x(\bar{x}, 0)(x - \bar{x}) + g_\sigma(\bar{x}, 0)\sigma$$
$$+ \frac{1}{2}g_{xx}(\bar{x}, 0)(x - \bar{x})^2 + g_{x\sigma}(\bar{x}, 0)(x - \bar{x})\sigma$$
$$+ \frac{1}{2}g_{\sigma\sigma}(\bar{x}, 0)\sigma^2,$$

$$h(x, \sigma) = h(\bar{x}, 0) + h_x(\bar{x}, 0)(x - \bar{x}) + h_\sigma(\bar{x}, 0)\sigma$$
$$+ \frac{1}{2}h_{xx}(\bar{x}, 0)(x - \bar{x})^2 + h_{x\sigma}(\bar{x}, 0)(x - \bar{x})\sigma$$
$$+ \frac{1}{2}h_{\sigma\sigma}(\bar{x}, 0)\sigma^2,$$

where, for notation convenience, we consider the scalar case only. We will follow Schmitt-Grohé and Uribe (2004) and derive an algorithm to solve for all the coefficients.[3] This algorithm also applies to the general high-dimensional case. We first note that

$$\bar{y} = g(\bar{x}, 0), \quad \bar{x} = h(\bar{x}, 0).$$

We then define

$$0 = F(x, \sigma)$$
$$\equiv Ef(g(h(x, \sigma) + \eta\sigma\varepsilon', \sigma), g(x, \sigma), h(x, \sigma) + \eta\sigma\varepsilon', x), \tag{2.30}$$

where we have substituted (2.29) into (2.27) and the expectation is taken with respect to ε'. Since $F(x, \sigma)$ is equal to zero for any values of (x, σ), we must have

$$F_{x^i\sigma^j}(x, \sigma) = 0 \quad \text{for any } i, j, x, \sigma,$$

---

3. The Matlab codes are publicly available on the website: http://www.columbia.edu/~mu2166/2nd_order.htm.

where $F_{x^i \sigma^j}$ denotes the partial derivative of F with respect to x taken i times and with respect to σ taken j times. We will use the equation above to derive other coefficients in the approximated solution.

We start with the first-order approximation. Let

$$F_x(\bar{x},0) = 0, \quad F_\sigma(\bar{x},0) = 0.$$

We then use (2.30) to compute

$$F_\sigma(\bar{x},0) = E\left\{f_{y'}\left[g_x(h_\sigma + \eta\varepsilon') + g_\sigma\right] + f_y g_\sigma + f_{x'}(h_\sigma + \eta\varepsilon')\right\}$$
$$= f_{y'}\left[g_x h_\sigma + g_\sigma\right] + f_y g_\sigma + f_{x'} h_\sigma = 0,$$

where all derivatives are evaluated at the non-stochastic steady state. This is a system of homogeneous linear equations for g_σ and h_σ. For a unique solution to exist, we must have

$$g_\sigma = h_\sigma = 0.$$

This result reflects the certainty equivalence principle in that the policy function in the first-order approximation is independent of the variance of the shock. Thus, linear approximation is not suitable to address the risk premium and welfare.

Next we use (2.30) to compute

$$F_x(\bar{x},0) = f_{y'} g_x h_x + f_y g_x + f_{x'} h_x + f_x = 0.$$

We can equivalently rewrite the preceding equation as

$$\begin{bmatrix} f_{x'} & f_{y'} \end{bmatrix} \begin{bmatrix} I \\ g_x \end{bmatrix} h_x = -\begin{bmatrix} f_x & f_y \end{bmatrix} \begin{bmatrix} I \\ g_x \end{bmatrix}. \tag{2.31}$$

Let $A = \begin{bmatrix} f_{x'} & f_{y'} \end{bmatrix}$, $B = -\begin{bmatrix} f_x & f_y \end{bmatrix}$, and $\hat{x}_t = x_t - \bar{x}$. Postmultiplying $\hat{x}_t$ on each side of (2.31) yields

$$A \begin{bmatrix} I \\ g_x \end{bmatrix} h_x \hat{x}_t = B \begin{bmatrix} I \\ g_x \end{bmatrix} \hat{x}_t. \tag{2.32}$$

Using the fact that $\hat{x}_{t+1} = h_x \hat{x}_t$ and $\hat{y}_t = g_x \hat{x}_t$ for the linearized nonstochastic solution, we obtain

$$A \begin{bmatrix} \hat{x}_{t+1} \\ \hat{y}_{t+1} \end{bmatrix} = B \begin{bmatrix} \hat{x}_t \\ \hat{y}_t \end{bmatrix}. \tag{2.33}$$

Notice that this equation is equivalent to equation (2.28). One could adopt the Klein method or the Sims method to solve this linear system. The solution would give h_x and g_x.

Now we turn to the second-order approximation. We compute

$$
\begin{aligned}
0 = F_{xx}\left(\bar{x},0\right) = &\; [f_{y'y}g_xh_x + f_{y'y}g_x + f_{y'x'}h_x + f_{y'x}]g_xh_x \\
&+ f_{y'}g_{xx}h_xh_x + f_{y'}g_xh_{xx} \\
&+ [f_{yy'}g_xh_x + f_{yy}g_x + f_{yx'}h_x + f_{yx}]g_x + f_y g_{xx} \\
&+ [f_{x'y'}g_xh_x + f_{x'y}g_x + f_{x'x'}h_x + f_{x'x}]h_x + f_{x'}h_{xx} \\
&+ f_{xy'}g_xh_x + f_{xy}g_x + f_{xx'}h_x + f_{xx}.
\end{aligned}
$$

Since we know the derivatives of f as well as the first derivatives of g and h evaluated at $(\bar{y},\bar{y},\bar{x},\bar{x})$, it follows that the preceding equation represents a system of $n \times n_x \times n_x$ linear equations for the same number of unknowns given by the elements of g_{xx} and h_{xx}.

Similarly we compute $g_{\sigma\sigma}$ and $h_{\sigma\sigma}$ by solving the equation $F_{\sigma\sigma}\left(\bar{x},0\right) = 0$. We compute

$$
\begin{aligned}
0 = F_{\sigma\sigma}\left(\bar{x},0\right) = &\; f_{y'}g_xh_{\sigma\sigma} + f_{y'y'}g_x\eta g_x\eta I \\
&+ f_{y'x'}\eta g_x\eta I + f_{y'}g_{xx}\eta\eta I + f_{y'}g_{\sigma\sigma} \\
&+ f_y g_{\sigma\sigma} + f_{x'}h_{\sigma\sigma} \\
&+ f_{x'y'}g_x\eta\eta I + f_{x'x'}\eta\eta I.
\end{aligned}
$$

This is a system of n linear equations for n unknowns $g_{\sigma\sigma}$ and $h_{\sigma\sigma}$.

Finally, we show that the cross derivatives $g_{\sigma x}$ and $h_{\sigma x}$ are equal to zero when evaluated at $(\bar{x},0)$. We compute

$$
0 = F_{\sigma x}\left(\bar{x},0\right) = f_{y'}g_xh_{\sigma x} + f_{y'}g_{\sigma x}h_x + f_y g_{\sigma x} + f_{x'}h_{\sigma x}.
$$

This is a system of $n \times n_x$ linear homogeneous equations for $n \times n_x$ unknowns $g_{\sigma x}$ and $h_{\sigma x}$. If a unique solution exists, then the solution must be equal to zero.

In summary, uncertainty matters in the second-order approximated solution only through the terms $\frac{1}{2}g_{\sigma\sigma}\left(\bar{x},0\right)\sigma^2$ and $\frac{1}{2}h_{\sigma\sigma}\left(\bar{x},0\right)\sigma^2$. In applications we typically set $\sigma = 1$ when Σ is "small." In principle, we can proceed to compute a third-order or even higher order approximate solution using the previous procedure. Because the algebra is highly involved, we omit the exposition here.

2.5   Numerical Solutions Using Dynare

Dynare can solve DSGE models in the form of (2.27). Using Dynare timing conventions, Dynare solves any stochastic model of the following general form:

$$E_t f\left(y_{t-1}^-, y_t, y_{t+1}^+, \varepsilon_t\right) = 0, \tag{2.34}$$

where y_t is a vector that contains endogenous variables, y_{t-1}^- is a subset of predetermined variables or variables with a lag, y_{t+1}^+ is a subset of variables with a lead, and ε_t is a vector of exogenous IID shocks with mean zero. This form is more general than that in (2.27), in that the former can incorporate a variable with both a one-period lead and a one-period lag. For example, for habit formation utility, the consumption Euler equation contains current consumption as well as consumption with one-period lead and lag. Thus consumption is both a predetermined and a non-predetermined variable and can be naturally incorporated in the Dynare form (2.34) but not in the form (2.27). One has to perform a change of variable to incorporate habit formation in (2.27).

The solution to (2.34) is given by the following form:

$$y_t = g\left(y_{t-1}^-, \varepsilon_t\right).$$

Dynare uses the perturbation method as in the previous section to deliver an approximate solution up to the third order. In particular, we introduce a perturbation scalar σ and then use Taylor expansions. Finally, we set $\sigma = 1$. The first-order approximate solution is given by

$$y_t = \bar{y} + g_y \hat{y}_{t-1}^- + g_u \varepsilon_t,$$

where $\hat{y}_{t-1}^- = y_{t-1}^- - \bar{y}$.

As in the deterministic case discussed in section 1.7, a Dynare program typically consists of five blocks. The preamble block and the model block are similar for both the deterministic and stochastic cases. The steady-state and initial values block is needed for the stochastic case because Dynare has to use the nonstochastic steady state as the perturbation point. The main differences between the two cases lie in the shocks block and the computation block.

We will use the following simple stochastic growth model as an example to illustrate how to work with Dynare:

$$\max_{\{C_t, N_t, K_{t+1}\}} E \sum_{t=0}^{\infty} \beta^t \left\{\ln\left(C_t\right) + \chi \ln\left(1 - N_t\right)\right\},$$

subject to

$$C_t + K_{t+1} - (1 - \delta) K_t = z_t K_t^\alpha N_t^{1-\alpha},$$ (2.35)

$$\ln z_t = \rho \ln z_{t-1} + \sigma \varepsilon_t.$$ (2.36)

The equilibrium system consists of the two first-order conditions

$$\frac{1}{C_t} = E_t \frac{\beta}{C_{t+1}} \left(z_{t+1} \alpha K_{t+1}^{\alpha-1} N_{t+1}^{1-\alpha} + 1 - \delta \right),$$

$$\frac{\chi C_t}{1 - N_t} = (1 - \alpha) z_t K_t^\alpha N_t^{-\alpha},$$

and the resource constraint (2.35) for three unknowns C_t, K_t, and N_t. We have to decide whether to use approximations in levels or in logs. If we use approximations in logs, we do the following transformation for any variable x_t:

$$lx_t = \ln(x_t) \quad \text{and} \quad x_t = \exp(lx_t).$$

We then rewrite the equilibrium system in terms of the transformed variables. Dynare will conduct approximations for these variables. Note that Dynare treats exogenous shocks (e.g., z_t) as endogenous variables. It treats the shock innovations as exogenous variables.

We will write a Dynare program for our example using approximations in levels.[4] We start with the first three blocks:

```
%---------------------------------------------
% 1. Preamble
%---------------------------------------------
var c k n z;
varexo e;
parameters beta chi delta alpha rho sigma;
alpha = 0.33;
beta = 0.99;
delta = 0.023;
chi = 1.75;
rho = 0.95;
sigma = 0.01;
%---------------------------------------------
% 2. Model
%---------------------------------------------
model;
```

---

4. The Dynare code is rbc0.mod.

```
(1/c) = beta*(1/c(+1))*(1+alpha*(k^(alpha-1))*exp(z(+1))
  *(n(+1))^(1-alpha)-delta);
chi*c/(1-n) = (1-alpha)*(k(-1)^alpha)*exp(z)*(n^(-alpha));
c+ k-(1-delta)*k(-1) = (k(-1)^alpha)*exp(z)*n^(1-alpha);
z = rho*z(-1)+e;
end;
%---------------------------------------------
% 3. Steady State and Initial Values
%---------------------------------------------
initval;
  k = 9;
  c = 0.76;
  n = 0.3;
  z = 0;
  e = 0;
end;
steady;
check;
```

Shocks Next we introduce the shocks block. For stochastic simulations the shocks block specifies the nonzero elements of the covariance matrix of the shocks of exogenous variables. The following commands may be used in this block:

`var VARIABLE_NAME; stderr EXPRESSION;`

  Specifies the standard error of a variable.

`var VARIABLE_NAME = EXPRESSION;`

  Specifies the variance of a variable.

`var VARIABLE_NAME, VARIABLE_NAME = EXPRESSION;`

  Specifies the covariance of two variables.

`corr VARIABLE_NAME, VARIABLE_NAME = EXPRESSION;`

  Specifies the correlation of two variables.
  For our example, we write the shocks block as:

```
%---------------------------------------------
% 4. Shocks Block
%---------------------------------------------
shocks;
var e = sigma^2;
end;
```

It is possible to mix deterministic and stochastic shocks to build models where agents know from the start of the simulation about future exogenous changes. In that case `stoch_simul` will compute the rational expectation solution adding future information to the state space (nothing is shown in the output of `stoch_simul`) and the command `forecast` will compute a simulation conditional on initial conditions and future information.

Here is an example:

```
varexo_det tau;
varexo e;
...
shocks;
var e; stderr 0.01;
var tau;
periods 1:9;
values -0.15;
end;
stoch_simul(irf=0);
forecast;
```

Computation   Now we turn to the computation block. The Dynare command used in this block is

```
stoch_simul (OPTIONS . . . ) [VARIABLE_NAME . . . ];
```

This command solves a stochastic (i.e., rational expectations) model using the perturbation method by Taylor approximations of the policy and transition functions around the steady state. Using this solution, it computes impulse response functions and various descriptive statistics (moments, variance decomposition, correlation and autocorrelation coefficients). For correlated shocks, the variance decomposition is computed as in the VAR literature through a Cholesky decomposition of the covariance matrix of the exogenous variables. When the shocks are correlated, the variance decomposition depends on the order of the variables in the `varexo` command.

The IRFs are computed as the difference between the trajectory of a variable following a shock at the beginning of period 1 and its steady-state value. Currently the IRFs are only plotted for 12 variables. Select the ones you want to see if your model contains more than 12 endogenous variables.

Variance decomposition, correlation, and autocorrelation are only displayed for variables with positive variance. Impulse response functions are only plotted for variables with response larger than 10^{-10}.

Variance decomposition is computed relative to the sum of the contribution of each shock. Normally this is, of course, equal to aggregate variance, but if a model generates very large variances, it may happen that due to numerical error, the two differ by a significant amount. Dynare issues a warning if the maximum relative difference between the sum of the contribution of each shock and aggregate variance is larger than 0.01 percent.

The covariance matrix of the shocks is specified in the shocks block. When a list of VARIABLE_NAME is specified, results are displayed only for these variables.

The command `stoch_simul` contains many options. Here I list a few commonly used options. The reader is referred to the *Dynare Reference Manual* for more options.

- `ar = INTEGER`: Order of autocorrelation coefficients to compute and to print. Default: 5.

- `drop = INTEGER`: Number of points dropped at the beginning of simulation before computing the summary statistics. Default: 100.

- `hp_filter = INTEGER`: Uses HP filter with = INTEGER before computing moments. Default: no filter.

- `irf = INTEGER`: Number of periods on which to compute the IRFs. Setting `irf=0` suppresses the plotting of IRF's. Default: 40.

- `relative_irf`: Requests the computation of normalized IRFs in percentage of the standard error of each shock.

- `linear`: Indicates that the original model is linear (put it rather in the model command).

- `nocorr`: Don't print the correlation matrix (printing them is the default).

- `nofunctions`: Don't print the coefficients of the approximated solution (printing them is the default).

- `nomoments`: Don't print moments of the endogenous variables (printing them is the default).

- `nograph`: Don't print the graphs. Useful for loops.

- `noprint`: Don't print anything. Useful for loops.

- `print`: Print results (opposite of noprint).

- `order = INTEGER`: Order of Taylor approximation. Acceptable values are 1, 2, and 3. Note that for third order, `k_order_solver` option is implied and only empirical moments are available (you must provide a value for `periods` option). Default: 2.

- `periods = INTEGER`: If different from zero, empirical moments will be computed instead of theoretical moments. The value of the option specifies the number of periods to use in the simulations. Values of the initval block, possibly recomputed by the command `steady`, will be used as starting point for the simulation. The simulated endogenous variables are made available to the user in a vector for each variable and in the global matrix `oo_.endo_simul`. Default: 0.

- `conditional_variance_decomposition = INTEGER`: See below.

- `conditional_variance_decomposition = [INTEGER1:INTEGER2]`: See below.

- `conditional_variance_decomposition = [INTEGER1 INTEGER2 ...]`: Computes a conditional variance decomposition for the specified period(s). Conditional variances are given by $\text{var}_t(y_{t+k})$. For period 1 the conditional variance decomposition provides the decomposition of the effects of shocks upon impact.

- `pruning`: Discard higher order terms when iteratively computing simulations of the solution, as in Kim et al. (2008).

- `partial_information`: Computes the solution of the model under partial information, along the lines of Pearlman, Currie, and Levine (1986). Agents are supposed to observe only some variables of the economy. The set of observed variables is declared using the `varobs` command. Note that if `varobs` is not present or contains all endogenous variables, then this is the full information case and this option has no effect.

For our example, we may write:

```
%---------------------------------------------
% 5. Computation Block
%---------------------------------------------
stoch_simul(hp_filter = 1600, order = 1);
```

Output and Results   The command `stoch_simul` produces the following results, which are stored in Matlab global variables starting with oo_.:

- **Model summary:** A count of the various variable types in your model (endogenous, jumpers, etc.).

- **Eigenvalues:** Displayed if the command `check` is used. The Blanchard–Kahn condition is checked.

- **Covariance matrix of exogenous shocks:** Should square with the values of the shock variances and co-variances you provided in the .mod file.

- **Policy and transition functions:** Coefficients of these functions stored up to third-order approximations and displayed on the screen up to second-order approximations. See below.
- **Moments of simulated variables:** Up to the fourth moments.
- **Correlation of simulated variables:** Contemporaneous correlations presented in a table.
- **Autocorrelation of simulated variables:** Up to the fifth lag, as specified in the options of `stoch_simul`.
- **Graphs of impulse response functions:** Up to 12 variables.

You can easily browse the global variables of output starting with oo_. in Matlab by either calling them in the command line, or using the workspace interface. Steady-state values are stored in `oo_.dr.ys` or `oo_.steady_state`. Impulse response functions are stored under the following nomenclature: "x_e" denotes the impulse response of variable x to shock e. Note that variables will always appear in the order in which you declare them in the preamble block of your .mod file.

Typology and Ordering of Variables Dynare distinguishes four types of endogenous variables:

- **Purely backward (or purely predetermined) variables:** Those that appear only at current and past periods in the model, but not in future periods (i.e., at t and $t-1$ but not $t+1$). The number of such variables is equal to `oo_.dr.npred` − `oo_.dr.nboth`.
- **Purely forward variables:** Those that appear only at current and future periods in the model, but not at past periods (i.e., at t and $t+1$ but not $t-1$). The number of such variables is stored in `oo_.dr.nfwrd`.
- **Mixed variables:** Those that appear at current, past, and future periods in the model (i.e., at t, $t-1$ and $t+1$). The number of such variables is stored in `oo_.dr.nboth`.
- **Static variables:** Those that appear only at current, not past or future periods in the model (i.e., only at t, not at $t+1$ or $t-1$). The number of such variables is stored in `oo_.dr.nstatic`.

Note that all endogenous variables fall into one of these four categories, since after the creation of auxiliary variables, all endogenous variables have at most one lead and one lag. We therefore have the following identity:

`oo_.dr.npred + oo_.dr.nfwrd + oo_.dr.nstatic = M_.endo_nbr`

Internally Dynare uses two orderings of the endogenous variables: the order of declaration (which is reflected in `M_.endo_names`) and an order based on the four types described above, which we will call the DR-order ("DR" stands for decision rule). Most of the time, the declaration order is used, but for elements of the decision rules, the DR-order is used.

The DR-order is the following: static variables appear first, then purely backward variables, then mixed variables, and finally purely forward variables. Within each category, variables are arranged according to the declaration order.

First-Order Approximation   The approximation has the form

$$y_t = \bar{y} + A\hat{y}_{t-1}^- + B\varepsilon_t,$$

where $\bar{y}$ is the deterministic steady-state value of y_t and $\hat{y}_{t-1}^- = y_{t-1}^- - \bar{y}^-$.

The coefficients of the decision rules are stored as follows:

- $\bar{y}$ is stored in `oo_.dr.ys`. The vector rows correspond to all endogenous variables in the declaration order.

- A is stored in `oo_.dr.ghx`. The matrix rows correspond to all endogenous variables in the DR-order. The matrix columns correspond to state variables in the DR-order.

- B is stored in `oo_.dr.ghu`. The matrix rows correspond to all endogenous variables in the DR-order. The matrix columns correspond to exogenous variables in the declaration order.

For our example, table 2.1 gives the first-order approximated policy and transition functions.

The row "constant" should give the steady-state values of the model. As an example, we write the consumption policy in the more familiar form:

$$C_t = 0.793902 + 0.041667\hat{K}_t + 0.306067\hat{z}_{t-1} + 0.322175\varepsilon_t,$$

or

$$\hat{C}_t = 0.041667\hat{K}_t + 0.322175\hat{z}_t,$$

where we have used the fact that $\hat{z}_t = 0.95\hat{z}_{t-1} + \varepsilon_t$.

Table 2.1
Policy and transition functions

	c	k	n	z
Constant	0.793902	10.269592	0.331892	0
$k(-1)$	0.041667	0.951446	−0.008169	0
$z(-1)$	0.306067	1.143748	0.226601	0.950000
e	0.322175	1.203945	0.238528	1.000000

Second-Order Approximation   The approximation has the form:

$$y_t = \bar{y} + \frac{1}{2}g_{\sigma\sigma} + A\hat{y}_{t-1}^- + B\varepsilon_t$$

$$+ \frac{1}{2}C\left(\hat{y}_{t-1}^- \otimes \hat{y}_{t-1}^-\right) + \frac{1}{2}D\left(\varepsilon_t \otimes \varepsilon_t\right) + F\left[\hat{y}_{t-1}^- \otimes \varepsilon_t\right],$$

where $g_{\sigma\sigma}$ is the shift effect of the variance of future shocks and $\otimes$ denotes the Kronecker product. The coefficients of the decision rules are stored in the variables described for the case of first-order approximations, plus the following variables:

- $g_{\sigma\sigma}$ is stored in `oo_.dr.ghs2`. The vector rows correspond to all endogenous variables in the DR-order.

- C is stored in `oo_.dr.ghxx`. The matrix rows correspond to all endogenous variables in the DR-order. The matrix columns correspond to the Kronecker product of the vector of state variables in the DR-order.

- D is stored in `oo_.dr.ghuu`. The matrix rows correspond to all endogenous variables in the DR-order. The matrix columns correspond to the Kronecker product of exogenous variables in the declaration order.

- F is stored in `oo_.dr.ghxu`. The matrix rows correspond to all endogenous variables in the DR-order. The matrix columns correspond to the Kronecker product of the vector of state variables (in the DR-order) by the vector of exogenous variables (in the declaration order).

We often refer to $y_s \equiv \bar{y} + 0.5g_{\sigma\sigma}$ as the **stochastic steady state**, which corrects for uncertainty. It is the steady state when we set the current shock $\varepsilon_t = 0$, but taking into account of future shocks. This is unlike the deterministic steady state in which shocks in all periods are shut down.

Third-Order Approximation   The approximation has the form

$$y_t = \bar{y} + G_0 + G_1 x_t + G_2\left(x_t \otimes x_t\right) + G_3\left(x_t \otimes x_t \otimes x_t\right),$$

where x_t is a vector consisting of the deviation from the steady state of the state variables (in the DR-order) at date $t-1$ followed by the exogenous variables at date t (in the declaration order). The coefficients of the decision rules are stored as follows:

- $\bar{y}$ is stored in `oo_.dr.ys`. The vector rows correspond to all endogenous variables in the declaration order.

- G_0 is stored in `oo_.dr.g_0`.

- G_1 is stored in `oo_.dr.g_1`.

- G_2 is stored in `oo_.dr.g_2`.

- G_3 is stored in `oo_.dr.g_3`.

2.6   Exercises

1. Consider the stochastic Cagan (1956) model:

$$m_t - p_t = -\alpha E_t \left(p_{t+1} - p_t \right), \quad \alpha > 0,$$

where m_t is the log of the nominal money supply and p_t is the log of the price level. Suppose that the money supply satisfies

$$m_{t+1} = \rho m_t + \varepsilon_{t+1}, \; \rho \in [0,1], \quad m_0 \text{ given,}$$

where ε_{t+1} is a white noise. Give conditions on the parameters such that there exists a unique stable solution for p_t. Derive this solution.

2. Modify the policy rule in Example 2.3.1 as follows:

   a. Set the policy rule as

   $$i_t = \delta \pi_t + \varepsilon_t.$$

   Prove that $\delta > 1$ is necessary and sufficient for the existence of a unique stable equilibrium. This condition is called the **Taylor principle**.

   b. Suppose that the policy rule is given by the **Taylor rule**

   $$i_t = \delta_\pi \pi_t + \delta_x x_t + \varepsilon_t.$$

   Derive conditions for the existence of a unique stable equilibrium.

3. For the example in section 2.5, write a Dynare program using approximations in logs. Plot impulse response functions for consumption C_t, investment I_t, output Y_t, hours N_t, capital K_t, wage w_t, and rental rate R_t. Compare the solutions using first-, second-, and third-order approximations.

3   Markov Processes

Economic data and economic models often have a recursive structure. A recursive structure is essential for researchers to use recursive methods to analyze dynamic problems and is also convenient for organizing time series data. To introduce a recursive structure, it is necessary to assume that exogenous shocks follow Markov processes. We are also interested in long-run properties of Markov processes induced by these exogenous shocks and economic agents' optimal behavior. In this chapter we provide a brief introduction to Markov processes and their convergence.[1] We first study Markov chains for which the state space is finite. We then study Markov processes with infinite state space. Finally, we discuss strong and weak convergence for general Markov processes.

Throughout this chapter we fix a probability space $(\Omega, \mathcal{F}, \Pr)$ and a measurable space $(\mathbb{X}, \mathcal{X})$.

Definition 3.0.1   *A stochastic process* $\{X_t\}_{t=0}^{\infty}$ *with the state space* $\mathbb{X}$ *is a **Markov process** if*

$$\Pr\left(X_{t+1} \in A | X_t = x_0, X_{t-1} = x_1, ..., X_{t-k} = x_k\right) = \Pr\left(X_{t+1} \in A | X_t = x_0\right)$$

for all $A \in \mathcal{X}$, *all* $x_0, x_1, ..., x_k \in \mathbb{X}$, *all* $0 \le k \le t$, *and all* $t \ge 0$. *If the probability above does not depend on* t, *the Markov process is **time homogeneous**.*

In this chapter we focus on time-homogeneous Markov processes only. We refer the reader to appendix D for a summary of some basic concepts and results in measure and probability theory that will be used in this chapter.

---

1. Our exposition draws heavily on the treatment in Lucas, Stokey, and Prescott (1989), Billingsley (1995), Shiryaev (1996), and Gallager (1996).

3.1   Markov Chains

If the state space $\mathbb{X}$ is countable or finite, then the Markov process $\{X_t\}$ is called a
Markov chain.[2] A Markov chain $\{X_t\}$ is characterized by three objects:

- A finite or countable state space $\mathbb{X}$. This set gives all possible values that x_t may
  take. Without loss of generality, we may simply assume that $\mathbb{X} = \{1, 2, ..., n\}$,
  where $n \leq \infty$.

- A **transition matrix** (or **stochastic matrix**) $P = \left(p_{ij}\right)_{n \times n}$, where

  $$p_{ij} = \Pr\left(X_{t+1} = j | X_t = i\right) \quad \text{and} \quad \sum_{k=1}^{n} p_{ik} = 1$$

  for all $i, j = 1, 2, ..., n$.

- An initial distribution $\pi_0 = (\pi_{01}, \pi_{02}, ..., \pi_{0n})$, where $\pi_{0i} = \Pr(x_0 = i)$ and
  $\sum_{i=1}^{n} \pi_{0i} = 1$.

Given a transition matrix P and an initial distribution π_0, there exists a unique
probability distribution $\Pr$ on $(\mathbb{X}^\infty, \mathcal{X}^\infty)$ such that there exists a Markov chain $\{X_t\}$
defined on this probability space and

$$\Pr(X_0 = i) = \pi_{0,i} \quad \text{and} \quad \Pr(X_{t+1} = j | X_t = i) = p_{ij}$$

for all $i, j \in \mathbb{X}$. A general version of this result is stated in theorem 3.2.3 below.

Given a transition matrix P, we can compute the probabilities of transition from
state i to state j in m steps, $m = 1, 2, 3, ...$. In particular, we can verify that if P is a
transition matrix, then so is P^m. If the initial state is i, then the probability distribution over states m periods ahead is given by the ith row of P^m. We denote by $p_{ij}^{(m)}$
the ith row and the jth column of P^m. The m-step transition probabilities satisfy the
Chapman–Kolmogorov equation:

$$P^{m+k} = P^k P^m \quad \text{or} \quad p_{ij}^{(m+k)} = \sum_{r=1}^{n} p_{ir}^{(k)} p_{rj}^{(m)} \quad \text{for any } m, k \geq 1. \tag{3.1}$$

It is convenient to use a directed graph to describe a Markov chain. In the graph
there is one node for each state and a directed arc for each nonzero transition probability. If $p_{ij} = 0$, then the arc from node i to node j is omitted. Since many important properties of a Markov chain depend only on which transition probabilities
are zero, the graph representation is an intuitive device for understanding these
properties. Figure 3.1 gives an example. We also give more examples below.

---

2. In the literature some researchers use the term "Markov chain" to refer to any Markov processes
   with a discrete-time parameter, regardless of the nature of the state space.

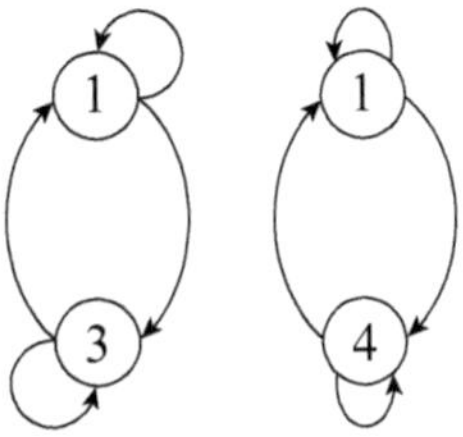

$$P = \begin{bmatrix} 1/3 & 0 & 2/3 & 0 \\ 0 & 1/4 & 0 & 3/4 \\ 1/2 & 0 & 1/2 & 0 \\ 0 & 1/4 & 0 & 3/4 \end{bmatrix}$$

Figure 3.1
Graphic representation of a Markov chain

Example 3.1.1 (Regime shifts) *Suppose that there are two states representing a boom and a recession, respectively. The transition matrix is given by*

$$P = \begin{bmatrix} p & 1-p \\ 1-q & q \end{bmatrix}, \quad p \in (0,1), \quad q \in (0,1).$$

The m-step transition matrix is given by

$$P^m = \frac{1}{2-p-q} \begin{bmatrix} 1-q & 1-p \\ 1-q & 1-p \end{bmatrix} + \frac{(p+q-1)^m}{2-p-q} \begin{bmatrix} 1-p & p-1 \\ q-1 & 1-p \end{bmatrix}.$$

Thus

$$\lim_{m \to \infty} P^m = \frac{1}{2-p-q} \begin{bmatrix} 1-q & 1-p \\ 1-q & 1-p \end{bmatrix}.$$

Example 3.1.2 (Cyclical moving subsets) *Suppose that the transition matrix is given by*

$$P = \begin{bmatrix} 0 & P_1 \\ P_2 & 0 \end{bmatrix},$$

where P_1 and P_2 are $k \times (n-k)$ and $(n-k) \times k$ transition matrices, respectively, each with strictly positive elements. Then

$$P^{2m} = \begin{bmatrix} (P_1 P_2)^m & 0 \\ 0 & (P_2 P_1)^m \end{bmatrix},$$

$$P^{2m+1} = \begin{bmatrix} 0 & (P_1 P_2)^m P_1 \\ (P_2 P_1)^m P_2 & 0 \end{bmatrix}.$$

Example 3.1.3 *Suppose that the transition matrix is given by*

$$P = \begin{bmatrix} 1-\alpha & \alpha/2 & \alpha/2 \\ 0 & 1/2 & 1/2 \\ 0 & 1/2 & 1/2 \end{bmatrix}, \quad \alpha \in (0,1).$$

Simple algebra gives

$$P^m = \begin{bmatrix} (1-\alpha)^m & \beta_m/2 & \beta_m/2 \\ 0 & 1/2 & 1/2 \\ 0 & 1/2 & 1/2 \end{bmatrix},$$

where $\beta_m = 1 - (1-\alpha)^m$. *Since* $\alpha \in (0,1)$, *it follows that*

$$\lim_{m \to \infty} P^m = \begin{bmatrix} 0 & 1/2 & 1/2 \\ 0 & 1/2 & 1/2 \\ 0 & 1/2 & 1/2 \end{bmatrix}.$$

Example 3.1.4 (Birth–death Markov chain) *Take a sequence of IID binary random variables* $\{b_t\}_{t\geq 1}$ *with* $\Pr(b_t = 1) = p$ *and* $\Pr(b_t = -1) = q = 1 - p$. *Let* $X_t = \max\{0, b_t + X_{t-1}\}$ *with* $X_0 = 0$. *The sequence* $\{X_t\}$ *is a special birth–death Markov chain. Its state space is* $\{0, 1, 2, ...\}$, *and its graphic representation is given in figure 3.2.*

Example 3.1.5 (Unrestricted one-dimensional random walk) *Consider a sequence of IID random variables* $\{w_t : t \geq 1\}$, *with* $\Pr(w_t = 1) = 0.5$ *and* $\Pr(w_t = -1) = 0.5$. *The unrestricted one-dimensional random walk* $\{X_t\}$ *is defined as* $X_t = X_{t-1} + w_t$, $X_0 = 0$. *Its state space is* $\{..., -2, -1, 0, 1, 2, ...\}$. *Its graphic representation is given in figure 3.3.*

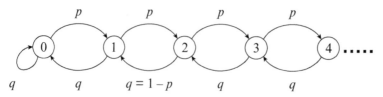

Figure 3.2
Graphic representation of the birth–death Markov chain

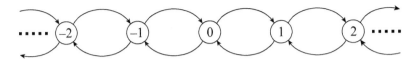

Figure 3.3
Graphic representation of the unrestricted one-dimensional random walk

Example 3.1.6 (Random walk with two barriers) *Suppose that there are four states* $\{1,2,3,4\}$ *with the transition matrix:*

$$P = \begin{bmatrix} 1 & 0 & 0 & 0 \\ q & 0 & p & 0 \\ 0 & q & 0 & p \\ 0 & 0 & 0 & 1 \end{bmatrix}.$$

*States 1 and 4 are **absorbing states** in the sense that once the chain enters one of the states, it stays there forever.*

In sections 3.1 and 3.2 we will focus on finite-state Markov chains. In section 3.3 we will briefly introduce countable-state Markov chains and highlight the key differences between these two cases.

3.1.1 Classification of States

This section, except where indicated otherwise, applies to Markov chains with both finite- and countable-state spaces. We begin with several definitions.

Definition 3.1.1 *A state j is **accessible** from state i (denoted $i \rightarrow j$) if $p_{ij}^{(m)} > 0$ for some $m \geq 1$. Two distinct states i and j **communicate** (denoted $i \leftrightarrow j$) if i is accessible from j and j is accessible from i. Let $i \leftrightarrow i$ regardless of whether $p_{ii}^{(m)} > 0$.*

The property of communicating is an equivalence relation because the following properties hold:

- $i \leftrightarrow i$ (reflexivity).
- $i \leftrightarrow j$ if and only if $j \leftrightarrow i$ (symmetry).
- $i \leftrightarrow k$ and $k \leftrightarrow j$ implies $i \leftrightarrow j$ (transitivity).

As a result the state space $\mathbb{X}$ can be completely divided into disjoint equivalence classes with respect to the equivalence relation $\leftrightarrow$. For the example of figure 3.1 there are two equivalent classes $\{1,3\}$ and $\{2,4\}$.

Definition 3.1.2   *A Markov chain is called* **irreducible** *if the state space consists of only one equivalence class of communication. It is called* **decomposable** *if there are at least two equivalence classes.*

By this definition, for an irreducible Markov chain with the transition matrix P, for any states i, j, there exists k such that $p_{ij}^{(k)} > 0$ (this k may depend on i, j). That is, all states communicate with each other. Sometimes this property is used to define irreducibility. If the matrix is decomposable, we can classify the equivalence classes according to whether the states in a class are recurrent or transient.

Definition 3.1.3   *For finite-state Markov chains a state i is called* **recurrent** *if whenever $i \to j$ for a state j, it must be $j \to i$. A state is called* **transient** *if it is not recurrent.*

According to this definition, a state i in a finite-state Markov chain is recurrent if there is no possibility of going to a state j from which there is no return. A state i is transient if there is some state j that is accessible from i but from which there is no possible return. For the example of figure 3.1, all states are recurrent. In examples 3.1.1 and 3.1.2, all states are recurrent. In example 3.1.3 state 1 is transient and states 2 and 3 are recurrent. examples 3.1.4 and 3.1.5 give two countable-state Markov chains. We will see in section 3.3 that the definition of recurrence for finite-state Markov chains is inadequate for the case with countable-state space. In section 3.3, we will propose a new definition.

Theorem 3.1.1   *(a) For finite-state Markov chains, either all states in an equivalence class are transient or all are recurrent. (b) The finite-state space can be partitioned into at least one recurrent classes and a set of transient states. (c) For an irreducible finite-state Markov chain, all states are recurrent.*

Proof

a. If there is no transient state in an equivalent class, then this class is recurrent. Suppose that there is a transient state i in a class such that $i \to j$ but $j \nrightarrow i$, and suppose that i and m are in the same class, meaning $i \leftrightarrow m$. Then $m \to i$ and $i \to j$, so $m \to j$. But $j \nrightarrow m$; otherwise, $j \to m \to i$, leading to a contradiction. Thus m is transient. Therefore all states in the class containing i are transient.

b. First, we show that there is at least one recurrent state so that there is at least one recurrent class. Suppose that state i_1 is transient. Then there is a state i_2 such that $i_1 \to i_2$ but $i_2 \nrightarrow i_1$. If i_2 is recurrent, then we are done. If i_2 is transient, then there is a state i_3 such that $i_2 \to i_3$ but $i_3 \nrightarrow i_2$ and $i_3 \nrightarrow i_1$. Continuing in this way, we obtain a directed graph that does not contain any cycle. Since the state space is finite, there is a last state j that does not have an outgoing arc. Such a node j must be recurrent because $p_{jj} = 1$ and $p_{jk} = 0$ for all $k \neq j$ by construction. Now all transient states form one class if there exists a transient state. The remaining states are recurrent and can be partitioned into disjoint classes of recurrent states using the equivalence relation $\leftrightarrow$.

c. By definition, an irreducible Markov chain has only one class. If this class is not recurrent, then there is there is a state i in this class and a state j outside this class such that $i \rightarrow j$ but not $j \nrightarrow i$. The state j belongs to another equivalence class, contradicting with the irreducibility of the Markov chain.   ∎

Remark 3.1.1 *Stokey, Lucas, and Prescott (1989) call a recurrent class an **ergodic set**. They define an ergodic set as a subset of states E if $\sum_{j \in E} p_{ij} = 1$ for each $i \in E$, and if no proper subset of E has this property. Exercise 1 asks readers to check that this definition is equivalent to our definition of a recurrent class for finite Markov chains.*

In terms of the graph of a Markov chain, a class is transient if there is some directed arc going from a node in the class to a node outside the class. Since an irreducible Markov chain has only one class, this class must be recurrent if the state space is finite. For the example of figure 3.1, $\{1, 3\}$ and $\{2, 4\}$ are two recurrent classes. In examples 3.1.1 and 3.1.2, all states are recurrent and the Markov chain is irreducible. The Markov chain in example 3.1.3 have two classes. One class consists of state 1 only and is transient. The other class consists of states 2 and 3 and is recurrent. For example 3.1.6, there are three classes $\{1\}, \{2, 3\}$, and $\{4\}$. The classes $\{1\}$ and $\{4\}$ are recurrent, but the class $\{2, 3\}$ is transient.

Next we classify states according to their periods.

Definition 3.1.4 *The **period** of a state, denoted $d(i)$, is the greatest common divisor of those values of m for which $p_{ii}^{(m)} > 0$. If the period is 1, the state is **aperiodic**, and if the period is at least 2, the state is **periodic**.*

By this definition, the state i is periodic with period $d(i)$ if a return to i is impossible except, in $d(i), 2d(i), 3d(i), ...$, steps, and $d(i) \geq 1$ is the greatest integer with this property. Clearly, this definition applies to recurrent states only. It also applies to both finite- and countable-state Markov chains. For the example of figure 3.1 and examples 3.1.1 and 3.1.4, all states are aperiodic. In example 3.1.3, the two recurrent states 2 and 3 are aperiodic. In examples 3.1.2 and 3.1.5, all states have period 2.

Theorem 3.1.2 *For any finite- or countable-state Markov chain, all states in the same class have the same period.*

Proof Let i and j be any distinct pair of states in a class. Then $i \leftrightarrow j$, and there is some r such that $p_{ij}^{(r)} > 0$ and some s such that $p_{ji}^{(s)} > 0$. Thus by the Chapman–Kolmogorov equation (3.1), $p_{ii}^{(r+s)} > 0$. By definition, $r + s$ must be divisible by $d(i)$. Let t be any integer such that $p_{jj}^{(t)} > 0$. By the Chapman–Kolmogorov equation (3.1), $p_{ii}^{(r+s+t)} > 0$. Thus $r + s + t$ must be divisible by $d(i)$, and thus t is divisible by $d(i)$. Since this is true for any t such that $p_{jj}^{(t)} > 0$, $d(j)$ is divisible by $d(i)$. By a symmetric argument, $d(i)$ is divisible by $d(j)$, so $d(i) = d(j)$.   ∎

We have classified each class of states for a finite-state Markov chain in terms of its period and in terms of whether it is recurrent or transient. In summary, we can reorder states so that a transition matrix can be written as follows:

$$
P = \begin{bmatrix}
A_1 & 0 & \cdots & 0 \\
0 & A_2 & \cdots & 0 \\
0 & 0 & \cdots & 0 \\
B_1 & B_2 & \cdots & A_k
\end{bmatrix},
$$

where $A_1, ..., A_{k-1}$ correspond to $k - 1$ classes of recurrent states. The last block corresponds to a set of transient states. Each submatrix A_i, $i = 1, ..., k - 1$, forms a transition matrix. The states corresponding to this matrix have the same period. We may further reorder states in a submatrix with period d so that it can be decomposed into d subclasses, as in example 3.1.2. In example 3.1.6, states $\{1\}$ and $\{4\}$ form two recurrent classes. States $\{2, 3\}$ form one transient class.

3.1.2   Stationary Distribution

Suppose that the initial distribution on the state space $\mathbb{X}$ is given by a row vector π_0. Then the distribution in period t is given by $\pi_t = \pi_0 P^t$. We are interested in long-run properties of Markov chains. That is, does π_t converge to a distribution? Does this convergence depend on the initial distribution π_0? We formally introduce the following definition to study these questions.

Definition 3.1.5   *An **invariant distribution** or **stationary distribution** for a Markov chain with transition matrix P is a distribution (row vector) π such that $\pi = \pi P$.*

The following theorem gives a sufficient condition for the existence and uniqueness of a stationary distribution.

Theorem 3.1.3   *For a finite-state Markov chain with the transition matrix P, if $p_{ij}^{(k)} > 0$ for some $k > 0$ and for all i, j, then the Markov chain has a unique stationary distribution π such that $\lim_{t \to \infty} p_{ij}^{(t)} = \pi_j > 0$ for all j and all i.*

Proof Fix any column j of P^t for all $t \geq 1$. Let $m_t = \min_i p_{ij}^{(t)}$ and $M_t = \max_i p_{ij}^{(t)}$. We will prove that:

1. the sequence $\{m_t\}$ is increasing;
2. the sequence $\{M_t\}$ is decreasing; and
3. $\Delta_t = M_t - m_t$ converges to zero exponentially fast.

To prove the first property, we apply the Chapman–Kolmogorov equation

$$m_{t+1} = \min_i \sum_v p_{iv} p_{vj}^{(t)} \geq \min_i \sum_v p_{iv} m_t = m_t.$$

The second property follows from a similar argument. To prove the third property, we temporarily suppose that all $p_{ij} > 0$. Let $\delta = \min_{i,j} p_{ij} > 0$. Since there are at least two states, it follows from $\sum_j p_{ij} \geq 2\delta$ that $\delta \leq 1/2$. Let l be the row such that $M_t = p_{lj}^{(t)}$. Then

$$m_{t+1} = \min_i p_{ij}^{(t+1)} = \min_i \sum_k p_{ik} p_{kj}^{(t)}$$

$$= \min_i p_{il} M_t + \sum_{k \neq l} p_{ik} p_{kj}^{(t)}$$

$$\geq \min_i p_{il} M_t + \sum_{k \neq l} p_{ik} m_t$$

$$= \min_i p_{il} M_t + (1 - p_{il}) m_t$$

$$\geq \delta M_t + (1 - \delta) m_t.$$

Similarly

$$M_{t+1} \leq \delta m_t + (1 - \delta) M_t.$$

Taking these two inequalities together yields

$$\Delta_{t+1} = M_{t+1} - m_{t+1}$$
$$\leq (1 - 2\delta)(M_t - m_t) = (1 - 2\delta) \Delta_t$$
$$\leq (1 - 2\delta)^{t+1}.$$

Letting $t \to \infty$, we find that m_t and M_t converge to a common limit, denoted by π_j. Since m_t is increasing, $\pi_j = \lim_t m_t \geq m_1 > 0$. For the case where $p_{ij}^{(k)} > 0$ for some $k > 0$, we consider m_{kt} and M_{kt}. Applying a similar argument, we can show that $M_{kt} - m_{kt} \leq (1 - 2\delta)^t$. Letting $t \to \infty$ gives the desired result as well. ∎

Since example 3.1.1 satisfies the assumption of the theorem, there exists a unique stationary distribution and each row of the limiting transition matrix gives the stationary distribution. Example 3.1.2 violates the assumption of the theorem. More concretely, let

$$P_1 = P_2 = \begin{bmatrix} 3/4 & 1/4 \\ 1/4 & 3/4 \end{bmatrix}.$$

Then as $m \to \infty$,

$$P^{2m} \to \begin{bmatrix} 1/2 & 1/2 & 0 & 0 \\ 1/2 & 1/2 & 0 & 0 \\ 0 & 0 & 1/2 & 1/2 \\ 0 & 0 & 1/2 & 1/2 \end{bmatrix} \quad \text{and}$$

$$P^{2m+1} \to \begin{bmatrix} 0 & 0 & 1/2 & 1/2 \\ 0 & 0 & 1/2 & 1/2 \\ 1/2 & 1/2 & 0 & 0 \\ 1/2 & 1/2 & 0 & 0 \end{bmatrix}.$$

Since we can check that $(1/4, 1/4, 1/4, 1/4)$ is the unique invariant distribution, the preceding theorem does not apply to this example.

When the dimension of the transition matrix is large, the condition in the theorem may be hard to check. The following theorem gives a simple equivalent condition.

Theorem 3.1.4 *A finite-state Markov chain is irreducible and aperiodic if and only if there exists $k_0 > 0$ such that $p_{ij}^{(k)} > 0$ for all i, j and all $k \geq k_0$.*

Proof The "if" part is trivial. We consider the "only if" part. Since the Markov chain is irreducible, there exists some $m \geq 1$ such that $p_{jj}^{(m)} > 0$ for some j. Define the set

$$S = \left\{ k : p_{jj}^{(k)} > 0, k \geq 1 \right\}.$$

By the Chapman–Kolmogorov equation, $p_{jj}^{(k+l)} \geq p_{jj}^{(k)} p_{jj}^{(l)}$. Thus, if $k, l \in S$, then $k + l \in S$. By a lemma in number theory, if a set of positive integers is closed under addition and has greatest common divisor 1, then it contains all integers exceeding some k_j (see appendix A21 of Billingsley 1995). We can apply this lemma because the Markov chain is aperiodic. Given i and j, there exists r_{ij} such that $p_{ij}^{(r_{ij})} > 0$ since the Markov chain is irreducible. For all $k > k_{ij} \equiv k_j + r_{ij}$, $p_{ij}^{(k)} \geq p_{ij}^{(r_{ij})} p_{jj}^{(k-r_{ij})} > 0$. Since the state space is finite, we can choose the largest among all k_{ij}, simply denoted k_0.   ∎

By definition, for an irreducible Markov chain there exists $k > 0$ such that $p_{ij}^{(k)} > 0$ for any i, j. However, this k may take different values for different i or j. The force of the theorem is that we can choose a k_0 common for all i, j such that $p_{ij}^{(k)} > 0$ for all $k > k_0$. The Markov chain in example 3.1.2 has period 2, which violates the assumption of theorem. As illustrated above, theorem 3.1.4 does not apply to this example.

For the general non-irreducible case, we can partition the state space into many classes of recurrent states and one class of transient states. Then each recurrent class is associated with an invariant distribution whose support is that recurrent class. All invariant distributions are linear combinations of those invariant distributions associated with recurrent classes. Thus, if there are at least two recurrent classes, then there are infinitely many invariant distributions. See theorem 11.1 in Stokey, Lucas, and Prescott (1989) for a more formal proof of this result.

The following result provides a sharper characterization and also gives the converse of theorem 3.1.3:

Theorem 3.1.5 *(a) A finite Markov chain has a limiting stationary distribution if and only if the Markov chain has a unique recurrent class and is aperiodic. (b) A finite Markov chain has a unique stationary distribution if and only if the Markov chain has a unique recurrent class.*

The proof follows from the previous two theorems. We omit it here. Theorems 11.2 and 11.4 in Stokey, Lucas, and Prescott (1989) are related to our theorem 3.1.5.

3.1.3 Countable-State Markov Chains

Countable-state Markov chains exhibit some types of behavior not possible for finite-state Markov chains. We use examples 3.1.4 and 3.1.5 to illustrate the new issues posed by countable-state spaces. For example 3.1.5 all states communicate with all other states and are thus in the same class. The chain is irreducible, and all states have period 2. The probability of each state approaches zero as time goes to infinity. These probabilities cannot form a steady-state distribution.

Next consider example 3.1.4. This chain is irreducible and aperiodic. For $p > 0.5$, transitions to the right occur with higher frequency than transitions to the left. Thus, reasoning heuristically, we expect that the state X_t at time t to drift to the right with increasing t. Given $X_0 = 0$, the probability $p_{0j}^{(l)}$ of being in state j at time l tends to zero for any fixed j with increasing l. Thus, a steady state cannot exist.

It is interesting to compare the markov chain in example 3.1.4 with the truncated finite-state Markov chain. In particular, suppose that there are k states $\{0, 1, ..., k-1\}$. Transition probabilities are given in figure 3.2. In addition, $p_{k-1,k-1} = p$. In this case exercise 3 asks readers to show that the stationary distribution $\pi = (\pi_0, \pi_1, ..., \pi_{k-1})$ is given by $\pi_i = (1 - \rho) \rho^i / (1 - \rho^k)$, where $\rho = p/q$ and $\rho \neq 1$. For $\rho = 1$, $\pi_i = 1/k$.

Now consider the limiting behavior as $k \to \infty$. On the one hand, for $\rho < 1$ ($p < 0.5$), $\pi_i \to (1 - \rho) \rho^i$ for all i, which we later interpret as the stationary distribution for the untruncated chain. On the other hand, for $\rho > 1$ ($p > 0.5$), $\pi_i \to 0$ for all i. So this limit cannot be a stationary distribution for the untruncated chain.

These two examples motivate us to redefine recurrence. To do so, we denote by τ_i the **first return time** of the Markov chain $\{X_t\}_{t=0}^{\infty}$ to the state i,

$$\tau_i = \min \{k \geq 1 : X_k = i\}.$$

Also we denote by $\Pr$ the probability distribution of $\{X_t\}$.

Definition 3.1.6   *The state i is called:*

- *positive recurrent if* $\Pr(\tau_i < \infty | X_0 = i) = 1$ *and* $E[\tau_i | X_0 = i] < \infty$;
- *null recurrent if* $\Pr(\tau_i < \infty | X_0 = i) = 1$ *and* $E[\tau_i | X_0 = i] = \infty$; *and*
- *transient if* $\Pr(\tau_i < \infty | X_0 = i) < 1$.

According to this definition, state i is positive (null) recurrent if, starting at i, the Markov chain eventually returns to i with certainty and also the mean return time is finite (infinite). State i is transient if there is a positive probability that the Markov chain started at state i eventually leaves this state. Given this new definition of recurrence, Parts a and b of theorem 3.1.1 are still true, but the proof must be modified (see lemma 1 in Shiryaev 1996, p. 575). In addition a recurrent class for countable state spaces is further classified into either positive recurrent or null recurrent. Part c is no longer true. For an irreducible countable-state Markov chain, all states can be either transient or recurrent (see theorem 8.3 in Billingsley 1995). For example 3.1.4, all states are transient if $p > 0.5$. If $p = 0.5$, it is possible to show that all states are null recurrent. The notion of period in definition 3.1.5 and theorem 3.1.2 still apply to countable-state Markov chains. Theorem 3.1.4 also applies, but the proof must be modified (see lemma 2 in Billingsley 1995, sec. 8). Theorem 3.1.3 does not apply and is modified below (see theorem 8.8 in Billingsley 1995):

Theorem 3.1.6   *For an irreducible and aperiodic Markov chain, there are three possibilities:*

a. *The chain is transient. For all i and j, $\lim_{k \to \infty} p_{ij}^{(k)} = 0$ and $\sum_k p_{ij}^{(k)} < \infty$.*

b. *The chain is null recurrent, but there exists no stationary distribution. For all i, j, $\lim_{k \to \infty} p_{ij}^{(k)} = 0$, but so slowly that $\sum_k p_{ij}^{(k)} = \infty$ and $E[\tau_j | X_0 = j] = \infty$.*

c. *The chain is positive recurrent, and there exists a unique stationary distribution π such that $\lim_{k \to \infty} p_{ij}^{(k)} = \pi_j = 1/E[\tau_j | X_0 = j] > 0$ for all i, j.*

Part c describes the intuitive meaning that the stationary probability of a state is equal to the long-run frequency of staying in this state. For a finite-state space, cases a and b cannot happen because $\sum_j p_{ij}^{(k)} = 1$. For a countable-state Markov chain, theorem 3.1.5 still holds provided that the recurrent class is replaced with the positive recurrent class (See Shiryaev 1996, thm. 4, p. 586).

3.2 General Markov Processes

General Markov processes can be conveniently characterized by transition functions, analogous to transition matrices for finite-state Markov chains. We fix measurable spaces $(\mathbb{X}, \mathcal{X})$ and $(\mathbb{Y}, \mathcal{Y})$.

Definition 3.2.1 *A function $P : \mathbb{X} \times \mathcal{Y} \to [0,1]$ is called a **stochastic kernel** if:*

a. for any $x \in \mathbb{X}$, $P(x, \cdot)$ is a probability measure on $(\mathbb{Y}, \mathcal{Y})$; and

b. for any $A \in \mathcal{Y}$, $P(\cdot, A)$ is an $\mathcal{X}$-measurable function.

*If the two spaces $(\mathbb{X}, \mathcal{X})$ and $(\mathbb{Y}, \mathcal{Y})$ are identical, then P is called a **transition function**.*

Given any time-homogeneous Markov process $\{X_t\}$ on a probability space $(\Omega, \mathcal{F}, \mathrm{Pr})$ with the state space $\mathbb{X}$, we can construct a transition function $P : \mathbb{X} \times \mathcal{X} \to [0,1]$ as follows:

$$P(x, A) = \mathrm{Pr}(X_{t+1} \in A | X_t = x), \quad (x, A) \in (\mathbb{X}, \mathcal{X}).$$

The interpretation is that $P(x, A)$ is the probability that the next period's state lies in the set A, given that the current state is x.

Next we consider composition of stochastic kernels. The following result is needed. Its proof is available in Stokey, Lucas, and Prescott (1989, p. 228).

Theorem 3.2.1 *Let $(\mathbb{W}, \mathcal{W})$, $(\mathbb{X}, \mathcal{X})$, and $(\mathbb{Y}, \mathcal{Y})$ be measurable spaces, and let P_1 and P_2 be stochastic kernels on $(\mathbb{W}, \mathcal{X})$ and $(\mathbb{X}, \mathcal{Y})$, respectively. Then there exists a unique stochastic kernel P_3 on $(\mathbb{W}, \mathcal{X} \times \mathcal{Y})$ such that*

$$P_3(w, A \times B) = \int_A P_2(x, B) P_1(w, dx)$$

for all $w \in \mathbb{W}$ and all $A \in \mathcal{X}, B \in \mathcal{Y}$

The kernel P_3 is often called the **direct product** of P_1 and P_2 and denoted $P_1 \otimes P_2$. The direct product gives the probability of landing in $A \times B$ when starting at the state w. It is equal to the probability of first going to a point $x \in A$ and then landing in B, integrated over all points in A. Given a transition function P, one can construct a corresponding time-homogeneous Markov process. We make use of theorem 3.2.1 and the following important result in probability theory

Theorem 3.2.2 (**Kolmogorov Extension Theorem**) *Suppose that $\mathbb{X}$ is a complete separable metric space.[3] Let $\{\mu_t\}$ be a sequence of probability measures on $\mathcal{X}^t$ such that*

$$\mu_t (A_1 \times \dots \times A_t) = \mu_{t+1} (A_1 \times \dots \times A_t \times \mathcal{X}) \tag{3.2}$$

for all t and all $A_i \in \mathcal{X}$. Then there exists a unique probability measure μ on $\mathcal{X}^\infty$ such that $\mu_t (A) = \mu (A \times \mathcal{X}^\infty)$ for each $A \in \mathcal{X}^t$.

Equation (3.2) is often called the **Kolmogorov consistency condition**. This condition and the theorem can be stated in terms of finite dimensional distributions. We refer to Shiryaev (1996, pp. 246–247) for a proof.

Theorem 3.2.3 *Let μ_0 be a probability measure on $\mathcal{X}$ and P be a transition function on $(\mathbb{X}, \mathcal{X})$. Suppose that $\mathbb{X}$ is a complete separable metric space. Then there exists a unique probability measure $\Pr$ on $(\mathbb{X}^\infty, \mathcal{X}^\infty)$ and a Markov process $\{X_t\}_{t=0}^\infty$ on $(\mathbb{X}^\infty, \mathcal{X}^\infty, \Pr)$ with the state space $\mathbb{X}$ such that (a) $\Pr (X_{t+1} \in A | X_t = x) = P (x, A)$ for all $(x, A) \in (\mathbb{X}, \mathcal{X})$ and (b) the distribution of X_0 is μ_0.*

Proof   Define a sequence of $\{\mu_t\}_{t=0}^\infty$ as follows:

$$\mu_t (A_0 \times A_1 \times \dots \times A_t)$$

$$= \int_{A_0} \int_{A_1} \dots \int_{A_{t-1}} P (x_{t-1}, A_t) P (x_{t-2}, dx_{t-1}) \dots P (x_0, dx_1) \mu_0 (dx_0)$$

for all $t \geq 0$ and all $A_i \in \mathcal{X}$ for all $i = 0, 1, \dots, t$. Repeatedly applying theorem 3.2.1, we can show that μ_t is a probability measure on $\mathcal{X}^{t+1}$. We can check that $\{\mu_t\}$ satisfies (3.2). By the Kolmogorov extension theorem, there exists a unique probability measure $\Pr$ on $(\mathbb{X}^\infty, \mathcal{X}^\infty)$. Define the sequence $\{X_t\}_{t=0}^\infty$ as

$$X_t (x_0, x_1, \dots, x_t, \dots) = x_t \tag{3.3}$$

for any $\{x_t\}_{t=0}^\infty \in \mathbb{X}^\infty$. Then we can verify that $\{X_t\}$ is the desired Markov process.   ∎

Remark 3.2.1   *The constructed probability space $(\mathbb{X}^\infty, \mathcal{X}^\infty, \Pr)$ is called **canonical**, and the construction given by (3.3) is called the **coordinate method** of constructing a stochastic process. This method is quite general and applies to continuous time (see Shiryaev 1996).*

An extension of the preceding theorem is the following:

Theorem 3.2.4 (**Tulcea theorem** on extending a measure and the existence of a stochastic process) *Let $(\Omega_n, \mathcal{F}_n), n = 0, 1, 2, \dots$, be any measurable spaces, and*

---

3. See appendix B for the definition of complete separable space.

let $\Omega = \Pi_{n=0}^{\infty}\Omega_n$ *and* $\mathcal{F} = \otimes_{n=0}^{\infty}\mathcal{F}_n$ *be the product measurable space. Suppose that a probability measure* Q_0 *is given on* $(\Omega_0, \mathcal{F}_0)$ *and that a sequence of stochastic kernels* $Q_n : (\Omega_0 \times \Omega_1 \times ... \times \Omega_n) \times \mathcal{F}_{n+1} \to [0,1], n \geq 1,$ *is given. Let*

$$P_n (A_0 \times A_1 \times ... \times A_n) = \int_{A_0} Q_0 (d\omega_0) \int_{A_1} Q_1 (\omega_0; d\omega_1)$$

$$... \int_{A_n} Q_n (\omega_0, \omega_1, ..., \omega_{n-1}; d\omega_n),$$

for all $A_i \in \mathcal{F}_i$, $n \geq 1$. *Then there exists a unique probability measure* $\Pr$ *on* $(\Omega, \mathcal{F})$ *such that*

$$\Pr (\omega : \omega_0 \in A_0, ..., \omega_n \in A_n) = P_n (A_0 \times A_1 \times ... \times A_n)$$

and there is a stochastic process $X = (X_0 (\omega), X_1 (\omega), ...)$ *such that*

$$\Pr (\omega : X_0 (\omega) \in A_0, ..., X_n (\omega) \in A_n) = P_n (A_0 \times A_1 \times ... \times A_n),$$

where A_i *are Borel sets for some measurable spaces* $(\mathbb{X}_i, \mathcal{X}_i)$.

Proof   See the proof of theorem 2 in Shiryaev (1996, pp. 249–51).   ∎

The following result is fundamental to the description of Markov processes.

Theorem 3.2.5   *Let* $\{X_t\}$ *be a time-homogeneous Markov process with the transition function* $P : \mathbb{X} \times \mathcal{X} \to [0,1]$. *Define n-step transitions recursively as follows:*

$$P^1 = P, \ P^n (a, A) = \int_{\mathbb{X}} P (x, A) P^{n-1} (a, dx), \tag{3.4}$$

where $(a, A) \in (\mathbb{X}, \mathcal{X})$. *Then* P^n *is a transition function for each* $n \geq 2$.

The interpretation is that $P^n (a, A)$ is the probability of going from the point a to the set A in exactly n periods. Equation (3.4) is called a Chapman–Kolmogorov equation, analogous to (3.1). Exercise 2 asks readers to prove this theorem and also the following result:

$$P^{m+n} (a, A) = \int_{\mathbb{X}} P^m (x, A) P^n (a, dx) \quad \text{for each } m, n \geq 1. \tag{3.5}$$

Next we introduce two important operators associated with a Markov process. Let $B (\mathbb{X}, \mathcal{X})$ denote the set of all bounded and $\mathcal{X}$-measurable functions on $\mathbb{X}$. Let $\mathcal{P} (\mathbb{X}, \mathcal{X})$ denote the set of all probability measures on $(\mathbb{X}, \mathcal{X})$

Definition 3.2.2   *The **Markov operator** T associated with the transition function* $P : \mathbb{X} \times \mathcal{X} \to [0,1]$ *is a map on* $B (\mathbb{X}, \mathcal{X})$ *such that*

$$Tf (x) = \int f (y) P (x, dy) \quad \text{for any } f \in B (\mathbb{X}, \mathcal{X}).$$

*The **adjoint operator** T^* of T is a map on $\mathcal{P}(\mathbb{X}, \mathcal{X})$ such that*

$$T^*\lambda(A) = \int P(x, A)\lambda(dx) \quad \text{for any } \lambda \in \mathcal{P}(\mathbb{X}, \mathcal{X}).$$

Exercise 4 asks readers to show that T is a self-map on $B(\mathbb{X}, \mathcal{X})$ and T^* is a self-map on $\mathcal{P}(\mathbb{X}, \mathcal{X})$. An intuitive property of T and T^* is that

$$\int (Tf)(x)\lambda(dx) = \int f(y)(T^*\lambda)(dy) = \int\int f(y)P(x, dy)\lambda(dx)$$

for any $f \in B(\mathbb{X}, \mathcal{X})$ and any $\lambda \in \mathcal{P}(\mathbb{X}, \mathcal{X})$. This equation gives the expected value of f next period, if λ is the probability measure over the current state and the conditional probability is $P(x, \cdot)$.

Let T^n and T^{*n} be the operators corresponding to the transitions P^n. It is straightforward to verify that

$$T^{(n+m)}f = (T^n)(T^m f), \quad f \in B(\mathbb{X}, \mathcal{X}),$$
$$T^{*(n+m)}\lambda = (T^{*n})(T^{*m}\lambda), \quad \lambda \in \mathcal{P}(\mathbb{X}, \mathcal{X}).$$

It follows that given any initial probability measure λ_0 on $(\mathbb{X}, \mathcal{X})$, we can define a sequence of probability measures $\{\lambda_n\}$ on $(\mathbb{X}, \mathcal{X})$ by

$$\lambda_n = T^*\lambda_{n-1} = T^{*n}\lambda_0.$$

The interpretation is that given the initial distribution λ_0, λ_n is the probability measure over the state in period n. As in the case of Markov chains, we define a fixed point π of T^* as an **invariant distribution** or **stationary distribution**. It satisfies the equation

$$\pi(A) = \int P(x, A)\pi(dx), \quad \text{all } A \in \mathcal{X}.$$

We will use the terms of invariant distribution and stationary distribution interchangeably below.

3.3   Convergence

We are interested in the existence and uniqueness of an invariant distribution π. Moreover, we are interested in the long-run stability of the Markov process, that is, whether or not $T^{*n}\lambda_0$ converges to π for any initial distribution λ_0. Unlike the finite-state case, the mode of convergence of a sequence of probability measures $\{\lambda_n\}$ is delicate. We need to introduce some metric to measure the distance between probability measures. We will study two metrics that induce two notions of convergence—strong and weak. The former implies the latter. Since the theory of strong convergence for Markov processes is developed in close analogy to the theory of Markov chains, we study it first.

3.3.1 Strong Convergence

We define the total variation distance on a set of probability measures $\mathcal{P}(\mathbb{X}, \mathcal{X})$ by

$$d_{TV}(\lambda_1, \lambda_2) = \sup_{A \in \mathcal{X}} |\lambda_1(A) - \lambda_2(A)|, \quad \lambda_1, \lambda_2 \in \mathcal{P}(\mathbb{X}, \mathcal{X}). \tag{3.6}$$

Intuitively, this is the largest possible difference between the probabilities that the two probability measures can assign to the same event. An important fact is that the space $\mathcal{P}(\mathbb{X}, \mathcal{X})$ endowed with the total variation distance is a complete metric space (see Stokey, Lucas, and Prescott 1989, lem. 11.8). Exercise 5 asks readers to show that the total variation distance in (3.6) can be written in terms of Radon–Nikodym derivatives:

$$\begin{aligned} d_{TV}(\lambda_1, \lambda_2) &= \frac{1}{2} \int \left| \frac{d\lambda_1}{d\nu} - \frac{d\lambda_2}{d\nu} \right| d\nu \\ &= 1 - \int \min\left(\frac{d\lambda_1}{d\nu}, \frac{d\lambda_2}{d\nu} \right) d\nu \\ &\equiv 1 - \lambda_1 \wedge \lambda_2, \end{aligned} \tag{3.7}$$

where $\nu = \lambda_1 + \lambda_2$ so that both λ_1 and λ_2 are absolutely continuous with respect to ν and $d\lambda_1/d\nu$ and $d\lambda_2/d\nu$ denote the Radon–Nikodym derivatives. In the second equality, we have used the fact that $|x - y| = x + y - 2\min(x, y)$.

Definition 3.3.1 *The sequence of probability measures $\{\lambda_n\}$ in $\mathcal{P}(\mathbb{X}, \mathcal{X})$ **converges strongly** to λ if $\lim_{n \to \infty} d_{TV}(\lambda_n, \lambda) = 0$.*

Remark 3.3.1 *There are several equivalent ways of defining strong convergence. Stokey, Lucas, and Prescott (1989) provide a good discussion on these definitions. Also see exercise 5 and appendix D.*

Theorem 3.3.1 below provides a sharp characterization of the stability of Markov processes in terms of strong convergence. This theorem needs the following condition, which appears in Onicescu (1969) and is discussed by Stokey, Lucas, and Prescott (1989).[4]

Condition M *There exists $\varepsilon > 0$ and an integer $N \geq 1$ such that for any $A \in \mathcal{X}$, either $P^N(x, A) \geq \varepsilon$ all $x \in \mathbb{X}$, or $P^N(x, A^c) \geq \varepsilon$, all $x \in \mathbb{X}$.*

---

4. Stokey, Lucas, and Prescott (1989) also discuss another condition due to Doeblin and its implications for the existence of invariant measures.

Theorem 3.3.1   *Let $\mathcal{P}(\mathbb{X}, \mathcal{X})$ be the space of probability measures on the measurable space $(\mathbb{X}, \mathcal{X})$ with the total variation distance, let P be a transition function on $(\mathbb{X}, \mathcal{X})$, and let T^* be the adjoint operator associated with P. If P satisfies Condition M for $N \geq 1$ and $\varepsilon > 0$, then there exists a unique probability measure π in $\mathcal{P}(\mathbb{X}, \mathcal{X})$ such that*

$$d_{TV}(T^{*Nk}\lambda_0, \pi) \leq (1 - \varepsilon)^k d_{TV}(\lambda_0, \pi) \tag{3.8}$$

for all $\lambda_0 \in \mathcal{P}(\mathbb{X}, \mathcal{X})$, $k = 1, 2, \dots$. Conversely, if (3.8) holds, then condition M is satisfied for some N and $\varepsilon > 0$.

Proof   We adapt the proof of theorem 11.12 in Stokey, Lucas, and Prescott (1989). Suppose that Condition M holds. We first show that T^{*N} is a contraction of modulus $(1 - \varepsilon)$ on the space $\mathcal{P}(\mathbb{X}, \mathcal{X})$ with the total variation distance. Define two measure $\bar{\lambda}_i$, $i = 1, 2$, as

$$\lambda_i = \lambda_1 \wedge \lambda_2 + d_{TV}(\lambda_1, \lambda_2)\,\bar{\lambda}_i.$$

By (3.7), we can verify that $\bar{\lambda}_i$ is a probability measure on $\mathcal{P}(\mathbb{X}, \mathcal{X})$. For any sets $A, A^c \in \mathcal{X}$, and without loss of generality, suppose that $P^N(x, A) \geq \varepsilon$ for all $x \in X$. Then

$$d_{TV}(T^{*N}\lambda_1, T^{*N}\lambda_2)$$

$$= d_{TV}(\lambda_1, \lambda_2) \sup_{A \in \mathcal{X}} \left| \int P^N(x, A)\,\bar{\lambda}_1(dx) - \int P^N(x, A)\,\bar{\lambda}_2(dx) \right|$$

$$\leq (1 - \varepsilon) d_{TV}(\lambda_1, \lambda_2).$$

Since $\mathcal{P}(\mathbb{X}, \mathcal{X})$ is a complete metric space with the total variation distance, the desired result follows from the **Contraction Mapping Theorem** (appendix B).

Conversely, suppose that (3.8) holds. Let $\delta_{\{x\}}$ denote the Dirac measure that puts a unit mass on $\{x\}$. Choosing any $x \in \mathbb{X}$, we show that

$$\left| P^{Nk}(x, A) - \pi(A) \right| \leq d_{TV}(P^{Nk}(x, \cdot), \pi(\cdot))$$

$$= d_{TV}(T^{*Nk}\delta_{\{x\}}, \pi)$$

$$\leq (1 - \varepsilon)^k d_{TV}(\delta_{\{x\}}, \pi)$$

$$\leq (1 - \varepsilon)^k.$$

Choose K sufficient large such that $(1 - \varepsilon)^K \leq 1/4$. Let $A, A^c \in \mathcal{X}$ be given, and without loss of generality, suppose that $\pi(A) \geq 1/2$. Then $\left| P^{Nk}(x, A) - \pi(A) \right| \leq 1/4$ implies that $P^{Nk}(x, A) \geq 1/4$. Condition M holds for $N_0 = NK$ and $\varepsilon_0 = 1/4$.   ∎

Meyn and Tweedie (1993) provide another condition for the stability of Markov processes.

Proof See the proof of theorem 12.12 in Stokey, Lucas, and Prescott (1989). ∎

In applications we are often interested in how the equilibrium system behaves when certain model parameters change. These parameters might affect exogenous shocks, preferences or technology. The result below studies how the long-run behavior changes when some parameters alter a transition function.

Let the state space $\mathbb{X} \subset \mathbb{R}^l$, with its Borel sets $\mathcal{X}$, and let the exogenous parameters be described by a vector $\theta \in \Theta \subset \mathbb{R}^m$. For each $\theta \in \Theta$, let P_θ be a transition function on $(\mathbb{X}, \mathcal{X})$, and let T_θ and T_θ^* be the operators associated with P_θ.

Theorem 3.3.6 *Assume that:*

a. $\mathbb{X}$ *is compact;*

b. *if* $\{(x_n, \theta_n)\}$ *is a sequence in* $\mathbb{X} \times \Theta$ *converging to* (x_0, θ_0), *then the sequence* $\{P_{\theta_n}(x_n, \cdot)\}$ *in* $\mathcal{P}(\mathbb{X}, \mathcal{X})$ *converges weakly to* $P_{\theta_0}(x_0, \cdot)$; *and*

c. *for each* $\theta \in \Theta$, T_θ^* *has a unique fixed point* $\mu_\theta \in \mathcal{P}(\mathbb{X}, \mathcal{X})$.

If $\{\theta_n\}$ *is a sequence in* Θ *converging to* θ_0, *then the sequence* $\{\mu_{\theta_n}\}$ *converges weakly to* μ_{θ_0}.

Proof See the proof of theorem 12.13 in Stokey, Lucas, and Prescott (1989). ∎

3.4 Exercises

1. Prove the statement in remark 3.1.1.

2. Prove theorem 3.2.5 and equation (3.5).

3. Derive the stationary distribution for the truncated finite-state birth–death Markov chain discussed in section 3.1.3.

4. Prove that T is a self-map on $B(\mathbb{X}, \mathcal{X})$ and T^* is a self-map on $\mathcal{P}(\mathbb{X}, \mathcal{X})$. Additionally, T and T^* satisfy

$$\int (Tf)(x) \, \lambda(dx) = \int f(y) \, (T^*\lambda)(dy) = \int \int f(y) \, P(x, dy) \, \lambda(dx).$$

5. Consider two measures $\lambda_1, \lambda_2 \in \mathcal{P}(\mathbb{X}, \mathcal{X})$. Show the following:
   a. For any $a < b$,

$$d_{TV}(\lambda_1, \lambda_2) = \frac{1}{b-a} \sup_{f: \mathbb{X} \to [a,b]} \left| \int f d\lambda_1 - \int f d\lambda_2 \right|.$$

b. If λ_1 and λ_2 have densities g and h, respectively, with respect to some measure ρ, then

$$d_{TV}(\lambda_1, \lambda_2) = 1 - \int \min(g, h)\, d\rho.$$

6. A transition matrix P is called **doubly stochastic** if

$$\sum_j p_{ij} = 1 \quad \text{for all } i, \text{ and}$$

$$\sum_i p_{ij} = 1 \quad \text{for all } j.$$

If a doubly stochastic chain has N states and is irreducible and aperiodic, compute its stationary distribution.

identical. We apply the Birkhoff theorem to $\{\tilde{X}_t\}$ using the function f defined earlier,

$$\lim_{N \to \infty} \frac{1}{N} \sum_{k=0}^{N-1} f\left(\theta^k \tilde{\omega}\right) = \tilde{E}\left[f\left(\tilde{\omega}\right) | \mathcal{I}\right], \quad \widetilde{\Pr}\text{-a.s.,} \tag{4.3}$$

where $\mathcal{I}$ is the σ-algebra of transformation invariant sets and $\tilde{E}$ is the expectation operator with respect to $\widetilde{\Pr}$. By definition, the σ-algebra of transformation-invariant sets is the same as the class of shift invariant sets. By construction, (4.3) is equivalent to (4.1). We can similarly prove (4.2). $\blacksquare$

Karlin and Taylor (1975) provide several equivalent formulations of ergodicity. We state their results below, which can be proved by applying the Birkhoff theorem.

Theorem 4.2.2 *Let* $\{X_t\} = (X_0, X_1, \dots)$ *be a real-valued stationary process on* $(\Omega, \mathcal{F}, \Pr)$. *The following conditions are equivalent:*

a. $\{X_t\}$ *is ergodic.*

b. *For every shift invariant set* A,

$$\Pr\{(X_0, X_1, \dots) \in A\} = 0 \quad or \quad 1.$$

c. *For every set* $A \in \mathcal{B}(\mathbb{R}^\infty)$,

$$\lim_{n \to \infty} \frac{1}{n} \sum_{j=1}^{n} \mathbf{1}_{\left\{(X_j, X_{j+1}, \dots) \in A\right\}} = \Pr\{(X_0, X_1, \dots) \in A\}, \quad \Pr\text{-a.s.}$$

d. *For every* $k = 1, 2, \dots$ *and every set* $A \in \mathcal{B}(\mathbb{R}^{k+1})$,

$$\lim_{n \to \infty} \frac{1}{n} \sum_{j=1}^{n} \mathbf{1}_{\left\{(X_j, X_{j+1}, \dots, X_{j+k}) \in A\right\}} = \Pr\{(X_0, X_1, \dots, X_k) \in A\}, \quad \Pr\text{-a.s.}$$

e. *For every* k *and every Borel measurable integrable function* ϕ,

$$\lim_{n \to \infty} \frac{1}{n} \sum_{j=1}^{n} \phi\left(X_j, X_{j+1}, \dots, X_{j+k}\right) = E\left[\phi\left(X_0, X_1, \dots, X_k\right)\right], \quad \Pr\text{-a.s.}$$

f. *For every Borel measurable function* $\phi : \mathbb{R}^\infty \to \mathbb{R}$ *with* $E\left[\|\phi\left(X_0, X_1, \dots\right)\|\right] < \infty$,

$$\lim_{n \to \infty} \frac{1}{n} \sum_{k=1}^{n} \phi\left(X_k, X_{k+1}, \dots\right) = E\left[\phi\left(X_0, X_1, \dots\right)\right], \quad \Pr\text{-a.s.}$$

Because ergodicity leads to laws of large numbers, it must be related to some sense of independence. The following result formalizes this intuition.

Definition 4.2.4 *A stationary process $\{X_t\}$ is **mixing** if for all sets $A, B \in B(\mathbb{R}^\infty)$,*

$$\lim_{n \to \infty} \Pr\{(X_1, X_2, ...) \in A \text{ and } (X_n, X_{n+1}, ...) \in B\}$$
$$= \Pr\{(X_1, X_2, ...) \in A\} \Pr\{(X_1, X_2, ...) \in B\}.$$

Loosely speaking, a stochastic process is mixing if any two collections of random variables partitioned far apart in the sequence are almost independently distributed.

Theorem 4.2.3 *A mixing process is ergodic.*

Proof Suppose that $\{X_t\}$ is mixing and $A = B$ is a shift invariant set. Then $(X_1, X_2, ...) \in B$ if and only if $(X_n, X_{n+1}, ...) \in B$. Applying the mixing condition yields

$$\Pr\{(X_1, X_2, ...) \in A\} = \Pr\{(X_1, X_2, ...) \in A \text{ and } (X_n, X_{n+1}, ...) \in A\}$$
$$\to [\Pr\{(X_1, X_2, ...) \in A\}]^2, \quad \text{as } n \to \infty.$$

The only possibility is $\Pr\{(X_1, X_2, ...) \in A\} = 0$ or 1. So $\{X_t\}$ is ergodic. ∎

We now present a **Central Limit Theorem** due to Gordin (1969) and Heyde (1974). Consider a stochastic process $\{X_t\}$ on probability space $(\Omega, \mathcal{F}, \Pr)$. Let L^2 be the Hilbert space of real-valued random variables with finite second moments. Let $\mathcal{F}_t$ be the σ-algebra generated by $\{X_k\}_{k=-\infty}^t$.

Theorem 4.2.4 *Let $\{X_t : -\infty < t < \infty\}$ be a stationary ergodic process with $EX_0^2 < \infty$ and write $S_n = \sum_{i=1}^n X_i$. If*

$$E\left[X_t | \mathcal{F}_{t-j}\right] \xrightarrow{L^2} 0, \quad \text{as } j \to \infty, \tag{4.4}$$

and

$$\sum_{j=0}^{\infty} \left(E\left[\xi_{tj}^2\right]\right)^{1/2} < \infty, \tag{4.5}$$

where $\xi_{tj} = E\left[X_t | \mathcal{F}_{t-j}\right] - E\left[X_t | \mathcal{F}_{t-j-1}\right]$, then

$$\frac{S_n}{\sqrt{n}} \xrightarrow{d} N(0, \sigma),$$

where

$$\lim_{n \to \infty} \frac{ES_n^2}{n} = \sigma^2 \equiv \sum_{k=-\infty}^{\infty} E[X_k X_0].$$

Condition (4.4) implies that $EX_t = 0$. Intuitively, as the conditional expectation is based on the information available at more and more distant points in the past, it should approach the unconditional expectation. Conditions (4.4) and (4.5) imply that σ^2 is well defined and finite.

The idea of the proof of the theorem is as follows. We can write

$$X_t = \sum_{j=0}^{J-1} \xi_{tj} + E\left[X_t | \mathcal{F}_{t-J}\right],$$

where ξ_{tj} is the revision made in forecasting X_t when information becomes available at time $t - j$. For any fixed j, the process $\{\xi_{tj}, \mathcal{F}_{t-j}\}$ is a martingale difference sequence because $E\left[\xi | \mathcal{F}_{t-j-1}\right] = 0$. Thus we have written X_t as a sum of martingale differences plus a remainder. We can show that the remainder vanishes asymptotically in L^2 and then apply a central limit theorem for stationary and ergodic martingale differences (Billingsley 1999) to establish the theorem.

4.3   Application to Stationary Markov Processes

In chapter 3 we showed that under certain conditions, a Markov process has a stationary distribution. However, there may be multiple stationary distributions. The goal of this section is to apply the Birkhoff ergodic theorem to characterize the set of stationary distributions. We then provide a strong law of large numbers for stationary Markov processes.

Fix a complete and separable metric space $\mathbb{X}$. To apply the Birkhoff ergodic theorem, we need to make Markov processes stationary. There are two ways to achieve this. First, theorem 3.2.3 shows that given a transition function P on a measurable space $(\mathbb{X}, \mathcal{X})$ and an initial distribution μ_0, we can construct a Markov process $\{X_t\}_{t=0}^{\infty}$ such that its associated conditional distribution is consistent with P. Given any stationary distribution π on $(\mathbb{X}, \mathcal{X})$, we can make the Markov process $\{X_t\}_{t=0}^{\infty}$ stationary by setting X_0 to follow the distribution π.

There is another way to make a Markov process stationary, which we will adopt below. The idea is to consider bi-infinite sequences. The space Ω is the set of all sequences $\{X_n : n = 0, \pm 1, \pm 2, \ldots\}$ and $\mathcal{F}$ is the corresponding product σ-algebra. That is, Ω is the countable product space $\mathbb{X}^{\mathbb{Z}}$, where $\mathbb{Z}$ is the set of all integers. We construct a probability measure $\mathbf{P}_\pi$ on $\mathbb{X}^{\mathbb{Z}}$ as follows: given a positive integer n, we define $\mathbf{P}_\pi^n$ on $\mathbb{X}^{2n+1}$ as

$$\mathbf{P}_\pi^n \left(A_{-n} \times \ldots \times A_n \right)$$
$$= \int_{A_{-n}} \int_{A_{-n+1}} \ldots \int_{A_n} P\left(x_{n-1}, dx_n\right) \ldots P\left(x_{-n}, dx_{-n+1}\right) \pi\left(dx_{-n}\right). \tag{4.6}$$

We can verify that $\mathbf{P}_\pi^n$ satisfies the Kolmogorov consistency condition so that it induces a unique probability measure $\mathbf{P}_\pi$ on $\mathbb{X}^{\mathbb{Z}}$ by the Kolmogorov extension theorem. We can then construct a Markov process $\{X_n\}_{-\infty}^{\infty}$ on the probability space $\left(\mathbb{X}^{\mathbb{Z}}, \mathcal{X}^{\mathbb{Z}}, \mathbf{P}_\pi\right)$. Exercise 3 asks readers to show that this Markov process is stationary and its marginal distribution for any X_n is π.

We define a shift operator θ on $\mathbb{X}^{\mathbb{Z}}$ as $\left(\theta^k x\right)(n) = x_{n+k}$ for any $k \in \mathbb{Z}$ and any $x = \{x_n\}$. It is a measurable transformation from $\mathbb{X}^{\mathbb{Z}}$ to $\mathbb{X}^{\mathbb{Z}}$. Then $\left(\mathbb{X}^{\mathbb{Z}}, \mathcal{X}^{\mathbb{Z}}, \mathbf{P}_\pi, \theta\right)$ form a dynamical system for every invariant distribution π. We will focus on this system below. The main result of this section is the following

Theorem 4.3.1 *Let $\mathcal{M}$ be the set of invariant measures for the transition function P. Then the dynamical system $\left(\mathbb{X}^{\mathbb{Z}}, \mathcal{X}^{\mathbb{Z}}, \mathbf{P}_\pi, \theta\right)$ is ergodic if and only if π is an extreme point of the convex set $\mathcal{M}$.*

To prove this theorem, we need some preliminary results. Let $\mathcal{F}_n^m = \sigma\left(x_k : n \le k \le m\right)$ where $\sigma\left(Y\right)$ denotes the σ-algebra generated by the random variable Y. Let $\mathcal{F}_\infty^\infty = \cap_{n \ge 1} \mathcal{F}_n^\infty$ and $\mathcal{F}_{-\infty}^{-\infty} = \cap_{n \ge 1} \mathcal{F}_{-\infty}^{-n}$.

Lemma 4.3.1 *Let $\mathcal{I}$ be the σ-algebra of shift invariant sets associated with the dynamical system $\left(\mathbb{X}^{\mathbb{Z}}, \mathcal{X}^{\mathbb{Z}}, \mathbf{P}_\pi, \theta\right)$. Then $\mathcal{I} \subset \mathcal{F}_0^0$, up to sets of $\mathbf{P}_\pi$-measure zero.*

Proof   For simplicity we assume that $\mathbb{X} = \mathbb{R}$. However, a similar argument can be applied to the general space $\mathbb{X}$. Let A be a shift invariant set. Then A can be approximated by sets A_k in σ-algebras corresponding to the coordinates from $[-k, k]$, $k \ge 1$. Formally, $A = \cap_{k \ge 0} B_k$, where

$$B_k = \left\{y \in \mathbb{X}^{\mathbb{Z}} : \exists x \in A \text{ with } x_n = y_n, \; \forall n \in [-k, k]\right\}.$$

Since A is shift invariant and θ is measure preserving, the sets $\theta^{\pm 2k} A_k$, $k \ge 1$, will approximate A just as well. Thus A belongs to the tail σ-algebras, the remote past and the remote future. That is, $A \in \tilde{\mathcal{F}}_\infty^\infty$ and $A \in \tilde{\mathcal{F}}_{-\infty}^{-\infty}$, where $\tilde{\mathcal{F}}_\infty^\infty$ and $\tilde{\mathcal{F}}_{-\infty}^{-\infty}$ are the completion of $\mathcal{F}_\infty^\infty$ and $\mathcal{F}_{-\infty}^{-\infty}$, respectively. By exercise 4, we have

$$\mathbf{P}_\pi\left(A|\mathcal{F}_0^0\right) = \mathbf{P}_\pi\left(A \cap A|\mathcal{F}_0^0\right) = \mathbf{P}_\pi\left(A|\mathcal{F}_0^0\right)\mathbf{P}_\pi\left(A|\mathcal{F}_0^0\right).$$

This implies that $\mathbf{P}_\pi\left(A|\mathcal{F}_0^0\right)$ is equal to zero or one. Thus $A \in \mathcal{F}_0^0$.   ∎

Proof of Theorem 4.3.1   Suppose first that $\pi \in \mathcal{M}$ is not extremal; that is, there exists an $\alpha \in (0, 1)$ and two distinct stationary distributions $\pi_1, \pi_2 \in \mathcal{M}$ such that $\pi = \alpha \pi_1 + (1 - \alpha) \pi_2$. Thus $\mathbf{P}_\pi = \alpha \mathbf{P}_{\pi_1} + (1 - \alpha) \mathbf{P}_{\pi_2}$. Assume, by contradiction, that $\left(\mathbb{X}^{\mathbb{Z}}, \mathcal{X}^{\mathbb{Z}}, \mathbf{P}_\pi, \theta\right)$ is ergodic so that $\mathbf{P}_\pi(A) = 0$ or 1 for every $A \in \mathcal{I}$. Thus $\mathbf{P}_{\pi_1}(A) = \mathbf{P}_{\pi_2}(A) = 0$, or $\mathbf{P}_{\pi_1}(A) = \mathbf{P}_{\pi_2}(A) = 1$. This means that $\left(\mathbb{X}^{\mathbb{Z}}, \mathcal{X}^{\mathbb{Z}}, \mathbf{P}_{\pi_1}, \theta\right)$ and $\left(\mathbb{X}^{\mathbb{Z}}, \mathcal{X}^{\mathbb{Z}}, \mathbf{P}_{\pi_2}, \theta\right)$ are also ergodic. By the Birkhoff ergodic theorem, for any bounded measurable function f on $\mathbb{X}^{\mathbb{Z}}$,

$$\lim_{n \to \infty} \frac{1}{n} \sum_{k=1}^{n} f\left(\theta^k x\right) = \int f(x) \mathbf{P}_{\pi_i}(dx), \quad \mathbf{P}_{\pi_i}\text{-a.s.}$$

Let E_i be the sets of points x such that the equality holds. Then $\mathbf{P}_{\pi_i}(E_i) = 1$ so that $\mathbf{P}_{\pi}(E_1) = \mathbf{P}_{\pi}(E_2) = 1$. Since f is arbitrary and since π_1 and π_2 are distinct, we can choose an f such that $\int f(x) \mathbf{P}_{\pi_1}(dx) \neq \int f(x) \mathbf{P}_{\pi_2}(dx)$. This implies that $E_1 \cap E_2 = \emptyset$, leading to $\mathbf{P}_{\pi}(E_1 \cup E_2) = 2$, a contradiction.

To prove the converse, suppose that $(\mathbb{X}^{\mathbb{Z}}, \mathcal{X}^{\mathbb{Z}}, \mathbf{P}_{\pi}, \theta)$ is not ergodic. We wish to show that there exist an $\alpha \in (0,1)$ and two distinct stationary distributions $\pi_1, \pi_2 \in \mathcal{M}$ such that $\pi = \alpha \pi_1 + (1 - \alpha) \pi_2$. By lemma 4.3.1, $A \in \mathcal{F}_0^0$ for any shift-invariant set in $\mathcal{X}^{\mathbb{Z}}$. Since we can label any time as time zero, we have $A \in \mathcal{F}_n^n$ for any $n \in \mathbb{Z}$. Thus there exists a set $A_1 \in \mathcal{X}$ such that $A = A_1^{\mathbb{Z}} \equiv \{(..., x_1, x_2, ...) \in \mathbb{X}^{\mathbb{Z}} : x_n \in A_1, n \in \mathbb{Z}\}$ up to a set of $\mathbf{P}_{\pi}$-measure zero. The set A_1 must be π-invariant.[2] Thus $\mathbf{P}_{\pi}(A) = \mathbf{P}_{\pi}\left(A_1^{\mathbb{Z}}\right) = \pi(A_1)$. Since we assume that $(\mathbb{X}^{\mathbb{Z}}, \mathcal{X}^{\mathbb{Z}}, \mathbf{P}_{\pi}, \theta)$ is not ergodic, there exists $\alpha \in (0,1)$ such that $\mathbf{P}_{\pi}(A) = \pi(A_1) = \alpha$. Furthermore we have $\pi(A_1^c) = 1 - \alpha$. The stationarity of π implies that $P(x, A_1^c) = 1$ for π-almost every $x \in A_1^c$. Define two measures on $(\mathbb{X}, \mathcal{X})$ as

$$\pi_1(B) = \frac{1}{\alpha} \pi(A_1 \cap B), \quad \pi_2(B) = \frac{1}{1 - \alpha} \pi(A_1^c \cap B), \quad \text{all } B \in \mathcal{X}.$$

Clearly, these two measures are stationary distributions.   ∎

From the proof of this theorem, we can relate our previous definition of ergodicity associated with $(\mathbb{X}, \mathcal{X}, P, \pi)$ in definition 3.3.5 to the present notion of ergodicity for the dynamical system $(\mathbb{X}^{\mathbb{Z}}, \mathcal{X}^{\mathbb{Z}}, \mathbf{P}_{\pi}, \theta)$. In particular, we have shown that $(\mathbb{X}^{\mathbb{Z}}, \mathcal{X}^{\mathbb{Z}}, \mathbf{P}_{\pi}, \theta)$ is ergodic if and only if the invariant distribution π is ergodic. It is also straightforward to show the following.

Corollary 4.3.1   *If a Markov process with the transition function P on $(\mathbb{X}, \mathcal{X})$ has a unique invariant distribution π, then π is ergodic.*

Finally, we introduce a strong law of large numbers for stationary Markov processes. Its proof follows from the Birkhoff ergodic theorem and theorem 4.3.1. We omit the details here.

Theorem 4.3.2   *Let $\mathbf{P}_{x_0}$ be the probability measure on $(\mathbb{X}^{\infty}, \mathcal{X}^{\infty})$ for the Markov process, with the transition function P on $(\mathbb{X}, \mathcal{X})$ starting at time zero from $x_0 \in \mathbb{X}$. Let f be a bounded measurable function on $\mathbb{X}$. Then for almost all x_0 with respect to any extremal*

---

2. This means that $P(x, A_1) = 1$ for π-almost every $x \in A_1$ (recall definition 3.3.5).

invariant distribution π on $(\mathbb{X}, \mathcal{X})$,

$$\lim_{N \to \infty} \frac{1}{N} \sum_{k=1}^{N} f(x_k) = \int f(y) \, \pi(dy)$$

for $\mathbf{P}_{x_0}$-almost every $\omega = (x_1, x_2, \ldots) \in \mathbb{X}^\infty$.

4.4   Exercises

1. Prove that the class of transformation invariant sets is a σ-algebra.

2. If θ is a measurable measure-preserving transformation, then

   $$Ef(\omega) = E[f(\theta\omega)]$$

   for a measurable and integrable function f on Ω.

3. Prove that the constructed process $\{X_n\}$ on $(\mathbb{X}^\mathbb{Z}, \mathcal{X}^\mathbb{Z}, \mathbf{P}_\pi)$ in section 4.3 is a stationary Markov process. In addition its marginal distribution for any X_n is π.

4. Prove that for any probability measure P on the product space $X \times Y \times Z$, and for any measurable and integrable function f, g, the following two equations are equivalent:

   $$E\left[f(x)g(z) \,|\, \mathcal{F}_y\right] = E\left[f(x) \,|\, \mathcal{F}_y\right] E\left[g(z) \,|\, \mathcal{F}_y\right],$$

   $$E\left[g(z) \,|\, \mathcal{F}_{x,y}\right] = E\left[g(z) \,|\, \mathcal{F}_y\right],$$

   where $\mathcal{F}_y$ is the σ-algebra generated by the projection onto Y and $\mathcal{F}_{x,y}$ is the σ-algebra generated by the projection onto $X \times Y$.

5. Prove theorems 4.2.2 and 4.3.2.

6. Prove that any two distinct ergodic invariant measures are mutually singular.

7. Let $X = (X_1, X_2, \ldots)$ be a Gaussian stationary sequence with $EX_n = 0$ and covariance $R_n = EX_{n+k}X_k$. Show that $\lim_{n \to \infty} R_n = 0$ is sufficient for X to be ergodic.

II Dynamic Optimization

Economic agents such as households, firms, and governments often face many choice problems. These choice problems are typically dynamic. For example, a household decides how much to consume today and how much to save for the future. A firm decides what amount of dividends to distribute today and how much to invest for the future. A worker decides whether to take a job offer today or to wait and search for a new job tomorrow. All these problems involve a cost–benefit trade-off between today and the future. In this part of the book, we discuss how to solve this type of problems. We focus on economic problems that have a recursive structure. We will formulate these problems as a Markov decision process model. We then apply a recursive approach—dynamic programming—to solve these problems. In chapter 5 we present the model setup and some examples. In chapter 6 we discuss the dynamic programming method for finite-horizon problems, while chapter 7 studies infinite-horizon problems. In chapter 8 we analyze linear-quadratic models. In chapter 9 we examine models with incomplete information. In chapter 10 we study numerical methods for solving dynamic programming problems.

5 Markov Decision Process Model

This chapter introduces the Markov decision process model and presents a variety of examples to illustrate the generality of this model.

5.1 Model Setup

Economic decisions can often be summarized as a problem in which a decision maker chooses an action to influence a stochastic dynamical system so as to maximize some criterion. To ensure a recursive structure, we formulate the framework by a Markov decision process, which consists of five elements: time, states, actions, stochastic kernels, and one-period rewards. A Markov decision process together with an optimality criterion is called a Markov decision problem. A Markov decision process and the associated decision problem form a Markov decision process model.

We now describe this model formally. Suppose that decisions are made at discrete points in time, denoted by $t \in \mathcal{T} \equiv \{0, 1, 2, ..., T\}$, where $T \leq \infty$. The decision time may not be the same as the calendar time. If $T < (=)\infty$, the decision process has a finite (infinite) horizon. At each time t, the system occupies a **state** s_t. The initial state s_0 is given. Denote the set of all possible states by $\mathbb{S}$, called the **state space**. Let $(\mathbb{S}, \mathcal{S})$ and $(\mathbb{A}, \mathcal{A})$ be some measurable spaces. After observing the state s_t, the decision maker chooses an **action** $a_t \in \mathbb{A}$. The constraints on this action are described by a nonempty-valued correspondence $\Gamma : \mathbb{S} \to \mathbb{A}$; that is, $\Gamma(s_t) \subset \mathbb{A}$ is the set of feasible actions given that the current state is $s_t \in \mathbb{S}$. Actions can be chosen randomly or deterministically. When the decision criterion function has kinks, random actions may be optimal. In game theory one can consider randomized actions to allow for mixed strategies. In this chapter we will focus on deterministic actions. In the end of this section, we will briefly introduce the model setup for randomized actions.

As a result of choosing action a_t at state s_t at time t, the decision maker receives a one-period reward $u_t(s_t, a_t)$. In addition the system state at time $t + 1$ is determined by the **stochastic kernel** $P_{t+1} : (\mathbb{S} \times \mathbb{A}) \times \mathcal{S} \to [0,1]$; that is, $P_{t+1}(s_t, a_t; \cdot)$ is the probability measure for states at time $t+1$ if the state and action at time t are s_t and a_t, respectively. Also, for any $B \in \mathcal{S}$, $P_{t+1}(\cdot, \cdot; B)$ is a measurable function on $\mathbb{S} \times \mathbb{A}$. Note that the decision maker's actions may affect the stochastic kernel.

The collection of objects

$$\left\{ \mathcal{T}, \ (\mathbb{S}, \mathcal{S}), \ (\mathbb{A}, \mathcal{A}), \ \Gamma, \ (P_t)_{t=1}^{T}, \ (u_t)_{t=0}^{T} \right\} \tag{5.1}$$

is called a **Markov decision process**. In our formulation we have assumed that $\mathbb{S}, \mathbb{A}$, and Γ are independent of time but that P_{t+1} and u_t may depend on time. For the infinite-horizon case we will assume that P_{t+1} and u_t are independent of time. In this case the Markov decision process is **stationary**. In finite-horizon decision processes, we will assume that no decision is made in the last period so that the terminal reward u_T is a function of the state only. We can refer to it as a salvage value, a scrap value, or a bequest value. In some economic problems we often assume that there is no reward from the terminal state x_T so that $u_T = 0$. In this case a constraint on the terminal state is often needed.[1]

In sum, a Markov decision process has the following essential features:

- The state system is governed by a Markov process (s_t).
- The stochastic kernels $(P_t)_{t=1}^{T}$ of this Markov process are affected by the decision maker's current actions, independent of future or past actions.
- The constraints correspondence Γ maps from a current state to a set of actions, independent of histories.
- The one-period rewards u_t are a function of current states and current actions, independent of histories. In the finite-horizon case the terminal reward is either zero or a function of state only.

Next we define the optimality criterion and formulate the Markov decision problem. Suppose that the initial state s_0 is given. Given this state, the decision maker chooses an action a_0. At time $t = 1$, the decision maker observes state s_1 and the past state and action (s_0, a_0). He then chooses an action a_1 contingent on this information. Since s_0 is known, we can ignore (s_0, a_0) in the information set. We then require the action a_1 be a measurable function of the history $s^1 = (s_1)$. Measurability is necessary for computing expected values. At time $t = 2$ the decision maker observes s_2 and (s_0, a_0, s_1, a_1). Since a_1 is a measurable function of s_1, it does not provide any new information; we can then write the history as $s^2 = (s_1, s_2)$ and require the action a_2 be a measurable function of s^2. In general, at any time $t \geq 1$, the decision maker observes the current state s_t and all the past states and

---

1. See section 6.6.2 for an example.

actions. His information is summarized by a history $s^t = (s_1, ..., s_t)$. He chooses an action a_t as a measurable function of this history s^t. His choice of the sequence of actions must satisfy some optimality criterion. In this chapter we assume that he maximizes total discounted expected rewards, where the expectation is over realizations of the states.

Formally, define the product measurable spaces $(\mathbb{S}^t, \mathcal{S}^t)$, $t = 1, ..., T$.

Definition 5.1.1 *A **plan** or **policy** π is a sequence of actions $(\pi_0, \pi_1, ..., \pi_{T-1})$ such that $\pi_0 \in \mathbb{A}$ and $\pi_t : \mathbb{S}^t \to \mathbb{A}$ is measurable for $t = 1, 2, ..., T - 1$. A plan π is **Markovian** if π_t is independent of states from time 0 to time $t - 1$, $t \geq 1$. It is **stationary** if π_t is independent of time t.*

Definition 5.1.2 *A plan $\pi = (\pi_0, \pi_1, ..., \pi_{T-1})$ is **feasible** from $s_0 \in \mathbb{S}$ if $\pi_0 \in \Gamma(s_0)$ and $\pi_t(s^t) \in \Gamma(s_t)$ for all $s^t \in \mathbb{S}^t$, $t = 1, 2, ..., T - 1$.*

Let $\Pi(s_0)$ denote the set of all feasible plans from s_0. Because of the measurability requirement, $\Pi(s_0)$ may be empty. We give the following sufficient condition to ensure nonemptiness of $\Pi(s_0)$.

Assumption 5.1.1 *The correspondence Γ has a **measurable selection**; that is, there exists a measurable function $h : \mathbb{S} \to \mathbb{A}$ such that $h(s) \in \Gamma(s)$, all $s \in \mathbb{S}$.*

Lemma 5.1.1 *Let $(\mathbb{S}, \mathcal{S}), (\mathbb{A}, \mathcal{A})$, and Γ be given. Under assumption 5.1.1, $\Pi(s_0)$ is nonempty for all $s_0 \in \mathbb{S}$.*

Proof Let h be a measurable selection of Γ. Define

$$\pi_0 = h(s_0), \quad \pi_t(s^t) = h(s_t),$$

for all $s^t \in \mathbb{S}^t$, $t = 1, 2, ..., T - 1$. Clearly, the plan $\pi = (\pi_0, \pi_1, ..., \pi_{T-1}) \in \Pi(s_0)$. ∎

Now we discuss how total discounted expected rewards are computed for a feasible plan. First, we maintain the following:

Assumption 5.1.2 *The discount factor is $\beta \in (0, 1)$.*

Next we define expectations. Given an initial state s_0, a feasible plan π from s_0, and the stochastic kernels P_t, $t = 1, ..., T$, define a probability measure on $\mathcal{S}^t$ as

$$\mu^t(s_0, B; \pi) = \int_{B_1} ... \int_{B_{t-1}} \int_{B_t} P_t\left(s_{t-1}, \pi_{t-1}(s^{t-1}); ds_t\right)$$
$$\times P_{t-1}\left(s_{t-2}, \pi_{t-2}(s^{t-2}); ds_{t-1}\right) ... P_1(s_0, \pi_0; ds_1), \tag{5.2}$$

for any $B = B_1 \times ... \times B_t \in \mathcal{S}^t$. By Tulcea's theorem 3.2.4, $\mu^t (s_0, \cdot \; ; \pi)$ is a well-defined probability measure on $\mathcal{S}^t$. Note that this measure depends on the policy π. We use this measure to compute expected rewards at each date. In the infinite-horizon case the sequence of measures $\mu^t (s_0, \cdot ; \pi)$, $t = 1, 2, ...$, induces a unique measure $\mu^\infty (s_0, \cdot ; \pi)$ on $\mathcal{S}^\infty$ by the Kolmogorov extension theorem.

We impose the following assumption for the finite-horizon case.

Assumption 5.1.3 *Let $T < \infty$. The one-period reward function $u_t : \mathbb{S} \times \mathbb{A} \to \mathbb{R}$ is measurable for $t = 0, 1, ..., T - 1$ and the terminal reward function $u_T : \mathbb{S} \to \mathbb{R}$ is measurable. For each $s_0 \in \mathbb{S}$ and each plan $\pi \in \Pi (s_0)$, $u_t \left(s_t, \pi_t \left(s^t \right) \right)$ is $\mu^t \left(s_0, ds^t; \pi \right)$ integrable.*

For the infinite-horizon case we require the sequences of one-period reward functions and stochastic kernels be time homogeneous or stationary.

Assumption 5.1.4 *Let $T = \infty$. At any date, the one-period reward function is $u : \mathbb{S} \times \mathbb{A} \to \mathbb{R}$ and the stochastic kernel is $P : (\mathbb{S} \times \mathbb{A}) \times \mathcal{S} \to [0, 1]$. For each $s_0 \in \mathbb{S}$ and each plan $\pi \in \Pi (s_0)$, $u \left(s_t, \pi_t \left(s^t \right) \right)$ is $\mu^t \left(s_0, ds^t; \pi \right)$ integrable, and the limit*

$$u (s_0, \pi_0) + \lim_{T \to \infty} \sum_{t=1}^{T} \beta^t \int u \left(s_t, \pi_t \left(s^t \right) \right) \mu^t \left(s_0, ds^t; \pi \right)$$

exists (although it may be plus or minus infinity).

Given the preceding assumptions, for any plan $\pi \in \Pi (s_0)$, we define the total discounted expected rewards for $T < \infty$ as

$$J_0^T (s_0, \pi) = u_0 (s_0, \pi_0) + \sum_{t=1}^{T-1} \beta^t \int u_t \left(s_t, \pi_t \left(s^t \right) \right) \mu^t \left(s_0, ds^t; \pi \right)$$

$$+ \beta^T \int u_T (s_T) \mu^T \left(s_0, ds^T; \pi \right). \tag{5.3}$$

If $T = \infty$, we define the total discounted expected rewards as

$$J (s_0, \pi) = u (s_0, \pi_0) + \lim_{T \to \infty} \sum_{t=1}^{T} \beta^t \int u \left(s_t, \pi_t \left(s^t \right) \right) \mu^t \left(s_0, ds^t; \pi \right). \tag{5.4}$$

We emphasize that for the finite-horizon case, discounting is not important because we can simply redefine u_t such that $\beta = 1$. But it is crucial for the infinite horizon case, as we will show in chapter 7. Here we maintain assumption 5.1.2 for both cases because we will study the connection between these two cases in chapter 7.

Assumptions 5.1.1, 5.1.3, and 5.1.4 ensure that $J_0^T (s, \cdot)$ and $J (s, \cdot)$ are well defined on the nonempty set $\Pi (s)$ for each initial state $s \in \mathbb{S}$. We can then define the optimality criterion as

$$V_0 (s) = \sup_{\pi \in \Pi(s)} J_0^T (s, \pi) \quad \text{if } T < \infty, \tag{5.5}$$

$$V (s) = \sup_{\pi \in \Pi(s)} J (s, \pi) \quad \text{if } T = \infty, \tag{5.6}$$

for each $s \in \mathbb{S}$. More precisely, we may write $V_0 (s)$ as $V_0^T (s)$ to indicate that the horizon is T. Whenever there is no risk of confusion, we will adopt the former notation.

We call the problem in (5.5) a **T-horizon Markov decision problem** and the problem in (5.6) an **infinite-horizon Markov decision problem**. The restriction "Markov" indicates that we focus on problems resulting from Markov decision processes. We call $V_0 : \mathbb{S} \to \mathbb{R} \cup \{\pm\infty\}$ the **value function** at date zero for the finite-horizon Markov decision problem and call $V : \mathbb{S} \to \mathbb{R} \cup \{\pm\infty\}$ the value function for the infinite-horizon Markov decision problem. That is, V_0 is the unique function satisfying the following three conditions:

1. If $|V_0 (s)| < \infty$, then:

   - for all $\pi \in \Pi (s)$,

     $$V_0 (s) \geq J_0^T (s, \pi);$$

   - for any $\varepsilon > 0$, there exists a feasible plan $\pi \in \Pi (s)$ such that

     $$V_0 (s) \leq J_0^T (s, \pi) + \varepsilon.$$

2. If $V_0 (s) = +\infty$, then there exists a sequence of plans (π^k) in $\Pi (s)$ such that $\lim_{k \to \infty} J_0^T (s, \pi^k) = +\infty$.

3. If $V_0 (s) = -\infty$, then $J_0^T (s, \pi) = -\infty$ for all $\pi \in \Pi (s)$.

An optimal plan $\pi^* \in \Pi (s)$ exists if it attains the supremum in that $V_0 (s) = J_0^T (s, \pi^*)$. If an optimal plan exists, then we can replace supremum with maximum in (5.5). Similar definitions apply to $V (s)$ in the infinite-horizon case. The following example illustrates that the supremum may be infinite and an optimal plan may not exist.

Example 5.1.1   *(a) Consider the static problem*

$$V_0 (s) = \sup_{a \in [s,2]} \frac{1}{a} + s, \quad a \neq 0.$$

If $s \in (0,2)$, then $V_0(s) = 1/s + s < \infty$ and $a^* = s$ attains the supremum. If $s < 0$, then $V_0(s) = +\infty$. No $a \in [s,2]$ attains this supremum.

(b) Consider $V_0(s) = \sup_{a \in (0,1)} a = 1$, $s \in \mathbb{S} = \mathbb{R}$. The value function is a finite constant. But no action $a \in (0,1)$ attains the supremum.

At this point we have completed the description of the Markov decision process model. This model includes deterministic decision problems as a special case. Thus we will not treat this case separately in this book. In the deterministic case the choice of actions determines the subsequent state with certainty. We can write the state transition as $s_{t+1} = f(s_t, a_t)$ for some function f. The stochastic kernels becomes

$$
P_{t+1}(s_t, a_t; B) = \begin{cases} 1 & \text{if } f(s_t, a_t) \in B, \\ 0 & \text{otherwise, } B \in \mathcal{S}. \end{cases}
$$

To close this section, we offer a few remarks on the model formulation. First, we have assumed that the criterion function is total discounted expected rewards. In operations research, researchers often consider other criterion functions, for example, the average expected rewards. We will not study this case in this book. Second, to explain some experimental evidence such as the **Allais paradox** and the **Ellsberg paradox**, researchers propose nonexpected utility models. Our model formulation does not include this case. Third, since we have assumed time-additive criterion functions, our model does not include dynamic choice problems with nonadditive criterion functions such as recursive utility. Chapter 20 will consider the last two cases.

Finally, we briefly introduce a very general setup with randomized actions. We refer readers to Bertsekas and Shreve (1978) for a more detailed treatment. Suppose that the initial state is unknown and drawn from the distribution P_0 on $\mathbb{S}$. Because actions may be randomized, the history at any date must include realizations of past actions. Define $\mathbb{H}_0 = \mathbb{S}$, $\mathbb{H}_t = \mathbb{H}_{t-1} \times \mathbb{A} \times \mathbb{S}$ and σ-algebra of $\mathbb{H}_t$, denoted $\mathcal{H}_t$. A date-t history is $h_t = (s_0, a_0, ..., a_{t-1}, s_t) \in \mathbb{H}_t$. An action at date t is a measurable mapping π_t that maps from $\mathbb{H}_t$ to the set of probability measures on $\mathbb{A}$. In addition, for feasibility, we require that $\Gamma(s) \in \mathcal{A}$ and $\pi_t(h_t)(\Gamma(s_t)) = 1$. A plan π is a sequence of actions π_t, $t = 0, 1, 2, ..., T$. Define the measurable space $(\mathbb{S}^t \times \mathbb{A}^t, \mathcal{S}^t \times \mathcal{A}^t)$ and the probability measure on this space given any plan π:

$$
\mu^t(ds_0, da_0, ..., ds_t, da_t; \pi) = P_0(ds_0) \pi_0(h_0)(da_0) P_1(s_0, a_0; ds_1) \pi_1(h_1)(da_1)
$$
$$
\times ... \times P_t(s_{t-1}, a_{t-1}; ds_t) \pi_t(h_t)(da_t),
$$

for $t = 0, 1, ..., T - 1$. In the finite-horizon case there is no action choice in the last period. Thus we have

$$\mu^T (ds_0, da_0, ..., ds_T; \pi)$$
$$= P_0 (ds_0) \pi_0 (h_0) (da_0) P_1 (s_0, a_0; ds_1) \pi_1 (h_1) (da_1) ... P_T (s_{T-1}, a_{T-1}; ds_T).$$

We use these measures to compute the total discounted expected rewards. In the infinite-horizon case, Tulcea's theorem implies that these measures induce a unique probability measure on the measurable space $(\mathbb{S}^\infty \times \mathbb{A}^\infty, \mathcal{S}^\infty \times \mathcal{A}^\infty)$, which is used to compute the total discounted expected rewards.

5.2 Examples

In this section we present some examples to illustrate our model formulation provided in the previous section. Some examples admit a variety of different interpretations and may have wide applicability.

5.2.1 Discrete Choice

If the action set $\mathbb{A}$ is finite, the Markov decision problem becomes a discrete choice problem. An example is the problem of optimal replacement of durable assets analyzed in Rust (1985, 1986). In this problem the state space is $\mathbb{S} = \mathbb{R}_+$. Time is denoted by $t = 0, 1, 2, ...$. The state s_t is interpreted as a measure of accumulated utilization of a durable good at time t. In particular, $s_t = 0$ means a brand new durable good. At each time t, a decision maker decides whether to keep or replace the durable. Let the action set be $\mathbb{A} = \{0, 1\}$, where $a_t = 0$ denotes the action of keeping the durable and $a_t = 1$ denotes the action of selling the durable at the scrap value P_c and replacing it with a new durable at a cost P_b. Suppose that the level of utilization follows an exponential distribution. We may write the densities of the stochastic kernels as

$$p (s_t, a_t; ds_{t+1}) = \begin{cases} 1 - \exp(-\lambda (ds_{t+1} - s_t)) & \text{if } a_t = 0 \text{ and } s_{t+1} \geq s_t, \\ 1 - \exp(-\lambda ds_{t+1}) & \text{if } a_t = 1 \text{ and } s_{t+1} \geq 0, \\ 0 & \text{otherwise.} \end{cases}$$

Assume that the cost of maintaining the durable at state s is $c(s)$ and the objective is to minimize the discounted expected cost of maintaining the durable over an infinite horizon. The discount factor is $\beta \in (0, 1)$. Since minimizing a function is equivalent to maximizing its negative, we can define the reward function as

$$u_t (s_t, a_t) = \begin{cases} -c(s_t) & \text{if } a_t = 0, \\ -(P_b - P_c) - c(0) & \text{if } a_t = 1. \end{cases}$$

5.2.2   Optimal Stopping

In the preceding discrete choice problem the decision maker's choice affects the evolution of the state system or its stochastic kernels. In a class of discrete choice problems, the so-called optimal stopping problems, the decision maker's choice does not affect the state system. Examples are abundant. An investor decides whether and when to invest in a project with exogenously given stochastic payoffs. A firm decides whether and when to enter or exit an industry. It may also decide whether and when to default on debt. A worker decides whether and when to accept a job offer or to quit his job. All these decisions share three characteristics. First, the decision is irreversible to some extent. Second, there is uncertainty about future rewards or costs. Third, decision makers have some flexibility in choosing the timing of the decision.

Now we formulate such problems. Time is denoted by $t = 0, 1, ..., T$, $T \leq \infty$. Uncertainty is generated by an exogenous Markov state process $(z_t)_{t \geq 0}$ taking values in some state space $\mathbb{Z}$. The transition function of $(z_t)_{t \geq 0}$ is given by $Q_t : \mathbb{Z} \times \mathcal{Z} \to [0,1]$, $t = 1, ..., T - 1$, where $(\mathbb{Z}, \mathcal{Z})$ is a measurable space. At any time t, after observing the exogenous state z_t, a decision maker decides whether to stop or to continue. His decision is irreversible in that if he chooses to stop, he will not make any choices in the future. Continuation at date t generates a payoff $f_t(z_t)$, while stopping at date t yields an immediate payoff $g_t(z_t)$ and zero payoff in the future, where f_t and g_t are functions that map $\mathbb{Z}$ into $\mathbb{R}$. The problem could have a finite horizon. In this case we assume that the terminal reward is $h(z_T)$ if the decision maker has not chosen to stop before. The decision maker is risk neutral and maximizes the total discounted payoffs with a discount factor $\beta \in (0, 1]$. In the infinite-horizon case we assume that f_t and g_t are independent of t.

To formulate the optimal stopping problem as a Markov decision problem, we introduce an additional state $\hat{s}$, representing stopping. This state is an absorbing state. Let $a = 1$ and $a = 0$ denote the actions of continuing and stopping, respectively. The Markov decision model consists of the following elements:

- Decision time:

$$\mathcal{T} = \{0, 1, ..., T\}, \quad T \leq \infty.$$

- States:

$$\mathbb{S} = \mathbb{Z} \cup \{\hat{s}\}.$$

- Actions:

$$\mathbb{A} = \{0, 1\}, \quad \Gamma(s) = \begin{cases} \{1, 0\} & \text{if } s \in \mathbb{Z}, \\ \{1\} & \text{if } s = \hat{s}. \end{cases}$$

- Rewards:

$$u_t(s,a) = \begin{cases} f_t(s) & \text{if } s \in \mathbb{Z}, \ a = 1, \\ g_t(s) & \text{if } s \in \mathbb{Z}, \ a = 0, \ t < T, \\ 0 & \text{if } s = \hat{s}, \end{cases}$$

$u_T(s) = h(s), \ s \in \mathbb{Z}, \ \text{if } T < \infty.$

- Stochastic kernels:

$P_{t+1}(s_t, a_t; B) = Q_{t+1}(s_t, B) \quad \text{if } s_t \in \mathbb{Z}, \ a_t = 1, \ B \in \mathcal{Z},$

$P_{t+1}(s_t, a_t; \hat{s}) = 1 \quad \text{if } s_t \in \mathbb{Z}, \ a_t = 0, \text{ or } s_t = \hat{s}, t < T,$

and $P_{t+1}(s_t, a_t; \cdot) = 0$, otherwise.

- Optimality criterion: maximization of total discounted expected rewards with discount factor $\beta \in (0,1)$.

In applications we only need to specify the Markov process (s_t) and the functions f_t, g_t, and h. We next consider some specific examples.

Option Exercise Consider an infinite-horizon irreversible investment problem. The state process $(z_t)_{t \geq 0}$ represents the stochastic project payoffs and has a time-homogeneous transition function Q. The decision maker is risk neutral. An investment project yields payoffs z_t if it is invested at date t. Investment costs a lump-sum value $I > 0$ at the time of the investment. If the decision maker chooses to wait, he receives nothing in the current period. Then he draws a new payoff in the next period and decides whether he should invest again. We can cast this problem into our framework by setting

$$g_t(z_t) = z_t - I, \tag{5.7}$$
$$f_t(z_t) = 0. \tag{5.8}$$

We may view this problem as an option exercise problem, in which the decision maker decides when to exercise an American call option on a stock. In this case s_t represents the stock price and I represents the strike price. The discount factor is equal to the inverse of the gross interest rate, $\beta = 1/(1+r)$.

Exit Exit is an important problem in industrial organization and macroeconomics.[2] We may describe a stylized infinite-horizon exit model as follows. Consider a firm in an industry. The Markov state process $(z_t)_{t \geq 0}$ with a stationary

---

2. See Hopenhayn (1992) for an industry equilibrium model of entry and exit.

transition function Q could be interpreted as a demand shock or a productivity shock. Staying in business at date t generates profits $\varphi(z_t)$ and incurs a fixed cost $c_f > 0$. The owner/manager may decide to exit and seek outside opportunities. Let the outside opportunity value be a constant $\xi > 0$. Then the problem fits into our framework by setting

$$g_t(z_t) = \xi, \tag{5.9}$$
$$f_t(z_t) = \varphi(z_t) - c_f. \tag{5.10}$$

Secretary Problem Cayley (1875) proposes a problem of how to play a lottery. This problem may be described as a secretary problem, which has been studied extensively in the fields of applied probability, statistics, decision theory, and auction theory. Here we follow Puterman's (1994) presentation closely. Consider an employer's decision to hire an individual to fill a vacancy for a secretarial position. There are N candidates or applicants for this job, with different abilities. Candidates are interviewed sequentially. After an interview the employer decides whether or not to offer the job to the current candidate. If he does not offer the job to this candidate, the candidate must seek employment elsewhere. The employer wishes to maximize the probability of giving an offer to the best candidate.

We formalize this problem in an abstract setting as follows. There are N objects that have different qualities. They are ranked from 1 to N, according to a decreasing order of quality. The true rankings are unknown to the decision maker. He observes the objects one at a time in a random order. He can either select the current object and terminate the search, or discard it and choose the next object. His objective is to maximize the probability of choosing the object ranked number 1.

To cast this problem in the optimal stopping model, we set the horizon $T = N$. The decision time $t = 1, 2, ..., N$ indexes the rank of a candidate and has nothing to do with the calendar time. The difficulty of this problem is how to model uncertainty generated by some Markov state process. We set the state space for this process as $\mathbb{Z} = \{0, 1\}$, where 1 denotes that the current object is the best object (rank closest to 1) seen so far, and 0 denotes that a previous object was better. The transition function of this state process is given by

$$Q_{t+1}(z_t, 1) = \frac{1}{t+1}, \quad Q_{t+1}(z_t, 0) = \frac{t}{t+1},$$

for each $z_t \in \mathbb{Z}$, $t = 1, 2, ..., N-1$. The interpretation is that given the date t state z_t, the probability that the $(t+1)$th candidate is the best candidate among the $t+1$ candidates seen so far is $1/(t+1)$. Note that this transition function is independent of the state z_t.

In any state the action $a = 0$ means select the current object (give an offer to the current candidate), and $a = 1$ means do not select the current object and continue the search (interview the next candidate).

Rewards are received only when stopping; that is, choosing action $a = 0$ at t. The probability of choosing the best candidate of N candidates given that he is the best of the first t candidates is given by

$$\Pr\left(\text{best of } N \mid \text{best of first } t\right)$$
$$= \frac{\Pr\left(\text{best of } N\right)}{\Pr\left(\text{best of first } t\right)} = \frac{1/N}{1/t} = \frac{t}{N}.$$

We can now define the rewards. We set $f_t(z_t) = 0$, $z_t \in \mathbb{Z}$, $g_t(0) = 0$, $g_t(1) = t/N$, and the terminal rewards, $h(0) = 0$ and $h(1) = 1$. To interpret the terminal rewards, we note that if the last object is the best, then the probability of choosing the best is 1; otherwise, it is 0.

5.2.3 Bandit Model

Consider a gambler's problem in which he chooses one of many arms of a slot machine to play. Each arm may give different winning probabilities unknown to the gambler. The gambler will choose the arm that yields the largest expected reward. This problem is often referred to as a multi-armed bandit problem. If the slot machine has only one arm, the problem is called a one-armed bandit problem. Typically there are two types of bandit problems according to the information available to the decision maker. In the first type, the decision maker has complete information about the underlying distribution of uncertainty and the structure of the system. In the other type, the decision maker has incomplete information about the system. For example, he may not know the type of the arms. He may learn about the unknown part of the system by observing past states and actions. In this chapter we focus on the first type of bandit problems. We discuss the second type in chapter 10.[3]

Now we formulate the bandit problem with full information in terms of the Markov decision model. Suppose that a decision maker observes the state of each of k Markov processes (k arms), at each date $t = 0, 1, ..., T$, $T \leq \infty$. Each Markov process $\left(s_t^i\right)_{t=0}^{T}$, $i = 1, 2, ..., k$, is characterized by a sequence of transition functions $Q_t^i : \mathbb{S}^i \times \mathcal{S}^i \to [0, 1]$, where $\left(\mathbb{S}^i, \mathcal{S}^i\right)$ is a measurable space, $t = 1, 2, ..., T - 1$. The decision maker chooses one of the Markov processes at each date. If he chooses process i at date t when the state is $s_t = \left(s_t^1, ..., s_t^k\right)$, then he receives a reward $u_t^i\left(s_t^i\right)$, which does not depend on other state processes. Moreover s_t^i moves to a state at date $t + 1$

---

3. See Berry and Fristedt (1985) and Gittins, Glazebrook, and Weber (2011) for a comprehensive study of the bandit model.

randomly according to the transition function Q_{t+1}^i, but the states of other processes remain frozen in that $s_{t+1}^j = s_t^j$ for all $j \neq i$. The decision maker's objective is to maximize the total discounted expected rewards from the selected process. We summarize the bandit model as follows:

- Decision time:

  $t = 0, 1, 2, \dots.$

- States:

  $\mathbb{S} = \mathbb{S}^1 \times \mathbb{S}^2 \times \dots \times \mathbb{S}^k.$

- Actions:

  $\mathbb{A} = \{1, 2, \dots, k\},\ \Gamma(s) = \mathbb{A},\ s \in \mathbb{S}.$

- Stochastic kernels:

  $$P_{t+1}\left(\left(s_t^1, \dots, s_t^k\right), a_t; B\right) = Q_{t+1}^i\left(s_t^i, B^i\right) \quad \text{if } a_t = i,$$

  for $\quad B = \left\{s_t^1\right\} \times \dots \times \left\{s_t^{i-1}\right\} \times B^i \times \left\{s_t^{i+1}\right\} \times \dots \times \left\{s_t^i\right\}$ and $B^i \in \mathcal{S}^i$. Moreover $P_{t+1}\left(\left(s_t^1, \dots, s_t^k\right), a_t; B\right) = 0$ for all other $B \in \mathcal{S}^1 \times \dots \times \mathcal{S}^k.$

- Rewards:

  $u_t(s_t, a_t) = u_t^i\left(s_t^i\right),\ s_t = \left(s_t^1, \dots, s_t^k\right) \in \mathbb{S} \quad \text{if } a_t = i.$

- Optimality criterion:

  $$\sup_{(a_t)} E\left[\sum_{t=0}^{T} \beta^t u_t(s_t, a_t)\right], \quad \beta \in (0, 1).$$

A crucial feature of the bandit problem is that when process i is chosen at time t, its state at time $t+1$ moves randomly while the states of other processes remain frozen. Thus, even though process i may be attractive at time t, it may draw a bad state at time $t+1$. At that state the decision maker may choose a different process. The bandit model is related to the optimal stopping model. Some optimal stopping problems may be viewed as a special case of the bandit model. For example, when there are two arms, one arm is represented by a deterministic constant process and the other arm is stochastic. Then this two-armed bandit problem is an optimal stopping problem. In general, if both arms are stochastic, then the decision maker may switch choices between these two arms depending on the state of the arms. It is not an optimal stopping problem.

There are many applications of the bandit model in economics and operations research, including task selection, search, resource allocation, and choice of R&D

processes, etc. Here we will describe the first two applications and also discuss some extensions of the bandit model. More applications are available for the bandit model with incomplete information. We will discuss this case in chapter 10.

Task Selection   Consider the task selection problem taken from Puterman (1994). A decision maker decides to take on one of k tasks at any date t. The state s_t^i represents the degree of completion of task i, $i = 1, 2, ..., k$. If the decision maker takes on task i, he receives an expected reward $u_t^i \left(s_t^i \right)$. He can receive a certain reward only if the task is completed. We can take $\mathbb{S}^i = [0, 1]$ and $s^i \in \mathbb{S}^i$, which represents the fraction of the task that has been completed. Working on a task for an additional period is likely to draw the decision maker closer to completion, but there is a chance that he falls behind. We can model $\left(s_t^i \right)$ as a Markov process. Let $p^i \left(C | s_t^i \right)$ be the conditional probability of completing task i given the state s_t^i, where C represents completion of the task. Let $u_t^i \left(s_t^i \right) = R^i p^i \left(C | s_t^i \right)$, where R^i represents the reward if task i is completed. Assume that the decision maker can work on only one task at any time. If he works on a given task, then other tasks are stopped at the previous state.

Search for the Best Alternative   Weitzman (1979) studies the following Pandora's problem. There are k closed boxes. Each box i, $1 \leq i \leq k$, contains an unknown reward x_i drawn from a distribution $F^i \left(x_i \right)$, independent of other boxes. It costs c_i to open box i and the reward is delivered after time t_i. The continuously compounded discount rate is r. So the reward is discounted at $\beta_i = e^{-r t_i}$. An outside value x_0 is available.

At each stage, Pandora decides whether to open a box and which box to open. If she chooses to stop searching, Pandora collects the maximum reward she has uncovered. If she continues to search, she pays the searching cost and waits for the reward to come. At the time when that reward is realized, she faces the same decision problem again. Pandora's objective is to maximize the total discounted expected rewards. The question is what is the optimal sequential search strategy of opening boxes.

Extensions   A natural extension of the preceding bandit model is to allow unchosen processes (arms) to change states between decision times. The effect of this extension is that we have to change the structure of stochastic kernels. This extended model is often called the restless bandits model. A second extension is to allow the number of arms to change over time. Instead, new arms arrive according to a Poisson process. A third extension is to allow switching costs when switching among different arms.

5.2.4   Optimal Control

In many applications it is more convenient to describe the evolution of the state system by difference equations instead of stochastic kernels. The decision maker's actions may affect these equations. This modeling framework is called the optimal control model. We now introduce this model.

Let $(\mathbb{X}, \mathcal{X})$, $(\mathbb{Z}, \mathcal{Z})$, and $(\mathbb{A}, \mathcal{A})$ be measurable spaces, where $\mathbb{X} \subset \mathbb{R}^{n_x}$, $\mathbb{Z} \subset \mathbb{R}^{n_z}$, and $\mathbb{A} \subset \mathbb{R}^{n_a}$. Suppose that the state s of the system consists of an endogenous state $x \in \mathbb{X}$ and an exogenous state $z \in \mathbb{Z}$, that is, $s = (x, z)$. Time is denoted by $t = 0, 1, 2, ..., T \leq \infty$. The initial state (x_0, z_0) is given. The exogenous state evolves according to a time-homogeneous Markov process with the stationary transition function $Q : \mathbb{Z} \times \mathcal{Z} \to [0, 1]$.[4] The endogenous state evolves according to the following difference equation:

$$x_{t+1} = \phi_t (x_t, a_t, z_t, z_{t+1}), \quad t = 0, 1, ..., T - 1, \ (x_0, z_0) \text{ given}, \tag{5.11}$$

where $\phi_t : \mathbb{X} \times \mathbb{A} \times \mathbb{Z} \times \mathbb{Z} \to \mathbb{X}$ is a measurable function. This equation is called the **state-transition equation**, and the function ϕ_t is called the **state-transition function**. After choosing an action $a_t \in \Gamma(x_t, z_t)$, the decision maker obtains reward $u_t(x_t, z_t, a_t)$. The action a_t is a vector of control variables.

If $T < \infty$, we may set a terminal reward $u_T(x_T, z_T)$, which may be interpreted as a scrap value or a bequest value. If there is no reward from the terminal state x_T, we may impose some additional constraint on x_T.[5] The decision maker's objective is to choose a feasible policy $(a_t)_{t=0}^{T-1}$ from (x_0, z_0) to maximize the total discounted expected reward:

$$\sup_{(a_t)_{t=0}^{T-1} \in \Pi(x_0, z_0)} E \left[\sum_{t=0}^{T-1} \beta^t u_t(x_t, z_t, a_t) + \beta^T u_T(x_T, z_T) \right] \tag{5.12}$$

subject to (5.11), where E is the expectation operator. The objective function in (5.12) is called the **Bolza form**. If $u_T = 0$ in (5.12), it is the **Lagrange form**. If $u_t = 0$ in (5.12) for $t = 0, 1, ..., T - 1$, it is called the **Mayer form**.

If $T = \infty$, we typically consider the time-homogeneous case in which $u_t = u$ and $\phi_t = \phi$. The decision maker's objective is to choose a feasible policy $(a_t)_{t=0}^{\infty}$ from (x_0, z_0) to maximize the total discounted expected reward:

$$\sup_{(a_t)_{t=0}^{\infty} \in \Pi(x_0, z_0)} E \left[\sum_{t=0}^{\infty} \beta^t u(x_t, z_t, a_t) \right] \tag{5.13}$$

---

4. The framework can be generalized to incorporate time-inhomogeneous Markov processes.
5. See section 6.6.2 for an example.

subject to

$$x_{t+1} = \phi(x_t, a_t, z_t, z_{t+1}), \quad t \geq 0, \ (x_0, z_0) \text{ given.} \tag{5.14}$$

The optimal control model fits in the Markov decision process model by defining transition kernels as

$$P_{t+1}(x_t, z_t, a_t; B_1 \times B_2) = \int 1_{B_2}(z_{t+1}) \, 1_{B_1}(\phi_t(x_t, a_t, z_t, z_{t+1})) \, Q(z_t, B_2),$$

where $B_1 \in \mathcal{X}$, $B_2 \in \mathcal{Z}$ and $1_A(y)$ is an indicator function that is equal to 1 if $y \in A$ and equal to 0 otherwise.

The state transition equation (5.11) or (5.14) can be generalized to contain past states and actions. This case can be cast into the present model by redefining states and controls in terms of vectors to take account of past states and controls. One could also include intratemporal constraints on the states and actions each period.

When the action set $\mathbb{A}$ is a finite set, the control problem is a discrete choice problem. When actions involve both discrete and continuous choices, the problem is often called a **mixed stopping and control problem**. Examples include inventory management and optimal investment with fixed costs. With fixed costs, the decision maker has to decide when to make adjustments as well as what size of adjustments to make. We will analyze such problems in chapter 8.6.

5.3   Exercises

1. (Job search) Consider McCall's (1970) job search model. An unemployed worker is searching for a job. Each period he draws one offer w from the same wage distribution F over $[0, B]$. If the worker rejects the offer, he receives unemployment compensation c this period and waits until next period to draw another offer from F. If the worker accepts the offer to work at w, he receives a wage of w each period forever. The worker's objective is to maximize the total discounted expected income. Formulate this problem as an optimal stopping problem.

2. (Put option) An American put option gives the holder the right to sell stocks at a specified price at any time up to its expiry date. Formulate the problem of when to exercise the put option as an optimal stopping problem.

3. (Secretary problem) Formulate a variant of the secretary problem in which the employer's objective is to maximize the probability of choosing one of the two best candidates.

4. (Pandora's problem) Formulate Pandora's problem analyzed by Weitzman (1979) as a bandit problem.

5. (Stochastic Ramsey growth model) Consider a social planner's resource allocation problem. His objective is to choose sequences of consumption (C_t), labor supply (N_t), and investment (I_t) so as to maximize a representative household's utility given by

$$E\left[\sum_{t=0}^{\infty} \beta^t u\left(C_t, 1 - N_t\right)\right], \quad \beta \in (0,1),$$

subject to the resource constraint

$$C_t + I_t = z_t F\left(K_t, N_t\right),$$
$$K_{t+1} = (1 - \delta) K_t + I_t,$$

where $u : \mathbb{R}_+ \times (0,1) \to \mathbb{R}$ is a v-NM utility function, $F : \mathbb{R}_+ \to \mathbb{R}$ is a production function, z_t represents productivity shocks that follow a Markov process with the transition function $Q : \mathbb{Z} \times \mathcal{Z} \to [0,1]$. Formulate this problem as an optimal control problem. Argue that one can choose C_t, I_t, and N_t as control variables or can choose K_{t+1} and N_t as control variables.

6. (Inventory management) Consider a manager's inventory management problem. Each period he has some amount of inventory. He also faces demand for his product. His sales are stochastic and are modeled as a Markov process. Sales generate revenues. The current inventory may not meet the demand. Thus the manager may place a new order to increase inventory. New orders incur a fixed cost and a variable cost. Maintaining inventories also incurs costs. The manager's objective is to choose an ordering policy so as to maximize the total discounted expected profits over an infinite horizon. Formulate this problem as an optimal control problem.

6   Finite-Horizon Dynamic Programming

The method of dynamic programming is best understood by studying finite-horizon problems first. These problems are often encountered in making life-cycle planning decisions on optimal consumption, savings, portfolio choice, and so forth. In this chapter we first solve a simple example to illustrate the idea of dynamic programming. We then present three main results in dynamic programming theory. Finally, we use the method of dynamic programming to solve some more complicated examples.

6.1   A Motivating Example

To explain the main idea of dynamic programming, we start with a deterministic example. Consider the following social planner's problem:

$$\max_{\{C_t, K_{t+1}\}} \sum_{t=0}^{T} \beta^t \ln(C_t) \tag{6.1}$$

subject to

$$C_t + K_{t+1} = K_t^\alpha, \quad t = 0, 1, ..., T, \; K_0 \text{ given.} \tag{6.2}$$

Here C_t and K_t represent consumption and capital, respectively. The discount factor is $\beta \in (0,1)$ and $\alpha \in (0,1)$ represents the capital share. In this problem the social planner makes a planning decision at time zero by choosing sequences of consumption and capital.

   A natural way to solve this problem is to use the resource constraint to substitute out (C_t) in the objective function. Then one can derive first-order conditions. Another way is to use the Lagrange method. One can also derive first-order conditions. Both ways give the following second-order difference equation:

$$\frac{1}{K_t^\alpha - K_{t+1}} = \beta \frac{1}{K_{t+1}^\alpha - K_{t+2}} \alpha K_{t+1}^{\alpha-1}, \quad t = 0, 1, ..., T - 1.$$

We need two boundary conditions. One boundary condition is the initial condition with given K_0. The other condition is the terminal condition $K_{T+1} = 0$. Using these two conditions, we obtain the following solution:

$$K_{t+1} = \alpha\beta \frac{1 - (\alpha\beta)^{T-t}}{1 - (\alpha\beta)^{T-t+1}} K_t^\alpha, \quad t = 0, 1, ..., T. \tag{6.3}$$

Next we consider another problem in which the social planner chooses a sequence $\{C_{t+j}, K_{t+j+1}\}_{j=0}^{T-t}$ at time t so as to maximize discounted utility from time t onward:

$$V_t(K_t) = \max \sum_{j=0}^{T-t} \beta^j \ln\left(C_{t+j}\right)$$

subject to a sequence of resource constraints in (6.2) starting from K_t. Here $V_t(K_t)$ is called the **value function** at date t. The original problem (6.1) is the special case with $t = 0$. Using the same method, we can derive

$$K_{t+1+j} = \alpha\beta \frac{1 - (\alpha\beta)^{T-t-j}}{1 - (\alpha\beta)^{T-t-j+1}} K_{t+j}^\alpha, \quad j = 0, 1, ..., T - t, \tag{6.4}$$

$$V_t(K_t) = \frac{\alpha(1 - (\alpha\beta)^{T-t+1})}{1 - \alpha\beta} \ln K_t + A_t, \tag{6.5}$$

where A_t satisfies the difference equation

$$A_t = \beta A_{t+1} + b_t, \quad A_T = 0,$$

$$b_t = \ln \frac{1 - \alpha\beta}{1 - (\alpha\beta)^{T-t+1}} \tag{6.6}$$

$$+ \frac{\alpha\beta\left(1 - (\alpha\beta)^{T-t}\right)}{1 - \alpha\beta} \left[\ln(\alpha\beta) + \ln \frac{1 - (\alpha\beta)^{T-t}}{1 - (\alpha\beta)^{T-t+1}}\right].$$

Note that the problem above is a deterministic optimal control problem. We may use the dynamic programming method. The idea of this method is to use backward induction. We start with the last period $t = T$. The planner solves the following problem:

$$\max \ln(C_T) \tag{6.7}$$

subject to (6.2) for $t = T$. Clearly, the solution is given by

$$C_T = K_T^\alpha, \quad K_{T+1} = 0,$$

Additionally $V_T(K_T) = \alpha \ln K_T$ given in (6.5) for $t = T$ is equal to the maximum value of problem (6.7).

At time $t = T - 1$ there are only two decision periods. The planner solves the following problem:

$$\max \ \ln(C_{T-1}) + \beta V_T(K_T) \tag{6.8}$$

subject to (6.2) for $t = T - 1$. The solution is given by

$$C_{T-1} = \frac{1}{1 + \alpha \beta} K_{T-1}^{\alpha}, \quad K_T = \frac{\alpha \beta}{1 + \alpha \beta} K_{T-1}^{\alpha}.$$

Furthermore we can verify that $V_{T-1}(K_{T-1})$ is equal to the maximum value of problem (6.8).

In general, at any time $t = 0, 1, ..., T - 1$, the planner knows that the maximized value of utility from time $t + 1$ onward is $V_{t+1}(K_{t+1})$ if the capital stock at $t + 1$ is K_{t+1}. The planner solves the following two-period problem:

$$\max_{C_t, K_{t+1}} \ \ln(C_t) + \beta V_{t+1}(K_{t+1})$$

subject to (6.2) at t. We obtain the solution for K_{t+1} given in (6.3). We can write the solution as $K_{t+1} = g_t(K_t)$, where the function g_t is called an optimal **decision rule** or **policy function**. In addition we can show that $V_t(K_t)$ given in (6.5) satisfies the equation

$$V_t(K_t) = \max_{C_t, K_{t+1}} \ \ln(C_t) + \beta V_{t+1}(K_{t+1}).$$

This equation is often called a **Bellman equation**. In the literature it is also called a **dynamic programming equation** or **optimality equation**. The problem in this equation is called a **dynamic programming problem**.

From the analysis above we observe the following properties: (1) The sequence of value functions obtained from the planning problem satisfies the Bellman equation from dynamic programming. (2) The optimal capital policy (plan) obtained from the planning problem is identical to those generated from the optimal policy functions obtained from dynamic programming. In addition the optimal plan made at time zero remains optimal at any future date t whenever the date$-t$ state K_t results from the initial optimal plan. In fact these properties are quite general and called the **Principle of Optimality**. This principle is stated in Bellman (1957, p. 83) as follows:

An optimal policy has the property that whatever the initial state and initial decision are, the remaining decisions must constitute an optimal policy with regard to the state resulting from the first decision.

Before formalizing this principle in the general Markov decision process model in section 6.3, we will explain the difficulty involved in stochastic models in the next section.

6.2 Measurability Problem

In stochastic models, measurability is necessary for computing expectations. This issue does not arise in deterministic models or stochastic models with countable state spaces. Unfortunately, measurability of value functions or policy functions on general uncountable state spaces may fail to hold for the dynamic programming method to work. We use a simple two-period optimization problem adapted from Bertsekas and Shreve (1978) as an example to illustrate this issue.

Suppose that a decision maker chooses a plan $\pi = (\pi_0, \pi_1)$ to solve the following problem:

$$V_0(s_0) = \sup_{\pi} \int u(s_1, \pi_1(s_1)) P(s_0, \pi_0; ds_1),$$

where $\pi_0 \in \mathbb{A}$ and $\pi_1 : \mathbb{S} \to \mathbb{A}$ is a measurable function. The measurability of π_1 is a necessary requirement for the computation of integration. Suppose that we use the method of dynamic programming to solve the problem above. We proceed by backward induction:

$$V_1^*(s_1) = \sup_{a_1 \in \mathbb{A}} u(s_1, a_1),$$

$$V_0^*(s_0) = \sup_{a_0 \in \mathbb{A}} \int V_1^*(s_1) P(s_0, a_0; ds_1).$$

Suppose that V_0, V_1^*, and V_0^* are finite functions. The Principle of Optimality implies that $V_0(s_0) = V_0^*(s_0)$. An informal proof of this result consists of the following two steps:

Step 1. For any plan π,

$$V_0^*(s_0) \geq \int V_1^*(s_1) P(s_0, \pi_0; ds_1) \geq \int u(s_1, \pi_1) P(s_0, \pi_0; ds_1).$$

Thus $V_0^*(s_0) \geq V_0(s_0)$.

Step 2. By the definition of supremum, given any $s_1 \in \mathbb{S}$, for any $\varepsilon > 0$, there exists $a_1^*(s_1) \in \mathbb{A}$ such that

$$u(s_1, a_1^*(s_1)) + \varepsilon \geq V_1^*(s_1). \tag{6.9}$$

Thus for any $a_0 \in \mathbb{A}$,

$$V_0(s_0) \geq \int u(s_1, a_1^*(s_1)) P(s_0, a_0; ds_1) \tag{6.10}$$

$$\geq \int V_1^*(s_1) P(s_0, a_0; ds_1) - \varepsilon. \tag{6.11}$$

Taking $\varepsilon \to 0$ and taking supremum over a_0, we deduce that $V_0(s_0) \geq V_0^*(s_0)$.

What goes wrong in the proof above? First, we need a_1^* to be measurable for the integration in (6.10) to make sense. But the measurable selection a_1^* in (6.9) may not exist. Second, we need V_1^* to be measurable for the integration in (6.11) to make sense. However, there are examples in which V_1^* may not be measurable. As Blackwell (1965) points out, the nonmeasurability of V_1^* stems from the fact that the projection of a Borel set in $\mathbb{R}^2$ on one of the axes need not be Borel measurable in the case where $\mathbb{S} = \mathbb{A} = \mathbb{R}$. For any $c \in \mathbb{R}$,

$$\{s_1 : V_1^*(s_1) < c\} = \text{proj}_{s_1}\{(s_1, a_1) : u(s_1, a_1) < c\},$$

where for any set $E \subset \mathbb{S} \times \mathbb{A}$,

$$\text{proj}_{s_1} E = \{s_1 : (s_1, a_1) \in E\}.$$

Even though $\{(s_1, a_1) : u(s_1, a_1) < c\}$ is a Borel set, $\{s_1 : V_1^*(s_1) < c\}$ need not be. There are several approaches to deal with the preceding two difficulties in the literature (see Bertsekas and Shreve 1978). Instead of getting into the complicated technical details, we simply sidestep these issues by imposing sufficient conditions in order to formalize the key idea of dynamic programming. For the model in section 6.4, all these conditions are satisfied so that we can apply the method of dynamic programming.

6.3   Principle of Optimality

Consider the Markov decision process model presented in chapter 5. In addition to studying the initial planning decisions, we also consider planning decisions at any future date $t = 1, 2, ..., T - 1$. Suppose that at date t the decision maker arrives at the history $s^t \in \mathbb{S}^t$. Imagine that at the history s^t and after experiencing a history of actions $(\pi_0, ..., \pi_{t-1}(s^{t-1}))$, the decision maker reconsiders his decision made initially at time zero. What is his new optimal plan at s^t? To formulate this problem, we need to consider **feasible plans from any history** s^t and their feasible **continuation plans** following s_{t+1}.

A feasible plan from history s^t, π^{s^t}, consists of a point $\pi_t^{s^t} \in \Gamma(s_t)$ and a sequence of measurable functions $\pi_{t+j}^{s^t} : \mathbb{S}^j \to \mathbb{A}$ satisfying $\pi_{t+j}^{s^t}(s_{t+1}^{t+j}) \in \Gamma(s_{t+j})$, for any $s_{t+1}^{t+j} \equiv (s_{t+1}, ..., s_{t+j}) \in \mathbb{S}^j$, $j = 1, 2, ..., T - t$. Denote the set of all feasible plans from history s^t by $\Pi(s^t)$. For $t = 0$, we set $s^0 = s_0$.

For any feasible plan from s^t, $\pi^{s^t} \in \Pi(s^t)$, we define its continuation plan following s_{t+1}, $C(\pi^{s^t}, s_{t+1})$, as

$$C_{t+1}\left(\pi^{s^t}, s_{t+1}\right) = \pi_{t+1}^{s^t}(s_{t+1}),$$

$$C_{t+j}\left(s_{t+2}^{t+j}; \pi^{s^t}, s_{t+1}\right) = \pi_{t+j}^{s^t}\left(s_{t+1}, s_{t+2}^{t+j}\right),$$

for any $s_{t+2}^{t+j} \in \mathbb{S}^{j-1}, j = 2, ..., T - t$. By definition, $C_{t+1}(\pi^{s^t}, s_{t+1})$ is a measurable function of s_{t+1}. Each $C_{t+j}(\cdot \; ; \pi^{s^t}, s_{t+1})$ is a measurable function on $\mathbb{S}^{j-1}$ and is also a measurable function of s_{t+1}. Since π^{s^t} is feasible, $C(\pi^{s^t}, s_{t+1})$ is also feasible by definition in that $C_{t+1}(\pi^{s^t}, s_{t+1}) \in \Gamma(s_{t+1})$ and $C_{t+j}(s_{t+2}^{t+j} \; ; \pi^{s^t}, s_{t+1}) \in \Gamma(s_{t+j})$. Thus $C_{t+1}(\pi^{s^t}, s_{t+1}) \in \Pi(s^{t+1})$.

Now we define the conditional probability measure on $\mathcal{S}^j$ given the history s^t and the feasible plan π^{s^t} from s^t

$$\mu_t^{t+j}\left(s^t, B; \pi^{s^t}\right) = \int_{B_1} \cdots \int_{B_j} P_{t+j}\left(s_{t+j-1}, \pi_{t+j-1}^{s^t}(s_{t+1}^{t+j-1}); ds_{t+j}\right)$$

$$\cdots P_{t+1}\left(s_t, \pi_t^{s^t}; ds_{t+1}\right), \tag{6.12}$$

where $B = B_1 \times \cdots \times B_j \in \mathcal{S}^j$, and $j = 1, 2, ..., T - t$. For $j = 1$ we set $\pi_{t+j-1}^{s^t}(s_{t+1}^{t+j-1}) = \pi_t^{s^t}$. Using these measures, we compute the sequence of discounted expected rewards resulting from any plan π^{s^t} from history s^t:

$$J_T^T\left(s^T\right) = u_T(s_T),$$

$$J_t^T\left(s^t, \pi^{s^t}\right) = u_t\left(s_t, \pi_t^{s^t}\right) \tag{6.13}$$

$$+ \sum_{j=1}^{T-t-1} \beta^j \int u_{t+j}\left(s_{t+j}, \pi_{t+j}^{s^t}(s_{t+1}^{t+j})\right) \mu_t^{t+j}(s^t, ds_{t+1}^{t+j}; \pi^{s^t})$$

$$+ \beta^{T-t} \int u_T(s_T) \mu_t^T\left(s^t, ds_{t+1}^T; \pi^{s^t}\right)$$

for $t = 0, 1, ..., T - 1$. Here we use ds_{t+1}^{t+j} to denote the integration with respect to $(s_{t+1}, ..., s_{t+j})$ on $\mathcal{S}^j$.

We are ready to write the decision maker's problem when arriving at any history s^t as follows:

$$V_t\left(s^t\right) = \sup_{\pi^{s^t} \in \Pi(s^t)} J_t^T\left(s^t, \pi^{s^t}\right), \quad t = 0, 1, ..., T - 1, \tag{6.14}$$

where $V_t : \mathbb{S}^t \to \mathbb{R} \cup \{\pm\infty\}$ is the value function at time t. Since at the terminal time, there is no decision to make, we set $V_T(s^T) = J_T^T(s^T) = u_T(s_T)$. The original Markov decision problem in (5.5) is a special case of the sequence problem (6.14) with $t = 0$.

In this book we will focus on the case where value functions always take on finite values because the value of infinity has no economic meaning. In view of the discussion in section 6.2, we will impose:

Assumption 6.3.1 *(a) The value function $V_t : \mathbb{S}^t \to \mathbb{R}$ is measurable. (b) For any $\varepsilon > 0$, there exists a plan π^{s^t} from history s^t such that*

$$J_t^T\left(s^t, \pi^{s^t}\right) + \varepsilon \geq V_t\left(s^t\right) \tag{6.15}$$

for $t = 1, 2, ..., T - 1$. In addition, as functions of s^t, $\pi_t^{s^t}$ is measurable and each $\pi_{t+j}^{s^t}(s_{t+1}^{t+j})$ is measurable for any fixed $s_{t+1}^{t+j} \in \mathbb{S}^j$, $j = 1, 2, ..., T - t - 1$.

By the definition of supremum, there exists a feasible π^{s^t} such that (6.15) holds. The added restriction of assumption 6.3.1 (b) is that π^{s^t} must satisfy certain measurability requirements.

The following lemma is fundamental for the Principle of Optimality.

Lemma 6.3.1 *Let the Markov decision process in (5.1) be given. Suppose that assumptions 5.1.1 through 5.1.3 hold. Then for any feasible plan π^{s^t} from $s^t \in \mathbb{S}^t$,*

$$J_t^T\left(s^t, \pi^{s^t}\right) = u_t(s_t, \pi_t^{s^t}) + \beta \int J_{t+1}^T(s^{t+1}, C(\pi^{s^t}, s_{t+1})) P_{t+1}(s_t, \pi_t^{s^t}; ds_{t+1}), \tag{6.16}$$

where $t = 0, 1, ..., T - 1$.

Proof Substituting equation (6.13) at $t + 1$ into the right-hand side of (6.16), we compute

$$u_t\left(s_t, \pi_t^{s^t}\right) + \beta \int J_{t+1}^T\left(s^{t+1}, C\left(\pi^{s^t}, s_{t+1}\right)\right) P_{t+1}\left(s_t, \pi_t^{s^t}; ds_{t+1}\right)$$

$$= u_t\left(s_t, \pi_t^{s^t}\right) + \beta \int u_{t+1}\left(s_{t+1}, \pi_{t+1}^{s^t}(s_{t+1})\right) P_{t+1}\left(s_t, \pi_t^{s^t}; ds_{t+1}\right)$$

$$+ \sum_{j=2}^{T-t-1} \beta^j \int \int u_{t+j}(s_{t+j}, \pi_{t+j}^{s^t}(s_{t+1}^{t+j}))$$

$$\times \mu_{t+1}^{t+j}(s^{t+1}, ds_{t+2}^{t+j}; C(\pi^{s^t}, s_{t+1})) P_{t+1}\left(s_t, \pi_t^{s^t}; ds_{t+1}\right)$$

$$+ \beta^{T-t} \int \int u_T(s_T) \mu_{t+1}^T\left(s^{t+1}, ds_{t+2}^T; C(\pi^{s^t}, s_{t+1})\right) P_{t+1}\left(s_t, \pi_t^{s^t}; ds_{t+1}\right)$$

$$= u_t\left(s_t, \pi_t^{s^t}\right) + \sum_{j=1}^{T-t-1} \beta^j \int u_{t+j}\left(s_{t+j}, \pi_{t+j}^{s^t}(s_{t+1}^{t+j})\right) \mu_t^{t+j}\left(s^t, ds_{t+1}^{t+j}; \pi^{s^t}\right)$$

$$+ \beta^{T-t} \int u_T(s_T) \mu_t^T\left(s^t, ds_{t+1}^T; \pi^{s^t}\right)$$

$$= J_t^T\left(s^t, \pi^{s^t}\right),$$

where the second equality follows from the definition of μ_t^{t+j} in (6.12). ∎

Equation (6.16) implies that the objective function has a recursive structure. This recursive structure together with the Markov decision process ensure that the sequence of value functions also has a recursive structure and is Markovian as the following theorem shows.

Theorem 6.3.1 *Let the Markov decision process in (5.1) be given. Let $(V_t)_{t=0}^T$ be the sequence of value functions for the sequence problem (6.14). Suppose that assumptions 5.1.1 to 5.1.3 and 6.3.1 hold. Then $(V_t)_{t=0}^T$ satisfies the **Bellman equation***

$$V_t\left(s^t\right) = \sup_{a_t \in \Gamma(s_t)} u_t\left(s_t, a_t\right) + \beta \int V_{t+1}\left(s^{t+1}\right) P_{t+1}\left(s_t, a_t; ds_{t+1}\right), \tag{6.17}$$

where $V_T\left(s^T\right) = u_T\left(s_T\right)$. In addition (V_t) is Markovian in that $V_t\left(s^t\right)$ does not depend on s^{t-1} for $t = 1, 2, ..., T$.

Proof In the terminal period T, there is no decision to make and thus $V_T\left(s^T\right) = u_T\left(s_T\right)$. Let $W_t\left(s^t\right)$ denote the right-hand side of (6.17). We first show that $W_t\left(s^t\right) \geq V_t\left(s^t\right)$. Consider any plan from s^t, $\pi^{s^t} \in \Pi\left(s^t\right)$. By the definition of V_{t+1}, we derive

$W_t\left(s^t\right)$

$$= \sup_{a_t \in \Gamma(s_t)} u_t\left(s_t, a_t\right) + \beta \int V_{t+1}\left(s^{t+1}\right) P_{t+1}\left(s_t, a_t; ds_{t+1}\right)$$

$$\geq \sup_{a_t \in \Gamma(s_t)} u_t\left(s_t, a_t\right) + \beta \int J_{t+1}^T\left(s^{t+1}, C(\pi^{s^t}, s_{t+1})\right) P_{t+1}\left(s_t, a_t; ds_{t+1}\right)$$

$$\geq u_t\left(s_t, \pi_t^{s^t}\right) + \beta \int J_{t+1}^T\left(s^{t+1}, C(\pi^{s^t}, s_{t+1})\right) P_{t+1}\left(s_t, \pi_t^{s^t}; ds_{t+1}\right)$$

$$= J_t^T\left(s^t, \pi^{s^t}\right),$$

where the first inequality uses the fact that $C(\pi^{s^t}, s_{t+1}) \in \Pi(s^{t+1})$, the second follows from the fact that $\pi_t^{s^t} \in \Gamma\left(s_t\right)$, and the last equality follows from lemma 6.3.1. Thus $W_t\left(s^t\right) \geq V_t\left(s^t\right)$.

Next we show that $W_t\left(s^t\right) \leq V_t\left(s^t\right)$. By assumption 6.3.1, for any $\varepsilon > 0$, there exists a plan from s^{t+1}, $\pi^{s^{t+1}} \in \Pi\left(s^{t+1}\right)$ such that

$$V_{t+1}\left(s^{t+1}\right) \leq J_{t+1}^T\left(s^{t+1}, \pi^{s^{t+1}}\right) + \varepsilon. \tag{6.18}$$

Besides, this plan satisfies certain measurability properties. For any action $a_t \in \Gamma\left(s_t\right)$, we construct a feasible plan $\pi^{s^t} \in \Pi\left(s^t\right)$ such that $\pi_t^{s^t} = a_t$ and $C(\pi_t^{s^t}, s_{t+1}) =$

$\pi^{s^{t+1}}$. By the definition of V_t, lemma 6.3.1, and (6.18), we obtain

$$V_t\left(s^t\right) \geq J_t^T\left(s^t, \pi^{s^t}\right)$$

$$= u_t\left(s_t, a_t\right) + \beta \int J_{t+1}^T\left(s^{t+1}, \pi^{s^{t+1}}\right) P_{t+1}\left(s_t, a_t; ds_{t+1}\right)$$

$$\geq u_t\left(s_t, a_t\right) + \beta \int V_{t+1}\left(s^{t+1}\right) P_{t+1}\left(s_t, a_t; ds_{t+1}\right) - \beta\varepsilon.$$

The measurability assumption on $\pi^{s^{t+1}}$ is needed to ensure the above integration makes sense. Since $a_t \in \Gamma\left(s_t\right)$ is arbitrary, we deduce that

$$V_t\left(s^t\right) \geq W_t\left(s^t\right) - \beta\varepsilon.$$

Letting $\varepsilon \to 0$, we obtain $V_t\left(s^t\right) \geq W_t\left(s^t\right)$. Combining with the first step, we have proved (6.17).

Finally, by definition, $V_T\left(s^T\right)$ is independent of s^{T-1}. Suppose that $V_{t+1}\left(s^{t+1}\right)$ is independent of s^t. Then it follows from (6.17) that $V_t\left(s^t\right)$ is independent of s^{t-1}. By induction, we conclude that $\left(V_t\right)$ is Markovian. ∎

Theorem 6.3.1 is often called the **Dynamic Programming Principle** in control theory. By this theorem, we may write the value function V_t as a function of s_t and rewrite the Bellman equation (6.17) as

$$V_t\left(s_t\right) = \sup_{a_t \in \Gamma\left(s_t\right)} u_t\left(s_t, a_t\right) + \beta \int V_{t+1}\left(s_{t+1}\right) P_{t+1}\left(s_t, a_t; ds_{t+1}\right). \tag{6.19}$$

If the supremum is attained, we denote the set of maximizers by $G_t\left(s_t\right)$ for any $s_t \in \mathbb{S}$. This way gives a policy correspondence G_t from $\mathbb{S}$ to $\mathbb{A}$. If each G_t is nonempty and if there exists a measurable selection from G_t, then we say that π is generated by $\left(G_t\right)_{t=0}^{T-1}$ from s_0 if it is formed in the following way. Let $\left(g_t\right)_{t=0}^{T-1}$ be a sequence of measurable selections from $\left(G_t\right)_{t=0}^{T-1}$, and define π by

$$\pi_0 = g_0\left(s_0\right),$$
$$\pi_t\left(s^t\right) = g_t\left(s_t\right), \quad \text{all } s^t \in \mathbb{S}^t, t = 1, ..., T-1.$$

By this construction, the plan π is Markovian.

Theorem 6.3.1 demonstrates that the value function from the Markov decision problem (5.5) can be computed by backward induction using the Bellman equation (6.17) or (6.19). A natural question is how to derive an optimal plan for the Markov decision problem using Bellman equations. The following theorem shows that any plan generated by the sequence of optimal policy correspondences associated with the Bellman equation (6.19) is an optimal plan for the Markov decision problem. In addition this optimal plan is Markovian.

Theorem 6.3.2 *Let the Markov decision process in (5.1) be given and assumptions 5.1.1 to 5.1.3 hold. Suppose that the solution V_t^* to the Bellman equation (6.19) is a finite and measurable function on $\mathbb{S}$ and that the associated optimal policy correspondence G_t is nonempty and permits a measurable selection, for each $t = 0, 1, ..., T - 1$. Then any Markovian plan π^* generated by (G_t) attains the supremum of (6.14), in that*

$$V_t^*(s_t) = J_t^T(s^t, \pi^{*s^t}) = V_t(s_t), \quad \text{all } s_t \in \mathbb{S}, \ t = 0, 1, ..., T - 1,$$

where π^{*s^t} is the plan from history s^t defined by $\pi_t^{*s^t} = \pi_t^*(s_t)$, $\pi_{t+j}^{*s^t}(s_{t+1}^{t+j}) = \pi_{t+j}^*(s_{t+j})$, $j = 1, ..., T - t - 1$.

Proof Consider any feasible plan from s^t, $\pi^{s^t} \in \Pi(s^t)$. By (6.19) and the given assumptions,

$V_t^*(s_t)$

$$= \sup_{a_t \in \Gamma(s_t)} u_t(s_t, a_t) + \beta \int V_{t+1}^*(s_{t+1}) P_{t+1}(s_t, a_t; ds_{t+1})$$

$$\geq u_t\left(s_t, \pi_t^{s^t}\right) + \beta \int V_{t+1}^*(s_{t+1}) P_{t+1}\left(s_t, \pi_t^{s^t}; ds_{t+1}\right)$$

$$= u_t\left(s_t, \pi_t^{s^t}\right) + \beta \int \left\{ \sup_{a_{t+1} \in \Gamma(s_{t+1})} [u_{t+1}(s_{t+1}, a_{t+1}) \right.$$

$$\left. + \beta \int V_{t+2}^*(s_{t+2}) P_{t+2}(s_{t+1}, a_{t+1}; ds_{t+2})] \right\} P_{t+1}\left(s_t, \pi_t^{s^t}; ds_{t+1}\right)$$

$$\geq u_t\left(s_t, \pi_t^{s^t}\right) + \beta \int [u_{t+1}\left(s_{t+1}, \pi_{t+1}^{s^t}(s_{t+1})\right)$$

$$+ \beta \int V_{t+2}^*(s_{t+2}) P_{t+2}\left(s_{t+1}, \pi_{t+1}^{s^t}(s_{t+1}); ds_{t+2}\right)] P_{t+1}\left(s_t, \pi_t^{s^t}; ds_{t+1}\right)$$

$$= u_t\left(s_t, \pi_t^{s^t}\right) + \beta \int u_{t+1}\left(s_{t+1}, \pi_{t+1}^{s^t}(s_{t+1})\right) \mu_t^{t+1}\left(s_t, ds_{t+1}; \pi^{s^t}\right)$$

$$+ \beta^2 \int \int V_{t+2}^*(s_{t+2}) \mu_t^{t+2}\left(s_t, ds_{t+1}, ds_{t+2}; \pi^{s^t}\right),$$

where the two inequalities follow from the feasibility of π^{s^t}, and the last equality follows from (6.12). Continuing in this way, we can show by induction that $V_t^*(s_t) \geq J_t^T\left(s^t, \pi^{s^t}\right)$ for any $\pi^{s^t} \in \Pi(s^t)$. Thus $V_t^*(s_t) \geq V_t(s_t)$. By assumption, we can replace the inequalities above by equalities if we set $\pi = \pi^*$. Thus $V_t^*(s_t) = J_t^T(s^t, \pi^{*s^t}) = V_t(s_t)$. ∎

The preceding theorem can be viewed as a **verification theorem** in control theory. The final result gives a partial converse of this theorem. It states that any optimal plan for the Markov decision problem can be generated by the sequence of optimal policy correspondences for the dynamic programming problem. This result ensures that the dynamic programming method finds all optimal plans for the Markov decision problem.

Theorem 6.3.3 *Let the Markov decision process in (5.1) be given and assumptions 5.1.1 to 5.1.3 hold. Suppose that the sequence of value functions $(V_t)_{t=0}^{T}$ satisfies the Bellman equation (6.17) and $V_t : \mathbb{S}^t \to \mathbb{R}$ is measurable for $t = 1, 2, ..., T$. Suppose that the associated optimal policy correspondence G_t is nonempty and permits a measurable selection for $t = 0, 1, ..., T-1$. Then any optimal plan $\pi^* \in \Pi(s_0)$ for problem (5.5) satisfies*

$$\pi_0^* \in G_0(s_0) \quad \text{and} \quad \pi_t^*(s^t) \in G_t(s_t), \quad \text{all } t, s^t.$$

Proof Since the sequence of value functions (V_t) satisfies the Bellman equation (6.17), it is sufficient to show that

$$V_0(s_0) = u_0(s_0, \pi_0^*) + \beta \int V_1(s_1) P_1(s_0, \pi_0^*; ds_1), \tag{6.20}$$

$$V_t(s^t) = u_t(s_t, \pi_t^*(s^t)) + \beta \int V_{t+1}(s^{t+1}) P_{t+1}(s_t, \pi_t^*(s^t); ds_{t+1}). \tag{6.21}$$

We derive these equations by forward induction.

Consider (6.20) first. Since π^* is an optimal plan,

$$V_0(s_0) = J_0^T(s_0, \pi^*) \geq J_0^T(s_0, \pi), \quad \text{all } \pi \in \Pi(s_0). \tag{6.22}$$

By lemma 6.3.1, we can rewrite the inequality above as

$$u_0(s_0, \pi_0^*) + \beta \int J_1^T(s_1, C(\pi^*, s_1)) P_1(s_0, \pi_0^*; ds_1) \tag{6.23}$$

$$\geq u_0(s_0, \pi_0) + \beta \int J_1^T(s_1, C(\pi, s_1)) P_1(s_0, \pi_0; ds_1),$$

for all $\pi \in \Pi(s_0)$.

Next choose a measurable selection g_t from G_t and define the plan $\pi^g \in \Pi(s_0)$ as follows:

$$\pi_0^g = \pi_0^*,$$
$$\pi_t^g(s^t) = g_t(s_t), \quad \text{all } s^t \in \mathbb{S}^t, \ t = 1, 2, ..., T-1.$$

Thus, for any $s_1 \in \mathbb{S}$, the continuation plan $C(\pi^g, s_1)$ is a plan generated by (G_t) from s_1. Replacing π by π^g in (6.23) gives

$$\int J_1^T(s_1, C(\pi^*, s_1)) P_1(s_0, \pi_0^*; ds_1) \geq \int J_1^T(s_1, C(\pi^g, s_1)) P_1(s_0, \pi_0^*; ds_1). \tag{6.24}$$

By theorem 6.3.2,

$$V_1(s_1) = J_1^T(s_1, C(\pi^g, s_1)) \geq J_1^T(s_1, \sigma) \tag{6.25}$$

for all $s_1 \in \mathbb{S}$, $\sigma \in \Pi(s^1)$. Since $C(\pi^*, s_1) \in \Pi(s^1)$, it follows that

$$J_1^T(s_1, C(\pi^g, s_1)) \geq J_1^T(s_1, C(\pi^*, s_1)), \quad \text{all } s_1 \in \mathbb{S}. \tag{6.26}$$

The two inequalities in (6.24) and (6.26) imply that

$$J_1^T(s_1, C(\pi^g, s_1)) = J_1^T(s_1, C(\pi^*, s_1)), \quad P_1(s_0, \pi_0^*; \cdot) \text{ - a.s.}$$

It then follows from (6.25) that

$$V_1(s_1) = J_1^T(s_1, C(\pi^*, s_1)), \quad P_1(s_0, \pi_0^*; \cdot) \text{ - a.s.} \tag{6.27}$$

Thus, by the optimality of π^*,

$$
\begin{aligned}
V_0(s_0) &= J_0^T(s_0, \pi^*) \\
&= u_0(s_0, \pi_0^*) + \beta \int J_1^T(s_1, C(\pi^*, s_1)) P_1(s_0, ds_1; \pi_0^*) \\
&= u_0(s_0, \pi_0^*) + \beta \int V_1(s_1) P_1(s_0, ds_1; \pi_0^*),
\end{aligned}
$$

where the second line follows from lemma 6.3.1. Since (V_t) satisfies the Bellman equation (6.19) at $t = 0$, the equation above implies that $\pi_0^* \in G_0(s_0)$.

Use an analogous argument, with (6.27) in place of (6.22) as the starting time, to show that (6.21) holds for $t = 1$, and continue by induction.   ∎

In this theorem we may impose assumption 6.3.1 to ensure that (V_t) satisfies the Bellman equation by theorem 6.3.1. If we know the solutions to problems (6.17) and (6.14) are unique, then theorem 6.3.2 guarantees that the dynamic programming method finds the unique solution to the Markov decision problem and theorem 6.3.3 is unnecessary.

Theorems 6.3.1 through 6.3.3 give the formal statement of the Principle of Optimality. Though theorem 6.3.1 is intuitive, its key assumption 6.3.1 is hard to check in applications. By contrast, the assumptions of theorem 6.3.2 can be easily verified by imposing certain continuity conditions as we show in the next section. Thus this theorem is widely used in applications.

6.4   Optimal Control

In this section we consider the optimal control model introduced in section 5.2.4. In this control model a state s can be decomposed into an endogenous state x and an exogenous state z. The exogenous state follows a time-homogeneous Markov process with the transition function Q. The endogenous state follows the dynamics in (5.14). The system transition function ϕ may be time dependent as in (5.11). All results in this section can be easily extended to this general case by suitably modifying assumptions. We consider the control problem in the Bolza form:

$$\sup_{(a_t)_{t=0}^{T-1} \in \Pi(x_0, z_0)} E\left[\sum_{t=0}^{T-1} \beta^t u_t(x_t, z_t, a_t) + \beta^T u_T(x_T, z_T)\right] \tag{6.28}$$

subject to (5.14).

The corresponding dynamic programming problem is given by

$$V_t(x_t, z_t) = \sup_{a_t \in \Gamma(x_t, z_t)} u_t(x_t, z_t, a_t) + \beta \int V_{t+1}(x_{t+1}, z_{t+1}) Q(z_t, dz_{t+1}) \tag{6.29}$$

subject to (5.14) and the terminal condition $V_T(x_T, z_T) = u_T(x_T, z_T)$. We will study the existence and properties of the solution to this problem and the connection to the control problem. We impose the following assumptions on the primitives of the model, $(\mathbb{X}, \mathcal{X})$, $(\mathbb{A}, \mathcal{A})$, $(\mathbb{Z}, \mathcal{Z})$, Q, Γ, ϕ, $(u_t)_{t=0}^{T}$, and β.

Assumption 6.4.1 $\mathbb{X}$ *is a convex Borel set in* $\mathbb{R}^{n_x}$, *with its Borel subsets* $\mathcal{X}$.

Assumption 6.4.2 $\mathbb{A}$ *is a convex Borel set in* $\mathbb{R}^{n_a}$, *with its Borel subsets* $\mathcal{A}$.

Assumption 6.4.3 *One of the following conditions holds:*

a. $\mathbb{Z}$ *is a countable set and* $\mathcal{Z}$ *is the σ-algebra containing all subsets of $\mathbb{Z}$; or*

b. $\mathbb{Z}$ *is compact Borel set in* $\mathbb{R}^{n_z}$, *with its Borel subsets* $\mathcal{Z}$, *and the transition function Q on $(\mathbb{Z}, \mathcal{Z})$ has the Feller property.*

The assumption that $\mathbb{Z}$ is compact may be dispensed with. See section 12.6 in Stokey, Lucas, and Prescott (1989).

Assumption 6.4.4 *The correspondence* $\Gamma : \mathbb{X} \times \mathbb{Z} \rightarrow \mathbb{A}$ *is nonempty, compact valued, and continuous.*

Assumption 6.4.5 *The state transition function* $\phi : \mathbb{X} \times \mathbb{A} \times \mathbb{Z} \times \mathbb{Z} \rightarrow \mathbb{X}$ *is continuous.*

Assumption 6.4.6 *The reward functions* $u_t : \mathbb{X} \times \mathbb{Z} \times \mathbb{A} \rightarrow \mathbb{R}$, $t = 0, 1, ..., T-1$, *and* $u_T : \mathbb{X} \times \mathbb{Z} \rightarrow \mathbb{R}$ *are continuous.*

If $\mathbb{Z}$ is a countable set, continuity on this set is in the sense of discrete topology. We may suppose that β satisfies assumption 5.1.2. But it is unnecessary for the finite-horizon case.

The following lemma is crucial for solving Bellman equations.

Lemma 6.4.1 *Let $(\mathbb{X}, \mathcal{X})$, $(\mathbb{A}, \mathcal{A})$, $(\mathbb{Z}, \mathcal{Z})$, Q, and ϕ satisfy assumptions 6.4.1, 6.4.2, 6.4.3, and 6.4.5. Then for any continuous function $f : \mathbb{X} \times \mathbb{Z} \to \mathbb{R}$, the function defined by*

$$h(x, a, z) = \int f(\phi(x, a, z, z'), z') Q(z, dz')$$

is also continuous.

Proof See the proof of lemmas 9.5 and 9.5′ in Stokey, Lucas, and Prescott (1989). ∎

Theorem 6.4.1 (Existence) *Let $(\mathbb{X}, \mathcal{X})$, $(\mathbb{A}, \mathcal{A})$, $(\mathbb{Z}, \mathcal{Z})$, Q, Γ, ϕ, $(u_t)_{t=0}^{T}$, and β satisfy assumptions 6.4.1 to 6.4.6 and 5.1.2. Then the solution to the Bellman equation (6.29), $V_t : \mathbb{X} \times \mathbb{Z} \to \mathbb{R}$, is continuous and the associated policy correspondence $G_t : \mathbb{X} \times \mathbb{Z} \to \mathbb{A}$ is nonempty, compact valued, and upper hemicontinuous for any $t = 0, 1, ..., T - 1$.*

Proof The proof is by induction. At $t = T - 1$, since $V_T = u_T$, the Bellman equation becomes

$$V_{T-1}(x_{T-1}, z_{T-1}) = \sup_{a \in \Gamma(x_{T-1}, z_{T-1})} u_{T-1}(x_{T-1}, z_{T-1}, a) \tag{6.30}$$
$$+ \beta \int u_T(\phi(x_{T-1}, a, z_{T-1}, z_T), z_T) Q(z_{T-1}, dz_T).$$

By assumptions 6.4.3, 6.4.6, and 6.4.5, it follows from lemma 6.4.1 that the expression in the second line of the equation above is continuous in (x_{T-1}, a, z_{T-1}). By assumptions, we can use the **Theorem of the Maximum** (appendix C) to deduce that V_{T-1} is continuous and the associated policy correspondence G_T is nonempty, compact valued, and upper hemicontinuous. Suppose that V_{t+1} is continuous. Then, applying lemma 6.4.1 and the theorem of the maximum to the problem in (6.29), we deduce that the conclusion in the theorem holds at time t. Thus it holds for any $t = 0, 1, ..., T - 1$.   ∎

By this theorem and the **Measurable Selection Theorem** (appendix D), each G_t permits a measurable selection. We can then apply theorem 6.3.2 to deduce that the function V_0 delivered by the Bellman equation is equal to the value function for the Markov decision problem at date zero and that any plan generated by (G_t) gives the optimal plan for this problem.

Now we provide some characterizations for (V_t, G_t). First, we impose assumptions to ensure the value function is concave.

Assumption 6.4.7 *For each $(z,a) \in \mathbb{Z} \times \mathbb{A}$, $u_T(\cdot,z) : \mathbb{X} \to \mathbb{R}$ is strictly increasing and $u_t(\cdot,z,a) : \mathbb{X} \to \mathbb{R}$ is strictly increasing for $t = 0,1,...,T-1$.*

Assumption 6.4.8 *For each $z \in \mathbb{Z}$, $\Gamma(\cdot,z) : \mathbb{X} \to \mathbb{A}$ is increasing in the sense that $x \leq x'$ implies $\Gamma(x,z) \subset \Gamma(x',z)$.*

Assumption 6.4.9 *For each $(a,z,z') \in \mathbb{A} \times \mathbb{Z} \times \mathbb{Z}$, $\phi(\cdot,a,z,z') : \mathbb{X} \to \mathbb{X}$ is increasing.*

Theorem 6.4.2 (Monotonicity) *Let $(\mathbb{X},\mathcal{X})$, $(\mathbb{A},\mathcal{A})$, $(\mathbb{Z},\mathcal{Z})$, Q, Γ, ϕ, $(u_t)_{t=0}^{T}$, and β satisfy assumptions 6.4.1 to 6.4.9 and 5.1.2. Then the solution to the Bellman equation (6.29), $V_t(\cdot,z) : \mathbb{X} \to \mathbb{R}$, is strictly increasing for each $z \in \mathbb{Z}$ and $t = 0,1,...,T$.*

Proof The proof is by induction. At time T, $V_T(\cdot,z) = u_T(\cdot,z)$ is strictly increasing for each $z \in \mathbb{Z}$. Let $x'_{T-1} > x_{T-1}$. Use the Bellman equation (6.30) at time $T-1$ to derive

$$V_{T-1}(x_{T-1},z_{T-1}) = u_{T-1}(x_{T-1},z_{T-1},a^*)$$
$$+ \beta \int u_T(\phi(x_{T-1},a^*,z_{T-1},z_T),z_T)\,Q(z_{T-1},dz_T)$$
$$< u_{T-1}(x'_{T-1},z_{T-1},a^*)$$
$$+ \beta \int u_T(\phi(x'_{T-1},a^*,z_{T-1},z_T),z_T)\,Q(z_{T-1},dz_T)$$
$$\leq \sup_{a \in \Gamma(x'_{T-1},z_{T-1})} u_{T-1}(x'_{T-1},z_{T-1},a)$$
$$+ \beta \int u_T(\phi(x'_{T-1},a,z_{T-1},z_T),z_T)\,Q(z_{T-1},dz_T)$$
$$= V_{T-1}(x'_{T-1},z_{T-1}),$$

where $a^* \in \Gamma(x_{T-1},z_{T-1})$ attains the supremum. The existence of a^* follows from theorem 6.4.1. The first inequality follows from assumptions 6.4.7 and 6.4.9. The second inequality follows from $a^* \in \Gamma(x'_{T-1},z_{T-1})$ by assumption 6.4.8. Suppose that $V_{t+1}(\cdot,z)$ is strictly increasing. We then apply the Bellman equation (6.29) at time t and follow the argument above to deduce that $V_t(\cdot,z)$ is strictly increasing. This completes the proof. ∎

Second, we impose assumptions to ensure that the value function is concave and the optimal policy correspondence is single valued.

Assumption 6.4.10 *For each $z \in \mathbb{Z}$, $u_T(\cdot,z)$ is strictly concave and*

$$u_t(\theta x + (1-\theta)x', z, \theta a + (1-\theta)a') \geq \theta u_t(x,z,a) + (1-\theta)u_t(x',z,a')$$

for all $(x,a),(x',a') \in \mathbb{X} \times \mathbb{A}$, all $\theta \in (0,1)$, and $t = 0,1,...,T-1$. The inequality is strict if $x \neq x'$.

Assumption 6.4.11 *For each $z \in \mathbb{Z}$ and all $x, x' \in \mathbb{X}$,*

$a \in \Gamma(x, z)$ *and* $a' \in \Gamma(x', z)$ *imply that*

$$\theta a + (1 - \theta) a' \in \Gamma(\theta x + (1 - \theta) x', z), \quad \text{all } \theta \in (0, 1).$$

Assumption 6.4.12 *For each $(z, z') \in \mathbb{Z}^2$, $\phi(\cdot, \cdot, z, z')$ is concave.*

Theorem 6.4.3 (Concavity) *Let $(\mathbb{X}, \mathcal{X})$, $(\mathbb{A}, \mathcal{A})$, $(\mathbb{Z}, \mathcal{Z})$, Q, Γ, ϕ, $(u_t)_{t=0}^{T}$, and β satisfy Assumptions 6.4.1 to 6.4.12 and 5.1.2. Let V_t be the solution to the Bellman equation (6.29) and G_t be the associated optimal policy correspondence, $t = 0, 1, ..., T - 1$. Then, for each $z \in \mathbb{Z}$, $V_t(\cdot, z) : \mathbb{X} \to \mathbb{R}$ is strictly concave and $G_t(\cdot, \cdot) : \mathbb{X} \times \mathbb{Z} \to \mathbb{A}$ is a single-valued continuous function.*

Proof The proof is by induction. At the terminal time T, $V_T(\cdot, z) = u_T(\cdot, z)$ is strictly concave by assumption 6.4.10. At $T - 1$, let $x_{T-1} \neq x'_{T-1} \in \mathbb{X}$. Define

$$x_{T-1}^{\theta} = \theta x_{T-1} + (1 - \theta) x'_{T-1} \quad \text{for } \theta \in (0, 1).$$

By assumption 6.4.1, $x_{T-1}^{\theta} \in \mathbb{X}$. Let $a^* \in \Gamma(x_{T-1}, z_{T-1})$ and $a' \in \Gamma(x'_{T-1}, z_{T-1})$ attain the supremum $V_{T-1}(x_{T-1}, z_{T-1})$ and $V_{T-1}(x'_{T-1}, z_{T-1})$, respectively. This is guaranteed by theorem 6.4.1. By assumption 6.4.11, $a^{\theta} = \theta a^* + (1 - \theta) a' \in \Gamma(x_{T-1}^{\theta}, z_{T-1})$. Use the Bellman equation (6.30) to deduce that

$$V_{T-1}\left(x_{T-1}^{\theta}, z_{T-1}\right) \geq u_{T-1}\left(x_{T-1}^{\theta}, z_{T-1}, a^{\theta}\right)$$

$$+ \beta \int u_T\left(\phi(x_{T-1}^{\theta}, a^{\theta}, z_{T-1}, z_T), z_T\right) Q\left(z_{T-1}, dz_T\right)$$

$$> \theta u_{T-1}\left(x_{T-1}, z_{T-1}, a^*\right) + (1 - \theta) u_{T-1}\left(x'_{T-1}, z_{T-1}, a'\right)$$

$$+ \beta \theta \int u_T\left(\phi(x_{T-1}, a^*, z_{T-1}, z_T), z_T\right) Q\left(z_{T-1}, dz_T\right)$$

$$+ \beta(1 - \theta) \int u_T\left(\phi(x'_{T-1}, a', z_{T-1}, z_T), z_T\right) Q\left(z_{T-1}, dz_T\right)$$

$$= \theta V_{T-1}\left(x_{T-1}, z_{T-1}\right) + (1 - \theta) V_{T-1}\left(x'_{T-1}, z_{T-1}\right),$$

where the second inequality follows from concavity of $u_{T-1}(\cdot, z_{T-1}, \cdot)$ and $u_T(\phi(\cdot, \cdot, z_{T-1}, z_T), z_T)$ by assumptions 6.4.7 and 6.4.10. Note that we need u_T to be monotonic for a composite of concave functions to be concave. This establishes concavity of $V_{T-1}(\cdot, z_{T-1})$. Suppose that $V_{t+1}(\cdot, z)$ is strictly concave. Then, by theorem 6.4.2, $V_{t+1}(\cdot, z)$ is strictly increasing. Applying the Bellman equation (6.29) at date t and the argument above, we deduce that $V_t(\cdot, z)$ is strictly concave. Because $V_t(\cdot, z)$ is strictly concave for all $t = 0, 1, ..., T$, the optimal policy correspondence is a single-valued continuous function. This completes the proof. ∎

If the assumptions in the theorem hold, then we write the optimal policy function as $g_t : \mathbb{X} \times \mathbb{Z} \to \mathbb{A}$. This policy function generates an optimal plan $(a_0, a_1, ..., a_{T-1})$ and optimal system dynamics $(x_0, x_1, ..., x_T)$ recursively as follows:

$$a_t \left(z^t \right) = g_t \left(x_t, z_t \right),$$
$$x_{t+1} \left(z^{t+1} \right) = \phi \left(x_t, a_t, z_t, z_{t+1} \right), \quad (x_0, z_0) \text{ given,}$$

where $z^t \in \mathbb{Z}^t$.

Third, we impose assumptions to ensure differentiability of the value function. For any set B in some Euclidean space, we use the notation $\text{int}(B)$ to denote the interior of B.

Assumption 6.4.13   *For each $z \in \mathbb{Z}$, $u_T (\cdot, z)$ is differentiable on the interior of $\mathbb{X}$ and $u_t (\cdot, z, \cdot)$ is continuously differentiable on the interior of $\mathbb{X} \times \mathbb{A}$, for $t = 0, 1, ..., T - 1$.*

Assumption 6.4.14   *For each $(z, z') \in \mathbb{Z} \times \mathbb{Z}$, $\phi (\cdot, \cdot, z, z')$ is differentiable on the interior of $\mathbb{X} \times \mathbb{A}$.*

Theorem 6.4.4   (Differentiability) *Let $(\mathbb{X}, \mathcal{X})$, $(\mathbb{A}, \mathcal{A})$, $(\mathbb{Z}, \mathcal{Z})$, Q, Γ, ϕ, $(u_t)_{t=0}^{T}$, and β satisfy assumptions 6.4.1 to 6.4.14 and 5.1.2. Let $x_t \in int(\mathbb{X})$ and $a_t = g_t (x_t, z_t) \in int(\Gamma (x_t, z_t))$ for each $z_t \in \mathbb{Z}$. Then $V_t (\cdot, z_t)$ is continuously differentiable on $int(\mathbb{X})$ and*

$$\frac{\partial V_t (x_t, z_t)}{\partial x} = \frac{\partial u_t (x_t, z_t, a_t)}{\partial x} + \beta E_t \frac{\partial V_{t+1} (x_{t+1}, z_{t+1})}{\partial x} \frac{\partial \phi (x_t, a_t, z_t, z_{t+1})}{\partial x} \tag{6.31}$$

for $t = 1, 2, ..., T - 1$, and

$$\frac{\partial V_T (x_T, z_T)}{\partial x} = \frac{\partial u_T (x_T, z_T)}{\partial x}, \tag{6.32}$$

where E_t is the expectation operator conditioned on (x_t, z_t) and x_{t+1} satisfies (5.14) with $a_t = g_t (x_t, z_t)$ for $t = 0, ..., T - 1$.

Proof   The proof is by induction. At time T, $V_T (x_T, z_T) = u_T (x_T, z_T)$. Let $x_{T-1} \in int(\mathbb{X})$ and $a_{T-1} = g_{T-1} (x_{T-1}, z_{T-1}) \in int(\Gamma (x_{T-1}, z_{T-1}))$. By assumption 6.4.4, there is some open neighborhood D of x_{T-1} such that $g_{T-1} (x_{T-1}, z_{T-1}) \in int(\Gamma (x, z_{T-1}))$, all $x \in D$. We define a function $W_{T-1} : D \to \mathbb{R}$ by

$$W_{T-1} (x) = u_{T-1} (x, z_{T-1}, g_{T-1}(x_{T-1}, z_{T-1}))$$
$$+ \beta \int u_T \left(\phi(x, g_{T-1} (x_{T-1}, z_{T-1}), z_{T-1}, z_T), z_T \right) Q (z_{T-1}, dz_T).$$

Then since $g_{T-1} (x_{T-1}, z_{T-1}) \in int(\Gamma (x, z_{T-1}))$, it follows from (6.30) that $W_{T-1} (x) \le V_{T-1} (x, z_{T-1})$ with equality at $x = x_{T-1}$. By assumptions 6.4.13 and 6.4.14, W_{T-1}

is differentiable. By the **Benveniste and Scheinkman theorem** (appendix C), $V_{T-1}(\cdot, z_{T-1})$ is differentiable at x_{T-1} and

$$\frac{\partial V_{T-1}(x_{T-1}, z_{T-1})}{\partial x} = \frac{\partial W_{T-1}(x_{T-1}, z_{T-1})}{\partial x}.$$

We then obtain equation (6.31). Suppose that $V_{t+1}(\cdot, z_{t+1})$ is continuously differentiable. We use the Bellman equation (6.29) at time t to construct a function $W_t(x)$. We use the same argument to conclude that $V_t(\cdot, z_t)$ is continuously differentiable and that its derivative at x_t satisfies equation (6.31). This completes the proof.   ■

Equation (6.31) is often referred to as the **envelope condition**. Note that we have not used the assumption that $\phi(x, a, z, z')$ is differentiable in a to derive this condition. We will use it to derive first-order conditions for the Bellman equation (6.29). By theorem 6.4.4 and assumptions 6.4.13 and 6.4.14, differentiating with respect to a_t yields

$$0 = \frac{\partial u_t(x_t, z_t, a_t)}{\partial a} + \beta E_t \frac{\partial V_{t+1}(x_{t+1}, z_{t+1})}{\partial x} \frac{\partial \phi(x_t, a_t, z_t, z_{t+1})}{\partial a} \tag{6.33}$$

for $t = 0, 1, ..., T-1$. Combining with the envelope condition (6.31) and (6.32) yields all the necessary conditions to solve for an optimal plan. At a first glance, these conditions are complicated because of the presence of the value function in each period. In the next section we will show that solving for value functions is not-necessary.

In the special case in which $\phi(x, a, z, z') = a$, we can simplify the solution significantly. We do not need V_t to be monotonic to establish concavity or differentiability. In this case assumptions 6.4.7 to 6.4.9 can be dispensed with. The first-order conditions become

$$0 = \frac{\partial u_t(x_t, z_t, x_{t+1})}{\partial a} + \beta E_t \frac{\partial u_{t+1}(x_{t+1}, z_{t+1}, x_{t+2})}{\partial x}$$

for $t = 0, 1, ..., T-2$, and

$$0 = \frac{\partial u_{T-1}(x_{T-1}, z_{T-1}, x_T)}{\partial a} + \beta E_{T-1} \frac{\partial u_T(x_T, z_T)}{\partial x}$$

for $t = T-1$. These equations are often called **Euler equations**. These equations are recursive and can be solved by backward induction to obtain a solution in the form $x_{t+1} = g_t(x_t, z_t)$, $t = 0, 1, ..., T-1$.

6.5   Maximum Principle

Pontryagin's Maximum Principle is originally proposed for continuous-time optimal control problems by Pontryagin et al. (1962). This principle is closely related to the Lagrange multiplier method and also applies to discrete-time optimal control problems. We now present this principle for the control problem (6.28) studied in section 6.4. In that section we used the dynamic programming method. Here we will study the relation between dynamic programming and the Maximum Principle.

To fix ideas, we simply assume that $\mathbb{X} = \mathbb{A} = \mathbb{R}$ and $\Gamma(x,z) = \mathbb{A}$ for all $(x,a) \in \mathbb{X} \times \mathbb{A}$. The analysis can be easily extended to the general multidimensional case. We write the Lagrangian form for problem (6.28) as

$$
L = E \sum_{t=0}^{T-1} \left[\beta^t u_t\left(x_t, z_t, a_t\right) - \beta^{t+1} \mu_{t+1}\left(x_{t+1} - \phi(x_t, a_t, z_t, z_{t+1})\right) \right]
$$
$$
+ E\beta^T u_T\left(x_T, z_T\right),
$$

where $\beta^{t+1}\mu_{t+1}$ is the discounted Lagrange multiplier associated with (5.14). Under assumptions 6.4.13 and 6.4.14, we can derive the first-order conditions for an interior solution. Specifically, differentiating with respect to a_t yields

$$
\frac{\partial u_t\left(x_t, z_t, a_t\right)}{\partial a} + \beta E_t \mu_{t+1} \frac{\partial \phi\left(x_t, a_t, z_t, z_{t+1}\right)}{\partial a} = 0 \tag{6.34}
$$

for $t = 0, 1, ..., T - 1$. Differentiating with respect to x_t yields

$$
\mu_t = \frac{\partial u_t\left(x_t, z_t, a_t\right)}{\partial x} + \beta E_t \mu_{t+1} \frac{\partial \phi\left(x_t, a_t, z_t, z_{t+1}\right)}{\partial x} \tag{6.35}
$$

for $t = 1, 2, ..., T - 1$, and

$$
\mu_T = \frac{\partial u_T\left(x_T, z_T\right)}{\partial x}. \tag{6.36}
$$

Define the **Hamiltonian function** as

$$
H_t\left(x_t, a_t, z_t, \mu_{t+1}\right) = u_t\left(x_t, z_t, a_t\right) + \beta E_t \mu_{t+1} \phi(x_t, a_t, z_t, z_{t+1}), \tag{6.37}
$$

and express the preceding first-order conditions as

$$
\frac{\partial H_t\left(x_t, a_t, z_t, \mu_{t+1}\right)}{\partial a} = 0, \quad t = 0, 1, ..., T - 1, \tag{6.38}
$$

$$
\frac{\partial H_t\left(x_t, a_t, z_t, \mu_{t+1}\right)}{\partial x} = \mu_t, \quad t = 1, 2, ..., T - 1. \tag{6.39}
$$

Combining with the state-transition equation (5.14) yields a system of $3T$ equations for $3T$ variables $(a_t, x_{t+1}, \mu_{t+1})_{t=0}^{T-1}$. This system gives the necessary conditions for optimality and can be solved recursively by backward induction. This result is called the **Maximum Principle**. Given suitable concavity conditions, the system of $3T$ equations is also sufficient for optimality. Here we state a result in the one-dimensional case. It can be easily generalized to the multidimensional case.

Theorem 6.5.1 (Sufficiency of the necessary conditions from the Maximum Principle) *Let* $\mathbb{X} = \mathbb{A} = \mathbb{R}$, $\Gamma(x, z) = \mathbb{A}$ *for all* $(x, a) \in \mathbb{X} \times \mathbb{A}$, *and let assumptions 5.1.2, 6.4.3, 6.4.13, and 6.4.14 hold. Let* $\left(x_{t+1}^*, a_t^*, \mu_{t+1}^*\right)_{t=0}^{T-1}$ *satisfy the system of 3T equations (5.14), (6.36), (6.38), and (6.39). Suppose that* $H_t\left(\cdot, \cdot, z_t, \mu_{t+1}^*\right)$ *is concave in* (x, a) *for each* $z_t \in \mathbb{Z}$ *and that* $u_T(\cdot, z_T)$ *is concave in* x *for each* $z_t \in \mathbb{Z}$. *Then* $(a_t^*)_{t=0}^{T-1}$ *is an optimal policy for problem (6.28).*

Proof   We wish to show that

$$D = E \sum_{t=0}^{T-1} \beta^t u_t \left(x_t^*, z_t, a_t^*\right) - E \sum_{t=0}^{T-1} \beta^t u_t \left(x_t, z_t, a_t\right)$$
$$+ E \beta^T u_T \left(x_T^*, z_T\right) - E \beta^T u_T \left(x_T, z_T\right)$$
$$\geq 0$$

for any feasible plan $(a_t)_{t=0}^{T-1}$ and the associated state process $(x_t)_{t=1}^T$ satisfying (5.14). Since both $(x_{t+1}, a_t)_{t=0}^{T-1}$ and $\left(x_{t+1}^*, a_t^*\right)_{t=0}^{T-1}$ satisfy the state-transition equation, we deduce that

$$D = E \sum_{t=0}^{T-1} \left[\beta^t u_t \left(x_t^*, z_t, a_t^*\right) - \beta^{t+1} \mu_{t+1}^* \left(x_{t+1}^* - \phi(x_t^*, a_t^*, z_t, z_{t+1})\right)\right]$$
$$- E \sum_{t=0}^{T-1} \left[\beta^t u_t \left(x_t, z_t, a_t\right) - \beta^{t+1} \mu_{t+1}^* \left(x_{t+1} - \phi(x_t, a_t, z_t, z_{t+1})\right)\right]$$
$$+ E \beta^T u_T \left(x_T^*, z_T\right) - E \beta^T u_T \left(x_T, z_T\right).$$

By the given assumptions, we obtain

$$D = E \sum_{t=0}^{T-1} \beta^t H_t \left(x_t^*, a_t^*, z_t, \mu_{t+1}^*\right) - E \sum_{t=0}^{T-1} \beta^t H_t \left(x_t, a_t, z_t, \mu_{t+1}\right)$$
$$- E \sum_{t=0}^{T-1} \beta^{t+1} \mu_{t+1}^* \left(x_{t+1}^* - x_{t+1}\right)$$
$$+ E \beta^T u_T \left(x_T^*, z_T\right) - E \beta^T u_T \left(x_T, z_T\right)$$
$$\geq E \sum_{t=0}^{T-1} \beta^t \frac{\partial H_t \left(x_t^*, a_t^*, z_t, \mu_{t+1}^*\right)}{\partial x} \left(x_t^* - x_t\right)$$
$$+ E \sum_{t=0}^{T-1} \beta^t \frac{\partial H_t \left(x_t^*, a_t^*, z_t, \mu_{t+1}^*\right)}{\partial a} \left(a_t^* - a_t\right)$$

$$- E \sum_{t=0}^{T-1} \beta^{t+1} \mu_{t+1}^* \left(x_{t+1}^* - x_{t+1} \right)$$

$$+ E \beta^T \frac{\partial u_T \left(x_T^*, z_T \right)}{\partial x} \left(x_T^* - x_T \right).$$

Rearranging terms and using (6.36), (6.38), (6.39), and $x_0^* = x_0$, we find that the right-hand side of the inequality above is equal to zero. Thus $D \geq 0$.   ∎

A set of sufficient conditions for $H_t \left(\cdot, \cdot, z_t, \mu_{t+1}^* \right)$ to be concave is the following: u_t is concave in (x, a) for $t = 0, 1, ..., T - 1$, u_T is concave in x, and ϕ is concave in (x, a). In addition $\mu_{t+1}^* \geq 0$ for $t = 0, 1, ..., T - 1$. If ϕ is linear in (x, a), then the last assumption on μ_{t+1}^* is not needed.

What is the relation between the Maximum Principle and dynamic programming? Let

$$\mu_t = \frac{\partial V_t \left(x_t, z_t \right)}{\partial x_t}, \quad t = 1, 2, ..., T,$$

where V_t is the value function defined in (6.29). The Lagrange multiplier μ_t is interpreted as the shadow value of the state. Then we can immediately see that equation (6.34) or (6.38) is equivalent to equation (6.33) and that equation (6.35) or (6.39) is equivalent to equation (6.31). The beauty of the Maximum Principle is that we do not need to study value functions directly, which are complicated objects as shown in the previous section. Instead, the Lagrange multipliers are the objects to solve for. Moreover this approach can easily handle additional intratemporal constraints on states or actions. One only needs to introduce additional Lagrange multipliers and then apply the Kuhn–Tucker theorem (appendix C) to derive first–order conditions.

In many economic problems the state-transition equation takes the following form:

$$x_{t+1} = \phi \left(x_t, a_t, z_t \right),$$

where x_{t+1} is nonstochastic conditioned on the current state and action. In this case we can replace the Lagrange multiplier $\beta^{t+1} \mu_{t+1}$ with $\beta^t \lambda_t$ in the Lagrangian form. The first-order conditions become

$$\frac{\partial u_t \left(x_t, z_t, a_t \right)}{\partial a} + \lambda_t \frac{\partial \phi \left(x_t, a_t, z_t, z_{t+1} \right)}{\partial a} = 0 \tag{6.40}$$

for $t = 0, 1, ..., T - 1$. Then

$$\lambda_t = \beta E_t \frac{\partial u_{t+1} \left(x_{t+1}, z_{t+1}, a_{t+1} \right)}{\partial x} + \beta E_t \lambda_{t+1} \frac{\partial \phi \left(x_{t+1}, a_{t+1}, z_{t+1} \right)}{\partial x}$$

for $t = 0, 1, ..., T - 2$, and

$$\lambda_{T-1} = E_{T-1}\left[u_T\left(x_T, z_T\right)\right].$$

6.6   Applications

In this section we analyze two Markov decision problems using the method of dynamic programming. The first problem is a classic optimal stopping problem, and the second is a classic optimal control problem.

6.6.1   Secretary Problem

Consider the secretary problem presented in section 5.2.2. Time is denoted by $t = 1, 2, ..., T = N$. Suppose that $N \geq 3$. The state space is $\{0, 1\}$. Let the value $V_t(1)$ be the maximum probability of choosing the best candidate, when the current candidate has the highest relative rank among the first t interviewed. Let $V_t(0)$ be the maximum probability of choosing the best candidate, when the current candidate does not have the highest relative rank among the first t interviewed.

We use the notation introduced in chapter 5.2.2. In the terminal time,

$$V_N(1) = h(1) = 1, \quad V_N(0) = h(0) = 0.$$

We write the Bellman equation as

$$V_t(1) = \max\left\{g_t(1), \ f_t(1) + Q_{t+1}(1,1)V_{t+1}(1) + Q_{t+1}(1,0)V_{t+1}(0)\right\}$$

$$= \max\left\{\frac{t}{N}, \ \frac{1}{t+1}V_{t+1}(1) + \frac{t}{t+1}V_{t+1}(0)\right\}$$

and

$$V_t(0) = \max\left\{g_t(0), \ f_t(0) + Q_{t+1}(0,1)V_{t+1}(1) + Q_{t+1}(0,0)V_{t+1}(0)\right\}$$

$$= \max\left\{0, \ \frac{1}{t+1}V_{t+1}(1) + \frac{t}{t+1}V_{t+1}(0)\right\}.$$

Note that $V_t \geq 0$. We deduce that

$$V_t(0) = \frac{1}{t+1}V_{t+1}(1) + \frac{t}{t+1}V_{t+1}(0), \tag{6.41}$$

$$V_t(1) = \max\left\{\frac{t}{N}, V_t(0)\right\}. \tag{6.42}$$

The following proposition characterizes an optimal policy.

Proposition 6.6.1 *It is optimal to interview τ candidates and subsequently choose the first candidate that is better than those τ candidates, where τ is given by*

$$\tau = \min\left\{t \geq 1 : \frac{1}{t} + \frac{1}{t+1} + \dots + \frac{1}{N-1} < 1\right\}. \tag{6.43}$$

Proof By (6.42), $V_t(1) \geq V_t(0)$ for all t. It follows from (6.41) that $V_t(0) \geq V_{t+1}(0)$. Thus there is a critical value τ such that $t/N \geq V_t(0)$ for all $t \geq \tau$ and $t/N \leq V_t(0)$ for all $t \leq \tau$. This implies that the best strategy is to wait till t candidates have being seen and then choose the first one that is the best so far. We now determine τ. For $t \geq \tau$, equation (6.41) implies that

$$V_t(0) = \frac{1}{t+1}\frac{t+1}{N} + \frac{t}{t+1}V_{t+1}(0) = \frac{1}{N} + \frac{t}{t+1}V_{t+1}(0).$$

Note that $V_N(0) = 0$. Solving this equation backward yields

$$V_t(0) = \frac{t}{N}\left(\frac{1}{t} + \frac{1}{t+1} + \dots + \frac{1}{N-1}\right), \quad t \geq \tau.$$

This equation gives τ defined in (6.43). ∎

We can write τ as a function of N. We would check that $\tau(4) = 1$. This means that the employer should first interview one candidate and then choose the next candidate that is better the first one. For N sufficiently large,

$$1 \simeq \frac{1}{\tau(N)} + \frac{1}{\tau(N)+1} + \dots + \frac{1}{N-1} \simeq \int_{\tau(N)}^{N} \frac{1}{x}dx.$$

Thus

$$\ln\frac{N}{\tau(N)} \simeq 1 \implies \frac{\tau(N)}{N} \simeq \frac{1}{e} \simeq 0.368.$$

This implies that with a large number of candidates, the employer should first interview about 36.8 percent of the candidates and then choose the first candidate who is better than those candidates.

6.6.2 A Consumption–Saving Problem

We consider a classical consumption–saving problem with uncertain labor income. A consumer is initially endowed with some savings. Each period he receives uncertain labor income. He then decides how much to consume and how much to save in order to maximize his discounted expected utility over a finite horizon.

We formulate this problem by the following Markov decision model:

$$\max E\left[\sum_{t=0}^{T}\beta^t u(c_t)\right]$$

subject to

$$c_t + a_{t+1} = Ra_t + y_t, \quad a_0 \geq 0 \text{ given,}$$

where $R > 0$ is the gross interest rate and c_t, a_t, and y_t represent consumption, savings, and labor income, respectively. Assume that $u'' < 0$, $u' > 0$ and $\lim_{c \to 0} u'(c) = \infty$. Assume that each y_t is independently and identically drawn from a distribution over $[y_{\min}, y_{\max}]$. Note that there is no reward from the terminal state a_{T+1}. We need to impose a constraint on a_{T+1}; otherwise, the consumer could borrow and consume an infinite amount. Thus we may impose a borrowing constraint of the form $a_{T+1} \geq -b_T$, where $b_T \geq 0$ represents a borrowing limit. In general, there may be borrowing constraints in each period because of financial market frictions:

$$a_{t+1} \geq -b_t \quad \text{for some } b_t \geq 0, \ t = 0, 1, ..., T,$$

where the borrowing limit b_t may be time and state dependent. Here we simply take an ad hoc constraint: $b_t = b \geq 0$.

Let $\hat{a}_t = a_t + b$. Define the cash on hand as $x_t = Ra_t + y_t + b$, which is the maximum that can be spent on consumption. Then we can rewrite the budget and borrowing constraints, respectively, as

$$x_{t+1} = R(x_t - c_t) + y_{t+1} - rb,$$

$$c_t + \hat{a}_{t+1} = x_t, \quad \hat{a}_{t+1} \geq 0.$$

By the Principle of Optimality, we consider the following dynamic programming problem:

$$V_t(x_t) = \max_{0 \leq \hat{a}_{t+1} \leq x_t} u(x_t - \hat{a}_{t+1}) + \beta E V_{t+1}(R\hat{a}_{t+1} + y_{t+1} - rb)$$

for $t = 0, 1, ..., T-1$, where the expectation is taken with respect to y_{t+1}. Clearly, in the last period $c_T = x_T$ and hence $V_T(x_T) = u(x_T)$. Note that the change above of variables reduces the dimension of the state space because we only need to consider one state variable, x_t, instead of two state variables, a_t and y_t. This method typically works for models with IID shocks but not for models with Markov shocks.

It is useful to define $n = T - t$, which is interpreted as an index for "time-to-go" following the terminology in Whittle (1982). We then rewrite the preceding Bellman equation as

$$v_0(x) = u(x),$$

$$v_n(x) = \max_{s \in [0,x]} u(x - s) + \beta E v_{n-1}(Rs + y - rb), \quad n = 1, ..., T.$$

We can apply the theory developed in section 6.4 to this problem. In particular, we deduce that v_n inherits the basic properties of u, that is, v_n is strictly increasing, strictly concave, and continuously differentiable on $\mathbb{R}_{++}$. In addition there exist optimal consumption and saving policy functions, $g_n(x)$ and $s_n(x) = x - g_n(x)$, respectively. The following properties can be proved:

- $v_n'(x)$ is increasing in n.
- $g_0(x) = x$ and $s_0(x) = 0$.
- $g_n(x)$ and $s_n(x)$ are continuous and increasing in x.
- $g_n(x)$ is decreasing in n and $s_n(x)$ is increasing in n.
- $g_n(x)$ and $s_n(x)$ satisfy the first-order and envelope conditions

$$v_n'(x) = u'(g_n(x)) \geq \beta RE\left[v_{n-1}'(Rs_n(x) + y - rb)\right],$$

with equality if $s_n(x) > 0$ for $n = 1, ..., T$.

Transforming to the original problem in terms of the calendar time, we write the consumption and saving functions at time t as $c_t(x) = g_{T-t}(x)$ and $\hat{a}_{t+1}(x) = s_{T-t}(x)$, respectively.

To compare with the deterministic case, let $c_t(x; y_{\min})$ denote the optimal consumption policy when $y_t = y_{\min}$ for $t = 0, 1, ..., T$. A similar interpretation applies to the notation $c_t(x; y_{\max})$. We then have the following result: $c_t(x; y_{\max}) \geq c_t(x) \geq c_t(x; y_{\min})$.

6.7 Exercises

1. Establish theorems 6.3.1 to 6.3.3 for the deterministic case by suitably modifying the assumptions. Compare these theorems to the stochastic case and discuss how the assumptions and proofs can be simplified without measurability restrictions.

2. Consider the example analyzed in section 6.1. Suppose that there is a multiplicative productivity shock z_t to the production function where (z_t) follows a Markov process with transition function Q. Solve the optimal consumption and investment policies.

3. Solve the secretary problem where the objective is to maximize the probability of choosing one of two best candidates, namely a candidate with rank 1 or 2.

4. Solve the secretary problem in which the objective is to maximize the expected rank of the candidate selected (note that 1 is the highest rank).

5. Prove the properties of the consumption and saving policy functions stated in section 6.6.2.

6. Formulate and analyze the stochastic consumption–saving problem in section 6.6.2 when labor income follows a general Markov process.

7. (Phelps 1962) Consider the stochastic consumption–saving problem analyzed in section 6.6.2. Suppose that there is no borrowing in that $b = 0$. Suppose that labor income $y_t = y$ is constant over time, but the interest rate is uncertain. The gross interest rate between time t and $t + 1$ is R_{t+1}, which is drawn independently and identically from some distribution. Analyze the properties of consumption and saving policies.

8. Consider the following deterministic consumption–saving problem:

$$\max \sum_{t=0}^{T} \beta^t \frac{c_t^{1-\gamma}}{1-\gamma}, \quad \gamma > 0,$$

subject to

$$c_t + a_{t+1} = Ra_t + y_t, \quad a_0 \text{ given,}$$

where $y_{t+1} = (1 + g) y_t$. There is no borrowing constraint. Explicitly solve this problem.

9. (Schechtman and Escudero 1977) Consider the following stochastic consumption–saving problem:

$$\max E \left[\sum_{t=0}^{T} \beta^t \left(-e^{-\gamma c_t} \right) \right], \quad \gamma > 0,$$

subject to

$$c_t + a_{t+1} = Ra_t + y_t, \quad a_0 \text{ given,}$$

where y_t is independently and identically distributed on $[y_{\min}, y_{\max}]$. Explicitly solve the optimal consumption and saving policies and the value function. Note that consumption can be negative for exponential utility.

10. (Levhari, Mirman, and Zilcha 1980) Suppose that we impose the constraints $c_t \geq 0$ and $a_{t+1} \geq 0$ in the problem above. Solve the optimal consumption and saving policies where $\beta R < 1$.

7 Infinite-Horizon Dynamic Programming

In this chapter we will study the infinite-horizon Markov decision process model introduced in chapter 5. The primitives of this model are $(\mathbb{S}, \mathcal{S})$, $(\mathbb{A}, \mathcal{A})$, Γ, P, u, and β. We will maintain assumptions 5.1.1 and 5.1.4. Unlike the finite-horizon case, the infinite-horizon model has a stationarity structure in that both the one-period rewards and the stochastic kernels for the state process are time homogeneous. Intuitively, we can view the infinite-horizon model as the limit of the finite-horizon model as the time horizon goes to infinity. As a result the theory developed in the previous chapter can be extended to the infinite-horizon case. In section 7.1 we formalize the Principle of Optimality and derive the Bellman equation for the infinite-horizon case. The difficulty of the infinite-horizon case is that there is no general theory to guarantee the existence of a solution to the Bellman equation. For bounded rewards we can use the powerful Contraction Mapping Theorem (appendix B) to deal with this issue. Section 7.2 studies models with bounded rewards. Section 7.3 analyzes the optimal control model with bounded and unbounded rewards. In section 7.4 we derive first-order conditions and transversality conditions.

7.1 Principle of Optimality

In this section we prove the infinite-horizon Principle of Optimality by establishing three theorems analogous to theorems 6.3.1 to 6.3.3. Recall that the value function $V : \mathbb{S} \to \mathbb{R} \cup \{\pm\infty\}$ is defined by

$$V(s) = \sup_{\pi \in \Pi(s)} J(s, \pi), \tag{7.1}$$

where $\Pi(s)$ is the set of feasible plans from initial state $s \in S$ and $J(s, \pi)$ is the total discounted expected rewards from π defined in (5.4). Also recall that under assumptions 5.1.1 and 5.1.4, this is a well-defined problem. We can make the following stronger assumption in order to establish that J has a recursive structure. This structure is important for dynamic programming.

Assumption 7.1.1   *If u takes on both signs, there is a collection of nonnegative, measurable functions $L_t : \mathbb{S} \to \mathbb{R}_+$, $t = 0, 1, \dots$, such that for all $\pi \in \Pi(s_0)$ and all $s_0 \in \mathbb{S}$,*

$$|u(s_0, \pi_0)| \le L_0(s_0), \quad |u(s_t, \pi_t(s^t))| \le L_t(s_0),$$

and

$$\sum_{t=0}^{\infty} \beta^t L_t(s_0) < \infty.$$

Lemma 7.1.1   *Let $(\mathbb{S}, \mathcal{S})$, $(\mathbb{A}, \mathcal{A})$, Γ, P, u, and β be given. Suppose that assumptions 5.1.1, 5.1.2, 5.1.4, and 7.1.1 hold. Then, for any $s_0 \in \mathbb{S}$ and any $\pi \in \Pi(s_0)$,*

$$J(s_0, \pi) = u(s_0, \pi_0) + \beta \int J(s_1, C(\pi, s_1)) P(s_0, \pi_0; ds_1),$$

where for each $s_1 \in \mathbb{S}$, $C(\pi, s_1)$ is the continuation plan of π following s_1.

Proof   By definition,

$$J(s_0, \pi) = u(s_0, \pi_0) + \beta \lim_{n \to \infty} \sum_{t=1}^{n} \beta^{t-1} \int u(s_t, \pi_t(s^t)) \mu^t(s_0, ds^t; \pi).$$

We compute the second term on the right-hand side of the equation above:

$$\lim_{n \to \infty} \sum_{t=1}^{n} \beta^{t-1} \int u(s_t, \pi_t(s^t)) \mu^t(s_0, ds^t; \pi)$$

$$= \lim_{n \to \infty} \int \{ u(s_1, \pi_1(s^1))$$

$$+ \sum_{t=2}^{n} \beta^{t-1} \int u(s_t, \pi_t(s^t)) \mu^{t-1}(s_1, ds_2^t; C(\pi, s_1)) \} P(s_0, \pi_0; ds_1)$$

$$= \int \lim_{n \to \infty} \{ u(s_1, \pi_1(s^1))$$

$$+ \sum_{t=2}^{n} \beta^{t-1} \int u(s_t, \pi_t(s^t)) \mu^{t-1}(s_1, ds_2^t; C(\pi, s_1)) \} P(s_0, \pi_0; ds_1)$$

$$= \int J(s_1, C(\pi, s_1)) P(s_0, \pi_0; ds_1),$$

where the first equality follows from the definition of μ^t in (5.2), the second from the Monotone Convergence Theorem if $u \ge 0$ or $u \le 0$, and from the Dominated

Convergence Theorem by assumption 7.1.1 if u takes on both signs, and the last from the definition of J. ∎

The following assumption is analogous to assumption 6.3.1.

Assumption 7.1.2 *(a) The value function $V : \mathbb{S} \to \mathbb{R}$ is measurable. (b) Given any $s \in \mathbb{S}$, for any $\varepsilon > 0$, there exists a plan from s, $\pi^s \in \Pi(s)$, such that*

$$J(s, \pi^s) + \varepsilon \geq V(s).$$

In addition, as functions of s, π_0^s, and $\pi_t^s(s_1^t)$ for any fixed $s_1^t \in \mathbb{S}^t$ are measurable, $t = 1, 2, \dots$.

A plan satisfying the measurability restriction in the above assumption is called a **global plan** in Stokey, Lucas, and Prescott (1989).

Theorem 7.1.1 (Dynamic Programming Principle) *Let $(\mathbb{S}, \mathcal{S})$, $(\mathbb{A}, \mathcal{A})$, Γ, P, u, and β be given. Suppose that assumptions 5.1.1, 5.1.2, 5.1.4, 7.1.1, and 7.1.2 hold. Then V satisfies the **Bellman equation**:*

$$V(s) = \sup_{a \in \Gamma(s)} u(s, a) + \int V(s') P(s, a; ds'). \tag{7.2}$$

Proof The proof consists of two steps. First, for any plan $\pi \in \Pi(s)$,

$$
\begin{aligned}
W(s) &\equiv \sup_{a \in \Gamma(s)} u(s, a) + \int V(s') P(s, a; ds') \\
&\geq \sup_{a \in \Gamma(s)} u(s, a) + \int J(s', C(\pi, s')) P(s, a; ds') \\
&\geq u(s, \pi_0) + \int J(s', C(\pi, s')) P(s, \pi_0; ds') \\
&= J(s, \pi).
\end{aligned}
$$

Thus $W(s) \geq V(s)$.

Second, by assumption 7.1.2, given any $s \in \mathbb{S}$ for any $\varepsilon > 0$, there exists a plan from s, $\pi^s \in \Pi(s)$ such that

$$J(s, \pi^s) + \varepsilon \geq V(s). \tag{7.3}$$

In addition, as functions of s, π_0^s and $\pi_t^s(s_1^t)$ for any fixed $s_1^t \in \mathbb{S}^t$ are measurable, $t = 1, 2, \dots$. For any $a \in \Gamma(s)$, define the plan $d = (a, d_1, d_2, \dots)$, where $C(d, s_1) = \pi^{s_1}$

for any $s_1 \in \mathbb{S}$. That is, $d_1(s_1) = \pi_0^{s_1}$ and $d_t(s_1, ..., s_t) = \pi_{t-1}^{s_1}(s_2, ..., s_t)$, $t = 2, 3 ....$ Assumption 7.1.2 implies that $d \in \Pi(s)$. Thus

$$V(s) \geq J(s, d)$$

$$= u(s, a) + \int J\left(s', \pi^{s'}\right) P(s, a; ds')$$

$$\geq u(s, a) + \int V(s') P(s, a; ds') - \beta\varepsilon,$$

where the second line follows from lemma 7.1.1 and the last line from (7.3). Taking the supremum over $a \in \Gamma(s)$ and letting $\varepsilon \to 0$, we obtain $V(s) \geq W(s)$. Combining the two steps above completes the proof.   ∎

Unlike in the finite-horizon case, the Bellman equation in the infinite-horizon case gives a nontrivial fixed point problem: To solve the problem on the right-hand side of (7.2), one needs to know the function V, which is also equal to the optimized value of this problem. We call this problem a **dynamic programming problem**. If there is a solution $a \in \Gamma(s)$ that attains the supremum in (7.2), we denote the set of all solutions as $G(s)$. This defines an optimal policy correspondence $G : \mathbb{S} \to \mathbb{A}$. If G permits a sequence of measurable selections $(g_t)_{t=0}^{\infty}$ (some selections may be identical), then we can define a plan π generated by G as follows:

$$\pi_0 = g_0(s_0), \quad \pi_t(s^t) = g_t(s_t), \quad s^t \in \mathbb{S}^t.$$

This plan is feasible from s_0 and is Markovian. If g_t is independent of t, then π is a stationary plan.

The following result demonstrates that under some conditions the solution to the Bellman equation (7.2) gives the value function for the Markov decision problem (7.1). Additionally any plan generated by the optimal policy correspondence from the dynamic programming problem is optimal for the Markov decision problem.

Theorem 7.1.2   (Verification) *Let $(\mathbb{S}, \mathcal{S})$, $(\mathbb{A}, \mathcal{A})$, Γ, P, u, and β be given. Suppose that assumptions 5.1.1, 5.1.2, 5.1.4, and 7.1.1 hold. Suppose that $V^* : \mathbb{S} \to \mathbb{R}$ is a measurable function satisfying the Bellman equation (7.2) and*

$$\lim_{n \to \infty} \beta^n \int V^*(s_n) \mu^n(s_0, ds^n; \pi) = 0 \tag{7.4}$$

for all $\pi \in \Pi(s_0)$ and all $s_0 \in \mathbb{S}$, where $\mu^t(s_0, \cdot; \pi)$ is defined in (5.2). Let G be the optimal policy correspondence associated with (7.2), and suppose that G is nonempty and permits a measurable selection. Then $V = V^*$ and any plan π^* generated by G attains the supremum in (7.1).

Proof   Given any $s_0 \in \mathbb{S}$, for any feasible plan $\pi \in \Pi(s_0)$, use the Bellman equation to derive

$$V^*(s_t) \geq u\left(s_t, \pi_t\left(s^t\right)\right) + \beta \int V^*(s_{t+1}) P\left(s_t, \pi_t\left(s^t\right); ds_{t+1}\right) \tag{7.5}$$

for $t = 0, 1, ..., n$. Multiplying by β^t and rearranging yield

$$\beta^t V^*(s_t) - \beta^{t+1} \int V^*(s_{t+1}) P\left(s_t, \pi_t\left(s^t\right); ds_{t+1}\right) \geq \beta^t u\left(s_t, \pi_t\left(s^t\right)\right).$$

Taking expectations with $\mu^t\left(s_0, ds^t; \pi\right)$ and summing over $t = 0, 1, ..., n - 1$, we obtain

$$V^*(s_0) - \beta^n \int V^*(s_n)\, \mu^n\left(s_0, ds^n; \pi\right) \geq \sum_{t=0}^{n-1} \beta^t \int u\left(s_t, \pi_t\left(s^t\right)\right) \mu^t\left(s_0, ds^t; \pi\right).$$

Taking limits as $n \to \infty$ and using (7.4), we deduce that

$$V^*(s_0) \geq J(s_0, \pi).$$

Since this is true for all $\pi \in \Pi(s_0)$, $V^*(s_0) \geq V(s_0)$. The equality is attained if we replace π by π^* because π^* is generated by G so that (7.5) becomes equality for all t at $\pi = \pi^*$.   ∎

Condition (7.4) is often called a **transversality condition**. It is trivially satisfied if V^* is bounded. To illustrate its usefulness if V^* is unbounded, we consider the following deterministic example:

$$\sup_{(c_t, a_{t+1})_{t=0}^{\infty}} \sum_{t=0}^{\infty} \beta^t c_t, \quad \beta = \frac{1}{R} \in (0, 1)$$

subject to

$$c_t + s_{t+1} = R s_t, \quad c_t \geq 0, \ s_0 > 0 \text{ given.}$$

Clearly, the consumer can borrow an infinite amount to approach an infinitely large value of discounted utility. Thus the value function is $V(s_0) = +\infty$ for any $s_0 > 0$.

Now consider the dynamic programming problem

$$V(s) = \sup_{c \geq 0} c + \beta V(Rs - c).$$

There are two solutions to this Bellman equation. One is $V^*(s) = +\infty$. The other is $\hat{V}^*(s) = Rs$. For the feasible plan $c_t = 0$ for all t, the asset holdings are $s_t = R^t s_0$ and $\beta^n \hat{V}^*(s_n) = s_0 > 0$. Thus the transversality condition (7.4) is violated for the solution $\hat{V}^*$.

We should emphasize that the transversality condition (7.4) is a sufficient condition, but not a necessary one. It is quite strong because it requires the limit to converge to zero for any feasible plan. This condition is often violated in many applications with unbounded rewards. For some special cases where an analytical solution to the Bellman equation is available, one can then verify the transversality condition (7.4) for the particular plan generated by the optimal policy function associated with the Bellman equation. If any feasible plan that violates the transversality condition is dominated by some feasible plan that satisfies this condition, then the following result, adapted from Stokey, Lucas, and Prescott (1989), guarantees that the solution to the Bellman equation is the value function and that the associated policy function generates an optimal plan.

Corollary 7.1.1 *Let $(\mathbb{S}, \mathcal{S})$, $(\mathbb{A}, \mathcal{A})$, Γ, P, u, and β be given. Suppose that assumptions 5.1.1, 5.1.2, 5.1.4, and 7.1.1 hold. Let V be the finite-value function for problem (5.6). Suppose that $V^* : \mathbb{S} \to \mathbb{R}$ is a measurable function satisfying the Bellman equation (7.2) and that the associated optimal policy correspondence G is nonempty and permits a measurable selection. Define $\hat{\Pi}(s)$ as the set of feasible plans π such that the transversality condition (7.4) holds, and define the function $\hat{V} : \mathbb{S} \to \mathbb{R}$ by*

$$\hat{V}(s) = \sup_{\pi \in \hat{\Pi}(s)} J(s, \pi), \quad \text{all } s \in \mathbb{S}.$$

Let $\pi^*(s) \in \Pi(s)$ be a plan generated by G. Suppose that

a. $\pi^*(s) \in \hat{\Pi}(s)$ all $s \in \mathbb{S}$, and

b. for any $s \in \mathbb{S}$ and $\pi \in \Pi(s)$, there exists $\hat{\pi} \in \hat{\Pi}(s)$ such that $J(s, \hat{\pi}) \geq J(s, \pi)$.

Then

$$V(s) = V^*(s) = \hat{V}(s) = J(s, \pi^*(s)) \quad \text{for all } s \in \mathbb{S}.$$

Proof   Since condition a holds, we can adapt the proof of theorem 7.1.2 to show that

$$V^*(s) = \hat{V}(s) = J(s, \pi^*(s)).$$

Since $\hat{\Pi}(s) \subset \Pi(s)$, $\hat{V}(s) \leq V(s)$. To show the reverse inequality, suppose that $\{\pi^k\}_{k=1}^{\infty}$ is a sequence in $\Pi(s)$ such that

$$\lim_{k \to \infty} J\left(s, \pi^k\right) = V(s).$$

Then by condition b, there is a sequence $\left\{\hat{\pi}^k\right\}_{k=1}^{\infty}$ such that $J\left(s,\hat{\pi}^k\right) \geq J\left(s,\pi^k\right)$. Thus

$$\lim_{k\to\infty} J\left(s,\hat{\pi}^k\right) \geq V\left(s\right).$$

So $\hat{V}\left(s\right) \geq V\left(s\right)$, completing the proof.   ∎

The following example illustrates this result by explicitly computing the value function. We call this method the value function approach.

Example 7.1.1 *Consider the infinite-horizon case of the example analyzed in section 6.1. We write the Bellman equation as*

$$V\left(K\right) = \max_{K',C\geq 0} \ln C + \beta V\left(K'\right) \tag{7.6}$$

subject to

$$C + K' = K^{\alpha}.$$

We can take the limit as the horizon $T \to \infty$ in (6.5) and (6.3) to obtain the value function

$$V\left(K\right) = \frac{1}{1-\beta}\left[\ln\left(1-\alpha\beta\right) + \frac{\beta}{1-\alpha\beta}\ln\left(\alpha\beta\right)\right] + \frac{\alpha}{1-\alpha\beta}\ln K$$

and the policy function

$$K' = g\left(K\right) = \alpha\beta K^{\alpha}.$$

Alternatively, given log utility, we could conjecture that the value function also takes a log form:

$$V\left(K\right) = A + B\ln K$$

for some constants A and B to be determined. We then would substitute this conjecture into the Bellman equation (7.6) to verify that this conjecture is correct and also to determine the constants A and B.

We use corollary 7.1.1 to verify that the solution above is optimal. First, we compute the policy $K_{t+1}^* = \alpha\beta K_t^{*\alpha}$ implied value:

$$V\left(K_t^*\right) = A + B\ln K_t^* = A + B\frac{1-\alpha^t}{1-\alpha}\ln\left(\alpha\beta\right) + B\alpha^t\ln\left(K_0\right).$$

Thus condition a in the corollary is satisfied since

$$\lim_{t\to\infty} \beta^t V\left(K_t^*\right) = 0. \tag{7.7}$$

To verify condition b in the corollary, we show that for any plan (K_t), either $J(K_0, (K_t)) = -\infty$ or it satisfies (7.7) (i.e., $(K_t) \in \hat{\Pi}(K_0)$) so that it is always dominated by (K_t^*). We note that $(K_t) \in \hat{\Pi}(K_0)$ if and only if

$$\lim_{t \to \infty} \beta^t \ln K_t = 0.$$

Suppose that this equation fails. Then the series on the right-hand side of the following equation must diverge:

$$J(K_0, (K_t)) = \sum_{t=0}^{\infty} \beta^t \ln C_t \leq \sum_{t=0}^{\infty} \beta^t \ln K_t^\alpha = \sum_{t=0}^{\infty} \alpha \beta^t \ln K_t.$$

However, this series is bounded above because we can use the resource constraint to show that

$$\ln K_t \leq \alpha^t \ln K_0.$$

Thus this series must diverge to $-\infty$, implying that $J(K_0, (K_t)) = -\infty$.

The final result is a partial converse of theorem 7.1.2. It ensures that any optimal plan for the Markov decision problem can be found by solving the dynamic programming problem in (7.2).

Theorem 7.1.3 *Let $(\mathbb{S}, \mathcal{S})$, $(\mathbb{A}, \mathcal{A})$, Γ, P, u, and β be given. Suppose that assumptions 5.1.1, 5.1.2, 5.1.4, and 7.1.1 hold. Suppose that the value function V is measurable and satisfies the Bellman equation (7.2). Suppose that the associated optimal policy correspondence G is nonempty and permits a measurable selection. Then any optimal plan $\pi^* \in \Pi(s_0)$ for problem (7.1) satisfies*

$$\pi_0^* \in G(s_0) \quad \text{and} \quad \pi_t^*(s^t) \in G(s_t), \quad \text{all } t, s^t.$$

Proof Since the value function V satisfies the Bellman equation (7.2), it is sufficient to show that

$$V(s_0) = u(s_0, \pi_0^*) + \beta \int V(s_1) P(s_0, \pi_0^*; ds_1), \tag{7.8}$$

$$V(s_t) = u(s_t, \pi_t^*(s^t)) + \beta \int V(s_{t+1}) P(s_t, \pi_t^*(s^t); ds_{t+1}). \tag{7.9}$$

We derive these equations by forward induction.
    Consider (7.8) first. Since π^* is an optimal plan,

$$V(s_0) = J(s_0, \pi^*) \geq J(s_0, \pi), \quad \text{all } \pi \in \Pi(s_0). \tag{7.10}$$

By lemma 7.1.1, we can rewrite the inequality above as

$$u\left(s_0, \pi_0^*\right) + \beta \int J\left(s_1, C(\pi^*, s_1)\right) P\left(s_0, \pi_0^*; ds_1\right)$$

$$\geq u\left(s_0, \pi_0\right) + \beta \int J\left(s_1, C(\pi, s_1)\right) P\left(s_0, \pi_0; ds_1\right) \tag{7.11}$$

for all $\pi \in \Pi\left(s_0\right)$.

Next choose a measurable selection g from G and define the plan $\pi^g \in \Pi\left(s_0\right)$ as follows:

$$\pi_0^g = \pi_0^*,$$
$$\pi_t^g\left(s^t\right) = g\left(s_t\right), \quad \text{all } s^t \in \mathbb{S}^t, \, t = 1, 2, ..., T-1.$$

Thus, for any $s_1 \in \mathbb{S}$, the continuation plan $C(\pi^g, s_1)$ is a plan generated by G from s_1. Replacing π by π^g in (7.11) gives

$$\int J\left(s_1, C(\pi^*, s_1)\right) P\left(s_0, \pi_0^*; ds_1\right) \geq \int J\left(s_1, C(\pi^g, s_1)\right) P\left(s_0, \pi_0^*; ds_1\right). \tag{7.12}$$

By theorem 7.1.2,

$$V\left(s_1\right) = J\left(s_1, C(\pi^g, s_1)\right) \geq J\left(s_1, \sigma\right) \tag{7.13}$$

for all $s_1 \in \mathbb{S}$, $\sigma \in \Pi\left(s^1\right)$. Since $C\left(\pi^*, s_1\right) \in \Pi\left(s^1\right)$, it follows that

$$J\left(s_1, C(\pi^g, s_1)\right) \geq J\left(s_1, C\left(\pi^*, s_1\right)\right), \quad \text{all } s_1 \in \mathbb{S}. \tag{7.14}$$

The two inequalities in (7.12) and (7.14) imply that

$$J\left(s_1, C(\pi^g, s_1)\right) = J\left(s_1, C\left(\pi^*, s_1\right)\right), \; P\left(s_0, \pi_0^*; \cdot\right)\text{-a.s.}$$

It then follows from (7.13) that

$$V\left(s_1\right) = J\left(s_1, C\left(\pi^*, s_1\right)\right), \; P\left(s_0, \pi_0^*; \cdot\right)\text{-a.s.} \tag{7.15}$$

Thus, by the optimality of π^*,

$$V\left(s_0\right) = J\left(s_0, \pi^*\right)$$

$$= u\left(s_0, \pi_0^*\right) + \beta \int J\left(s_1, C(\pi^*, s_1) P\left(s_0, ds_1; \pi_0^*\right)\right.$$

$$= u\left(s_0, \pi_0^*\right) + \beta \int V\left(s_1\right) P\left(s_0, ds_1; \pi_0^*\right),$$

where the second line follows from lemma 7.1.1. Since V satisfies the Bellman equation (7.2), the equation above implies that $\pi_0^* \in G\left(s_0\right)$.

We can use an analogous argument, with (7.15) in place of (7.10) as the starting time, to show that (7.9) holds for $t = 1$, and continue by induction. ∎

Theorems 7.1.1 through 7.1.3 constitute the main theory of infinite-horizon dynamic programming and formalize the Principle of Optimality in the infinite-horizon case. As in the finite-horizon case, one difficulty in applying these theorems is how to check measurability. A difficulty arising only in the infinite-horizon case is showing the existence of a solution to the fixed-point problem in the Bellman equation (7.2). In the next section we will impose certain continuity assumptions for bounded rewards to resolve both difficulties. For unbounded rewards, there is no general solution to the second difficulty. We will provide some recent results in section 7.3.2.

7.2   Bounded Rewards

Consider the Markov decision process model with the primitives $(\mathbb{S}, \mathcal{S})$, $(\mathbb{A}, \mathcal{A})$, Γ, P, u, and β. Our objective is to study the existence of a solution to the Bellman equation (7.2). We focus on the Borel case in which assumptions 6.4.1 and 6.4.2 hold. In addition we impose the following:

Assumption 7.2.1   *The reward function $u : \mathbb{S} \times \mathbb{A} \to \mathbb{R}$ is bounded and continuous.*

Assumption 7.2.2   *The correspondence $\Gamma : \mathbb{S} \to \mathbb{A}$ is nonempty, compact valued, and continuous.*

Assumption 7.2.3   *The stochastic kernel P satisfies the property that*

$$\int f(s') P(s, a; ds')$$

is continuous in (s, a) for any bounded and continuous function $f : \mathbb{S} \to \mathbb{R}$.

These assumptions allow us to use the powerful Contraction Mapping Theorem to find a fixed point of some operator or mapping. To apply this theorem, we need to introduce a Banach space and a contraction mapping. We consider the set of bounded and continuous functions on $\mathbb{S}$ endowed with the sup norm. Denote this set by $C(\mathbb{S})$. The sup norm is defined as

$$\|f\| = \sup_{s \in \mathbb{X}} |f(s)|, \quad f \in C(\mathbb{S}).$$

This set is a Banach space by theorem 3.1 in Stokey, Lucas, and Prescott (1989).

Define a **Bellman operator** T on $C(\mathbb{S})$ by

$$(Tf)(s) = \sup_{a \in \Gamma(s)} u(s, a) + \beta \int f(s') P(s, a; dz') \tag{7.16}$$

for any $f \in C(\mathbb{S})$. Then the solution to the Bellman equation (7.19) is a fixed point of T in that $V = TV$.

Theorem 7.2.1   (Existence) *Let* $(\mathbb{S}, \mathcal{S})$, $(\mathbb{A}, \mathcal{A})$, Γ, P, u, *and* β *satisfy assumptions 5.1.2, 6.4.1, 6.4.2, and 7.2.1–7.2.3. Then there exists a unique solution* $V \in C(\mathbb{S})$ *to the Bellman equation (7.2) and the associated policy correspondence* G *is nonempty, compact valued and upper hemicontinuous.*

Proof   For each $f \in C(\mathbb{S})$, the problem in (7.16) is to maximize a continuous function over the compact set $\Gamma(s)$. Thus the maximum is attained. Since both u and f are bounded, Tf is bounded. It follows from the Theorem of the Maximum (appendix C) that Tf is continuous in (x, z). Thus $T : C(\mathbb{S}) \to C(\mathbb{S})$. We use assumption 5.1.2 to verify that the conditions in the **Blackwell theorem** (appendix B) are satisfied so that T is a contraction. Since $C(\mathbb{S})$ is a Banach space, it follows from the Contraction Mapping Theorem (appendix B) that T has a unique fixed point $V \in C(\mathbb{S})$. Finally, we apply the Theorem of the Maximum to deduce the stated properties of G.   ∎

By this theorem and the Measurable Selection Theorem (appendix D), G permits a measurable selection. We can then apply theorem 7.1.2 to deduce that the solution V to the Bellman equation is equal to the value function for the Markov decision problem at date zero and any plan generated by G gives an optimal Markov plan for this problem.

The contraction property of the Bellman operator T gives a globally convergent algorithm to solve the value function. In addition it allows us to formalize the intuitive result that the solution to an infinite-horizon problem is the limit of that to a finite-horizon problem.

Theorem 7.2.2   (Convergence) *Suppose that* $(\mathbb{S}, \mathcal{S})$, $(\mathbb{A}, \mathcal{A})$, Γ, P, u, *and* β *satisfy assumptions 5.1.2, 6.4.1, 6.4.2, and 7.2.1–7.2.3. Let* V *be the unique solution to the Bellman equation (7.2). Let* V_0^N *be the value function for the N-horizon Markov decision problem (5.5):*

$$V_0^N(s) = \sup_{\pi \in \Pi(s)} J_0^N(s; \pi), \quad any\ s \in \mathbb{S},$$

where J_0^N is defined in (5.3) with $u_t = u$, $t = 0, 1, \ldots, N - 1$, and $u_N = 0$. Then

$$\|T^n v_0 - V\| \le \beta^n \|v_0 - V\|, \quad n = 1, 2, \ldots, \tag{7.17}$$

$$\lim_{N \to \infty} T^N v_0 = \lim_{N \to \infty} V_0^N = V. \tag{7.18}$$

for any $v_0 \in C(\mathbb{S})$.

Proof   Equation (7.17) follows from the Contraction Mapping Theorem. Thus $\lim_{N \to \infty} T^N v_0$ for any $v_0 \in C(\mathbb{S})$. By the definition of T and theorem 6.3.2, we can verify that $V_t^N = T^{N-t}0$, for $t = 0, 1, ..., N - 1$, where 0 is a function that is equal to 0 for any $s \in \mathbb{S}$. Thus

$$\lim_{N \to \infty} V_0^N = \lim_{N \to \infty} T^N 0 = V.$$

This completes the proof.   ∎

This convergence theorem connects the finite- and infinite-horizon problems. In terms of notations, we use V_t^N to denote the value function at any time t for an N-period problem. At time t, the decision maker faces an $(N - t)$ horizon. Thus $V_t^N = V_0^{N-t}$. In the proof, we show that $v_n = T^n 0 = V_{N-n}^N = V_0^n$, where n is the horizon or the time to go. Similar notations apply to the policy functions.

7.3   Optimal Control

In order to provide sharper characterizations of the value function and the optimal policy correspondence, we study the infinite-horizon optimal control model introduced in section 5.2.4. In this model the state space is $\mathbb{S} = \mathbb{X} \times \mathbb{Z}$. The set $\mathbb{X}$ is the set of possible values for the endogenous state variable, and $\mathbb{Z}$ is the set of possible values for the exogenous shock. The primitives of this model are $(\mathbb{X}, \mathcal{X})$, $(\mathbb{A}, \mathcal{A})$, $(\mathbb{Z}, \mathcal{Z})$, Q, Γ, ϕ, u, and β.

The control problem is given by (5.13) and (5.14). We will study the associated dynamic programming problem:

$$V(x, z) = \sup_{a \in \Gamma(x, z)} u(x, z, a) + \beta \int V(\phi(x, a, z, z'), z') Q(z, dz'). \tag{7.19}$$

The associated Bellman operator T on $C(\mathbb{S})$ is defined by

$$(Tf)(x, z) = \sup_{a \in \Gamma(x, z)} u(x, z, a) + \beta \int f(\phi(x, a, z, z'), z') Q(z, dz') \tag{7.20}$$

for any $f \in C(\mathbb{S})$. We will use this operator extensively to study the existence and properties of the solution to the Bellman equation.

7.3.1   Bounded Rewards

For bounded rewards, we can use the powerful Contraction Mapping Theorem to analyze dynamic programming problems as we have shown in section 7.2. As in that section we require that the reward function be continuous. Given $\mathbb{S} = \mathbb{X} \times \mathbb{Z}$, we replace assumption 7.2.1 by

Assumption 7.3.1 *The reward function $u : \mathbb{X} \times \mathbb{Z} \times \mathbb{A} \to \mathbb{R}$ is bounded and continuous.*

Using lemma 6.4.1 and theorem 7.2.1, we immediately obtain the following:

Theorem 7.3.1 (Existence) *Let* $(\mathbb{X}, \mathcal{X})$, $(\mathbb{A}, \mathcal{A})$, $(\mathbb{Z}, \mathcal{Z})$, Q, Γ, ϕ, u, *and* β *satisfy assumptions 5.1.2 6.4.1–6.4.5, and 7.3.1. Then there exists a unique solution* $V \in C(\mathbb{S})$ *to the Bellman equation (7.19), and the associated policy correspondence G is nonempty, compact valued, and upper hemicontinuous.*

Now we can study the properties of the solution (V, G). As in the finite-horizon case we focus on the properties of monotonicity, concavity, and differentiability. First, we consider monotonicity.

Assumption 7.3.2 *For each* $(z, a) \in \mathbb{Z} \times \mathbb{A}$, $u(\cdot, z, a) : \mathbb{X} \to \mathbb{R}$ *is strictly increasing.*

Theorem 7.3.2 (Monotonicity) *Let* $(\mathbb{X}, \mathcal{X})$, $(\mathbb{A}, \mathcal{A})$, $(\mathbb{Z}, \mathcal{Z})$, Q, Γ, ϕ, β, *and* u *satisfy assumptions 5.1.2 6.4.1–6.4.5, 6.4.8, 6.4.9, 7.3.1, and 7.3.2. Then the solution to the Bellman equation (7.19),* $V(\cdot, z) : \mathbb{X} \to \mathbb{R}$, *is strictly increasing for each* $z \in \mathbb{Z}$.

Proof Let $C'(\mathbb{S}) \subset C(\mathbb{S})$ be the subset of bounded continuous functions f on $\mathbb{S} = \mathbb{X} \times \mathbb{Z}$ that are increasing in x, and let $C''(\mathbb{S})$ be the subset of functions that are strictly increasing in x. Since $C'(\mathbb{S})$ is a closed subspace of the complete metric space $C(\mathbb{S})$, by the **Closed-Subspace Theorem** (appendix B), it is sufficient to show that T maps an element in $C'(\mathbb{S})$ into $C''(\mathbb{S})$. This can be done by applying an argument similar to that in the proof of theorem 6.4.2.   ∎

Second, we consider concavity by replacing assumption 6.4.10 with the following:

Assumption 7.3.3 *For each* $z \in \mathbb{Z}$,

$$u(\theta x + (1 - \theta) x', z, \theta a + (1 - \theta) a') \geq \theta u(x, z, a) + (1 - \theta) u(x', z, a')$$

for all $(x, a), (x', a') \in \mathbb{X} \times \mathbb{A}$ *and all* $\theta \in (0, 1)$. *The inequality is strict if* $x \neq x'$.

Theorem 7.3.3 (Concavity) *Let* $(\mathbb{X}, \mathcal{X})$, $(\mathbb{A}, \mathcal{A})$, $(\mathbb{Z}, \mathcal{Z})$, Q, Γ, ϕ, β, *and* u *satisfy assumptions 5.1.2, 6.4.1–6.4.5, 6.4.8, 6.4.9, 6.4.12, 7.3.1, 7.3.2, and 7.3.3. Let V be the solution to the Bellman equation (7.19) and G be the associated optimal policy correspondence. Then, for each* $z \in \mathbb{Z}$, $V(\cdot, z) : \mathbb{X} \to \mathbb{R}$ *is strictly concave and* $G(\cdot, \cdot) : \mathbb{X} \times \mathbb{Z} \to \mathbb{A}$ *is a single-valued continuous function.*

Proof Let $C'(\mathbb{S}) \subset C(\mathbb{S})$ be the set of bounded continuous functions f on $\mathbb{S} = \mathbb{X} \times \mathbb{Z}$ that are concave in x, and let $C''(\mathbb{S})$ be the subset of functions that are strictly concave in x. Since $C'(\mathbb{S})$ is a closed subspace of the complete metric space $C(\mathbb{S})$, by the Closed Subspace Theorem, it is sufficient to show that T maps an element in $C'(\mathbb{S})$ into $C''(\mathbb{S})$. This can be done by applying an argument similar to that in the proof of theorem 6.4.3. $\blacksquare$

If the assumptions in the preceding theorem hold, then we write the optimal policy function as $g : \mathbb{X} \times \mathbb{Z} \to \mathbb{A}$. This policy function generates an optimal plan $(a_0, a_1, ...)$ and optimal system dynamics $(x_0, x_1, ...)$ recursively as follows:

$$a_t \left(z^t \right) = g \left(x_t, z_t \right)$$
$$x_{t+1} \left(z^{t+1} \right) = \phi \left(x_t, a_t, z_t, z_{t+1} \right), \quad (x_0, z_0) \text{ given,}$$

where $z^t \in \mathbb{Z}^t$.

To establish differentiability, we replace assumptions 6.4.13 and 6.4.14 with the following:

Assumption 7.3.4 *For each* $z \in \mathbb{Z}$, $u(\cdot, z, \cdot)$ *is continuously differentiable on the interior of* $\mathbb{X} \times \mathbb{A}$.

Assumption 7.3.5 *The system transition function* $\phi(x, a, z, z') = a$ *is independent of* (x, z, z').

Assumption 7.3.5 seems strong. But it is often satisfied in applications because one may perform a suitable change of variables such that $x' = a$. Given this assumption, the Bellman equation (7.19) becomes

$$V(x, z) = \sup_{x' \in \Gamma(x, z)} u(x, z, x') + \beta \int V(x', z') Q(z, dz'). \tag{7.21}$$

This is the problem extensively studied in Stokey, Lucas, and Prescott (1989). We call this class of control problems the **Euler class**.

Theorem 7.3.4 (Differentiability) *Let* $(\mathbb{X}, \mathcal{X})$, $(\mathbb{A}, \mathcal{A})$, $(\mathbb{Z}, \mathcal{Z})$, Q, Γ, ϕ, β, *and* u *satisfy assumptions 5.1.2, 6.4.1–6.4.4, 6.4.11, and 7.3.3–7.3.5. Let* $V : \mathbb{X} \times \mathbb{Z} \to \mathbb{R}$ *be the solution to (7.21) and* $g : \mathbb{X} \times \mathbb{Z} \to \mathbb{R}$ *be the associated optimal policy function. Let* $x_0 \in int(\mathbb{X})$ *and* $g(x_0, z_0) \in int(\Gamma(x_0, z_0))$ *for some* $z_0 \in \mathbb{Z}$. *Then* $V(\cdot, z_0)$ *is continuously differentiable at* x_0 *and*

$$V_x(x_0, z_0) = u_x(x_0, z_0, g(x_0, z_0)). \tag{7.22}$$

Proof By theorems 7.3.1 and 7.3.3, the solution for V and g exists and V is strictly concave. Let $x_0 \in int(\mathbb{X})$ and $g(x_0, z_0) \in int(\Gamma(x_0, z_0))$. By assumption 6.4.4, there is some open neighborhood D of x_0 such that $g(x_0, z_0) \in int(\Gamma(x, z_0))$, all $x \in D$. We define $W : D \to \mathbb{R}$ by

$$W(x) = u(x, z_0, g(x_0, z_0)) + \beta \int V(g(x_0, z_0), z') Q(z_0, dz').$$

Then since $g(x_0, z_0) \in \text{int}(\Gamma(x, z_0))$, it follows from (7.21) that $W(x) \leq V(x, z_0)$ with equality at $x = x_0$. By assumptions 7.3.4, W is differentiable. By the Benveniste–Scheinkman theorem, $V(\cdot, z_0)$ is differentiable at x_0 and

$$\frac{\partial V(x_0, z_0)}{\partial x} = \frac{\partial W(x_0)}{\partial x}.$$

We then obtain equation (7.22).   ■

Finally, we show that not only does the sequence of value functions in the finite-horizon problem converge to the value function in the infinite-horizon problem but also the sequence of policy functions.

Theorem 7.3.5   (Convergence) *Let* $(\mathbb{X}, \mathcal{X})$, $(\mathbb{A}, \mathcal{A})$, $(\mathbb{Z}, \mathcal{Z})$, Q, Γ, ϕ, β, *and* u *satisfy assumptions 5.1.2, 6.4.1–6.4.5, 6.4.8, 6.4.9, 6.4.12, 7.3.1, 7.3.2, and 7.3.3. Let V be the solution to the Bellman equation (7.19) and g be the associated optimal policy function. Let $C'(\mathbb{S}) \subset C(\mathbb{S})$ be the set of bounded and continuous functions that are concave on X. Let $v_0 \in C'(\mathbb{S})$ and define (v_n, g_n) by*

$$v_n = T^n v_0$$

and

$$g_n(x, z) = \arg \max_{a \in \Gamma(x, z)} u(x, z, a) + \beta \int v_n(\phi(x, a, z, z'), z') Q(z, dz')$$

for $n = 1, 2, \dots$. *Then* $g_n \to g$ *pointwise. If* $\mathbb{X}$ *and* $\mathbb{Z}$ *are compact, then the convergence is uniform.*

Proof   The proof is analogous to that of theorem 9.9 in Stokey, Lucas, and Prescott (1989). We omit it here.   ■

As in theorem 7.2.2 we can relate the result above to that in the finite-horizon case. We have the relation $T^n 0 = V_{N-n}^N = V_0^n$. Intuitively, $T^n 0$ is equal to the value function at time $N - n$ for an N-period problem with the terminal reward $u_N = 0$. It is also equal to the value function for the n-horizon problem with the terminal reward $u_n = 0$, and g_n is equal to the associated initial policy function. As the horizon or the time-to-go $n \to \infty$, the sequence of n-horizon policy functions (g_n) converges to the infinite-horizon policy function g.

7.3.2   Unbounded Rewards

For Markov decision problems with unbounded rewards, there is no general theory for dynamic programming to work. One difficulty is that there is no general fixed-point theorem to guarantee the existence of a solution to the Bellman equation. The Contraction Mapping Theorem cannot be simply applied to the set of unbounded and continuous functions because the sup norm on this set is not well defined. We could apply other fixed point theorems such as the Schauder fixed-point theorem or the Tarski fixed-point theorem to find a fixed point. However, there is no general theorem to guarantee its uniqueness and global convergence. Another difficulty is that the transversality condition (7.4) often fails for some feasible plans, so theorem 7.1.2 does not apply. In this case, corollary 7.1.1 is useful. Stokey, Lucas, and Prescott (1989) give several examples to illustrate this result. In chapter 8 we will provide more examples. Here we introduce an approach based on weighted norm.

A natural idea to apply the Contraction Mapping Theorem to unbounded and continuous functions is to restrict to a subset of these functions. Each function in this subset is bounded by some function and thus one can define a sup norm weighted by this function. Under this weighted sup norm, the subset is a complete metric space. As a result, if one can construct a contraction mapping in this space, one can apply the Contraction Mapping Theorem. This idea appears in the mathematics literature (e.g., Wessels 1977) and is extended by Boyd (1990) in economics. Recently Durán (2000, 2003) further extends this approach.

To formalize it, let $\varphi : \mathbb{S} \to \mathbb{R}_{++}$ be a continuous function. Define $C_\varphi(S)$ as the set of continuous functions such that $\sup_{s \in \mathbb{S}} |f(s)/\varphi(s)| < \infty$, for any $f \in C_\varphi(\mathbb{S})$. We call φ a **weight function** and define a **weighted sup norm** by

$$\|f\|_\varphi = \sup_{s \in \mathbb{S}} \left| \frac{f(s)}{\varphi(s)} \right|, \quad f \in C_\varphi(\mathbb{S}). \tag{7.23}$$

In exercise 1, the reader is asked to show that this is a well-defined norm and that $C_\varphi(\mathbb{S})$ endowed with this norm is a Banach space.

Now we need to check that the Bellman operator is a contraction under the weighted sup norm. The following theorem analogous to the Blackwell Theorem is useful.

Theorem 7.3.6 *Let the operator $T : C_\varphi(\mathbb{S}) \to C_\varphi(\mathbb{S})$ be such that*

a. *(monotonicity) $f \le g$ implies $Tf \le Tg$;*

b. *(discounting) $T(f + a\varphi) \le Tf + \theta a\varphi$ for some constant $\theta \in (0,1)$ and any constant $a > 0$;*

c. *(one-period weighted boundedness) $T0 \in C_\varphi(\mathbb{S})$.*

Then T is a contraction with modulus θ and has a unique fixed point in $C_\varphi(\mathbb{S})$.

Proof Since $f, g \in C_\varphi(\mathbb{S})$, $f \le g + |f - g| \le g + \|f - g\|_\varphi \varphi$. By conditions a and b,

$$Tf \le T\left(g + \|f - g\|_\varphi \varphi\right) \le Tg + \theta \|f - g\|_\varphi \varphi.$$

Similarly $Tg \leq Tf + \theta \|f - g\|_\varphi \varphi$. Thus

$$\|Tf - Tg\|_\varphi \leq \theta \|f - g\|_\varphi,$$

and T is a contraction with modulus θ. For any $f \in C_\varphi(\mathbb{S})$, setting $g = 0$ yields

$$Tf \leq T0 + \theta \|f\|_\varphi \varphi \leq \|T0\|_\varphi \varphi + \theta \|f\|_\varphi \varphi.$$

Thus $\|Tf\|_\varphi < \infty$ by (c). By the Contraction Mapping Theorem, T has unique fixed point in $C_\varphi(\mathbb{S})$. ∎

   Conditions a and b ensure that T is a contraction. Condition c ensures that $\|Tf\|_\varphi < \infty$ so that T is a self-map. This result is often called the **Weighted Contraction Mapping Theorem**. The following example illustrates this theorem.

Example 7.3.1 *Consider the deterministic AK model*

$$\max_{(C_t, K_{t+1})_{t=0}^\infty} \sum_{t=0}^\infty \beta^t C_t^\gamma, \quad \gamma \in (0,1),$$

subject to

$$C_t + K_{t+1} = AK_t, \quad A > 0, \ K_0 > 0 \ given.$$

Define the value function for this problem as $V(K)$. Clearly, it is an unbounded function. Note that the utility function is homogeneous of degree γ and the constraint set is linearly homogeneous. We choose the weight function $\varphi(K) = K^\gamma$, $K \geq 0$.[1] For any continuous function $f : \mathbb{R}_+ \to \mathbb{R}$ that is homogeneous of degree γ, define the weighted sup norm, $\|f\|_\varphi = \sup_{k \geq 0} |f(k)/k^\gamma| = |f(1)| < \infty$. Let $C_\varphi(\mathbb{R}_+)$ be the space of all such functions. Define the Bellman operator T on this space:

$$Tf(K) = \max_{y \in [0, AK]} (AK - y)^\gamma + \beta f(y), \ f \in C_\varphi(\mathbb{R}_+).$$

We now verify that T is a contraction under the weighted sup norm $\|\cdot\|_\varphi$. First, T satisfies monotonicity. Second, we derive

$$\begin{aligned}
T(f + a\varphi)(K) &= \max_{y \in [0, AK]} (AK - y)^\gamma + \beta f(y) + \beta a y^\gamma \\
&\leq \max_{y \in [0, AK]} (AK - y)^\gamma + \beta f(y) + \beta a (AK)^\gamma \\
&= Tf(K) + \beta A^\gamma a \varphi(K).
\end{aligned}$$

Thus, if $\beta A^\gamma < 1$, then T satisfies discounting. Third, we compute

$$T0(K) = \max_{C \in [0, AK]} C^\gamma = A^\gamma K^\gamma = A^\gamma \varphi(K).$$

---

1. This function is equal to zero only if $K = 0$. But it is still a well-defined weight function for homogeneous functions if we use the convention that $K^\gamma / K^\gamma = 1$ for $K = 0$.

Thus $T0 \in C_\varphi(\mathbb{R}_+)$. We conclude that if $\beta A^\gamma < 1$, then T is a contraction mapping and has a unique fixed point in $C_\varphi(\mathbb{R}_+)$.

Alvarez and Stokey (1998) consider general dynamic programming problems with a similar homogeneity property. They show that the Weighted Contraction Mapping Theorem can be applied to general cases with positive degree of homogeneity. Durán (2000, 2003) extends the weighted norm approach to general problems without the homogeneity property. His idea does not rely on the Weighted Contraction Mapping Theorem because the conditions in this theorem are hard to verify in some applications. He imposes conditions on the weight function to directly verify that the Bellman operator is a contraction.

To explain his idea, we consider the deterministic model

$$\max_{(x_{t+1})} \sum_{t=0}^{\infty} \beta^t u(x_t, x_{t+1}), \quad x_0 \text{ given}, \tag{7.24}$$

subject to $x_{t+1} \in \Gamma(x_t)$, $t = 0, 1, \dots$. We impose the following:

Assumption 7.3.6 *The function $u : \mathbb{X} \times \mathbb{X} \to \mathbb{R}$ is continuous, where $\mathbb{X} \subset \mathbb{R}^{n_x}$.*

Assumption 7.3.7 *The correspondence $\Gamma : \mathbb{X} \to \mathbb{X}$ is nonempty, compact-valued, and continuous.*

We define the Bellman operator

$$Tf(x) = \sup_{y \in \Gamma(x)} u(x, y) + \beta f(y). \tag{7.25}$$

We let φ be a weight function and consider the space $C_\varphi(\mathbb{X})$ endowed with the weighted sup norm $\|\cdot\|_\varphi$. Our objective is to give conditions such that T is a contraction and a self-map on this space so that a unique fixed point exists.

First, in exercise 2, the reader is asked to show the following:

$$|Tf - Tg|(x) \leq \beta \sup_{x' \in \Gamma(x)} |f(x') - g(x')|$$

$$= \beta \sup_{x' \in \Gamma(x)} \frac{|f(x') - g(x')|}{\varphi(x')} \frac{\varphi(x')}{\varphi(x)} \varphi(x)$$

$$\leq \beta \sup_{x' \in \Gamma(x)} \frac{\varphi(x')}{\varphi(x)} \|f - g\|_\varphi \varphi(x). \tag{7.26}$$

Thus, if

$$\beta \sup_{x' \in \Gamma(x)} \frac{\varphi(x')}{\varphi(x)} \leq \theta < 1 \quad \text{for all } x \in \mathbb{X}, \tag{7.27}$$

then T is a contraction with the modulus θ under the weighted sup norm. Next, we need to show that T maps a function in $C_\varphi(\mathbb{X})$ into itself. The key step is to verify that $\|Tf\|_\varphi < \infty$ if $\|f\|_\varphi < \infty$. Setting $g = 0$ in (7.26) yields

$$Tf(x) \le \theta \|f\|_\varphi \, \varphi(x) + T0(x) \le \theta \|f\|_\varphi \, \varphi(x) + \|T0\|_\varphi \, \varphi(x).$$

Thus, if we can show that

$$\|T0\|_\varphi < \infty, \tag{7.28}$$

then

$$\|Tf\|_\varphi \le \theta \|f\|_\varphi + \|T0\|_\varphi < \infty.$$

Finally, we need to verify continuity. This is routine. To conclude, (7.27) and (7.28) are the key conditions for the application of the Contraction Mapping Theorem to T under the norm $\|\cdot\|_\varphi$. This result can be applied to models without homogeneity properties. The following example illustrates this result.

Example 7.3.2 *We modify the previous example to incorporate nonhomogeneous technology. Let the production function be $F(x) = Ax + x^\alpha$, $A > 1$ and $\alpha \in (0,1)$. Then one-period utility is $u(x,y) = (Ax + x^\alpha - y)^\gamma$. Take the weight function $\varphi(x) = 1 + (Ax + x^\alpha)^\gamma$. To check condition (7.27), we compute*

$$\beta \sup_{y \in [0, Ax + x^\alpha]} \frac{1 + (Ay + y^\alpha)^\gamma}{1 + (Ax + x^\alpha)^\gamma} \le \beta \frac{1 + (Az + z^\alpha)^\gamma}{1 + z^\gamma}$$

$$\le \lim_{z \to \infty} \beta \frac{1 + (Az + z^\alpha)^\gamma}{1 + z^\gamma},$$

$$= \beta A^\gamma,$$

where $z = Ax + x^\alpha \ge 0$. We assume that $\beta A^\gamma < 1$. To check condition (7.28), we compute

$$T0(x) = \sup_{y \in [0, Ax + x^\alpha]} (Ax + x^\alpha - y)^\gamma < \varphi(x).$$

It is straightforward to extend the preceding approach to stochastic models (see Durán 2003). As Durán (2000) points out, it is not easy to apply this approach to models with reward functions that are bounded above but unbounded below. Alvarez and Stokey (1998) also point out this difficulty and propose solutions for homogeneous functions. To see the issue, we consider the AK model in example 7.3.1 with log utility: $u(x,y) = \ln(Ax - y)$. To ensure one-period boundedness, we could set $\varphi(x) = 1 + |\ln(Ax)|$. However, condition (7.27) can never be satisfied.

Other approaches to the case of unbounded returns include the non–contraction-based method of Le Van and Morhaim (2002) and the k-local contraction method of Rincon-Zapatero and Rodriguez-Palmero (2003) and Matkowski and Nowak (2011).

7.4   The Maximum Principle and Transversality Conditions

Consider the optimal control problem studied in the previous section. For simplicity, we assume that $\mathbb{X} \subset \mathbb{R}_+$ and $\mathbb{A} \subset \mathbb{R}$ are convex. To present the infinite-horizon Maximum Principle, we write the Lagrangian form as

$$L = E \sum_{t=0}^{\infty} \left[\beta^t u \left(x_t, z_t, a_t \right) - \beta^{t+1} \mu_{t+1} \left(x_{t+1} - \phi(x_t, a_t, z_t, z_{t+1}) \right) \right], \tag{7.29}$$

where $\beta^{t+1} \mu_{t+1}$ is the discounted Lagrange multiplier associated with (5.14).[2] Under assumptions 7.3.4 and 6.4.14, we can derive the first-order conditions for an interior solution:

$$a_t : u_a \left(x_t, z_t, a_t \right) + \beta E_t \mu_{t+1} \phi_a \left(x_t, a_t, z_t, z_{t+1} \right) = 0, \quad t \geq 0,$$

$$x_t : \mu_t = u_x \left(x_t, z_t, a_t \right) + \beta E_t \mu_{t+1} \phi_x \left(x_t, a_t, z_t, z_{t+1} \right), \quad t \geq 1.$$

Define the Hamiltonian function as

$$H \left(x_t, a_t, z_t, \mu_{t+1} \right) = u \left(x_t, z_t, a_t \right) + \beta E_t \mu_{t+1} \phi(x_t, a_t, z_t, z_{t+1}),$$

and express the preceding first-order conditions as

$$\frac{\partial H \left(x_t, a_t, z_t, \mu_{t+1} \right)}{\partial a} = 0, \quad t \geq 0, \tag{7.30}$$

$$\frac{\partial H \left(x_t, a_t, z_t, \mu_{t+1} \right)}{\partial x} = \mu_t, \quad t \geq 1. \tag{7.31}$$

To study the connection with dynamic programming, we consider the Bellman equation (7.19). Given suitable differentiability assumptions, we derive the first-order condition for a:

$$0 = u_a \left(x, z, a \right) + \beta \int V_x \left(\phi(x, a, z, z'), z' \right) \phi_a(x, a, z, z') Q \left(z, dz' \right).$$

The envelope condition is given by

$$V_x \left(x, z \right) = u_x \left(x, z, a \right)$$
$$+ \beta \int V_x \left(\phi(x, a, z, z'), z' \right) \phi_x(x, a, z, z') Q \left(z, dz' \right).$$

---

2. As discussed in section 6.5, if the state transition equation is $x_{t+1} = \phi \left(x_t, a_t, z_t \right)$, then we would replace $\beta^{t+1} \mu_{t+1}$ with $\beta^t \lambda_t$.

After setting $\mu_t = V_x(x_t, z_t)$, we can see that the two conditions given above are equivalent to (7.30) and (7.31). The Lagrange multiplier μ_t is interpreted as the shadow value of the state. As in the finite-horizon case the beauty of the Maximum Principle is that the Lagrange multiplier is the object of study instead of the value function. As studied in the last section, analyzing the existence and properties of the value function is nontrivial, especially for unbounded reward functions. By contrast, unbounded reward functions do not pose any difficulty for the Maximum Principle to work.[3]

Next we turn to the first-order conditions. Suppose that we can use (7.30) to solve for a_t as a function of x_t, z_t and μ_{t+1}. We then substitute this solution into equation (7.31) and the state transition equation (5.14) to obtain a system of two first-order nonlinear difference equations for $(x_{t+1}, \mu_{t+1})_{t=0}^{\infty}$. We need two boundary conditions to obtain a solution. One boundary condition is the initial value for x_0. Unlike in the finite-horizon case analyzed in section 6.5 where we have a terminal condition for μ_T, there is no well-defined terminal condition in the infinite-horizon case. Instead, the second boundary condition is in the form of the **transversality condition**:

$$\lim_{T \to \infty} E\left[\beta^T \mu_T x_T\right] = 0. \tag{7.32}$$

The interpretation is that the discounted shadow value of the state variable must be zero at infinity. Intuitively, this condition prevents overaccumulation of wealth. One should not be confused with the **no–Ponzi–game condition**, which is also called a transversality condition in the literature. The no–Ponzi-game condition prevents the overaccumulation of debt as we show in section 8.3. It is a restriction on the choice set of feasible plans. But the transversality condition (7.32) is an optimality condition for a given choice set. In section 8.3 we will show that these two conditions are closely related given first-order conditions.

Now we state a sufficiency result for the one-dimensional case.

Theorem 7.4.1 (Sufficiency of the necessary condition from the Maximum Principle and the transversality condition) *Let $\mathbb{X} \subset \mathbb{R}_+$ and $\mathbb{A} \subset \mathbb{R}$ be convex. Suppose that assumptions 5.1.2, 6.4.3, 6.4.12, 6.4.14, and 7.3.3, and 7.3.4 hold. Let $\left(x_{t+1}^*, a_t^*, \mu_{t+1}^*\right)_{t=0}^{\infty}$ satisfy (5.14), (7.30), (7.31), and (7.32). Suppose that $a_t^*\left(z^t\right) \in int(\Gamma\left(x_t^*\left(z^t\right), z_t\right))$, $x_t^* \in int\,\mathbb{X}$, and $\mu_{t+1}^* \geq 0$ for $t \geq 0$. Then (a_t^*) is an optimal plan.*

Proof We define

$$D_T \equiv E \sum_{t=0}^{T} \beta^t u_t\left(x_t^*, z_t, a_t^*\right) - E \sum_{t=0}^{T} \beta^t u_t\left(x_t, z_t, a_t\right)$$

---

3. See Chow (1997) for extensive applications of the Maximum Principle to economics.

for any feasible plan $(a_t)_{t=0}^{\infty}$ and the associated state process $(x_t)_{t=1}^{\infty}$ satisfying (5.14). Since both $(x_{t+1}, a_t)_{t=0}^{\infty}$ and $(x_{t+1}^*, a_t^*)_{t=0}^{\infty}$ satisfy the state transition equation, we rewrite the preceding equation as

$$
D_T = E \sum_{t=0}^{T} \left[\beta^t u_t \left(x_t^*, z_t, a_t^* \right) - \beta^{t+1} \mu_{t+1}^* \left(x_{t+1}^* - \phi(x_t^*, a_t^*, z_t, z_{t+1}) \right) \right]
$$

$$
- E \sum_{t=0}^{T} \left[\beta^t u_t \left(x_t, z_t, a_t \right) - \beta^{t+1} \mu_{t+1}^* \left(x_{t+1} - \phi(x_t, a_t, z_t, z_{t+1}) \right) \right].
$$

By our assumptions, we have

$$
D_T = E \sum_{t=0}^{T} \beta^t H_t \left(x_t^*, a_t^*, z_t, \mu_{t+1}^* \right) - E \sum_{t=0}^{T} \beta^t H_t \left(x_t, a_t, z_t, \mu_{t+1}^* \right)
$$

$$
- E \sum_{t=0}^{T} \beta^{t+1} \mu_{t+1}^* \left(x_{t+1}^* - x_{t+1} \right)
$$

$$
\geq E \sum_{t=0}^{T} \beta^t \frac{\partial H_t \left(x_t^*, a_t^*, z_t, \mu_{t+1}^* \right)}{\partial x} \left(x_t^* - x_t \right)
$$

$$
+ E \sum_{t=0}^{T} \beta^t \frac{\partial H_t \left(x_t^*, a_t^*, z_t, \mu_{t+1}^* \right)}{\partial a} \left(a_t^* - a_t \right)
$$

$$
- E \sum_{t=0}^{T} \beta^{t+1} \mu_{t+1}^* \left(x_{t+1}^* - x_{t+1} \right).
$$

Rearranging terms and using (7.30), (7.31), and $x_0^* = x_0$, we obtain

$$
D_T \geq -E \beta^{T+1} \mu_{T+1}^* \left(x_{T+1}^* - x_{T+1} \right).
$$

Since $\mu_{T+1}^* \geq 0$ and $x_{T+1} \geq 0$, we deduce that

$$
D_T \geq -E \beta^{T+1} \mu_{T+1}^* x_{T+1}^*.
$$

Taking limit as $T \to \infty$ and using the transversality condition (7.32), we obtain the desired result.   ∎

Note that if ϕ is linear in (x, a), then the assumption of $\mu_{t+1}^* \geq 0$ is not needed. The assumption that $\mathbb{X} \subset \mathbb{R}_+$ is typically satisfied in many economic problems. For example, the capital stock as a state variable is always nonnegative. In many problems we can make a suitable change of variables such that the state variables become nonnegative. For example, in the consumption-saving model analyzed in section 6.6.2, we can choose either modified asset holdings $\hat{a}_t = a_t + b \geq 0$ or cash on hand $x_t \geq 0$ as the state variable.

To prove the necessity of the transversality condition is quite difficult. In the next section we analyze this issue for a special class of control problems—the Euler class.

7.5 Euler Equations and Transversality Condition

In this section we consider the following Euler class of stochastic optimal control problems analyzed in section 7.3:

$$\max_{(x_{t+1})_{t=0}^{\infty}} \ J\left(x_0, z_0, (x_{t+1})_{t=0}^{\infty}\right) \equiv E\left[\sum_{t=0}^{\infty} \beta^t u\left(x_t, z_t, x_{t+1}\right)\right] \tag{7.33}$$

subject to $x_{t+1}\left(z^t\right) \in \Gamma\left(x_t\left(z^{t-1}\right), z_t\right)$ for all $z^t \in \mathbb{Z}^t$, $t = 0, 1, \dots$, and (x_0, z_0) given. Under suitable differentiability assumptions, we can derive first-order necessary conditions for (7.33).

We can use two ways to derive these conditions. First, we may use the dynamic programming approach. Consider the associated dynamic programming problem (7.21). Under suitable differentiability assumptions, we can derive the first-order conditions for an interior solution:

$$u_a\left(x, z, g\left(x, z\right)\right) + \beta \int V_x\left(g(x, z), z'\right) Q\left(z, dz'\right) = 0,$$

where $x' = g(x, z)$ is the optimal policy function. Combining with the envelope condition (7.22) yields the Euler equation:

$$0 = u_a\left(x, z, g\left(x, z\right)\right) + \beta \int u_x\left[g(x, z), z', g(g(x, z))\right] Q\left(z, dz'\right).$$

This is a functional equation for the optimal policy function g. If we set $x_t^* = x$, $z_t = z$, and $x_{t+1}^* = g\left(x_t^*, z_t\right)$, we obtain the Euler equation in the sequence form:

$$u_a\left(x_t^*, z_t, x_{t+1}^*\right) + \beta E_t u_x\left(x_{t+1}^*, z_{t+1}, x_{t+2}^*\right) = 0, \quad t \geq 0, \tag{7.34}$$

where E_t is the conditional expectation operator given the information available at time t. Both forms of Euler equations are useful for numerical analysis studied later.

Another way of deriving Euler equations is to note that if the plan $(x_{t+1}^*)_{t=0}^{\infty}$ is optimal, then x_{t+1}^* must solve the following problem:

$$\max_y \ u\left(x_t^*, z_t, y\right) + \beta E_t u\left(y, z_{t+1}, x_{t+2}^*\right)$$

subject to

$$y \in \Gamma\left(x_t^*, z_t\right), \quad x_{t+2}^* \in \Gamma\left(y, z_{t+1}\right).$$

The idea is that a small variation of x_{t+1}^* should not improve the total expected reward. This idea underlies the classical **variational approach** to optimal control. It is also related to the Maximum Principle studied in the last section.

Unlike in the finite-horizon case, we cannot solve Euler equations simply by backward induction because we do not have an explicit terminal condition. Instead, the terminal condition for the infinite-horizon case is typically in the form of the so-called transversality condition:

$$\lim_{T \to \infty} E\left[\beta^T u_a\left(x_T^*, z_T, x_{T+1}^*\right) \cdot x_{T+1}^*\right] = 0. \tag{7.35}$$

To understand the intuition behind this condition, we start with a finite-horizon social planner's problem:

$$\sup_{(c_t)_{t=0}^T} E\left[\sum_{t=0}^T \beta^t u\left(c_t\right)\right]$$

subject to

$$x_{t+1} = z_t F\left(x_t\right) - c_t, \quad t = 0, 1, ..., T, \quad (x_0, z_0) \text{ given,}$$

where $x_t \geq 0$ represents capital stock. In the last period, the planner solves the problem:

$$\max_{x_{T+1}} E\left[\beta^T u\left(z_T F(x_T) - x_{T+1}\right)\right].$$

Clearly, there must be a terminal condition that constrains the capital stock x_{T+1}. Otherwise, the planner will make x_{T+1} as large (small) as possible if $u' < (>)0$. Given the assumption that $u' \geq 0$ and $x_{T+1} \geq 0$, we obtain the first-order condition for x_{T+1} as

$$E\left[\beta^T u'\left(c_T^*\right)\right] \geq 0, \quad \text{with inequality if } x_{T+1}^* = 0.$$

We rewrite it as

$$E\left[\beta^T u'\left(c_T^*\right) \cdot x_{T+1}^*\right] = 0. \tag{7.36}$$

This is the transversality condition in the finite-horizon case. The economic meaning is that the expected discounted shadow value of the terminal state (e.g., capital or wealth) must be zero. Note that we have used the inner product notation in (7.36) to anticipate that we will consider the multidimensional case below.

In the infinite-horizon case, one can take the limit of (7.36) to obtain (7.35). Using the Euler equation (7.34), we can rewrite (7.35) as

$$\lim_{T\to\infty} E\left[\beta^T u_x\left(x_T^*, z_T, x_{T+1}^*\right)\cdot x_T^*\right] = 0. \tag{7.37}$$

This form has no counterpart in the finite-horizon case or in the continuous-time case. Note that from the analysis in the previous section and the envelope condition for the Euler class, we deduce that $\mu_T = V_x\left(x_T^*, z_T\right) = u_x\left(x_T^*, z_T, x_{T+1}^*\right)$. It follows that (7.37) is a special case of (7.32).

Researchers used to believe that it is nontrivial to prove the necessity of the transversality condition (see Weitzman 1973; Ekeland and Scheinkman 1986). Kamihigashi (2000) simplifies the proof significantly. We now consider one of his results.

Theorem 7.5.1 (Necessity of the transversality condition) *Let $\mathbb{X} \subset \mathbb{R}^{n_x}$ be a convex set and contains the origin. Let $0 \in \Gamma\left(0, z\right)$ for any $z \in \mathbb{Z}$. Suppose that assumptions 6.4.3, 6.4.11, and 7.3.2–7.3.4 hold. Let $\left(x_{t+1}^*\right)_{t=0}^\infty$ be an interior optimal plan that gives a finite discounted expected reward $J\left(x_0, z_0, \left(x_{t+1}^*\right)\right)$. Suppose that $J\left(x_0, z_0, \left(\xi x_{t+1}^*\right)\right)$ is also finite for some $\xi \in [0, 1)$. Then $\left(x_{t+1}^*\right)_{t=0}^\infty$ satisfies the Euler equation (7.34) and the transversality condition (7.35).*

Proof We have outlined the proof of the necessity of the Euler equation. We focus on the transversality condition. The key is to use the following result: let $f : [0, 1] \to \mathbb{R} \cup \{-\infty\}$ be a concave function with $f(1) > -\infty$. Then for any $\gamma \in [0, 1)$ and $\lambda \in [\gamma, 1)$,

$$\frac{f(1) - f(\lambda)}{1 - \lambda} \leq \frac{f(1) - f(\gamma)}{1 - \gamma}. \tag{7.38}$$

To prove this, we let $\alpha = (1 - \lambda) / (1 - \gamma) \in (0, 1]$. By concavity of f, $f(\lambda) \geq \alpha f(\gamma) + (1 - \alpha) f(1)$. We then obtain the inequality above.

Now fix any integer $T \geq 0$. By the convexity assumption of $\mathbb{X}$ and Γ and the assumption that $0 \in \Gamma(0, z)$ for any $z \in \mathbb{Z}$, $\{x_0, x_1^*, ..., x_T^*, \lambda x_{T+1}^*, \lambda x_{T+2}^*, ...\}$ is a feasible plan for some $\lambda \in [\xi, 1)$. By optimality,

$$0 \geq E\left\{\beta^T u\left(x_T^*, z_T, \lambda x_{T+1}^*\right) - \beta^T u\left(x_T^*, z_T, x_{T+1}^*\right)\right.$$
$$\left. + \sum_{t=T+1}^\infty \left[\beta^t u\left(\lambda x_t^*, z_t, \lambda x_{t+1}^*\right) - \beta^t u\left(x_t^*, z_t, x_{t+1}^*\right)\right]\right\}.$$

By assumption 7.3.3, $u\left(\lambda x_t^*, z_t, \lambda x_{t+1}^*\right)$ is a concave function of λ. Use (7.38) with $\gamma = \xi$ to derive

$$
E\beta^T \frac{u\left(x_T^*, z_T, \lambda x_{T+1}^*\right) - u\left(x_T^*, z_T, x_{T+1}^*\right)}{1-\lambda}
$$

$$
\leq E \sum_{t=T+1}^{\infty} \beta^t \frac{u\left(x_t^*, z_t, x_{t+1}^*\right) - u\left(\lambda x_t^*, z_t, \lambda x_{t+1}^*\right)}{1-\lambda}
$$

$$
\leq E \sum_{t=T+1}^{\infty} \beta^t \frac{u\left(x_t^*, z_t, x_{t+1}^*\right) - u\left(\xi x_t^*, z_t, \xi x_{t+1}^*\right)}{1-\xi}.
$$

Since $\left(x_{t+1}^*\right)$ is an interior solution, taking $\lambda \to 1$ yields

$$
0 \leq -E\beta^T u_a\left(x_T^*, z_T, x_{T+1}^*\right) \cdot x_{T+1}^*
$$

$$
\leq E \sum_{t=T+1}^{\infty} \beta^t \frac{u\left(x_t^*, z_t, x_{t+1}^*\right) - u\left(\xi x_t^*, z_t, \xi x_{t+1}^*\right)}{1-\xi},
$$

where the first inequality follows from assumptions 7.3.2 and 7.3.4 and the Euler equation. The last term in the equation above converges to zero as $T \to \infty$ by the assumption that $J\left(x_0, z_0, \left(\xi x_{t+1}^*\right)\right)$ and $J\left(x_0, z_0, \left(x_{t+1}^*\right)\right)$ are finite. Letting $T \to \infty$ yields the transversality condition (7.37).   ■

The idea of the proof is simple. If we proportionally shift down the continuation plan at any date by a small amount, and if this results in a feasible plan that reduces the optimal total discounted expected reward by a finite value, then the transversality condition is necessary. This condition is easy to check for models with a homogeneity property or models with a bounded reward function. From the proof we can see that some assumptions can be weakened. For example, we can weaken assumption 6.4.3 and allow a general stochastic process for the shock (z_t).

Note that if we can apply the preceding argument to each component of the state vector, then the transversality condition (7.35) applies to all components of the state vector. As a result we obtain n_x equations as terminal boundary conditions. The Euler equation gives a system of n_x second-order difference equations. Given n_x initial conditions and n_x terminal transversality conditions, we can solve this system. We call this method the Euler equation approach.

Let us turn to the sufficiency part. Its proof is similar to that of theorem 7.4.1.

Theorem 7.5.2 (Sufficiency of the Euler and transversality conditions) *Let $\mathbb{X} \subset \mathbb{R}_+^{n_x}$ be convex and suppose that assumptions 6.4.3 and 7.3.2–7.3.4 hold. If the plan $\left(x_{t+1}^*\right)_{t=0}^{\infty}$ with $x_{t+1}^*\left(z^t\right) \in int(\Gamma\left(x_t^*\left(z^{t-1}\right), z_t\right))$ for any $z^t \in \mathbb{Z}^t$ satisfies the Euler equation (7.34) and the transversality condition (7.35), then it is optimal for problem (7.33).*

Proof   Consider any feasible plan $(x_t) \in \Pi(x_0, z_0)$ and any integer $T \geq 0$. We compute

$$D_T \equiv E \sum_{t=0}^{T} \beta^t \left[u\left(x_t^*, z_t, x_{t+1}^*\right) - u\left(x_t, z_t, x_{t+1}\right) \right]$$

$$\geq E \sum_{t=0}^{T} \beta^t \left[u_x\left(x_t^*, z_t, x_{t+1}^*\right) \cdot \left(x_t^* - x_t\right) + u_a\left(x_t^*, z_t, x_{t+1}^*\right) \cdot \left(x_{t+1}^* - x_{t+1}\right) \right]$$

$$= E \sum_{t=0}^{T-1} \beta^t \left[u_a\left(x_t^*, z_t, x_{t+1}^*\right) + \beta u_x\left(x_{t+1}^*, z_{t+1}, x_{t+2}^*\right) \right] \cdot \left(x_{t+1}^* - x_{t+1}\right)$$

$$+ E \beta^T u_a\left(x_T^*, z_T, x_{T+1}^*\right) \cdot \left(x_{T+1}^* - x_{T+1}\right),$$

where the inequality follows from assumption 7.3.3 and the last equality follows from $x_0^* = x_0$. Using the Euler equation (7.34), we deduce that the first expectation on the right-hand side of the last equation is zero. By assumption 7.3.2 and the Euler equation, we deduce that $u_a < 0$. It follows from $x_{T+1} \geq 0$ that

$$D_T \geq E \beta^T u_a\left(x_T^*, z_T, x_{T+1}^*\right) \cdot x_{T+1}^*.$$

Taking limit as $T \to \infty$ yields

$$\lim_{T \to \infty} E \sum_{t=0}^{T} \beta^t \left[u\left(x_t^*, z_t, x_{t+1}^*\right) - u\left(x_t, z_t, x_{t+1}\right) \right] \geq 0.$$

Thus $J\left(x_0, z_0, \left(x_{t+1}^*\right)\right) \geq J\left(x_0, z_0, \left(x_{t+1}\right)\right)$, establishing the desired result.   ∎

Let us consider an example to illustrate the previous theorems.

Example 7.5.1   (Phelps 1962; Levhari and Srinivasan 1969) *Say we have the following consumption–saving problem:*

$$\max_{(c_t)} E \sum_{t=0}^{\infty} \beta^t \frac{c_t^{1-\gamma}}{1-\gamma}, \quad \gamma > 0, \neq 1,$$

subject to

$$x_{t+1} = R_{t+1}\left(x_t - c_t\right), \quad x_{t+1} \geq 0, \ x_0 > 0 \ given,$$

where $R_{t+1} > 0$ is identically and independently drawn from some distribution. There is no labor income. We interpret $\gamma = 1$ as log utility. We can derive the Euler equation and the transversality condition:

$$c_t^{-\gamma} = \beta E \left[R_{t+1} c_{t+1}^{-\gamma} \right],$$

$$\lim_{t \to \infty} E \left[\beta^t c_t^{-\gamma} x_t \right] = 0.$$

Suppose that the consumption policy is given by $c_t = Ax_t$, where $A \in (0,1)$ is a constant to be determined. Substituting this conjecture into the Euler equation and using the budget constraint, we obtain

$$A^{-\gamma} x_t^{-\gamma} = \beta E \left[R_{t+1} A^{-\gamma} R_{t+1}^{-\gamma} (x_t - Ax_t)^{-\gamma} \right].$$

Solving yields

$$A = 1 - \left(\beta E \left[R_{t+1}^{1-\gamma} \right] \right)^{1/\gamma}. \tag{7.39}$$

For log utility ($\gamma = 1$), we obtain $A = 1 - \beta$. In general, for $A \in (0,1)$, we need to assume that

$$0 < \left(\beta E \left[R_{t+1}^{1-\gamma} \right] \right)^{1/\gamma} < 1.$$

Now we show that the consumption policy is optimal by verifying the transversality condition. Using the budget constraint and policy function, we derive

$$E \left[\beta^t c_t^{-\gamma} x_t \right] = E \left[\beta^t A^{-\gamma} x_t^{1-\gamma} \right] = E \left[\beta^t A^{-\gamma} R_t^{1-\gamma} (1-A)^{1-\gamma} x_{t-1}^{1-\gamma} \right]$$

$$= \ldots = \beta^t A^{-\gamma} (1-A)^{t(1-\gamma)} x_0^{1-\gamma} E \left[\Pi_{s=1}^t R_s^{1-\gamma} \right].$$

Since R_t is IID, it follows from (7.39) that the transversality condition is satisfied for $A \in (0,1)$.

7.6   Exercises

1. Prove that $C_\varphi (\mathbb{X})$ is a complete metric space when endowed with the weighted sup norm defined in (7.23).

2. Let T be the Bellman operator defined in (7.25). Prove that

   $$|Tf - Tg| (x) \le \beta \sup_{x' \in \Gamma(x)} |f(x') - g(x')|,$$

   for any continuous functions f, g on $\mathbb{X}$.

3. Replace the production function in example 7.3.1 so that the constraint correspondence is $\Gamma(K) = [0, AK + K^\alpha]$, $A > 1$, and $\alpha \in (0,1)$. Use the weighted norm approach to analyze the existence of a solution to the Bellman equation.

4. Consider the deterministic Ramsey growth model

   $$\max \sum_{t=0}^{\infty} \beta^t u(C_t)$$

subject to

$$C_t + K_{t+1} = f(K_t), \quad K_0 \text{ given.}$$

Assume that f is continuous and strictly increasing. Additionally assume that $f(0) = 0$ and that there exists some x_m such that $x \leq f(x) \leq x_m$ for all $0 \leq x \leq x_m$, and $f(x) < x$ for all $x > x_m$. Prove that one can restrict the state space to $\mathbb{X} = [0, x_m]$. This exercise illustrates that even though the reward function is unbounded, one can choose a suitable compact state space to transform the problem into a problem with a bounded reward.

5. Consider the stochastic growth model

$$\max E \left[\sum_{t=0}^{\infty} \beta^t \ln(C_t) \right]$$

subject to

$$C_t + K_{t+1} = z_t K_t^\alpha, \quad K_0 \text{ given,}$$

where z_t follows a Markov process with transition function Q. Derive the optimal consumption and investment policies and the value function using the Euler equation approach or the value function approach. Verify they are indeed optimal.

6. Use the value function approach to derive the optimal consumption policy and the value function in example 7.5.1, and verify that the solution is optimal.

7. (Schechtman and Escudero 1977) Let $T \to \infty$ in exercise 9 of chapter 6. Solve the limit consumption and saving policies. Prove that limit policies are optimal for the infinite-horizon case, and derive the value function.

8. (Phelps 1962) Consider the model in exercise 7 of chapter 6. Let the utility function be $u(c) = c^{1-\gamma}/(1-\gamma)$. Solve the consumption policy in the finite-horizon case. Then let the time horizon go to infinity and derive the consumption policy for the infinite-horizon case. Prove that the limit policy is optimal.

9. Solve for the value function in example 7.5.1. Relate the value function to the transversality condition (7.4) and the transversality condition (7.35).

8   Applications

In this chapter we study six economic problems to illustrate how the theory developed previously can be applied. We focus on stochastic models. For some problems we also consider their deterministic counterparts.

8.1   Option Exercise

Consider the option exercise problem presented in section 5.2.2, which belongs to the class of optimal stopping problems. For simplicity, assume that the lump-sum investment payoff is drawn independently and identically from the distribution F over $[0, B]$, where $B > I$. We write the Bellman equation as

$$V(z) = \max \left\{ \beta \int V(z') \, dF(z'), z - I \right\},$$

where the maximization is over two choices: (1) make the investment and obtain profits $z - I$, or (2) wait and draw a new payoff from distribution F next period. The function V represents option value. By the dynamic programming theory developed in section 7.3.1, we can immediately show that there exists a unique solution V to the Bellman equation. In addition it is increasing and convex (see figure 8.1).

As this figure shows, there exists a unique threshold value z^* such that the decision maker chooses to invest whenever the project payoff exceeds z^* for the first time. The value function V satisfies

$$V(z) = \begin{cases} z - I, & z > z^*, \\ \beta \int_0^B V(z') \, dF(z'), & z \leq z^*. \end{cases}$$

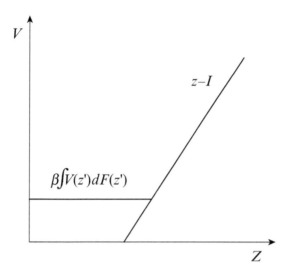

Figure 8.1
Option value. Plotted is the value function $V(z)$ for the irreversible project investment problem.

At z^* we obtain

$$V(z^*) = \beta \int_0^B V(z')\, dF(z') = z^* - I$$

$$= \beta \int_0^{z^*} (z^* - I)\, dF(z') + \beta \int_{z^*}^B (z' - I)\, dF(z')$$

$$= \beta \int_0^B (z^* - I)\, dF(z') + \beta \int_{z^*}^B (z' - z^*)\, dF(z').$$

Thus the threshold value is determined by the equation

$$z^* - I = \frac{\beta}{1 - \beta} \int_{z^*}^B (z' - z^*)\, dF(z').$$

We can verify that there exists a unique solution in $(0, B)$ to this equation. From the equation we see that $z^* > I$. According to the net present value rule often used in capital budgeting, the investment threshold is equal to I. With irreversibility, the decision maker forgoes some projects with positive net present values because there is option value of waiting.

It is straightforward to derive the probability distribution of the waiting time until the project is invested. Let $\lambda = F(z^*)$ be the probability that the project is not invested. Let N be the random variable for "length of time until the project is invested." Then we can compute $\Pr(N = j) = (1 - \lambda)\lambda^j$. We can also compute the mean waiting time to invest as $E[N] = 1/(1 - \lambda)$. The mean waiting time increases with the threshold z^*. Thus z^* fully characterizes the investment timing.

What will happen if the investment project becomes riskier? We use second-order stochastic dominance to characterize the riskiness of two distributions with the same mean. Say distribution F_1 is riskier than distribution F_2 in the sense of second-order stochastic dominance if

$$\int x dF_1(x) = \int x dF_2(x) \quad \text{and} \quad \int u(x) dF_1(x) \le \int u(x) dF_2(x)$$

for any concave and increasing function u. Another equivalent definition is in terms of mean preserving spreads. We refer to Rothschild and Stiglitz (1970) and Green, Mas-Colell, and Whinston (1995) for a detailed discussion.

Now suppose that there are two projects that generate identical mean payoffs. Suppose that project 2 is riskier than project 1. Then by the convexity of the value function, we can easily show that the decision maker prefers the riskier project 2 instead of the safer project 1. This seemingly counterintuitive result follows from the fact that the decision maker receives payoffs only from the tail of the distribution. He does not exercise the investment option for bad payoff realizations. This result underlies the key idea of the asset substitution (or risk-shifting) problem identified by Jensen and Meckling (1976). Jensen and Meckling (1976) point out that equityholders or managers with limited liability have incentives to make excessively risky investments at the expense of bondholders.

We can restate the preceding result in terms of the investment timing: an increase in risk in terms of second-order stochastic dominance induces the decision maker to delay investment. In chapter 20 we will argue that there is a distinction between risk and uncertainty and that this distinction matters for the analysis of the investment timing (see also Miao and Wang 2011).

We should mention that McCall's (1970) job search model is similar to the investment problem (see exercise 1 of chapter 5). Each period a worker draws one wage offer w from the same distribution F. He may reject the offer and receive unemployment compensation c. Then he waits until next period to draw another offer from F. Alternatively, the worker accepts the offer to work at w and receives w each period forever. The Bellman equation for the worker's problem is

$$V(w) = \max \left\{ c + \beta \int V(w') dF(w'), \frac{w}{1 - \beta} \right\}.$$

Stokey, Lucas, and Prescott (1989) and Ljungqvist and Sargent (2004) provide an extensive analysis of this problem and its various extensions.

8.2   Discrete Choice

Consider the discrete choice problem analyzed by Rust (1985, 1986) and presented in section 5.2.1. We write the Bellman equation as

$$V(s) = \max\{-c(s) + \beta \int_s^\infty V(s')\lambda \exp(-\lambda(s'-s))\,ds',$$

$$-(P_b - P_c) - c(0) + \beta \int_0^\infty V(s')\lambda \exp(-\lambda s')\,ds'\},$$

where the state variable s represents the accumulated utilization of a durable good. The first expression in the curly bracket represents the value from maintaining the durable, and the second represents the value from replacing the durable with a new one. The decision maker chooses the maximum of these two values. Assume that $c(s)$ is a bounded, continuously differentiable, and strictly increasing function. By the dynamic programming theory with bounded reward, we can show that V is decreasing and continuous (see figure 8.2).

Since $P_b > P_c$, it is never optimal to replace the new durable when $s = 0$. Note that the value of replacing the durable is constant. Let s^* be the smallest value such that the decision maker is indifferent between maintaining and replacing. Differentiating the Bellman equation on the region $(0, s^*)$ yields

$$V'(s) = -c'(s) + \lambda c(s) + \lambda(1-\beta)V(s). \tag{8.1}$$

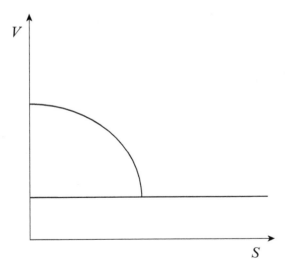

Figure 8.2
Value function. Plotted is the value function $V(s)$ for the discrete choice problem.

This is a first-order differential equation. It is called a **free boundary value problem** since the boundary condition is endogenous at the point s^*. To derive this condition, we note that

$$V(0) = -c(0) + \beta \int_0^\infty V(s') \lambda \exp(-\lambda s') \, ds'.$$

Thus, at s^*,

$$\begin{aligned} V(s^*) &= -(P_b - P_c) - c(0) + \beta \int_0^\infty V(s') \lambda \exp(-\lambda s') \, ds' \\ &= -(P_b - P_c) + V(0). \end{aligned}$$

Additionally

$$\begin{aligned} V(s^*) &= -c(s^*) + \beta \int_{s^*}^\infty V(s') \lambda \exp(-\lambda(s' - s^*)) \, ds' \\ &= -c(s^*) + \beta \int_{s^*}^\infty V(s^*) \lambda \exp(-\lambda(s' - s^*)) \, ds' \\ &= -c(s^*) + \beta V(s^*). \end{aligned}$$

It follows that

$$V(s^*) = \frac{-c(s^*)}{1 - \beta}, \quad V(0) = (P_b - P_c) - \frac{c(s^*)}{1 - \beta}. \tag{8.2}$$

We can then solve the differential equation (8.1) and the trigger value s^* subject to the two boundary conditions in (8.2). The solution is given by

$$V(s) = \max \left\{ \frac{-c(s^*)}{1 - \beta}, \frac{-c(s)}{1 - \beta} + \int_s^{s^*} \frac{c'(y)}{1 - \beta} \left[1 - \beta e^{-\lambda(1-\beta)(y-s)} \right] dy \right\},$$

and s^* is the unique solution to

$$P_b - P_c = \int_0^{s^*} \frac{c'(z)}{1 - \beta} \left[1 - \beta e^{-\lambda(1-\beta)z} \right] dz.$$

The decision maker's optimal policy is to replace the old durable with a new one whenever $s > s^*$. Unlike the option exercise problem analyzed in the last section, the problem is not over after replacement. Rather, when the accumulated utilization of the new durable rises over time and exceeds s^*, the decision maker replaces this durable with a second new one. This process is repeated. This problem is called a **regenerative optimal stopping problem**.

8.3   Consumption and Saving

We consider the following infinite-horizon consumption-saving problem:

$$\max_{(c_t)} E\left[\sum_{t=0}^{\infty}\beta^t u\left(c_t\right)\right], \quad \beta \in (0,1),$$

subject to

$$c_t + a_{t+1} = Ra_t + y_t, \tag{8.3}$$

$$c_t \geq 0, \, a_{t+1} \geq -b, \quad (a_0, y_0) > 0 \text{ given.} \tag{8.4}$$

Here c_t, a_t, and y_t represent consumption, asset holdings, and that labor income at time t, respectively. Assume that the gross interest rate $R > 1$ and that the utility function u satisfies the usual conditions: $u' > 0$, $u'' < 0$, $\lim_{c\to 0} u'(c) = \infty$, and $\lim_{c\to\infty} u'(c) = 0$. Let y_t follow a Markov process with transition function Q. Suppose that its support is $[y_{\min}, y_{\max}] \subset \mathbb{R}_+$. This implies that the present value of labor income is finite almost surely.

The constant $b \geq 0$ represents an exogenous borrowing limit. Without any constraint on borrowing, the consumer can achieve any consumption level by borrowing and rolling over debt. In this way his utility level approaches infinity. This strategy is often called a **Ponzi game** or **Ponzi scheme**. To rule out this strategy, the following no–Ponzi-game condition is often imposed:

$$\lim_{T\to\infty} \frac{a_{T+1}}{R^T} \geq 0. \tag{8.5}$$

To see what will happen if this condition is violated, we use the budget constraint (8.3) to derive

$$\sum_{t=0}^{T} \frac{c_t}{R^t} + \frac{a_{T+1}}{R^T} = Ra_0 + \sum_{t=0}^{T} \frac{y_t}{R^t}. \tag{8.6}$$

Taking limits as $T \to \infty$, we find that if (8.5) is violated, then the present value of consumption exceeds the sum of the present value of labor income and initial wealth because the consumer's debt is never repaid. For example, the consumer can keep rolling over his initial debt, say $a_1 < 0$, at the interest rate $r = R - 1$ so that his debt grows at the interest rate $a_{T+1} = R^t a_1$. We then have

$$\lim_{T\to\infty} \frac{a_{T+1}}{R^T} = \lim_{T\to\infty} \frac{R^T a_1}{R^T} = a_1 < 0.$$

The following result is adapted from Aiyagari (1994).

Theorem 8.3.1 *Let $R = 1 + r > 1$. Suppose that (y_t) has support $[y_{\min}, y_{\max}] \subset \mathbb{R}_+$. If $a_{t+1} \geq -b$ for all $t \geq 0$ and any $b \geq 0$, then the no–Ponzi-game condition (8.5) holds. Conversely, if the no–Ponzi-game condition (8.5) holds, then*

$$a_t \geq -\frac{y_{\min}}{r} \quad a.s. \text{ for } t \geq 0.$$

Proof First, let $a_{t+1} \geq -b$ for all $t \geq 0$. It follows from (8.6) that

$$Ra_0 + \sum_{t=0}^{T} \frac{y_t}{R^t} = \sum_{t=0}^{T} \frac{c_t}{R^t} + \frac{a_{T+1}}{R^T} \geq \sum_{t=0}^{T} \frac{c_t}{R^t} - \frac{b}{R^T}.$$

Taking limit as $T \to \infty$, we obtain

$$Ra_0 + \sum_{t=0}^{\infty} \frac{y_t}{R^t} \geq \sum_{t=0}^{\infty} \frac{c_t}{R^t}.$$

Using (8.6) again yields

$$\frac{a_{T+1}}{R^T} = Ra_0 + \sum_{t=0}^{T} \frac{y_t}{R^t} - \sum_{t=0}^{T} \frac{c_t}{R^t}.$$

Taking limit as $T \to \infty$ yields (8.5).

Now let (8.5) hold. Suppose that $a_t = -(y_{\min}/r) - \varepsilon$ for some $\varepsilon > 0$ and for some t with positive probability. By assumption, there is a positive probability that $y_t \leq y_{\min} + r\varepsilon/2$. Using (8.3) and $c_t \geq 0$, we derive $a_{t+1} \leq -y_{\min}/r + r\varepsilon/2 - (1 + r)\varepsilon$. Repeatedly using this argument, we deduce that

$$a_{t+n} \leq -\frac{y_{\min}}{r} + \frac{r\varepsilon}{2} \left[1 + (1 + r) + \ldots + (1 + r)^{n-1} \right] - (1 + r)^n \varepsilon,$$

with positive probability. Then, with positive probability,

$$\frac{a_{t+n}}{(1 + r)^n} \leq -\frac{1}{(1 + r)^n} \left(\frac{y_{\min}}{r} + \frac{\varepsilon}{2} \right) - \frac{\varepsilon}{2} < -\frac{\varepsilon}{2}.$$

Thus, with positive probability, $\lim_{n \to \infty} \left[(a_{t+n})/(1 + r)^n \right] < 0$, contradicting with (8.5). ■

Following Aiyagari (1994), we call $y_{\min}/r$ the natural debt limit. This is the largest debt level that is feasible for the consumer to repay almost surely. If $b > y_{\min}/r$, then the borrowing constraint will never be binding. One can impose more stringent debt limits. Here we assume that $b < y_{\min}/r$ in (8.4).

As in section 6.6.2 it is more convenient to redefine variables. Let $\hat{a}_t = a_t + b$. Define the cash on hand or the disposable resource as $x_t = Ra_t + y_t + b$. Then we can rewrite the budget and borrowing constraints as

$$x_{t+1} = R(x_t - c_t) + y_{t+1} - rb,$$

$$c_t + \hat{a}_{t+1} = x_t, \quad \hat{a}_{t+1} \geq 0, \ x_0 \geq 0 \text{ given.}$$

By the Maximum Principle, we can derive the Euler inequality

$$u'(c_t) \geq \beta R E_t [u'(c_{t+1})] \quad \text{with equality if } \hat{a}_{t+1} > 0, \tag{8.7}$$

and the transversality condition

$$\lim_{t \to \infty} E\beta^t u'(c_t) x_t = 0. \tag{8.8}$$

These conditions are also sufficient for optimality.

We can also write the associated Bellman equation as

$$V(x_t, y_t) = \max_{\hat{a}_{t+1} \in [0, x_t]} u(x_t - \hat{a}_{t+1})$$
$$+ \beta E_t [V(R\hat{a}_{t+1} + y_{t+1} - rb, y_{t+1})].$$

If (y_t) is IID, then y_t is not a state variable and x_t is the only state variable. In this case we can write the value function as $V(x)$. When u is unbounded, the analysis of the Bellman equation above is nontrivial. One approach followed by Schechtman and Escudero (1977) and Sotomayor (1984) is to first study the truncated finite-horizon problem as in section 6.6.2, and then to analyze the limit as the horizon goes to infinity. Here we simply assume that there exists a unique solution V to the Bellman equation and that V inherits properties of u in that $V(x)$ is strictly increasing, strictly concave, and continuously differentiable in x. Additionally the envelope condition, $V'(x) = u'(c)$, holds. We write the consumption and saving policy functions as $c(x)$ and $\hat{a}(x)$. From the envelope condition and concavity of V, we can see that $c(x)$ is strictly increasing in x. Properties of the consumption and saving policies depend on uncertainty in the income process and the relation between the discount factor β and the interest rate R. The intuition is simple. Uncertainty affects consumption smoothing and precautionary savings across states and over time. Discounting also affects consumption smoothing over time even without uncertainty.

8.3.1   Deterministic Income

Suppose that y_t is deterministic for each t. In the analysis below we consider three cases. In the first two cases, we suppose that $y_t = y > rb$ for all t. The Bellman equation is given by

$$V(x) = \max_{\hat{a} \in [0,x]} u(x - \hat{a}) + \beta V(R\hat{a} + y - rb). \tag{8.9}$$

We allow u to be unbounded.

Case 1 $\beta R < 1$.

This case was analyzed by Schechtman and Escudero (1977) and Stokey, Lucas, and Prescott (1989). In this case the consumer is so impatient that he prefers to consume more in early periods. If he has low wealth, then he prefers to borrow and so may exhaust the borrowing limit. Thus the initial wealth level plays an important role. We conjecture that there are critical levels $x_0^* < x_1^* < x_2^* < \dots$ for the cash on hand such that if $x \in [x_{t-1}^*, x_t^*]$ with $x_{-1}^* = y - rb$, then the consumer will not exhaust the borrowing limit from periods 0 to $t - 1$ and will exhaust the borrowing limit from period t onward for $t \geq 0$. We will construct a consumption–saving plan based on this conjecture and verify that this plan is optimal. We will also characterize the value function explicitly.

First, consider $t = 0$. Note that $u'(x)$ is continuous and decreasing in x. Since $u'(y - rb) > \beta R u'(y - rb)$ and $u'(\infty) = 0 < \beta R u'(y - rb)$, there exists a unique value $x_0^* > y - rb$ such that

$$u'(x_0^*) = \beta R u'(y - rb). \tag{8.10}$$

Then, for any $x \in [x_{-1}^*, x_0^*)$,

$$u'(x) > u'(x_0^*) = \beta R u'(y - rb).$$

We can define the consumption and saving policies by

$$f_0(x) = x, \; g_0(x) = 0 \text{ for } x \in [x_{-1}^*, x_0^*], \tag{8.11}$$

which satisfy the Euler inequality above. Since $x' = R(x - f_0(x)) + y - rb = y - rb < x_0^*$, we deduce that $f_0(x') = x'$ and $g_0(x') = 0$. This means that if the consumer's initial cash on hand $x_0 \in [x_{-1}^*, x_0^*]$, then he will always exhaust the borrowing limit ($a_{t+1} = -b$, $t \geq 0$) and will consume all his labor income net of interest payments on debt ($c_0 = x_0 = Ra_0 + y + b$ and $c_t = y - rb$, $t \geq 1$). This plan is optimal because it satisfies the Euler inequality (8.7) and the transversality condition (8.8). Given this plan, we can compute the value function explicitly as

$$V_0(x) = u(x) + \frac{\beta}{1 - \beta} u(y - rb), \quad x \in [x_{-1}^*, x_0^*].$$

By the deterministic version of theorem 7.1.1, it satisfies the Bellman equation (8.9). Moreover it satisfies the envelope condition $V_0'(x) = u'(x)$ for $x \in [x_{-1}^*, x_0^*]$.

Next consider $t = 1$. We conjecture that for initial cash on hand x in some interval $[x_0^*, x_1^*]$, the consumer's optimal plan is to consume part of his disposable resources in period 0 and to save the remaining $\hat{a} > 0$ such that his cash on hand in the next period $z = R\hat{a} + y - rb$ is in the interval $[x_{-1}^*, x_0^*]$. As a result, from period $t = 1$ on, the consumer follows the plan described previously for the case in which $t = 0$.

We first need to determine the value x_1^*. Because $u'(0) = \infty$ and $u'(\infty) = 0$, it can be verified that there exists a unique solution $x > (z - y + rb)/R$ to the equation

$$u'\left(x - \frac{z - y + rb}{R}\right) = \beta R u'(z) = \beta R V_0'(z) \tag{8.12}$$

for any $z \in [x_{-1}^*, x_0^*]$. Define this solution x as a function of z, $x = h_0(z)$ for $z \in [x_{-1}^*, x_0^*]$. Because u' is continuous and strictly decreasing, we can check that h_0 is continuous and strictly increasing. From equations (8.10) and (8.12) we see that as $z \to x_{-1}^* = y - rb$, $h_0(z) \to x_0^*$. Define $x_1^* = \lim_{z \to x_0^*} h_0(z) > x_0^*$. Then $h_0 : [x_{-1}^*, x_0^*] \to [x_0^*, x_1^*]$.

Now we can verify that the previously conjectured plan is optimal. We define the initial saving and consumption policies, respectively, by

$$g_1(x) = \frac{h_0^{-1}(x) - y + rb}{R}, \quad f_1(x) = x - g_1(x), \quad \text{for } x \in [x_0^*, x_1^*],$$

which deliver cash on hand in the next period $z = h_0^{-1}(x_0) \in [x_{-1}^*, x_0^*]$. From period 1 on, the consumer follows the plan for $t = 0$ with initial cash on hand $h_0^{-1}(x_0) \in [x_{-1}^*, x_0^*]$. Because we can show that (1) the initial policies satisfy the Euler equation (8.12) between periods 0 and 1, (2) the plan from period 1 on also satisfies the Euler inequality, and (3) the transversality condition holds, we conclude that the constructed plan from time 0 is indeed optimal. This plan gives the value function

$$V_1(x) = u(f_1(x)) + \beta V_0\left(h_0^{-1}(x)\right), \quad x \in [x_0^*, x_1^*].$$

By construction, it satisfies

$$V_1(x) = \max_{\hat{a} \in [0,x]} u(x - \hat{a}) + \beta V_0(R\hat{a} + y - rb), \quad x \in [x_0^*, x_1^*].$$

By the envelope condition, $V_1'(x) = u'(f_1(x))$ for $x \in [x_0^*, x_1^*]$. As in section 6.4, we can show that V_1 inherits properties of V_0 in that V_1 is strictly increasing and strictly concave.

In general, for any $t \geq 1$, suppose that we obtain the following:

- A sequence of nontrivial intervals $[x_{s-1}^*, x_s^*]$ for $s = 0, 1, \ldots, t$.

- A sequence of continuous and strictly increasing functions,

$$h_{s-1} : [x^*_{s-2}, x^*_{s-1}] \rightarrow [x^*_{s-1}, x^*_s],$$

  with $h_{s-1}(x^*_{s-2}) = x^*_{s-1}$ and $h_{s-1}(x^*_{s-1}) = x^*_s$, for $s = 1, .., t$.
- A sequence of savings and consumption policies $g_s(x)$ and $f_s(x)$ for $x \in [x^*_{s-1}, x^*_s]$, $s = 0, 1, ..., t$.
- A sequence of value functions $V_s : [x^*_{s-1}, x^*_s] \rightarrow \mathbb{R}$ for $s = 0, 1, ..., t$.

These functions satisfy the following equations:

$$u'\left(h_s(z) - \frac{z - y + rb}{R}\right) = \beta R u'\left(z - \frac{h^{-1}_{s-1}(z) - y + rb}{R}\right)$$

$$= \beta R V'_s(z), \quad z \in [x^*_{s-1}, x^*_s],$$

$$g_s(x) = \frac{h^{-1}_{s-1}(x) - y + rb}{R}, \quad f_s(x) = x - g_s(x), \quad x \in [x^*_{s-1}, x^*_s],$$

$$V_s(x) = u(f_s(x)) + \beta V_{s-1}\left(h^{-1}_{s-1}(x)\right), \quad x \in [x^*_{s-1}, x^*_s],$$

for $s = 0, 1, ..., t$. Each value function V_s is strictly increasing, strictly concave, and satisfies the envelope condition $V'_s(x) = u'(f_s(x))$ for $x \in [x^*_{s-1}, x^*_s]$. At each critical value x^*_s, $h_s(x^*_s) = h_{s+1}(x^*_s)$, $g_s(x^*_s) = g_{s+1}(x^*_s)$, $V_s(x^*_s) = V_{s+1}(x^*_s)$, and $V'_s(x^*_s) = V'_{s+1}(x^*_s)$ for $s = 0, 1, ..., t-1$.

Now, at $s = t + 1$, we define another function $h_t(z)$ as the unique solution to the equation

$$u'\left(h_t(z) - \frac{z - y + rb}{R}\right) = \beta R u'\left(z - \frac{h^{-1}_{t-1}(z) - y + rb}{R}\right) \tag{8.13}$$

$$= \beta R V'_t(z)$$

for $z \in [x^*_{t-1}, x^*_t]$. The last equality follows from the envelope condition for $z \in [x^*_{t-1}, x^*_t]$ and $f_t(z) = z - \left[h^{-1}_{t-1}(z) - y + rb\right]/R$. Since V_t is strictly concave on $[x^*_{t-1}, x^*_t]$, the function h_t is strictly increasing on $[x^*_{t-1}, x^*_t]$. By definition, $h_t(x^*_{t-1}) = x^*_t$. Define $x^*_{t+1} = h_t(x^*_t)$. Setting $z = x^*_t$ in equation (8.13) and using $h^{-1}_{t-1}(x^*_t) = x^*_{t-1}$ and $\beta R < 1$, we obtain

$$u'\left(x^*_{t+1} - \frac{x^*_t - y + rb}{R}\right) = \beta R u'\left(x^*_t - \frac{x^*_{t-1} - y + rb}{R}\right)$$

$$< u'\left(x^*_t - \frac{x^*_{t-1} - y + rb}{R}\right)$$

$$< u'\left(x^*_t - \frac{x^*_t - y + rb}{R}\right).$$

Thus $x_{t+1}^* > x_t^*$. It follows that $h_t : [x_{t-1}^*, x_t^*] \to [x_t^*, x_{t+1}^*]$.

Define saving and consumption policies as

$$g_{t+1}(x) = \frac{h_t^{-1}(x) - y + rb}{R} > 0, \quad f_{t+1}(x) = x - g_{t+1}(x), \tag{8.14}$$

for any initial cash on hand $x \in (x_t^*, x_{t+1}^*]$. Because in period 1 these policies deliver cash on hand, $z = h_t^{-1}(x) \in (x_{t-1}^*, x_t^*]$, from period 1 on the consumer will follow the consumption and saving plans starting from initial cash on hand $z \in (x_{t-1}^*, x_t^*]$. Continuing by backward induction, we deduce that the consumer will not exhaust the borrowing limit until period t, and his borrowing will always reach the limit from period $t + 1$ on. Given these policies, we compute the value function as

$$V_{t+1}(x) = u(f_{t+1}(x)) + \beta V_t \left(h_t^{-1}(x) \right), \quad x \in [x_t^*, x_{t+1}^*].$$

By construction, it satisfies the equation

$$V_{t+1}(x) = \max_{\hat{a} \in [0,x]} u(x - \hat{a}) + \beta V_t(R\hat{a} + y - rb), \ x \in [x_t^*, x_{t+1}^*].$$

As in the analysis in section 6.4, we can show that V_{t+1} is strictly increasing, strictly concave, and satisfies the envelope condition, $V_{t+1}'(x) = u'(f_{t+1}(x))$ for $x \in [x_t^*, x_{t+1}^*]$. Additionally we can show that $V_t(x_t^*) = V_{t+1}(x_t^*)$ and $V_t'(x_t^*) = V_{t+1}'(x_t^*)$.

By induction, we can define the consumption, saving, and value functions, respectively, on the whole state space $[y - rb, \infty)$ by

$$c(x) = f_t(x), \quad \hat{a}(x) = g_t(x), \quad V(x) = V_t(x), \quad \text{if } x \in [x_{t-1}^*, x_t^*],$$

for any $t \geq 0$. We can verify that the value function satisfies the Bellman equation (8.9). We can also verify that for any initial cash on hand $x_0 \geq y - rb$, the following sequences

$$\hat{a}_{t+1} = \hat{a}(x_t), \ c_t = x_t - \hat{a}(x_t),$$

$$x_{t+1} = R\hat{a}(x_t) + y - rb, \quad t \geq 0,$$

give optimal consumption and saving plans, respectively.

In terms of dynamics, starting from any initial wealth level, there is a finite time T such that consumption c_t, savings a_{t+1}, and cash on hand x_t all decrease until period T, and after period T they are constant over time in that $c_t = x_t = y - rb$ and $a_{t+1} = -b$ for $t > T$.

Case 2 $\beta R > 1$.

In this case the consumer is so patient that he prefers to save and postpone consumption. We claim that the borrowing constraint is never binding. Suppose, to the contrary, that at time t the borrowing constraint is binding in that $\hat{a}_{t+1} = 0$. Then $x_{t+1} = y - rb$. By the Euler inequality and the envelope condition,

$$V'(x_t) \geq \beta R V'(x_{t+1}) > V'(x_{t+1}),$$

where the last inequality follows from $\beta R > 1$. Because V is strictly concave, $x_t < x_{t+1}$. By the budget constraint, $x_t = R\hat{a}_t + y - rb \geq y - rb = x_{t+1}$, a contradiction.

What are the limiting properties of the optimal consumption and saving plans? By the Euler equation,

$$u'(c_t) = \beta R u'(c_{t+1}) > u'(c_{t+1}).$$

It follows that $c_t < c_{t+1}$. Thus (c_t) is an increasing sequence and hence has a limit as $t \to \infty$. Suppose that $\lim_{t \to \infty} c_t = c^* < \infty$. Then taking limit in the Euler equation above as $t \to \infty$, we obtain $u'(c^*) = \beta R u'(c^*)$, which contradicts with $\beta R > 1$. Thus $\lim c_t = \infty$. This also implies that $\lim x_t = \lim \hat{a}_{t+1} = \infty$ by the budget constraint.

Case 3 $\beta R = 1$.

In this case we assume that y_t is deterministic but may not be constant over time. Without borrowing constraints, the consumer would enjoy a constant consumption stream. In the presence of borrowing constraints, his current consumption is less than the future whenever he currently exhausts the borrowing limit. Formally, by the Euler inequality,

$$u'(c_t) \geq u'(c_{t+1}) \quad \text{with inequality if } \hat{a}_{t+1} = 0.$$

Thus either $c_t = c_{t+1}$ or $c_t < c_{t+1}$ when $\hat{a}_{t+1} = 0$. When $\hat{a}_{t+1} = 0$, $x_{t+1} = y - rb$. Suppose that the consumer arrives in period t and is borrowing constrained. If he knows that the borrowing constraint will never bind again in the future, he would find it optimal to choose the highest sustainable constant consumption level, given by the annuity value of the income stream (net of interest payments on debt) starting from period t,

$$A_t = r \sum_{j=1}^{\infty} R^{-j}(y_{t+j} - rb).$$

Chamberlain and Wilson (2000) show that the impact of the borrowing constraint will never vanish until the consumer reaches the period with the highest annuity value of the remainder of the income process in that

$$c^* \equiv \lim_{t \to \infty} c_t = \sup_t A_t \equiv A^*,$$

where (c_t) is an optimal plan. We now formally prove this result.

We first show that $c^* \le A^*$. Suppose, to the contrary, that $c^* > A^*$. Then there is a t such that the consumer is borrowing constrained in period $t-1$ so that $\hat{a}_t = 0$, $x_t = y_t - rb$, and $c_j > A_t$ for all $j \ge t$. Thus there is a τ sufficiently large such that

$$0 < \sum_{j=t}^{\tau} R^{t-j} \left(c_j - y_j + rb \right) = R^{t-\tau} \left(c_\tau - x_\tau \right),$$

where the equality uses $x_t = y_t - rb$ and successive iterations on the budget constraint. This is a contradiction because $c_\tau \le x_\tau$.

To show that $c^* \ge A^*$, suppose, to the contrary, that $c^* < A^*$. Then there is an A_t such that $c_j < A_t$ for all $j \ge t$, and hence

$$\sum_{j=t}^{\infty} R^{t-j} c_j < \sum_{j=t}^{\infty} R^{t-j} A_t = \sum_{j=t}^{\infty} R^{t-j}(y_j - rb)$$

$$\le x_t + \sum_{j=t+1}^{\infty} R^{t-j}(y_j - rb),$$

where the last inequality uses the inequality $x_t \ge y_t - rb$. Thus there is an $\varepsilon > 0$ and $\tau^* > t$ such that for all $\tau > \tau^*$,

$$\sum_{j=t}^{\tau} R^{t-j} c_j < x_t + \sum_{j=t+1}^{\tau} R^{t-j}(y_j - rb) - \varepsilon.$$

Using the budget constraint repeatedly, we obtain

$$R^{t-\tau} c_\tau < R^{t-\tau} x_\tau - \varepsilon,$$

or equivalently,

$$c_\tau < x_\tau - R^{\tau-t}\varepsilon.$$

We can then construct an alternative feasible consumption plan (c_j') such that $c_j' = c_j$ for all $j \ne \tau^*$ and $c_j' = c_j + \varepsilon$ for $j = \tau^*$. This plan yields higher utility than the plan (c_j), which is a contradiction.

We next consider two examples taken from Ljungqvist and Sargent (2004) to illustrate the preceding result.

Example 8.3.1 *Assume that $a_0 = 0$, $b = 0$, and the labor income stream $\{y_t\} = \{y_h, y_l, y_h, y_l, ...\}$, where $y_h > y_l > 0$. The present value of the labor income is*

$$\sum_{t=0}^{\infty} \frac{y_t}{(1+r)^t} = \frac{y_h + y_l/R}{1 - R^{-2}}.$$

The annuity value $\bar{c}$ that has the same present value as the labor income stream is given by

$$\frac{R\bar{c}}{r} = \frac{y_h + y_l/R}{1 - R^{-2}} \quad or \quad \bar{c} = \frac{y_h + y_l/R}{1 + 1/R}.$$

Consuming $\bar{c}$ each period satisfies the Euler equation. Using the budget constraint, we can find the associated savings plan: $a_{t+1} = (y_h - y_l) R / (1 + R)$ for even t and $a_{t+1} = 0$ for odd t.[1]

Example 8.3.2   *Assume that $a_0 = 0$, $b = 0$, and the labor income stream $\{y_t\} = \{y_l, y_h, y_l, y_h, y_l, ...\}$, where $y_h > y_l > 0$. The solution is $c_0 = y_l$ and $a_1 = 0$, and from period 1 on, the solution is the same as in the previous example. Hence the consumer is borrowing constrained in the first period only.*

In the case of constant labor income $y_t = y$ for all t, the policies $c_t = y + ra_0$ and $a_{t+1} = a_0, t \geq 0$, for any initial asset holdings $a_0 \geq -b$, satisfy the Euler equation and the transversality condition. Thus they are optimal. This means that it is optimal to roll over the initial asset (or debt) level forever.

8.3.2   Stochastic Income

We now suppose that the labor income y_t follows an IID process. We will show that the limiting behavior of the consumption and saving policies is quite different from that in the deterministic case. We first establish some properties of consumption and saving policies.

Lemma 8.3.1   *Let $\beta \in (0,1)$ and $R > 0$. Define $x_{\min} = y_{\min} - rb$. The consumption policy function $c(x)$ is strictly increasing for $x \geq x_{\min}$ and the saving policy function $\hat{a}(x)$ satisfies*

$$0 \leq \hat{a}(x') - \hat{a}(x) < x' - x \quad all\ x_{\min} \leq x < x',$$

with equality if and only if $\hat{a}(x') = \hat{a}(x) = 0$.

Proof   By the envelope condition, $V'(x) = u'(c(x))$. It follows from the strict concavity of V that c is strictly increasing.

Given any $x \geq x_{\min} = y_{\min} - rb$, define the function f by

$$f(s;x) = u'(x - s) - \beta REV'(Rs + y - rb), \quad s \geq 0, \tag{8.15}$$

where the expectation E is taken with respect to the stochastic labor income y. Let $x' > x$. We consider two cases. First, suppose that $\hat{a}(x) = 0$. Then $\hat{a}(x') \geq \hat{a}(x) = 0$.

---

1. Note that $a_{t+1} = 0$ does not necessarily imply that the consumer is borrowing constrained. If and only if the Lagrange multiplier associated with the borrowing constraint is positive, the consumer is borrowing constrained.

If $\hat{a}(x') = 0$, then the result is trivial. Consider $\hat{a}(x') > 0$. Suppose that $\hat{a}(x') \geq x' - x > 0$. Then, by the Euler equation at x' and the strict concavity of u and V,

$$
\begin{aligned}
0 &= u'(x' - \hat{a}(x')) - \beta REV'(R\hat{a}(x') + y - rb) \\
&\geq u'(x) - \beta REV'(R(x' - x) + y - rb) \\
&> u'(x) - \beta REV'(y - rb),
\end{aligned}
$$

which contradicts the Euler inequality at x since $\hat{a}(x) = 0$.

In the second case, $\hat{a}(x) > 0$. So we use the Euler equation at x to deduce that $f(\hat{a}(x); x') < f(\hat{a}(x); x) = 0$. Moreover

$$
\begin{aligned}
f(\hat{a}(x) &+ x' - x; x') \\
&= u'(x - \hat{a}(x)) - \beta REV'(R\hat{a}(x) + R(x' - x) + y - rb) \\
&= \beta REV'(R\hat{a}(x) + y - rb) - \beta REV'(R\hat{a}(x) + R(x' - x) + y - rb) \\
&> 0.
\end{aligned}
$$

Since $f(s; x')$ is strictly increasing in s, it follows from the Intermediate Value Theorem that there exists a unique solution $\hat{a}(x') \in (\hat{a}(x), \hat{a}(x) + x' - x)$ to the equation $f(s; x') = 0$ for each $x' > x$. ∎

Lemma 8.3.1 implies that whenever the borrowing constraint does not bind, then the consumption and saving functions are strictly increasing and have slopes less than 1. From the proof we observe that this result holds for the deterministic case and is also independent of whether $\beta R > 1, = 1$ or < 1.

Case 1 $\beta R < 1$.

Similar to the deterministic case, the optimal consumption, savings and cash on hand sequences under uncertainty will settle down to a steady state. However, this steady state does not imply constant paths, but implies the existence of a stationary distribution. Before establishing this result formally, we present two lemmas.

Lemma 8.3.2   (Schechtman and Escudero 1977) *Let $\beta R < 1$. Suppose that $x_{\min} \equiv y_{\min} - rb > 0$. Then there is an $\hat{x} > x_{\min}$ such that if $x_t \leq \hat{x}$, then $\hat{a}_{t+1} = 0$, and if $x_t > \hat{x}$, then $\hat{a}_{t+1} > 0$.*

Proof   Suppose that the borrowing constraint is never binding. Then by the Euler equation and the envelope condition,

$$
V'(x_t) = \beta RE_t[V'(x_{t+1})] \leq \beta RV'(x_{\min}) < V'(x_{\min}),
$$

where the first inequality follows from the concavity of V. Letting $x_t \to x_{\min}$ leads to a contradiction. Thus there exits a t and $\bar{x}_t \geq x_{\min}$ such that $\hat{a}_{t+1} = 0$ and the

Euler inequality

$$u'(\bar{x}_t) > \beta RE_t V'(y_{t+1} - rb) > 0$$

is satisfied. Since $u'(\infty) = 0$, and u' is continuous and strictly decreasing, there exists a unique $\hat{x} > \bar{x}_t$ such that $u'(\hat{x}) = \beta RE_t V'(y_{t+1} - rb)$. For any $x_t < \hat{x}$ it follows that the Euler inequality holds: $u'(x_t) > \beta RE_t V'(y_{t+1} - rb)$. Thus, for any $x_t \leq \hat{x}$, the consumer must exhaust the borrowing limit in that $c_t = x_t$ and $\hat{a}_{t+1} = 0$. If $x_t > \hat{x}$, then $u'(x_t) < \beta RE_t V'(y_{t+1} - rb)$, implying that $\hat{a}_{t+1} > 0$. ■

This result is similar to that in the deterministic case. The key intuition is that high discounting of the future induces the consumer to borrow more and consume more in the present relative to the future. If his wealth is sufficiently low, he will exhaust his borrowing limit. Figure 8.3 plots consumption and assets as functions of cash on hand.

Lemma 8.3.3 (Schechtman and Escudero 1977) *Let $\beta R < 1$. If*

$$-\frac{cu''(c)}{u'(c)} < \gamma$$

for all c sufficiently large for some $\gamma > 0$, then there exists an x^* such that if $x_t > x^*$, then $x_{t+1} < x_t$.

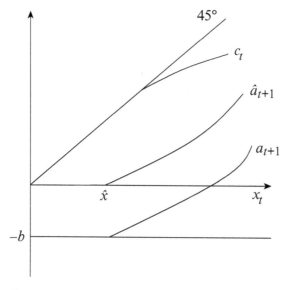

Figure 8.3
Policy functions. Plotted are consumption and assets as functions of cash on hand.

Proof Recall that the consumption and saving policy functions are $c(x)$ and $\hat{a}(x)$, respectively. If $\hat{a}(x)$ is bounded in that $\hat{a}(x) \leq K$ for all $x \geq x_{\min} = y_{\min} - rb$. Then we take $x^* = RK + y_{\max} - rb$. It follows that $x_{t+1} = R\hat{a}(x_t) + y_{t+1} - rb \leq RK + y_{\max} - rb = x^*$. Thus, if $x_t > x^*$, then $x_{t+1} \leq x^* < x_t$.

Now suppose that $\hat{a}(x)$ is unbounded as $x \to \infty$. Using the envelope condition and the concavity of V, we derive that for x_t sufficiently large

$$\frac{E_t V'(x_{t+1})}{V'(y_{\max} - rb + R\hat{a}(x_t))} \leq \frac{V'(y_{\min} - rb + R\hat{a}(x_t))}{V'(y_{\max} - rb + R\hat{a}(x_t))}$$

$$= \frac{u'(c(y_{\min} - rb + R\hat{a}(x_t)))}{u'(c(y_{\max} - rb + R\hat{a}(x_t)))}$$

$$\leq \left[\frac{c(y_{\max} - rb + R\hat{a}(x_t))}{c(y_{\min} - rb + R\hat{a}(x_t))} \right]^\gamma,$$

where γ is the upper bound of $-cu''(c)/u'(c)$.[2] By definition,

$$c(y_{\max} - rb + R\hat{a}(x_t)) = c(y_{\min} - rb + R\hat{a}(x_t)) + y_{\max} - y_{\min}.$$

Thus

$$1 \leq \frac{E_t V'(x_{t+1})}{V'(y_{\max} - rb + R\hat{a}(x_t))} \leq \left[1 + \frac{y_{\max} - y_{\min}}{c(y_{\min} - rb + R\hat{a}(x_t))} \right]^\gamma. \tag{8.16}$$

We first show that $c(x)$ goes to infinity as $x \to \infty$ if $\hat{a}(x) \to \infty$. When $\hat{a}(x_t) \to \infty$ as $x_t \to \infty$, the borrowing constraint will not bind at x_t when x_t is sufficiently large. In this case the Euler inequality holds as an equality:

$$u'(c(x_t)) = \beta R E_t u'(c(x_{t+1})).$$

If $\lim_{x \to \infty} c(x) = \bar{c} > 0$, then taking the limit as $x_t \to \infty$ yields $x_{t+1} = R\hat{a}(x_t) + y_{t+1} - rb \to \infty$ and hence the Euler equation above implies that $u'(\bar{c}) = \beta R u'(\bar{c})$, leading to a contradiction. Thus we must have $\lim_{x \to \infty} c(x) = \infty$. It follows from (8.16) that

$$\lim_{x_t \to \infty} \frac{E_t V'(x_{t+1})}{V'(y_{\max} - rb + R\hat{a}(x_t))} = 1.$$

Choose a positive $\varepsilon < (1 - \beta R)/(\beta R)$, and note that there exists a sufficiently large x^* such that for $x_t > x^*$, $EV'(x_{t+1})/V'(y_{\max} - rb + R\hat{a}(x_t)) < 1 + \varepsilon$. Using the Euler equation, we write

$$V'(x_t) = \beta R E_t V'(x_{t+1}) < (1 + \varepsilon) \beta R V'(y_{\max} - rb + R\hat{a}(x_t))$$

$$\leq V'(y_{\max} - rb + R\hat{a}(x_t)).$$

---

2. If $-cu''(c)/u'(c) \leq \gamma$ for all $c > c_0$, then $u'(c)/u'(c_0) \geq (c_0/c)^\gamma$ for all $c > c_0$.

It follows from the concavity of V that if $x_t \geq x^*$, then $x_t > y_{\max} - rb + R\hat{a}(x_t) \geq x_{t+1}$.

∎

Lemma 8.3.3 implies that whenever the cash on hand is larger than a critical value x^*, then the cash on hand in the next period will fall. Let $x_{\max}$ denote the smallest critical values that satisfy the property in this lemma. Then the cash on hand in the long run will settle down in the closed interval $[x_{\min}, x_{\max}]$ as illustrated in figure 8.4.

Exercise 9 asks the reader to show that $x_{\max} > x_{\min}$ and $x_{\max}$ is the largest value such $R\hat{a}(x_{\max}) + y_{\max} - rb = x_{\max}$.

Proposition 8.3.1   (Schechtman and Escudero 1977; Clarida 1987; Aiyagari 1994) *Let $\beta R < 1$. Let y_t be independently and identically drawn from the distribution μ, satisfying*

$$\mu([a,b]) \geq \alpha[a,b] \quad \text{for any } [a,b] \subset [y_{\min}, y_{\max}].$$

Suppose that $-cu''(c)/u'(c) < \gamma$ for all c sufficiently large for some $\gamma > 0$. Then there exists a unique stable stationary distribution over the support $[x_{\min}, x_{\max}]$ for (x_t). Further the stationary distribution is continuous (in the weak convergence topology) in the parameters R and b.

Proof   The Markov process (x_t) defined by

$$x_{t+1} = R\hat{a}(x_t) + y_{t+1} - rb$$

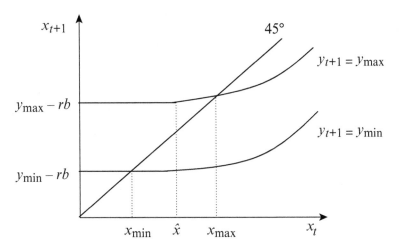

Figure 8.4
Evolution of cash on hand. Plotted is x_{t+1} as a function of x_t for the largest and the lowest income levels.

induces a transition function P on the state space $[x_{\min}, x_{\max}]$. We will apply theorems 3.3.5 and 3.3.6. We can easily verify that the transition function is monotone and satisfies the Feller property. The key is to verify that it satisfies the mixing condition in that there exists $\bar{x}$ and $\varepsilon > 0$ such that $P^n(x_{\min}, [\bar{x}, x_{\max}]) \geq \varepsilon$ and $P^n(x_{\max}, [x_{\min}, \bar{x}]) \geq \varepsilon$ for n sufficiently large.

Define the sequence $\{\varphi_n(x, y)\}$ by

$$\varphi_0(x, y) = x,$$
$$\varphi_{n+1}(x, y) = R\hat{a}(\varphi_n(x, y)) + y - rb.$$

That is, $\varphi_n(x, y)$ is the cash on hand at the beginning of period n if x is the initial cash on hand, the labor income takes the constant value y each period, and the saving policy $\hat{a}$ is followed each period. Since $\varphi_n(x, y)$ is increasing in y, we deduce that

$$P^n(x, [\varphi_n(x, y_{\max} - \delta), \varphi_n(x, y_{\max})]) \geq \alpha^n \delta^n,$$
$$P^n(x, [\varphi_n(x, y_{\min}), \varphi_n(x, y_{\min} + \delta)]) \geq \alpha^n \delta^n,$$

for all $0 < \delta < y_{\max} - y_{\min}$ and all $n \geq 1$.

Since

$$\varphi_0(x_{\min}, y_{\max}) = x_{\min} < y_{\max} - rb = \varphi_1(x_{\min}, y_{\max}),$$

it follows by induction that $\{\varphi_n(x_{\min}, y_{\max})\}$ is a strictly increasing sequence. Since it is bounded by $x_{\max}$, it converges to a limit $\xi < x_{\max}$. Similarly $\lim_{n \to \infty} \varphi_n(x_{\min}, Ey)$ exists. We choose this limit as $\bar{x}$. Since $\varphi_n(x_{\min}, y_{\max}) > \varphi_n(x_{\min}, Ey)$, it follows that $\xi \geq \bar{x}$. If $\xi = \bar{x}$, then by continuity of $\hat{a}$,

$$\xi = R\hat{a}(\xi) + y_{\max} - rb$$
$$= \bar{x} = R\hat{a}(\bar{x}) + Ey - rb,$$

which contradicts $y_{\max} > Ey$. Thus we must have $\xi > \bar{x}$. This allows us to choose N sufficiently large such that $\varphi_N(x_{\min}, y_{\max}) > \bar{x}$, and $\delta > 0$ sufficiently small such that $\varphi_N(x_{\min}, y_{\max} - \delta) > \bar{x}$. Then

$$P^N(x_{\min}, [\bar{x}, x_{\max}])$$
$$\geq P^N(x_{\min}, [\varphi_N(x_{\min}, y_{\max} - \delta), \varphi_N(x_{\min}, y_{\max})]) \geq \alpha^N \delta^N > 0.$$

A similar argument applies to $x_0 = x_{\max}$:

$$P^N(x_{\max}, [x_{\min}, \bar{x}]) \geq \alpha^N \delta^N > 0.$$

The rest of the proof is routine.   ∎

This is a remarkable result and is the foundation for the incomplete markets models of Bewley (1980) and Aiyagari (1994).

Case 2 $\beta R > 1$.

In the deterministic case we showed that (c_t) is an increasing sequence and hence has a limit. In the stochastic case, a stochastic process (M_t) with the property $M_t \geq (\leq)E_t[M_{t+1}]$, analogous to monotonicity in the deterministic case, is called a supermartingale (submartingale). Chamberlain and Wilson (2000) analyze the long-run behavior of consumption and savings using the powerful Supermartingale Convergence Theorem. Let $M_t = \beta^t R^t u'(c_t) \geq 0$. It follows from the Euler inequality that $\{M_t\}$ is a nonnegative supermartingale. By the **Supermartingale Convergence Theorem** (appendix D), $\{M_t\}$ converges to a nonnegative limit. If $\beta R > 1$, then we must have $\lim_t u'(c_t) = 0$, and hence $\lim_t c_t = \infty$. By the budget constraint, we also have $\lim_t x_t = \infty$ and $\lim_t \hat{a}_{t+1} = \infty$.

Sotomayor (1984) proves a stronger result when labor income is an IID process.

Proposition 8.3.2 (Sotomayor 1984) *Let $\beta R > 1$. (a) Let $\lim_{x \to \infty} \hat{a}(x) = \infty$. (b) If $-cu''(c)/u'(c) < \gamma$ for all c sufficiently large for some $\gamma > 0$, then there exists an $\tilde{x}$ such that if $x_t > \tilde{x}$, then $x_{t+1} > x_t$.*

Proof (a) Suppose, to the contrary, that $\lim_{x \to \infty} \hat{a}(x) = k < \infty$. Then by the Euler inequality,

$$V'(x_t) \geq \beta R E_t V'(y_{t+1} - rb + R\hat{a}(x_t)).$$

Taking the limit as $x_t \to \infty$ yields

$$\lim_{x_t \to \infty} V'(x_t) \geq \beta R E_t V'(y_{t+1} - rb + Rk) > 0.$$

Let $\lim_{x_t \to \infty} V'(x_t) = K > 0$. Then, when x is larger than $y_{\max} - rb + Rk$, it follows from the concavity of V that

$$K \geq \beta R E_t V'(y_{t+1} - rb + Rk) \geq \beta R V'(x).$$

Letting $x \to \infty$ yields $K \geq \beta R K$, a contradiction with $\beta R > 1$.

(b) Using the concavity of u and the assumption, we have

$$\frac{E_t u'(c(y_{t+1} - rb + Ra(x_t))}{u'(c(y_{\min} - rb + R\hat{a}(x_t)))}$$
$$\geq \frac{u'(c(y_{\max} - rb + R\hat{a}(x_t)))}{u'(c(y_{\min} - rb + R\hat{a}(x_t)))} \geq \left(\frac{c(y_{\min} - rb + R\hat{a}(x_t))}{c(y_{\max} - rb + R\hat{a}(x_t))}\right)^{\gamma},$$

for x_t sufficiently large. Using part (a) and a similar argument in the proof of lemma 8.3.3, we can deduce that

$$\frac{E_t u'\left(c(y_{t+1} - rb + R\hat{a}\left(x_t\right))\right)}{u'\left(c(y_{\min} - rb + R\hat{a}\left(x_t\right))\right)} \geq 1 \quad \text{as } x_t \to \infty.$$

Thus there exists an $\tilde{x}$ sufficiently large such that when $x_t > \tilde{x}$,

$$V'\left(x_t\right) = \beta R E_t V'\left(x_{t+1}\right) > E_t u'\left(c(y_{t+1} - rb + R\hat{a}\left(x_t\right))\right)$$
$$\geq V'\left(y_{\min} - rb + R\hat{a}\left(x_t\right)\right),$$

where the first inequality follows from the envelope condition and $\beta R > 1$. It follows from the concavity of V that $x_t < y_{\min} - rb + R\hat{a}\left(x_t\right) \leq x_{t+1}$.

∎

Case 3 $\beta R = 1$.

Chamberlain and Wilson (2000) show that consumption also converges to infinity almost surely for $\beta R = 1$ for very general stochastic labor income processes if the discounted present value of labor income is sufficiently stochastic. Sotomayor (1984) and Aiyagari (1994) provide a simple proof in the IID case. When $\beta R = 1$, the Supermartingale Convergence Theorem does not necessarily imply that $u'\left(c_t\right)$ converges to zero. Suppose that $u'\left(c_t\right)$ converges to a positive limit so that c_t converges to a finite limit almost surely. Then x_t also converges to a finite limit almost surely. Since the set of sample paths for which there are infinitely many t such that $y_{t+1} = y_{\min}$ and $y_{t+1} = y_{\max}$ both have probability one, we assume that the sample paths on which x_t converges also have this property. This contradicts the budget constraint $x_{t+1} = R\hat{a}\left(x_t\right) + y_{t+1} - rb$ given the continuity of $\hat{a}$.

Compared to the deterministic case, this limiting result is remarkable. As discussed by Chamberlain and Wilson (2000), the economic intuition behind this result is hard to explain. The key argument relies on the powerful Supermartingale Convergence Theorem.

Sotomayor (1984) argues that although $\lim_t x_t = \infty$ for both $\beta R > 1$ and $\beta R = 1$, the convergence behavior is different. Unlike the case of $\beta R > 1$, there is no initial level of cash on hand from which the optimal sequence of cash on hand is increasing. Intuitively, when x_t is sufficiently large, the borrowing constraint does not bind at x_t. Then by the Euler equation and the envelope condition,

$$V'\left(x_t\right) = \beta R E_t V'\left(x_{t+1}\right) = E_t V'\left(R\hat{a}\left(x_t\right) + y_{t+1} - rb\right)$$
$$\leq V'\left(R\hat{a}\left(x_t\right) + y_{\min} - rb\right).$$

Thus $x_t \geq R\hat{a}\left(x_t\right) + y_{\min} - rb$. A similar argument shows that $x_t \leq R\hat{a}\left(x_t\right) + y_{\max} - rb$. Thus unless $x_t = R\hat{a}\left(x_t\right) + y_{\min} - rb$ for all large x_t, there is a positive probability that $x_t > R\hat{a}(x_t) + y_{\min} - rb$, and hence there is a positive probability that $x_t > x_{t+1} = R\hat{a}(x_t) + y_{t+1} - rb$.

Lemma 8.3.4 (Sotomayor 1984) *Let $\beta R = 1$. There is no $\tilde{x}$ such that for all $x > \tilde{x}$, $x = R\hat{a}(x) + y_{\min} - rb$.*

Proof If there exists an $\tilde{x}$ such that $x = R\hat{a}(x) + y_{\min} - rb$. Then for x large enough,

$$V'(R\hat{a}(x) + y_{\min} - rb) = V'(x) = EV'(R\hat{a}(x) + y - rb),$$

where the second equality follows from the Euler inequality and the expectation is taken with respect to the random variable y. The equation above cannot hold for strictly concave V. ∎

8.4 Consumption/Portfolio Choice

In this previous section the agent can trade only one risk-free asset. This section studies the case in which the agent can trade a portfolio of assets. Suppose that there are J risky stocks and one riskless one-period bond. Stock j pays dividends D_{jt} and has price P_{jt} in period t. The gross return on the bond between periods t and $t+1$ is given by R^f_{t+1}. We can write down the budget constraint as

$$C_t + \sum_{j=1}^{J} P_{jt}\psi_{jt} + B_t = \sum_{j=1}^{J}(P_{jt} + D_{jt})\psi_{jt-1} + R^f_t B_{t-1},$$

where ψ_{jt} denotes the stock holdings in period t and B_t denotes the bond holdings in terms of consumption units in period t. We can define financial wealth as

$$W_t = \sum_{j=1}^{J}(P_{jt} + D_{jt})\psi_{jt-1} + R_t B_{t-1}.$$

Define the fraction of wealth after consumption invested in stock j as

$$\pi_{jt} = \frac{P_{jt}\psi_{jt}}{W_t - C_t}.$$

By the budget constraint, we then have

$$\frac{B_t}{W_t - C_t} = 1 - \sum_{j=1}^{J}\pi_{jt}.$$

By the analysis above, we can rewrite the budget constraint as

$$W_{t+1} = \sum_{j=1}^{J} \left(P_{jt+1} + D_{jt+1} \right) \psi_{jt} + R_{t+1}^f B_t$$

$$= \sum_{j=1}^{J} \frac{P_{jt+1} + D_{jt+1}}{P_{jt}} P_{jt} \psi_{jt} + R_{t+1}^f B_t$$

$$= \sum_{j=1}^{J} R_{jt+1} P_{jt} \psi_{jt} + R_{t+1}^f B_t$$

$$= R_{wt+1} \left(W_t - C_t \right), \tag{8.17}$$

where R_{jt+1} and R_{wt+1} are the return on stock j and the portfolio return, respectively, defined as

$$R_{jt+1} \equiv \frac{P_{jt+1} + D_{jt+1}}{P_{jt}}, \quad R_{wt+1} \equiv R_{t+1}^f + \sum_{j=1}^{J} \pi_{jt} \left(R_{jt+1} - R_{t+1}^f \right).$$

In a consumption/portfolio choice problem, the return processes $\{R_{jt+1}\}$ and $\{R_{t+1}^f\}$ are exogenously given. The agent's problem is to choose consumption $\{C_t\}$ and portfolios $\{\pi_{jt+1}\}$ to solve the following problem:

$$\max \; E \sum_{t=0}^{\infty} \beta^t u \left(C_t \right)$$

subject to (8.17). We may impose some portfolio constraints or a transversality condition to rule out Ponzi schemes.[3] Suppose that these constraints do not bind. The Bellman equation is given by

$$V_t \left(W_t \right) = \max_{C_t, \pi_{jt}} u \left(C_t \right) + \beta E_t V_{t+1} \left(R_{wt+1} \left(W_t - C_t \right) \right),$$

where $V_t \left(W_t \right)$ is the agent's value function. We have suppressed other state variables that drive the dynamics of returns. Suppose that V_t is differentiable and concave. This needs primitive assumptions on u. The first-order conditions are given by

$$C_t : u' \left(C_t \right) = \beta E_t V_{t+1}' \left(R_{wt+1} \left(W_t - C_t \right) \right) R_{wt+1},$$

$$\pi_{jt} : 0 = E_t V_{t+1}' \left(R_{wt+1} \left(W_t - C_t \right) \right) \left(W_t - C_t \right) \left(R_{jt+1} - R_{t+1}^f \right).$$

---

3. See chapter 13 for an in-depth analysis.

The envelope condition is given by

$$V_t'(W_t) = \beta E_t V_{t+1}'(R_{wt+1}(W_t - C_t)) R_{wt+1}.$$

Combining the preceding conditions, we obtain

$$u'(C_t) = \beta E_t u'(C_{t+1}) R_{wt+1} = V_t'(W_t),$$

$$0 = E_t u'(C_{t+1}) \left(R_{jt+1} - R_{t+1}^f \right).$$

Hence we obtain the following set of Euler equations:

$$E_t \left[\frac{\beta u'(C_{t+1})}{u'(C_t)} R_{t+1}^f \right] = 1,$$

$$E_t \left[\frac{\beta u'(C_{t+1})}{u'(C_t)} R_{jt+1} \right] = 1, \quad j = 1, 2, ..., J.$$

These equations give testable restrictions on asset returns. In an equilibrium model one can assume that consumption and dividends are exogenously given but asset returns are endogenous. Chapter 13 analyzes this issue.

8.5 Inventory

Inventory control is a classical problem in operations research and is also important in economics. This problem typically involves both fixed and variable costs and belongs to the class of the mixed stopping and control problems. Our presentation below follows Scarf (1959) and Iglehart (1963) closely. Suppose that a firm has an inventory stock x_t of some good at the beginning of period t. It may sell the good to meet the exogenous stochastic market demand $z_{t+1} \geq 0$ at the end of period t. Suppose that the demand $\{z_{t+1}\}$ is IID with distribution φ. After observing x_t and z_t and before observing z_{t+1}, the firm may order $d_t \geq 0$ units of the good to increase its inventory stock. Then the law of motion of the inventory stock is given by

$$x_{t+1} = x_t + d_t - z_{t+1}, \quad x_0 \text{ given.} \tag{8.18}$$

We allow x_t to take negative values. Negative stocks represent debt to suppliers or backlogging. Sales of z_{t+1} generates profits $R(z_{t+1}) \geq 0$. Storage of x_t incurs costs $\Phi(x_t) \geq 0$. Placing an order of size d_t costs $C(d_t) \geq 0$. Assume that future cash flows are discounted by $\beta \in (0,1)$. The firm's problem is given by

$$\max_{(d_t) \geq 0} E \sum_{t=0}^{\infty} \beta^t [R(z_{t+1}) - \Phi(x_t) - C(d_t)] \tag{8.19}$$

subject to (8.18), where the expectation is taken with respect to (z_t).

What makes this problem special is the specification of the order cost function $C(d)$. Suppose that

$$C(d) = \begin{cases} 0 & \text{if } d = 0, \\ c + pd & \text{if } d > 0, \end{cases}$$

where c represents fixed costs and p represents proportional costs. The presence of fixed costs makes the analysis of the problem in (8.19) difficult. We will use the dynamic programming method to analyze it. Observe that this problem is equivalent to minimizing discounted expected costs. It is also convenient to define $y_t = x_t + d_t$, which represents the stock immediately after order and before sales. Moreover we define the expected holding and storage costs by

$$L(y_t) = \beta E\Phi(x_{t+1}) = \beta E\Phi(y_t - z_{t+1}),$$

where E is the expectation operator for the random variable z.

Assumption 8.5.1 *The function* $L : \mathbb{R} \to \mathbb{R}_+$ *is convex and* **coercive** *in that* $\lim_{|y| \to \infty} L(y) = +\infty$.

After a change of variables, we write the cost minimization problem as

$$\min_{(y_t)} E \sum_{t=0}^{\infty} \beta^t \left[L(y_t) + C(y_t - x_t) \right] \tag{8.20}$$

subject to $x_{t+1} = y_t - z_{t+1}$, $y_t \geq x_t$, $t \geq 0$, and x_0 is given. The Bellman equation for this problem is given by

$$V(x) = \min_{y \geq x} L(y) + C(y - x) + \beta E V(y - z), \tag{8.21}$$

where E is the expectation operator for the random variable z. Note that the reward function for this problem, $L(y) + C(y - x)$, is bounded below by zero but unbounded above. We cannot apply the dynamic programming theory for bounded rewards developed earlier. We will study corresponding finite-horizon problems and take the limit as the horizon goes to infinity.

Define the Bellman operator by

$$Tf(x) = \min_{y \geq x} L(y) + c\mathbf{1}_{y > x} + p \cdot (y - x) + \beta E f(y - z)$$

for any nonnegative function $f : \mathbb{R} \to \mathbb{R}_+$. Here $\mathbf{1}_{y > x}$ is an indicator function. The sequence of finite-horizon problems is given by $f_n(x) = T^n f_0(x)$, $n = 1, 2, ...$, where we set $f_0 = 0$. To get a quick idea about the nature of the solution, we consider the single-period case:

$$f_1(x) = \min_{y \geq x} L(y) + c\mathbf{1}_{y > x} + p \cdot (y - x).$$

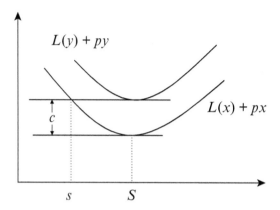

Figure 8.5
Optimality of the (s, S) policy. Illustrated is the solution for the one-period problem.

Figure 8.5 illustrates that the optimal ordering policy takes the (s, S) form. The stock level S minimizes the function $L(y) + py$. At the point $s < S$, the firm is indifferent between placing an order $S - s$ and not ordering such that $L(S) + c + pS = L(s) + ps$. For $x < s$, $L(S) + c + pS < L(x) + px$. Thus it is optimal for the firm to order $S - x$. For $x > s$ and any $y \geq x$, $L(y) + c + py > L(x) + px$. It is not optimal for the firm to place any order $y - x$. This form of the ordering policy is called **the** (s, S) **form.**

8.5.1 Finite-Horizon Problem

Let us generalize the intuition above to a dynamic setting. The n-period problem is given by

$$f_n(x) = \min_{y \geq x} \ L(y) + c\mathbf{1}_{y > x} + p \cdot (y - x) + \beta E f_{n-1}(y - z), \tag{8.22}$$

where $f_0 = 0$. We can rewrite it as

$$f_n(x) = \min \ \{L(x) + \beta E f_{n-1}(x - z),$$
$$\min_{y \geq x} \ L(y) + c + p \cdot (y - x) + \beta E f_{n-1}(y - z)\}.$$

This problem is a mixed control and stopping problem in that the firm first decides whether and when to order (stopping), and if it decides to order, then it chooses how much to order (control).

Define

$$G_n(y) = L(y) + py + \beta E f_{n-1}(y - z).$$

If it is optimal to order from x to $y > x$, then $G_n(x) > c + G_n(y)$, and this y must minimize $G_n(y)$. Let S_n be the smallest minimizer if there are many. If $G_n(y)$ decreases to a minimum and then increases (e.g., $G_n(y)$ is convex), then there is a solution $s_n < S_n$ to the equation

$$G_n(s_n) = c + G_n(S_n). \tag{8.23}$$

At the stock level s_n, the firm is indifferent between ordering and not. If $x < s_n$, the firm should place an order $S_n - x$ to bring the stock to S_n. Thus it is natural that the optimal ordering policy takes the (s, S) form.

The problem of the argument above is that $G_n(y)$ may not be convex, and there may be multiple local minimizers as can be verified by numerical examples even if $L(x)$ is strictly convex. To prove the optimality of the (s, S) policy, we need the notion of c-convexity introduced by Scarf (1959).

Definition 8.5.1 *Let $c \geq 0$, and let $h : \mathbb{R} \to \mathbb{R}$ be a differentiable function. Say that h is c-convex if*

$$c + h(x + a) - h(x) - ah'(x) \geq 0 \quad \text{for all } a > 0. \tag{8.24}$$

If differentiability is not assumed, then the inequality above is replaced with

$$c + h(x + a) - h(x) - a\frac{h(x) - h(x - b)}{b} \geq 0 \tag{8.25}$$

for all $a, b > 0$.

Lemma 8.5.1 *If h is a differentiable c-convex function, then*

$$c + h(y) - h(x) - (y - x)h'(u) \geq 0$$

for all $y > x > u$.

Proof We consider two cases.
Case 1 $h(u) - h(x) + (x - u)h'(u) \leq 0$.
In this case

$$c + h(y) - h(x) - (y - x)h'(u)$$
$$\geq c + h(y) - h(x) - \frac{y - x}{x - u}[h(x) - h(u)] \geq 0,$$

where the last inequality follows from (8.25).
Case 2 $h(u) - h(x) + (x - u)h'(u) > 0$.
We then have

$$c + h(y) - h(x) - (y - x)h'(u)$$
$$> c + h(y) - h(u) - (x - u)h'(u) - (y - x)h'(u) \geq 0,$$

where the last inequality follows from (8.24).   ∎

Additional properties of c-convex functions are as follows:

1. Convex function is 0-convex and any c-convex function is also c'-convex for $c' > c \geq 0$.
2. If $h(x)$ is c-convex, then $h(x+a)$ is also c-convex for all $a \in \mathbb{R}$.
3. If f is c-convex and g is b-convex, then $\alpha f + \gamma g$ is $(\alpha c + \gamma b)$-convex for $\alpha, \gamma > 0$.

An important property of c-convexity is that it is impossible that in three consecutive sub-intervals (x_1, x_2), (x_2, x_3), (x_3, x_4), the optimal policy is not to order, to order and not to order, respectively, as illustrated in figure 8.6.

Suppose the contrary. Then there is a local maximizer in the interval (x_2, x_3). Let x^* be one of the maximizers. By the c-convexity of $G_n(y)$,

$$0 \leq c + G_n(S_2) - G_n(x^*) - \frac{(S_2 - x^*)[G_n(x^*) - G_n(x^* - b)]}{b}$$
$$\leq c + G_n(S_2) - G_n(x^*), \quad b > 0,$$

which is a contradiction.

The following lemma demonstrates the optimal policy must be of the (s, S) form.

Lemma 8.5.2 *If $G_n(y)$ is continuous, c-convex, and coercive, then the following (s, S) policy is optimal:*

$$d_n(x) = \begin{cases} 0 & \text{if } x > s_n, \\ S_n - x & \text{if } x \leq s_n, \end{cases}$$

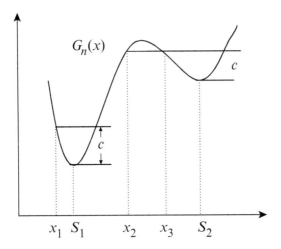

Figure 8.6
Minimization of $G_n(x)$

where S_n is a global minimizer of $G_n(y)$ and s_n is the smallest solution to (8.23) such that $s_n < S_n$.

Proof   Since G_n is continuous and coercive, there exists a minimizing point of G_n. Let S_n be such a point. Let s_n be the smallest value such that (8.23) holds. For all $x < s_n$, it follows from the definition of c-convexity that

$$c + G_n(S_n) \geq G_n(s_n) + \frac{S_n - s_n}{s_n - x}(G_n(s_n) - G_n(x)).$$

Thus $G_n(s_n) \leq G_n(x)$. Since $x < s_n$ and s_n is the smallest value such that (8.23) holds, we must have $G_n(x) > G_n(s_n) = G_n(S_n) + c$. Thus, for all $x < s_n$, it is optimal to order $S_n - x$.

Now we can show that $G_n(x) \leq G_n(y) + c$ for all x, y with $s_n \leq x \leq y$. This is true for $x = y$, $x = S_n$ or $x = s_n$. There remain two other possibilities: $S_n < x < y$ and $s_n < x < S_n$. If $S_n < x < y$, then by c-convexity,

$$c + G_n(y) \geq G_n(x) + \frac{y - x}{x - S_n}(G_n(x) - G_n(S_n))$$
$$\geq G_n(x).$$

If $s_n < x < S_n$, then

$$G_n(s_n) = c + G_n(S_n) \geq G_n(x) + \frac{S_n - x}{x - s_n}(G_n(x) - G_n(s_n)).$$

Thus $G_n(s_n) \geq G_n(x)$. It follows that

$$G_n(y) + c \geq G_n(S_n) + c = G_n(s_n) \geq G_n(x_n).$$

We conclude that it is optimal not to order for all $x > s_n$.   ∎

We can also prove that $G_n(x)$ is decreasing for $x < s_n$. Let $x_1 < x_2 < s_n$. We have

$$c + G_n(S_n) \geq G_n(x_2) + \frac{S_n - x_2}{x_2 - x_1}(G_n(x_2) - G_n(x_1)).$$

Since $G_n(x_2) > G_n(S_n) + c$, we must have $G_n(x_2) < G_n(x_1)$.

The following lemma completes the proof of the optimality of (s, S) policy for the finite-horizon problem by showing that $G_n(x)$ is indeed c-convex for all $n \geq 1$.

Lemma 8.5.3   *Suppose that assumption 8.5.1 holds. Then $G_n(x)$ is c-convex for all $n \geq 1$.*

Proof   We prove by induction. By definition, $f_0(x) = 0$ and $G_1(x) = L(x) + px$. Clearly, $G_1(x)$ is c-convex. Suppose that $G_n(x)$ is c-convex. Using the previous lemma, we obtain that for $x > s_n$,

$$f_n(x) = -px + G_n(x),$$

which is c-convex. For $x < s_n$,

$$f_n(x) = L(S_n) + c + p(S_n - x) + \beta E f_{n-1}(S_n - z)$$
$$= c - px + G_n(S_n).$$

Consider two cases. If $x < x + a < s_n$, then $f_n(x)$ is linear in x and is c-convex. If $x < s_n < x + a$, then

$$c + f_n(x + a) - f_n(x) - a\frac{f_n(x) - f_n(x - b)}{b}$$
$$= c + [-p(x + a) + G_n(x + a)] - [c - px + G_n(S_n)]$$
$$- a\frac{[c - px + G_n(S_n)] - [c - p(x - b) + G_n(S_n)]}{b}$$
$$= G_n(x + a) - G_n(S_n) \geq 0,$$

where the inequality follows from the fact that S_n is the global minimizer of G_n. Thus $f_n(x)$ is c-convex.

By the properties of c-convex functions, $f_n(x - z)$ and $E f_n(x - z)$ and $\beta E f_n(x - z)$ are all c-convex functions. Thus $G_{n+1}(x)$ is c-convex. ∎

8.5.2 Infinite-Horizon Problem

We now study the convergence of the sequence of solutions to the finite-horizon problems. We need to exploit additional properties of the finite-horizon problems. In doing so, we impose an assumption:

Assumption 8.5.2 *The function $L(x)$ is differentiable.*

From the proof of the previous lemma and equation (8.23),

$$f_n(x) = \begin{cases} -px + G_n(s_n) & \text{if } x \leq s_n, \\ -px + G_n(x) & \text{if } x > s_n. \end{cases} \tag{8.26}$$

Moreover each f_n is continuous. Since $L(x)$ is differentiable, we can prove the following results by induction:

1. Each function $f_n(x)$ is differentiable except at the point $x = s_n$ where the left and right-hand derivatives exist:

$$f_n'(x) = \begin{cases} -p & \text{if } x \leq s_n, \\ -p + G_n'(x) & \text{if } x > s_n. \end{cases} \tag{8.27}$$

2. Each function $G_n(y)$ is differentiable:

$$G_n'(y) = L'(y) + p + \beta E f_{n-1}'(y - z).$$

Now we establish bounds for the sequences of $\{s_n\}$ and $\{S_n\}$. The following lemma shows that $\{S_n\}$ is bounded below.

Lemma 8.5.4 *Suppose that assumptions 8.5.1 and 8.5.2 hold. Then* $S_1 \leq S_n$, $n = 2, 3, \dots$.

It is sufficient to prove inductively that $G'_n(x) < 0$ for $x < S_1$. We leave the proof as an exercise. The lemma below shows that $\{S_n\}$ is bounded above.

Lemma 8.5.5 *Suppose that assumptions 8.5.1 and 8.5.2 hold. $S_n \leq M < \infty$ for all* $n = 1, 2, \dots$.

Proof For all $a > 0$,

$$G_n(x+a) - G_n(x) = pa + L(x+a) - L(x)$$
$$+ \beta \int_0^\infty \left[f_{n-1}(x+a-z) - f_{n-1}(x-z) \right] \varphi(z)\, dz.$$

Dividing the integral into two regions, we obtain

$$G_n(x+a) - G_n(x) = pa + L(x+a) - L(x) - pa\beta \int_{\max\{x+a-s_{n-1},0\}}^\infty \varphi(z)\, dz$$
$$+ \beta \int_0^{\max\{x+a-s_{n-1},0\}} \left[f_{n-1}(x+a-z) - f_{n-1}(x-z) \right] \varphi(z)\, dz.$$

Since f_{n-1} is c-convex, it follows from lemma 8.5.1 that

$$\int_0^{\max\{x+a-s_{n-1},0\}} \left[f_{n-1}(x+a-z) - f_{n-1}(x-z) \right] \varphi(z)\, dz$$
$$\geq \int_0^{\max\{x+a-s_{n-1},0\}} \left[-c + af'_{n-1}(x - \max\{x+a-s_{n-1},0\}) \right] \varphi(z)\, dz$$
$$= \int_0^{\max\{x+a-s_{n-1},0\}} \left[-c - ap \right] \varphi(z)\, dz,$$

where we have used (8.27). Thus we obtain

$$G_n(x+a) - G_n(x) \geq L(x+a) - L(x) - c.$$

Since $L(x)$ is convex and $\lim_{|x|\to\infty} L(x) = \infty$, there exist M_1 and M_2 such that when $x > M_1$ and $a > M_2$, $L(x+a) - L(x) - c > 0$. Suppose that $S_n > M_1 + M_2$. Then letting $x + a = S_n$, we find that $G_n(S_n) - G_n(x) > 0$. This contradicts the fact that S_n minimizes $G_n(x)$. Thus $S_n \leq M_1 + M_2 \equiv M$. ∎

Clearly, since $s_n < S_n \leq M$, $\{s_n\}$ is bounded above. The following lemma shows that s_n is also bounded below.

Lemma 8.5.6 *Suppose that assumptions 8.5.1 and 8.5.2 hold. $2s_1 - S_1 < s_n$ for all $n = 2, 3, \dots$.*

Proof The result is obtained by inductively proving that $G'_n(x) \leq -c/(S_1 - s_1)$ for $x \leq s_1$ and all $n \geq 1$. For $n = 1$, the cord connecting the two points $(s_1, G_1(s_1))$ and $(S_1, G_1(S_1))$ has slope $-c/(S_1 - s_1)$. Since $G_1(x) = px + L(x)$ is convex, $G'_1(x) \leq -c/(S_1 - s_1)$. Suppose that $G'_n(x) \leq -c/(S_1 - s_1)$ for $x \leq s_1$. Then, since $f'_n(x) \leq -c$ for $x \leq s_1$, it follows that

$$G'_{n+1}(x) \leq G'_1(x) - \beta c < -\frac{c}{S_1 - s_1} \quad \text{for } x \leq s_1.$$

By the Mean Value Theorem, there exists a $\xi \in [s_1 - (S_1 - s_1), s_1]$ such that

$$G_n(S_n) \leq G_n(s_1) = G_n(s_1 - (S_1 - s_1)) + G_n(\xi)(S_1 - s_1)$$
$$< G_n(s_1 - (S_1 - s_1)) - c,$$

where the first inequality follows from the fact that S_n minimizes $G_n(x)$ and the second from the previous claim. From these inequalities we know that at the stock level $s_1 - (S_1 - s_1)$, it is optimal for the firm to place an order so that $s_1 - (S_1 - s_1) < s_n$, for $n = 2, 3, \dots$. ∎

Given the bounds above, we can prove:

Proposition 8.5.1 *Suppose that assumptions 8.5.1 and 8.5.2 hold. Then $\{f_n(x)\}$ and $\{G_n(x)\}$ converge monotonically to finite limits, and the convergence is uniform for all x in any finite interval. The limit functions $f(x)$ and $G(x)$ are continuous.*

Proof Define

$$T(y, x, f) = C(y - x) + L(y) + \beta Ef(y - z),$$

and let $y_n(x)$ be a minimizing value of y, as a function of x in the finite-horizon problem (8.22). Then (8.22) becomes

$$f_n(x) = \min_{y \geq x} T(y, x, f_{n-1}) = T(y_n, x, f_{n-1}).$$

Using the optimality properties of y_n and y_{n+1}, we obtain

$$T(y_{n+1}, x, f_n) - T(y_{n+1}, x, f_{n-1}) \leq f_{n+1}(x) - f_n(x)$$
$$\leq T(y_n, x, f_n) - T(y_n, x, f_{n-1})$$

or expressed as

$$|f_{n+1}(x) - f_n(x)| \leq \max\{|T(y_n, x, f_n) - T(y_n, x, f_{n-1})|,$$
$$|T(y_{n+1}, x, f_n) - T(y_{n+1}, x, f_{n-1})|\}.$$

Expanding $T(\cdot, \cdot, \cdot)$ and cancelling terms yields

$$|f_{n+1}(x) - f_n(x)|$$

$$\leq \max \left\{ \begin{array}{l} \beta \left| \int_0^\infty [f_n(y_n - z) - f_{n-1}(y_n - z)] \varphi(z) \, dz \right|, \\ \beta \left| \int_0^\infty [f_n(y_{n+1} - z) - f_{n-1}(y_{n+1} - z)] \varphi(z) \, dz \right| \end{array} \right\}.$$

Now choose two positive constants A and B such that $-A \leq 2s_1 - S_1$ and $B \geq M$, where M is given in lemma 8.5.5. Then the inequality above implies that

$$\max_{-A \leq x \leq B} |f_{n+1}(x) - f_n(x)| \leq \beta \max_{-A \leq x \leq B} \int |f_n(x - z) - f_{n-1}(x - z)| \varphi(z) \, dz,$$

where we have used the fact that $-A \leq y_n(x) \leq B$ for $-A \leq x \leq B$ and $n = 1, 2, \ldots$. From lemma 8.5.6, $s_n > -A$. By equation (8.26), $f_n(x) = px + G_n(s_n)$ for $x \leq -A < s_n$. Thus we can deduce that

$$\max_{-A \leq x \leq B} |f_{n+1}(x) - f_n(x)| \leq \beta \max_{-A \leq x \leq B} |f_n(x) - f_{n-1}(x)|.$$

Iterating this inequality yields

$$\max_{-A \leq x \leq B} |f_{n+1}(x) - f_n(x)| \leq \beta^n \max_{-A \leq x \leq B} |f_1(x)|, \quad n = 1, 2, \ldots.$$

Hence the series $\sum_{n=0}^\infty [f_{n+1}(x) - f_n(x)]$ converges absolutely and uniformly for all x in the interval $-A \leq x \leq B$. Since $\{f_n(x)\}$ is an increasing sequence in n for each fixed x and A and B can be chosen arbitrarily large, we know that $f_n(x)$ converges monotonically and uniformly for all x in any finite interval. Since the functions $f_n(x)$ are continuous and the convergence is uniform, the limit function $f(x)$ is also continuous. By the definition of $G_n(x)$, we immediately obtain the result for $\{G_n(x)\}$. ∎

Proposition 8.5.2 *Suppose that assumptions 8.5.1 and 8.5.2 hold. Then the limit function $f(x)$ satisfies the Bellman equation (8.21).*

Proof   Since convergence to $f(\cdot)$ is monotone,

$$f_n(x) = \min_{y \geq x} T(y, x, f_{n-1}) \leq \min_{y \geq x} T(y, x, f).$$

On the one hand, letting $n \to \infty$ yields

$$f(x) \leq \min_{y \geq x} T(y, x, f).$$

On the other hand, monotone convergence implies that

$$f(x) \geq \min_{y \geq x} T(y, x, f_n).$$

Since $S_n \leq M < \infty$, we can choose a constant $N > M$ such that the inequality above is equivalent to

$$f(x) \geq \min_{N \geq y \geq x} T(y, x, f_n).$$

This allows us to take the limit by interchanging the limiting, minimum and integration operations, though the proof is tedious. Thus we have $f(x) = \min_{y \geq x} T(y, x, f)$. ∎

The following result characterizes the limiting behavior of $\{s_n\}$ and $\{S_n\}$. The proof is left as an exercise.

Proposition 8.5.3 *Suppose that assumptions 8.5.1 and 8.5.2 hold. Then the sequences $\{s_n\}$ and $\{S_n\}$ contain convergent subsequences. Every limit point of the sequence $\{S_n\}$ is a point at which the function*

$$G(x) = px + L(x) + \beta Ef(x - z)$$

attains its minimum. If $G(x)$ has a unique minimum point, the sequence $\{S_n\}$ converges. Furthermore $G(x)$ is c-convex and any limit point s of the sequence $\{s_n\}$ satisfies $G(S) + c = G(s)$, where S is a limit point of the sequence $\{S_n\}$. The optimal ordering policy for the infinite horizon problem is of the (s, S) form:

$$d(x) = \begin{cases} 0 & \text{if } x > s, \\ S - x & \text{if } x \leq s. \end{cases}$$

Note that $G(x)$ may have multiple minimizers. If there is a unique minimizer, then $\{S_n\}$ will converge to it. Finally, we state a uniqueness result for the Bellman equation. The proof is nontrivial and is omitted here. Interested readers may consult Iglehart (1963).

Proposition 8.5.4 *Suppose that assumptions 8.5.1 and 8.5.2 hold. If $F(x)$ is a solution to the Bellman equation (8.21), which is bounded in any finite interval and is such that for some y $\inf_{x \leq y} F(x) > -\infty$, then $F(x) = f(x)$.*

What is the limiting property of the stochastic process $\{x_t\}$? From the optimal (s, S) policy, we find that the sequence of inventory stocks $\{x_t\}$ satisfies

$$x_{t+1} = \begin{cases} x_t - z_{t+1} & \text{if } s < x_t \leq S, \\ S - z_{t+1} & \text{if } x_t \leq s. \end{cases}$$

Iglehart (1963) shows that $\{x_t\}$ has a stationary distribution that can be characterized explicitly using renewal theory for stochastic processes. A simple way to prove the existence of a stationary distribution is to apply theorem 3.3.1 by verifying Condition M. We have left this analysis as an exercise.

8.6   Investment

We first present neoclassical theory and Q theory in the deterministic case. Introducing uncertainty to these theories does not change their essence. We then present models with fixed and/or proportional adjustment costs. In these models uncertainty plays an important role in investment decisions and will be explicitly incorporated.[4]

8.6.1   Neoclassical Theory

Consider a firm's investment decisions. The firm uses capital and labor inputs to produce output according to the production function $F : \mathbb{R}_+^2 \to \mathbb{R}_+$. Assume that $F(0, \cdot) = F(\cdot, 0) = 0$, $F_1 > 0$, $F_2 > 0$, $F_{11} < 0$, $F_{22} < 0$, $\lim_{K \to 0} F_1(K, L) = \infty$, $\lim_{L \to 0} F_1(K, L) = \infty$, and $\lim_{K \to \infty} F_1(K, L) = 0$. The firm hires labor at the wage rate w_t. Suppose that it rents capital at the rental rate R_{kt}. The firm's objective is to maximize discounted present value of profits:

$$\max_{(K_{t+1}, L_t)} \sum_{t=0}^{\infty} \beta^t [F(K_t, L_t) - w_t L_t - R_{kt} K_t],$$

where $\beta = 1/(1 + r)$ and r is the interest rate. This problem reduces to maximizing static profits. The solution is such that

$$F_1(K_t, L_t) = R_{kt} \quad \text{and} \quad F_2(K_t, L_t) = w_t.$$

In reality, most capital is not rented, but is owned by firms that use it. We now present the problem if the firm owns capital and makes investment decisions

$$\max_{(K_{t+1}, L_t)} \sum_{t=0}^{\infty} \beta^t [F(K_t, L_t) - w_t L_t - I_t] \tag{8.28}$$

subject to

$$K_{t+1} = (1 - \delta) K_t + I_t, \quad K_0 > 0 \text{ given,} \tag{8.29}$$

where I_t represents investment spending and $\delta \in (0, 1)$ represent the depreciation rate. Let $\beta^t Q_t$ be the Lagrange multiplier associated with (8.29). The variable Q_t

---

4. See Dixit and Pindyck (1994) for an extensive study of investment under uncertainty.

represents the shadow price of capital. The first-order conditions are

$$Q_t = 1, \quad Q_t = \beta(1 - \delta + F_1(K_{t+1}, L_{t+1})).$$

Thus

$$F_1(K_{t+1}, L_{t+1}) = r + \delta.$$

Thus, if the rental rate R_k is equal to $r + \delta$, then the above two problems give identical solutions.

It is convenient to define operating profits net of labor costs only as

$$\pi(K_t) = \max_{L_t} F(K_t, L_t) - w_t L_t.$$

Then by the envelope condition, $\pi'(K_t) = F_1(K_t, L_t)$. For the Cobb–Douglas production function $F(K, L) = K^{\alpha_k} L^{\alpha_l}$, we can derive that

$$\pi(K_t) = K_t^{\alpha_k/(1-\alpha_l)} \left(\frac{\alpha_l}{w_t}\right)^{\alpha_l/(1-\alpha_l)} (1 - \alpha_l) \equiv A_t K_t^{\alpha_k/(1-\alpha_l)}.$$

We can assume that w_t is a fixed constant and hence A_t is constant too. If the production function has constant returns to scale $\alpha_k + \alpha_l = 1$, then $\pi(K) = AK$. If the production function has increasing (decreasing) returns to scale $\alpha_k + \alpha_l > (<)1$, then $\pi(K)$ is convex (concave).

8.6.2 Q Theory

The neoclassical investment theory implies that capital demand is determined by the static condition that the marginal product of capital is equal to the user cost of capital. This condition has two undesirable problems. First, investment and capital are too responsive to exogenous shocks. Second, there is no mechanism through which expectations about the future affect investment demand. To modify this theory, we now introduce the Q **theory of investment** developed by Abel (1980, 1982), Hayashi (1982), and Summers (1981).[5]

The key idea of the Q theory is that investment incurs convex adjustment costs. Following Lucas (1967), Gould (1968), and Treadway (1969), assume that these costs reduce firm profits directly. These costs may reflect costs of installing capital and training workers. Assume that the adjustment cost function $\Psi : \mathbb{R} \times \mathbb{R}_+ \to \mathbb{R}_+$ satisfies $\Psi_1 > 0$, $\Psi_{11} > 0$, $\Psi_2 \leq 0$, and $\Psi(0, \cdot) = 0$. The firm's problem is given by

$$\max_{(I_t, K_{t+1})} \sum_{t=0}^{\infty} \beta^t [\pi(K_t) - I_t - \Psi(I_t, K_t)]$$

---

5. See Lucas (1967), Gould (1969), Uzawa (1969), and Treadway (1969) for early studies of investment with adjustment costs.

subject to (8.29). Let $\beta^t Q_t$ be the Lagrange multiplier associated with (8.29). The first-order conditions are given by

$$1 + \Psi_1 (I_t, K_t) = Q_t, \tag{8.30}$$

$$Q_t = \beta[\pi' (K_{t+1}) - \Psi_2 (I_{t+1}, K_{t+1})] + \beta(1 - \delta)Q_{t+1}. \tag{8.31}$$

The transversality condition is given by

$$\lim_{T \to \infty} \beta^T Q_T K_{T+1} = 0. \tag{8.32}$$

From equation (8.31), we derive that

$$Q_t = \sum_{j=1}^{\infty} \beta^j (1 - \delta)^{j-1} \left[\pi' (K_{t+j}) - \Psi_2 (I_{t+j}, K_{t+j}) \right], \tag{8.33}$$

where we have used the condition

$$\lim_{T \to \infty} \beta^T (1 - \delta)^T Q_{T+1} = 0,$$

which follows from the transversality condition (8.32). Equation (8.33) shows that Q is equal to the present value of undepreciated marginal revenue product of capital net of changes in adjustment costs due to changes in the capital stock. This equation indicates that Q summarizes all relevant information about the future profitability of investment. Equation (8.30) shows that investment increases with Q, and Q is a sufficient statistic for investment decisions.

Q has a natural economic interpretation. A unit increase in the firm's capital stock raises the present value of profits by Q and thus raises the value of the firm by Q. In a sense, Q is the market value of a marginal unit of capital. Since we have assumed that the purchase price of capital is 1, Q is also the ratio of the market value of a marginal unit of capital to its replacement cost. It is often referred to as **Tobin's marginal** Q (Tobin 1969). **Tobin's average** Q is defined as the ratio of the total market value of the firm to the replacement cost of its total capital stock. Marginal Q is unobservable in the data. To test the Q theory of investment, one must use a proxy for marginal Q.

Hayashi (1982) shows that if the production function has constant returns to scale and the adjustment cost function is linearly homogeneous, then marginal Q is equal to average Q. Since the latter is observable in the data, one can then use average Q to replace marginal Q to test the Q theory of investment. We now prove Hayashi's result formally.

Let $\pi (K) = AK$. By equation (8.31) and linear homogeneity of Ψ,

$$Q_t = \beta \left[\pi' (K_{t+1}) - \frac{\Psi (I_{t+1}, K_{t+1}) - I_{t+1} \Psi_1 (I_{t+1}, K_{t+1})}{K_{t+1}} \right]$$
$$+ \beta(1 - \delta) Q_{t+1}.$$

Using equation (8.30) yields

$$
\begin{aligned}
Q_t &= \beta \left[\pi'(K_{t+1}) - \frac{\Psi(I_{t+1}, K_{t+1}) - I_{t+1}Q_{t+1} + I_{t+1}}{K_{t+1}} \right] + \beta(1-\delta)Q_{t+1} \\
&= \beta \left[\pi'(K_{t+1}) - \frac{\Psi(I_{t+1}, K_{t+1}) + I_{t+1} - (K_{t+2} - (1-\delta)K_{t+1})Q_{t+1}}{K_{t+1}} \right] \\
&\quad + \beta(1-\delta)Q_{t+1} \\
&= \beta \left[\frac{AK_{t+1} - \Psi(I_{t+1}, K_{t+1}) - I_{t+1}}{K_{t+1}} \right] + \beta \frac{K_{t+2}Q_{t+1}}{K_{t+1}}.
\end{aligned}
$$

Thus

$$
Q_t K_{t+1} = \beta[AK_{t+1} - \Psi(I_{t+1}, K_{t+1}) - I_{t+1}] + \beta K_{t+2}Q_{t+1}.
$$

Iterating forward and using the transversality condition, we obtain

$$
Q_t K_{t+1} = \sum_{j=1}^{\infty} \beta^j \left[\pi\left(K_{t+j}\right) - I_{t+j} - \Psi\left(I_{t+j}, K_{t+j}\right) \right].
$$

The expression on the right-hand side of the equation above represents the total (ex-dividend) market value of the firm or (ex-dividend) equity value. Thus we have proved Hayashi's result.

An alternative way of introducing adjustment costs is suggested by Uzawa (1969). He leaves (8.28) unchanged but changes (8.29) as follows:

$$
K_{t+1} = (1-\delta)K_t + \Phi(I_t, K_t), \tag{8.34}
$$

where Φ represents the adjustment cost function. In this formulation I units of investment do not turn into I units of capital, but Φ units. Assume that Φ satisfies $\Phi_1 > 0$, $\Phi_{11} < 0$ and $\Phi(0, \cdot) = 0$. Exercise 14 asks the reader to show that both this formulation and the previous one deliver similar results.

8.6.3 Augmented Adjustment Costs

There is ample empirical evidence that documents irreversibility and lumpiness of investment in the data. To model this behavior, we follow Abel and Eberly (1994) and Cooper and Haltiwanger (2006) and introduce an **augmented adjustment cost function** given by

$$
C(I, K) = \begin{cases} p_b I + \phi(K) + \Psi(I, K) & \text{if } I > 0, \\ 0 & \text{if } I = 0, \\ p_s I + \phi(K) + \Psi(I, K) & \text{if } I < 0, \end{cases}
$$

where $p_b > p_s \geq 0$ represent purchase and sale prices, respectively, $\phi(K)$ represents fixed costs of adjusting capital, and $\Psi(I, K)$ represents convex adjustment costs. The difference between the purchase and sale prices reflects transactions costs. Assume that fixed costs may depend on the size of the firm measured by K. Assume that the convex adjustment cost function Ψ satisfies previous assumptions and also $\Psi_1(0, K) = 0$.

The firm's optimization problem is given by

$$\max_{(I_t)} E \sum_{t=0}^{\infty} \beta^t \left[\pi(K_t, z_t) - p_b I_t \mathbf{1}_{I_t \geq 0} - p_s I_t \mathbf{1}_{I_t \leq 0} - \phi(K_t) \mathbf{1}_{I_t \neq 0} - \Psi(I_t, K_t) \right],$$

where $\mathbf{1}$ is the indicator function and (z_t) represents profitability shocks and follows a Markov process with transition function P. Given any state (K, z), the firm has three options: (1) take inaction and let capital depreciate and obtain value $V^i(K, z)$, (2) buy capital and obtain value $V^b(K, z)$, (3) sell capital and obtain value $V^s(K, z)$. The firm chooses the best among these three and obtains value $V(K, z)$. The Bellman equation is given by

$$V(K, z) = \max \left\{ V^i(K, z), V^b(K, z), V^s(K, z) \right\}, \tag{8.35}$$

where

$$V^i(K, z) = \pi(K, z) + \beta E[V((1 - \delta) K, z') \,|\, z],$$

$$V^b(K, z) = \max_{I > 0} \pi(K, z) - p_b I - \phi(K) - \Psi(I, K) + \beta E[V(K', z') \,|\, z]$$

subject to (8.29),

$$V^s(K, z) = \max_{I < 0} \pi(K, z) - p_s I - \phi(K) - \Psi(I, K) + \beta E[V(K', z') \,|\, z]$$

subject to (8.29).

Here $E[\cdot | z]$ represents the conditional expectation operator over z' given z.

This problem is similar to the inventory problem analyzed earlier. It is difficult to analyze given Markov shocks.[6] To provide transparent intuition, we will proceed heuristically. Interested readers are invited to make the arguments below more rigorous.[7] From the Bellman equation we observe that optimal investment

---

6. Miao and Wang (2009, 2011a) provide a tractable model under the assumption of constant returns to scale.

7. Under some conditions the continuous time version of the investment problem has a closed-form solution.

I^* solves the following problem:

$$\varphi(K,z) = \max_I \beta E[V((1-\delta)K + I, z') \,|z] - \beta E[V((1-\delta)K, z') \,|z]$$
$$-p_s I 1_{I<0} - p_b I 1_{I>0} - \phi(K) 1_{\{I \neq 0\}} - \Psi(I,K). \tag{8.36}$$

Suppose that V is differentiable in K.[8] Using a Taylor approximation up to the first order around $I = 0$, we rewrite the problem above as

$$\varphi(K,z) \simeq \max_I \beta E[V_1((1-\delta)K, z') \,|z] I$$
$$-p_s I 1_{I<0} - p_b I 1_{I>0} - \phi(K) 1_{\{I \neq 0\}} - \Psi(I,K)$$
$$= \max_I QI - p_s I 1_{I<0} - p_b I 1_{I>0} - \phi(K) 1_{\{I \neq 0\}} - \Psi(I,K)$$
$$\equiv \psi(Q, K),$$

where we define marginal Q at zero investment as

$$Q = \beta E[V_1((1-\delta)K, z') \,|z]. \tag{8.37}$$

We analyze two cases. First, consider the case without fixed costs $\phi(K) = 0$. The first-order conditions for I in the problem above are given by[9]

$$p_b + \Psi_1(I^*, K) = Q \text{ and } I^* > 0 \quad \text{if } Q > p_b, \tag{8.38}$$

$$I^* = 0 \quad \text{if } p_s \leq Q \leq p_b, \tag{8.39}$$

$$p_s + \Psi_1(I^*, K) = Q \quad \text{and} \quad I^* < 0 \quad \text{if } Q < p_s. \tag{8.40}$$

These conditions deliver a modified Q theory in the sense that optimal investment is weakly increasing in Q. Optimal investment is in one of three regimes (positive, zero, and negative investment), depending on the value of Q relative to two critical values p_b and p_s. Figure 8.7 illustrates the function $\psi(Q, K)$ for a fixed K.

Using equation (8.37), we obtain a boundary $K = K^b(z)$ determined by the equation

$$p_b = \beta E[V_1((1-\delta)K, z') \,|z]. \tag{8.41}$$

On this boundary, the firm is indifferent between buying capital and taking inaction. If V is concave, V_1 increases with z', and the transition function P of (z_t) is monotone, then $K^b(z)$ increases with z. Below this boundary, $Q > p_b$ and the firm buys capital such that the target investment level satisfies equation (8.38). We say

---

8. Clearly, there are kinks in V due to fixed costs or transactions costs.
9. More precisely, the first-order conditions for (8.36) implies that $Q = \beta E[V_1((1-\delta)K + I, z') \,|z]$.

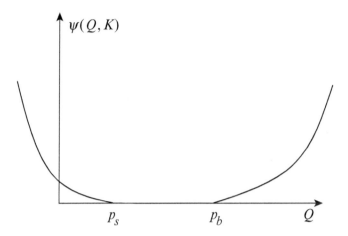

Figure 8.7
Reward to investing. Plotted is the function $\psi(Q,K)$ for a fixed value of K in the case without fixed costs.

that states (K,z) below the boundary $K^b(z)$ are in the "buy region." Similarly there is a boundary $K = K^s(z)$ determined by the equation

$$p_s = \beta E\left[V_1\left((1-\delta)K, z'\right)|z\right]. \tag{8.42}$$

Above this boundary, $Q < p_s$ and the firm sells capital such that the target disinvestment level satisfies equation (8.40). We say that states (K,z) above the boundary $K^s(z)$ are in the "sell region." Within these two boundaries, the firm does not invest or disinvest. This is the "inaction region." Whenever the firm faces a large positive (negative) shock z such that the state (K,z) moves outside the inaction region, the firm responds by buying (selling) capital to bring the state into the inaction region.

Note that without fixed costs, there is no investment lumpiness in that investment responds to profitability shocks continuously. There is no discrete jump of investment. Figure 8.8 illustrates the three regions of states (K,z) and the property of the solution.

In the special case of $p_s = 0$, equation (8.42) cannot hold. Then it is never optimal for the firm to make negative investment. This implies that investment is fully irreversible. When $p_b > p_s > 0$, investment is partially irreversible.

Example 8.6.1   *Consider the following static investment problem:*

$$\psi(Q) = \max_I \ QI - p_b I 1_{I>0} - p_s I 1_{I<0} - \frac{I^2}{2} - \phi 1_{I\neq 0}.$$

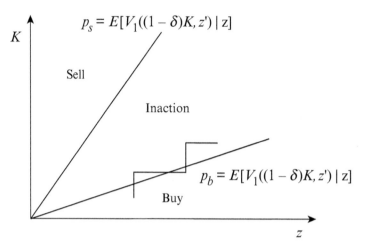

Figure 8.8
Three regions of states for (K, z). Plotted are the two boundaries that partition the state space into the buy region, sell region, and inaction region in the case without fixed costs.

If there is no fixed cost $\phi = 0$, the optimal investment level is given by

$$I^* = \begin{cases} Q - p_b > 0 & \text{if } Q > p_b, \\ 0 & \text{if } p_s \leq Q \leq p_b, \\ Q - p_s < 0 & \text{if } Q < p_s. \end{cases}$$

The corresponding profits are given by

$$\psi(Q) = \begin{cases} \frac{1}{2}(Q - p_b)^2 & \text{if } Q > p_b, \\ 0 & \text{if } p_s \leq Q \leq p_b, \\ \frac{1}{2}(Q - p_s)^2 & \text{if } Q < p_s. \end{cases}$$

In the presence of fixed costs $\phi > 0$, we must subtract ϕ from the preceding equation. To ensure nonnegative profits, the new investment policy is given by

$$I^* = \begin{cases} Q - p_b > 0 & \text{if } Q > p_b + 2\sqrt{\phi}, \\ 0 & \text{if } p_s - 2\sqrt{\phi} \leq Q \leq p_b + 2\sqrt{\phi}, \\ Q - p_s < 0 & \text{if } Q < p_s - 2\sqrt{\phi}. \end{cases}$$

Next consider the case of fixed costs $\phi(K) > 0$. Although equations (8.38) to (8.40) are still first-order necessary conditions, they are not sufficient for optimality. As figure 8.9 illustrates, the presence of fixed costs shifts the previous $\psi(Q, K)$

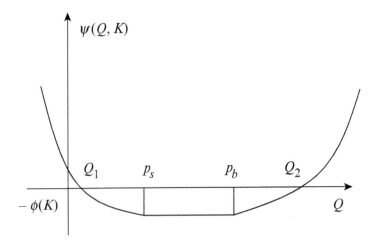

Figure 8.9
Reward to investing. Plotted is the function $\psi\,(Q,K)$ for a fixed value of K in the presence of fixed costs.

curve down by $\phi\,(K)$. The new curve crosses the horizontal axis at two points Q_1 and Q_2. The new investment rule is given by

$$p_b + \Psi_1\,(I^*,K) = Q \text{ and } I^* > 0 \quad \text{if } Q > Q_2, \tag{8.43}$$

$$I^* = 0 \quad \text{if } Q_1 \leq Q \leq Q_2, \tag{8.44}$$

$$p_s + \Psi_1\,(I^*,K) = Q \quad \text{and} \quad I^* < 0 \quad \text{if } Q < Q_1. \tag{8.45}$$

When $Q = Q_2$ $(Q = Q_1)$, the firm is indifferent between buying (selling) and taking inaction. We can derive these boundaries more explicitly using the Bellman equation (8.35). The buy boundary $K^b\,(z)$ is the maximal solution K to the equation

$$V^i\,(K,z) = V^b\,(K,z) \tag{8.46}$$

for each z. Similarly the equation

$$V^i\,(K,z) = V^s\,(K,z) \tag{8.47}$$

determines a sale boundary $K^s\,(z)$. It is intuitive that the firm will buy capital if $K < K^b\,(z)$, sell capital if $K > K^s\,(z)$, and take inaction, otherwise. These two boundaries are increasing functions of z and partition the state space for (K,z) into three regions as in figure 8.8. The presence of fixed costs widens the inaction region.

Equivalently, the two boundaries are determined by the maximal and minimal solutions to the equation $\varphi\,(K,z) = 0$. In the case without fixed costs $\phi\,(K) = 0$, $\varphi\,(K,z) \simeq \psi\,(Q,K)$. Thus conditions (8.41) and (8.42) are consistent with (8.46) and (8.47). We may view the former as the differential form of the boundary conditions.

In the presence of fixed costs $\phi(K) > 0$, the boundary conditions cannot take a differential form. In this case investment exhibits lumpiness in that it may have discrete jumps. As illustrated in figure 8.9, between p_b and Q_2 investment returns are not sufficient to cover the fixed costs. The firm must refrain from investment until Q is sufficiently large. When Q just exceeds Q_2, optimal investment jumps up discretely. The target investment (or disinvestment) level satisfies equation (8.43) (or 8.45). When there is no transactions cost in that $p_b = p_s$, these two equations collapse to a single one.

8.7 Exercises

1. Consider the McCall's (1970) job search model analyzed in section 8.1. Suppose that the wage offer follows a Markov process with transition function Q. Write down the Bellman equation and characterize the solution.

2. Suppose that each period there is probability α that the worker is fired in the McCall's (1970) job search model. After the worker is fired, he has to wait for one period and start to search for a new job in the next period. The job offer is still drawn from the previous wage distribution. Write down the Bellman equation for this case and characterize the solution.

3. Prove lemma 8.5.4.

4. Prove proposition 8.5.3.

5. Let $\{x_t\}$ be the sequence of optimal inventory levels for the inventory control model analyzed in section 8.5. Show that it is a Markov process and derive its transition function. Prove that it has a unique stationary distribution.

6. Consider the inventory model in section 8.5. Suppose that the fixed distribution for the demand z_t has density $\lambda e^{-\lambda z}$, $z \geq 0$. Characterize s and S.

7. Suppose that there is no fixed cost ($c = 0$) in the inventory control problem analyzed in section 8.5. Show that $s = S$ and s satisfies the equation

$$p(1 - \beta) + L'(s) = 0.$$

8. Consider the following deterministic consumption–saving problem

$$\max \sum_{t=0}^{\infty} \beta^t \frac{c_t^{1-\gamma}}{1 - \gamma}$$

subject to

$$c_t + a_{t+1} = Ra_t + y_t, \quad a_0 \text{ given,}$$

and a no-Ponzi-game condition (natural borrowing constraint). Here y_t is deterministic labor income. Derive the optimal consumption–saving policy. Give conditions such that the value function is finite. Study properties of the optimal consumption and saving plans for the cases of $\beta R > 1$, $\beta R < 1$, and $\beta R = 1$.

9. Consider the stochastic consumption–saving problem in the case of $\beta R < 1$ analyzed in section 8.3.2. Prove that $x_{max} > x_{min}$ and x_{max} is the largest value such that $R\hat{a}\,(x_{max}) + y_{max} - rb = x_{max}$.

10. (Levhari, Mirman, and Zilcha 1980) Consider the following consumption–saving problem:

$$\max_{0 \le c_t \le x_t} E \sum_{t=0}^{\infty} -\beta^t e^{-\gamma c_t}$$

subject to

$$x_{t+1} = R(x_t - c_t) + y_{t+1}, \quad x_0 \text{ given}, \ \beta R < 1.$$

Characterize the optimal consumption–saving policies for two cases: (a) $y_t = y$ is constant over time; (b) y_t is IID and drawn from a fixed distribution.

11. (Schechtman and Escudero 1977) Explicitly solve the optimal consumption–saving policies for the following problem:

$$\max_{c_t} E \left[\sum_{t=0}^{\infty} -\beta^t e^{-\gamma c_t} \right]$$

subject to

$$x_{t+1} = R(x_t - c_t) + y_{t+1}, \quad a_0 \text{ given},$$

$$y_{t+1} = \rho y_t + \varepsilon_{t+1},$$

where ε_{t+1} is independently and identically drawn from a fixed distribution over a bounded support. Let $\rho = 0$. Show that there is no stationary distribution for (x_t).

12. Use the Bellman equation to derive Hayashi's result. Interpret marginal Q in terms of the value function.

13. Consider the following investment problem:

$$\max \sum_{t=0}^{\infty} \beta^t \left[AK_t - I_t - \frac{I_t^2}{2K_t} \right]$$

subject to

$$K_{t+1} = I_t + (1 - \delta) K_t.$$

Solve for the optimal investment policy and the value of the firm. Give conditions such that the value function is finite.

14. Consider Uzawa's formulation of convex adjustment costs in equation (8.34). Derive the optimal investment policy and formulate the Q theory of investment in this framework.

9 Linear-Quadratic Models

Linear-quadratic models have two essential features: quadratic reward functions and linear constraints. As we will show, these models deliver linear decision rules and quadratic value functions. Thus they are tractable in applications. These models can also be used to approximate and solve nonlinear models. In this chapter we first explain how to solve linear-quadratic control models. We then study optimal policy under commitment and under discretion using a linear-quadratic framework. Finally, we introduce robust control within the linear-quadratic framework.

9.1 Controlled Linear State-Space System

We are given a fixed probability space with a filtration $\{\mathcal{F}_t\}_{t=0}^{\infty}$. On this space we define a process of conditionally homoskedastic martingale differences $\{\varepsilon_t\}_{t=1}^{\infty}$, which satisfies the following:

Assumption 9.1.1 *The process $\{\varepsilon_t\}_{t=1}^{\infty}$ satisfies*

a. $E[\varepsilon_{t+1}|\mathcal{F}_t] = 0$;

b. $E[\varepsilon_{t+1}\varepsilon'_{t+1}|\mathcal{F}_t] = I$.

Consider the controlled linear system

$$x_{t+1} = Ax_t + Bu_t + C\varepsilon_{t+1}, \tag{9.1}$$

where x_t is $n_x \times 1$ vector of state variables, u_t is $n_u \times 1$ vector of control variables adapted to $\{\mathcal{F}_t\}$, and ε_t is $n_\varepsilon \times 1$ vector of random variables satisfying assumption 9.1.1. Here A, B, and C are conformable matrices. Note that x_t may contain exogenous state variables that are independent of controls. Equation (9.1) is often called a **state-transition equation**. The state vector x_t may be partially observable in that it is not $\mathcal{F}_t$-measurable. An unobservable state is called a **hidden state**. Let $\mathcal{F}_t$ be generated by the observation n_y-vector y_t, which satisfies

$$y_t = Gx_t + Hu_{t-1} + D\varepsilon_t, \tag{9.2}$$

where G, H, and D are conformable matrices. We call equation (9.2) a **measurement equation**. The preceding two equations constitute a **state-space representation**. When the processes $\{x_t\}$ and $\{\varepsilon_t\}$ are adapted to $\{\mathcal{F}_t\}$, the decision maker possess full information and the measurement equation can be ignored. Otherwise, the system is partially observed.

In this section we introduce some important concepts for the controlled linear system when A, B, C, D, G, and H are independent of time. These concepts may be valid when they are time dependent. First, we consider stability.

Definition 9.1.1 *The pair of matrices (A, B) is **stabilizable** if there is a matrix H such that $A + BH$ is stable.*

The motivation of this definition is the following. Take a control $u_t = Hx_t$ so that the transition equation reduces to

$$x_{t+1} = (A + BH)x_t + C\varepsilon_{t+1}.$$

Then the deterministic steady state $\bar{x} = 0$ will be stable if and only if $A + BH$ is stable, meaning (A, B) is stabilizable. This condition can be verified by choosing a trivial control law.

Next we say that the system (9.1) is **controllable** if, given an arbitrary initial value x_0, one can choose values $u_0, u_1, ..., u_{r-1}$ such that x_r has an arbitrarily prescribed value for any $r > 0$. This definition is equivalent to the following (see Whittle 1982, thm. 4.3.1):

Definition 9.1.2 *The pair of matrices (A, B) is **controllable** if*

$$\sum_{j=0}^{n_x-1} A^j BB' (A')^j > 0,$$

where $M > 0$ means M is positive definite for any square matrix M.

Note that controllability implies stabilizability. But the converse is not true. For example, let A be a stability matrix and set $B = 0$. Clearly, this system is stabilizable, but not controllable. This example shows that the concept of controllability applies to endogenous states affected by controls only. It does not apply to exogenous states.

In the case of partial information, the state-space representation (9.1) and (9.2) is called **observable** if x_0 can be determined from the knowledge of $y_0, y_1, .., y_r; u_0,$

$u_1, .., u_{r-1}; \varepsilon_0, \varepsilon_1, ..., \varepsilon_r$ for any initial value x_0 and for any $r > 0$. This definition is equivalent to the following (see Whittle 1982, thm. 4.4.1):

Definition 9.1.3   *The pair of matrices (A, G) is* **observable** *if*

$$\sum_{j=0}^{n_x-1} (A')^j G'GA^j > 0.$$

We now introduce the last concept.

Definition 9.1.4   *The pair of matrices (A, G) is* **detectable** *if there is a matrix J such that $A - JG$ is stable.*

The motivation of this definition is the following. Let $\hat{x}_{t+1|t}$ be the estimate of x_{t+1} given information y^t. Under some conditions, we will show in section 10.1.1 that $\hat{x}_{t+1|t}$ satisfies the system

$$\hat{x}_{t+1|t} = A\hat{x}_{t|t-1} + Bu_t + AKa_t, \tag{9.3}$$

where $a_t = y_t - E\left[y_t | y^{t-1}\right] = G\left(x_t - \hat{x}_{t|t-1}\right) + D\varepsilon_t$. Define $\Delta_t = x_t - \hat{x}_{t|t-1}$. Then subtracting equation (9.3) from equation (9.1) yields

$$\Delta_{t+1} = (A - AKG)\Delta_{t-1} + C\varepsilon_{t+1} - AKD\varepsilon_t.$$

Note that Δ_t is stable if and only if $A - AKG$ is stable. Thus detectability implies that one can find an updating rule of type (9.3) that will asymptotically yield a correct estimate of the state.

9.2   Finite-Horizon Problems

In what follows, we focus on the case of full information and ignore the measurement equation (9.2). In the next chapter we will study the case of partial information and incorporate the measurement equation. We first consider the nonstationary finite-horizon problem:

$$\max_{\{u_t\}} -E\left[\sum_{t=0}^{T-1} \beta^t (x_t'Q_tx_t + u_t'R_tu_t + 2x_t'S_tu_t) + \beta^T x_T'P_Tx_T\right], \quad \beta \in (0, 1],$$

subject to

$$x_{t+1} = A_tx_t + B_tu_t + C_t\varepsilon_{t+1},$$

where A_t, B_t, C_t, Q_t, R_t, and S_t are deterministic matrices that depend on t only. Suppose that $\{\varepsilon_t\}$ satisfies assumption 9.1.1.

For any two symmetric matrices M and N, say that $M \geq N$ if $M - N$ is positive semidefinite and $M > N$ if $M - N$ is positive definite.

Proposition 9.2.1 *Suppose that*

$$\begin{bmatrix} Q_t & S_t \\ S_t' & R_t \end{bmatrix}$$

and P_T are positive semidefinite and that $R_t > 0$ for $t < T$. Then:

a. *The value function takes the form*

$$V_t(x_t) = -x_t' P_t x_t - d_t, \tag{9.4}$$

where $P_t \geq 0$ and satisfies

$$
\begin{aligned}
P_t = Q_t &+ \beta A_t' P_{t+1} A_t \\
&- (\beta A_t' P_{t+1} B_t + S_t)(R_t + \beta B_t' P_{t+1} B_t)^{-1}(\beta B_t' P_{t+1} A_t + S_t')
\end{aligned}
\tag{9.5}
$$

for $t < T$, and d_t satisfies

$$d_t = \beta tr(P_{t+1} C_t C_t') + \beta d_{t+1}, \quad t < T, \, d_T = 0. \tag{9.6}$$

b. *The optimal control is*

$$u_t = -F_t x_t, \tag{9.7}$$

where

$$F_t = (R_t + \beta B_t' P_{t+1} B_t)^{-1}(S_t' + \beta B_t' P_{t+1} A_t), \quad t < T. \tag{9.8}$$

Proof The proof is by induction. At time T, $V_T(x_T) = -x_T' P_T x_T$. Suppose that (9.4) holds at time $t + 1 < T$. Consider time t. By the Bellman equation,

$$V_t(x_t) = \max_{u_t} - (x_t' Q_t x_t + u_t' R_t u_t + 2x_t' S_t u_t) + \beta E_t V_{t+1}(x_{t+1}),$$

where E_t denotes the conditional expectation operator given information $\mathcal{F}_t$. Noting that $E_t \varepsilon_{t+1} = 0$ and

$$
\begin{aligned}
E_t \varepsilon_{t+1}' C_t' P_{t+1} C_t \varepsilon_{t+1} &= tr\left(E_t \varepsilon_{t+1}' C_t' P_{t+1} C_t \varepsilon_{t+1}\right) \\
&= E_t tr\left(P_{t+1} C_t \varepsilon_{t+1} \varepsilon_{t+1}' C_t'\right) \\
&= tr\left(P_{t+1} C_t C_t'\right),
\end{aligned}
$$

we can compute

$$
E_t V_{t+1}(x_{t+1})
$$
$$
= -E_t \left(A_t x_t + B_t u_t + C_t \varepsilon_{t+1} \right)' P_{t+1} \left(A_t x_t + B_t u_t + C_t \varepsilon_{t+1} \right) - d_{t+1}
$$
$$
= -\left(A_t x_t + B_t u_t \right)' P_{t+1} \left(A_t x_t + B_t u_t \right) - E_t \varepsilon_{t+1}' C_t' P_{t+1} C_t \varepsilon_{t+1} - d_{t+1}
$$
$$
= -\left(A_t x_t + B_t u_t \right)' P_{t+1} \left(A_t x_t + B_t u_t \right) - \mathrm{tr}\left(P_{t+1} C_t C_t' \right) - d_{t+1}.
$$

Substituting this equation into the Bellman equation above and taking the first-order condition,[1] we obtain

$$
\left(R_t + \beta B_t' P_{t+1} B_t \right) u_t = -\left(S_t' + \beta B_t' P_{t+1} A_t \right) x_t.
$$

This gives (9.7) and (9.8). Since $R_t > 0$ and $P_{t+1} \geq 0$, $\left(R_t + \beta B_t' P_{t+1} B_t \right)$ is also positive definite. We can then derive

$$
u_t = -\left(R_t + \beta B_t' P_{t+1} B_t \right)^{-1} \left(S_t' + \beta B_t' P_{t+1} A_t \right) x_t.
$$

Substituting this decision into the the Bellman equation and matching coefficients yield (9.4) to (9.6). ∎

Decision rule (9.7) is called a **feedback** or **closed-loop control** in that u_t depends on the current state x_t. An **open-loop control** may be expressed as $u_t = u^*(x_0, t)$ for which actions are determined by the clock rather than by the current state. These two forms may not be equivalent. Equation (9.5) is called a **Riccati equation**, which is of fundamental importance for our later analyses. To understand this equation, we need to know that P_t satisfies

$$
P_t = \min_{F_t} \; Q_t - F_t' S_t' - S_t F_t + F_t' R_t F_t \tag{9.9}
$$
$$
+ \beta \left(A_t - B_t F_t \right)' P_{t+1} \left(A_t - B_t F_t \right),
$$

where the minimization is in the sense of positive definiteness. The minimizer F_t is given by (9.8).

From the analysis above, we observe that uncertainty through the matrix C_t does not affect the linear decision rule (9.7) and (9.8). It also does not affect the matrix P_t in (9.5). It only affects the constant term d_t. We state the observation as follows:

Certainty Equivalence Principle　The decision rule that solves the stochastic optimal linear-quadratic problem is identical with the decision rule for the corresponding deterministic linear-quadratic problem.

---

1. We use the following differential rules: $\partial x' A x / \partial x = (A + A') x$, $\partial y' B z / \partial y = B z$, and $\partial y' B z / \partial z = B' y$.

By this principle, we can solve for the decision rules using the corresponding deterministic model. This principle is very useful for us to study linear-quadratic control problems.

Note that we have assumed that the return function is "centered." In the uncentered case

$$r(x,u) = -E \sum_{t=0}^{T-1} \left\{ (x_t - x^*)' Q_t (x_t - x^*) + (u_t - u^*)' R_t (u_t - u^*) \right.$$

$$\left. + (x_t - x^*)' S_t (u_t - u^*) + (x_T - x^*)' P_T (x_T - x^*) \right\},$$

where x^* and u^* are some constants. One way to deal with this case is to adopt the augmented state vector $[x', 1]'$. We can then conduct the previous analysis using this augmented state vector. The other way is to perform a change of variables by defining $\tilde{x}_t = x_t - x^*$ and $\tilde{u}_t = u_t - u^*$. We can then rewrite the state transition equation and conduct a similar analysis.

9.3   Infinite-Horizon Limits

Consider the following infinite-horizon stochastic linear regulator problem:

$$\max_{\{u_t\}} \quad -E \sum_{t=0}^{\infty} \beta^t (x_t' Q x_t + u_t' R u_t + 2x_t' S u_t), \quad \beta \in (0,1],$$

subject to (9.1), where the matrices $Q, R, S, A, B,$ and C are time homogeneous. In economic applications we often impose the following side condition (see Hansen and Sargent 2008):

$$E\left[\sum_{t=0}^{\infty} \beta^t (u_t \cdot u_t + x_t \cdot x_t) \right] < \infty. \tag{9.10}$$

Condition (9.10) is a stability condition that ensures that u_t and x_t cannot grow at a rate exceeding $1/\sqrt{\beta}$. This condition is not required in standard control problems but may be useful in some economic problems because it is related to the transversality condition.

To study the infinite-horizon problem above, we will analyze the infinite-horizon limits of a sequence of corresponding finite-horizon problems. Let

$$P(s) = P_t, \quad F(s) = F_t, \quad d(s) = d_t, \quad s = T - t,$$

where $P_t, F_t,$ and d_t are given in proposition 9.2.1 for the time-homogeneous case. By this proposition, we obtain

$$P(s) = \mathcal{T}(P(s-1)) = \mathcal{T}^s(P(0)),$$

where $\mathcal{T}$ is an operator defined by

$$\mathcal{T}(P) = Q + \beta A'PA - (S + \beta A'PB)(R + \beta B'PB)^{-1}(S' + \beta B'PA). \tag{9.11}$$

Moreover

$$F(s) = (R + \beta B'P(s-1)B)^{-1}(S' + \beta B'P(s-1)A).$$

Our goal is to show that $P(s)$ has a limit P as $s \to \infty$, and hence $F(s)$ and $d(s)$ have limits F and d, respectively. These limits give the value function and the optimal policy function for the infinite-horizon problem.

For ease of exposition, we will assume that the matrix S has been normalized to zero. This can be done by a suitable change of variables. Also we will consider the deterministic case by the certainty equivalence principle. In this case the constant term in the value function vanishes. We can then write the value function for the s-horizon problem as

$$V_s(x) = -x'P(s)x.$$

Proposition 9.3.1   *Suppose that (a) $Q > 0$, (b) $R > 0$, and (c) $\left(\sqrt{\beta}A, \sqrt{\beta}B\right)$ is either controllable or stabilizable. Then the Riccati equation,*

$$P = \mathcal{T}(P), \tag{9.12}$$

has a unique positive semidefinite solution P. $P(s) \to P$ for any finite, positive semidefinite $P(0)$.

Proof   Let $P(0) = 0$. Then, by (9.11), $P(1) = Q$. Thus $V_1(x) = -x'P(1)x < 0 = V_0(x)$. By the Bellman equation, we deduce that $V_{s+1}(x) < V_s(x)$ for any s. Thus $P(s+1) > P(s)$ for any s. We next show that $\{P(s)\}$ is bounded above and hence has a finite positive semidefinite limit P.

To demonstrate boundedness, we only need to show that a policy can be found that incurs a finite infinite-horizon value for any initial value x_0. In the controllable case, one achieves this by choosing a control u bringing x to zero in a finite number of steps, and by holding u (and so x) zero thereafter. In the stabilizable case, one chooses $u_t = Kx_t$, where K is such that $\sqrt{\beta}(A + BK)$ is a a stable matrix. Define $\Gamma = A + BK$. Then $x_t = \Gamma^t x_0$, $u_t = K\Gamma^t x_0$. The infinite-horizon objective function under this control takes a finite value

$$-E\sum_{t=0}^{\infty} \beta^t x_0'(\Gamma')^t (Q + K'RK)\Gamma^t x_0.$$

The limit P is positive semidefinite and satisfied (9.12), which is rewritten as

$$P = Q + F'RF + \beta\Gamma'P\Gamma, \tag{9.13}$$

where

$$F = (R + \beta B'PB)^{-1} \beta B'PA, \quad \Gamma = A - BF.$$

Consider the function $V(x) = -x'Px$ and a sequence $x_t = \left(\sqrt{\beta}\Gamma\right)^t x_0$:

$$V(x_{t+1}) - V(x_t)$$
$$= -x'_{t+1}Px_{t+1} + x'_t Px_t$$
$$= -\beta x'_t \Gamma' P\Gamma x_t + x'_t (Q + F'RF + \beta \Gamma' P\Gamma) x_t$$
$$= x'_t (Q + F'RF) x_t \geq 0.$$

$V(x_t)$ increases to a finite limit because $\{V(x_t)\}$ is bounded above by zero. Thus

$$x'_t (Q + F'RF) x_t \to 0, \tag{9.14}$$

which implies that $x_t \to 0$. Since x_0 is arbitrary, this implies that $\left(\sqrt{\beta}\Gamma\right)^t \to 0$. Thus, by (9.13),

$$P = \sum_{j=0}^{\infty} \left(\sqrt{\beta}\Gamma'\right)^j (Q + F'RF) \left(\sqrt{\beta}\Gamma\right)^j.$$

Note that for arbitrary finite positive semidefinite $P(0)$,

$$P(s) = T^s(P(0)) \geq T^s(0) \to P.$$

Comparing the maximal s-horizon reward with that incurred by using the stationary rule $u_t = -Fx_t$, we deduce the reverse inequality

$$P(s) \leq \sum_{j=0}^{s-1} \beta^j (\Gamma')^j (Q + F'RF) \Gamma^j + (\Gamma')^s P(0) \Gamma^s \to P.$$

The two equations above imply that $P(s) \to P$ for any finite positive semidefinite $P(0)$.

Finally, we prove uniqueness. If $\hat{P}$ is another solution for (9.12), then

$$\hat{P} = T\left(\hat{P}\right) = T^s\left(\hat{P}\right) \to P.$$

This completes the proof.   ∎

Proposition 9.3.2 *Proposition 9.3.1 still holds if condition a is weakened to $Q = L'L$, where $\left(\sqrt{\beta}A, L\right)$ is either observable or detectable.*

Proof   Let $x_t = \left(\sqrt{\beta}\Gamma\right)^t x_0$. Relation (9.14) becomes

$$(Lx_t)'(Lx_t) + (Fx_t)'R(Fx_t) \to 0,$$

which implies that $Fx_t \to 0$ and $Lx_t \to 0$. Using $x_{t+1} = \sqrt{\beta}\,(A - BF)\,x_t$, we deduce that x_t will enters a system such that

$$Lx_t = 0 \text{ and } x_{t+1} = \sqrt{\beta}Ax_t. \tag{9.15}$$

The observability condition implies that the relation above can hold only if x_t is a constant zero. The detectability condition implies that we can find an H such that $\sqrt{\beta}A - HL$ is a stable matrix. By equation (9.15),

$$x_{t+1} = \left(\sqrt{\beta}A - HL\right)x_t.$$

Thus $x_t \to 0$, implying that $\sqrt{\beta}\Gamma$ is a stable matrix. The rest of the proof is the same as that for proposition 9.3.1.   ∎

Note that we can replace the detectability or observability condition with the side condition (9.10) in the preceding proposition. We now turn to the general case under uncertainty where $S \neq 0$. The value function is given by

$$V(x) = -x'Px - d,$$

where P is a positive semidefinite matrix solution to equation (9.12) and $T(P)$ is given by (9.11). Additionally d is a constant,

$$d = (1 - \beta)^{-1}\beta\mathrm{tr}(PCC').$$

The optimal decision rule is given by

$$u = -Fx, \tag{9.16}$$

where

$$F = (R + \beta B'PB)^{-1}(S' + \beta B'PA). \tag{9.17}$$

Now we discuss three numerical methods to solve the linear-quadratic control problem in the centered case.

9.3.1   Value Function Iteration

We may first solve the truncated finite-horizon problem and then take limit to obtain the infinite-horizon solution. Proposition 9.3.1 gives an algorithm. The Matlab program olrp.m can be used to solve the discounted linear-quadratic control problem.

9.3.2   Policy Improvement Algorithm

We may use (9.9) to rewrite the Riccati equation as

$$P = Q + F'RF - SF - F'S' + \beta(A - BF)'P(A - BF).$$

Starting for an initial F_0 for which the eigenvalues of $A - BF_0$ are less than $1/\sqrt{\beta}$ in modulus, the algorithm iterates on the two equations:

$$P_j = Q + F_j'RF_j - SF_j - F_j'S' + \beta(A - BF_j)'P_j(A - BF_j),$$

$$F_{j+1} = \left(R + \beta B'P_jB\right)^{-1}\left(S' + \beta B'P_jA\right).$$

The first equation is a **discrete Lyapunov** or **Sylvester** equation, which is to be solved for P_j. If the eigenvalues of the matrix $A - BF_j$ are bounded in modulus by $1/\sqrt{\beta}$, then a solution to this equation exists. There are several methods available for solving this equation. See Anderson et al. (1996) and chapter 5 in Ljungqvist and Sargent (2004).

9.3.3   Lagrange Method

The Lagrange method is not only useful for computations, it also delivers insights about the connections between stability and optimality. The Lagrange multipliers play an important role as the shadow price. Form the Lagrangian

$$-E\sum_{t=0}^{\infty}\beta^t\left\{\begin{array}{c} x_t'Qx_t + u_t'Ru_t + 2x_t'Su_t \\ -2\beta\lambda_{t+1}'\left(x_{t+1} - Ax_t - Bu_t - \varepsilon_{t+1}\right) \end{array}\right\},$$

where $2\beta^{t+1}\lambda_{t+1}$ is the Lagrange multiplier associated with the linear constraint. First-order conditions with respect to $\{u_t, x_t\}$ are

$$u_t: \ Ru_t + S'x_t + \beta B'E_t\lambda_{t+1} = 0,$$

$$x_t: \ \lambda_t = Qx_t + Su_t + \beta A'E_t\lambda_{t+1}.$$

Combining with the linear constraint, we obtain the following linear system:

$$\begin{bmatrix} I & 0 & 0 \\ 0 & 0 & -\beta B' \\ 0 & 0 & \beta A' \end{bmatrix}\begin{bmatrix} E_t x_{t+1} \\ E_t u_{t+1} \\ E_t \lambda_{t+1} \end{bmatrix} = \begin{bmatrix} A & B & 0 \\ S' & R & 0 \\ -Q & -S & I \end{bmatrix}\begin{bmatrix} x_t \\ u_t \\ \lambda_t \end{bmatrix}.$$

We can solve this system using the Klein method discussed in section 2.3.2. In this system x_t is a vector of predetermined or backward-looking variables according to definition 2.3.4, and u_t and λ_t are vectors of non-predetermined or forward-looking variables. Anderson et al. (1996) and Ljungqvist and Sargent (2004) discuss several numerical methods based on the assumption that Q is invertible. This assumption is not needed for the Klein method.

The Lagrange multiplier has important economic meaning. By the envelope condition, we can show that

$$\frac{\partial V(x_t)}{\partial x_t} = Qx_t + Su_t + \beta A' E_t \lambda_{t+1} = \lambda_t, \quad t \geq 0.$$

Thus we have $\lambda_t = Px_t$, which is interpreted as the shadow price of x_t.

9.4   Optimal Policy under Commitment

Suppose that the equilibrium system can be summarized by the following state space form:

$$D \begin{bmatrix} z_{t+1} \\ E_t y_{t+1} \end{bmatrix} = A \begin{bmatrix} z_t \\ y_t \end{bmatrix} + Bu_t + \begin{bmatrix} C \\ 0 \end{bmatrix} \varepsilon_{t+1}, \tag{9.18}$$

where $z_0 = \bar{z}_0$ is exogenously given. Here z_t is an $n_z \times 1$ vector of predetermined variables in the sense of definition 2.3.4, y_t is an $n_y \times 1$ vector of non-predetermined or forward-looking variables, u_t is an $n_u \times 1$ vector of instrument or control variables chosen by a government, and ε_{t+1} is a vector of exogenous shocks that are white noise with an identity covariance matrix. We typically use z_t to represent the state of the economy, which may include productivity shocks, preference shocks, or capital stock. Note that z_t may include a component of unity in order to handle constants. The vector y_t represents endogenous variables such as consumption, inflation rate, and output. Examples of instruments u_t include interest rates and money growth rates.

The matrices A, B, C, and D are conformable with the vectors above. We assume that the matrix D can be partitioned conformably as

$$D = \begin{bmatrix} I & 0 \\ D_{21} & D_{22} \end{bmatrix}.$$

Note that we allow the matrix D to be singular. In this case the equilibrium system in (9.18) may contain intratemporal optimality conditions.

Define the period loss function be

$$L_t = \frac{1}{2} [z_t', y_t'] \begin{bmatrix} Q_{zx}, & Q_{zy} \\ Q_{zy}', & Q_{yy} \end{bmatrix} \begin{bmatrix} z_t \\ y_t \end{bmatrix} + \frac{1}{2} u_t' R u_t + [z_t', y_t'] \begin{bmatrix} S_z \\ S_y \end{bmatrix} u_t, \tag{9.19}$$

where the matrix

$$Q = \begin{bmatrix} Q_{zx}, & Q_{zy} \\ Q_{zy}', & Q_{yy} \end{bmatrix}$$

is symmetric positive semidefinite. The policy maker's objective is to choose $\{z_t, y_t, u_t\}$ so as to minimize the following discounted loss function

$$E\left[\sum_{t=0}^{\infty} \beta^t L_t\right]$$

subject to (9.18). In this problem the policy maker is committed to choose $\{z_t, y_t, u_t\}$ at time zero and will not reoptimize in the future. This problem is also called a **Ramsey problem**.

Example 9.4.1   *Consider the following basic New Keynesian model:*

$$\pi_t = \kappa x_t + \beta E_t \pi_{t+1} + z_t, \tag{9.20}$$

$$x_t = E_t x_{t+1} - \frac{1}{\gamma}\left(i_t - E_t \pi_{t+1} - r_t^n\right), \tag{9.21}$$

where

$$z_{t+1} = \rho_z z_t + \varepsilon_{z,t+1},$$
$$\hat{Y}^f_{t+1} = \rho_y \hat{Y}^f_t + \varepsilon_{y,t+1},$$
$$r_t^n = -\ln\beta + \gamma\left(E_t^f \hat{Y}_{t+1} - \hat{Y}^f_t\right).$$

In the preceding equations π_t is the inflation rate, x_t is the output gap, y_t^f is the output under flexible prices, i_t is the nominal interest rate, z_t is a cost-push shock, and r_t^n is the **natural rate of interest**. *The vector of forward-looking variables is $(\pi_t, x_t)'$. The vector of predetermined variables is $(1, z_t, y_t^f, r_t^n)$. The vector of instruments is i_t. The one-period loss function is*

$$L_t = \frac{1}{2}\left(\pi_t - \pi^*\right)^2 + \frac{1}{2}\lambda x_t^2,$$

where π^* is the inflation target. We use unity in the state vector to handle the constant π^*.

To solve the Ramsey problem, we append (9.18) a block associated with u_t:

$$\bar{D}\begin{bmatrix} z_{t+1} \\ E_t y_{t+1} \\ E_t u_{t+1} \end{bmatrix} = \bar{A}\begin{bmatrix} z_t \\ y_t \\ u_t \end{bmatrix} + \begin{bmatrix} C \\ 0 \end{bmatrix}\varepsilon_{t+1},$$

where

$$\bar{D} = \begin{bmatrix} I & 0 & 0 \\ 0 & D & 0 \end{bmatrix}, \quad \bar{A} = \begin{bmatrix} A & B \end{bmatrix}.$$

We write

$$
L_t = \frac{1}{2} \begin{bmatrix} z_t' & y_t' & u_t' \end{bmatrix} W \begin{bmatrix} z_t \\ y_t \\ u_t \end{bmatrix},
$$

where

$$
W = \begin{bmatrix} Q_{zz} & Q_{zy} & S_z \\ Q_{zy}' & Q_{yy} & S_y \\ S_z' & S_y' & R \end{bmatrix}.
$$

Form the Lagrangian expression:

$$
E \sum_{t=0}^{\infty} \beta^t \left\{ L_t + \beta \begin{bmatrix} \mu_{zt+1}', \mu_{yt+1}' \end{bmatrix} \left(\bar{D} \begin{bmatrix} z_{t+1} \\ E_t y_{t+1} \\ E_t u_{t+1} \end{bmatrix} - \bar{A} \begin{bmatrix} z_t \\ y_t \\ u_t \end{bmatrix} - \begin{bmatrix} C \\ 0 \end{bmatrix} \varepsilon_{t+1} \right) \right\}
$$

$$
+ \mu_{z0}' \bar{D} (z_0 - \bar{z}_0)
$$

$$
= E \sum_{t=0}^{\infty} \beta^t \left\{ L_t + \beta \begin{bmatrix} \mu_{zt+1}', \mu_{yt+1}' \end{bmatrix} \left(\bar{D} \begin{bmatrix} z_{t+1} \\ y_{t+1} \\ u_{t+1} \end{bmatrix} - \bar{A} \begin{bmatrix} z_t \\ y_t \\ u_t \end{bmatrix} - \begin{bmatrix} C \\ 0 \end{bmatrix} \varepsilon_{t+1} \right) \right\}
$$

$$
+ \mu_{z0}' \bar{D} (z_0 - \bar{z}_0),
$$

where $\beta^{t+1} \begin{bmatrix} \mu_{zt+1}', \mu_{yt+1}' \end{bmatrix}$ is the vector of Lagrange multipliers associated with the constraint (9.18). Note that μ_{zt+1} is measurable with respect to date $t+1$ information and corresponds to z_{t+1}, but μ_{yt+1} is measurable with respect to date t information and corresponds to y_t. In other words, μ_{zt} is non-predetermined and μ_{yt} is predetermined. We set $\mu_{y0} = 0$ to indicate that there are no past promises to keep. First-order conditions with respect to z_t, y_t, and u_t are given by

$$
\begin{bmatrix} z_t' & y_t' & u_t' \end{bmatrix} W + \begin{bmatrix} \mu_{zt}' & \mu_{yt}' \end{bmatrix} \bar{D} - \beta E_t \begin{bmatrix} \mu_{zt+1}' & \mu_{yt+1}' \end{bmatrix} \bar{A} = 0
$$

for $t \geq 0$. Note that at time 0, z_0 is given exogenously, but y_0 is chosen endogenously. Thus the Lagrange multiplier corresponding to z_0, μ_{z0}, must be endogenously determined, while the Lagrange multiplier corresponding to y_0 is set as $\mu_{y0} = 0$.

Combining the first-order conditions with (9.18) yields

$$
\begin{bmatrix} \overline{D} & 0 \\ 0 & \beta\overline{A}' \end{bmatrix}
\begin{bmatrix} z_{t+1} \\ E_t y_{t+1} \\ E_t u_{t+1} \\ E_t \mu_{zt+1} \\ \mu_{yt+1} \end{bmatrix}
=
\begin{bmatrix} \overline{A} & 0 \\ W & \overline{D}' \end{bmatrix}
\begin{bmatrix} z_t \\ y_t \\ u_t \\ \mu_{zt} \\ \mu_{yt} \end{bmatrix}
+
\begin{bmatrix} C \\ 0 \end{bmatrix}
\varepsilon_{t+1}.
\tag{9.22}
$$

Taking conditional expectations given information at date t yields a form as in (2.11).

As discussed in section 2.3, there are many methods to solve this system. Here we adopt the Klein method as discussed in Söderlind (1999).[2] An important advantage of this method is that it allows the matrix D to be singular. Define the $(n_z + n_y) \times 1$ vector of predetermined variables k_t and the $(n_y + n_z + n_u) \times 1$ vector of non-predetermined variables λ_t by

$$
k_t = \begin{bmatrix} z_t \\ \mu_{yt} \end{bmatrix}, \quad \lambda_t = \begin{bmatrix} y_t \\ u_t \\ \mu_{zt} \end{bmatrix},
$$

where k_0 is exogenously given and $\mu_{y0} = 0$. We reorder equations in (9.22) and rewrite it as

$$
J \begin{bmatrix} E_t k_{t+1} \\ E_t \lambda_{t+1} \end{bmatrix} = H \begin{bmatrix} k_t \\ \lambda_t \end{bmatrix}
$$

for some conformable matrices J and H. In general, J can be singular. As we show in chapter 2, the preceding system has a unique saddle path solution as long as a stability condition and a rank condition is satisfied. The solution for the original system is in the following form:

$$
z_{t+1} = A_{zz} z_t + A_{z\mu_y} \mu_{yt} + C\varepsilon_{t+1},
$$
$$
\mu_{yt+1} = A_{\mu_y z} z_t + A_{\mu_y \mu_y} \mu_{yt}, \quad z_0 \text{ given}, \ \mu_{y0} = 0,
$$

for the predetermined variables and the Lagrange multipliers corresponding to the forward-looking variables, and

$$
y_t = A_{yz} z_t + A_{y\mu_y} \mu_{yt},
$$
$$
u_t = A_{uz} z_t + A_{u\mu_y} \mu_{yt},
$$
$$
\mu_{zt} = A_{\mu_z z} z_t + A_{\mu_z \mu_y} \mu_{yt},
$$

---

2. See Currie and Levine (1985, 1993) and Backus and Driffill (1986) for other methods.

for the forward-looking and control variables and the Lagrange multipliers associated with the predetermined variables.[3] In the preceding form, the vector of Lagrange multipliers μ_{yt} associated with the forward-looking variables y_t is a state vector, which makes the solution recursive.

The optimal policy under commitment is generally time inconsistent in the sense that if the policy maker can reoptimize in the future, then he may choose a different sequence of policy rules than the one chosen in period 0. Formally, suppose that the policy maker decides to reoptimize in period t. Then we can derive first-order conditions with respect to x_s and u_s for $s \geq t$. By a similar argument to that analyzed above, we must have $\mu_{yt} = 0$ because y_t is freely chosen. This value of μ_{yt} is likely to be different from the value chosen by the policy maker when he optimizes in period 0.

Example 9.4.2   *Consider the following basic New Keynesian model:*

$$\pi_t = \kappa x_t + \beta E_t \pi_{t+1} + z_t, \tag{9.23}$$

$$x_t = E_t x_{t+1} - \frac{1}{\gamma}(i_t - E_t \pi_{t+1} - r_t^n), \tag{9.24}$$

where π_t is the inflation rate, $x_t = y_t^a - y_t^f$ is the output gap, defined as the actual output relative to the equilibrium level of output under flexible prices, i_t is the nominal interest rate, r_t^n is the natural rate of interest and z_t is a cost-push shock. Suppose that $\{z_t\}$ follows the following process:

$$z_{t+1} = \rho z_t + \varepsilon_{t+1}, \quad z_0 = \bar{z}_0,$$

where ε_{t+1} is IID with variance Σ. The policy maker's optimal policy under commitment is to choose $\{x_t, \pi_t, i_t\}$ to solve the following problem:

$$\min \frac{1}{2} E \sum_{t=0}^{\infty} \beta^t \left[\pi_t^2 + \lambda (x_t - x^*)^2 \right]$$

subject to (9.23) and (9.24), where x^* is the target level of the output gap. Since i_t does not enter the objective function, we can ignore equation (9.24). We form the Lagrangian:

$$E \sum_{t=0}^{\infty} \beta^t \left\{ \begin{array}{l} \frac{1}{2}\pi_t^2 + \frac{1}{2}\lambda(x_t - x^*)^2 - \beta\mu_{zt+1}(z_{t+1} - \rho z_t - \varepsilon_{t+1}) \\ -\beta\mu_{xt+1}(\kappa x_t + \beta\pi_{t+1} + z_t - \pi_t) - \mu_{z0}(z_0 - \bar{z}_0) \end{array} \right\},$$

---

3. See Paul Söderlind's link http://home.datacomm.ch/paulsoderlind/ for Matlab and Octave codes of solving optimal policy with commitment and discretion in a general linear-quadratic framework.

where $\beta^{t+1}\mu_{xt+1}$ is the Lagrange multiplier associated with (9.23). First-order conditions with respect to $\{\pi_t, x_t, z_t\}$ are given by[4]

$$\pi_t : \ \pi_t + \beta E_t\mu_{xt+1} - \beta\mu_{xt} = 0, \tag{9.25}$$

$$x_t : \ \lambda(x_t - x^*) - \beta\kappa E_t\mu_{xt+1} = 0, \tag{9.26}$$

$$z_t : \ -\beta E_t\mu_{xt+1} + \beta\rho E_t\mu_{zt+1} - \mu_{zt} = 0, \tag{9.27}$$

for all $t \geq 0$, where $\mu_{x0} = 0$. Note that μ_{xt} is predetermined so that $E_t\mu_{xt+1} = \mu_{xt+1}$. Combining these conditions with (9.23) yields the following form in terms of a system of linear rational expectations equilibrium:

$$
\begin{bmatrix} 1 & 0 & 0 & 0 & 0 \\ 0 & \beta & 0 & 0 & 0 \\ 0 & \beta\kappa & 0 & 0 & 0 \\ 0 & \beta & 0 & 0 & 0 \\ 0 & -\beta & 0 & 0 & \beta\rho \end{bmatrix}
\begin{bmatrix} E_t z_{t+1} \\ E_t\mu_{xt+1} \\ E_t x_{t+1} \\ E_t\pi_{t+1} \\ E_t\mu_{zt+1} \end{bmatrix}
$$

$$
= \begin{bmatrix} \rho & 0 & 0 & 0 & 0 \\ 0 & \beta & 0 & -1 & 0 \\ 0 & 0 & \lambda & 0 & 0 \\ -1 & 0 & -\kappa & 1 & 0 \\ 0 & 0 & 0 & 0 & 1 \end{bmatrix}
\begin{bmatrix} z_t \\ \mu_{xt} \\ x_t \\ \pi_t \\ \mu_{zt} \end{bmatrix}
- \begin{bmatrix} 0 \\ 0 \\ \lambda x^* \\ 0 \\ 0 \end{bmatrix}.
$$

The predetermined variables are z_t and μ_{xt} and the non-predetermined variables are π_t, x_t, and μ_{zt}. We can then use the Klein method to solve this system. Note that the Lagrange multiplier μ_{zt} is not useful for solving other variables.

We can solve this simple problem analytically. Using (9.25) and (9.26) to solve for π_t and x_t, respectively, and then substituting them into (9.23), we obtain

$$E_t\left\{\beta\mu_{xt+2} - \left(1 + \beta + \frac{\kappa^2}{\lambda}\right)\mu_{xt+1} + \mu_{xt}\right\} = \frac{\kappa}{\beta}x^* + \frac{z_t}{\beta}, \tag{9.28}$$

where $\mu_{x0} = 0$. The characteristic equation of this second-order difference equation is

$$\beta a^2 - \left(1 + \beta + \frac{\kappa^2}{\lambda}\right)a + 1 = 0, \tag{9.29}$$

which has two real roots:

$$0 < a_1 < 1 < a_2.$$

---

4. Note that z_t is exogenous and that the first-order condition with respect to this variable has no meaning. But we will see below that this condition does not affect the solution.

We use the lag operator method discussed in section 2.2.1 to solve (9.28):

$$\beta \left(\mathbf{L}^{-1} - a_1 \right) \left(\mathbf{L}^{-1} - a_2 \right) \mu_{xt} = \frac{\kappa}{\beta} x^* + \frac{z_t}{\beta},$$

where $\mathbf{L}^{-j} X_t = E_t X_{t+j}$. *Thus*

$$\left(\mathbf{L}^{-1} - a_1 \right) \mu_{xt} = \frac{1}{\beta} \frac{1}{\mathbf{L}^{-1} - a_2} \left(\frac{\kappa}{\beta} x^* + \frac{z_t}{\beta} \right).$$

Since μ_{xt} *is predetermined without any prediction error,* $E_t \mu_{xt+1} = \mu_{xt+1}$, *we obtain*

$$\mu_{xt+1} - a_1 \mu_{xt} = \frac{-1}{\beta^2 a_2} \frac{1}{1 - \mathbf{L}^{-1} a_2^{-1}} \left(\kappa x^* + z_t \right)$$

$$= \frac{-1}{\beta^2 a_2} \sum_{j=0}^{\infty} a_2^{-j} \left(\kappa x^* + E_t z_{t+j} \right).$$

Thus

$$\mu_{xt+1} = a \mu_{xt} - \frac{a}{\beta} \left(\frac{\kappa x^*}{1 - \beta a} + \frac{z_t}{1 - \beta a \rho} \right),$$

where we have defined $a = a_1$ *and used the fact that* $a_2 = \beta^{-1} a_1^{-1}$. *Given* $\mu_{x0} = 0$, *the equation above determines* $\{\mu_{xt}\}$. *Equations (9.25) to (9.27) then determine* π_t, x_t, *and* μ_{zt} *for* $t \geq 0$.

9.5 Optimal Discretional Policy

In the discretional case the policy maker reoptimizes each period and the sequence of policy rules are time consistent. To solve for an **optimal discretional policy**, we focus on a linear Markov perfect equilibrium in which we take the predetermined variable z_t as the state variable and the public's reaction and the policy rule in period t are linear functions of the state variable z_t:

$$y_t = M z_t, \quad u_t = -F z_t, \tag{9.30}$$

where M and F are matrices to be determined.

Definition 9.5.1 *A pair of linear rules in (9.30) is a **Markov perfect equilibrium** if (a) given* $E_t y_{t+1} = f(z_t)$ *for some function* f, $u_t = -F z_t$ *and* $y_t = M z_t$ *solve the Bellman equation*

$$J(z_t) = \min_{u_t, y_t} L_t + \beta E_t \left[J(z_{t+1}) \right] \tag{9.31}$$

subject to (9.18); (b) $f(z_t) = M E_t [z_{t+1}]$.

Part (a) states that the policy maker takes the private sector's expectations as given and solves for the decision rules. Part (b) states that the decision rule for y must be consistent with the private sector's expectations. Clearly, this equilibrium is a fixed point and multiple equilibria can exist.

To solve for a linear Markov perfect equilibrium, we use the method of successive approximations by backward induction as in Oudiz and Sachs (1985), Backus and Driffill (1986), and Söderlind (1999). Consider the corresponding finite-horizon problem. In period t the policy maker expects that the public's reaction function in period $t + 1$ is

$$y_{t+1} = M_{t+1} z_{t+1}, \tag{9.32}$$

where M_{t+1} is some conformable matrix. The policy maker's problem in period t is given by the Bellman equation:

$$J_t(z_t) = \min_{u_t} L_t + \beta E_t \left[J_{t+1}(z_{t+1}) \right] \tag{9.33}$$

subject to (9.18) and (9.32). Because this is a linear-quadratic control problem, we conjecture that the value function in period t takes the following quadratic form:

$$J_t(z_t) = \frac{1}{2} z_t' V_t z_t + \frac{1}{2} v_t, \tag{9.34}$$

where V_t is a matrix and v_t is a scalar.

We proceed with the following three steps.

Step 1. Partitioning matrices in (9.18) conformably and using equations (9.18) and (9.32), we derive

$$y_{t+1} = M_{t+1} z_{t+1} = M_{t+1} \left(A_{zz} z_t + A_{zy} y_t + B_z u_t + \varepsilon_{t+1} \right). \tag{9.35}$$

Partitioning matrices in (9.18) conformably yields

$$D_{yy} E_t y_{t+1} = A_{yz} z_t + A_{yy} y_t + B_y u_t. \tag{9.36}$$

Taking conditional expectations and premultiplying D_{yy} on the two sides of equation (9.35), we use equation (9.36) to derive

$$A_{yz} z_t + A_{yy} y_t + B_y u_t = D_{yy} M_{t+1} \left(A_{zz} z_t + A_{zy} y_t + B_z u_t \right).$$

Assuming that the matrix $A_{yy} - D_{yy} M_{t+1} A_{zy}$ is invertible, we can then use the preceding equation to solve for

$$y_t = H_{zt} z_t + H_{ut} u_t, \tag{9.37}$$

where

$$H_{zt} = \left(A_{yy} - D_{yy}M_{t+1}A_{zy}\right)^{-1}\left(D_{yy}M_{t+1}A_{zz} - A_{yz}\right),$$
$$H_{ut} = \left(A_{yy} - D_{yy}M_{t+1}A_{zy}\right)^{-1}\left(D_{yy}M_{t+1}B_z - B_y\right).$$

Substituting (9.37) into the upper block of (9.18), we obtain the new system dynamics:

$$z_{t+1} = A_t^* z_t + B_t^* u_t + \varepsilon_{t+1}, \quad z_t \text{ given}, \tag{9.38}$$

where

$$A_t^* = A_{zz} + A_{zy}H_{zt},$$
$$B_t^* = B_z + A_{zy}H_{ut},$$

Step 2. We rewrite the return function in (9.19) as

$$
\begin{aligned}
L_t &= \frac{1}{2}z_t' Q_{zz} z_t + \frac{1}{2}y_t' Q_{yy} y_t + z_t' Q_{zy} y_t + \frac{1}{2}u_t' R u_t + z_t' S_z u_t + y_t' S_y u_t \\
&= \frac{1}{2}z_t' Q_t^* z_t + \frac{1}{2}u_t' R_t^* u_t + z_t' S_t^* u_t,
\end{aligned}
$$

where

$$Q_t^* = Q_{zz} + H_{zt}' Q_{yy} H_{zt} + 2Q_{zy}H_{zt},$$
$$R_t^* = R + H_{ut}' Q_{yy} H_{ut} + H_{ut}' S_y,$$
$$S_t^* = Q_{zy}H_{ut} + S_z + H_{zt}S_y.$$

Step 3. Substituting the conjectured value function (9.34) and the preceding return function into the Bellman equation (9.33), we obtain the following control problem:

$$
\begin{aligned}
\frac{1}{2}z_t' V_t z_t + \frac{1}{2}v_t = \min_{u_t} \ & \frac{1}{2}z_t' Q_t^* z_t + \frac{1}{2}u_t' R_t^* u_t + z_t' S_t^* u_t \\
& + \frac{1}{2}\beta E_t \left[z_{t+1}' V_{t+1} z_{t+1} + v_{t+1}\right],
\end{aligned}
\tag{9.39}
$$

subject to (9.38), where z_0 is given. The first-order condition with respect to u_t gives

$$u_t = -F_t z_t, \tag{9.40}$$

where

$$F_t = \left(R_t^* + \beta B_t^{*'} V_{t+1} B_t^*\right)^{-1}\left(S_t^{*'} + \beta B_t^{*'} V_{t+1} A_t^*\right).$$

Substituting (9.40) back into the Bellman equation (9.39) and using (9.38), we obtain

$$V_t = Q_t^* + F_t' R_t^* F_t - 2S_t^* F_t + \beta \left(A_t^* - B_t^* F_t \right)' V_{t+1} \left(A_t^* - B_t^* F_t \right). \tag{9.41}$$

Also we obtain a recursive equation for v_t:

$$v_t = \beta \mathrm{tr}\left(V_{t+1} \Sigma \right) + \beta v_{t+1}.$$

Substituting (9.40) into (9.37) yields

$$y_t = \left(H_{zt} - H_{ut} F_t \right) z_t.$$

Thus we have the updated value

$$M_t = H_{zt} - H_{ut} F_t. \tag{9.42}$$

Now we start with an initial guess of a positive semidefinite matrix V_{t+1} and any matrix M_{t+1}. We obtain the updated matrices V_t and M_t using equations (9.41) and (9.42) and other related equations given above. Iterating this process until convergence gives V and M in a Markov perfect equilibrium. Additionally v_t converges to v in the value function and F_t converges to F, which gives the stationary policy rule.

Example 9.5.1 *Consider again the canonical New Keynesian model discussed in example 9.4.2. We now solve for the optimal discretional policy. There is no predetermined endogenous state variable. The only state variable is the exogenous shock z_t. Thus the discretionary policy solves the following static problem:*

$$\min \frac{1}{2} \pi_t^2 + \frac{\lambda}{2} \left(x_t - x^* \right)^2$$

subject to

$$\pi_t = \kappa x_t + \beta \pi_t^e + z_t,$$

where π_t^e is the expected inflation that is taken as given by the policy maker. The solution of this problem is given by

$$\pi_t = \frac{\lambda}{\kappa^2 + \lambda} \left(\kappa x^* + \beta \pi_t^e + z_t \right). \tag{9.43}$$

A Markov perfect equilibrium is a pair of functions $\pi(z_t)$ and $\pi^e(z_t)$ such that (a) $\pi(z_t) = \pi_t$ in (9.43) when $\pi_t^e = \pi^e(z_t)$ and (b) $\pi^e(z_t) = E_t \pi(z_{t+1})$. Using (9.43) yields

$$\pi_t = \frac{\lambda}{\kappa^2 + \lambda} \left(\kappa x^* + \beta E_t \pi_{t+1} + z_t \right).$$

We can then solve for the discretionary inflation rate:

$$\pi_t = \frac{\lambda}{\kappa^2 + \lambda} \sum_{j=0}^{\infty} \beta^j \left(\frac{\lambda}{\kappa^2 + \lambda} \right)^j \left[\kappa x^* + E_t z_{t+j} \right].$$

9.6 Robust Control

An optimal control problem can be written as the following standard form:

$$\max_{\{u_t\}} E \sum_{t=0}^{\infty} \beta^t r(x_t, u_t), \quad \beta \in (0,1),$$

subject to

$$x_{t+1} = f(x_t, u_t, \varepsilon_{t+1}), \quad x_0 \text{ given,} \tag{9.44}$$

where r is a reward or return function, f is a state transition function, x_t is a state vector, u_t is a control vector, and ε_t is a vector of possibly serially correlated random variables. An implicit assumption of this setup is that the decision maker fully trusts his model in that the expectation operator E is taken with respect to the probability measure P underlying the stochastic process $\{\varepsilon_t\}$. In economics this means that the decision maker has rational expectations because his subjective beliefs coincide with the objective probability measure.

Control theorists and applied mathematicians have sought ways to relax the assumption that the decision maker trusts his model. They formulate **robust control theory** in order to take into account the fact that the model may be misspecified.[5] Lars Hansen and Thomas Sargent have extended this theory so that it can be applied to economics.[6] In this section we provide a brief introduction of their work. In chapter 20 we will discuss the connection with the literature on ambiguity aversion in decision theory.

9.6.1 Belief Distortions and Entropy

The decision maker's information set at date t is given by x_0 and $\varepsilon^t = (\varepsilon'_1, ..., \varepsilon'_t)$. For simplicity, we assume that ε_t is IID and drawn from a distribution with density $\pi(\varepsilon)$. This density induces a probability measure P on the full state space of the model. The decision maker views this model as an approximation and fears

---

5. See Zhou, Doyle, and Glover (1996) for an introduction to robut control theory.
6. See Hansen and Sargent (2008) for a comprehensive treatment.

that the model is misspecified. He believes that ε_{t+1} is drawn from an alternative distribution with density $\hat{\pi}\left(\varepsilon|\varepsilon^t\right)$. Form the likelihood ratio:

$$m_{t+1} = \frac{\hat{\pi}\left(\varepsilon_{t+1}|\varepsilon^t\right)}{\pi\left(\varepsilon_{t+1}\right)}.$$

Clearly,

$$E\left[m_{t+1}|\varepsilon^t\right] = \int \frac{\hat{\pi}\left(\varepsilon|\varepsilon^t\right)}{\pi\left(\varepsilon\right)}\pi\left(\varepsilon\right)d\varepsilon = 1,$$

where we use E to denote the expectation operator with respect to the reference measure P.

Set $M_0 = 1$ and define

$$M_{t+1} = m_{t+1}M_t = \Pi_{j=1}^{t+1}m_j.$$

The random variable M_t is the ratio of the distorted joint density to the reference joint density of ε^t conditioned on x_0 and evaluated at the random vector ε^t. The process $\{M_t\}$ is a martingale and induces a distorted measure Q on the full state space. For any Borel function $\varphi\left(\varepsilon^t\right)$ of ε^t, we can compute its expectation with respect to the distorted belief Q as

$$E^Q\left[\varphi\left(\varepsilon^t, x_0\right)\right] = E\left[M_t\varphi\left(\varepsilon^t, x_0\right)\right].$$

We use **relative entropy** to measure discrepancies between two probability measures P and Q. It is defined as

$$E^Q\left[\ln\left(\left.\frac{dQ}{dP}\right|_{\varepsilon^t}\right)\right] = E\left[M_t \ln M_t\right],$$

where $dQ/dP|_{\varepsilon^t}$ denotes the Radon–Nikodym derivative of Q with respect to P when restricted to the σ-algebra generated by ε^t. Clearly, relative entropy is non-negative and equal to zero if and only if $M_t = 1$ or $Q = P$. We can decompose relative entropy as

$$E\left[M_t \ln M_t\right] = \sum_{j=0}^{t-1} E\left[M_j E\left(m_{j+1}\ln m_{j+1}|\varepsilon^j\right)\right],$$

where $E\left[m_{t+1}\ln m_{t+1}|\varepsilon^t\right]$ is the conditional relative entropy of a perturbation to the one-step transition density associated with the approximating model. Discounted entropy over an infinite horizon can be expressed as

$$(1-\beta)\sum_{j=0}^{\infty}\beta^j E\left[M_j \ln M_j\right] = \beta\sum_{j=0}^{\infty}\beta^j E\left[M_j E(m_{j+1}\ln m_{j+1}|\varepsilon^j)\right].$$

To express the idea that model P is a good approximation when Q actually generates the data, we restrain the approximation errors by the entropy constraint

$$\beta \sum_{j=0}^{\infty} \beta^j E \left[M_j E(m_{j+1} \ln m_{j+1} | \varepsilon^j) \right] \leq \eta_0, \tag{9.45}$$

where η_0 represents the size of errors.

9.6.2   Two Robust Control Problems

To acknowledge model misspecification, it is natural to formulate the following problem:

$$\max_{\{u_t\}} \min_{\{m_{t+1}\}} E^Q \sum_{t=0}^{\infty} \beta^t r \left(x_t, u_t \right)$$

subject to (9.44) and (9.45). The interpretation is the following. The decision maker may use a distorted belief Q induced by a sequence of one-step likelihood ratios $\{m_{t+1}\}$ to evaluate discounted rewards. He is averse to model uncertainty. He chooses a distorted belief that minimizes the discounted expected rewards given the entropy constraint (9.45). He then chooses an optimal control $\{u_t\}$ based on this worst-case distorted belief. Hansen and Sargent (2008) call the formulation above the **constrained problem**. They also propose a related **multiplier problem**, which is more tractable in applications:

$$\max_{\{u_t\}} \min_{\{m_{t+1}\}} E^Q \sum_{t=0}^{\infty} \beta^t r \left(x_t, u_t \right) + \beta \theta E^Q \left\{ \sum_{t=0}^{\infty} \beta^t E \left[m_{t+1} \ln m_{t+1} | \varepsilon^t \right] \right\}$$

subject to (9.44). One may view θ as the Lagrange multiplier associated with the entropy constraint (9.45). The parameter θ captures concerns about robustness. Following Hansen and Sargent (2008), we may rewrite the multiplier problem above as

$$\max_{\{u_t\}} \min_{\{m_{t+1}\}} E \sum_{t=0}^{\infty} \beta^t M_t \left\{ r \left(x_t, u_t \right) + \beta \theta E \left[m_{t+1} \ln m_{t+1} | \varepsilon^t \right] \right\} \tag{9.46}$$

subject to (9.44) and

$$M_{t+1} = m_{t+1} M_t \text{ and } E \left[m_{t+1} | \varepsilon^t \right] = 1.$$

When θ goes to infinity, the penalty of distortions is so large that no distortion is optimal. In this case the multiplier problem converges to the standard control problem under the reference probability measure P. When θ becomes smaller, the decision maker is more concerned about model misspecification. We will show in chapter 20 that θ can also be interpreted as a parameter for ambiguity aversion. A smaller θ means a larger degree of ambiguity aversion.

Note that θ cannot be arbitrarily small. There is a lower bound $\underline{\theta}$ called a **break-down point** beyond which it is fruitless to seek more robustness. This is because if the minimizing agent is sufficiently unconstrained, then he can push the objective function to $-\infty$.[7] We will assume that $\theta > \underline{\theta}$ throughout this section.

9.6.3   Recursive Formulation

We can formulate the multiplier problem (9.46) recursively. We conjecture the value function takes the form $W(M, x) = MV(x)$. Substituting the constraints, we write the Bellman equation as

$$MV(x) = \max_{u} \min_{m(\varepsilon)} M\{r(x, u) + \beta \int [m(\varepsilon) V(f(x, u, \varepsilon)) + \theta m(\varepsilon) \ln m(\varepsilon)] \pi(\varepsilon) d\varepsilon\}$$

subject to $E[m(\varepsilon)] = 1$. Thus we obtain

$$V(x) = \max_{u} r(x, u) + \beta \min_{m(\varepsilon)} \int (m(\varepsilon) V(f(x, u, \varepsilon)) + \theta m(\varepsilon) \ln m(\varepsilon)) \pi(\varepsilon) d\varepsilon.$$

The first-order condition for the minimization problem gives

$$\ln m^*(\varepsilon) = \frac{-V(f(x, u, \varepsilon))}{\theta} + \lambda,$$

where λ is chosen such that $E[m(\varepsilon)] = 1$. Thus

$$m^*(\varepsilon) = \frac{\exp(-V(f(x, u, \varepsilon))/\theta)}{\int \exp(-V(f(x, u, \varepsilon))/\theta) \pi(\varepsilon) d\varepsilon}. \tag{9.47}$$

Under the minimizing m^*, we compute

$$\mathcal{R}(V)(x, u) \equiv \int (m^*(\varepsilon) V(f(x, u, \varepsilon)) + \theta m^*(\varepsilon) \ln m^*(\varepsilon)) \pi(\varepsilon) d\varepsilon$$

$$= -\theta \ln \left[\int \exp \left(\frac{-V(f(x, u, \varepsilon))}{\theta} \right) \pi(\varepsilon) d\varepsilon \right], \tag{9.48}$$

where $\mathcal{R}$ is an operator that adjusts the value function. The expression on the second line of the equation above is the risk-sensitive adjustment to the value

---

7. See chapter 8 of Hansen and Sargent (2008) for more discussions on the breakdown point.

function. We can reinterpret $1/\theta$ as a parameter that enhances risk aversion. Now the multiplier problem becomes

$$V(x) = \max_u \; r(x,u) + \beta \mathcal{R}(V)(x,u).$$ (9.49)

This problem is identical to a **risk-sensitive control problem** in which there is no concern about model misspecification. If there is no choice of optimal control, the recursive equation above defines a recursive utility function. This utility model is a special case of recursive utility studied by Epstein and Zin (1989). It is also studied by Hansen and Sargent (1995) in a linear-quadratic setting.

9.6.4 Linear-Quadratic Model with Gaussian Disturbances

Consider a linear-quadratic setting studied in section 9.3 in which the state transition equation is given by (9.1). Let

$$r(x,u) = -\frac{1}{2}\left(x'Qx + u'Ru + 2x'Su\right).$$

Suppose that the disturbances $\{\varepsilon_t\}$ is an IID Gaussian process. In this setting the value function for the multiplier problem is quadratic and takes the form

$$V(x) = -\frac{1}{2}x'Px - \frac{d}{2}.$$ (9.50)

By equation (9.47), we can compute the worst-case likelihood ratio:

$$m^*(\varepsilon) \propto \exp\left[\frac{1}{2\theta}\varepsilon'C'PC\varepsilon + \frac{1}{\theta}\varepsilon'C'P'(Ax+Bu)\right],$$

where $\propto$ means "proportional." When the reference density π is a standard normal density, we can compute the worst-case distorted density:

$$\pi^*(\varepsilon) = \pi(\varepsilon)m^*(\varepsilon) \propto \exp\left[-\frac{1}{2}\varepsilon'\left(I - \frac{1}{\theta}C'PC\right)\varepsilon \right.$$
$$\left. + \varepsilon'\left(I - \frac{1}{\theta}C'PC\right)(\theta I - C'PC)^{-1}C'P(Ax+Bu)\right].$$

Thus $\pi^*(\varepsilon)$ is also a normal density with mean $(\theta I - C'PC)^{-1}C'P(Ax+Bu)$ and covariance matrix $(I - \theta^{-1}C'PC)^{-1}$. In this computation we must assume that the matrix $(I - \theta^{-1}C'PC)$ is nonsingular. This means that θ must exceed a cutoff value $\underline{\theta}$. Such a value is called the **breakdown point**.

Next we compute the adjustment to the value function in (9.48):

$$
\mathcal{R}\left(V\right)(x,u) = \int V\left(f\left(x,u,\varepsilon\right),u\right)\pi^{*}\left(\varepsilon\right)d\varepsilon + \theta\int\pi^{*}\left(\epsilon\right)\ln\left(\frac{\pi^{*}\left(\varepsilon\right)}{\pi\left(\varepsilon\right)}\right)d\varepsilon
$$

$$
= -\frac{1}{2}\left(Ax+Bu\right)'\left[P+PC\left(\theta I - C'PC\right)^{-1}C'P\right]\left(Ax+Bu\right)
$$

$$
-\frac{d}{2}-\frac{\theta}{2}\ln\det\left(I-\frac{1}{\theta}C'PC\right)^{-1}.
$$

Alternatively, we can compute this adjustment directly using the expression in the second line of equation (9.48).

We define an operator $\mathcal{D}$ by

$$
\mathcal{D}\left(P\right) = P + PC\left(\theta I - C'PC\right)^{-1}C'P.
$$

Using this operator, substituting the conjecture in (9.50) and the expression for $\mathcal{R}\left(V\right)$ into (9.49), we obtain

$$
-\frac{1}{2}x'Px - \frac{d}{2} = \max_{u}\ -\frac{1}{2}x'Qx - \frac{1}{2}u'Ru - x'Su
$$

$$
-\beta\frac{1}{2}\left(Ax+Bu\right)'\mathcal{D}\left(P\right)\left(Ax+Bu\right)
$$

$$
-\frac{\beta d}{2}-\frac{\beta\theta}{2}\ln\det\left(I-\frac{1}{\theta}C'PC\right)^{-1}.
$$

Now, using the first-order condition, we can solve for the optimal control:

$$
u = -Fx, \tag{9.51}
$$

where

$$
F = \left(R+\beta B'\mathcal{D}(P)B\right)^{-1}\left(S'+\beta B'\mathcal{D}(P)A\right). \tag{9.52}
$$

Substituting this decision rule back into the Bellman equation above and matching coefficients, we obtain

$$
P = \mathcal{T}\circ\mathcal{D}\left(P\right), \tag{9.53}
$$

where the operator $\mathcal{T}$ is defined as

$$
\mathcal{T}(P) = Q + \beta A'PA \tag{9.54}
$$

$$
-\left(S+\beta A'PB\right)\left(R+\beta B'PB\right)^{-1}\left(S'+\beta B'PA\right),
$$

$$
d = \left(1-\beta\right)^{-1}\beta\theta\ln\det\left(I-\frac{1}{\theta}C'PC\right)^{-1}. \tag{9.55}
$$

Note that the operator $\mathcal{T}$ is identical to that in (9.11) for the standard control problem.

In summary, we use equations (9.53) and (9.54) to solve for P. A simple value function iteration algorithm as in section 9.3 may be applied. We then use equation (9.55) to determine the constant term in the value function. Finally, we use equations (9.51) and (9.52) to solve for the robust decision rule.

9.6.5 Relative Entropy and Normal Distributions

We have shown that the worst-case distribution is normal. It is useful to compute the relative entropy for normal distributions. Suppose that π is a multivariate standard normal distribution and that $\hat{\pi}$ is normal with mean w and nonsingular covariance Σ. Our objective is to compute the relative entropy

$$\int \hat{\pi}(\varepsilon) \ln \frac{\hat{\pi}(\varepsilon)}{\pi(\varepsilon)} d\varepsilon.$$

First, we compute the log likelihood ratio

$$\ln \frac{\hat{\pi}(\varepsilon)}{\pi(\varepsilon)} = \frac{1}{2} \left[-(\varepsilon - w)' \Sigma^{-1} (\varepsilon - w) + \varepsilon'\varepsilon - \ln \det \Sigma \right].$$

Next we compute

$$\int \frac{1}{2} (\varepsilon - w)' \Sigma^{-1} (\varepsilon - w) \hat{\pi}(\varepsilon) d\varepsilon = \frac{1}{2} \mathrm{tr}(I).$$

Using the fact that

$$\frac{1}{2}\varepsilon'\varepsilon = \frac{1}{2} w'w + \frac{1}{2} (\varepsilon - w)' (\varepsilon - w) + w'(\varepsilon - w),$$

we compute

$$\frac{1}{2} \int \varepsilon'\varepsilon \hat{\pi}(\varepsilon) d\varepsilon = \frac{1}{2} w'w + \frac{1}{2} \mathrm{tr}(\Sigma).$$

Combining terms yields

$$\int \hat{\pi}(\varepsilon) \ln \frac{\hat{\pi}(\varepsilon)}{\pi(\varepsilon)} d\varepsilon = \frac{1}{2} w'w - \frac{1}{2} \ln \det \Sigma + \frac{1}{2} \mathrm{tr}(\Sigma - I). \tag{9.56}$$

The first term on the right-hand side measures the mean distortion and the last two terms measure the distortion of variances.

9.6.6   Modified Certainty Equivalence Principle

In doing the computation, it is convenient to solve a deterministic problem with the state-transition equation

$$x_{t+1} = Ax_t + Bu_t + Cw_t,$$

where we have replaced the stochastic shock by a distorted mean w. To solve for the worst-case distortion, we consider the following minimization problem:

$$\min_{w} \; -\frac{1}{2}(Ax + Bu + Cw)'P(Ax + Bu + Cw) + \frac{\theta}{2}w'w.$$

In this problem relative entropy is not well defined. We could use instead (9.56) and consider the penalty of distortions in the mean. The solution for w then is

$$w^* = (\theta I - C'PC)^{-1}C'P(Ax + Bu).$$

This is identical to the mean distortion of the worst-case normal distribution $\pi^*(\varepsilon)$ discussed earlier. The minimized objective function is

$$-\frac{1}{2}(Ax + Bu)'\left[P + PC(\theta I - C'PC)^{-1}C'P\right](Ax + Bu),$$

which is identical to the stochastic robust adjustment to the value function coming from the quadratic form in $(Ax + Bu)$.

The difference between this deterministic problem and the stochastic problem is that the distorted covariance matrix for the worst-case normal distribution and the constant term in the adjusted value function are not present in the deterministic problem. However, neither object affects the computation of the robust decision rule and the matrix P in the value function. This is the modified certainty equivalence studied by Hansen and Sargent (2005a). We should emphasize that unlike the standard control problem, the volatility matrix C affects both the decision rule and the matrix P in the deterministic robust control problem.

9.7   Exercises

1. One can normalize $S = 0$ in the control problem. Show that this can be achieved by adopting the transformed control variable $\tilde{u}_t = u_t + R^{-1}Sx_t$, where we assume that R is nonsingular.

2. Solve the following uncentered control problem:

$$\max_{\{u_t\}} \; -E\sum_{t=0}^{\infty}\beta^t(x_t - x^*)'\begin{bmatrix} Q & S \\ S' & R \end{bmatrix}(u_t - u^*), \quad \beta \in (0,1],$$

subject to

$$x_{t+1} = Ax_t + Bu_t + C\varepsilon_{t+1}, \quad x_0 \text{ given,} \tag{9.57}$$

where x^* and u^* are exogenously given.

3. Show that as $\theta \to \infty$, the solution for the multiplier problem in (9.52) to (9.55) converges to the solution to the standard control problem without robustness.

4. (Hall 1978) Consider the following consumption–saving problem:

$$\max \; - E \sum_{t=0}^{\infty} \beta^t (c_t - b)^2, \quad \beta \in (0,1),$$

subject to

$$c_t + a_{t+1} = Ra_t + y_t,$$

$$y_t = \mu_y (1 - \rho) + \rho y_{t-1} + \sigma_y \varepsilon_t,$$

where $b, \mu_y > 0$, $R > 1$, $|\rho| < 1$, and ε_t is IID Gaussian. Use $x_t = [1 \; a_t \; y_t]'$ as the state vector. Solve for the optimal consumption rule.

5. Let the robustness parameter be θ and consider the multiplier problem for the consumption–saving choices above. Solve for the robust consumption rule.

10 Control under Partial Information

Economic agents often possess limited information. In addition economic information is often noisy possibly because of measurement errors. In this chapter we study control problems under partial (or imperfect) information. To do this, we first study how to estimate hidden states given observations.

10.1 Filters

Filtering is a procedure of estimating hidden states based on observable data. We first present the Kalman filter in a linear-Gaussian framework. We then study nonlinear filters.

10.1.1 Kalman Filter

We consider the following linear **state-space representation**:

$$x_{t+1} = A_t x_t + B_t u_t + C_t \varepsilon_{t+1}, \tag{10.1}$$

$$y_t = G_t x_t + H_{t-1} u_{t-1} + D_t \varepsilon_t, \tag{10.2}$$

where x_t is an $n_x \times 1$ state vector, y_t is an $n_y \times 1$ observation (or measurement) vector, u_t is an $n_u \times 1$ control vector, $\{\varepsilon_t\}$ is an IID sequence of Gaussian vectors with $E\varepsilon_t\varepsilon_t' = I$, A_t, B_t, C_t, D_t, G_t, and H_t are conformable matrices with known but possibly time-varying elements.[1] Assume that x_0 is Gaussian $N(x_0, \Sigma_0)$ and is independent of all other random variables. Let $\mathcal{F}_t = \{y_0, y_1, ..., y_t\}$ be the information set at date t and let u_t be adapted to $\mathcal{F}_t$. Equation (10.1) is called the **state-transition equation** and equation (10.2) is called the **measurement equation**. Note that we allow the errors in these two equations to be correlated, though the uncorrelated case is often considered in applications.

---

1. See Hamilton (1994), Kim and Nelson (1999), and Ljungqvist and Sargent (2004) for various applications of the Kalman filter.

In econometrics, the state-space representation is often written as

$$x_{t+1} = Ax_t + C\varepsilon_{t+1}, \tag{10.3}$$

$$y_t = Gx_t + Hz_t + D\varepsilon_t, \tag{10.4}$$

where z_t is an $n_z \times 1$ vector of exogenous or predetermined variables. Let $\mathcal{F}_t = \{y_0, y_1, ..., y_t, z_0, z_1, ..., z_t\}$. Assume that z_t is independent of x_s and ε_s for any $s \geq t$. The matrices $A, C, D, G,$ and H may be unknown and need to be estimated based on observations $\{y_0, ..., y_T\}$ and $\{z_0, ..., z_T\}$. In this chapter we focus on the representation in (10.1) and (10.2). The representation in (10.3) and (10.4) can be viewed as a special case.

We adopt the following notations:

- $\hat{x}_{t|s} = E[x_t|\mathcal{F}_s]$ and $\hat{y}_{t|s} = E[y_t|\mathcal{F}_s]$ for $s \leq t$,
- $\Sigma_{t|t} = E\left[(x_t - \hat{x}_{t|t})(x_t - \hat{x}_{t|t})' | \mathcal{F}_t\right],$
- $\Sigma_{t|t-1} = E\left[(x_t - \hat{x}_{t|t-1})(x_t - \hat{x}_{t|t-1})' | \mathcal{F}_{t-1}\right],$
- $\Omega_{t|t-1} = E\left[(y_t - \hat{y}_{t|t-1})(y_t - \hat{y}_{t|t-1})' | \mathcal{F}_{t-1}\right].$

Because of the assumption of Gaussian random variables, we can treat the conditional variance-covariance matrices above as the unconditional variance-covariance matrices. Moreover, given information $\mathcal{F}_t$, x_t is distributed according to $N\left(\hat{x}_{t|t}, \Sigma_{t|t}\right)$, x_{t+1} is distributed according to $N\left(\hat{x}_{t+1|t}, \Sigma_{t+1|t}\right)$, and y_{t+1} is distributed according to $N\left(G_{t+1}\hat{x}_{t+1|t} + H_t u_t, \Omega_{t+1|t}\right)$.

Example 10.1.1 (Labor income process) *Guvenen (2007) considers the following dynamics for the log labor income process:*

$$y_t = \alpha + \beta t + z_t + v_t, \tag{10.5}$$

$$z_t = \rho z_{t-1} + \eta_t, \tag{10.6}$$

where α and β are unknown parameters and z_t is a hidden state representing the persistent component of labor income. The information set at date t is y^t. Assume that $\{v_t\}$, $\{\eta_t\}$, α, β, and z_0 are Gaussian and independent of each other. We can express the system above as the state-space representation

$$x_{t+1} \equiv \begin{bmatrix} \alpha \\ \beta \\ z_{t+1} \end{bmatrix} = \begin{bmatrix} 1 & & \\ & 1 & \\ & & \rho \end{bmatrix} \begin{bmatrix} \alpha \\ \beta \\ z_t \end{bmatrix} + \begin{bmatrix} 0 & 0 \\ 0 & 0 \\ 1 & 0 \end{bmatrix} \begin{bmatrix} \eta_{t+1} \\ v_{t+1} \end{bmatrix}$$

$$= Ax_t + C\varepsilon_{t+1},$$

and

$$y_t = \begin{bmatrix} 1 & t & 1 \end{bmatrix} \begin{bmatrix} \alpha \\ \beta \\ z_t \end{bmatrix} + \begin{bmatrix} 0 & 1 \end{bmatrix} \begin{bmatrix} \eta_t \\ v_t \end{bmatrix} = G_t x_t + D\varepsilon_t.$$

The Kalman filter gives the following recursive forecasting procedure. Suppose that we know $\hat{x}_{t|t-1}$ and $\hat{y}_{t|t-1}$ at date t. After observing y_t, the Kalman filter gives the estimate $\hat{x}_{t|t}$ using the linear equation:

$$\hat{x}_{t|t} = \hat{x}_{t|t-1} + K_t \left(y_t - \hat{y}_{t|t-1} \right), \tag{10.7}$$

where K_t is called a **Kalman gain**, which measures how much $\hat{x}_{t|t-1}$ is updated based on the error in predicting y_t. This error is often called an **innovation,** denoted by $a_t = y_t - \hat{y}_{t|t-1}$. The variance-covariance matrix of the innovation is given by

$$\Omega_{t|t-1} = E\left[a_t a_t'\right] = E\left[\left(G_t \left(x_t - \hat{x}_{t|t-1} \right) + D_t \varepsilon_t \right) \left(G_t \left(x_t - \hat{x}_{t|t-1} \right) + D_t \varepsilon_t \right)' \right]$$
$$= G_t \Sigma_{t|t-1} G_t' + D_t D_t' + G_t C_t D_t' + D_t C_t' G_t', \tag{10.8}$$

where we have used the fact that

$$E\left[\left(x_t - \hat{x}_{t|t-1} \right) \varepsilon_t' \right] = E\left[\left(A_{t-1} x_{t-1} + B_{t-1} u_{t-1} + C_t \varepsilon_t - \hat{x}_{t|t-1} \right) \varepsilon_t' \right]$$
$$= C_t. \tag{10.9}$$

The optimal Kalman gain K_t minimizes the sum of variances of the estimation errors:

$$E\left[(x_t - \hat{x}_{t|t})'(x_t - \hat{x}_{t|t}) \right].$$

We will show below that the solution is given by

$$K_t = \left(\Sigma_{t|t-1} G_t' + C_t D_t' \right) \Omega_{t|t-1}^{-1}. \tag{10.10}$$

The intuition behind the formula for K_t is the following. If there is a large error in forecasting x_t using past information y^{t-1} (i.e., $\Sigma_{t|t-1}$ is large), then the Kalman filter will give a larger weight to new information (i.e., K_t is large). If new information is noisy (i.e., $\Omega_{t|t-1}$ is large), the Kalman filter will give a large weight to the old prediction (i.e., K_t is small).

Since $\hat{x}_{t+1|t} = A_t \hat{x}_{t|t} + B_t u_t$ and $\hat{y}_{t+1|t} = G_{t+1} \hat{x}_{t+1|t} + H_t u_t$, we can then move to date $t+1$ and use the previous procedure again. To make this procedure work, we need to update $\Sigma_{t|t-1}$. In doing so, we first compute

$$\Sigma_{t+1|t} = E\left[\left(A_t \left(x_t - \hat{x}_{t|t} \right) + C\varepsilon_{t+1} \right) \left(A_t \left(x_t - \hat{x}_{t|t} \right) + C_t \varepsilon_{t+1} \right)' \right]$$
$$= A_t \Sigma_{t|t} A_t' + C_t C_t'.$$

We then compute

$$
\begin{aligned}
\Sigma_{t|t} &= E\left[\left(x_t - \hat{x}_{t|t}\right)\left(x_t - \hat{x}_{t|t}\right)'\right]\\
&= E\left[\left(x_t - \hat{x}_{t|t-1} - K_t a_t\right)\left(x_t - \hat{x}_{t|t-1} - K_t a_t\right)'\right]\\
&= E\left[\left((I - K_t G_t)\left(x_t - \hat{x}_{t|t-1}\right) - K_t D_t \varepsilon_t\right) \times \left((I - K_t G_t)\left(x_t - \hat{x}_{t|t-1}\right) - K_t D_t \varepsilon_t\right)'\right]\\
&= (I - K_t G_t)\, \Sigma_{t|t-1}\,(I - K_t G_t)' + K_t D_t D_t' K_t'\\
&\quad - E\left[(I - K_t G_t)\left(x_t - \hat{x}_{t|t-1}\right)\varepsilon_t' D_t' K_t'\right]\\
&\quad - E\left[K_t D_t \varepsilon_t\left(x_t - \hat{x}_{t|t-1}\right)'(I - K_t G_t)'\right],
\end{aligned}
$$

where we have used (10.7) in the second equality, the definition of innovation in the third equality, and (10.8) in the last equality. We have to compute

$$
\begin{aligned}
&E\left[(I - K_t G_t)\left(x_t - \hat{x}_{t|t-1}\right)\varepsilon_t' D_t' K_t'\right]\\
&\quad = E\left[(I - K_t G_t)\left(A_{t-1} x_{t-1} + B_{t-1} u_{t-1} + C_t \varepsilon_t - \hat{x}_{t|t-1}\right)\varepsilon_t' D_t' K_t'\right]\\
&\quad = (I - K_t G_t)\, C_t D_t' K_t'.
\end{aligned}
$$

Similarly we can compute $E\left[D_t \varepsilon_t\left(x_t - \hat{x}_{t|t-1}\right)'(I - K_t G_t)'\right]$. We then obtain

$$
\begin{aligned}
\Sigma_{t|t} &= (I - K_t G_t)\, \Sigma_{t|t-1}\,(I - K_t G_t)' + K_t D_t D_t' K_t'\\
&\quad - (I - K_t G_t)\, C_t D_t' K_t' - K_t D_t C_t'\,(I - K_t G_t)'.
\end{aligned}
\tag{10.11}
$$

We can use (10.11) to understand how we obtain the optimal Kalman gain matrix in (10.10). Minimizing $E\left[(x_t - \hat{x}_{t|t})'(x_t - \hat{x}_{t|t})\right]$ is equivalent to minimizing the trace of $\Sigma_{t|t}$. Taking the first-order condition using (10.11) yields

$$
\begin{aligned}
0 = \frac{\partial \operatorname{tr}\left(\Sigma_{t|t}\right)}{\partial K_t} &= -2\left(\Sigma_{t|t-1} G_t' + C_t D_t'\right)\\
&\quad + 2K_t\left(G_t \Sigma_{t|t-1} G_t' + D_t D_t' + G_t C_t D_t' + D_t C_t' G_t'\right).
\end{aligned}
$$

Solving gives the optimal Kalman gain matrix K_t in (10.10). Plugging this equation and (10.8) into (10.11) yields

$$
\Sigma_{t|t} = (I - K_t G_t)\, \Sigma_{t|t-1} - K_t D_t C_t'.
$$

One can derive (10.7) using a probabilistic approach. By the Projection Theorem,

$$\hat{x}_{t|t} = \hat{x}_{t|t-1} + \text{Cov}(x_t, y_t | y^{t-1}) \left[\text{Var}(y_t | y^{t-1}) \right]^{-1} (y_t - \hat{y}_{t|t-1}). \qquad (10.12)$$

We then compute

$$\begin{aligned}
\text{Cov}(x_t, y_t | y^{t-1}) &= E\left[(x_t - \hat{x}_{t|t-1})(y_t - \hat{y}_{t|t-1})' \right] \\
&= E\left[(x_t - \hat{x}_{t|t-1})(G_t(x_t - \hat{x}_{t|t-1}) + D_t \varepsilon_t)' \right] \\
&= \Sigma_{t|t-1} G_t' + C_t D_t',
\end{aligned}$$

$$\text{Var}(y_t | y^{t-1}) = E\left[(y_t - \hat{y}_{t|t-1})(y_t - \hat{y}_{t|t-1})' \right] = \Omega_{t|t-1}.$$

The Kalman gain is given by

$$K_t = \text{Cov}(x_t, y_t | y^{t-1}) \left[\text{Var}(y_t | y^{t-1}) \right]^{-1}.$$

Now we summarize the Kalman filter algorithm as follows:

Step 1. Initialization:

$$\Sigma_{0|-1} = \Sigma_0, \ \hat{x}_{0|-1} = \hat{x}_0.$$

We can set initial values at the steady-state values such that

$$\hat{x}_0 = A\hat{x}_0$$

and

$$\Sigma_0 = A\Sigma_0 A' + Q.$$

Step 2. At date t, start with $\hat{x}_{t|t-1}$ and $\Sigma_{t|t-1}$. After observing y_t, we compute the following:

$$\Omega_{t|t-1} = G_t \Sigma_{t|t-1} G_t' + D_t D_t' + G_t C_t D_t' + D_t C_t' G_t',$$

$$K_t = \left(\Sigma_{t|t-1} G_t' + C_t D_t' \right) \Omega_{t|t-1}^{-1}.$$

$$\hat{x}_{t|t} = \hat{x}_{t|t-1} + K_t \left(y_t - G_t \hat{x}_{t|t-1} - H_{t-1} u_{t-1} \right),$$

$$\Sigma_{t|t} = (I - K_t G_t) \Sigma_{t|t-1} - K_t D_t C_t',$$

$$\Sigma_{t+1|t} = A_t \Sigma_{t|t} A_t' + C_t C_t',$$

$$\hat{x}_{t+1|t} = A_t \hat{x}_{t|t} + B_t u_t.$$

Step 3. We obtain $\hat{x}_{t+1|t}$ and $\Sigma_{t+1|t}$ and go to step 2, starting with date $t+1$.

We can rewrite the Kalman filter in a fully recursive form:

$$\hat{x}_{t+1|t} = A_t\hat{x}_{t|t-1} + B_tu_t + A_tK_ta_t,$$

where the innovation $a_t = y_t - G_t\hat{x}_{t|t-1} - H_{t-1}u_{t-1}$ is independently and normally distributed with mean zero and covariance matrix $\Omega_{t|t-1}$, and $\Sigma_{t+1|t}$ satisfies the recursive equation:

$$\Sigma_{t+1|t} = A_t\left[(I - K_tG_t)\Sigma_{t|t-1} - K_tD_tC_t'\right]A_t' + C_tC_t'$$

$$= A_t\Sigma_{t|t-1}A_t + C_tC_t' - A_t\left(G_t\Sigma_{t|t-1} + D_tC_t'\right)'\Omega_{t|t-1}^{-1}\left(G_t\Sigma_{t|t-1} + D_tC_t'\right)A_t',$$

where we have used equation (10.10). This is a Riccati equation for $\Sigma_{t+1|t}$.

Alternatively, we can rewrite the Kalman filter as

$$\hat{x}_{t+1|t+1} = \hat{x}_{t+1|t} + K_{t+1}a_{t+1} = A_t\hat{x}_{t|t} + B_tu_t + K_{t+1}a_{t+1},$$

and $\Sigma_{t|t}$ satisfies the recursion

$$\Sigma_{t+1|t+1} = (I - K_{t+1}G_{t+1})\Sigma_{t+1|t} - K_{t+1}D_{t+1}C_{t+1}'$$

$$= (I - K_{t+1}G_{t+1})\left(A_t\Sigma_{t|t}A_t' + C_tC_t'\right) - K_{t+1}D_{t+1}C_{t+1}'.$$

For infinite-horizon models we typically consider a time-homogeneous setup in which A_t, B_t, C_t, D_t, G_t, and H_t are all independent of t. We then often use the long-run stationary Kalman filter in which $\Sigma_t \to \Sigma$ and $K_t \to K$. The law of motion for the Kalman filter is stationary, so we can build it into stationary dynamic models using a recursive approach.

Below we provide some examples to illustrate the application of the Kalman filter.

Example 10.1.2   (Muth's 1960 example) *Muth (1960) studies the model*

$$x_{t+1} = x_t + \eta_{t+1},$$

$$y_t = x_t + v_t,$$

where x_t, y_t are scalar stochastic processes, and $\{\eta_t\}$, $\{v_t\}$ are mutually independent IID Gaussian processes with mean zeros and variances $E\eta_t^2 = Q$, $Ev_t^2 = R$. Here x_t is a hidden state and y_t is observable. The initial condition is that x_0 is Gaussian with mean $\hat{x}_0$ and variance Σ_0. Applying the Kalman filter gives

$$K_t = \frac{\Sigma_{t|t-1}}{\Sigma_{t|t-1} + R},$$

$$\Sigma_{t+1|t} = \frac{\Sigma_{t|t-1}(R + Q) + QR}{\Sigma_{t|t-1} + R}.$$

As $t \to \infty$, $\Sigma_{t|t-1} \to \Sigma$, and $K_t \to K$. Thus we obtain

$$\hat{x}_{t+1|t} = (1 - K)\,\hat{x}_{t|t-1} + Ky_t.$$

This is a version of Cagan's adaptive expectations formula. Thus Muth (1960) has constructed stochastic processes such that the adaptive expectations formula above is optimal.

In the special scalar case where $\eta_t = Q = 0$, we can set $x_t = \theta$ for all t. Define $m_t = E\left[\theta|y^t\right] = \hat{x}_{t+1|t}$ and $\sigma_{t+1} = E\left(\theta - m_t\right)^2 = \Sigma_{t+1|t}$. From the result above, we obtain

$$m_t = (1 - K_t)\,m_{t-1} + K_t y_t,$$
$$K_t = \frac{\sigma_t}{\sigma_t + R},$$
$$\sigma_t = \frac{\sigma_{t-1} R}{\sigma_{t-1} + R}.$$

We can write the innovation in the form

$$m_{t+1} = m_t + K_{t+1} a_{t+1}$$
$$\qquad = m_t + \sqrt{K_{t+1}\sigma_{t+1}}\,\xi_{t+1},$$

where ξ_{t+1} is a standard IID normal random variable. Here we have used the fact that the variance of a_{t+1} is equal to $\sigma_{t+1} + R$. Thus the variance of $K_{t+1} a_{t+1}$ is $K_{t+1}^2\left(\sigma_{t+1} + R\right) = K_{t+1}\sigma_{t+1}$.

Example 10.1.3   (Estimating long-run productivity growth) *Edge, Laubach, and Williams (2007) and Gilchrist and Saito (2008) consider the following filtering problem in dynamic stochastic general equilibrium models. Assume that agents observe the level of labor productivity, but not its persistent and transitory components. We denote by z_t the log of total factor productivity, and by x_t its expected growth rate. Assume that z_t and x_t follow:*

$$x_t = (1 - \rho)g + \rho x_{t-1} + \eta_t,$$
$$z_t = z_{t-1} + x_t + v_t,$$

where $\{\eta_t\}$ and $\{v_t\}$ are mutually independent IID Gaussian processes with $E\eta_t = Ev_t = 0$, $E\eta_t^2 = \sigma_\eta^2$, and $Ev_t^2 = \sigma_v^2$. Let $\hat{x}_{t|t} = E\left[x_t|z_0, ..., z_t\right]$. Let $y_t = z_t - z_{t-1}$. Applying the stationary Kalman filter gives

$$\hat{x}_{t+1|t+1} = \rho\hat{x}_{t|t} + (1 - \rho)g + Ka_{t+1},$$

where

$$a_{t+1} = z_{t+1} - z_t - \rho\hat{x}_{t|t} - (1 - \rho)g.$$

The Kalman gain is given by

$$K = \frac{\Sigma}{\Sigma + \sigma_v^2},$$

and the stationary covariance matrix $\Sigma = E\left(x_t - \hat{x}_{t|t-1}\right)^2$ *satisfies*

$$\Sigma = \rho^2 \left(1 - \Sigma\left(\Sigma + \sigma_v^2\right)^{-1}\right)\Sigma + \sigma_\eta^2.$$

Solving this equation yields

$$\Sigma = \frac{\sigma_v^2}{2}\left[-\left(1 - \rho^2 - \phi\right) + \sqrt{\left(1 - \rho^2 - \phi\right)^2 + 4\phi}\right],$$

where $\phi = \sigma_\eta^2 / \sigma_v^2$. *It follows that*

$$K = 1 - \frac{2}{2 - \left(1 - \rho^2 - \phi\right) + \sqrt{\left(1 - \rho^2 - \phi\right)^2 + 4\phi}}.$$

We can also compute the variance of the innovation:

$$Ea_t^2 = \Sigma + \sigma_v^2.$$

Thus conditional on z^t, $\hat{x}_{t+1|t+1}$ *is normally distributed with mean* $\rho\hat{x}_{t|t} + (1 - \rho)g$ *and variance* $K^2\left(\Sigma + \sigma_v^2\right) = K\Sigma$.

Edge, Laubach, and Williams (2007) and Gilchrist and Saito (2008) *apply this filter to dynamic stochastic general equilibrium models.*

Example 10.1.4   (Likelihood function) *Suppose that we observe a sequence of data* y^T *generated by the state-space system (10.1) and (10.2). We write down its log-likelihood density as*

$$\ln p\left(y^T|\theta\right) = \sum_{t=1}^{T} \ln p\left(y_t|y^{t-1},\theta\right)$$

$$= -\frac{n_y T}{2}\ln(2\pi) - \sum_{t=1}^{T}\frac{1}{2}\ln\left|\Omega_{t|t-1}\right| - \frac{1}{2}\sum_{t=1}^{T}a_t'\Omega_{t|t-1}^{-1}a_t,$$

where θ *is a vector of model parameters,* $a_t = y_t - \hat{y}_{t|t-1}$ *is the innovation and* $\Omega_{t|t-1}$ *is given by (10.8).*

10.1.2   Hidden Markov Chain

Consider an N-state Markov chain $\{x_t\}_{t=0}^{\infty}$. We represent the state space in terms of the unit vector $\{e_1, e_2, ..., e_N\}$, where e_i is the ith N-dimensional unit (column) vector. Let the transition matrix be P, with (i,j) element

$$p_{ij} = \Pr\left(x_{t+1} = e_j | x_t = e_i\right).$$

Given this formulation, we have

$$E\left[x_{t+1}|x_t\right] = P'x_t.$$

We then obtain the state transition equation:

$$x_{t+1} = P'x_t + v_{t+1},\tag{10.13}$$

where $\{v_t\}$ is a martingale difference process adapted to x^t, since $E\left[v_{t+1}|x_t\right] = 0$. To compute its conditional second moment, we use (10.13) to derive that

$$x_{t+1}x'_{t+1} = P'x_t\left(P'x_t\right)' + P'x_tv'_{t+1} + v_{t+1}x'_tP + v_{t+1}v'_{t+1}$$

and

$$x_{t+1}x'_{t+1} = \text{diag}(x_{t+1}) = \text{diag}\left(P'x_t\right) + \text{diag}\left(v_{t+1}\right),$$

where $\text{diag}(x_{t+1})$ is a diagonal matrix whose diagonal entries are the elements of x_{t+1}. Thus

$$v_{t+1}v'_{t+1} = \text{diag}\left(P'x_t\right) + \text{diag}\left(v_{t+1}\right)$$
$$- \left[P'x_t\left(P'x_t\right)' + P'x_tv'_{t+1} + v_{t+1}x'_tP\right].$$

It follows that

$$E\left[v_{t+1}v'_{t+1}|x_t\right] = \text{diag}\left(P'x_t\right) - P'\text{diag}\left(x_t\right)P.$$

We next introduce a measurement equation. Suppose that x_t is not observed but that a noisy signal of x_t, denoted by y_t, is observed. Let y_t take values in the set $\{\xi_1, \xi_2, ..., \xi_M\}$, where ξ_i is the ith M-dimensional unit vector. Define the $N \times M$ matrix $Q = (q_{ij})$ by

$$\Pr\left(y_t = \xi_j|x_t = e_i\right) = q_{ij}.$$

It follows that

$$E\left[y_t|x_t\right] = Q'x_t.$$

We can then write the measurement equation as

$$y_t = Q'x_t + w_t,\tag{10.14}$$

where $\{w_t\}$ is a martingale difference process satisfying $E\left[w_t|x_t\right] = 0$ and

$$E\left[u_tu'_t|x_t\right] = \text{diag}(Q'x_t) - Q'\,\text{diag}(x_t)\,Q.$$

Our goal is to give a recursive formula for computing the conditional (posterior) distribution of the hidden state. By Bayes's rule,

$$\pi_t\left(e_i|y^t\right) \equiv \Pr\left\{x_t = e_i|y^t\right\} = \frac{\Pr\left(x_t = e_i, y_t|y^{t-1}\right)}{\Pr\left(y_t|y^{t-1}\right)}$$

$$= \frac{\sum_{x_{t-1}} \Pr\left(y_t|x_t = e_i\right)\Pr\left(x_t = e_i|x_{t-1}\right)\Pr\left(x_{t-1}|y^{t-1}\right)}{\sum_{x_t}\sum_{x_{t-1}} \Pr\left(y_t|x_t\right)\Pr\left(x_t|x_{t-1}\right)\Pr\left(x_{t-1}|y^{t-1}\right)}.$$

It follows that

$$\pi_t\left(e_i|y^{t-1}, y_t = \xi_j\right) = \frac{\sum_s q_{ij}p_{si}\pi_{t-1}\left(e_s|y^{t-1}\right)}{\sum_i\sum_s q_{ij}p_{si}\pi_{t-1}\left(e_s|y^{t-1}\right)},$$

where $y_t = \xi_j$ is the value of y_t. The interpretation is that given the conditional distribution $\pi_{t-1}\left(\cdot|y^{t-1}\right)$ at date $t-1$ and after observing the signal $y_t = \xi_j$, the conditional distribution of the hidden state at date t is given by $\pi_t\left(\cdot|y^{t-1}, y_t = \xi_j\right)$. We may set the prior distribution of x_0 as the stationary distribution π^{ss}. Thus

$$\pi_0\left(e_i|y_0 = \xi_j\right) = \Pr\left(x_0 = e_i|y_0 = \xi_j\right)$$

$$= \frac{\Pr\left(y_0 = \xi_j|x_0 = e_i\right)\Pr\left(x_0 = e_i\right)}{\sum_i \Pr\left(y_0 = \xi_j|x_0 = e_i\right)\Pr\left(x_0 = e_i\right)}$$

$$= \frac{q_{ij}\pi_i^{ss}}{\sum_i q_{ij}\pi_i^{ss}}.$$

10.1.3   Hidden Markov–Switching Model

Consider the hidden regime–switching model in which the state transition equation is given by (10.13) and the measurement equation is given by

$$y_t = h\left(x_t, \varepsilon_t\right),$$

where ε_t is IID. An example is the following:

$$\Delta \ln C_t = \kappa\left(x_t\right) + \varepsilon_t,$$

where $\Delta \ln C_t$ is consumption growth, $x_t \in \{e_1, e_2\}$, $\kappa\left(e_i\right) = \kappa_i$, and ε_t is IID $N\left(0, \sigma^2\right)$. In this example, x_t describes hidden economic regimes. The expected growth rates of consumption are different in the two regimes.

Let

$$f\left(x, y\right) = \Pr\left(h\left(x, \varepsilon\right) = y\right) = \Pr\left(y_t = y|x_t = x\right).$$

Define the conditional (posterior) distribution of the hidden state as

$$\pi_t\left(e_i|y^t\right) = \Pr\left(x_t = e_i|y^t\right), \quad \pi_t\left(e_i|y^{t-1}\right) = \Pr\left(x_t = e_i|y^{t-1}\right).$$

Our goal is to derive a recursive formula for computing these conditional distributions. First, we compute

$$\pi_t\left(e_i|y^{t-1}\right) = \Pr\left(x_t = e_i|y^{t-1}\right) = \sum_{x_{t-1}} \Pr\left(x_t = e_i|y^{t-1}, x_{t-1}\right) \Pr\left(x_{t-1}|y^{t-1}\right)$$

$$= \sum_{x_{t-1}} \Pr\left(x_t = e_i|x_{t-1}\right) \Pr\left(x_{t-1}|y^{t-1}\right) = \sum_j p_{ji}\pi_{t-1}\left(e_j|y^{t-1}\right).$$

We then compute

$$\pi_t\left(e_i|y^t\right) = \Pr\left(x_t = e_i|y^t\right) = \frac{\Pr\left(y_t|x_t = e_i, y^{t-1}\right) \Pr\left(x_t = e^i|y^{t-1}\right)}{\sum_j \Pr\left(y_t|x_t = e_j, y^{t-1}\right) \Pr\left(x_t = e_j|y^{t-1}\right)}$$

$$= \frac{f\left(x, y_t\right) \pi_t\left(e_i|y^{t-1}\right)}{\sum_j f\left(e_j, y_t\right) \pi_t\left(e_j|y^{t-1}\right)}.$$

The interpretation is that given date $t-1$ conditional distribution $\pi_{t-1}\left(\cdot|y^{t-1}\right)$ and after observing y_t at date t, we can use the above equations to compute the conditional distribution $\pi_t\left(\cdot|y^t\right)$ and $\pi_t\left(e_i|y^{t-1}\right)$ at date t. We may set the initial prior distribution $\pi_0\left(e_i|y^{-1}\right)$ as the stationary distribution of the Markov chain.

10.2 Control Problems

For simplicity, consider a finite-horizon problem. Suppose that the state x_t is not perfectly observable at date t. Instead, the decision maker observes a noisy signal y_t about x_t. He then chooses an action u_t. The information set at date t is given by y^t. We make some assumptions about the stochastic structure: (1) The prior distribution of x_0 is given. (2) Given the past states, signals, and actions, the conditional distribution of x_{t+1} satisfies $\Pr\left(x_{t+1}|x^t, y^t, u^t\right) = \Pr\left(x_{t+1}|x_t, u_t\right)$. (3) The conditional distribution of the signal y^t satisfies $\Pr\left(y_t|x^t, u^t, y^{t-1}\right) = \Pr\left(y_t|x_t, u_{t-1}\right)$. These assumptions are typically satisfied for the state-space representation. The objective is to maximize the following expected total rewards:

$$E\left[\sum_{t=0}^{T-1} \beta^t r\left(x_t, u_t, t\right) + \beta^T R\left(x_T\right)\right],$$

where R is a terminal reward function.

Given the assumptions above, we can compute

$$\Pr\left(x_{t+1}, y_{t+1}|x^t, y^t, u^t\right) = \Pr\left(y_{t+1}|x_{t+1}, x^t, y^t, u^t\right) \Pr\left(x_{t+1}|x^t, y^t, u^t\right)$$

$$= \Pr\left(y_{t+1}|x_{t+1}, u_t\right) \Pr\left(x_{t+1}|x_t, u_t\right).$$

Define the posterior distribution as

$$P_t(x_t) = \Pr\left(x_t | y^t, u^{t-1}\right).$$

We can show that

$$P_{t+1}(x_{t+1}) = \Pr\left(x_{t+1} | y^{t+1}, u^t\right) = \frac{\Pr\left(x_{t+1}, y_{t+1} | y^t, u^t\right)}{\Pr\left(y_{t+1} | y^t, u^t\right)}$$

$$= \frac{\sum_{x_t} \Pr\left(x_{t+1}, x_t, y_{t+1} | y^t, u^t\right)}{\sum_{x_{t+1}} \sum_{x_t} \Pr\left(x_{t+1}, x_t, y_{t+1} | y^t, u^t\right)}$$

$$= \frac{\sum_{x_t} \Pr\left(x_t | y^t, u^t\right) \Pr\left(x_{t+1}, y_{t+1} | x_t, y^t, u^t\right)}{\sum_{x_{t+1}} \sum_{x_t} \Pr\left(x_{t+1}, x_t, y_{t+1} | y^t, u^t\right)}$$

$$= \frac{\sum_{x_t} P_t(x_t) \Pr\left(x_{t+1}, y_{t+1} | x_t, u_t\right)}{\sum_{x_{t+1}} \sum_{x_t} P_t(x_t) \Pr\left(x_{t+1}, y_{t+1} | x_t, u_t\right)}.$$

This equation gives a recursive equation for linking today's posterior distribution of the hidden state P to tomorrow's P^*. Using this distribution as a state variable, we can then establish the following dynamic programming equation:

$$V(P, t) = \max_u \sum_x P(x) r(x, u, t)$$

$$+ \beta \sum_x \sum_y \sum_z P(z) a_t(x, y | z, u) V(P^*, t+1),$$

where $V(P, t)$ is the value function for $t = 0, 1, ..., T - 1$, and

$$V(P, T) = \sum_x P(x) R(x), a_t(x, y | z, u) = \Pr\left(x_{t+1} = x, y_{t+1} = y | x_t = z, u_t = u\right).$$

In applications, the posterior distribution is an infinite-dimensional object. This makes the general control problem under partial information hard to solve numerically. In some special cases such as normal distributions or discrete states, the posterior distribution is finite-dimensional. For example, for the linear state-space representation, the Kalman filter implies that the posterior distribution of the hidden state is Gaussian. Hence we can use the conditional mean and conditional variance to summarize this distribution.

Example 10.2.1 (Life-cycle consumption–saving problem, Guvenen 2007) *Guvenen (2007) studies a life-cycle consumption–saving problem when a household's log labor income follows the process in (10.5) and (10.6). The household* *observes past income data but does not observe $\alpha, \beta,$ and z. It solves the following problem:*

$$\max_{\{c_t, s_{t+1}\}} E \sum_{t=0}^{T} \beta^t U(c_t)$$

subject to the budget constraint:

$$c_t + s_{t+1} = Rs_t + \exp(y_t), \quad s_{t+1} \geq 0. \tag{10.15}$$

To solve this problem, we first derive the state-space representation as in example 10.1.1 and then apply the Kalman filter to derive the recursion:

$$\hat{x}_{t+1|t} = A\hat{x}_{t|t-1} + AK_t\left(y_t - G_t\hat{x}_{t|t-1}\right). \tag{10.16}$$

Finally, we can write the dynamic programming problem as follows:

$$V_{T+1} = 0,$$

and for $t = 0, 1, ..., T,$

$$V_t\left(s_t, y_t, \hat{x}_{t|t-1}\right) = \max_{c_t, a_{t+1}} U(c_t) + \beta E\left[V_{t+1}\left(s_{t+1}, y_{t+1}, \hat{x}_{t+1|t}\right) | s_t, y_t, \hat{x}_{t|t-1}\right]$$

subject to (10.15) and (10.16). Note that the conditional expectation is with respect to y_{t+1} only. The conditional distribution of y_{t+1} is $N\left(G_t\hat{x}_{t+1|t}, \Omega_{t+1|t}\right)$. For a general utility function U, there is no analytical solution. One has to use a numerical method to solve this dynamic problem. Note that we have used $(y_t, \hat{x}_{t|t-1})$ as state variables. Alternatively, we can use $\hat{x}_{t|t}$ as a state variable.

10.3 Linear-Quadratic Control

Consider the following linear-quadratic control problem:

$$\max_{\{u_t\}} -E \sum_{t=0}^{\infty} \beta^t r(x_t, u_t), \quad \beta \in (0, 1],$$

subject to

$$x_{t+1} = Ax_t + Bu_t + \eta_{t+1},$$
$$y_t = Gx_t + v_t,$$

where

$$r(x, u) = \frac{1}{2}\left(x'Qx + u'Ru + 2x'Su\right).$$

Assume that $\{\eta_t\}$ and $\{v_t\}$ are IID Gaussian processes and independent of each other and that x_0 is Gaussian and independent of other random variables. The decision maker observes only y^t at date t.

In the case of full information studied in section 9.3, we have shown that the value function takes the form:

$$V(x_t) = -\frac{1}{2}x_t'Px_t + \text{constant},$$

where P satisfies equation (9.12), and the optimal policy is given by

$$u_t = -Fx_t, \tag{10.17}$$

where F is given by (9.17). We will show that under partial information, the value function takes the form:

$$V(\hat{x}_{t|t}) = -\frac{1}{2}\hat{x}_{t|t}'P\hat{x}_{t|t} + \text{constant},$$

where P also satisfies (9.12). However, the constant term may be different from that in the full information case. We will also show that the optimal policy is given by

$$u_t = -F\hat{x}_{t|t},$$

where F satisfies (9.17). This result is a form of **certainty equivalence**: the optimal control is obtained by substituting the estimate of the state $\hat{x}_{t|t}$ for the actual state x_t in the decision rule for the full information optimal control.

We now sketch a proof. The first step is to apply the long-run stationary Kalman filter to obtain the estimate $\hat{x}_{t|t}$. Then conjecture

$$V(\hat{x}_{t|t}) = -\frac{1}{2}\hat{x}_{t|t}'P\hat{x}_{t|t} + \text{constant}.$$

Define

$$\Delta_t \equiv x_t - \hat{x}_{t|t} = Ax_{t-1} + \eta_t - A\hat{x}_{t-1|t-1} - Ka_t.$$

It is independent of control u_t since $E\left[(x_t - \hat{x}_{t|t})u_t\right] = 0$. We first compute

$$E_t\left[(x_t'Qx_t + u_t'Ru_t + 2x_t'Su_t)\right]$$
$$= E_t\left[\left((\hat{x}_{t|t} + \Delta_t)'Q(\hat{x}_{t|t} + \Delta_t) + u_t'Ru_t + 2(\hat{x}_{t|t} + \Delta_t)'Su_t\right)\right]$$
$$= \left(\hat{x}_{t|t}'Q\hat{x}_{t|t} + u_t'Ru_t + 2\hat{x}_{t|t}'Su_t\right) + ...,$$

where we use the notation "+..." to denote terms independent of the control u_t. Here E_t denotes the conditional expectation operator given information y^t. Next we compute

$$E_t \left[\hat{x}'_{t+1|t+1} P \hat{x}_{t+1|t+1} \right]$$

$$= E_t \left[(x_{t+1} - \Delta_{t+1})' P (x_{t+1} - \Delta_{t+1}) \right]$$

$$= E_t \left[x'_{t+1} P x_{t+1} \right] - 2 E_t \left[\Delta'_{t+1} P x_{t+1} \right] + E_t \left[\Delta'_{t+1} P \Delta_{t+1} \right]$$

$$= E_t \left[x'_{t+1} P x_{t+1} \right] - 2 E_t \left[\Delta'_{t+1} P (A x_t + B u_t + \eta_{t+1}) \right] + E_t \left[\Delta'_{t+1} P \Delta_{t+1} \right]$$

$$= E_t \left[(A x_t + B u_t + \eta_{t+1})' P (A x_t + B u_t + \eta_{t+1}) \right] + \dots$$

$$= E_t \left[(A x_t + B u_t)' P (A x_t + B u_t) \right] + \dots$$

$$= E_t \left[(A \hat{x}_{t|t} + B u_t)' P (A \hat{x}_{t|t} + B u_t) \right] + \dots.$$

We then solve the problem

$$V\left(\hat{x}_{t|t}\right) = \max_{u_t} E_t \left[-\frac{1}{2} \left(x'_t Q x_t + u'_t R u_t + 2 x'_t S u_t \right) \right]$$

$$- \frac{\beta}{2} E_t \left[\hat{x}'_{t+1|t+1} P \hat{x}_{t+1|t+1} \right] + \dots$$

$$= \max_{u_t} \; -\frac{1}{2} \left(\hat{x}'_{t|t} Q \hat{x}_{t|t} + u'_t R u_t + 2 \hat{x}'_{t|t} S u_t \right)$$

$$+ \beta E_t \left[-\frac{1}{2} \left(A \hat{x}_{t|t} + B u_t \right)' P \left(A \hat{x}_{t|t} + B u_t \right) \right] + \dots.$$

Clearly, this is the full-information problem in which the state is $\hat{x}_{t|t}$. Following the same analysis as in section 9.3 delivers the desired result.

10.4   Exercises

1. Let

$$y_t = \mu + \varepsilon_t + b \varepsilon_{t-1}.$$

Write down the state-space representation.

2. Consider example 10.1.1. Set $\alpha = \beta = 0$. Assume that ρ is unknown and normally distributed with mean $\mu_\rho \in (0,1)$ and variance σ_ρ^2. Derive the Kalman filter.

3. Let $x_t = \theta$ for all t and $y_t = \theta + v_t$. Assume that θ is Gaussian with mean μ and variance Σ_0. Derive the Kalman filter. What happens in the long run?

4. There is another way of writing the state-space representation:

$$x_{t+1} = Ax_t + Bu_t + C\varepsilon_t,$$
$$y_t = Gx_t + Hu_{t-1} + D\varepsilon_t.$$

Derive the Kalman filter for this formulation.

5. Derive the Kalman filter for the state-space representation (10.3) and (10.4).

6. Consider examples 10.1.1 and 10.2.1. Set $\alpha = \beta = 0$ and $u(c) = -\exp(-\gamma c)/\gamma$.

   a. Derive the Kalman filter.

   b. Let $T = 1$. Solve the dynamic programming problem.

   c. Solve the dynamic programming problem for any finite T.

   d. If we use $\hat{x}_{t|t}$ as a state variable instead of $\hat{x}_{t|t-1}$, how do we write down the Bellman equation?

11   Numerical Methods

Quantitative answers are often needed for many economic problems. For example, how much do technology shocks contribute to business cycles? What is the impact of a major tax reform on the macroeconomy? To provide quantitative answers, numerical solutions are needed. In this chapter we present some widely used numerical methods for solving dynamic programming problems and equilibrium systems. The reader is referred to Judd (1998), Miranda and Fackler (2002), and Adda and Cooper (2003) for other textbook treatments of numerical methods in economics and finance.[1]

11.1   Numerical Integration

Computing expected values is necessary in economic problems under uncertainty. This section studies how to numerically compute integral $\int_D f(x) \, dx$, where $f : \mathbb{R}^n \to \mathbb{R}$ is an integrable function over the domain D. There are several numerical methods as detailed by Judd (1998). In this section we focus on the Gaussian quadrature method. We start with the one-dimensional case and then discuss the multidimensional case.

11.1.1   Gaussian Quadrature

The idea of the quadrature method is to approximate the integral by summation:

$$\int_a^b f(x) \, dx \simeq \sum_{i=1}^n w_i f(x_i),$$

---

1. Miranda and Fackler (2002) provide an excellent toolbox CompEcon downloadable from the website: http://www4.ncsu.edu/unity/users/p/pfackler/www/compecon/. This toolbox can be used to solve many problems described in this chapter.

where x_i's are **quadrature nodes** and w_i's are **quadrature weights**. Newton–Cotes methods are an example of the quadrature method. The Gaussian quadrature method is constructed with respect to a specific weight function w. For a given order of approximation, this method chooses the nodes $x_1, x_2, ..., x_n$ and weights $w_1, w_2, ..., w_n$ so as to satisfy the following $2n$ conditions:

$$\int_a^b x^k w(x)\, dx = \sum_{i=1}^n w_i x_i^k, \quad k = 0, 1, ..., 2n - 1.$$

The integral approximation is then computed by forming the prescribed weighted sum of function values at the prescribed nodes:

$$\int_a^b f(x) w(x)\, dx = \sum_{i=1}^n w_i f(x_i).$$

Thus, if the function f can be approximated by polynomials accurately, then the Gaussian quadrature method will give an accurate approximation to the integral. When the weight function w is a density function, Gaussian quadrature has a straightforward interpretation. It essentially discretizes a continuous random variable as a discrete random variable with mass points x_i and probabilities w_i.

Computing the n-degree Gaussian quadrature nodes and weights is nontrivial because it requires solving $2n$ nonlinear equations. The CompEcon toolbox provided by Miranda and Fackler (2002) contains efficient numerical programs for computing Gaussian quadrature nodes and weights for different weight functions, including the most known probability distribution functions such as the uniform, normal, lognormal, exponential, gamma, and beta distributions.

The following is a list of some well-known quadrature.

- Gauss–Legendre quadrature. The weight function is $w(x) = 1$. Gauss–Legendre quadrature computes integral $\int_{-1}^1 f(x)\, dx$. A change of variables can compute integrals in any bounded interval and hence infinite intervals,

$$\int_a^b f(x)\, dx \simeq \frac{b-a}{2} \sum_{i=1}^n w_i f\left(\frac{(x_i + 1)(b - a)}{2} + a \right).$$

- Gauss–Chebyshev quadrature. This method computes

$$\int_{-1}^1 f(x) \left(1 - x^2\right)^{-1/2} dx \simeq \frac{\pi}{n} \sum_{i=1}^n f(x_i),$$

where

$$x_i = \cos\left(\frac{2i - 1}{2n} \pi \right), \quad i = 1, 2, ..., n.$$

- Gauss–Hermite quadrature. This method computes

$$\int_{-\infty}^{\infty} f(x) e^{-x^2} dx \simeq \sum_{i=1}^{n} w_i f(x_i).$$

This quadrature is very useful to compute integrals with respect to normal distributions:

$$Ef(Y) = \pi^{-1/2} \sum_{i=1}^{n} w_i f\left(\sqrt{2}\sigma x_i + \mu\right),$$

where Y is normal with mean μ and variance σ^2.

- Gauss–Laguerre quadrature. This method computes

$$\int_{0}^{\infty} e^{-x} f(x) dx \simeq \sum_{i=1}^{n} w_i f(x_i).$$

It is useful to compute present values

$$\int_{a}^{\infty} e^{-ry} f(y) dy \simeq \frac{e^{-ra}}{r} \sum_{i=1}^{n} w_i f\left(\frac{x_i}{r} + a\right).$$

11.1.2 Multidimensional Quadrature

Suppose that we want to compute the d-dimensional integral $\int_{[a,b]^d} f(x) dx$. We can use the product rule based on any one-dimensional quadrature rule. Let x_i^j, w_i^j, $i = 1, \ldots, n_j$, be one-dimensional quadrature points and weights in dimension j. The product rule gives the approximation

$$\sum_{i_1=1}^{n_1} \cdots \sum_{i_d=1}^{n_d} w_{i_1}^1 w_{i_2}^2 \cdots w_{i_d}^d f\left(x_{i_1}^1, x_{i_2}^2, \ldots, x_{i_d}^d\right).$$

For Gaussian quadrature, if w^j is a scalar weight function in dimension j, then let

$$W(x) = \Pi_{j=1}^{d} w^j(x_j).$$

Gaussian quadrature computes the integral $\int_{[a,b]^d} f(x) W(x) dx$ using the preceding approximation. We can apply a change of variables to compute the integral in any interval. A difficulty of the product approach is the curse of dimensionality. See Judd (1998) for a discussion of a nonproduct approach.

11.2   Discretizing AR(1) Processes

In economic problems, exogenous shocks are often modeled as a Markov process. When solving stochastic dynamic programming problems, we need to compute expected values with respect to the shocks. If a shock follows a discrete Markov chain, then expected values are just a simple summation. However, if a shock follows an autoregressive process of order one (AR(1)) process, then computing expectations is cumbersome. In the last section, we discussed how to compute numerical integration. In this section, we introduce two methods proposed by Tauchen (1986) and Tauchen and Hussey (1991) to approximate an AR(1) process by a discrete Markov chain.

Consider the following AR(1) process:

$$z_{t+1} = \mu(1-\rho) + \rho z_t + \sigma \varepsilon_{t+1}, \tag{11.1}$$

where μ and ρ are the unconditional mean and autocorrelation of z_t, respectively, and ε_t is IID standard normal. Without loss of generality, we set $\mu = 0$. The unconditional standard deviation of z_t is $\sigma_z = \sigma/\sqrt{1-\rho^2}$. Our goal is to construct a discrete Markov chain with the state space $\{z^i\}_{i=1}^{N}$ and the transition matrix $\pi = (\pi_{ij})$ that approximates $\{z_t\}$. Making N larger, the discrete Markov chain approximation becomes more accurate.

11.2.1   Tauchen (1986) Method

The method of Tauchen (1986) consists of the following steps:[2]

Step 1. Choose a discrete state space with N equally spaced points:

$$\left(z^i\right)_{i=1}^{N} = \left\{ z_{\min}, z_{\min} + \frac{z_{\max} - z_{\min}}{N-1}, ..., z_{\min} + \frac{N-2}{N-1}(z_{\max} - z_{\min}), z_{\max} \right\},$$

where

$$z_{\max} = m\sigma_z, \ z_{\min} = -m\sigma_z.$$

In practice, setting $m = 3$ or 4 is sufficient.

Step 2. Choose N intervals:

$$I_1 = \left(-\infty, z_{\min} + \frac{z_{\max} - z_{\min}}{2(N-1)} \right),$$

$$I_2 = \left(z_{\min} + \frac{z_{\max} - z_{\min}}{2(N-1)}, z_{\min} + \frac{3(z_{\max} - z_{\min})}{2(N-1)} \right), ...,$$

---

2. The Matlab code `markovappr.m` implements this method.

$$I_{N-1} = \left(z_{\min} + \frac{(2N-5)\,(z_{\max} - z_{\min})}{2\,(N-1)}, z_{\min} + \frac{(2N-3)\,(z_{\max} - z_{\min})}{2\,(N-1)} \right),$$

$$I_N = \left(z_{\min} + \frac{(2N-3)\,(z_{\max} - z_{\min})}{2\,(N-1)}, \infty \right).$$

Step 3. Determine transition probabilities:

$$\pi_{ij} = \Pr\left(z_{t+1} \in I_j \,|\, z_t = z^i \right).$$

By (11.1), these transition probabilities can be easily computed.

11.2.2   Tauchen–Hussey (1991) Method

The method of Tauchen and Hussey (1991) is related to the Gauss–Hermite quadrature method discussed earlier.[3] Suppose that we want to compute the conditional expectation:

$$E\left[v\left(z'\right) | z\right] = \int_{-\infty}^{\infty} v\left(z'\right) f\left(z'|z\right) dz',$$

where $f\left(\cdot|z\right)$ is the conditional density of z_{t+1} given $z_t = z$. Using the Gauss–Hermite method, we can approximate this integral as

$$\int v\left(z'\right) f\left(z'|z\right) dz' \simeq \pi^{-1/2} \sum_{j=1}^{N} w_j v\left(\sqrt{2}\sigma x_j + \rho z \right),$$

where x_j and w_j are the Gauss–Hermite nodes and weights, respectively. The problem of this approach is that this approximation depends continuously on z. Tauchen and Hussey (1991) propose the following transformation:

$$\int v\left(z'\right) f\left(z'|z\right) dz' = \int v\left(z'\right) \frac{f\left(z'|z\right)}{f\left(z'|0\right)} f\left(z'|0\right) dz' = \frac{1}{\sqrt{\pi}} \sum_{j=1}^{N} w_j v\left(z^j\right) \frac{f\left(z^j|z\right)}{f\left(z^j|0\right)},$$

where $z^j = \sqrt{2}\sigma x_j$. Thus

$$E\left[v\left(z'\right) | z^i\right] \simeq \sum_{j=1}^{N} \tilde{\pi}_{ij} v\left(z^j\right),$$

where

$$\tilde{\pi}_{ij} = \pi^{-1/2} w_j \frac{f\left(z^j|z^i\right)}{f\left(z^j|0\right)}.$$

---

3. The Matlab program `tauch_hussey.m` implements this method. The code `gauss_herm.m` is needed.

Note that we may have

$$\sum_{j=1}^{N} \tilde{\pi}_{ij} \neq 1.$$

We can then normalize

$$\pi_{ij} = \frac{\tilde{\pi}_{ij}}{\sum_{j=1}^{N} \tilde{\pi}_{ij}},$$

and take the approximation,

$$E\left[v\left(z'\right)|z^{i}\right] \simeq \sum_{j=1}^{N} \pi_{ij} v\left(z^{j}\right).$$

Note that this is not the Gauss–Hermite approximation of the integral. But as N is sufficiently large, $\sum_{j=1}^{N} \tilde{\pi}_{ij}$ converges to one. Thus we can use the discrete Markov chain with the state space $\{z^1, z^2, ..., z^N\}$ and the transition matrix (π_{ij}) to approximate the AR(1) process.

11.2.3   Simulating a Markov Chain

Suppose that $\{z_t\}$ is a Markov chain with the state space $\{z^1, z^2, ..., z^N\}$ and the transition matrix (π_{ij}). We want to simulate this Markov chain to generate a series for $t = 0, 1, 2, ..., T$. Start in period $t = 0$, and suppose that z_0 is initialized at some z^i. Next we have to assign values for z_t, $t = 1, 2, ..., T$. The following steps describe an algorithm:[4]

Step 1. Compute the cumulative distribution of the Markov chain Π^c. That is,

$$\Pi_{ij}^{c} = \sum_{k=1}^{j} \pi_{ik}$$

is the probability that the Markov chain is in a state lower or equal to j given that it was in state i in period $t - 1$.

Step 2. Set the initial state, and simulate T random numbers from a uniform distribution over $[0, 1]$: $\{p_t\}_{t=1}^{T}$.

Step 3. Assume that the Markov chain was in state i in $t - 1$, and find the index j such that

$$\Pi_{i(j-1)}^{c} < p_t \leq \Pi_{ij}^{c} \quad \text{for } j \geq 2.$$

Then z^j is the state in period t. If $p_t \leq \pi_{i1}$, then z^1 is the state in period t.

---

4. The Matlab code `markovsimul.m` implements this algorithm.

11.3 Interpolation

Function approximations are an important step in solving computational problems. Generally speaking, there are three methods to approximate a given function f. The first method is based on a local approximation using data of f around a particular point x^*. The Taylor expansion theorem is the main theory behind this method. The perturbation method discussed in chapters 1 and 2 and in section 11.4 belongs to this category. The second approximation method uses global properties of f. For example, an L^p approximation finds a function g that is close to f over some domain in the L^p norm. This approximation method typically requires too much information to be feasible in applications. The third approximation method is interpolation, which uses a finite set of data to fit the function f. In particular, it uses n conditions to determine n free parameters. There is also a method, called regression, that lies between L^p approximation and interpolation in that it uses m conditions to fix n parameters where $m > n$. This method is more stable but requires more information than interpolation, and it is less accurate than the L^p approximation.

In this section we focus on the interpolation method.[5] We start with the one-dimensional case to explain the key idea. Consider a continuous function $f : [a, b] \rightarrow \mathbb{R}$. The objective of interpolation is to approximate f by $\hat{f}$,

$$\hat{f}(x) = \sum_{j=1}^{n} c_j \phi_j(x),$$

where n is called the **degree of interpolation** or **the degree of approximation**, $\phi_1, \phi_2, ...,$ and ϕ_n are linearly independent **basis functions**, and $c_1, c_2, ...,$ and c_n are **basis coefficients**.

The first step in implementing the interpolation method is to choose suitable basis functions. There are two ways of specifying basis functions. The **spectral method** uses basis functions which are almost everywhere nonzero on $[a, b]$. Typically these functions are polynomials. The **finite element method** uses basis functions that are nonzero only on small subdomains of $[a, b]$. These functions are typically splines. In the next two subsections we will discuss these two types of basis functions.

The second step in implementing the interpolation method is to determine basis coefficients $c_1, ..., c_n$. A natural way to solve these n coefficients is to use n data points (x_i, y_i), where $y_i = f(x_i)$ is known, such that $\hat{f}(x_i) = y_i$, $i = 1, 2, .., n$. That is,

---

5. The CompEcon toolbox designed by Miranda and Fackler (2002) contains many useful Matlab programs for implementing the approximation methods discussed in this section.

we solve the following system of n equations:

$$\sum_{j=1}^{n} c_j \phi_j(x_i) = f(x_i), \quad i = 1, ..., n.$$

We can rewrite it in a matrix form:

$$\Phi c = y,$$

where $\Phi_{ij} = \phi_j(x_i)$. This equation is called the **interpolation equation** and the matrix Φ is called the **interpolation matrix**. The points $x_1, x_2, ..., x_n$ are called **interpolation nodes**. The choice of the degree of interpolation and the interpolation nodes are important for an accurate approximation.

When the number m of interpolation nodes exceeds the number n of basis coefficients, we cannot use the interpolation equation. Instead, we can use the **least squares method** or the **regression method** by solving the following problem:

$$\min_{\{c_i\}} \sum_{i=1}^{m} \left[f(x_i) - \sum_{j=1}^{n} c_j \phi_j(x_i) \right]^2, \quad m > n.$$

This problem leads to the solution

$$c = (\Phi'\Phi)^{-1} \Phi'y,$$

which is equivalent to the the interpolation equation if $m = n$ and Φ is invertible.

Interpolation conditions may not be limited to data on function values. The information about function derivatives can also be used to solve for the basis coefficients.

11.3.1   Orthogonal Polynomials

A natural family of basis functions is the **monomial basis** $\{1, x, x^2, x^3...\}$. The interpolation matrix Φ is given by

$$\Phi = \begin{bmatrix} 1 & x_1 & ... & x_1^{n-1} \\ 1 & x_2 & ... & x_2^{n-1} \\ ... \\ 1 & x_n & ... & x_n^{n-1} \end{bmatrix}.$$

This matrix is ill-conditioned, and hence interpolation using this basis yields a large rounding error. One reason is that the monomial basis functions are not mutually orthogonal.

Definition 11.3.1   *A weighting function $w(x)$ on $[a,b]$ is any function that is positive and has a finite integral over $[a,b]$. Given a weighting function $w(x)$, define an inner product for integrable functions on $[a,b]$,*

$$<f,g>_w = \int_a^b f(x)g(x)w(x)\,dx.$$

The family of functions $\{\phi_j\}$ on $[a,b]$ is mutually orthogonal with respect to $w(x)$ if

$$<\phi_i,\phi_j>_w = 0, \quad i \ne j.$$

The inner product induces a norm

$$\|f\|_w = <f,f>_w,$$

and hence a natural metric.

The following is a list of commonly used orthogonal basis functions:

- Legendre polynomials. The nth Legendre polynomial is

$$P_n(x) = \frac{(-1)^n}{2^n n!} \frac{d^n}{dx^n} \left[(1-x^2)^n \right], \quad P_0(x) = 1,\ x \in [-1,1].$$

  The weighting function is $w(x) = 1$ on $[-1,1]$. We can use the transformation $z = 2(x-a)/(b-a) - 1$ to define functions on any bounded interval $[a,b]$.

- Chebyshev polynomials. The nth Chebyshev polynomial on $[-1,1]$ is defined recursively:

$$T_0(x) = 1,\ T_1(x) = x,\ T_2(x) = 2x^2 - 1,$$
$$T_n(x) = 2xT_{n-1}(x) - T_{n-2}(x).$$

  The weighting function is $w(x) = (1-x^2)^{-1/2}$. One can also equivalently define

$$T_n(x) = \cos(n \arccos(x)).$$

- Laguerre polynomials. The nth member is

$$L_n(x) = \frac{e^x}{n!} \frac{d^n}{dx^n} \left(x^n e^{-x} \right), \quad L_0(x) = 1,\quad x \in [0,\infty).$$

  The weighting function is $w(x) = e^{-x}$ on $[0,\infty)$. Laguerre polynomials are used to approximate functions of time in deterministic models.

- Hermite polynomials. The nth member is

$$H_n(x) = (-1)^n e^{x^2} \frac{d^n}{dx^n} \left(e^{-x^2} \right), \quad H_0(x) = 1,\quad x \in (-\infty, \infty).$$

The weight function is $w(x) = e^{-x^2}$. Hermite polynomials are often used to approximate functions of normal random variables.

We will focus on Chebyshev polynomials because they possess some desirable properties. The roots of $T_n(x)$ on $[-1,1]$ are given by

$$x_k = \cos\left(\frac{\pi(2k-1)}{2n}\right), \quad k = 1, 2, \ldots, n.$$

$T_n(x)$ has $n+1$ extrema at

$$x = \cos\left(\frac{\pi k}{n}\right), \quad k = 0, 1, \ldots, n.$$

At all maxima, $T_n(x) = 1$ and at all minima, $T_n(x) = -1$. Figure 11.1 illustrates nine Chebyshev polynomial basis functions up to nine degrees on the unit interval.

The Chebyshev polynomials have a discrete orthogonality property. If x_k ($k = 1, 2, \ldots, m$) are the m roots of $T_m(x)$, and if $i, j < m$, then

$$\sum_{k=1}^{m} T_i(x_k) T_j(x_k) = \begin{cases} 0 & \text{if } i \neq j, \\ m/2 & \text{if } i = j \neq 0, \\ m & \text{if } i = j = 0. \end{cases}$$

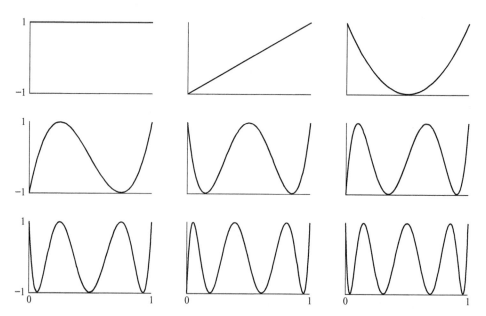

Figure 11.1
Chebychev polynomial basis functions up to nine degrees on the unit interval.

Using this property, we now compute the basis coefficients $c_1, c_2, ..., c_n$ when the basis functions are given by

$$\phi_j(x) = T_{j-1}(x), \quad j = 1, ..., n.$$

A suitable choice of interpolation nodes is critical for a good approximation. We will choose the n roots of $T_n(x)$, $\{x_1, x_2, ..., x_k\}$, as the interpolation nodes. We can then compute $\Phi'\Phi = \text{diag}(n,, n/2, n/2, ..., n/2)$. Using the least squares formula $c = (\Phi'\Phi)^{-1}\Phi'y$ and the discrete orthogonality property, we can derive

$$c_j = \frac{\sum_{k=1}^{n} f(x_k) T_{j-1}(x_k)}{\sum_{k=1}^{n} T_{j-1}(x_k)^2} = \begin{cases} \frac{1}{n} \sum_{k=1}^{n} f(x_k) T_{j-1}(x_k) & \text{for } j = 1, \\[2mm] \frac{2}{n} \sum_{k=1}^{n} f(x_k) T_{j-1}(x_k) & \text{for } j \geq 2. \end{cases}$$

We then obtain the **Chebyshev interpolant**:

$$I_{n-1}^{f}(x) = \sum_{i=1}^{n} c_i T_{i-1}(x).$$

One can also check that I_{n-1}^{f} and f are exactly matched at the n roots of $T_n(x)$.

The following theorem from Rivlin (1990, p. 14) guarantees that interpolation at the zeros of Chebyshev polynomials lead to asymptotically valid approximations of f.

Theorem 11.3.1 (Chebyshev interpolation theorem) *Suppose that function* $f : [-1, 1] \to R$ *is k times continuously differentiable for some $k \geq 1$. Let I_n^{f} be the degree n Chebyshev interpolant of f. Then there is some d_k such that for all n,*

$$\left\| f - I_n^{f} \right\|_{\infty} \leq \left(\frac{2}{\pi} \ln(n+1) + 2 \right) \frac{d_k}{n^k} \left\| f^{(k)} \right\|_{\infty},$$

where $\|\cdot\|_{\infty}$ is the uniform norm.

This theorem says that the Chebyshev interpolant converges to f rapidly as we increase the degree of interpolation. Note that interpolation at uniformly spaced nodes does not necessarily converge as we use more points. Thus the Chebyshev interpolant is extremely useful whenever the approximated function is smooth.

We may use more interpolation nodes to construct a Chebyshev interpolation of lower degree. Suppose that n is large so that I_n^{f} approximates f almost perfectly. Consider the truncated approximation:

$$I_{m-1}(x) = \sum_{i=1}^{m} c_i T_{i-1}(x), \quad m << n, \tag{11.2}$$

where the terms for $k = m + 1, ..., n$ are dropped from I_{n-1}^f. Since $T_k(x)$ is bounded between -1 and 1, the difference between I_{n-1}^f and I_{m-1} is bounded by the sum of the dropped terms c_k for $k = m + 1, ..., c_n$. Since the coefficients are rapidly decreasing, the difference is dominated by $c_{m+1}T_m(x)$. Thus the truncated approximation I_{m-1} is almost the same as the minimax polynomial that (among all polynomials of the same degree) has the smallest maximum deviation from the true function f. In this sense, the Chebyshev polynomial interpolation is almost the most accurate approximation. See section 6.7 of Judd (1998) for a more formal discussion and for an equivalent Chebyshev regression algorithm to compute (11.2).

11.3.2   Splines

Chebyshev polynomials interpolation works well for well-behaved smooth functions. For functions that have kinks or regions of high curvatures, it seems better to use spline approximations (or more general finite element methods). The idea of constructing a spline interpolation is to first divide the domain into nonintersecting subdomains called **elements**. The function is approximated by some polynomials on each subdomain. The local approximations are then patched together to get a global approximation. A function $\phi(x)$ on $[a, b]$ is a **spline of order** k if ϕ is C^{k-2} on $[a, b]$ and there is a grid of points (called **nodes** or **breaks**), $a = x_0 < x_1 < ... < x_n = b$, such that ϕ is a polynomial of order at most $k - 1$ on each subinterval $[x_i, x_{i+1}]$ $i = 0, 1, ..., n - 1$. Note that a spline of order 2 (or **linear spline**) is a piecewise linear function.

A **cubic spline** ϕ (that is of order 4) has the following properties: (1) $\phi(x_i) = f(x_i) = y_i$, $i = 0, 1, ..., n$. (2) On each subinterval $[x_i, x_{i+1}]$, $\phi(x) = a_i + b_i x + c_i x^2 + d_i x^3$, $i = 0, 1, ..., n - 1$. (3) $\lim_{x \uparrow x_i} \phi(x_i) = \lim_{x \downarrow x_i} \phi(x_i)$, $\lim_{x \uparrow x_i} \phi'(x_i) = \lim_{x \downarrow x_i} \phi'(x_i)$, and $\lim_{x \uparrow x_i} \phi''(x_i) = \lim_{x \downarrow x_i} \phi''(x_i)$. There are $4n - 2$ conditions for $4n$ coefficients. We need two additional restrictions. The **natural spline** imposes $\phi''(x_0) = \phi''(x_n) = 0$. The **Hermite spline** imposes $\phi'(x_0) = f'(x_0)$ and $\phi'(x_n) = f'(x_n)$ (called the **clamped end condition**) if those derivatives are known. Cubic splines can approximate an almost smooth function with kinks or with small regions of high curvatures. The **not-a-knot end condition** requires that $\lim_{x \uparrow x_1} \phi'''(x) = \lim_{x \downarrow x_1} \phi'''(x)$ and $\lim_{x \uparrow x_{n-1}} \phi'''(x) = \lim_{x \downarrow x_{n-1}} \phi'''(x)$. The Matlab spline toolbox uses the not-a-knot condition as the default and the Hermite spline as an option.

There are two approaches to representing a spline. A **pp-form** of a polynomial spline of order k provides a description in terms of its breaks $x_0, x_1, ..., x_n$ and the local polynomial coefficients c_{ji} of its n pieces,

$$p_j(x) = \sum_{i=1}^{k} (x - x_{j-1})^{k-i} c_{ji}, \quad j = 1, ..., n.$$

The **B-form** of a spline of order k is a linear combination of some basis splines or **B-splines** of the required order k. A B-spline is a spline function that has a minimal support with respect to a given degree, smoothness, and domain partition. de Boor (1978) shows that every spline function of a given degree, smoothness, and domain partition can be uniquely represented as a linear combination of B-splines of that same degree and smoothness, and over that same partition. We now construct B-splines following the method of de Boor (1978). Define the **knots** $\xi_1 = \xi_2 = \ldots = \xi_k < \xi_{k+1} < \ldots < \xi_{k+n} = \ldots = \xi_{k+n+k-1}$, with $\xi_{k+i} = x_i, i = 0, 1, \ldots, n$, and the jth B-spline of order k for these knots:

$$B_{j1}(x) = \begin{cases} 1 & \text{if } x \in [\xi_j, \xi_{j+1}), \\ 0 & \text{else,} \end{cases}$$

and

$$B_{jk}(x) = \frac{x - \xi_j}{\xi_{j+k-1} - \xi_j} B_{j,k-1}(x) + \frac{\xi_{j+k} - x}{\xi_{j+k} - \xi_{j+1}} B_{j+1,k-1}(x),$$

for $j = 1, 2, \ldots, n + k - 1$. Note that $B_{jk}(x)$ is a nonnegative piecewise polynomial of degree $k - 1$ and is zero outside the interval $[\xi_j, \xi_{j+k}]$. We can then write the B-form of a spline of order k as

$$\phi(x) = \sum_{j=1}^{n+k-1} B_{jk}(x) a_j,$$

where the coefficients a_j are called **de Boor points** or **control points**.

As an example, the B-spline of order 2 with knots $\xi_1 = \xi_2 = x_0 < \xi_3 = x_1 < \ldots < x_n = \xi_{n+2} = \xi_{n+3}$ is given by

$$B_{j2}(x) = \begin{cases} \frac{\xi_{j+1} - x}{\xi_{j+1} - \xi_j} & \text{if } x \in [\xi_j, \xi_{j+1}] \text{ if } \xi_j < \xi_{j+1}, \\ \frac{x - \xi_{j+1}}{\xi_{j+2} - \xi_{j+1}} & \text{if } x \in [\xi_{j+1}, \xi_{j+2}] \text{ if } \xi_{j+1} < \xi_{j+2}, \\ 0 & \text{otherwise,} \end{cases}$$

for $j = 1, 2, \ldots, n + 1$. These are linear splines and are also called **tent** functions. Figure 11.2 illustrates $9 = n + k - 1$ pieces of linear B-splines (order $k = 2$) with $n + 1 = 9$ equally spaced breakpoints on the unit interval. Figure 11.3 illustrates $9 = n + k - 1$ pieces of cubic B-splines (order $k = 4$) with $n + 1 = 7$ equally spaced breakpoints on the unit interval.

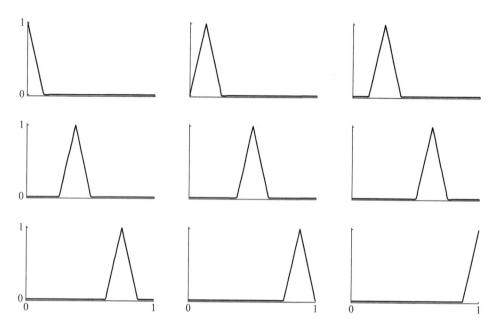

Figure 11.2
Linear B-splines with nine equally spaced breakpoints $\{0, 1/8, 1/4, 3/8, 1/2, 5/8, 3/4, 7/8, 1\}$

In many applications, preserving the shape of the approximating functions is important. For example, when approximating value functions, keeping concavity is important. Schumaker (1983) proposes a shape-preserving quadratic spline.[6] See Judd (1998 p. 231) for an introduction of this construction of this spline.

11.3.3   Multidimensional Approximation

Consider the problem of interpolating a d-variate function f on a d-dimensional interval

$$I = \{(x_1, x_2, ..., x_d) : a_i \leq x_i \leq b_i, i = 1, 2, ..., d\}.$$

Let $\{\phi_{ij} : j = 1, 2, ..., n_i\}$ be an n_i-degree univariate basis for real-valued functions defined on $[a_i, b_i]$, and let $\{x_{ij} : j = 1, 2, ..., n_i\}$ be a sequence of n_i interpolation nodes for the interval $[a_i, b_i]$. Then an $n = \Pi_{i=1}^d n_i$ degree interpolation on I may be constructed using the basis functions:

$$\phi_{j_1 j_2 ... j_d}(x_1, x_2, ..., x_d) = \phi_{1j_1}(x_1) \phi_{2j_2}(x_2) ... \phi_{dj_d}(x_d)$$

---

6. Leonardo Rezende wrote a Matlab program `schumaker.m` to compute this spline. Use the Matlab command `ppval` to evaluate the spline.

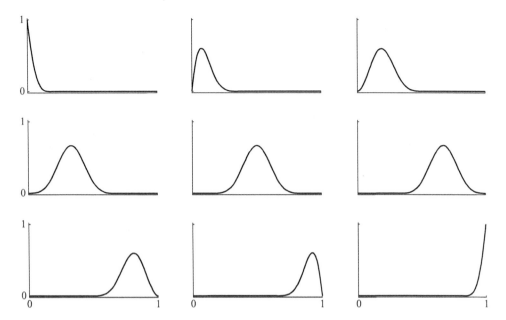

Figure 11.3
Cubic B-splines with seven equally spaced breakpoints $\{0, 1/6, 1/3, 1/2, 2/3, 5/6, 1\}$

for $i = 1, ..., d$ and $j_i = 1, 2, ..., n_i$. An approximation for f in the tensor product basis takes the form

$$\hat{f}(x_1, x_2, ..., x_d) = \sum_{j_1=1}^{n_1} \sum_{j_2=1}^{n_2} ... \sum_{j_d=1}^{n_d} c_{j_1...j_d} \phi_{j_1 j_2...j_d}(x_1, x_2, ..., x_d).$$

In tensor notation,

$$\hat{f}(x_1, x_2, ..., x_d) = [\phi_d(x_d) \otimes \phi_{d-1}(x_{d-1}) \otimes ... \otimes \phi_1(x_1)] c,$$

where c is an $n \times 1$ column vector and each ϕ_i is the $1 \times n_i$ row vector of basis functions over dimension i. When evaluated at n interpolation nodes, the equation above can be written in the matrix form

$$\Phi c = y,$$

where $\Phi = \Phi_d \otimes \Phi_{d-1} \otimes ... \otimes \Phi_1$ is the $n \times n$ interpolation matrix, each Φ_i is an $n_i \times n_i$ univariate basis matrix, and y is the $n \times 1$ vector containing the values of f at the n interpolation nodes, properly stacked. If each Φ_d is invertible, then

$$c = \left[\Phi_d^{-1} \otimes \Phi_{d-1}^{-1} \otimes ... \otimes \Phi_1^{-1} \right] y.$$

For orthogonal polynomials, we can use least squares to compute $c = (\Phi'\Phi)^{-1}\Phi'y$ when the number of nodes exceeds the degree of interpolation.

Now we take an example from Miranda and Fackler (2002) to illustrate the tensor product basis. Consider a two-dimensional basis built from univariate monomial bases with $n_1 = 3$ and $n_2 = 2$. Then the vectors of basis functions for each dimension are

$$\phi_1(x_1) = \begin{bmatrix} 1 & x_1 & x_1^2 \end{bmatrix}, \quad \phi_2(x_2) = \begin{bmatrix} 1 & x_2 \end{bmatrix}.$$

The full basis functions are listed in the vector:

$$\phi(x) = \begin{bmatrix} 1 & x_2 \end{bmatrix} \otimes \begin{bmatrix} 1 & x_1 & x_1^2 \end{bmatrix} = \begin{bmatrix} 1 & x_1 & x_1^2 & x_2 & x_1x_2 & x_1^2x_2 \end{bmatrix}.$$

Construct a grid of nodes from the univariate nodes $x_1 = \{0,1,2\}$ and $x_2 = \{0,1\}$. Then

$$\Phi_1 = \begin{bmatrix} 1 & 0 & 0 \\ 1 & 1 & 1 \\ 1 & 2 & 4 \end{bmatrix}, \quad \Phi_2 = \begin{bmatrix} 1 & 0 \\ 1 & 1 \end{bmatrix},$$

and

$$\Phi = \Phi_2 \otimes \Phi_1 = \begin{bmatrix} 1 & 0 & 0 & 0 & 0 & 0 \\ 1 & 1 & 1 & 0 & 0 & 0 \\ 1 & 2 & 4 & 0 & 0 & 0 \\ 1 & 0 & 0 & 1 & 0 & 0 \\ 1 & 1 & 1 & 1 & 1 & 1 \\ 1 & 2 & 4 & 1 & 2 & 4 \end{bmatrix}.$$

Stacking the interpolation nodes yields

$$X = \begin{bmatrix} 0 & 0 \\ 1 & 0 \\ 2 & 0 \\ 0 & 1 \\ 1 & 1 \\ 2 & 1 \end{bmatrix}.$$

Let $y_i = f(z_i)$ where z_i is the ith row of the matrix X. We then obtain the vector y.

The tensor product approach suffers from the curse of dimensionality when the dimension is high. Judd (1998) recommends to use complete polynomial bases; see Judd (1988, p. 239).

11.4   Perturbation Methods

As Judd (1998) points out, the basic idea of perturbation methods is to formulate a general problem, find a special case with a known solution, and then use the special case and its solution as a reference point for computing approximate solutions to the nearby general problem. The foundation of this approach is the implicit function theorem and the Taylor expansion theorem. An application of this approach familiar in economics is the linearization and second-order approximation methods in solving deterministic and stochastic nonlinear difference equations. Perturbation methods have in fact wide applications in economics, including performing comparative statics and solving difference or differential equations.

In this section we take an example from Hansen, Heaton, and Li (2008) to illustrate the method. Consider a representative agent with the following recursive utility (Kreps and Porteus 1978; Epstein and Zin 1989):

$$V_t = \left[(1 - \beta) C_t^{1-\rho} + \beta \mathcal{R}_t \left(V_{t+1} \right)^{1-\rho} \right]^{1/(1-\rho)}, \tag{11.3}$$

where

$$\mathcal{R}_t \left(V_{t+1} \right) = \left[E_t \left(V_{t+1}^{1-\gamma} \right) \right]^{1/(1-\gamma)}.$$

Here the parameter γ measures the degree of risk aversion and $1/\rho$ measures elasticity of intertemporal substitution (EIS). We will discuss general recursive utility in chapter 20. Aggregate consumption follows the dynamics

$$\ln \frac{C_{t+1}}{C_t} = \mu_c + x_t + \sigma_c \varepsilon_{c,t+1},$$

$$x_{t+1} = \rho x_t + \sigma_x \varepsilon_{x,t+1},$$

where $\varepsilon_{c,t}$ and $\varepsilon_{x,t}$ are IID standard normals and mutually independent. Our objective is to compute the utility value V_t.

We will derive a closed-form expression for V_t in the special case with unitary EIS $\rho = 1$. We will use the perturbation method to derive an approximate solution for V_t for the general case with $\rho \neq 1$.

To do so, we rewrite (11.3) as

$$\frac{V_t}{C_t} = \left[(1 - \beta) + \beta \mathcal{R}_t \left(\frac{V_{t+1}}{C_{t+1}} \frac{C_{t+1}}{C_t} \right)^{1-\rho} \right]^{1/(1-\rho)},$$

and define

$$v_t = \ln \left(\frac{V_t}{C_t} \right) \quad \text{and} \quad c_t = \ln C_t.$$

We then have

$$v_t = \frac{1}{1-\rho} \ln\left((1-\beta) + \beta \exp\left[(1-\rho) \, \mathcal{Q}_t \, (v_{t+1} + c_{t+1} - c_t)\right]\right), \qquad (11.4)$$

where

$$\mathcal{Q}_t \, (v_{t+1}) = \frac{1}{1-\gamma} \ln E_t \exp\left[(1-\gamma) \, v_{t+1}\right].$$

When $\rho = 1$, we can show that

$$v_t = \beta \mathcal{Q}_t \, (v_{t+1} + c_{t+1} - c_t)$$

$$= \frac{\beta}{1-\gamma} \ln E_t \exp\left[(1-\gamma) \, (v_{t+1} + c_{t+1} - c_t)\right], \qquad (11.5)$$

and guess that

$$v_t = Ax_t + \mu_v, \qquad (11.6)$$

where A and μ_v are constants to be determined.

This conjecture helps us compute

$$\ln E_t \exp\left[(1-\gamma) \, (v_{t+1} + c_{t+1} - c_t)\right]$$
$$= \ln E_t \exp\left[(1-\gamma) \, (Ax_{t+1} + \mu_v + \mu_c + x_t + \sigma_c \varepsilon_{c,t+1})\right]$$
$$= \ln E_t \exp\left[(1-\gamma) \, (A\rho x_t + A\sigma_x \varepsilon_{x,t+1} + \mu_v + \mu_c + x_t + \sigma_c \varepsilon_{c,t+1})\right]$$
$$= (1-\gamma) \left[(A\rho + 1) \, x_t + \mu_v + \mu_c\right] + \frac{(1-\gamma)^2}{2} \left[(A\sigma_x)^2 + \sigma_c^2\right].$$

Substituting the expression above and our conjecture into (11.5) and matching coefficients, we find that

$$A = \frac{\beta}{1 - \beta\rho},$$

$$\mu_v = \frac{\beta}{1-\beta} \left[\mu_c + \frac{1-\gamma}{2} \left(\left(\frac{\beta\sigma_x}{1-\beta\rho}\right)^2 + \sigma_c^2\right)\right].$$

We can now use the perturbation method to solve for v_t when $\rho \neq 1$. Let $v_t = v_t \, (\rho)$. By Taylor expansion, the approximate solution is

$$v_t \, (\rho) \simeq v_t \, (1) + (\rho - 1) \, v_t' \, (1).$$

We intend to find $v_t \, (1)$ and $v_t' \, (1)$. So we use (11.4) to define a functional equation

$$0 = F \, (v_t \, (\rho), v_{t+1} \, (\rho), \rho)$$
$$\equiv \ln\left((1-\beta) + \beta \exp\left[(1-\rho) \, \mathcal{Q}_t \, (v_{t+1} \, (\rho) + c_{t+1} - c_t)\right]\right)$$
$$- (1-\rho) \, v_t \, (\rho).$$

Taking derivatives with respect to ρ yields

$$0 = \frac{\beta \exp\left[(1-\rho)\, \mathcal{Q}_t\left(v_{t+1}\left(\rho\right) + c_{t+1} - c_t\right)\right]}{(1-\beta) + \beta \exp\left[(1-\rho)\, \mathcal{Q}_t\left(v_{t+1}\left(\rho\right) + c_{t+1} - c_t\right)\right]}$$
$$\times \left[(1-\rho)\, \hat{E}_t v'_{t+1}\left(\rho\right) - \mathcal{Q}_t\left(v_{t+1}\left(\rho\right) + c_{t+1} - c_t\right)\right]$$
$$- (1-\rho)\, v'_t\left(\rho\right) + v_t\left(\rho\right),$$

where $\hat{E}_t$ is a twisted expectation with density

$$\frac{\exp\left[(1-\gamma)\left(v_{t+1}\left(\rho\right) + c_{t+1} - c_t\right)\right]}{E_t \exp\left[(1-\gamma)\left(v_{t+1}\left(\rho\right) + c_{t+1} - c_t\right)\right]}.$$

Evaluating at $\rho = 1$, we find that $v_t\left(1\right)$ and $v_{t+1}\left(1\right)$ satisfy equation (11.5). Thus $v_t\left(1\right)$ is given by (11.6). Next, taking derivatives with respect to ρ again in the equation above and evaluating at $\rho = 1$, we find that

$$v'_t\left(1\right) = \frac{-\beta\left(1-\beta\right)}{2}\left[\mathcal{Q}_t\left(v_{t+1}\left(1\right) + c_{t+1} - c_t\right)\right]^2 + \beta \tilde{E}_t\left[v'_{t+1}\left(1\right)\right], \tag{11.7}$$

where $\tilde{E}_t$ is the expectation operator with respect to the density

$$\frac{\exp\left[(1-\gamma)\left(v_{t+1}\left(1\right) + c_{t+1} - c_t\right)\right]}{E_t \exp\left[(1-\gamma)\left(v_{t+1}\left(1\right) + c_{t+1} - c_t\right)\right]}.$$

We now guess that

$$v'_t\left(1\right) = -\frac{A_d}{2}x_t^2 + B_d x_t + \mu_d.$$

Substituting this conjecture into (11.7) and matching coefficients, we can determine the coefficients A_d, B_d and μ_d. Exercise 2 asks you to complete the explicit solution.

11.5 Projection Methods

Consider the following functional equation:

$$F\left(f\right) = 0,$$

where $f : D \subset \mathbb{R}^N \to \mathbb{R}^M$ and F maps the function space $\mathfrak{F}$ of all such f to itself. The operator F may encode equilibrium conditions. For ease of exposition, we consider the case of $M = 1$ only. Since an analytical solution is typically not available, an approximated solution to f is needed. A natural approximation is to take a linear combination of some basis functions,

$$\hat{f}\left(x\right) = \sum_{j=1}^{n} c_j \phi_j\left(x\right).$$

The goal of the projection method is to determine the degree of approximation n, the vector of basis coefficients $\mathbf{c} = \{c_1, c_2, ..., c_n\}$, and the basis functions $\{\phi_1, \phi_2, ..., \phi_n\}$. As Judd (1992, 1998) explains, the projection method typically consists of the following 5 steps.

Step 1. Choose basis functions, ϕ_i, $i = 1, 2, ...$, and an inner product, $< \cdot, \cdot >$, on $\mathfrak{F}$.

  The basis functions should be flexible, capable of yielding a good approximation for the solution, and the inner products should induce useful norms on the spaces. We have discussed this issue in section 11.3. Next we decide how many basis elements to use and how to implement F.

Step 2. Choose a degree of approximation n for f, a computable approximation $\hat{F}$ of F, and a collection of n functions on $\mathfrak{F}$, $p_i : D \rightarrow \mathbb{R}, i = 1, ..., n$.

  One may start with a small value of n and increase it until some diagnostic test indicates that little is gained by continuing. Whenever possible, we choose $\hat{F} = F$. The functions p_i are the projection directions or weighting functions.

Step 3. For a guess $\mathbf{c}$, compute the approximation

$$\hat{f}(x; \mathbf{c}) = \sum_{j=1}^{n} c_j \phi_j(x)$$

and the residual function

$$R(x; \mathbf{c}) = \hat{F}\left(\hat{f}(x; \mathbf{c})\right).$$

  The initial guess of $\mathbf{c}$ should reflect some initial knowledge about the solution. After the initial guess, further guesses are generated in steps 4 and 5, where we see how we use the inner product, $< \cdot, \cdot >$, to measure how the approximation is close to the true solution.

Step 4. For each guess of $\mathbf{c}$, compute the n projections,

$$P_i(\mathbf{c}) = < R(\cdot; \mathbf{c}), p_i(\cdot) >, \quad i = 1, 2..., n.$$

Step 5. By iterating over steps 3 and 4, find $\mathbf{c}$ that sets the n projections $P_i(\mathbf{c})$ equal to zero.

  Different choices of the p_i lead to different implementations of the projection method:

• *Collocation method*   This method uses the following projection directions:

$$p_i(x) = \begin{cases} 1 & \text{if } x = x_i, \\ 0 & \text{if } x \neq x_i, \end{cases} \quad \text{for } i = 1, ..., n,$$

where the points $x_1, ..., x_n$ are selected **collocation nodes** on D. It follows from the projection equation,

$$P_i(\mathbf{c}) = <R(\cdot; \mathbf{c}), p_i(\cdot)> = 0,$$

that

$$R(x_i; \mathbf{c}) = 0, \quad i = 1, ..., n.$$

Thus, by a suitable choice of collocation nodes, one solves the system above of n equations for n basis coefficients $(c_1, c_2, ..., c_n)$.

Orthogonal collocation chooses the n roots of the $(n+1)$th basis function as collocation points.[7] The basis functions are orthogonal with respect to the inner product. Chebyshev polynomial basis functions are especially useful. Suppose that we have found a $\mathbf{c}$ such that $R(x_i; \mathbf{c}) = 0, i = 1, 2, ..., n$, where the x_i's are the n roots of $T_n(x)$. As long as $R(x; \mathbf{c})$ is smooth in x, the Chebyshev interpolation theorem says that these zero conditions force $R(x; \mathbf{c})$ to be close to zero for all x and that these are the best possible points to use if we are to force $R(x; \mathbf{c})$ to be close to zero. In practice, the performance of the orthogonal collocation method is surprisingly good.

- **Least squares method** This method chooses projections directions:

$$p_i(x) = \frac{\partial R(x; \mathbf{c})}{\partial c_i}, \quad i = 1, 2, ..., n.$$

It is equivalent to solving the following problem:

$$\min_{\mathbf{c}} <R(\cdot; \mathbf{c}), R(\cdot; \mathbf{c})>.$$

- **Galerkin method** This method chooses basis functions as projection directions:

$$p_i(x) = \phi_i(x), \quad i = 1, 2, ..., n.$$

These lead to the projection condition

$$P_i(\mathbf{c}) = <R(\cdot; \mathbf{c}), \phi_i(\cdot)> = 0, \quad i = 1, 2, ..., n.$$

- **Method of moments** This method chooses the first n polynomials as projection directions:

$$p_i(x) = x^{i-1}, \quad i = 1, 2, ..., n.$$

---

7. Note that the first basis function is typically equal to 1 and the $(n+1)$th basis function has degree n leading polynomial term and hence exactly n roots.

These lead to the projection condition:

$$P_i(\mathbf{c}) = <R(x; \mathbf{c}), x^{i-1}> = 0, \quad i = 1, 2, ..., n.$$

Choosing the projection directions is critical since the major computational task is the computation of the projection conditions. The collocation method is fastest in this regard since it evaluates $R(\cdot; \mathbf{c})$ at n points and solves a system of n nonlinear algebraic equations. More generally, the projections will involve integration when evaluating inner products $<R(\cdot; \mathbf{c}), p_i(\cdot)>$. Numerical quadrature techniques are often used to compute integration. As explained previously, a typical quadrature formula approximates $\int_a^b f(x) g(x) dx$ with a finite sum, $\sum_i f(x_i) w_i$, where the x_i's are the quadrature nodes and the w_i's are the weights. Since these formulas also evaluate $R(\cdot; \mathbf{c})$ at just a finite number of points, quadrature-based projection techniques are essentially weighted collocation methods. The advantage of quadrature formulas over collocation is that information at more points is used to compute the approximation, hopefully yielding a more accurate approximation of the projections.

There are many root-finding algorithm to solve the projection conditions $P_i(\mathbf{c}) = 0$. A good initial guess is critical for convergence. In applications, one typically uses a known solution to a special case as an initial guess or a linear approximation as an initial guess.

Now we use the following simple stochastic growth model as an example to illustrate the projection method:

$$\max E\left[\sum_{t=0}^{\infty} \beta^t u(C_t)\right]$$

subject to

$$C_t + K_{t+1} = f(K_t, z_t),$$

$$\ln z_{t+1} = \rho \ln z_t + \sigma \varepsilon_{t+1},$$

where $\{\varepsilon_t\}$ is IID standard normal and $f(k, z) = zk^\alpha + (1 - \delta)k$. The equilibrium condition consists of the Euler equation:

$$u'(f(K_t, z_t) - K_{t+1}) = \beta E_t u'(f(K_{t+1}, z_{t+1}) - K_{t+2}) f'(K_{t+1}, z_{t+1}), \tag{11.8}$$

and a transversality condition. We seek a stable solution in the form

$$K_{t+1} = g(K_t, z_t).$$

To reduce nonlinearity, we use the Euler equation to define the functional equation as

$$0 = f(k,z) - g(k,z) - (u')^{-1}\left(\beta \int I(k,z,\varepsilon)\frac{\exp\left(-\varepsilon^2/2\right)}{\sqrt{2\pi}}d\varepsilon\right) \equiv F(g)(k,z),$$

where we define

$$I(k,z,\varepsilon) \equiv u'\left(f(g(k,z),\exp(\rho\ln z + \sigma\varepsilon)) - g(g(k,z),\exp(\rho\ln z + \sigma\varepsilon))\right)$$
$$\times f'(g(k,z),\exp(\rho\ln z + \sigma\varepsilon)).$$

Since the operator F involves integration without an explicit solution, we need to use an approximation $\hat{F}$ of F. We can use the Gauss–Hermite quadrature to approximate

$$\int I(k,z,\varepsilon)\frac{\exp\left(-\varepsilon^2/2\right)}{\sqrt{2\pi}}d\varepsilon \approx \pi^{-1/2}\sum_{j=1}^{m_\varepsilon} I\left(k,z,\sqrt{2}\varepsilon_j\right)w_j,$$

where w_j and ε_j are Gauss–Hermite quadrature weights and points, respectively. We choose Chebyshev polynomials as the basis functions. Thus we need to truncate the domain such that

$$(k,z) \in [k_m,k_M] \times [z_m,z_M],$$

where $[k_m,k_M]$ must contain the deterministic steady-state value of capital, and we then set

$$z_m = \exp\left(\frac{-4\sigma}{\sqrt{1-\rho^2}}\right) \quad \text{and} \quad z_M = \exp\left(\frac{4\sigma}{\sqrt{1-\rho^2}}\right).$$

For Chebyshev polynomials, we choose the inner product

$$<f,g>_w = \int\int f(k,z)g(k,z)w(k,z)\,dkdz,$$

where

$$w(k,z) = \left[1-\left(\frac{2k-k_m-k_M}{k_M-k_m}\right)^2\right]^{-1/2}\left[1-\left(\frac{2z-z_m-z_M}{z_M-z_m}\right)^2\right]^{-1/2}.$$

We use the tensor product approximation

$$\hat{g}(k,z;\mathbf{c}) = \sum_{i=1}^{n_k}\sum_{j=1}^{n_z} c_{ij}\phi_{ij}(k,z),$$

where $n_k \times n_z$ is the degree of approximation and

$$\phi_{ij}(k,z) = T_{i-1}\left(\frac{2k - k_m - k_M}{k_M - k_m}\right) T_{j-1}\left(\frac{2z - z_m - z_M}{z_M - z_m}\right).$$

Now we can write the residual function as

$$R(k,z;\mathbf{c}) = f(k,z) - \hat{g}(k,z;\mathbf{c}) - (u')^{-1}\left(\beta \pi^{-1/2} \sum_{j=1}^{m_\varepsilon} I\left(k, z, \sqrt{2}\varepsilon_j;\mathbf{c}\right) w_j\right),$$

where

$$I(k,z,\varepsilon;\mathbf{c})$$
$$= u'(f(\hat{g}(k,z;\mathbf{c}), \exp(\rho \ln z + \sigma\varepsilon)) - \hat{g}(\hat{g}(k,z;\mathbf{c}), \exp(\rho \ln z + \sigma\varepsilon);\mathbf{c})).$$

Once we obtain the residual function, we can proceed to compute $\mathbf{c}$ numerically using one of the implementation methods above. Judd (1992, 1998) shows that the orthogonal collocation method performs well in terms of speed and accuracy. Finally, we should check that the solution is stable. This is easy to do for deterministic models. But it seems hard to check for stochastic models. One way is to check whether the ergodic set for the endogenous state is compact.

We can use other basis functions, for example, piecewise polynomials or splines. This leads to the finite element method. We refer to McGrattan (1996) for details on this method.

11.6   Numerical Dynamic Programming

From the standpoint of computation, there is an important distinction between discrete dynamic programming problems, whose state and control variables can take only a finite number of possible values, and continuous dynamic programming problems, whose state and control variables can take a continuum of possible values. This section will focus on the latter problems, since the methods for solving discrete dynamic programming problem have been well-developed in the operations research literature (e.g., Bertsekas 1987; Porteus 1980; Puterman 1990, 1994). There are two basic strategies for solving continuous dynamic programming problems numerically: (1) discrete approximation and (2) smooth approximation. Discrete approximation methods solve a discrete dynamic problem that approximates the original continuous dynamic programming problem over a finite grid of points in the state space and the action space. Smooth approximation methods use continuous or smooth functions to approximate the value function or the policy function. These methods are typically more efficient, but less reliable, than the discrete approximation methods. The reader is referred to chapter 12 of Judd (1998) and Rust (1996) for more discussions on numerical dynamic programming.

We will use a simple infinite-horizon stochastic growth model to illustrate different numerical methods. We will not treat finite-horizon problems separately. Solving a finite-horizon problem may be an intermediate step. The dynamic programming problem is given by

$$V(K,z) = \max_{C,K'>0} u(C) + \beta E\left[V(K',z')|z\right] \tag{11.9}$$

subject to

$$C + K' = f(K,z),$$

$$\ln z' = \rho \ln z + \sigma \varepsilon',$$

where ε_t is IID standard normal.

11.6.1 Discrete Approximation Methods

The first step to apply a discrete approximation method is to discretize the state space. This requires one to truncate the state space to a compact set because many dynamic programming problems in economics have unbounded state spaces. As long as the truncated state space is sufficiently large, the truncated problem can approximate the original problem arbitrarily closely. For the stochastic growth model discussed above, we choose the truncated endogenous state space as $[k_{\min}, k_{\max}]$. We take a small positive value as $k_{\min}$ and require $k_{\max}$ to be larger than the deterministic steady-state value of capital. We put grid points on $[k_{\min}, k_{\max}]$, $k_{\min} = k_1 < k_2 < ... < k_{n_k} = k_{\max}$. These points are equally spaced. But for problems with kinks, we could put more points on the domain with kinks. We then obtain the discretized space $\mathcal{K} = \{k_1, k_2, ..., k_{n_k}\}$.

For the exogenous shock, we define $s_t = \ln z_t$. Then $\{s_t\}$ is an AR(1) process. To approximate this process, we use either the Tauchen (1986) method or the Tauchen and Hussey (1991) method to derive the discretized Markov chain with the state space $\mathcal{S} = \{s_1, s_2, ..., s_{n_z}\}$ and the transition matrix (π_{ij}).

Now the original problem is transformed to a discretized dynamic programming problem:

$$V(k_m, s_i) = \max_{k' \in \mathcal{K}} u\left(f(k_m, \exp(s_i)) - k'\right) + \beta \sum_{j=1}^{n_z} \pi_{ij} V(k', s_j) \tag{11.10}$$

for $m = 1, 2, ..., n_k$ and $i = 1, 2, ..., n_z$. There are two algorithms to solve this problem.

Value Function Iteration   The first method is to iterate on the value function. It is often called the **value function iteration method** or the method of successive approximations. This means that we define the Bellman operator B on the space of bounded functions on $\mathcal{K} \times \mathcal{S}$ into itself:

$$Bv\left(k_m, s_i\right) = \max_{k' \in \mathcal{K}} u\left(f\left(k_m, \exp\left(s_i\right)\right) - k'\right) + \beta \sum_{j=1}^{n_z} \pi_{ij} v\left(k', s_j\right). \tag{11.11}$$

The solution to (11.10) is the fixed point $V = BV$. The Contracting Mapping Theorem ensures that there is a unique fixed point. To solve for this fixed point, we start with an arbitrary guess V_0 and iterate the Bellman operator

$$V_n = B\left(V_{n-1}\right) = B^n V_0.$$

Note that in the case where we set $V_0 = 0$, this method is equivalent to solving an approximate finite-horizon problem by backward induction. The Contraction Mapping Theorem guarantees the convergence of this algorithm; in particular, the contraction property implies that $||V - V_n||$ converges to zero at a geometric rate.

Policy Function Iteration   The second method iterates on the policy function. This method starts by choosing an arbitrary initial policy, g_0. Note that g_0 takes $n_k \times n_z$ discrete values. Next a policy evaluation step is carried out to compute the value function implied by the stationary decision rule g_0. This is effectively to solve the following linear system:

$$V_0\left(k_m, s_i\right) = u\left(f\left(k_m, \exp\left(s_i\right)\right) - g_0\left(k_m, s_i\right)\right) + \beta \sum_{j=1}^{n_z} \pi_{ij} V_0\left(g_0\left(k_m, s_i\right), s_j\right) \tag{11.12}$$

for the $n_k \times n_z$ values of V_0. Once the solution V_0 is obtained, a policy improvement step is used to generate an updated policy g_1:

$$g_1\left(k_m, s_i\right) = \arg\max_{k' \in \mathcal{K}} u\left(f\left(k_m, \exp\left(s_i\right)\right) - k'\right) + \beta \sum_{j=1}^{n_z} \pi_{ij} V_0\left(k', s_j\right).$$

Given g_1, we could continue the cycle of policy valuation and policy improvement steps until the first iteration n such that $g_n = g_{n-1}$ (or alternatively $V_n = V_{n-1}$). Since such a g_n satisfies the Bellman equation (11.10), it is optimal.

The policy function iteration method is much faster than the value function iteration method. The reason is closely connected to the very rapid quadratic convergence rates of Newton's method for nonlinear equations. Indeed Puterman and Brumelle (1979) show that policy iteration is a form of the Newton–Kantorovich method for finding a zero to the nonlinear mapping $F : \mathbb{R}^{n_k n_z} \to \mathbb{R}^{n_k n_z}$ defined by $F\left(V\right) = \left(I - B\right) V$.

We could use the modified policy iteration method to speed up the policy evaluation step. Instead of solving for the large linear system, we would use successive approximations to approximate the solution to (11.12). We would define an operator

$$\hat{B}V_0\left(k_m, s_i\right) = u\left(f\left(k_m, \exp\left(s_i\right)\right) - g_0\left(k_m, s_i\right)\right) + \beta\sum_{j=1}^{n_z}\pi_{ij}V_0\left(g_0\left(k_m, s_i\right), s_j\right).$$

Then the solution to the linear system is a fixed point $V_0 = \hat{B}V_0$. We would iterate on $\hat{B}$ for a small number of times to obtain an approximation of V_0.

Multigrid Method   In the previous two methods, we fixed the discretized the state space. In order to get an accurate solution, a large state space is needed that will slow down the speed. Chow and Tsitsiklis (1991) propose a multigrid method that makes convergence much faster. The idea of this method is very simple. We start with a coarse grid and get the solution to the discretized dynamic programming. Then we double the number of grid points to obtain a finer grid. In this grid we solve the discretized dynamic programming using the solution from the previous grid as an initial guess. We repeat this step until convergence.

11.6.2   Smooth Approximation Methods

The discrete approximation methods require the choice of the endogenous states to lie in the grid. Moreover many grid points are needed to get an accurate solution. Thus these methods are inefficient. A natural strategy to deal with this issue is to use value function interpolation. This method consists of the following steps.

Step 1. Discretize the endogenous state space $k_{\min} = k_1 < k_2 < ... < k_{n_k} = k_{\max}$. Discretize the AR(1) process for $\{s_t\}$ to obtain a Markov chain with state space $S = \{s_1, s_2, ..., s_{n_z}\}$ and transition matrix $\left(\pi_{ij}\right)$.

Step 2. Start with an initial guess $V_0\left(k_m, s_i\right)$ for $m = 1, 2, ..., n_k$ and $i = 1, 2, ..., n_z$. Use one of the interpolation methods introduced in section 11.3 to get an approximate $\hat{V}_0$ on $[k_{\min}, k_{\max}] \times S$.

Step 3. Compute

$$V_1\left(k_m, s_i\right) = \max_{k' \in [k_{\min}, k_{\max}]} u\left(f\left(k_m, \exp\left(s_i\right)\right) - k'\right) + \beta\sum_{j=1}^{n_z}\pi_{ij}\hat{V}_0\left(k', s_j\right).$$

Step 4. Update V_0 by V_1 and go to step 2. Keep iterating until convergence.

This method is a simple variation of the discrete value function iteration method and requires much fewer grid points to get an accurate solution with faster convergence. This method, however, still suffers from the problem of slow convergence due to the discrete state space. Next we introduce two more efficient methods based on polynomial approximations.

Projection Methods   Projection methods approximate the value function by a linear combination of some basis functions on a truncated state space $[k_{min}, k_{max}] \times [s_{min}, s_{max}]$:

$$\hat{V}(k,s;\mathbf{c}) = \sum_{i=1}^{d_k} \sum_{j=1}^{d_z} c_{ij} \phi_{ij}(k,s),$$

where c_{ij} are basis coefficients and ϕ_{ij} are basis functions. Define the residual function as

$$R(k,s;\mathbf{c}) = \hat{V}(k,s;\mathbf{c}) - B\hat{V}(k,s;\mathbf{c}),$$

where

$$B\hat{V}(k,s;\mathbf{c}) = \max_{k' \in [k_{min}, k_{max}]} u\left(f(k,\exp(s)) - k'\right) + E\left[\hat{V}(k',s';\mathbf{c})\,|s\right].$$

We can use the Gauss quadrature method to derive numerical integration for the conditional expectation. We then obtain an approximate residual function, and hence we can apply one of the implementations of the projection methods discussed earlier to solve for $\mathbf{c}$.

Parameterized Expectations Approach   The parameterized expectations approach (PEA) was introduced by Marcet (1988) and den Haan and Marcet (1990) and has been refined by Christiano and Fisher (2000). Here we will present the refinement of Christiano and Fisher (2000), which borrows ideas from the projection methods and approximates the conditional expectation from the Euler equation by polynomials. This method is especially useful for models with occasionally binding constraints.

   Following Christiano and Fisher (2000), we use the stochastic growth model with irreversible investment as an example. We introduce the constraint

$$K' \geq (1-\delta)K, \tag{11.13}$$

into the previous dynamic programming problem (11.9). We can write the first-order conditions as

$$u'\left(f(k,z) - g(k,z)\right) - h(k,z) = \beta \int m\left(g(k,z), z'; g, h\right) q(z'|z)\, dz',$$

$$h(k,z)\left(g(k,z) - (1-\delta)k\right) = 0,$$

$$g(k,z) - (1-\delta)k \geq 0,\ h(k,z) \geq 0,$$

where

$$m (k',z';g,h) \equiv u' (f (k',z') - g (k',z')) f' (k',z') - h (k',z') (1 - \delta) \geq 0. \tag{11.14}$$

Here $g (k,z)$ is the policy function for the next-period capital stock, $h (k,z)$ is the Lagrange multiplier associated with the constraints (11.13), and $q (z'|z)$ is the conditional density implied by the AR(1) shock process. The inequality in (11.14) reflects the fact that m is the derivative of the value function and the value function is increasing in the capital stock. The conditions above combined with the transversality condition are sufficient for optimality. We can use the projection methods to solve for g and h. This means that we have to approximate these two functions by polynomials.

PEA simplifies the solution in that we need to approximate only one function. To achieve this goal, we write the first-order conditions as

$$u' (f (k,z) - \tilde{g} (k,z)) = \beta \int m (g (k,z), z'; g, h) q (z'|z) dz',$$

$$g (k,z) = \begin{cases} \tilde{g} (k,z) & \text{if } \tilde{g} (k,z) \geq (1 - \delta) k, \\ (1 - \delta) k & \text{otherwise,} \end{cases}$$

$$h (k,z) = u' (f (k,z) - g (k,z)) - \beta \int m (g (k,z), z'; g, h) q (z'|z) dz'.$$

Define the functional equation:

$$0 = F (e) (k,z) \equiv e (k,z) - \beta \int m (g (k,z), z'; g, h) q (z'|z) dz',$$

where

$$g (k,z) = \max \left\{ (1 - \delta) k, f (k,z) - (u')^{-1} (e (k,z)) \right\},$$

$$h (k,z) = u' (f (k,z) - g (k,z)) - e (k,z),$$

and m is defined in (11.14). The goal is to approximate the function $e (k,z)$ by polynomials. We can then apply the projection methods to solve the functional equation above for $e (k,z)$.

As Christiano and Fisher (2000) point out, an important advantage of PEA is that the conditional expectation, $e (k,z)$, is a relatively smooth function because expectations smooth out some kinks. Thus this method performs better than the usual projection methods to approximate g and h in terms of both speed and accuracy.

11.7   Exercises

1. Use the CompEcon toolbox to construct the 5- and 20-degree approximants of
   the functions $f(x) = |x|^{0.6}$ and $f(x) = (1 + 2x^2)^{-1}$ on the interval $[-1, 1]$ using
   each of the following interpolation methods. For each method and degree of
   approximation, plot the approximation error and the approximant.
   a. Uniform grid, monomial basis polynomial approximant.
   b. Chebyshev node, Chebyshev basis polynomial approximant.
   c. Uniform node, linear spline.
   d. Uniform node, cubic spline.

2. Complete the solution for the example in section 11.4.

3. Introduce endogenous labor choice to the stochastic growth model

$$\max_{C_t, N_t, K_{t+1}} E \sum_{t=0}^{\infty} \beta^t \frac{\left(C_t^{\theta} (1 - N_t)^{1-\theta} \right)^{1-\gamma}}{1 - \gamma}$$

   subject to

$$C_t + K_{t+1} = (1 - \delta) K_t + z_t K_t^{\alpha} N_t^{1-\alpha},$$

$$\ln z_{t+1} = \rho \ln z_t + \sigma \varepsilon_{t+1}.$$

   Let $\theta = 0.8$, $\gamma = 2$, $\alpha = 0.33$, $\rho = 0.95$, $\sigma = 0.01$, $\delta = 0.025$, and $\beta = 0.99$. Use the
   following methods to solve the model in Matlab:
   a. The discrete value function iteration method.
   b. The discrete policy function iteration method.
   c. The value function interpolation method implemented by cubic spline or
      Chebyshev polynomials.
   d. The projection method based on the Euler equation, implemented by the
      orthogonal collocation using Chebyshev polynomials.
   e. The projection method based on the value function, implemented by the
      orthogonal collocation using Chebyshev polynomials.

12 Structural Estimation

Most economic data are generated using economic decision rules and state processes. There are two ways to determine from the data what parameter values an economic agent used in the decision rules and state processes. First, there is a reduced-form estimation method. By this method the parameters can be estimated directly by specifying functional forms for decision rules or state transition equations, independent of behavioral theory. Second, there is a structural method. Here one first studies an agent's optimization problem using dynamic programming, and then simulates the model to generate the model predicted data. The model predicted data are compared to the actual data to uncover structural parameters using certain estimation methods from econometrics. The structural estimation method has been applied widely in many fields of economics, including macroeconomics, finance, industrial organization, and labor economics. We refer the reader to Adda and Cooper (2003) for a textbook treatment of this methodology and to Rust (1996) for an excellent survey.

In this chapter we will explore three widely used estimation methods based on structural models. For our model, we will assume that the model generates a sequence of $\mathbb{R}^r$-valued data $\{x(\omega_t, \theta)\}_{t=1}^{T}$, where $\theta \in \Theta \subset \mathbb{R}^k$ is a k-dimensional vector of parameters and ω_t is a history of shocks. Further we will assume that the observed data are generated by this model at the "true" value of the parameters, denoted by θ_0, and at the "true" value of shocks, denoted by ω_t^0. Our goal is to estimate the vector of parameters θ_0 from the observed data and make statistical inferences.

12.1 Generalized Method of Moments

The generalized method of moments (GMM), formalized by Hansen (1982), is an estimation method that exploits the sample moment counterparts of population moment conditions (or orthogonality conditions) of the data-generating model.

As Hansen (2008) points out, GMM estimators have become widely used for the following reasons:

- GMM estimators have large sample properties that are easy to characterize in ways that facilitate comparison. In particular, properties such as consistency, efficiency, and asymptotic distribution are relatively easy to establish.
- GMM estimators can be constructed without specifying the full data-generating process, unlike the maximum likelihood estimator. This characteristic has been exploited in analyzing partially specified economic models, in studying potentially misspecified dynamic models designed to match target moments, and in constructing stochastic discount factor models that link asset pricing to sources of macroeconomic risk.

Textbook treatments of GMM estimation with a wide array of applications include Cochrane (2001), Arellano (2003), Hall (2005), and Singleton (2006). Hall (2005) also includes a nice Matlab toolbox, downloadable from the website, http://www.kostaskyriakoulis.com/gmmgui.html.

12.1.1   Estimation

Suppose that the model is correctly specified as a vector of moment condition:

$$g\left(\theta_0\right) \equiv E\left[h\left(x_t, \theta_0\right)\right] = 0, \tag{12.1}$$

where $\theta_0 \in \Theta$ and h has $q \geq k$ coordinates. We do not consider the case of misspecification in which there is no $\theta \in \Theta$ such that the (12.1) holds. We make the following assumptions:

Assumption 12.1.1 $\{x_t\}_{t=-\infty}^{\infty}$ *is a strictly stationary process.*

Assumption 12.1.2 h *is continuous in θ and $E\left[h\left(x_t, \theta\right)\right]$ is finite and continuous in $\theta \in \Theta$.*

Assumption 12.1.3   (Global identification) *On the parameter space Θ,*

$$E\left[h\left(x_t, \theta\right)\right] = 0 \quad \text{if and only if} \quad \theta = \theta_0.$$

The model is typically partially specified in that the parameter θ_0 is not sufficient to write down a likelihood function. Other parameters are needed to pin down the probability model underlying the data-generating process. Examples include the following:

1. Linear and nonlinear versions of instrumental variables estimators as in Sargan (1958), Sargan (1959), and Amemiya (1974).

2. Rational expectations models as in Hansen and Singleton (1982) and Hayashi and Sims (1983).

3. Security market pricing of aggregate risks as described, for example, by Cochrane (2001), and Singleton (2006).

4. Matching and testing target moments of possibly misspecified models as described by, for example, Christiano and Eichenbaum (1992) and Hansen and Heckman (1996).

When the law of large numbers applies, we can replace the population moment by the empirical moment:

$$g_T(\theta) \equiv \frac{1}{T} \sum_{t=1}^{T} h(x_t, \theta).$$

The GMM estimator $\hat{\theta}_T$ is obtained by solving the following problem:

$$\min_{\theta \in \Theta} \; Q_T(\theta) \equiv g_T(\theta)' W_T g_T(\theta),$$

where W_T satisfies:

Assumption 12.1.4 W_T *is a $q \times q$ positive semidefinite weighting matrix and converges in probability to a positive definite matrix of constants W.*

The first-order conditions for the minimization problem above are given by

$$\left[\frac{\partial g_T}{\partial \theta}(\hat{\theta}_T) \right]' W_T g_T(\hat{\theta}_T) = 0. \tag{12.2}$$

For linear models, these conditions could be solved to obtain a closed-form solution for $\hat{\theta}_T$ as a function of the data. For nonlinear models, this is typically impossible and numerical methods are needed.

Example 12.1.1   *For the consumption/portfolio model studied in chapter 8.3, the Euler equation is given by*

$$u'(C_t) = \beta E_t R_{jt+1} u'(C_{t+1}).$$

We can define

$$h(C_t, C_{t+1}, R_{jt+1}, \theta) = \frac{\beta R_{jt+1} u'(C_{t+1})}{u'(C_t)} - 1,$$

where θ represents parameters in the utility function, such as β and γ when $u(c) = c^{1-\gamma}/(1-\gamma)$. We then obtain the moment condition (12.1). The Euler equation *delivers more restrictions. For any variable z_t that belongs to the information set at date t, we also have the following orthogonality condition:*

$$Eh\left(C_t, C_{t+1}, R_{jt+1}, z_t, \theta\right) = E\left\{z_t\left[\beta R_{jt+1}u'\left(C_{t+1}\right)/u'\left(C_t\right) - 1\right]\right\} = 0.$$

Hansen and Singleton (1982) use the GMM method to estimate this problem.

12.1.2   Asymptotic Properties

To apply some Laws of Large Numbers and the Central Limit Theorem, presented section 4.2, we impose the following:

Assumption 12.1.5   *The stochastic process $\{x_t : -\infty < t < \infty\}$ is ergodic.*

We also need the next two technical conditions:

Assumption 12.1.6 Θ *is compact.*

Assumption 12.1.7 $E\left[\sup_{\theta \in \Theta} \|h\left(x_t, \theta\right)\|\right] < \infty.$

We can now state the consistency result.

Theorem 12.1.1   *Under assumptions 12.1.1 through 12.1.7, the GMM estimator $\hat{\theta}_T \xrightarrow{p} \theta_0$.*

The proof can be found in Hall (2005, p. 68). The idea is simple. Consider the minimization of the population analog to $Q_T\left(\theta\right)$:

$$Q_0\left(\theta\right) \equiv E\left[h\left(x_t, \theta\right)\right]' WE\left[h\left(x_t, \theta\right)\right].$$

By the global identification condition and the positive definiteness of W, $Q_0\left(\theta\right)$ has a unique minimizer θ_0. Intuitively, if $\hat{\theta}_T$ minimizes $Q_T\left(\theta\right)$ and $Q_T\left(\theta\right)$ converges in probability to $Q_0\left(\theta\right)$ whose unique minimum is at θ_0, then $\hat{\theta}_T$ must converge to θ_0 in probability.

To derive the asymptotic distribution of the GMM estimator, we need to derive a closed-form representation for $\sqrt{T}\left(\hat{\theta}_T - \theta_0\right)$. This can be derived from the Mean Value Theorem

$$g_T\left(\hat{\theta}_T\right) = g_T\left(\theta_0\right) + \frac{\partial g_T}{\partial \theta}\left(\bar{\theta}_T\right)\left(\hat{\theta}_T - \theta_0\right), \tag{12.3}$$

where $\bar{\theta}_T = \lambda_T \theta_0 + \left(1 - \lambda_T\right)\hat{\theta}_T$ for some $\lambda_T \in [0, 1]$. We thus need to impose an assumption:

Assumption 12.1.8   *(a) The derivative matrix $\partial h\left(x_t, \theta\right)/\partial\theta$ exists and is continuous for each x_t; (b) θ_0 is an interior point of Θ; (c) $E\left[\partial h\left(x_t, \theta\right)/\partial\theta\right]$ exists and is finite.*

Premultiplying (12.3) by $\left[\partial g_T\left(\hat{\theta}_T\right)/\partial\theta\right]' W_T$ yields

$$\left[\frac{\partial g_T}{\partial\theta}\left(\hat{\theta}_T\right)\right]' W_T g_T\left(\hat{\theta}_T\right)$$

$$= \left[\frac{\partial g_T}{\partial\theta}\left(\hat{\theta}_T\right)\right]' W_T g_T\left(\theta_0\right) + \left[\frac{\partial g_T}{\partial\theta}\left(\hat{\theta}_T\right)\right]' W_T \frac{\partial g_T\left(x_t,\bar{\theta}_T\right)}{\partial\theta}\left(\hat{\theta}_T - \theta_0\right).$$

By the first-order conditions (12.2), the expression on the left-hand side of the equation above is equal to zero. We can then derive

$$\sqrt{T}\left(\hat{\theta}_T - \theta_0\right) = -M_T\sqrt{T}g_T\left(\theta_0\right),$$

where

$$M_T = \left(\left[\frac{\partial g_T}{\partial\theta}\left(\hat{\theta}_T\right)\right]' W_T \frac{\partial g_T}{\partial\theta}\left(\bar{\theta}_T\right)\right)^{-1}\left[\frac{\partial g_T}{\partial\theta}\left(\hat{\theta}_T\right)\right]' W_T.$$

We need to know the asymptotic behavior of $\sqrt{T}g_T\left(\theta_0\right)$, which follows from the Central Limit Theorem 4.2.4. To apply this theorem, it is necessary to assume that the second-moment matrices of the sample moment satisfy certain restrictions.

Assumption 12.1.9   (a) $E\left[h\left(x_t,\theta_0\right)h'\left(x_t,\theta_0\right)\right]$ is finite and (b) the limit

$$\lim_{T\to\infty} Var\left[\sqrt{T}g_T\left(\theta_0\right)\right] = S$$

is a finite positive definite matrix.

Note that the matrix S is the long-run covariance matrix of $h\left(x_t,\theta_0\right)$, which is different from the contemporaneous covariance matrix $E\left[h\left(x_t,\theta_0\right)h'\left(x_t,\theta_0\right)\right]$.

Lemma 12.1.1   Under assumptions 12.1.1, 12.1.5, and 12.1.9, $\sqrt{T}g_T\left(\theta_0\right) \xrightarrow{d} N\left(0,S\right)$.

We need M_T to converge, and hence we impose the following technical condition:

Assumption 12.1.10   (a) $E\left[\partial h\left(x_t,\theta\right)/\partial\theta\right]$ is continuous on some neighborhood N_ϵ of θ_0. (b)

$$\sup_{\theta\in N_\epsilon}\left\|\frac{1}{T}\sum_{t=1}^{T}\frac{\partial h\left(x_t,\theta\right)}{\partial\theta} - E\left[\frac{\partial h\left(x_t,\theta\right)}{\partial\theta}\right]\right\| \xrightarrow{p} 0.$$

We can now state the following result:

Theorem 12.1.2   *Under assumptions 12.1.1 through 12.1.10,*

$$\sqrt{T}\left(\hat{\theta}_T - \theta_0\right) \xrightarrow{d} N\left(0, MSM'\right),$$

where

$$M \equiv \left(G_0'WG_0\right)^{-1}G_0'W, \quad G_0 \equiv E\left[\partial h\left(x_t, \theta_0\right)/\partial\theta\right].$$

12.1.3   Weighting Matrix and Covariance Matrix Estimation

The principle of choosing a weighting matrix W is that more accurate (less noisy) moment conditions should be weighted more than the less accurate (more noisy or uncertain) ones. The accuracy of the moment conditions can be measured by the variance covariance matrix. We thus set $W = S^{-1}$. In this case

$$\sqrt{T}\left(\hat{\theta}_T - \theta_0\right) \xrightarrow{d} N\left(0, \left(G_0'S^{-1}G_0\right)^{-1}\right),$$

and the estimator is the most efficient one in the class of all asymptotically normal estimators. Efficiency in this case means that such an estimator will have the smallest possible covariance matrix.

Empirically, we need consistent estimates for G_0 and S. We can take the sample average as the consistent estimate for G_0. The consistent estimate for S is more complicated. We will use the heteroscedasticity and autocorrelation covariance (HAC) matrix estimator. To present this estimator, we first use the definition to derive

$$S = \lim_{T\to\infty} Var\left[\sqrt{T}g_T\left(\theta_0\right)\right] = \lim_{T\to\infty} Var\left[T^{-1/2}\sum_{t=1}^{T}h_t\right]$$

$$= \lim_{T\to\infty} E\left[\begin{array}{c}\left(T^{-1/2}\sum_{t=1}^{T}h_t - E\left[T^{-1/2}\sum_{t=1}^{T}h_t\right]\right) \\ \times \left(T^{-1/2}\sum_{t=1}^{T}h_t - E\left[T^{-1/2}\sum_{t=1}^{T}h_t\right]\right)'\end{array}\right],$$

where we define $h_t = h\left(x_t, \theta_0\right)$. Simplifying yields

$$S = \lim_{T\to\infty} E\left[T^{-1}\sum_{t=1}^{T}\sum_{s=1}^{T}\left(h_t - Eh_t\right)\left(h_s - Eh_s\right)'\right].$$

The stationarity assumption implies that

$$E\left[\left(h_t - Eh_t\right)\left(h_{t-j} - Eh_{t-j}\right)'\right] = \Gamma_j$$

for all t. Thus

$$S = \Gamma_0 + \lim_{T\to\infty}\sum_{j=1}^{T-1}\frac{T-j}{T}\left(\Gamma_j + \Gamma_j'\right) = \Gamma_0 + \sum_{i=1}^{\infty}\left(\Gamma_i + \Gamma_i'\right).$$

Table 12.1
Kernels for three common HAC estimators

Name	Authors	Kernel $\omega_{i,T}$
Bartlett	Newey and West (1987)	$1 - a_i$ for $a_i \leq 1$ 0 for $a_i > 1$
Parzen	Gallant (1987)	$1 - 6a_i^2 + 6a_i^3$ for $0 \leq a_i \leq 0.5$ $2\left(1 - a_i\right)^3$ for $0.5 < a_i \leq 1$ 0 for $a_i > 1$
Quadratic spectral	Andrews (1991)	$\frac{25}{12\pi^2 d_i^2}\left[\frac{\sin(m_i)}{m_i} - \cos\left(m_i\right)\right]$

Note: $a_i = i/b_T + 1$; $d_i = i/b_T$; $m_i = 6\pi d_i/5$.

The class of heteroscedasticity autocorrelation covariance (HAC) matrices consists of estimators of the form

$$\hat{S}_{HAC} = \hat{\Gamma}_0 + \sum_{i=1}^{T-1} \omega_{i,T}\left(\hat{\Gamma}_i + \hat{\Gamma}'_i\right),$$

where $\omega_{i,T}$ is known as the kernel (or weight) and

$$\hat{\Gamma}_j = T^{-1} \sum_{t=j+1}^{T} h\left(x_t, \hat{\theta}_T\right) h\left(x_{t-j}, \hat{\theta}_T\right)', \quad j = 0, 1, ..., T-1,$$

is the sample autocovariance. The kernel must be carefully chosen to ensure the twin properties of consistency and positive semidefiniteness.

The three most popular choices in the econometrics literature are given in table 12.1.

In the table b_T is called the bandwidth, which must be nonnegative. This parameter controls the number of autocovariances included in the HAC estimator when either a Bartlett or Parzen kernel is used. In these two cases, b_T must be an integer, but no such restriction is required for the quadratic spectral kernel.

12.1.4 Overidentifying Restrictions

When the number of moment conditions q is greater than the dimension of the parameter vector k, the model is said to be overidentified. When $q = k$, we say the model is exactly identified. Overidentification allows us to check whether the model's moment conditions match the data well. We use the so-called J-test. The null hypothesis is $H_0 : E\left[h\left(x_t, \theta_0\right)\right] = 0$.

Construct the J-statistic

$$J_T = T g_T\left(\hat{\theta}_T\right)' \hat{S}_T g_T\left(\hat{\theta}_T\right), \tag{12.4}$$

where $\hat{\theta}_T$ is the GMM estimator and $\hat{S}_T$ is a consistent estimate of S. Hansen (1982) shows that under the null, $J_T \xrightarrow{d} \chi^2 (q - k)$ for $q > k$.

12.1.5 Implementation

In principle, one should take $W = S^{-1}$ as the weighting matrix. However, S is unknown before we derive an estimator $\hat{\theta}_T$. Several approaches exist to deal with this issue, the first one being the most popular:

- *Two-step feasible GMM*   Step 1: Take $W = I$ (the identity matrix), and compute a preliminary GMM estimate $\hat{\theta}_{(1)}$. This estimator is consistent for θ_0 although not efficient. Step 2: Estimate

$$\hat{\Gamma}_j = \left[\frac{1}{T} \sum_{t=j+1}^{T} h(x_t, \hat{\theta}_{(1)}) h(x_{t+j}, \hat{\theta}_{(1)})' \right]^{-1} , \quad j = 0, 1, \ldots, T-1,$$

where we have plugged in our first-step preliminary estimate $\hat{\theta}_{(1)}$. Estimate

$$\hat{S}_T = \hat{\Gamma}_0 + \sum_{i=1}^{T-1} \omega_{i,T} \left(\hat{\Gamma}_i + \hat{\Gamma}_i' \right).$$

It is a consistent estimator of S. If we compute $\hat{\theta}$ with weighting matrix $W = \hat{S}_T^{-1}$, the estimator will be asymptotically efficient.

- *Iterated GMM*   Essentially the same procedure as two-step GMM, except that the matrix $\hat{W}_T$ is recalculated several times in step 2 by iteration. Asymptotically no improvement can be achieved through such iterations, although certain Monte Carlo experiments suggest that finite-sample properties of this estimator are slightly better.

- *Continuously updating GMM*   Estimate $\hat{\theta}$ simultaneously with estimating the weighting matrix W:

$$\hat{\theta} = \arg\min_{\theta \in \Theta} \left[\frac{1}{T} \sum_{t=1}^{T} h(x_t, \theta) \right]' S_T(\theta)^{-1} \left[\frac{1}{T} \sum_{t=1}^{T} h(x_t, \theta) \right],$$

where

$$S_T(\theta) = \Gamma_{0,T}(\theta) + \sum_{i=1}^{T-1} \omega_{i,T} \left(\Gamma_{i,T}(\theta) + \Gamma_{i,T}'(\theta) \right),$$

$$\Gamma_j(\theta) = T^{-1} \sum_{t=j+1}^{T} h(x_t, \theta) h(x_{t-j}, \theta)', \quad j = 0, 1, \ldots, T-1.$$

In Monte Carlo experiments this method demonstrated a better performance than the traditional two-step GMM. The estimator has smaller median bias (although fatter tails), and the J-test for overidentifying restrictions in many cases was more reliable.

12.1.6 Relation to Other Estimation Methods

GMM encompasses many estimation methods in econometrics, with suitable choices of moment conditions as illustrated below.

- Ordinary least squares (OLS):

$$E\left[x_t \left(y_t - x_t'\beta\right)\right] = 0.$$

- Instrumental variables regression (IV):

$$E\left[z_t \left(y_t - x_t'\beta\right)\right] = 0,$$

where z_t represents instrumental variables uncorrelated with error terms.

- Nonlinear least squares (NLS):

$$E\left[\frac{\partial g\left(x_t, \beta\right)}{\partial \beta} \cdot \left(y_t - g\left(x_t, \beta\right)\right)\right] = 0.$$

12.2 Maximum Likelihood

The maximum likelihood method is one of the most popular ways to estimate the parameter θ that specifies a probability function $\Pr\left(X = x|\theta\right)$ of a discrete stochastic variable X (or a probability density function $f\left(x|\theta\right)$ of a continuous stochastic variable X) based on the observations $x_1, ..., x_T$, which are independently sampled from the distribution.

12.2.1 Estimation

Unlike the GMM approach, the maximum likelihood (ML) method requires one to know the full distribution of the data-generating process. Suppose that the observable data $\{x_1, ..., x_T\}$ are independently and identically drawn from a pdf $f\left(\cdot, \theta\right)$ given a parameter θ. The joint distribution is given by

$$f\left(x_1, ..., x_T|\theta\right) = \prod_{t=1}^{T} f\left(x_t, \theta\right).$$

The maximum likelihood method is designed to maximize the likelihood function for the entire sample:

$$L\left(\theta|x_1, ..., x_T\right) = f\left(x_1, ..., x_T|\theta\right).$$

In practice, it is often more convenient to work with the logarithm of the likelihood function, called the log-likelihood:

$$\max_{\theta \in \Theta} \ln L (\theta | x_1, ..., x_T) = \sum_{t=1}^{T} \ln f (x_t, \theta).$$

Example 12.2.1 *Consider the job search problem studied in chapter 8.1. Suppose that job offers are independently and identically drawn from fixed known distribution F. The Bellman equation is given by*

$$V (w) = \max \left\{ \frac{w}{1 - \beta}, \ c + \beta \int V (w') \, dF (w') \right\}.$$

There is a cutoff value $w^* (\theta)$ such that the worker takes the job offer w if and only if $w \geq w^* (\theta)$, where θ represents the parameters c and β. The reservation wage $w^* (\theta)$ is unobservable. But we can compute it numerically given any parameter value θ. We can then compute the likelihood of observing a worker i accepting a job for the first time after t_i periods:

$$L_i (\theta) = (1 - F (w^* (\theta))) [F (w^* (\theta))]^{t_i - 1}.$$

Say we observe durations t_i for N workers. Then the likelihood of the sample is given by

$$L (\theta) = \prod_{i=1}^{N} L_i (\theta).$$

12.2.2   Asymptotic Properties

Suppose that f is differentiable and concave in θ. The first-order condition for the log-likelihood function is given by

$$\sum_{t=1}^{T} \frac{\partial \ln f (x_t, \theta)}{\partial \theta} = 0.$$

The population analogue is given by

$$E \left[\frac{\partial \ln f (x_t, \theta)}{\partial \theta} \right] = 0.$$

This moment condition implies that the maximum likelihood estimator can be viewed as a GMM estimator with $h (x_t, \theta) = \partial \ln f (x_t, \theta) / \partial \theta$. We can then apply the results derived in the previous section. We list these properties without explicitly stating relevant conditions and proofs

- Consistency:

$$\hat{\theta}_T \xrightarrow{p} \theta_0.$$

- Asymptotic normality:

$$\sqrt{T}\left(\hat{\theta}_T - \theta_0\right) \xrightarrow{d} N\left(0, I\left(\theta_0\right)^{-1}\right),$$

where

$$I\left(\theta\right) \equiv -E\left[\frac{\partial^2}{\partial\theta\partial\theta'} \ln L\left(\theta\right)\right],$$

is the Fisher information matrix. By the information matrix equality,

$$I\left(\theta\right) = -E\left[\frac{\partial^2}{\partial\theta\partial\theta'} \ln L\left(\theta\right)\right] = E\left[\left(\frac{\partial \ln L\left(\theta\right)}{\partial\theta}\right)' \frac{\partial \ln L\left(\theta\right)}{\partial\theta}\right].$$

- Asymptoptic efficiency: The maximum likelihood estimator achieves the Cramer–Rao lower bound when the sample size tends to infinity. This means that no asymptotically unbiased estimator has lower asymptotic mean-squared error than the maximum likelihood estimator.
- Invariance: The maximum likelihood estimator of $\gamma_0 = c\left(\theta_0\right)$ is $c\left(\hat{\theta}\right)$ if c is a continuously differentiable function.

12.2.3 Hypothesis Testing

We consider maximum likelihood estimation of a parameter θ and a test of the hypothesis $H_0 : c\left(\theta\right) = 0$. There are three approaches to testing H_0:

- *Likelihood ratio test* If the restriction $c\left(\theta\right) = 0$ is valid, then imposing it should not lead to a large reduction in the log-likelihood function. Therefore we base the test on the log ratio, $2\ln\left(L_U/L_R\right)$, where L_U is the value of the likelihood function at the unconstrained value of θ and L_R is the value of the likelihood function at the restricted estimate.
- *Wald test* If the restriction is valid, then $c\left(\hat{\theta}_T\right)$ should be close to zero because the ML estimator is consistent. Therefore the test is based on $c\left(\hat{\theta}_T\right)$. We reject the hypothesis if this value is significantly different from zero. The Wald statistic is given by

$$W = c\left(\hat{\theta}_T\right)' \left[\lim_T \text{Var}\left(c\left(\hat{\theta}_T\right)\right)\right]^{-1} c\left(\hat{\theta}_T\right),$$

where $\hat{\theta}_T$ is the ML estimate without the restriction.

- *Lagrange multiplier test* If the restriction is valid, then the restricted estimator should be near the point that maximizes the log-likelihood. Therefore the slope of the log-likelihood function should be near zero at the restricted estimator.

The test is based on the slope of the log-likelihood at the point where the function is maximized subject to the restriction. The test statistic is given by

$$
LM = \left(\frac{\partial \ln L \left(\hat{\theta}_R \right)}{\partial \theta} \right)' \left[I \left(\hat{\theta}_R \right) \right]^{-1} \left(\frac{\partial \ln L \left(\hat{\theta}_R \right)}{\partial \theta} \right),
$$

where $\hat{\theta}_R$ is the ML estimator under the restriction.

These three tests are asymptotically equivalent under the null hypothesis because the asymptotic distributions for these tests are chi-squared with degrees of freedom equal to the number of restrictions imposed. But they can behave rather differently in a small sample. Unfortunately, their small-sample properties are unknown, except in a few special cases. Thus the choice among them is typically made on the basis of ease of computation. The likelihood ratio test requires calculation of both restricted and unrestricted estimators. If both are simple to compute, then this way to proceed is convenient. The Wald test requires only the unrestricted estimator, and the Lagrange multiplier test requires only the restricted estimator. In some problems, one of these estimators may be much easier to compute than the other. For example, a linear model is simple to estimate but becomes nonlinear and cumbersome if a nonlinear constraint is imposed. In this case the Wald statistic might be preferable. Alternatively, restrictions sometimes remove nonlinearities, which would make the Lagrange multiplier test simpler. For a textbook treatment of these tests, we refer the reader to Greene (2011) among others.

12.3   Simulation-Based Methods

In many applications moment conditions are difficult to construct explicitly. To deal with this issue, researchers develop estimation methods based on simulation. This field is growing. Here we focus on only a few methods. For more in-depth discussions and applications of these methods, we refer the reader to Gouriéroux and Monfort (1996) and Adda and Cooper (2003).

Example 12.3.1   *Consider the job search problem studied previously, but where the wage offers are serially correlated. The Bellman equation is given by*

$$
V \left(w \right) = \max \left\{ \frac{w}{1 - \beta}, \ c + \beta \int V \left(w' \right) dF \left(w' | w \right) \right\}.
$$

where $F \left(w' | w \right)$ is the conditional distribution of the next-period wage offer given the current wage, w. Let w^* be the reservation wage. The probability of waiting t periods to accept a job offer is given by

$$
P_t = \Pr \left(w_1 < w^*, ..., w_{t-1} < w^*, w_t > w^* \right).
$$

When the job offers are IID, we can compute this probability easily. But if (w_t) is serially correlated, then this probability is difficult to compute numerically. Simulated methods can overcome this problem.

12.3.1   Simulated Method of Moments

The simulated method of moments (SMM) is developed by McFadden (1989), Lee and Ingram (1991), and Duffie and Singleton (1993). It is a simulation-based GMM. Let $\{x(w_t, \theta_0)\}_{t=1}^{T}$ be a sequence of observed data. Let $\{x(w_t^s, \theta)\}_{t=1}^{T}$ be a sequence of simulated data for $s = 1, 2, ..., S$ and for a given parameter value θ. The simulations are done by fixing θ and by using the TS draws of the shocks w_t^s. We simply write $x_t^s(\theta) = x(w_t^s, \theta)$. Denote by $m(x_t)$ a q-dimensional vector of functions of the observed data.[1] The estimator for the SMM is defined as

$$\hat{\theta}_{ST} = \arg\min_{\theta \in \Theta} \left[\sum_{t=1}^{T} \left(m(x_t) - \frac{1}{S} \sum_{s=1}^{S} m(x_t^s(\theta)) \right) \right]' W_T$$

$$\times \left[\sum_{t=1}^{T} \left(m(x_t) - \frac{1}{S} \sum_{s=1}^{S} m(x_t^s(\theta)) \right) \right],$$

where W_T is a weighting matrix. If we define

$$h(x_t, \theta) = m(x_t) - \frac{1}{S} \sum_{s=1}^{S} m(x_t^s(\theta)), \tag{12.5}$$

then SMM is a special case of GMM. We can then apply the results developed for GMM.

Example 12.3.2   *Consider the job search model with serially correlated wage offers. Suppose that we have a data set of N workers for which we observe the durations of their search, D_i, $i = 1, ..., N$. Given a vector of parameters θ that describes the model, such as the discount factor, the unemployment benefit, or the parameters in the distribution function, we can solve the model numerically and compute the reservation wage. Next we can simulate a series of wage offers and determine the duration for this particular draw of the wage offers. We can repeat this step in order to construct S data sets, each containing N simulated durations.*

To identify the parameters of the model, we can, for instance, use the mean duration and the variance of the duration. Both of these moments would be calculated from the observed data set and the simulated data. If we want to identify

---

1. For example, $m(x) = (x, x^2)'$ if one wants to match the mean and the variance of the process.

more than two parameters, we can try to characterize the distribution of the dura-
tion better and include, for instance, the fraction of workers at the end of the first,
second, and third periods.

Asymptotic Properties   Using results for GMM discussed earlier, we can establish these properties as $T \to \infty$ for fixed S.

- Consistency:

$$\hat{\theta}_{ST} \xrightarrow{p} \theta_0.$$

- Asymptotic normality:

$$\sqrt{T}\left(\hat{\theta}_{ST} - \theta_0\right) \xrightarrow{d} N(0, Q_S),$$

where

$$Q_S = \left(1 + \frac{1}{S}\right) [B'WB]^{-1} B'W\Sigma WB [B'WB]^{-1}$$

and

$$B \equiv E\left[\frac{\partial m\left(x_t^s\left(\theta_0\right)\right)}{\partial \theta}\right] \quad \text{for all } s, t,$$

$$\Sigma \equiv \lim_{T \to \infty} \text{Var}\left(\frac{1}{\sqrt{T}}\left[\frac{1}{T}\sum_{t=1}^{T}\left(m\left(x_t\right) - Em\left(x_t^s\left(\theta_0\right)\right)\right)\right]\right).$$

- Optimal weighting matrix:

$$W = \left[\left(1 + \frac{1}{S}\right)\Sigma\right]^{-1}.$$

Under this matrix

$$\sqrt{T}\left(\hat{\theta}_{ST} - \theta_0\right) \xrightarrow{d} N\left(0, \left(1 + \frac{1}{S}\right)[B'\Sigma^{-1}B]^{-1}\right).$$

Empirically, we can use any consistent estimates for B and Σ. In particular, we can use HAC estimator $\hat{\Sigma}_{ST}$ for Σ discussed earlier. We can use J-statistic defined in (12.4) to test overidentifying restrictions:

$$J_{ST} = Tg_T\left(\hat{\theta}_{ST}\right)' \hat{\Sigma}_{ST}g_T\left(\hat{\theta}_{ST}\right) \xrightarrow{d} \chi^2(q - k), \tag{12.6}$$

where g_T is defined for the function h given in (12.5) with $\theta = \hat{\theta}_T$.

When S approaches to infinity, the covariance matrix of the SMM estimator converges to that of the GMM estimator. In practice, the SMM requires a large number of simulations to compute the standard errors of the estimator, even if the estimator is consistent for a fixed number of simulations.

12.3.2 Simulated Maximum Likelihood

In applications there may not exist an explicit form of the likelihood function. Sometimes the likelihood function is hard to compute analytically. We can then use the simulated maximum likelihood (SML) method to approximate the likelihood function. Suppose that the process x_t is independently and identically drawn from the distribution $f(\cdot|\theta)$. The log-likelihood function is given by

$$l(\theta) = \sum_{t=1}^{T} \ln f(x_t, \theta).$$

Let $\tilde{f}(\theta|x_t, \omega_t)$ be an unbiased simulator of $f(x_t, \theta)$ in that

$$E_\omega \tilde{f}(\theta|x_t, \omega_t) = \lim_{s \to \infty} \frac{1}{S} \sum_{s=1}^{S} \tilde{f}(\theta|x_t, \omega_t^s) = f(x_t, \theta).$$

The SML estimator is defined as

$$\hat{\theta}_{ST} = \arg\max_{\theta \in \Theta} \sum_{t=1}^{T} \ln \frac{1}{S} \sum_{s=1}^{S} \tilde{f}(\theta|x_t, \omega_t^s).$$

We can also construct simulated log-likelihood similarly.

The SML estimator is consistent when both T and S approach infinity, but is inconsistent if S is fixed. When both T and S approach infinity and when $\sqrt{T}/S \to 0$,

$$\sqrt{T}\left(\hat{\theta}_{ST} - \theta_0\right) \xrightarrow{d} N\left(0, I^{-1}(\theta_0)\right),$$

where the matrix $I(\theta_0)$ can be approximated by

$$-\frac{1}{T} \sum_{t=1}^{T} \frac{\partial^2 \ln\left(1/S \sum_{s=1}^{S} \tilde{f}\left(\hat{\theta}_{ST}|x_t, \omega_t^s\right)\right)}{\partial\theta\partial\theta'}.$$

12.3.3 Indirect Inference

When the model is too complex to write down the likelihood function, the indirect inference method can be used. This method first estimates a simpler auxiliary model both on the observed data and on simulated data. It then tries to find the values of structural parameters that bring the auxiliary parameters from the simulated data as close as possible to the one obtained on observed data.

Consider the likelihood of the auxiliary model $\phi(x_t, \beta)$, where β is a vector of auxiliary parameters. The ML estimator computed from the observed data is defined by

$$\hat{\beta}_T = \arg\max_{\beta} \psi_T((x_t), \beta) \equiv \sum_{t=1}^{T} \ln \phi(x_t, \beta).$$

Suppose that there is a link between the true value of the auxiliary parameter β_0 and the structural parameter θ. This link is described by a binding function $b(\theta)$ (Gouriéroux, Monfort, and Renault 1993). If this function is known, we can invert it to compute θ from the estimated auxiliary parameter. Unfortunately, this function is usually unknown. Simulations can help.

The model is simulated by taking independent draws for the shock ω_t^s. This gives S artificial data sets of length T: $\{x_1^s(\theta),...,x_T^s(\theta)\}$, $s = 1,2,...,S$. The auxiliary model is then estimated by SML using the simulated data:

$$\hat{\beta}_T^s(\theta) = \arg\max_{\beta} \ \psi_T((x_t^s(\theta)),\beta) = \sum_{t=1}^{T} \ln\phi(x_t^s(\theta),\beta).$$

Define $\hat{\beta}_{ST}$ the average value of the auxiliary parameters over all simulations:

$$\hat{\beta}_{ST}(\theta) = \frac{1}{S}\sum_{s=1}^{S} \hat{\beta}_T^s(\theta).$$

The indirect inference estimator is the solution to

$$\hat{\theta}_{ST} = \arg\min_{\theta \in \Theta} \ \left[\hat{\beta}_T - \hat{\beta}_{ST}(\theta)\right]' W_T \left[\hat{\beta}_T - \hat{\beta}_{ST}(\theta)\right],$$

where W_T is a positive definite weight matrix which converges to a constant positive definite matrix W.

Example 12.3.3 *Consider the job search model with serially correlated wage offers. The likelihood of the structural model is intractable, but we can find an auxiliary model that is easier to estimate. As the data set consists of durations, a natural auxiliary model is the standard duration model. Suppose that we choose an exponential model that is a simple and standard model of duration characterized by a constant hazard equal to β. The probability of observing a particular duration D_i for individual i is $\beta e^{-\beta D_i}$. The log-likelihood of observing a set of durations D_i, $i = 1,...,N$, is*

$$\ln L = \sum_{i=1}^{N} \ln\left(\beta e^{-\beta D_i}\right).$$

Maximizing it with respect to β yields

$$\hat{\beta}_T = \sum_{i=1}^{N} \frac{D_i}{N}.$$

In this case the auxiliary parameter is estimated as the average duration in the data set. Given a structural parameter θ in our model, we can construct by simulation S data sets containing N observations. For each artificial data set s, we can estimate the auxiliary *duration model to obtain* $\hat{\beta}_T^s(\theta)$. *We then use the procedure above to find an estimator* $\hat{\theta}_{ST}$ *such that the auxiliary parameters on both observed and simulated data are as close as possible. Note that with the simple auxiliary model that we use, the indirect inference procedure turns out to be the same as the simulated method of moments because we are matching the average duration.*

We have used the exponential duration model for simplicity of exposition. This model has only one parameter, so we can identify at best only one structural parameter. To estimate more structural parameters, we need to estimate a duration model with a more flexible hazard.

Gallant and Tauchen (1996) develop an efficient method of moments (EMM) method based on the use of an auxiliary model. Instead of matching a set of auxiliary parameters, they propose to minimize the score of the auxiliary model. This score is the first derivative of the likelihood of the auxiliary model defined by

$$
m\left(\theta, \hat{\beta}_T\right) = \frac{1}{S} \sum_{s=1}^{S} \frac{1}{T} \sum_{t=1}^{T} \frac{\partial}{\partial \beta} \ln \phi\left(x_t^s(\theta), \hat{\beta}_T\right).
$$

The estimator for the structural parameters is given by

$$
\hat{\theta}_{ST} = \arg \min_{\theta \in \Theta} m\left(\theta, \hat{\beta}_T\right)' W m\left(\theta, \hat{\beta}_T\right).
$$

Asymptotic Properties   For a fixed number of simulations S, as T goes to infinity,

$$
\sqrt{T}\left(\hat{\theta}_{ST} - \theta_0\right) \xrightarrow{d} N\left(0, Q_S(W)\right), \tag{12.7}
$$

where

$$
Q_S(W) = \left(1 + \frac{1}{S}\right)\left[\left(\frac{\partial b(\theta_0)}{\partial \theta}\right)' W \frac{\partial b(\theta_0)}{\partial \theta}\right]^{-1} \left(\frac{\partial b(\theta_0)}{\partial \theta}\right)' W J_0^{-1}
$$

$$
\times (I_0 - K_0) J_0^{-1} W \left(\frac{\partial b(\theta_0)}{\partial \theta}\right)' \left[\left(\frac{\partial b(\theta_0)}{\partial \theta}\right)' W \frac{\partial b(\theta_0)}{\partial \theta}\right]^{-1},
$$

and

$$
J_0 \equiv \operatorname*{p\,lim}_T -\frac{\partial^2 \psi_T\left((x_t), \beta_0\right)}{\partial \beta \partial \beta'},
$$

$$
I_0 \equiv \lim_T \operatorname{Var}\left[\sqrt{T}\frac{\partial \psi_T\left((x_t), \beta_0\right)}{\partial \beta}\right],
$$

$$
K_0 \equiv \lim_T \operatorname{Var}\left[E\left(\sqrt{T}\frac{\partial \psi_T\left((x_t), \beta_0\right)}{\partial \beta} \mid (z_t)\right)\right],
$$

where (z_t) is the component of (x_t) whose distribution is independent of θ. Since the binding function $b(\theta)$ may not be known explicitly, we want to find an observable expression to replace $\partial b(\theta_0)/\partial \theta$. Suppose that

$$\psi_T\left(\left(x_t^s(\theta)\right), \beta\right) \xrightarrow{a.s.} \psi_\infty(\theta, \beta),$$

and that $b(\theta)$ satisfies the first-order condition:

$$\frac{\partial \psi_\infty(\theta, b(\theta))}{\partial \beta} = 0.$$

Differentiate with respect to θ to obtain

$$\frac{\partial b'(\theta_0)}{\partial \theta} = J_0^{-1} \frac{\partial^2 \psi_\infty(\theta_0, b(\theta_0))}{\partial \beta \partial \theta'}.$$

The optimal weighting matrix that minimizes the variance of the estimator is given by

$$W^* = J_0 (I_0 - K_0)^{-1} J_0.$$

In this case the covariance matrix of the estimator becomes

$$Q_S(W^*) = \left(1 + \frac{1}{S}\right) \left[\left(\frac{\partial b(\theta_0)}{\partial \theta}\right)' W^* \frac{\partial b(\theta_0)}{\partial \theta}\right]^{-1},$$

or equivalently,

$$Q_S(W^*) = \left(1 + \frac{1}{S}\right) \left[\frac{\partial^2 \psi_\infty(\theta_0, b(\theta_0))}{\partial \theta \partial \beta'} (I_0 - K_0)^{-1} \frac{\partial^2 \psi_\infty(\theta_0, b(\theta_0))}{\partial \beta \partial \theta'}\right]^{-1}.$$

In practice, $b(\theta_0)$ can be approximated by $\hat{\beta}_{ST}\left(\hat{\theta}_{ST}\right)$. A consistent estimator of $I_0 - K_0$ is given by

$$\widehat{I_0 - K_0} = \frac{T}{S} \sum_{s=1}^{T} (W_s - \bar{W})(W_s - \bar{W})',$$

where

$$W_s = \frac{\partial \psi_T\left(\left(x_t^s\left(\hat{\theta}_{ST}\right)\right), \hat{\beta}_{ST}\right)}{\partial \beta}, \quad \bar{W} = \sum_{s=1}^{S} W_s.$$

A global specification test can be applied using the following statistic:

$$\xi_T = \frac{TS}{1+S} \min_\theta \left[\hat{\beta}_T - \hat{\beta}_{ST}(\theta)\right]' W_T \left[\hat{\beta}_T - \hat{\beta}_{ST}(\theta)\right],$$

which follows asymptotically $\chi^2(q - k)$.

12.4   Exercises

1. Consider the coin-tossing example. The probability of heads is p. Denote the realization of the tth toss by x_t, which is equal to 1 if heads and 0 if tails. After N independent tosses, observe data $\{x_1, ..., x_N\}$. Write down the likelihood of observing $\{x_1, ..., x_N\}$. Find the ML estimate of p.

2. In random sampling from the exponential distribution $f(x) = \theta \exp(-x\theta)$, $x \geq 0$, $\theta > 0$, find the maximum likelihood estimator of θ and obtain the asymptotic distribution of this estimator.

3. Use the job search model to simulate some data. Suppose that the wage offer is independently drawn from a lognormal distribution with mean μ and variance σ^2. Suppose that $\mu = 1$, $\sigma^2 = 2$, and $c = 0.5$. The structural parameter to be estimated is β. Let the true value is $\beta_0 = 0.98$. Construct the likelihood of the sample and plot it against different possible values of β. Find the ML estimate of β by varying the sample size T.

4. Construct a computer program to implement the procedure outlined in example 12.3.2 based on the parameter values in exercise 3. First use the mean and variance of the duration as moments. Then increase the number of moments for the fraction of workers after the first and second period. Find the SMM estimate of β. As the model is overidentified, test the overidentification restrictions.

III   Equilibrium Analysis

In this part we apply the tools developed in previous chapters to analyze a variety of equilibrium models widely used in macroeconomics and finance. They range from finite-horizon overlapping generations models to infinite-horizon exchange and production models, from complete markets models to incomplete markets models, from perfectly competitive models to monopolistically competitive models, and from competitive equilibrium models to search and matching models. We introduce analytical methods to explore model properties as well as numerical methods to investigate empirical and quantitative implications.

13 Complete Markets Exchange Economies

This chapter studies competitive equilibria for a pure exchange infinite-horizon economy with stochastic endowments. This economy is a benchmark for studying consumption, risk sharing, and asset pricing. We describe two market structures: an Arrow–Debreu structure with complete markets in dated contingent claims all traded at time zero, and a sequential trading structure with short-lived or long-lived securities. For the latter structure we consider various securities including stocks, bonds, and one-period Arrow securities. We also study various equilibrium concepts. We will focus on complete markets without any trading frictions. In this regard we establish that the two market structures imply identical equilibrium consumption allocations that are Pareto optimal. Conversely, we show that a Pareto optimal allocation can be supported in a competitive equilibrium. We also introduce portfolio constraints and study asset price bubbles.

13.1 Uncertainty, Preferences, and Endowments

Time is denoted by $t = 0, 1, 2, \ldots$. Uncertainty is captured by a finite state space $\mathbb{S} = \{1, 2, \ldots, S\}$. In each period t there is a realization of a stochastic event $s_t \in \mathbb{S}$. The history of events (or node) up until time t is denoted by $s^t = (s_0, s_1, \ldots, s_t)$. Each node s^t has a unique immediate predecessor, denoted by s^{t-1}. Its immediate successor is denoted by s^t_+. Let $s^T | s^t$ denote the history at T following s^t. The unconditional probability of observing a particular sequence of events s^t is given by a probability measure $\Pr(s^t)$. The conditional probability of observing s^t given the realization of s^τ is denoted $\Pr(s^t | s^\tau)$. Assume that $s^0 = s_0$ is given so that $\Pr(s_0) = 1$. An **adapted process** x is a sequence of functions $\{x_t\}_{t=0}^{\infty}$ such that each x_t maps the history s^t into some Euclidean space. Let L_∞ be the space of real-valued bounded adapted processes, $L_\infty = \{x : \sup_{t,s^t} |x_t(s^t)| < \infty\}$. Let L_1 be the space of real-valued summable adapted processes, $L_1 = \{x : \sum_{t,s^t} |x_t(s^t)| < \infty\}$.

There is one consumption good in the economy. Consumption lies in the set $L_{\infty+}$ of nonnegative processes in L_∞. There are I agents named $i = 1, 2, ..., I$. Agent i owns endowment $y^i \in L_{\infty+}$. Let $\bar{y} = \sum_i y^i$ denote the aggregate endowment. When we introduce financial assets later, agents may be endowed with some financial assets. A consumption plan for agent i is denoted by $c^i = \{c_t^i(s^t)\}_{t=0}^\infty \in L_{\infty+}$. Agent i derives utility from c^i according to the discounted expected utility

$$U^i(c^i) = \sum_{t=0}^\infty \sum_{s^t} \beta^t u^i(c_t^i(s^t)) \Pr(s^t), \tag{13.1}$$

where the discount factor $\beta \in (0, 1)$ is common to all agents and u^i satisfies the following:

Assumption 13.1.1 *For each i, u^i is strictly increasing, twice continuously differentiable, strictly concave, and satisfies the usual Inada condition.*

This assumption may be stronger than needed for some of the results derived below.

13.2   Pareto Optimum

An allocation $(c^1, ..., c^I)$ is **feasible** if

$$\sum_i c_t^i(s^t) = \sum_i y_t^i(s^t). \tag{13.2}$$

An allocation $(c^1, ..., c^I)$ is **Pareto optimal** (or **efficient**) if there is no feasible allocation $(\hat{c}^1, ..., \hat{c}^I)$ such that $U^i(\hat{c}^i) \geq U^i(c^i)$ for all i with at least one strict inequality. Imagine that there is a social planner that attaches a nonnegative Pareto weight λ_i to agent i and chooses allocations $c^i, i = 1, 2, ..., I$, to maximize

$$\sum_i \lambda_i U^i(c^i)$$

subject to (13.2).

Proposition 13.2.1 *An allocation is Pareto optimal if and only if it solves the social planner problem discussed above for some nonzero weight in $\mathbb{R}_+^I$.*

Proof   We first prove the "only if" part. Suppose that $(c^1, ..., c^I)$ is Pareto optimal. For any allocation x, let $U(x) = (U^1(x^1), ..., U^I(x^I))$. Define

$$\mathcal{U} = \{U(x) - U(c) - z : x \in \mathfrak{F},\ z \in \mathbb{R}_+^I\} \subset \mathbb{R}^I,$$

where $\mathfrak{F}$ is the set of feasible allocations. Define $\mathcal{Y} = \{y \in \mathbb{R}_+^I : y \neq 0\}$. Since U is convex by the concavity of utility functions and $\mathcal{Y} \cap \mathcal{U} = \varnothing$ by Pareto optimality, the **Separating Hyperplane Theorem** (appendix B) implies that there is a nonzero vector $\lambda \in \mathbb{R}^I$ such that $\lambda \cdot z \leq \lambda \cdot y$ for each $y \in \mathcal{Y}$ and $z \in \mathcal{U}$. Since $0 \in \mathcal{U}$, we know that $\lambda \geq 0$.

We next prove the "if" part. Suppose that $(c^1, ..., c^I)$ solves the social planner problem. If it is not Pareto optimal, then there is a feasible allocation $(\hat{c}^1, ..., \hat{c}^I)$ such that $U^i(\hat{c}^i) \geq U^i(c^i)$ for all i with at least one strict inequality. Suppose that there exists an i such that $U^i(\hat{c}^i) > U^i(c^i)$ and $\lambda^i > 0$. Then the allocation $(\hat{c}^1, ..., \hat{c}^I)$ gives higher weighted utility, a contradiction! Suppose that for all i such that $U^i(\hat{c}^i) > U^i(c^i)$, we have $\lambda^i = 0$. We then decrease $\hat{c}^i$ a little but raise some other agent j's consumption $\hat{c}^j$ with $\lambda^j > 0$ so that the feasibility condition still holds. We can make agent j strictly better off, a contradiction. ∎

Using first-order conditions, we can derive

$$\frac{u^{i\prime}\left(c_t^i\left(s^t\right)\right)}{u^{j\prime}\left(c_t^j\left(s^t\right)\right)} = \frac{\lambda^j}{\lambda^i},$$

which implies that

$$c_t^i\left(s^t\right) = \left(u^{i\prime}\right)^{-1}\left(\lambda_i^{-1}\lambda_1 u^{1\prime}\left(c_t^1\left(s^t\right)\right)\right). \tag{13.3}$$

Substituting this equation into the feasibility condition (13.2) yields

$$\sum_i \left(u^{i\prime}\right)^{-1}\left(\lambda_i^{-1}\lambda_1 u^{1\prime}\left(c_t^1\left(s^t\right)\right)\right) = \sum_i y_t^i\left(s^t\right). \tag{13.4}$$

This is one equation in $c_t^1\left(s^t\right)$. It shows that $c_t^1\left(s^t\right)$ is a function of the aggregate endowment only. It follows from (13.3) that any agent's consumption is also a function of the aggregate endowment only. If the aggregate endowment is determined by an aggregate Markov state variable, then individual consumption is a function of the state only. There is no history dependence in consumption allocation.

13.3 Time 0 Trading

There is a complete set of dated state-contingent claims to consumption. Agents trade these claims at time 0, after s_0 is realized. They can exchange claims on time-t consumption, contingent on history s^t at price $q_t^0\left(s^t\right)$. The superscript 0 refers to the date at which trades occur, while the subscript t refers to the date that deliveries are to be made. We call $\{q_t^0\left(s^t\right)\}$ an **Arrow–Debreu state price** process. Normalize $q_0^0\left(s^0\right) = 1$.

Agent i's budget constraint is given by

$$\sum_{t=0}^{\infty} \sum_{s^t} q_t^0\left(s^t\right) c_t^i\left(s^t\right) \leq \sum_{t=0}^{\infty} \sum_{s^t} q_t^0\left(s^t\right) y_t^i\left(s^t\right). \tag{13.5}$$

For this budget constraint to be well-defined, we need q^0 to be in L_1.

Definition 13.3.1 *An Arrow–Debreu equilibrium consists of a price system* $\left\{q_t^0\left(s^t\right)\right\}_{t=0}^{\infty} \in L_1$ *and a consumption allocation* $\left(c^1, c^2, ..., c^I\right) \in \left(L_{\infty+}\right)^I$ *such that* c^i *solves agent i's problem of maximizing (13.1) subject to (13.5) and markets clear in that (13.2) holds.*

Let μ^i be the Lagrange multiplier associated with (13.5). First-order conditions give

$$\beta^t u^{i\prime}\left(c_t^i\left(s^t\right)\right) \Pr\left(s^t\right) = \mu^i q_t^0\left(s^t\right). \tag{13.6}$$

By normalization, we deduce that $\mu^i = u^{i\prime}\left(c_0^i\left(s^0\right)\right)$. Thus the Arrow–Debreu state price is given by

$$q_t^0\left(s^t\right) = \frac{\beta^t u^{i\prime}\left(c_t^i\left(s^t\right)\right) \Pr\left(s^t\right)}{u^{i\prime}\left(c_0^i\left(s^0\right)\right)}. \tag{13.7}$$

Using (13.6) yields

$$\frac{u^{i\prime}\left(c_t^i\left(s^t\right)\right)}{u^{j\prime}\left(c_t^j\left(s^t\right)\right)} = \frac{\mu^i}{\mu^j}. \tag{13.8}$$

Thus

$$c_t^i\left(s^t\right) = \left(u^{i\prime}\right)^{-1}\left\{u^{1\prime}\left(c_t^1\left(s^t\right)\right) \frac{\mu^i}{\mu^1}\right\}. \tag{13.9}$$

By the feasibility condition,

$$\sum_i \left(u^{i\prime}\right)^{-1}\left\{u^{1\prime}\left(c_t^1\left(s^t\right)\right) \frac{\mu^i}{\mu^1}\right\} = \sum_i y_t^i\left(s^t\right). \tag{13.10}$$

This equation is similar to (13.4). Comparing first-order conditions, we conclude that an Arrow–Debreu equilibrium allocation is a particular Pareto optimal allocation, one that sets the Pareto weights $\lambda_i = \mu_i^{-1}$, $i = 1, 2, ..., I$. Moreover, at the competitive equilibrium allocation, the **shadow prices** $\xi_t\left(s^t\right)$ for the associated planning problem (i.e., the Lagrange multipliers associated with the feasibility constraint) equal the Arrow–Debreu state prices $q_t^0\left(s^t\right)$. This result reflects the two welfare theorems to be presented later.

Example 13.3.1   (Risk sharing) *Suppose that the one-period utility function takes the following form:*

$$u^i(c) = \frac{c^{1-\gamma}}{1-\gamma}$$

for all i, where $\gamma > 0$ represents the coefficient of constant relative risk aversion. Equation (13.8) implies that

$$c_t^i(s^t) = c_t^j(s^t)\left(\frac{\mu_i}{\mu_j}\right)^{-1/\gamma}.$$

This equation shows that individual consumption is perfectly correlated. In addition we can show that

$$c_t^i(s^t) = \frac{(\mu_i)^{-1/\gamma}}{\sum_i (\mu_i)^{-1/\gamma}}\bar{y}_t(s^t),$$

which implies that individual consumption is a constant fraction of the aggregate endowment.

13.3.1   Equilibrium Computation

The following Negishi algorithm (Negishi 1960) allows us to solve the Arrow–Debreu equilibrium:

1. Fix a positive value for one μ^i, say μ^1 throughout the algorithm. Guess some positive values for the remaining μ^i's. Then solve equations (13.9) and (13.10) for a candidate consumption allocation $c_t^i(s^t)$, $i = 1, 2, ..., I$.
2. Use (13.6) for any household i to solve for the price system $\{q_t^0(s^t)\}$.
3. For $i = 1, 2, ..., I$, check the budget constraint (13.5). For those i's for which the cost of consumption exceeds the value of their endowment, raise μ^i, while for those i's for which the reverse inequality holds, lower μ^i.
4. Iterate until convergence on steps 1 through 3.

Multiplying all of the μ^i's by a positive scalar changes the scale of the price system. That is why we are free to normalize as we have in step 1. According to the algorithm above, $q_0^0(s^0) \neq 1$ in general.

13.3.2   Two Welfare Theorems

We now present the two welfare theorems that are the cornerstone in economics. Here we consider pure exchange economies only. We refer the reader to the book by Stokey, Lucas, and Prescott (1989) who treat the general production economies.

We restrict attention to discounted expected utility in (13.1). But the two welfare theorems hold for more general preferences. The First Welfare Theorem formalizes Adam Smith's idea of the "invisible hand."

Theorem 13.3.1 (First Welfare Theorem) *Suppose that u^i is strictly increasing for all i. If $\left((c^i)_{i=1}^I, q^0 \right)$ is an Arrow–Debreu equilibrium, then the allocation $(c^i)_{i=1}^I$ is Pareto optimal.*

The assumption for this theorem is rather weak. Only the assumption of monotonicity of each u^i is needed.

Theorem 13.3.2 (Second Welfare Theorem) *Suppose that u^i is continuous and strictly concave. If the allocation $(c^i)_{i=1}^I$ is Pareto optimal, then there exists an Arrow–Debreu state price process q^0 such that $\left((c^i)_{i=1}^I, q^0 \right)$ is an Arrow–Debreu equilibrium.*

The proof of the Second Welfare Theorem is nontrivial and consists of three steps. Here we provide an outline of these steps and leave the details to the reader. In step 1 we use the **Hahn–Banach theorem** (appendix B) to show the existence of a continuous linear functional $\phi : L_{\infty+} \to \mathbb{R}$ such that $U^i(\hat{c}^i) \geq U^i(c^i)$ implies $\phi(\hat{c}^i) \geq \phi(c^i)$. This means that c^i is the cost-minimizing choice over the set of consumption weakly preferred to c^i. Note that the linear functional ϕ on $L_{\infty+}$ need not have an inner product representation because it need not lie in L_1. We thus proceed to the next step.

In step 2 we show that one can replace ϕ by another continuous linear functional ψ such that ψ has an inner product representation. Since utility is strictly increasing, $\phi \geq 0$. It follows from the **Yosida–Hewitt theorem** (appendix D) that there exists a unique decomposition, $\phi = \phi_c + \phi_f$, where $\phi_c \in L_{1+}$ and ϕ_f is a nonnegative purely finitely additive measure (sometimes called a pure charge). Furthermore $\phi_f(x) = 0$ whenever $x \in L_{\infty+}$ has only a finite number of nonzero components. Suppose that $\phi_f(c^i) > 0$. Let $\alpha > 0$ be such that $\alpha\phi_c(\mathbf{1}) < \phi_f(c^i)$, where $\mathbf{1}$ denotes the deterministic consumption plan of one unit good in each node.

Let $x^T = (x_0, ..., x_T, 0, 0, ...)$ denote the truncated consumption plan of $x \in L_{\infty+}$. Say a utility function $U : L_{\infty+} \to \mathbb{R}$ satisfies **Mackey continuity** if $U(x) > U(x')$ implies that $U(x^T) > U(x')$ for T sufficiently large. This is a continuity requirement on preferences to the effect that sufficiently distant consumption is discounted in a very weak sense so that it does not affect the ranking of consumption. The continuous expected discounted utility function satisfies this requirement.

By monotonicity and Mackey continuity of utility, there exists T large enough such that $\left(c^i + \alpha \mathbf{1}\right)^T \succ c^i$, where $\mathbf{1}$ denotes the consumption plan that gives 1 unit of good in all histories. Now

$$\phi\left(c^i + \alpha \mathbf{1}\right)^T = \phi_c\left(c^i + \alpha \mathbf{1}\right)^T + \phi_f\left(c^i + \alpha \mathbf{1}\right)^T$$
$$= \phi_c\left(c^i + \alpha \mathbf{1}\right)^T \leq \phi_c\left(c^i + \alpha \mathbf{1}\right)$$
$$= \phi_c\left(c^i\right) + \alpha \phi_c\left(\mathbf{1}\right) < \phi\left(c^i\right).$$

But this contradicts step 1. Thus we must have $\phi_f\left(c^i\right) = 0$. It follows that for any $\hat{c}^i \in L_{\infty+}$ such that $U^i\left(\hat{c}^i\right) \geq U\left(c^i\right)$,

$$\phi_c\left(\hat{c}^i\right) \leq \phi\left(\hat{c}^i\right) \leq \phi\left(c^i\right) = \phi_c\left(c_t^i\right).$$

In step 3 we show that c^i is also a utility-maximizing choice for all i given the budget set $\{\hat{c}^i \in L_{\infty+} : \phi_c\left(\hat{c}^i\right) \leq \phi_c\left(c^i\right)\}$. In this step we use the assumption that for each i, there is a cheaper consumption plan $\bar{c}^i \in L_{\infty+}$ such that $\phi_c\left(\bar{c}^i\right) < \phi_c\left(c^i\right)$. This assumption is satisfied whenever c^i is an interior solution because we can pick $\bar{c}^i = 0$. Under this assumption we deduce that for any $\hat{c}^i \in \{\hat{c}^i \in L_{\infty+} : \phi_c\left(\hat{c}^i\right) \leq \phi_c\left(c^i\right)\}$,

$$\phi_c\left(c_\lambda^i\right) = \lambda \phi_c\left(\hat{c}^i\right) + (1 - \lambda)\phi_c\left(\bar{c}^i\right) < \phi_c\left(c^i\right)$$

for $\lambda \in (0, 1)$. It follows from step 2 that $U^i\left(c_\lambda^i\right) < U^i\left(c^i\right)$. Thus, by continuity, $U^i\left(\hat{c}^i\right) = \lim_{\lambda \to 1} U^i\left(c_\lambda^i\right) \leq U^i\left(c^i\right)$.

13.3.3 Asset Pricing

In an Arrow–Debreu economy with complete markets, one can price an asset by breaking it into a sequence of history-contingent claims, evaluating each component of that sequence with the associated Arrow–Debreu price $q_t^0\left(s^t\right)$. The asset is viewed as redundant in the sense that it offers a bundle of history-contingent dated claims, each component of which has already been priced by the market. For example, consider an asset with a stream of payoffs $\{d_t\left(s^t\right)\}_{t=0}^{\infty} \in L_{\infty+}$. The price of this asset at date zero is given by

$$p_0\left(s^t\right) = \sum_{j=1}^{\infty} \sum_{s^{t+j}|s^t} q_{t+j}^0\left(s^{t+j}\right) d_{t+j}\left(s^{t+j}\right).$$

The price of this asset at date t is given by

$$p_t\left(s^t\right) = \frac{1}{q_t^0\left(s^t\right)} \sum_{j=1}^{\infty} \sum_{s^{t+j}|s^t} q_{t+j}^0\left(s^{t+j}\right) d_{t+j}\left(s^{t+j}\right).$$

For the discounted expected utility (13.1), q_t^0 is given in (13.7). Note that it is important that $q^0 \in L_1$ for the prices above be well-defined. The Arrow–Debreu approach to asset pricing requires strong assumptions: it assumes complete frictionless markets. In section 13.8 we will present some other asset-pricing models that apply to more general environments.

13.4   Sequential Trading

The Arrow–Debreu market structure is an idealized theoretical benchmark that cannot capture the trading of financial assets such as stocks and bonds in actual economies. In this subsection we study a market structure with sequential trading of financial assets. We also introduce trading frictions and study asset-pricing implications.

13.4.1   Investment Opportunities

Suppose that financial markets open sequentially. Each period there are J securities available for trade. A portfolio of agent i at node s^t is a $J \times 1$ vector of security holdings $\theta_t^i\left(s^t\right) \in \mathbb{R}^J$. A trading strategy of agent i is an adapted process of portfolios $\left\{\theta_t^i\left(s^t\right)\right\}$. Let Θ denote the set of trading strategies. Security j's price at node s^t is denoted by $p_{jt}\left(s^t\right) \in \mathbb{R}_{++}$. Let $p\left(s^t\right) = \left(p_1\left(s^t\right), ..., p_J\left(s^t\right)\right)^\mathsf{T}$. Any security j traded at s^t can be characterized by one-period payoff $f_{j,t+1}\left(s^{t+1}\right) \in \mathbb{R}_+$ to be delivered in date $t+1$ for all $s^{t+1}|s^t$. Let $f_{t+1}\left(s^t, s_{t+1}\right) = \left[f_{1,t+1}\left(s^t, s_{t+1}\right), ..., f_{J,t+1}\left(s^t, s_{t+1}\right)\right]^\mathsf{T}$ be the $J \times 1$ vector of payoffs. We stack these vectors for all $s_{t+1} \in \mathbb{S}$ in a $J \times S$ payoff matrix $D_{t+1}\left(s^t\right)$. Note that we do not specify when the securities are initially issued since what we care about is how to price assets given future payoffs.

Given the J securities, agent i's budget constraint is given by

$$c_t^i\left(s^t\right) + p_t\left(s^t\right) \cdot \theta_t^i\left(s^t\right) \leq f_t\left(s^t\right) \cdot \theta_{t-1}^i\left(s^{t-1}\right) + y_t^i\left(s^t\right), \tag{13.11a}$$

$$c_0^i\left(s^0\right) + p_0\left(s^0\right) \cdot \theta_0^i\left(s^0\right) \leq p_0\left(s^0\right) \cdot \theta_{-1}^i + y_0^i\left(s^0\right), \tag{13.11b}$$

for all $t > 0$, where $\theta_{-1}^i \in \mathbb{R}_+^J$ is the exogenously given portfolio of securities.

We now give some examples of securities to be analyzed later.

Arrow Securities   A unit of Arrow security traded at node s^t gives one unit of consumption good at node $\left(s^t, s_{t+1}\right)$ and zero at other nodes for some $s_{t+1} \in \mathbb{S}$. Each $s_{t+1} \in \mathbb{S}$ indexes one particular Arrow security. In total there are S distinct Arrow securities. Suppose that agents trade these securities at each node. Agent i's budget constraint is given by

$$c_t^i\left(s^t\right) + \sum_{s_{t+1} \in \mathbb{S}} Q_t\left(s_{t+1}|s^t\right) a_t^i\left(s^t, s_{t+1}\right) \leq a_{t-1}^i\left(s^t\right) + y_t^i\left(s^t\right), \quad t \geq 0, \tag{13.12}$$

where $a^i_{-1}(s^0)$ is the exogenously given initial holdings of Arrow securities, $Q_t(s_{t+1}|s^t)$ represents the price of the Arrow security at node s^t that delivers one unit of consumption good at node (s^t, s_{t+1}) and zero at other nodes, and $a^i_t(s^t, s_{t+1})$ represents the holdings of that Arrow security at node s^t.

Risk-Free Bonds and Stocks   A stock traded at s^t has ex-dividend price $p_t(s^t)$ and delivers a stream of dividends $d_\tau(s^\tau)$ for all $s^\tau|s^t$ and $\tau > t$. We can describe the stock's payoff flow by a one-period payoff: $f_{t+1}(s^{t+1}) = p_{t+1}(s^{t+1}) + d_{t+1}(s^{t+1})$. A one-period risk-free bond traded at s^t delivers a unit of consumption good at any node $s^{t+1}|s^t$ and zero at all other nodes. Its payoff is given by $f_{t+1}(s^{t+1}) = 1$ for each $s^{t+1}|s^t$. A two-period risk-free bond traded at s^t delivers a unit of consumption good at each node $s^{t+2}|s^t$ and zero at all other nodes. We may equivalently describe this security as the one that delivers payoff $f_{t+1}(s^{t+1}) = q_{1,t+1}(s^{t+1})$ for each $s^{t+1}|s^t$, where $q_{1,t+1}(s^{t+1})$ is the price of a one-period risk-free bond at node $s^{t+1}|s^t$.

Call Option   A call option on the stock traded at s^t has the strike price k at some future time $T > t$. The payoff of the option is given by $\max\{p_T(s^T) - k, 0\}$ at each node $s^T|s^t$ and by zero at all other nodes, where $p_T(s^T)$ is the stock price at node $s^T|s^t$. The equivalent one-period payoff is given by the price $p^c_{t+1}(s^{t+1})$ of the call option traded at $s^{t+1}|s^t$ that has the strike price k at T, for all $s^{t+1}|s^t$.

13.4.2   Ponzi Scheme and Portfolio Constraints

Before defining competitive equilibrium under sequential trading, we discuss a particular kind of trading strategy. A **Ponzi scheme** is a trading strategy that allows an agent to keep rolling over debt in order to raise his wealth and hence his utility. Formally, a trading strategy $\{\Delta_t(s^t)\}$ is a Ponzi scheme if

$$p_0(s^0) \cdot \Delta_0(s^0) < 0$$

and

$$p_t(s^t) \cdot \Delta_t(s^t) = f_t(s^t) \cdot \Delta_{t-1}(s^{t-1}) \quad \text{for all } s^t, t > 0.$$

Without any portfolio constraint, a Ponzi scheme makes an agent achieve infinite utility. To ensure finite utility, one has to impose some assumption to rule out Ponzi schemes. One can impose some sort of portfolio constraint (e.g., borrowing constraints, short-sales constraints, and debt constraints) or transversality condition (e.g., see Magill and Quinzii 1994):

- The debt constraint is given by

$$f_{t+1}(s^{t+1}) \cdot \theta^i_t(s^t) \geq -\bar{D}^i_{t+1}(s^{t+1}), \quad \text{all } s^{t+1}|s^t, \text{ all } s^t, \tag{13.13}$$

  where $\bar{D}^i_{t+1}(s^{t+1}) \geq 0$ may be endogenous and agent specific.

- The borrowing constraint is given by

$$p_t\left(s^t\right) \cdot \theta_t^i\left(s^t\right) \geq -\bar{B}_t^i\left(s^t\right), \quad \text{all } s^t, \tag{13.14}$$

  where $\bar{B}_t^i\left(s^t\right) \geq 0$ may be endogenous and agent specific.
- The short-sales constraint is given by

$$\theta_t^i\left(s^t\right) \geq -\bar{h}_t^i\left(s^t\right), \quad \text{all } s^t, \tag{13.15}$$

  where $\bar{h}_t^i\left(s^t\right) \geq 0$ may be endogenous and agent specific.

Let $\Theta^{DC}\left(p,f\right)$, $\Theta^{BC}\left(p,f\right)$, and $\Theta^{SC}\left(p,f\right)$ denote the set of admissible trading strategies that satisfy debt constraints, borrowing constraints and short-sales constraints, respectively. In this chapter we focus on the case where the limits on borrowing, debt, or short sales are sufficiently loose so that the portfolio constraints never bind in equilibrium. Later we will show how such limits can be imposed and then introduce the transversality condition.

13.4.3   Radner Equilibrium

Let the aggregate security supply be

$$\bar{\theta}_{-1} = \sum_i \theta_{-1}^i.$$

Definition 13.4.1 *A Radner equilibrium with debt constraints consists of* $\left(\left(c^i,\theta^i\right)_{i=1}^I, p\right)$ *such that: (i) Given the price system p, $\left(c^i,\theta^i\right)$ solves agent i's problem of maximizing (13.1) subject to (13.11), and (13.13). (ii) Markets clear,*

$$\sum_{i=1}^I c_t^i\left(s^t\right) = \bar{y} + \bar{\theta}_{-1} \cdot \left(f_t\left(s^t\right) - p_t\left(s^t\right)\right),$$

$$\sum_i \theta_t^i\left(s^t\right) = \bar{\theta}_{-1}.$$

A Radner equilibrium with borrowing constraints or short-sales constraints can be defined similarly. When the security supply is zero, the market-clearing condition is identical with the feasibility condition (13.2). In this case we will study the connection between Radner equilibrium, Arrow–Debreu equilibrium, and Pareto optimum. We will also analyze the case where some assets are in positive supply. For example, stocks are in positive supply and provide dividends for consumption.

13.4.4   Arbitrage and State Prices

Given a price-payoff pair (p,f), a trading strategy θ is an **arbitrage** opportunity if

$$p_0\left(s^0\right) \cdot \theta_0\left(s^0\right) \le 0$$

and

$$f_t\left(s^t\right) \cdot \theta_{t-1}\left(s^{t-1}\right) - p_t\left(s^t\right) \cdot \theta_t\left(s^t\right) \ge 0, \quad \text{all } s^t \text{ and } t > 0,$$

with at least one strict inequality. By definition, a Ponzi scheme is an arbitrage opportunity. A trading strategy θ is a **one-period arbitrage** opportunity given (p,f) at s^t if

$$p_t\left(s^t\right) \cdot \theta_t\left(s^t\right) \le 0$$

and

$$f_{t+1}\left(s^{t+1}\right) \cdot \theta_t\left(s^t\right) \ge 0, \quad \text{all } s^{t+1}|s^t,$$

with at least one strict inequality. If there is no arbitrage, then there is no one-period arbitrage at any node s^t. The converse may not be true.

We are interested in arbitrage opportunities on a subset of trading strategies. Define the recession set for the set of admissible trading strategies $\Theta^a\left(p,f\right)$ as

$$R\left(\Theta^a\left(p,f\right)\right) = \{\theta \in \Theta : \Theta^a\left(p,f\right) + \lambda\theta \subset \Theta^a\left(p,f\right), \; \forall\lambda > 0\}.$$

Here a may stand for DC, BC, or SC. It may also stand for other types of portfolio constraints that are not treated in this book.

Theorem 13.4.1 *If u^i is strictly increasing and if agent i's problem of maximizing (13.1) subject to (13.11) and $\theta^i \in \Theta^a\left(p,f\right)$ has a solution, then he has no arbitrage opportunity given (p,f) on the recession set $R\left(\Theta^a\left(p,f\right)\right)$.*

The proof of this theorem is left as an exercise. Next we introduce the **First Fundamental Theorem of Asset Pricing**.

Theorem 13.4.2 *The price-payoff pair (p,f) admits no one-period arbitrage on $R\left(\Theta^a\left(p,f\right)\right)$, $a \in \{DC, BC\}$, at any node s^t if and only if there is a strictly positive state-price process $\{q_t^0\left(s^t\right)\}$ such that*

$$p_t\left(s^t\right) = \frac{1}{q_t^0\left(s^t\right)} \sum_{s^{t+1}|s^t} q_{t+1}^0\left(s^{t+1}\right) f_{t+1}\left(s^{t+1}\right), \quad \text{all } s^t. \tag{13.16}$$

Proof The recession sets for debt constraints and borrowing constraints are given by

$$R\left(\Theta^{DC}(p,f)\right) = \{\theta \in \Theta : f_{t+1} \cdot \theta_t \geq 0, \text{ all } t \geq 0\},$$

$$R\left(\Theta^{BC}(p,f)\right) = \{\theta \in \Theta : p_t \cdot \theta_t \geq 0, \text{ all } t \geq 0\}.$$

By definition, there is no $\theta_t\left(s^t\right) \in \mathbb{R}^J$ such that

$$\theta_t\left(s^t\right)^{\mathsf{T}}\left[-p_t\left(s^t\right), f_{t+1}\left(s^t, 1\right), ..., f_{t+1}\left(s^t, S\right)\right]_{J \times (S+1)} > 0$$

at any s^t. By **Stiemke's lemma** (appendix C), there exist $S+1$ strictly positive values $q_t^0\left(s^t\right)$, $q_{t+1}^0\left(s^t, 1\right)$, ..., and $q_{t+1}^0\left(s^t, S\right)$ such that

$$\left[-p_t\left(s^t\right), f_{t+1}\left(s^t, 1\right), ..., f_{t+1}\left(s^t, S\right)\right]\begin{bmatrix} q_t^0\left(s^t\right) \\ q_{t+1}^0\left(s^t, 1\right) \\ ... \\ q_{t+1}^0\left(s^t, S\right) \end{bmatrix} = 0.$$

This completes the proof.   ∎

Equation (13.16) is called the **no-arbitrage pricing equation**. In this equation, only the ratio $q_{t+1}^0\left(s^{t+1}\right)/q_t^0\left(s^t\right)$ is restricted. We thus normalize $q_t^0\left(s^0\right) = 1$. Define the **state-price deflator** $\{\pi_t\}$ as

$$\pi_t\left(s^t\right) = q_t^0\left(s^t\right)/\Pr\left(s^t\right), \tag{13.17}$$

and the **stochastic discount factor** $\{M_t\}$ as

$$M_{t+1} = \frac{\pi_{t+1}}{\pi_t}.$$

Then the following pricing formula obtains

$$p_t = \frac{1}{\pi_t}E_t\left[\pi_{t+1}f_{t+1}\right] = E_t\left[M_{t+1}f_{t+1}\right], \tag{13.18}$$

where E_t is the conditional expectation operator given the information available up to date t. In the literature, one can call π a **state-price density** or a **marginal-rate-of-substitution** process, and call M a **pricing kernel** process. We emphasize that theorem 13.4.2 does not imply that π or q^0 lies in L_1. As a result the present value of a payoff stream discounted by π or q^0 might not be finite. This is related to asset price bubbles discussed later.

Since the recession set for $\Theta^{SC}(p,f)$ is given by

$$R\left(\Theta^{SC}(p,f)\right) = \{\theta \in \Theta : \theta_t \geq 0, \text{ all } t \geq 0\},$$

the no-arbitrage pricing equation (13.16) does not apply to an economy with short-sales constraints. Using an extension of Stiemke's lemma for convex cones shows that (13.16) holds as an inequality (e.g., see Huang 2002).

13.4.5 Complete Markets
Financial markets are **(dynamically) complete** at the price-payoff pair (p,f) if for any bounded process $\{x_t(s^t)\}_{t=1}^{\infty}$, there is some trading strategy θ such that

$$f_t\left(s^t\right) \cdot \theta_{t-1}\left(s^{t-1}\right) - p_t\left(s^t\right) \cdot \theta_t\left(s^t\right) = x_t\left(s^t\right) \quad \text{all } s^t, \; t \geq 1,$$

where $\theta_{-1} = 0$. Complete markets means that any payoff process x starting at date 1 can be attained by investing $\theta_0(s^0)$ at date 0 and continually trading subsequently. Exercise 8 asks the reader to prove that financial markets are complete at (p,f) if and only if the $J \times S$ payoff matrix $D_{t+1}(s^t)$ has rank S at each node s^t. The completeness of markets depends on the security price process p. This dependence makes the proof of the existence of an equilibrium a nontrivial issue.

Theorem 13.4.3 *If financial markets are complete at (p,f) and there is no arbitrage opportunity on $R\left(\Theta^a(p,f)\right)$, $a \in \{DC, BC\}$, then there exists a unique state price process up to a positive scaling factor.*

Proof Define the S-column vector:

$$x_{t+1}\left(s^t\right) = \left[\frac{q_{t+1}^0\left(s^t,1\right)}{q_t^0\left(s^t\right)}, \ldots, \frac{q_{t+1}^0\left(s^t,S\right)}{q_t^0\left(s^t\right)}\right]^{\mathsf{T}}.$$

Rewrite (13.16) as

$$p_t\left(s^t\right) = D_{t+1}\left(s^t\right) x_{t+1}\left(s^t\right).$$

Since the $J \times S$ payoff matrix $D_{t+1}(s^t)$ has rank S, the matrix $D_{t+1}(s^t)^{\mathsf{T}} D_{t+1}(s^t)$ is invertible. Thus we can solve for $x_{t+1}(s^t)$:

$$x_{t+1}\left(s^t\right) = \left[D_{t+1}\left(s^t\right)^{\mathsf{T}} D_{t+1}\left(s^t\right)\right]^{-1} D_{t+1}\left(s^t\right)^{\mathsf{T}} p_t\left(s^t\right)$$

for any s^t. Given the normalization $q_0(s^0) = 1$, we then obtain a unique solution $\{q_t^0(s^t)\}$. ∎

A canonical setup of complete markets is the one with a complete set of Arrow securities. The budget constraint is given by (13.12). We also introduce debt (or solvency) constraints to rule out Ponzi schemes:

$$a_t^i\left(s^t, s_{t+1}\right) \geq -\bar{D}_{t+1}^i\left(s^t, s_{t+1}\right), \quad \text{all } t \geq 0,$$

where the debt limit $\bar{D}^i$ is loose enough so that the debt constraints never bind in equilibrium. Using first-order conditions, we can compute the Arrow security price of one unit of date $t+1$ consumption, contingent on the realization s_{t+1} at $t+1$, given the history s^t:

$$Q_t\left(s_{t+1}|s^t\right) = \frac{\beta u^{i\prime}\left(c_{t+1}^i\left(s^{t+1}\right)\right)}{u^{i\prime}\left(c_t^i\left(s^t\right)\right)} \Pr\left(s^{t+1}|s^t\right).$$

Under complete markets the equation above does not depend on i. The relation between the Arrow–Debreu state price $\left\{q_t^0\left(s^t\right)\right\}$ and the Arrow security price $\left\{Q_t\left(s_{t+1}|s^t\right)\right\}$ is as follows:

$$q_{t+1}^0\left(s^{t+1}\right) = Q_t\left(s_{t+1}|s^t\right) q_t^0\left(s^t\right), \quad q_0^0\left(s^0\right) = 1.$$

13.4.6   Equilibrium with Transversality Condition

To study the relation among the Pareto optimum, Arrow–Debreu equilibrium, and Radner equilibrium with debt constraints, we introduce another concept of equilibrium: equilibrium with transversality condition. Though this equilibrium notion is less intuitive than an equilibrium with borrowing or debt constraints, it is useful for proving existence of the latter type of equilibrium, especially in the case of incomplete markets (Magill and Quinzii 1994).

Suppose that markets are complete and the price-payoff pair (p, f) admits no arbitrage. Then there exists a unique state price deflator π. Multiplying by π_t on the two sides of the date-t budget constraints (13.11), taking conditional expectations, and summing up, we obtain

$$E_t \sum_{j=0}^{T} \pi_{t+j} c_{t+j}^i + E_t \pi_{t+T} p_{t+T} \cdot \theta_{t+T}^i \leq \pi_t f_t \cdot \theta_{t-1}^i + E_t \sum_{j=0}^{T} \pi_{t+j} y_{t+j}^i \tag{13.19}$$

for $t > 0$, where we have used equation (13.16). At date 0, we have

$$E \sum_{t=0}^{T} \pi_t c_t^i + E \pi_T p_T \cdot \theta_T^i \leq \pi_0 p_0 \cdot \theta_{-1}^i + E \sum_{t=0}^{T} \pi_t y_t^i. \tag{13.20}$$

Given the following transversality condition,

$$\lim_{T \to 0} E\left[\pi_T p_T \cdot \theta_T^i\right] = 0, \tag{13.21}$$

we take limits as $T \to \infty$ in (13.19) and (13.20) to obtain

$$E \sum_{t=0}^{\infty} \pi_t c_t^i \leq \pi_0 p_0 \cdot \theta_{-1}^i + E \sum_{t=0}^{\infty} \pi_t y_t^i, \tag{13.22}$$

$$E_t \sum_{j=0}^{\infty} \pi_{t+j} c_{t+j}^i \leq \pi_t f_t \cdot \theta_{t-1}^i + E_t \sum_{j=0}^{\infty} \pi_{t+j} y_{t+j}^i, \quad t > 0. \tag{13.23}$$

We are ready to introduce the following:

Definition 13.4.2 *A competitive equilibrium with transversality condition consists of* $\left((c^i, \theta^i)_{i=1}^{I}, \pi, p \right) \in (L_{\infty+})^I \times \Theta^I \times L_{1++} \times (L_{\infty+})^J$ *such that:*

a. *given* (π, p), *for each* i, (c^i, θ^i) *solves agent* i's *problem of maximizing (13.1) subject to (13.11) and (13.21);*

b. *given* π, *for each* i, c^i *solves agent* i's *problem of maximizing (13.1) subject to (13.22);*

c. (π, p) *satisfies (13.18); and*

d. *markets clear, meaning (13.2) holds and* $\sum_i \theta_t^i = \bar{\theta}_{-1}$.

Conditions (a) and (d) are standard. However, π must be restricted in condition (a). This restriction is given in conditions (b) and (c).

To relate to the Pareto optimality and the Arrow–Debreu equilibrium studied earlier, we suppose that all assets are in zero supply, that is, $\bar{\theta}_{-1} = 0$. Moreover we suppose that each agent's initial asset holdings are also zero, that is, $\theta_{-1}^i = 0$ for all i. By definition, any allocation in a competitive equilibrium with transversality condition is an Arrow–Debreu equilibrium allocation and hence is Pareto optimal.

We can claim that any Pareto optimal allocation can be supported in a competitive equilibrium with transversality condition. To prove this result, we observe that equation (13.22) is equivalent to the Arrow–Debreu budget constraint (13.5) given $\theta_{-1}^i = 0$. We then apply the Second Welfare Theorem to show that the Pareto optimal allocation can be supported by an Arrow–Debreu state price $q^0 \in L_{1++}$ or a state price deflator $\pi \in L_{1++}$ in an Arrow–Debreu equilibrium. Thus conditions (b) and (c) in definition 13.4.2 hold. Now it remains to verify condition (a). We need to show that the Arrow–Debreu budget constraints (13.22) with $\theta_{-1}^i = 0$ and the sequential budget constraints (13.11) with transversality condition (13.21) give identical consumption plans. We have demonstrated earlier that any consumption plan satisfying the sequential budget constraints (13.11) with the transversality condition (13.21) also satisfies the Arrow–Debreu budget constraints (13.22) with $\theta_{-1}^i = 0$. To show the converse, we apply the definition of complete markets to establish the existence of a trading strategy θ^i such that $f_t \cdot \theta_{t-1}^i - p_t \cdot \theta_t^i = c_t^i - y_t^i$.

13.4.7　Natural Debt Limit

In this subsection we derive the tightest debt (borrowing) limit such that it is never reached in equilibrium. Such a limit is often called a **natural debt (borrowing) limit** and the corresponding portfolio constraints are called **natural debt (borrowing) constraints**. Consider complete markets with a unique state price deflator π. Since consumption must be nonnegative, it follows from (13.23) that

$$f_t \cdot \theta_{t-1}^i \geq -\frac{1}{\pi_t} E_t \sum_{j=0}^{\infty} \pi_{t+j} y_{t+j}^i, \quad t \geq 1. \tag{13.24}$$

This means that agent i's debt cannot exceed his present value of current and future endowments. We can set the debt limit as

$$\bar{D}_t^i = \frac{1}{\pi_t} E_t \sum_{j=0}^{\infty} \pi_{t+j} y_{t+j}^i, \quad t \geq 1.$$

Under this debt limit the debt constraint will never bind if optimal consumption is strictly positive.

To derive the natural borrowing limit, we use (13.18) and (13.24) to show that

$$\theta_{t-1}^i \cdot p_{t-1} = \frac{1}{\pi_{t-1}} E_{t-1} \left[\pi_t f_t \cdot \theta_{t-1}^i \right] \geq -\frac{1}{\pi_{t-1}} E_{t-1} \sum_{j=0}^{\infty} \pi_{t+j} y_{t+j}^i$$

for all $t \geq 1$. This inequality means that agent i's borrowing cannot exceed his present value of future endowments, which gives the natural borrowing limit $\bar{B}_t^i$.

When the price process p is bounded, we can use the previous inequalities to derive the tightest limit on short sales such that it is never reached in equilibrium.

13.5　Equivalence of Equilibria

In this section we establish equivalence of various equilibrium concepts. This result allows us to establish the existence of an equilibrium with nonbinding debt or borrowing constraints using the existence of an equilibrium with transversality condition. In this subsection we suppose that all assets are in zero supply and $\theta_{-1}^i = 0$ for all i.

Theorem 13.5.1　*Suppose that markets are complete at the price-payoff pair (p, f). Then $\left((c^i, \theta^i)_{i=1}^I, p \right)$ is a Radner equilibrium with nonbinding debt or borrowing constraints if and only if there exists a state price deflator $\pi \in L_1$ such that $\left((c^i, \theta^i)_{i=1}^I, \pi, p \right)$ is a competitive equilibrium with transversality condition.*

Before proving this theorem, we note that there exist economies for which an equilibrium with transversality condition is not an equilibrium with debt or borrowing constraints as shown by the following example.

Example 13.5.1 (Magill and Quinzii 1994) *Consider a deterministic economy with two agents. Their utility functions are given by*

$$U^1(c) = c_0, \quad U^2(c) = \sum_{t=1}^{\infty} \frac{2}{t^2} \sqrt{c_t},$$

and their endowments are given by

$$y^1 = (0, 1, 1, ...), \quad y^2 = \left(\sum_{t=1}^{\infty} \frac{1}{t^2}, 0, 0, ... \right).$$

Agent 1 derives utility only at date 0 so that he has an incentive to borrow against his future endowments in order to consume at zero. The Arrow–Debreu equilibrium is given by

$$c^{1*} = y^2, \quad c^{2*} = y^1, \quad \pi_0 = 1, \quad \pi_t = \frac{1}{t^2}.$$

If there is a one-period bond at each date, then the competitive equilibrium with transversality condition has the same allocation $\left(c^{1*}, c^{2*} \right)$, *trading strategy*

$$\theta_t^1 = -(t+1)^2 \sum_{n=t+1}^{\infty} \frac{1}{n^2}, \quad t \geq 0,$$

and bond price

$$p_0 = 1, p_t = \frac{t^2}{(t+1)^2}, \quad t > 0.$$

The transversality condition is satisfied, since

$$\pi_T p_T \theta_T^1 = - \sum_{n=T+1}^{\infty} \frac{1}{n^2} \to 0 \quad as \ T \to \infty.$$

However, agent 1's borrowing is unlimited, since

$$p_T \theta_T^1 = - \sum_{s=1}^{\infty} \frac{T^2}{(T+s)^2} \to -\infty \quad as \ T \to \infty.$$

Thus the equilibrium with transversality condition is not a Radner equilibrium with borrowing constraints. The intuition is the following. The Arrow–Debreu prices (after date 1) are determined by the marginal utility of agent 2. Since agent 2 becomes *progressively more patient as time evolves—in that $t^2/(t+1)^2$ increases with t—the present value at date T of agent 1's endowments,*

$$\sum_{s=1}^{\infty} \frac{\pi_{T+s}}{\pi_T} = \sum_{s=1}^{\infty} \frac{T^2}{(T+s)^2},$$

tends to infinity as $T \to \infty$. It is the fact that the present value of agent 1's future income keeps growing and that gives him the right to go progressively deeper into debt.

The example above illustrates that it is important to impose an assumption that prevents agents from becoming progressively more patient and precludes the phenomenon of agents going progressively deeper into debt.

Assumption 13.5.1   (Uniform lower bound on impatience) *For any i, any node s^t and any κ^i, there exists $\alpha^i \in (0,1)$ independent of s^t such that for any consumption plan c^i, the consumption plan of replacing $c_t^i(s^t)$ with $c_t^i(s^t) + \kappa^i \bar{y}_t(s^t)$ and replacing $c_\tau^i(s^\tau)$ with $\alpha^i c_\tau^i(s^\tau)$ for all $s^\tau | s^t$ is preferred to the plan c^i.*

This assumption is satisfied by continuous discounted expected utility.

Proof of Theorem 13.5.1 (Sketch)   First sketch the proof of the "if" part. Let $\left(\left(c^i, \theta^i \right)_{i=1}^I, \pi, p \right)$ be a competitive equilibrium with transversality condition. Construct a trading strategy as follows. Given the market-clearing condition, there exists an agent i such that $p_t \theta_t^i > 0$ at each node s^t. Scale down the trading strategy θ^i to $\alpha^i \theta^i$ starting from the node s^t on, where α^i is given in assumption 13.5.1. Consider the consumption plan $\hat{c}^i$ which is obtained from c^i by replacing c_t^i with $c_t^i(s^t) + \left(1 - \alpha^i \right) p_t(s^t) \cdot \theta_t^i(s^t)$ at node s^t and replacing $c_\tau^i(s^\tau)$ with $\alpha^i c_\tau^i(s^\tau)$ for all $s^\tau | s^t$, $\tau > t$. This plan is budget feasible since at node s^t,

$$c_t^i + \left(1 - \alpha^i \right) p_t \cdot \theta_t^i + \alpha^i p_t \cdot \theta_t^i \leq f_t \cdot \theta_{t-1}^i + y_t^i,$$

and at node $s^\tau | s^t$,

$$\alpha^i c_\tau^i(s^\tau) + \alpha^i p_\tau(s^\tau) \cdot \theta_\tau^i(s^\tau) \leq \alpha^i f_\tau(s^\tau) \cdot \theta_{\tau-1}^i(s^{\tau-1}) + y_\tau^i(s^\tau).$$

It follows from the assumption of the uniform lower bound on impatience that $\left(1 - \alpha^i \right) p_t \cdot \theta_t^i < \kappa^i \bar{y}_t$. Define $\alpha = \max_i \alpha^i$. Then

$$p_t \cdot \theta_t^i < \frac{\kappa^i \bar{y}_t}{1 - \alpha} \quad \text{for all } i.$$

Since $\sum_i p_t \cdot \theta_t^i = 0$, it follows that

$$p_t \cdot \theta_t^i > -\frac{(I-1)\,\kappa^i \bar{y}_t}{1-\alpha} \quad \text{for all } i.$$

Thus (c^i, θ^i) is budget feasible and satisfies the borrowing constraint. Since any bounded process $\{p_t \cdot \theta_t^i\}$ satisfies the transversality condition

$$\lim_{T \to \infty} \left[\pi_T p_T \cdot \theta_T^i \right] = 0,$$

the constraint set in the equilibrium with borrowing constraint is contained in the constraint set in the equilibrium with transversality condition. Thus (c^i, θ^i) is also optimal in the former set and hence $\left((c^i, \theta^i)_{i=1}^{I}, p \right)$ is an equilibrium with nonbinding borrowing constraints. It is easy to see that it is also an equilibrium with nonbinding debt constraints.

Next we sketch the proof of the "only if" part, which is quite technical. For a complete proof, see Magill and Quinzii (1994, 1996). Let $\left((c^i, \theta^i)_{i=1}^{I}, p \right)$ be an equilibrium with nonbinding borrowing constraints. Since (c^i, θ^i) is optimal given the budget constraints and borrowing constraints, a separation argument gives the existence of a price functional P^i on $L_{\infty+}$, which separates the preferred set $\mathcal{U}^i = \{ \hat{c}^i \in L_{\infty+} : U^i(\hat{c}^i) > U^i(c^i) \}$ from the budget set with debt constraints. The set $\mathcal{U}^i$ has a nonempty interior in the norm topology. Mackey continuity of utility implies that P^i can be replaced by a linear functional in L_1. The absence of arbitrage implies the existence of a state price deflator $\pi \in L_1$ that satisfies (13.18). Complete markets deliver a unique π, which pins down P^i. Note that the budget set with borrowing constraints is contained in the budget set with transversality condition, which is contained in the Arrow–Debreu budget set given price P^i. Since c^i is in all these sets, and since by the separation argument, c^i is optimal in the largest Arrow–Debreu budget set, it is also optimal in the budget set with transversality condition. Thus $\left((c^i, \theta^i)_{i=1}^{I}, \pi, p \right)$ is a competitive equilibrium with transversality condition. ∎

13.6   Asset Price Bubbles

By backward induction, there is no bubble on assets with finite maturity. Thus we focus on assets with infinite maturity. Since the equilibria exhibited in the existence proof are often obtained by taking limits of equilibria of truncated finite economies, they have the property that all assets are priced at their fundamental values. It is natural to ask whether this property holds for all possible equilibria. It turns out that the crucial condition depends on whether an asset is in zero supply and whether the present value of aggregate endowments is finite.

Suppose that all J securities are stocks with payoffs $f_t = p_t + d_t$. Suppose that markets are complete and π denotes the unique state price deflator. Then the no-arbitrage pricing equation is given by

$$p_t = \frac{1}{\pi_t} E_t \pi_{t+1} (p_{t+1} + d_{t+1}).$$

Solving this equation forward by repeated substitution yields

$$p_t = \frac{1}{\pi_t} \sum_{j=1}^{T} E_t \pi_{t+j} d_{t+j} + \frac{1}{\pi_t} E_t \pi_{t+T} p_{t+T}.$$

Define the **fundamental value** of the stocks with dividends $\{d_t\}$ as

$$v_t(d) = \frac{1}{\pi_t} \sum_{j=1}^{\infty} E_t \left[\pi_{t+j} d_{t+j} \right].$$

Define an **asset price bubble** as

$$b_t = p_t - v_t(d).$$

That is, an asset price bubble is equal to the difference between the market price of the asset and its fundamental value (i.e., the present value of its payoffs). This definition applies to the case when the asset payoffs are exogenously given. This case also happens in pure exchange economies. The definition also applies unambiguously to an intrinsically useless asset like money whose payoffs are zero. But it is problematic when asset payoffs are endogenous in production economies (see Miao and Wang 2011b, c, 2012a, b); Miao, Wang, and Xu 2013; Miao, Wang, and Xu 2013).

By definition,

$$b_t = \lim_{T \to \infty} \frac{1}{\pi_t} E_t \left[\pi_{t+T} p_{t+T} \right].$$

It is straightforward to show that the bubble satisfies the following properties:

$$0 < b_t \leq p_t,$$

$$b_t = \frac{1}{\pi_t} E_t \left[\pi_{t+1} b_{t+1} \right]. \tag{13.25}$$

We call the second property the **discounted martingale property**. One could view the bubble as a separate asset traded in the market. This asset is intrinsically useless and does not deliver any payoffs. Equation (13.25) is a no-arbitrage pricing equation for the bubble.

The following theorem gives sufficient conditions for the nonexistence of a bubble due to Santos and Woodford (1997). It generalizes the Santos–Woodford result by including debt constraints. Unlike Santos and Woodford (1997), it restricts attention to complete markets. Using assumption 13.5.1, it is possible to extend the result to incomplete market economies.

Theorem 13.6.1 *Let p be a Radner equilibrium price system under debt or borrowing constraints. Suppose that markets are complete at p, and let π be the unique state price deflator. If the present value of the aggregate endowment is finite,*

$$E\sum_{t=0}^{T}\pi_t\bar{y}_t < \infty,$$

then there is no bubble on any asset with positive supply.

Proof We have shown that equation (13.22) holds when the present value of the aggregate endowment is finite. Summing over all i yields

$$\sum_{i}E\sum_{t=0}^{\infty}\pi_t c_t^i + \bar{\theta}_{-1} \cdot \lim_{T\to\infty}E\pi_T p_T \le \pi_0 p_0 \cdot \bar{\theta}_{-1} + E\sum_{t=0}^{\infty}\pi_t\bar{y}_t. \qquad (13.26)$$

Suppose that there is a bubble on an asset with positive supply. Then

$$\sum_{i}E\sum_{t=0}^{\infty}\pi_t c_t^i < \pi_0 p_0 \cdot \bar{\theta}_{-1} + E\sum_{t=0}^{\infty}\pi_t\bar{y}_t. \qquad (13.27)$$

This means that for at least one agent i,

$$E\sum_{t=0}^{\infty}\pi_t c_t^i < \pi_0 p_0 \cdot \theta_{-1}^i + E\sum_{t=0}^{\infty}\pi_t y_t^i.$$

This contradicts agent i's optimality. ∎

The intuition behind the absence of a bubble is the following. The aggregate wealth in the economy is equal to the aggregate financial wealth from stock holdings plus the aggregate human wealth from the present value of the total endowment. Suppose that there is a bubble on the stock with positive supply. Then the aggregate wealth is spent in financing total consumption and in holding the bubble. Thus there exists an agent such that he must hold part of the bubble so that his present value of consumption is strictly less than his financial and human wealth. But this contradicts his optimality.

The preceding theorem shows that a necessary condition for the existence of a bubble is that either the present value of the aggregate endowment is infinity or the asset is in zero supply. To illustrate these conditions, we consider two examples. The first example shows that a bubble exists for an asset with zero supply.

Example 13.6.1   (Kocherlakota 1992) *Consider a deterministic economy. There is only one stock for trading. Suppose that $\theta^i_{-1} = 0$ for all i and that $\left((c^i, \theta^i)_{i=1}^{I}, p \right)$ is an equilibrium with natural borrowing constraints such that*

$$p_t = \frac{1}{\pi_t} \sum_{s=t+1}^{\infty} \pi_s d_s,$$

where $\pi \in L_1$ is the unique state price deflator. We claim that $\left((\hat{c}^i, \hat{\theta}^i)_{i=1}^{I}, \hat{p} \right)$ is also an equilibrium with natural borrowing constraints, where

$$\hat{c}^i_t = c^i_t, \ \hat{p}_t = p_t + \frac{\eta}{\pi_t}, \ \hat{\theta}^i_t = \theta^i_t \frac{p_t}{\hat{p}_t}$$

for any $\eta \geq 0$. The bubble component is $b_t = \eta/\pi_t$. Note that

$$\frac{\pi_t}{\pi_{t+1}} = \frac{\hat{p}_{t+1} + d_{t+1}}{\hat{p}_t} = \frac{p_{t+1} + d_{t+1}}{p_t}.$$

We can then check that

$$\hat{c}^i_t + \hat{p}_t \hat{\theta}^i_t = c^i_t + p_t \theta^i_t \leq (p_t + d_t) \theta^i_{t-1} + y^i_t$$

$$= \frac{p_t + d_t}{p_{t-1}} \theta^i_{t-1} p_{t-1} + y^i_t = \frac{\hat{p}_t + d_t}{\hat{p}_{t-1}} \theta^i_{t-1} p_{t-1} + y^i_t$$

$$= (\hat{p}_t + d_t) \hat{\theta}^i_{t-1} + y^i_t, \ t > 0,$$

$$\hat{c}^i_0 + \hat{p}_0 \hat{\theta}^i_0 = c^i_0 + p_0 \theta^i_0 \leq y^i_0.$$

The natural borrowing constraints are identical. Finally, we check that the transversality condition holds:

$$\lim_{t \to \infty} \pi_t \hat{p}_t \hat{\theta}^i_t = \lim_{t \to \infty} \pi_t p_t \theta^i_t = 0.$$

This example also illustrates that $\left((\hat{c}^i, \hat{\theta}^i)_{i=1}^{I}, \pi, \hat{p} \right)$ is an equilibrium with transversality condition, as established in theorem 13.5.1.

The following example shows that a bubble exists on an asset with positive supply in the case of infinite present value of aggregate endowments.

Example 13.6.2 (Werner 2012) *Consider a deterministic economy. There are two agents with an identical utility function:*

$$\sum_{t=0}^{\infty} \beta^t \ln c_t^i, \quad i = 1, 2.$$

There is only one asset that delivers zero payoff (money), and hence its fundamental value is zero. The budget constraints are given by

$$c_t^i + p_t \theta_t^i = p_t \theta_{t-1}^i + y_t^i,$$

where $\theta_{-1}^1 = 1$ and $\theta_{-1}^2 = 0$. Both agents face short sales constraints

$$\theta_t^i \geq -1, \quad t \geq 0.$$

The endowments are given by

$$y^1 = (B, A, B, A, \ldots), \quad y^2 = (A, B, A, B, \ldots),$$

where $A > B > 0$. Agent 1 initially has fewer endowments and one unit of the asset. He prefers to sell the asset to exchange for initial consumption. Agent 2 initially has more endowments, but no asset. He prefers to save and lend by buying the asset. There is an equilibrium with

$$p_t = \frac{1}{3}\eta > 0,$$

where

$$\eta = \frac{\beta A - B}{\beta + 1} \quad \text{for } \beta A > B.$$

The equilibrium consumption and asset holdings are given by

$$c^1 = (B + \eta, A - \eta, B + \eta, A - \eta, \ldots),$$
$$c^2 = (A - \eta, B + \eta, A - \eta, B + \eta, \ldots),$$

and

$$\theta^1 = (-1, 2, -1, 2, \ldots), \quad \theta^2 = (2, -1, 2, -1, \ldots).$$

For the initial budget constraints to hold, we set the initial endowments as

$$y_0^1 = B + \frac{1}{3}\eta, \quad y_0^2 = A - \frac{1}{3}\eta.$$

The transversality condition holds. The state price is given by

$$\pi_{t+1} = \frac{p_t}{p_{t+1}}\pi_t = \pi_t = \pi_0 = 1.$$

Thus the present value of aggregate endowments is $\sum_{t=0}^{\infty} \pi_t \left(y_t^1 + y_t^2\right) = \infty$. In this example, π is not in L_1.

There is another equilibrium in which $p = 0$. The asset has no value and hence no trade occurs. The bubbly equilibrium occurs when the short-sales constraint binds infinitely often.

13.7   Recursive Formulation

In applications a recursive structure is useful to summarize the effects of past events and current information by a limited number of state variables. To formulate a recursive structure, suppose that uncertainty is generated by a Markov chain $\{s_t\}$. Let $\Pr\left(s_{t+1}|s^t\right) = \Pr\left(s_{t+1}|s_t\right)$. We then have

$$\Pr\left(s^t\right) = \Pr\left(s_t|s_{t-1}\right)\Pr\left(s_{t-1}|s_{t-2}\right)...\Pr\left(s_1|s_0\right).$$

Assume that agents' endowments in period t are time-invariant measurable functions of s_t, $y_t^i\left(s^t\right) = y^i\left(s_t\right)$, for each i. There are J stocks available for trading with the dividends vector $d_t\left(s^t\right) = d\left(s_t\right)$. Markets may be incomplete. We also consider debt constraints with debt limit $\bar{D}_t\left(s^t\right) = \bar{D}\left(s_t\right)$. Since markets may be incomplete and there are trading frictions, there may not exist perfect consumption insurance. Thus the equilibrium stock price may depend on wealth distribution. We conjecture that the price is given by $p_t\left(s^t\right) = p\left(\mathbf{w}_t, s_t\right)$, where $\mathbf{w}_t = \left(w_t^1, w_t^2, ..., w_t^I\right)$ denotes a wealth distribution. The wealth distribution is a state variable and its evolution is governed by

$$\mathbf{w}' = G\left(\mathbf{w}, s, s'\right) \tag{13.28}$$

for some function $G = \left(G^1, G^2, ..., G^I\right)$ to be determined in equilibrium. But each agent i takes it as given.

We can then write agent i's problem by dynamic programming:

$$V^i\left(w^i;\mathbf{w},s\right) = \max_{(c,\theta)\in\mathbb{R}\times\mathbb{R}^J} u^i\left(c\right) + \beta\sum_{s'} V^i\left(w^{i\prime},s'\right)\Pr\left(s'|s\right) \tag{13.29}$$

subject to (13.28) and

$$c + p\left(\mathbf{w},s\right)\cdot\theta \le w^i + y\left(s\right),$$
$$w^{i\prime} = \left(p\left(\mathbf{w}',s'\right) + d\left(s'\right)\right)\cdot\theta,$$
$$w^{i\prime} \ge -\bar{D}\left(s'\right),$$

where a variable with a prime denotes its value in the next period.

Definition 13.7.1   *A recursive competitive equilibrium with debt constraints consists of value functions, $V^i\left(w^i;\mathbf{w},s\right)$, consumption functions $c^i\left(w^i;\mathbf{w},s\right)$, and portfolio-holding functions $\theta^i\left(w^i;\mathbf{w},s\right)$ for $i=1,2,...,I$, a price function $p\left(\mathbf{w},s\right)$, and a law of motion $G\left(\mathbf{w},s,s\right)$ such that (a) given G and p, $\left(c^i,\theta^i\right)$ solves agent i's dynamic programming problem (13.29); (b) markets clear,*

$$\sum_i h^i\left(w^i;\mathbf{w},s\right) = \sum_i y^i\left(s\right) + \sum_j d_j\left(s\right),$$

$$\sum_i g^i\left(w^i;\mathbf{w},s\right) = 1;$$

and (c) the law of motion for the wealth distribution is consistent with equilibrium in that

$$G^i\left(\mathbf{w},s,s'\right) = \left(p\left(G\left(\mathbf{w},s,s'\right),s'\right) + d\left(s'\right)\right)\cdot\theta^i\left(w^i;\mathbf{w},s\right)\quad\textit{for all } i.$$

Note that as a state variable, we can use the distribution of portfolio holdings instead of the wealth distribution. We can also remove one agent's wealth or portfolio holdings from the list of state variables using market-clearing conditions. When markets are complete and when there is no trading friction, there exists perfect consumption insurance in that each agent's consumption is a function of aggregate consumption and hence a function of the aggregate shock. The price is also a function of the aggregate shock only. We can then remove the wealth distribution as a state variable in the definition of recursive equilibrium.

It is nontrivial to establish the existence of a recursive competitive equilibrium with natural state variables. It may even not exist (see Kubler and Schmedders 2002). One way to deal with this issue is to include a large set of state variables (see Duffie et al. 1994).

13.8   Asset Pricing

By the First Fundamental Theorem of Asset Pricing, if any asset-payoff pair (p_j, f_j) admits no arbitrage, then there exists a stochastic discount factor (SDF) M such that

$$p_{jt} = E_t \left[M_{t+1} f_{j,t+1} \right].$$

Define the return on this asset as

$$R_{j,t+1} = \frac{f_{j,t+1}}{p_{jt}}.$$

We then have

$$E_t \left[M_{t+1} R_{j,t+1} \right] = 1. \tag{13.30}$$

This form is often used in empirical work. It applies to any asset. In particular, the risk-free rate satisfies

$$R_{f,t+1} = \frac{1}{E_t \left[M_{t+1} \right]},$$

and the conditional expected excess return on any risky asset j satisfies

$$E_t \left[\left(R_{j,t+1} - R_{f,t+1} \right) M_{t+1} \right] = 0.$$

It follows that

$$E_t \left[R_{j,t+1} - R_{f,t+1} \right] = \frac{ -\text{Cov}_t \left(M_{t+1}, R_{j,t+1} - R_{f,t+1} \right) }{ E_t \left[M_{t+1} \right] }. \tag{13.31}$$

The intuition behind this equation is as follows. An asset commands a risk premium when it is negatively correlated with the SDF. It has low returns when the SDF is large, that is, when marginal utility is high. In equilibrium, investors must be compensated for holding the risky asset when it does poorly in bad times. During bad times, investors' marginal utility is high and their wealth is most valuable.

Since $\text{Cov}_t \left(M_{t+1}, R_{j,t+1} - R_{f,t+1} \right) \geq -\sigma_t \left(M_{t+1} \right) \sigma_t \left(R_{j,t+1} - R_{f,t+1} \right)$, it follows that

$$\frac{ \sigma_t \left(M_{t+1} \right) }{ E_t \left[M_{t+1} \right] } \geq \frac{ E_t \left[R_{j,t+1} - R_{f,t+1} \right] }{ \sigma_t \left(R_{j,t+1} - R_{f,t+1} \right) },$$

where $\sigma_t(x)$ denotes the conditional volatility of x. The inequality above says that the **Sharpe ratio** for asset j—the asset's risk premium divided by its volatility— puts a lower bond on the **market price of risk,** defined as the volatility of the SDF divided by its mean. The tightest bond is obtained by finding the risky asset, or portfolio of assets, with the highest Sharpe ratio.

Since the SDF M is not observable in the data, one needs to specify an economic model to recover M. We consider three models below.[1]

13.8.1   Capital Asset-Pricing Model

We start with the **capital asset-pricing model (CAPM)** of Sharpe (1964) and Lintner (1965). Suppose that the SDF is linearly related to the return on a market portfolio or wealth portfolio:

$$M_{t+1} = a + bR_{m,t+1}.$$

In exercises 9 and 10 the reader is asked to show that this relation can hold under a variety of primitive assumptions on preferences and technology. From (13.31) we can derive

$$E_t \left[R_{m,t+1} - R_{f,t+1} \right] = \frac{-b Var_t \left(R_{m,t+1} \right)}{E_t \left[M_{t+1} \right]},$$

$$E_t \left[R_{j,t+1} - R_{f,t+1} \right] = \frac{-b \, \mathrm{Cov}_t \left(R_{m,t+1}, R_{j,t+1} \right)}{E_t \left[M_{t+1} \right]}.$$

It follows that

$$E_t \left[R_{j,t+1} - R_{f,t+1} \right] = \beta_{jt} E_t \left[R_{m,t+1} - R_{f,t+1} \right],$$

where

$$\beta_{jt} = \frac{\mathrm{Cov}_t \left[R_{j,t+1}, M_{t+1} \right]}{Var_t \left(M_{t+1} \right)}$$

describes the quantity of risk. It gives the regression coefficient of the asset return j on the market portfolio return.

13.8.2   Factor-Pricing Model

Suppose that the SDF is linearly related to a finite number of independent factors with zero mean, $F_1, ..., F_K$,

$$M_{t+1} = a + \sum_{k=1}^{K} b_{kt} F_{k,t+1}. \tag{13.32}$$

---

1. See Duffie (2001) and Cochrane (2005) for a comprehensive treatment of asset-pricing theory. See Campbell, Low, and MacKinlay (1997) for a summary of recent work on empirical implementations.

We can compute

$$-\text{Cov}_t\left(M_{t+1}, R_{j,t+1} - R_{f,t+1}\right) = -\sum_k b_{kt}\text{Cov}_t\left(F_{k,t+1}, R_{j,t+1}\right)$$

$$= -\sum_k b_{kt}\text{Var}_t\left(F_{k,t+1}\right)\frac{\text{Cov}_t\left(F_{k,t+1}, R_{j,t+1}\right)}{\text{Var}_t\left(F_{k,t+1}\right)}.$$

We define beta, "the quantity of risk," and the "price of risk" of the kth factor as

$$\beta_{jkt} = \frac{\text{Cov}_t\left(F_{k,t+1}, R_{j,t+1}\right)}{\text{Var}_t\left(F_{k,t+1}\right)}, \quad \lambda_{kt} = \frac{-b_{kt}\,\text{Var}_t\left(F_{k,t+1}\right)}{E_t\left(M_{t+1}\right)},$$

respectively. We then obtain the factor-pricing model using (13.31):

$$E_t\left[R_{j,t+1} - R_{f,t+1}\right] = \sum_k \beta_{jkt}\lambda_{kt}.$$

Ross (1976) shows that the linear relation in (13.32) can be delivered from the statistical characterization of asset returns in terms of factor decomposition.

13.8.3   Consumption-Based Capital Asset-Pricing Model

In this section, we present a **consumption-based capital asset-pricing model** (**CCAPM**) (Lucas 1978; Breeden 1979). There is a representative agent with utility function given by

$$E\sum_{t=0}^{\infty}\beta^t u\left(c_t\right).$$

There is a risk-free bond with zero supply and a stock with one share supply. The stock pays aggregate consumption C as dividends. In this case the SDF is given by

$$M_{t+1} = \frac{\beta u'\left(C_{t+1}\right)}{u'\left(C_t\right)}.$$

Suppose that the joint conditional distribution of the stock return and the SDF is lognormal and homoskedastic. By (13.30), we can derive that

$$r_{f,t+1} = -E_t m_{t+1} - \frac{\sigma_m^2}{2}, \tag{13.33}$$

$$E_t\left[r_{j,t+1} - r_{f,t+1}\right] + \frac{\sigma_j^2}{2} = -\sigma_{jm}, \tag{13.34}$$

where

$$m_t = \ln M_t,$$
$$r_{jt} = \ln R_{jt},$$
$$\sigma_j^2 = \text{Var}\left(r_{j,t+1} - E_t r_{j,t+1}\right),$$
$$\sigma_m^2 = \text{Var}\left(m_{t+1} - E_t m_{t+1}\right),$$
$$\sigma_{jm} = \text{Cov}\left(r_{j,t+1} - E_t r_{j,t+1}, m_{t+1} - E_t m_{t+1}\right).$$

Assume that

$$u\left(c\right) = \frac{c^{1-\gamma}}{1-\gamma},$$

and that consumption growth satisfies

$$\Delta c_{t+1} = \ln \frac{C_{t+1}}{C_t} = g_c + \sigma_c \varepsilon_{t+1},$$

where $c_t = \ln C_t$ and ε_t is IID normal. We then obtain that

$$m_{t+1} = \ln \beta - \gamma \Delta c_{t+1}.$$

Equations (13.33) and (13.34) become

$$r_{f,t+1} = -\ln \beta + \gamma g_c - \frac{\gamma^2 \sigma_c^2}{2}, \tag{13.35}$$

$$E_t\left[r_{j,t+1} - r_{f,t+1}\right] + \frac{\sigma_j^2}{2} = \gamma \sigma_{jc}, \tag{13.36}$$

where $\sigma_{jc} = \text{Cov}\left(r_{j,t+1} - E_t r_{j,t+1}, \varepsilon_{t+1}\right)$.

Equation (13.35) says that the risk-free rate decreases with the subjective discount factor β, increases with expected consumption growth, and decreases with the variance of consumption growth. When β is higher, the representative agent is more patient and hence consumes less today and saves more for the future, leading to a lower interest rate. When consumption growth is higher, the interest rate must be higher to induce the agent to save more and consume less today. This effect increases with γ, which should be interpreted as the inverse of the **elasticity of intertemporal substitution** (EIS). A larger EIS implies that a small interest rate response is needed to induce a given change in consumption growth. The last term in (13.35) reflects the precautionary saving effect. Higher risk aversion or higher consumption growth risk causes a larger precautionary saving effect, inducing the interest rate to be lower. This effect is quantitatively small since consumption growth is smooth in the data.

Equation (13.36) shows that the expected excess stock return (equity premium) is determined by the product of the risk aversion parameter and the covariance between the stock return and consumption growth.[2]

Mehra and Prescott (1985) implement the CCAPM model above empirically and find that an implausibly large risk aversion parameter is needed to explain the equity premium in the US data. This is called the **equity premium puzzle**. Equation (13.36) gives the intuition behind the puzzle. In the data the covariance between the stock return and the consumption growth is small. A larger γ is needed to match high the equity premium in the data (about 6 percent). However, a high γ implies a large risk-free rate by equation (13.35). This generates the **risk-free rate puzzle** pointed out by Weil (1989) since the the risk-free rate is quantitatively small in the data.

13.9   Exercises

1. (Existence of a representative agent) Define for each $\lambda \in \mathbb{R}_+^I$ the utility function $u_\lambda : \mathbb{R}_+ \to \mathbb{R}$ by

$$u_\lambda (x) = \sup_{(c^1,\dots,c^I)} \sum_i \lambda_i u^i \left(c^i \right) \tag{13.37}$$

   subject to

$$\sum_i c^i = x.$$

   Suppose that $\left((c^i, \theta^i)_{i=1}^I, p \right)$ is an equilibrium with nonbinding debt constraints and zero asset supply and that markets are complete. Then there exists some nonzero $\lambda \in \mathbb{R}_+^I$ such that $(\bar{y}, p)$ is a no-trade equilibrium for the representative agent economy in which the agent has utility function U_λ and endowment $\bar{y}$. Given such λ and $\bar{y}$, problem (13.37) is solved by the equilibrium consumption allocation $(c^i)_{i=1}^I$.

2. Suppose that the aggregate endowment is constant over time. Solve for the Pareto optimal allocation.

3. Prove theorem 13.4.1.

4. Consider the following three transversality conditions:

$$\lim_{T\to\infty} E \left[\beta^{T+1} u^{i\prime} \left(c_{T+1}^i \right) \left(f_{T+1} \cdot \theta_T^i + \bar{D}_{T+1}^i \right) \right] = 0, \tag{13.38}$$

---

2. We ignore the Jensen inequality term $\sigma_j^2/2$.

$$\lim_{T \to \infty} E \left[\beta^T u^{i\prime} \left(c_T^i \right) \left(p_T \cdot \theta_T^i + \bar{B}_T^i \right) \right] = 0, \tag{13.39}$$

$$\lim_{T \to \infty} E \left[\beta^T u^{i\prime} \left(c_T^i \right) p_T \cdot \left(\theta_T^i + \bar{h}_T^i \right) \right] = 0, \tag{13.40}$$

for the three economies with debt constraints (13.13), with borrowing constraints (13.14), and with short-sales constraints (13.15), respectively. Derive the first-order conditions for a Radner equilibrium $\left(\left(c^i, \theta^i \right)_{i=1}^I, p \right)$ for each of these three economies. Prove that these first-order conditions together with the corresponding transversality conditions in (13.38), (13.39), and (13.40) are necessary and sufficient to characterize an equilibrium.

5. (Kocherlakota 1992) Consider a deterministic economy with only one asset (stock) in zero supply. Suppose that $u^i(c) = c^{1-\gamma} / (1 - \gamma)$ for all i and $\theta_{-1}^i \neq 0$ for some i. Show that there is a continuum of equilibria indexed by $\eta \geq 0$ in which

$$c_t^i = s^i(\eta) \, \bar{y}_t,$$

$$\pi_t = \beta^t \left(\frac{\bar{y}_t}{\bar{y}_0} \right)^{-\gamma},$$

$$q_t = \frac{1}{\pi_t} \sum_{s=t+1}^{\infty} \pi_s d_s + \frac{\eta}{\pi_t},$$

$$\theta_t^i = \frac{1}{\pi_t q_t} \left\{ \sum_{s=0}^{t} \pi_s \left(y_s^i - c_s^i \right) + \theta_{-1}^i \left(-v_0 + d_0 + \eta \right) \right\},$$

where

$$s^i(\eta) = \frac{1}{\sum_{t=0}^{\infty} \pi_t \bar{y}_t} \left\{ \sum_{t=0}^{\infty} \pi_t y_t^i + \theta_{-1}^i \left(-v_0 + d_0 + \eta \right) \right\},$$

and

$$v_0 = \frac{1}{\pi_0} \sum_{s=1}^{\infty} \pi_s d_s.$$

6. (Kocherlakota 1992) Let $u^i(c) = c^{1-\gamma} / (1 - \gamma)$ for all i $\theta_{-1}^i = 0$ for all i, and $d_t = 0$ for all t. There is equilibrium where $q_t = 0$. Show that there is a continuum of equilibria indexed by $\eta > 0$ where

$$\pi_t = \beta^t \left(\frac{\bar{y}_t}{\bar{y}_0} \right)^{-\gamma},$$

$$q_t = \frac{\eta}{\pi_t} > 0,$$

$$c_t^i = s^i \bar{y}_t, \quad \text{with } s^i = \frac{\sum_{t=0}^{\infty} \pi_t y_t^i}{\sum_{t=0}^{\infty} \pi_t \bar{y}_t},$$

$$\theta_t^i = \sum_{s=0}^{t} \frac{\pi_s \left(y_s^i - c_s^i \right)}{\pi_t q_t}.$$

Additionally, the consumption allocation is Pareto optimal.

7. (Kocherlakota 2008) Consider an economy with a representative agent having utility

$$U(c) = \sum_{t=0}^{\infty} \sum_{s^t} \Pr(s^t) \beta^t u\left(c_t\left(s^t\right)\right).$$

The agent is endowed with a constant endowment y, a single long-lived asset with constant dividend d and zero complete Arrow securities. He faces the budget constraint

$$c_t\left(s^t\right) + a_t\left(s^t\right) p_t\left(s^t\right) + \sum_{s^{t+1}|s^t} q_t\left(s^{t+1}\right) b_t\left(s^{t+1}\right)$$

$$\leq y + a_{t-1}\left(s^{t-1}\right) \left(p_t\left(s^t\right) + d\right) + b_{t-1}\left(s^t\right)$$

and the debt constraint

$$a_t\left(s^t\right) \left(p_{t+1}\left(s^{t+1}\right) + d\right) + b_t\left(s^{t+1}\right) \geq -\overline{D}_{t+1}\left(s^{t+1}\right),$$

where the debt limit is given by $D_{t+1}\left(s^{t+1}\right) = y/\left(1 - \beta\right)$. Prove that the equilibrium prices are given by

$$q_t\left(s^t\right) = \beta \Pr\left(s^t|s^{t-1}\right), \quad p_t\left(s^t\right) = \frac{\beta d}{1 - \beta}.$$

Now we perturb the debt limit and define $\overline{D}_t\left(s^t\right) = y/\left(1 - \beta\right) - B_t\left(s^t\right)$, where B satisfies $B_t = \beta E_t B_{t+1}$. Prove that there exists an equilibrium in which $p_t\left(s^t\right) = \beta d/\left(1 - \beta\right) + B_t\left(s^t\right)$.

8. Prove that financial markets are complete at (p, f) if and only if the $J \times S$ payoff matrix $D_{t+1}\left(s^t\right)$ has rank S at each node s^t.

9. Consider the CCAPM in which the representative agent has log utility. Show that the SDF, $M_{t+1} = 1/R_{w,t+1}$, where $R_{w,t+1}$ is the return on the wealth portfolio.

10. Consider a static CCAPM with exponential utility and normality distributed returns. Derive the CAPM.

14 Neoclassical Growth Models

Neoclassical growth theory is the cornerstone of modern macroeconomics. This theory was developed independently by Solow (1956) and Swan (1956) and is used to study long-run economic growth. The Solow–Swan model explains long-run economic growth by looking at productivity, capital accumulation, population growth, and technological progress. In the Solow–Swan model the saving rate is exogenously given. Ramsey (1928) develop a model in which national savings could be endogenously chosen from household utility maximization. Cass (1965) and Koopmans (1965) modify the Ramsey model by incorporating population growth and technical progress as in the Solow–Swan model, giving birth to the optimal growth model, also named the Ramsey–Cass–Koopmans model or simply the Ramsey model. Brock and Mirman (1972) introduce uncertainty into the Ramsey model. Kydland and Prescott (1982) take the stochastic optimal growth model to US data and study how much technology shocks can explain business cycles quantitatively. They argue that growth and fluctuations can be studied in the same neoclassical growth framework and pioneer the real business cycles theory. In this chapter we first consider the deterministic models. We then turn to real business cycle models. Last, we discuss some empirical strategies of how to take models to the data.

14.1 Deterministic Models

14.1.1 A Basic Ramsey Model

In a basic deterministic Ramsey model there is no government. There is population growth and technological growth. We first study the Arrow–Debreu equilibrium in which markets for contingent claims open at date zero. We then consider two sequential market arrangements depending on who owns capital stock in the economy. Finally, we study a social planner's problem.

Arrow–Debreu Equilibrium   There is a continuum of households of measure unity. Each household consists of identical members whose size grows at gross rate g_n. The initial size is normalized to one. Each household derives utility from consumption and leisure according to the utility function

$$\sum_{t=0}^{\infty} \beta^t g_n^t u\left(c_t, n_t\right),\tag{14.1}$$

where $\beta \in (0,1)$ is the subjective discount factor and c_t and n_t represent a household member's consumption and labor, respectively. Assume that

$$u_c > 0, \quad u_{cc} < 0, \quad \lim_{c \to 0} u\left(c, \cdot\right) = \infty, \quad u_n < 0, \quad u_{nn} < 0.$$

There is a continuum of identical firms of measure unity. Each firm combines capital and labor to produce output using a constant-returns-to-scale production function. Due to the constant-returns-to-scale technology we only need to consider a single aggregate firm. Let the aggregate production function be given by

$$Y_t = F\left(K_t, A_t N_t\right),$$

where Y_t, K_t, N_t, and A_t represent aggregate output, aggregate capital, aggregate labor demand, and technical progress, respectively. Here $A_t N_t$ represents effective labor. Technical progress that enters in this fashion is known as **labor augmenting** or **Harrod neutral**.[1] Technology growth at the gross rate g_a so that $A_t = g_a^t$. Assume that F is homogeneous of degree one and satisfies

$$F\left(0, \cdot\right) = F\left(\cdot, 0\right) = F\left(0, 0\right) = 0,$$

$$F_1 > 0, \quad F_2 > 0, \quad F_{11} < 0, \quad F_{22} < 0,$$

$$\lim_{K \to 0} F_1\left(K, 1\right) = \infty, \quad \lim_{K \to \infty} F\left(K, 1\right) = 0.$$

Suppose that households own all factors of production and all shares in firms and that these endowments are equally distributed across households. Each period households sell capital and supply labor to firms and buy goods produced by firms, consuming some and accumulating the rest as capital. Assume that firms hire labor and rent capital from households to produce output, sell output,

---

1. If technology enters in the form $Y = F(AK, N)$, technical progress is capital augmenting. If it enters in the form $Y = AF(K, N)$, technical progress is Hicks neutral. For the Cobb–Douglas production function, all three forms of technical progress are equivalent and consistent with balanced growth. For all other production functions the only form of technical progress consistent with balanced growth is labor augmenting.

and pay out profits to households. All transactions take place in a single once-and-for-all market that meets in period 0. Prices and quantities are determined simultaneously at date 0. After this market is closed, at future dates agents simply deliver the quantities of factors and goods they have contracted to sell and receive those they have contracted to buy according to the contracted prices.

Let q_t^0 be the date zero Arrow–Debreu price of a claim in terms of consumption goods to be delivered at date t. Let w_t and R_{kt} be the wage rate and the rental rate at date t. Then the budget constraint is given by

$$\sum_{t=0}^{\infty} q_t^0 \left(g_n^t c_t + g_n^t i_t \right)$$

$$= \sum_{t=0}^{\infty} q_t^0 \left(R_{kt} k_t g_n^t + w_t n_t g_n^t \right) + \Pi,$$

where Π represents the present value of profits from firms. A representative household chooses sequences of $\{c_t, i_t, n_t\}$ so as to maximize utility (14.1) subject to the budget constraint above and the capital accumulation equation

$$g_n k_{t+1} = (1 - \delta) k_t + i_t, \quad k_0 \text{ given,} \tag{14.2}$$

where $\delta \in (0,1)$ is the capital depreciation rate.

The first-order conditions from the household's optimization problem are given by

$$c_t : \beta^t u_c \left(c_t, n_t \right) = \lambda q_t^0,$$

$$n_t : -\beta^t u_n \left(c_t, n_t \right) = \lambda q_t^0 w_t,$$

$$k_{t+1} : q_t^0 = q_{t+1}^0 \left(R_{k,t+1} + 1 - \delta \right),$$

where λ is the Lagrange multiplier associated with the budget constraint.

Each firm solves the following problem:

$$\Pi = \max_{\{K_t, N_t\}} \sum_{t=0}^{\infty} q_t^0 \left[F \left(K_t, A_t N_t \right) - R_{kt} K_t - w_t N_t \right],$$

where K_t and N_t represent aggregate capital and aggregate labor, respectively, demanded by firms. The first-order conditions are given by

$$F_K \left(K_t, A_t N_t \right) = R_{kt}, \quad A_t F_N \left(K_t, A_t N_t \right) = w_t. \tag{14.3}$$

The firm makes zero profit so that $\Pi = 0$, because of the constant-returns-to-scale technology.

An Arrow–Debreu equilibrium consists of sequences of per capita quantities $\{c_t, i_t, n_t, k_{t+1}\}$, aggregate quantities $\{C_t, I_t, N_t, K_{t+1}\}$, and prices $\{q_t^0, w_t, R_{kt}\}$ such that (1) given prices, the sequences $\{c_t, i_t, n_t, k_{t+1}\}$ solve the household's problem; (2) given prices, $\{K_t, N_t\}$ solves the firm's problem; and (3) markets clear in that

$$C_t = g_n^t c_t, \ K_t = g_n^t k_t, \tag{14.4a}$$

$$I_t = g_n^t i_t, \ N_t = g_n^t n_t, \tag{14.4b}$$

$$K_{t+1} = (1 - \delta) K_t + I_t, \tag{14.4c}$$

$$C_t + I_t = F(K_t, A_t N_t). \tag{14.4d}$$

We focus on the equilibrium that is consistent with balanced growth in that all aggregate variables in the steady state must grow at constant rates (some rates could be zero). To satisfy this property, King, Plosser, and Rebelo (1988) show that the utility function must satisfy

$$u(c, n) = \frac{c^{1-\sigma} v(n)}{1 - \sigma} \quad \text{for } \sigma \in (0, 1) \text{ or } \sigma > 1, \tag{14.5}$$

or

$$u(c, n) = \ln c + v(n) \quad \text{for } \sigma = 1, \tag{14.6}$$

for some function v.

Given this class of utility functions, we can show that Y_t, K_t, I_t, and C_t all grow at the gross rate $g_a g_n$ in the steady state. Moreover the wage rate grows at the rate g_a and the rental rate of capital R_{kt} is constant in the steady state. Define a detrended variable as $\tilde{x}_t = g_a^{-t} x_t$ for $x_t = k_t, i_t, c_t,$ or w_t. Using the first-order conditions for the household's problem and for the firm's problem, we can then characterize the equilibrium system as

$$g_a^\sigma u_c(\tilde{c}_t, n_t) = \beta u_c(\tilde{c}_{t+1}, n_{t+1})(R_{k,t+1} + 1 - \delta),$$

$$\frac{-u_n(\tilde{c}_t, n_t)}{u_c(\tilde{c}_t, n_t)} = \tilde{w}_t,$$

$$R_{kt} = F_K(\tilde{k}_t, n_t), \ \tilde{w}_t = F_N(\tilde{k}_t, n_t),$$

$$g_n g_a \tilde{k}_{t+1} = (1 - \delta) \tilde{k}_t + \tilde{i}_t,$$

$$\tilde{c}_t + \tilde{i}_t = F(\tilde{k}_t, n_t) = Y_t g_a^{-t} g_n^{-t}.$$

Sequential Equilibrium: Households Own Capital   The market structure in the Arrow–Debreu equilibrium is unrealistic in that there is a single big market opening only at date zero. We now consider the market arrangement in which agents trade sequentially. Suppose that households own capital and make consumption, investment, and labor supply decisions each period. Households receive income from firms by renting capital and supplying labor. Households also own firms and earn profits Π_t. A representative household's budget constraint is given by

$$c_t + i_t = R_{kt}k_t + w_t n_t + \Pi_t,$$

where i_t, k_t, R_{kt}, and w_t represent investment, capital, the rental rate, and the wage rate, respectively. Since the firm rents capital and hires labor each period, it solves the following static problem:

$$\Pi_t = \max_{K_t, N_t} F(K_t, A_t N_t) - R_{kt}K_t - w_t N_t.$$

A sequential competitive equilibrium consists of sequences of per capita quantities $\{c_t, i_t, n_t, k_{t+1}\}$, aggregate quantities $\{C_t, I_t, N_t, K_{t+1}\}$, and prices $\{w_t, R_{kt}\}$ such that (1) given prices, the sequences $\{c_t, i_t, n_t, k_{t+1}\}$ solve the household's problem; (2) given prices, $\{K_t, N_t\}$ solve the firm's problem; and (3) markets clear in that the conditions in (14.4) hold.

From the household's optimization problem, we can derive the first-order conditions:

$$u_c(c_t, n_t) = \beta u_c(c_{t+1}, n_{t+1})(R_{k,t+1} + 1 - \delta), \tag{14.7}$$

$$\frac{-u_n(c_t, n_t)}{u_c(c_t, n_t)} = w_t, \tag{14.8}$$

and the transversality condition:

$$\lim_{t \to \infty} \beta^t u_c(c_t, n_t) k_{t+1} = 0. \tag{14.9}$$

The first-order conditions from the firm's problem are the same as in equation (14.3). After detrending, we can easily show that the equilibrium system in this subsection is identical to that in the previous subsection.

Sequential Equilibrium: Firms Own Capital   Consider a different sequential market arrangement in which firms own capital and make investment decisions. Households own firms and trade firm shares in a stock market. Each household chooses consumption $\{c_t\}$, share holdings $\{\psi_{t+1}\}$, and labor supply $\{n_t\}$ so as to maximize utility (14.1) subject to the budget constraint

$$g_n^t c_t + \psi_{t+1}(V_t - D_t) = \psi_t V_t + w_t g_n^t n_t,$$

where V_t is the cum-dividends stock market value of the firm and D_t represents dividends.

There is a continuum of identical firms of measure unity. Each firm chooses labor and investment so as to maximize its stock market value at any time t:

$$V_t = \max_{\{I_{t+j}, N_{t+j}\}} \sum_{j=0}^{\infty} M_{t,t+j} D_{t+j}$$

subject to

$$D_{t+j} = F\left(K_{t+j}, A_{t+j} N_{t+j}\right) - w_{t+j} N_{t+j} - I_{t+j},$$

$$K_{t+j+1} = (1 - \delta) K_{t+j} + I_{t+j}, \tag{14.10}$$

where $M_{t,t+j}$ is the discount factor or the pricing kernel. $M_{t,t+j}$ gives the date t value of a claim that delivers one unit of consumption good in date $t+j$. Normalize $M_{t,t} = 1$.

A sequential competitive equilibrium consists of sequences of quantities, $\{c_t, n_t, \psi_{t+1}\}$ and $\{K_{t+1}, N_t, I_t\}$, and prices $\{V_t, w_t, M_{t,t+j}\}$ such that households and firms optimize and markets clear,

$$\psi_t = 1, \quad C_t = g_n^t c_t, \quad N_t = g_n^t n_t,$$

$$C_t + I_t = F(K_t, A_t N_t).$$

To analyze this equilibrium, we first note that the pricing kernel $M_{t,t+j}$ comes from the household's optimization problem. The first-order condition with respect to share holdings gives

$$u_c(c_t, n_t)(V_t - D_t) = \beta u_c(c_{t+1}, n_{t+1}) V_{t+1}.$$

Thus we obtain an asset pricing equation:

$$V_t = D_t + \frac{\beta u_c(c_{t+1}, n_{t+1})}{u_c(c_t, n_t)} V_{t+1}. \tag{14.11}$$

Solving this equation forward yields

$$V_t = \sum_{j=0}^{\infty} \frac{\beta^j u_c(c_{t+j}, n_{t+j})}{u_c(c_t, n_t)} D_{t+j}, \tag{14.12}$$

where we have used the transversality condition to rule out bubbles:

$$\lim_{j \to \infty} \beta^j u_c(c_{t+j}, n_{t+j}) V_{t+j} = 0. \tag{14.13}$$

Equation (14.12) states that the stock price is equal to the discounted present value of future dividends. To derive condition (14.13), we use the transversality condition from the household problem:

$$\lim_{t \to \infty} \beta^t u_c (c_t, n_t) \, \psi_{t+1} (V_t - D_t) = 0.$$

Using the equilibrium condition $\psi_{t+1} = 1$ and equation (14.11) delivers (14.13). Equation (14.12) implies that the pricing kernel is equal to the intertemporal marginal rate of substitution:

$$M_{t,t+j} = \frac{\beta^j u_c \left(c_{t+j}, n_{t+j}\right)}{u_c \left(c_t, n_t\right)}.$$

From the firm's optimization problem, we can derive the first-order conditions for N_t as in (14.3) and for I_t and K_{t+1}:

$$I_t : \ Q_t = 1,$$

$$K_{t+1} : \ Q_t = M_{t,t+1} \left[F_K \left(K_{t+1}, A_{t+1} N_{t+1}\right) + (1 - \delta) Q_{t+1}\right], \tag{14.14}$$

where $Q_{t+j} M_{t,t+j}$ is the Lagrange multiplier associated with the capital accumulation equation (14.10). Here Q_t is Tobin's marginal Q, which represents the marginal value of the firm following an additional unit increase in the installed capital. Thus Q_t may also be interpreted as the price of capital. More formally, we can write the firm's problem by dynamic programming:

$$V_t (K_t) = \max_{I_t, K_{t+1}} D_t + M_{t,t+1} V_{t+1} (K_{t+1})$$

subject to (14.10), where $V_t (K_t)$ is the value of the firm with capital K_t. Let Q_t be the Lagrange multiplier associated with (14.10). By the envelope theorem,

$$Q_t = M_{t,t+1} \frac{\partial V_{t+1} (K_{t+1})}{\partial K_{t+1}}.$$

Because there is no adjustment cost in the model, $Q_t = 1$. We can then show that equations (14.7) and (14.14) are equivalent. Consequently we can show that the equilibrium allocations implied by the two different sequential market arrangements are identical.

This decentralization is very useful for studying asset pricing questions. For example, equation (14.11) implies that the (gross) return on capital or the stock return is given by

$$\frac{V_{t+1}}{V_t - D_t} = \frac{u_c (c_t, n_t)}{\beta u_c (c_{t+1}, n_{t+1})} = R_{k,t+1} + 1 - \delta,$$

where we have used equation (14.7). This return is also equal to the risk-free rate if households can trade risk-free bonds.

Social Planner's Problem   We have considered three decentralized market arrangements.[2] We have shown that they imply identical equilibrium allocations. Are these allocations Pareto optimal? To answer this question, we consider a social planner's problem in which the social planner chooses consumption, labor, and investment so as to maximize a representative household's utility subject to the resource constraint:

$$\max_{c_t, n_t, i_t} \sum_{t=0}^{\infty} \beta^t g_n^t u\left(c_t, n_t\right)$$

subject to

$$g_n^t c_t + g_n^t i_t = F\left(g_n^t k_t, A_t g_n^t n_t\right) = Y_t,$$
$$g_n k_{t+1} = (1 - \delta) k_t + i_t.$$

We can derive the first-order conditions:

$$u_c\left(c_t, n_t\right) = \beta u_c\left(c_{t+1}, n_{t+1}\right) \left[F_K\left(k_{t+1}, A_{t+1}n_{t+1}\right) + 1 - \delta\right],$$

$$\frac{-u_n\left(c_t, n_t\right)}{u_c\left(c_t, n_t\right)} = F_N\left(k_t, A_t n_t\right),$$

$$c_t + i_t = F\left(k_t, A_t n_t\right),$$

and the transversality condition given by (14.9). Defining detrended variables as in the previous analysis, we can show that

$$g_a^\sigma u_c\left(\tilde{c}_t, n_t\right) = \beta u_c\left(\tilde{c}_{t+1}, n_{t+1}\right) \left[F_K\left(\tilde{k}_{t+1}, n_{t+1}\right) + 1 - \delta\right],$$

$$\frac{-u_n\left(\tilde{c}_t, n_t\right)}{u_c\left(\tilde{c}_t, n_t\right)} = F_N\left(\tilde{k}_t, n_t\right),$$

$$\tilde{c}_t + \tilde{i}_t = F\left(\tilde{k}_t, n_t\right),$$

$$g_n g_a \tilde{k}_{t+1} = (1 - \delta) \tilde{k}_t + \tilde{i}_t.$$

Comparing with the equilibrium systems derived earlier, we can see that the competitive equilibrium allocations are Pareto optimal. Conversely, we can also find equilibrium prices to support the Pareto optimal allocation for different market arrangements.

---

2. There exist other market arrangements that give identical equilibrium allocations. See Stokey, Lucas, and Prescott (1989) and Ljungqvist and Sargent (2004) for examples.

Recursive Competitive Equilibrium   Prescott and Mehra (1980) develop an alternative approach to summarize competitive equilibrium behavior. This approach defines equilibrium by time-invariant decision rules and other functions that characterize prices and state transitions, rather than by sequences of quantities and prices. These decision rules specify current actions as a function of a limited number of state variables which fully summarize the effects of past decisions and current information. Knowledge of these state variables provides the economic agents with a full description of the economy's current state. The state transition equation determines the state in the next period, giving rise to a recursive structure of the equilibrium. This type of equilibrium is called a **recursive competitive equilibrium**. It is natural for this recursive approach to apply the powerful dynamic programming theory developed earlier to analyze both theoretical issues and empirical questions. It has become the workhorse in modern macroeconomics. The idea of defining an equilibrium in a recursive approach has been applied to define **recursive equilibrium** for noncompetitive economies.

In order to apply the concept of recursive competitive equilibrium, the equilibrium decision rules must be time invariant. Because the previously presented Ramsey model features long-run growth, one has to detrend variables suitably. For ease of exposition, we will consider the special case without long-run growth to illustrate the equilibrium concept. Suppose $g_a = g_n = 1$.

We consider the market arrangement in which households own capital. The equilibrium rental rate and wage rate are functions of the aggregate state, the aggregate capital stock K. From the firm's optimization problem, we can show that these functions satisfy

$$F_K(K, N) = R_k(K), \quad F_N(K, N) = W(K). \tag{14.15}$$

Next we write a household's decision problem by dynamic programming:

$$V(k, K) = \max_{c, n, k'} u(c, n) + \beta V(k', K')$$

subject to

$$c + k' - (1 - \delta)k = kR_k(K) + W(K)n,$$

$$K' = G(K). \tag{14.16}$$

Here k is the individual state of the capital stock. Because prices depend on the aggregate state and households take equilibrium sequences of prices as given when making decisions, the aggregate state K enters each household's dynamic programming problem. Additionally households must form rational expectations about the transition of the aggregate state, which is given by (14.16). This transition or law of motion determines the evolution of prices.

A recursive competitive equilibrium consists of the value function $V(k,K)$, decision rules $c = g^c(k,K)$, $n = g^n(k,K)$, $k' = g(k,K)$, the law of motion for K in (14.16), and price functions $R_k(K)$ and $W(K)$ such that (1) given the price functions and the law of motion for K, the value function and decision rules solve the household's dynamic programming problem; (2) price functions satisfy (14.15); (3) markets clear in that

$$k = K, \quad k' = K', \quad g(K,K) = G(K), \quad c = C, \quad n = N,$$

$$K' - (1-\delta)K + C = F(K,N).$$

Because all households are identical, the individual choices must be equal to the aggregate choices in equilibrium. Additionally the individual law of motion for capital must be consistent with the aggregate law of motion in equilibrium.

Given a recursive competitive equilibrium, equilibrium sequences of prices and quantities can be naturally generated. One can show that these sequences are equivalent to those in the sequential competitive equilibrium analyzed earlier. Conversely, one can often show that a sequential competitive equilibrium can be characterized recursively. But sometimes it can be nontrivial to represent a sequential competitive equilibrium in a recursive way. The difficulty comes from the selection of state variables. We will see later that selecting suitable state variables for some problems needs ingenious thinking.

14.1.2   Incorporating Fiscal Policy

In this subsection we use the deterministic growth model to study fiscal policy. We abstract from long-run growth. Consider the decentralization in which firms own capital and make investment decisions. Consider a tax system in which households pay dividend taxes, capital gains taxes, consumption taxes, and labor income taxes. The treatment of capital gains taxes is complicated because these taxes are realization based rather than accrual based. Moreover the capital gains tax rate is usually lower than the dividend tax rate. Hence firms have an incentive to repurchase shares instead of paying dividends. This requires that we introduce some frictions in the model to limit share repurchases. To avoid this complication, we follow King (1977), Auerbach (1979), Bradford (1981), and McGrattan and Prescott (2005) and assume that dividend and capital gains taxes together are modeled as distribution taxes.

The representative household's problem is given by

$$\max_{\{C_t, N_t, \psi_{t+1}\}} \sum_{t=0}^{\infty} \beta^t u(C_t, N_t) \tag{14.17}$$

subject to

$$(1 + \tau_t^s) C_t + \psi_{t+1} \left(V_t - \left(1 - \tau_t^d \right) D_t \right) + \frac{B_{t+1}}{R_t}$$
$$= \psi_t V_t + (1 - \tau_t^n) w_t N_t + B_t - T_t, \ t \geq 0,$$

where τ_t^s, τ_t^d, and τ_t^n are the tax rates on consumption, distribution, and labor income, respectively. Here B_t represents holdings of riskless government bonds and T_t represents lump-sum taxes. First-order conditions are given by

$$C_t : u_C (C_t, N_t) = (1 + \tau_t^s) \Lambda_t,$$

$$N_t : -u_N (C_t, N_t) = (1 - \tau_t^n) \Lambda_t w_t,$$

$$\psi_{t+1} : \Lambda_t \left(V_t - \left(1 - \tau_t^d \right) D_t \right) = \beta \Lambda_{t+1} V_{t+1},$$

$$B_{t+1} : \Lambda_t = \beta \Lambda_{t+1} R_t,$$

where $\beta^t \Lambda_t$ is the Lagrange multiplier associated with the budget constraint at time t.

The representative firm's problem is given by

$$V_t = \max_{\{I_t, K_{t+1}\}} \left(1 - \tau_t^d \right) D_t + \frac{\beta \Lambda_{t+1}}{\Lambda_t} V_{t+1}$$

subject to

$$D_t = (1 - \tau_t^c) (F (K_t, N_t) - w_t N_t) - I_t + \tau_t^c \delta K_t,$$

$$K_{t+1} = (1 - \delta) K_t + I_t, \tag{14.18}$$

where τ_t^c is the corporate income tax rate. First-order conditions are given by

$$I_t : Q_t = 1 - \tau_t^d, \tag{14.19}$$

$$K_{t+1} : Q_t = \frac{\beta \Lambda_{t+1}}{\Lambda_t} \left[\begin{array}{l} (1 - \delta) Q_{t+1} + \left(1 - \tau_{t+1}^d \right) \tau_{t+1}^c \delta \\ + \left(1 - \tau_{t+1}^d \right) \left(1 - \tau_{t+1}^c \right) F_K (K_{t+1}, N_{t+1}) \end{array} \right], \tag{14.20}$$

where Q_t represents the price of capital (Tobin's marginal Q).

The government budget constraint is given by

$$G_t + B_t = \frac{B_{t+1}}{R_t} + \tau_t^s C_t + \tau_t^d D_t + \tau_t^c (F (K_t, N_t) - w_t N_t) + \tau_t^n w_t N_t + T_t.$$

To close the model, we impose the market clearing condition $\psi_t = 1$ and the resource constraint

$$C_t + I_t + G_t = F (K_t, N_t) = Y_t.$$

McGrattan and Prescott (2005) prove the following result.

Proposition 14.1.1   *Ex-dividends equity value satisfies*

$$V_t - \left(1 - \tau_t^d\right) D_t = \left(1 - \tau_t^d\right) K_{t+1}.$$

Proof   Multiplying K_{t+1} on the two sides of equation (14.20) yields

$$Q_t K_{t+1} = \frac{\beta \Lambda_{t+1}}{\Lambda_t} \left[\begin{array}{l} (1 - \delta) Q_{t+1} K_{t+1} + \left(1 - \tau_{t+1}^d\right) \tau_{t+1}^c \delta K_{t+1} \\ + \left(1 - \tau_{t+1}^d\right) \left(1 - \tau_{t+1}^c\right) F_K \left(K_{t+1}, N_{t+1}\right) K_{t+1} \end{array} \right]$$

$$= \frac{\beta \Lambda_{t+1}}{\Lambda_t} \left(1 - \tau_{t+1}^d\right) \left(1 - \tau_{t+1}^c\right) \left(F \left(K_{t+1}, N_{t+1}\right) - w_{t+1} N_{t+1}\right)$$

$$+ \frac{\beta \Lambda_{t+1}}{\Lambda_t} \left[Q_{t+1} \left(K_{t+2} - I_{t+1}\right) + \left(1 - \tau_{t+1}^d\right) \tau_{t+1}^c \delta K_{t+1} \right]$$

$$= \frac{\beta \Lambda_{t+1}}{\Lambda_t} \left(1 - \tau_{t+1}^d\right) \left(1 - \tau_{t+1}^c\right) \left(F \left(K_{t+1}, N_{t+1}\right) - w_{t+1} N_{t+1}\right)$$

$$+ \frac{\beta \Lambda_{t+1}}{\Lambda_t} \left[Q_{t+1} K_{t+2} - \left(1 - \tau_{t+1}^d\right) I_{t+1} + \left(1 - \tau_{t+1}^d\right) \tau_{t+1}^c \delta K_{t+1} \right]$$

$$= \frac{\beta \Lambda_{t+1}}{\Lambda_t} \left(D_{t+1} + Q_{t+1} K_{t+2}\right),$$

where the second equality follows from the substitution of the capital accumulation equation and the linear homogeneity of F, the third equality follows from (14.19), and the last equality follows from the definition of dividends D_{t+1}. Given the transversality condition,

$$\lim_{T \to \infty} \beta^T \Lambda_T Q_T K_{T+1} = 0,$$

we find that

$$Q_t K_{t+1} = \sum_{j=1}^{\infty} \frac{\beta^j \Lambda_{t+j}}{\Lambda_t} D_{t+j}.$$

Thus $Q_t K_{t+1}$ is the ex-dividend equity value.   ∎

What is the impact of changes in the distribution tax rate? Consider a permanent tax change in τ^d when all tax rates are constant over time. Suppose that lump-sum taxes are levied to balance the government budget. In this case equations (14.19) and (14.20) imply that

$$1 = \frac{\beta \Lambda_{t+1}}{\Lambda_t} \left[(1 - \delta) + \tau^c \delta + (1 - \tau^c) F_K \left(K_{t+1}, N_{t+1}\right)\right]. \tag{14.21}$$

Thus the distribution tax does not change investment decisions, but it changes the price of capital and hence equity value. More strikingly, it does not affect the equilibrium allocation. When other distortionary taxes are levied to balance the government budget, the change in the distribution tax will be distortionary.

Notice that the result above depends on an implicit assumption that firms finance investment by retained earnings so that $D_t > 0$ for all t. When $D_t < 0$, investors must inject new equity to firms. That is, firms must rely on external new equity to finance investment. New equity changes capital gains and hence triggers capital gains taxes in the US tax system. Introducing both capital gains taxes and dividend taxes separately, one can show that dividend taxes affect investment (Poterba and Summers 1985). Gourio and Miao (2010) document empirical evidence that in the cross section some firms use external equity financing and some firms use internal financing. They then build a model with firm heterogeneity in idiosyncratic productivity shocks. They calibrate the model and study the long-run quantitative impact of the 2003 dividend and capital gains tax reform. Gourio and Miao (2011) study transitional dynamics when the tax reform is temporary.

In the model above, we have assumed that lump-sum taxes are available so that whenever there is a change in tax rates, we use lump-sum taxes as a residual to balance the government budget. When there is no lump-sum tax, we have to either adjust some particular tax or government expenditures to balance the government constraint. Since this adjustment is arbitrary, there could be many equilibria.

14.2 A Basic RBC Model

Real business cycle (RBC) theory is pioneered by Kydland and Prescott (1982) and Long and Plosser (1983). The basic idea of this theory is to introduce uncertainty into the neoclassical growth model. The resulting stochastic growth framework is then used to study business cycles quantitatively. This theory argues that technology shocks account for most of business cycles. Though this view is highly debated, RBC theory provides a profound methodological contribution and has become the cornerstone for business cycle analysis. In particular, the use of a quantitative analysis of dynamic stochastic general equilibrium (DSGE) models has become a standard procedure. In this section we first present a basic RBC model and then discuss various extensions in the next section. We refer the reader to King and Rebelo (1999) for an excellent survey of the RBC theory.

We introduce uncertainty into the basic Ramsey model in the form of aggregate total factor productivity (TFP) shocks. We emphasize that our previous analysis regarding Pareto optimality and decentralized competitive equilibrium still applies to the stochastic case. We ignore long-run growth and consider some specific functional forms. We start by the social planner's problem given by

$$\max_{\{C_t,N_t,I_t\}} E \sum_{t=0}^{\infty} \beta^t \left[\ln C_t + \chi \ln (1 - N_t) \right] \qquad (14.22)$$

subject to

$$C_t + I_t = z_t K_t^\alpha N_t^{1-\alpha} = Y_t, \tag{14.23}$$

$$K_{t+1} = (1 - \delta) K_t + I_t, \tag{14.24}$$

$$\ln z_t = \rho \ln z_{t-1} + \sigma \varepsilon_t, \quad \varepsilon_t \sim IID\,N(0,1), \tag{14.25}$$

where χ measures the utility weight on leisure, and the technology shock $\{z_t\}$ is modeled as an AR(1) process. The optimal allocation $\{C_t, N_t, K_{t+1}, I_t, Y_t\}$ satisfies the following system of nonlinear difference equations:

$$\frac{1}{C_t} = E_t \frac{\beta}{C_{t+1}} \left[\alpha z_{t+1} K_{t+1}^{\alpha-1} N_{t+1}^{1-\alpha} + 1 - \delta \right], \tag{14.26}$$

$$\frac{\chi C_t}{1 - N_t} = (1 - \alpha) z_t K_t^\alpha N_t^{-\alpha}, \tag{14.27}$$

and (14.23) and (14.24). The usual transversality condition also holds. In a decentralized equilibrium in which households own capital and make real investment, the rental rate and the wage rate are given by

$$R_{kt} = \alpha z_t K_t^{\alpha-1} N_t^{1-\alpha} \quad \text{and} \quad w_t = (1 - \alpha) z_t K_t^\alpha N_t^{-\alpha}.$$

The next step is to parameterize the model and solve the model numerically. The RBC approach advocates a calibration methodology. This method assigns parameter values based on either long-run steady-state relationships or moments from other studies such as microeconomic evidence.

14.2.1   Steady State

Now we solve for the nonstochastic steady state in which $z_t = 1$ for all t. We use X to denote the steady-state value of a variable X_t. By the Euler equation (14.26),

$$1 = \beta \left[\alpha K^{\alpha-1} N^{1-\alpha} + 1 - \delta \right].$$

It follows that

$$\frac{K}{N} = \left(\frac{\alpha}{1/\beta - (1 - \delta)} \right)^{1/(1-\alpha)}.$$

Hence the equilibrium factor prices are given by

$$R_{kt} = \alpha \frac{Y}{K} = \alpha \left(\frac{K}{N} \right)^{\alpha-1}, \quad w_t = (1 - \alpha) \left(\frac{K}{N} \right)^\alpha.$$

By (14.24),

$$I = \delta K = \frac{\delta K}{N} N.$$

Thus, given N, we can solve for I and also

$$Y = \left(\frac{K}{N}\right)^\alpha N.$$

Finally, the steady-state consumption C comes from the resource constraint (14.23).

Note that we have not used the equilibrium condition (14.27). We will use this equation to solve for χ:

$$\chi = (1 - \alpha) \left(\frac{K}{N}\right)^\alpha \frac{1 - N}{C}. \tag{14.28}$$

The idea is that given other parameter values, there is a one-to-one mapping between χ and N. Here we are using a reverse engineering approach to calibrate a parameter using an endogenous variable as the input. This approach is very useful for complicated models because we have avoided solving a system of nonlinear equations for endogenous variables given exogenous parameter values.

14.2.2 Calibration

We are ready to assign parameter values. One period corresponds to a quarter. First, we set $\alpha = 0.33$, which is consistent with the fact that average labor share of income is about 2/3 in the United States. We set $\beta = 0.99$, implying that the annual interest rate is $4(1/\beta - 1) = 4$ percent. Set $\delta = 0.025$, implying that the annual depreciation rate is about 10 percent. Take $N = 0.33$, implying that households work 8 hours out of 24 hours a day. Given this value of N and other calibrated parameter values, we can pin down the parameter $\chi = 1.75$ and also solve for all other steady-state values.[3]

We can use Solow residuals $\{SR_t\}$ for the US data constructed below to estimate the parameters ρ and σ in two steps. First, we estimate the equation by OLS:

$$SR_t = \beta_0 + \beta_1 t + u_t. \tag{14.29}$$

Next we estimate the residuals by OLS:

$$u_t = \rho u_{t-1} + \sigma \varepsilon_t, \tag{14.30}$$

where u_t corresponds to $\ln z_t$ in the basic RBC model. We then obtain $\rho = 0.99$ and $\sigma = 0.0089$. Alternatively, we can use the HP filtered data to estimate (14.25).

14.2.3 Log-Linearized System

Once parameter values are assigned, the model can be solved numerically. There are many different methods to solve this model as discussed in previous chapters. It turns out that the log-linearization method is extremely useful in terms of

---

3. The Matlab code for calibration is calibration.m.

balancing between speed and accuracy (see Aruoba, Fernández-Villaverde, and Rubio-Ramírez 2006). Dynare can get the log-linearized solution in a second. Before doing this, we perform log-linearization by hand in order to understand the workings of the RBC model. We use $\hat{X}_t$ to denote log deviation from the steady state.

Start with equation (14.27). Taking logarithms and total differentiation on the two sides of this equation yields

$$\hat{C}_t + \frac{N}{1-N}\hat{N}_t = \hat{z}_t + \alpha\hat{K}_t - \alpha\hat{N}_t.$$

Solving yields

$$\hat{N}_t = \frac{1}{\alpha+\zeta}\hat{z}_t + \frac{\alpha}{\alpha+\zeta}\hat{K}_t - \frac{1}{\alpha+\zeta}\hat{C}_t. \tag{14.31}$$

where $\zeta \equiv N/(1-N)$.

Substituting (14.24) into (14.23) and taking total differentiation, we obtain

$$dC_t + dK_{t+1} - (1-\delta)dK_t$$
$$= K^\alpha N^{1-\alpha}dz_t + \alpha K^{\alpha-1}N^{1-\alpha}dK_t + (1-\alpha)K^\alpha N^{-\alpha}dN_t.$$

Thus

$$C\hat{C}_t + K\hat{K}_{t+1} - (1-\delta)K\hat{K}_t$$
$$= K^\alpha N^{1-\alpha}\hat{z}_t + \alpha K^\alpha N^{1-\alpha}\hat{K}_t + (1-\alpha)K^\alpha N^{1-\alpha}\hat{N}_t.$$

Solving for $\hat{K}_{t+1}$ yields

$$\hat{K}_{t+1} = \frac{Y}{K}\left[\hat{z}_t + \alpha\hat{K}_t + (1-\alpha)\hat{N}_t\right] - \frac{C}{K}\hat{C}_t + (1-\delta)\hat{K}_t$$
$$= \frac{1}{\beta}\hat{K}_t + \frac{Y}{K}\left[\hat{z}_t + (1-\alpha)\hat{N}_t\right] - \frac{C}{K}\hat{C}_t,$$

where we have used the steady-state Euler equation

$$1 = \beta\left(\alpha\frac{Y}{K} + 1 - \delta\right).$$

Substituting equation (14.31) for $\hat{N}_t$ yields

$$\hat{K}_{t+1} = \left(\frac{1}{\beta} + \frac{1-\alpha}{\alpha+\zeta}\alpha\frac{Y}{K}\right)\hat{K}_t + \frac{Y}{K}\left(\frac{1+\zeta}{\zeta+\alpha}\right)\hat{z}_t - \left(\frac{C}{K} + \frac{1-\alpha}{\alpha+\zeta}\frac{Y}{K}\right)\hat{C}_t. \tag{14.32}$$

Total differentiation of the Euler equation yields

$$
-\frac{dC_t}{C^2} = -E_t \frac{\beta dC_{t+1}}{C^2} \left[\alpha K^{\alpha-1} N^{1-\alpha} + 1 - \delta\right]
$$

$$
+ E_t \frac{\beta}{C} \left[\alpha K^{\alpha-1} N^{1-\alpha} dz_{t+1} + \alpha\left(\alpha-1\right) K^{\alpha-2} N^{1-\alpha} dK_{t+1}\right]
$$

$$
+ E_t \frac{\beta}{C} \alpha\left(1-\alpha\right) K^{\alpha-1} N^{-\alpha} dN_{t+1}.
$$

It follows that

$$
-\hat{C}_t = -E_t \hat{C}_{t+1} + \beta\alpha \frac{Y}{K} E_t \left[\hat{z}_{t+1} + \left(\alpha-1\right) \hat{K}_{t+1} + \left(1-\alpha\right) \hat{N}_{t+1}\right].
$$

Substituting $\hat{N}_{t+1}$ using (14.31) yields

$$
-\hat{C}_t = -E_t \hat{C}_{t+1} + \beta\alpha \frac{Y}{K} E_t \left[\hat{z}_{t+1} + \left(\alpha-1\right) \hat{K}_{t+1}\right]
$$

$$
+ \left(1-\alpha\right) \beta\alpha \frac{Y}{K} E_t \left[\frac{1}{\alpha+\zeta} \hat{z}_{t+1} + \frac{\alpha}{\alpha+\zeta} \hat{K}_{t+1} - \frac{1}{\alpha+\zeta} \hat{C}_{t+1}\right].
$$

Simplifying yields

$$
-\hat{C}_t = -\left[1 + \left(1-\alpha\right) \beta\alpha \frac{Y}{K} \frac{1}{\alpha+\zeta}\right] E_t \hat{C}_{t+1} + \beta\alpha \frac{Y}{K} \frac{1+\zeta}{\alpha+\zeta} E_t \hat{z}_{t+1}
$$

$$
- \beta\alpha\left(1-\alpha\right) \frac{Y}{K} \frac{\zeta}{\alpha+\zeta} E_t \hat{K}_{t+1}. \tag{14.33}
$$

Equations (14.32) and (14.33) combined with the shock process in (14.25) constitute a linear system of difference equations for $\{\hat{C}_t, \hat{K}_{t+1}\}$. To analyze this system, we plot the phase diagram for the corresponding deterministic system:

$$
\hat{K}_{t+1} - \hat{K}_t = \left(\frac{1}{\beta} - 1 + \frac{1-\alpha}{\alpha+\zeta} \alpha \frac{Y}{K}\right) \hat{K}_t + \frac{Y}{K}\left(\frac{1+\zeta}{\zeta+\alpha}\right) \hat{z}_t - \left(\frac{C}{K} + \frac{1-\alpha}{\alpha+\zeta} \frac{Y}{K}\right) \hat{C}_t, \tag{14.34}
$$

$$
\hat{C}_{t+1} - \hat{C}_t = \left(1-\alpha\right) \beta\alpha \frac{Y}{K} \frac{1}{\alpha+\zeta} \hat{C}_{t+1} + \beta\alpha \frac{Y}{K} \frac{1+\zeta}{\alpha+\zeta} \hat{z}_{t+1}
$$

$$
- \beta\alpha\left(1-\alpha\right) \frac{Y}{K} \frac{\zeta}{\alpha+\zeta} \hat{K}_{t+1}.
$$

First, consider the isocline $\Delta\hat{C}_t = \hat{C}_{t+1} - \hat{C}_t = 0$:

$$
\hat{C}_{t+1} = \frac{1+\zeta}{1-\alpha} \hat{z}_{t+1} - \zeta \hat{K}_{t+1}.
$$

Figure 14.1 plots this equation after one-period lag. This line is downward sloping.

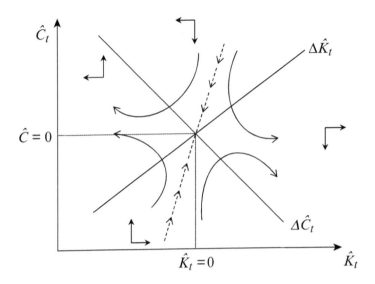

Figure 14.1
Phase diagram for the log-linearized basic RBC model

Next consider the isocline $\Delta\hat{K}_t = \hat{K}_{t+1} - \hat{K}_t = 0$:

$$\hat{C}_t = \left(\frac{C}{K} + \frac{1-\alpha}{\alpha+\zeta}\frac{Y}{K}\right)^{-1}\left[\left(\frac{1}{\beta} - 1 + \frac{1-\alpha}{\alpha+\zeta}\alpha\frac{Y}{K}\right)\hat{K}_t + \frac{Y}{K}\left(\frac{1+\zeta}{\zeta+\alpha}\right)\hat{z}_t\right]. \tag{14.35}$$

This line is upward sloping.

We now find the saddle path. When $\hat{K}_t$ is above the isocline $\hat{C}_t = \hat{C}_{t+1}$, $\hat{C}_t$ is expected to fall because high $\hat{K}_t$ implies low marginal product of capital and hence a low interest rate. When $\hat{C}_t$ is above the isocline $\hat{K}_{t+1} = \hat{K}_t$, $\hat{K}_t$ is expected to fall because households save less. Hence there is a saddle path converging to the steady state. Given any initial state for $\hat{K}_0$ and $\hat{z}_0$, there is a unique solution $\hat{C}_0$ that must lie on the saddle. We can determine the whole paths for $\hat{C}_t$ and $\hat{K}_t$. We can also determine other equilibrium variables $\hat{N}_t$, $\hat{w}_t$, $\hat{R}_{kt}$, $\hat{I}_t$, and $\hat{Y}_t$.

Consider first $\hat{N}_t$. Instead of using (14.31), it is more instructive to look at the labor market. From equation (14.27) the labor supply is

$$\frac{\chi C_t}{1 - N_t} = w_t. \tag{14.36}$$

Thus labor supply increases with w_t and decreases with C_t. The dependence on consumption captures the wealth effect. The log-linearized labor supply equation is given by

$$\frac{N}{1-N}\hat{N}_t = -\hat{C}_t + \hat{w}_t.$$

This curve is upward sloping. The log-linearized labor demand equation is given by

$$\hat{w}_t = \hat{z}_t + \alpha \hat{K}_t - \alpha \hat{N}_t. \tag{14.37}$$

This curve is downward sloping. The intersection point gives the equilibrium $\hat{N}_t$ and $\hat{w}_t$ as illustrated in figure 14.2. Once we know $\hat{C}_t$ and $\hat{z}_t$, we can determine $\hat{N}_t$ and $\hat{w}_t$ since $\hat{K}_t$ is predetermined.

After deriving $\hat{N}_t$, we can determine equilibrium output using the log-linearized equation

$$\hat{Y}_t = \alpha \hat{K}_t + (1 - \alpha) \hat{N}_t + \hat{z}_t.$$

We can also determine the rental rate R_{kt}. Since $R_{kt} = \alpha z_t K_t^{\alpha-1} N_t^{1-\alpha} = \alpha Y_t / K_t$, we get

$$\hat{R}_{kt} = \hat{Y}_t - \hat{K}_t.$$

Finally, we can solve for financial returns using the decentralization in which firms own capital and make investment. As in the deterministic case, we can show

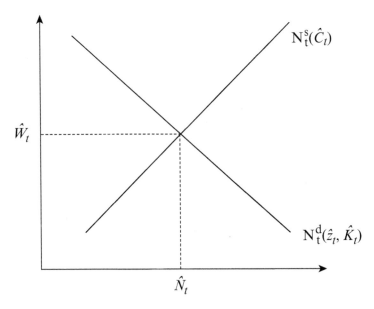

Figure 14.2
Labor market equilibrium for the log-linearized basic RBC model

that the ex-dividend stock return is given by

$$R_t^s = R_{kt} + 1 - \delta \implies \hat{R}_t^s = \frac{R_k}{R_k + 1 - \delta} \hat{R}_{kt}.$$

Turn to the risk-free rate or the interest rate r_{t+1}^f which satisfies the Euler equation

$$\frac{1}{C_t} = \beta E_t \frac{1 + r_{t+1}^f}{C_{t+1}}.$$

Total differentiation yields

$$\frac{-dC_t}{C^2} = \beta E_t \left[\left(1 + r^f\right) \frac{-dC_{t+1}}{C^2} + \frac{d\left(1 + r_{t+1}^f\right)}{C} \right].$$

For the interest rate it is awkward to use percentage deviation from the steady state dr_{t+1}^f / r^f. For example, when the interest rate goes up from 1 to 4 percent, the interest rate rises by three percentage points, but rises relatively by 300 percent. Thus, without risk of confusion, we define

$$\hat{r}_{t+1}^f \equiv r_{t+1}^f - r^f \simeq \frac{d\left(1 + r_{t+1}^f\right)}{1 + r^f}.$$

In terms of gross interest rate $R_{t+1}^f = 1 + r_{t+1}^f$, we then have

$$\hat{R}_{t+1}^f = \frac{dR_{t+1}^f}{R^f} \simeq R_{t+1}^f - R^f = \hat{r}_{t+1}^f.$$

Given this definition and noting that r_{t+1}^f is known at date t, we obtain the log-linearized Euler equation

$$\hat{r}_{t+1}^f = E_t \hat{C}_{t+1} - \hat{C}_t.$$

This implies that the change in the interest rate reflects the expected change in consumption. Finally, we can derive investment simply from the resource constraint.

14.2.4   Business Cycle Statistics and Model Results
Business cycle statistics focus primarily on volatility, comovement (or cyclicality), and persistence. Volatility refers to the standard deviation of an HP-filtered series. Cyclicality refers to the contemporaneous correlation of a series with GDP. Persistence refers to the first-order autocorrelation of a series. It is also

interesting to examine how strongly a series is correlated with output led or lagged a number of periods, so as to say something about which series are "lagging indicators" and which series are "leading indicators."

The series that we are most interested in are output, consumption, investment, total hours worked, the real wage rate, and the real interest rate. Moreover we will look at average labor productivity (the ratio of output to total hours worked), the price level, stock returns, and total factor productivity (TFP). The price level is not in the basic RBC model, but it will appear in extended models. All series except for interest rate and stock returns are HP filtered.

The sample period covers the first quarter of 1948 through the fourth quarter of 2010. All series (with the exception of TFP, the price level, the interest rate, and the stock return) are expressed in per capita terms after dividing by the civilian non-institutional population aged 16 and over. The civilian non-institutional population aged 16 and over is downloaded from the Federal Reserve Bank of St. Louis. All series are in logs. All nominal series (except for the price level) are deflated by the price level. The price level is measured as the implicit price deflator for GDP from table 1.1.9 downloaded from the Bureau of Economic Analysis (BEA). The nominal GDP, consumption, and investment are taken from NIPA table 1.1.5 downloaded from the BEA. Consumption is measured as the sum of nondurable and services consumption. Investment is measured as total private fixed investment plus consumption expenditures on durable goods (durable goods should be thought of as investment because they provide benefits in the future, just like new physical capital does).

Total hours are measured as total hours in the nonfarm business sector, from the Bureau of Labor Statistics (BLS). Labor productivity is output per hour in the nonfarm business sector, from the BLS. Wages are measured as real compensation per hour in the nonfarm business sector, from the BLS. The nominal interest rate is measured as the three month Treasury Bill rate. The aggregate stock returns are measured as the value weighted return from NYSE, AMEX, and NASDAQ. Both the nominal interest rate and the stock return are taken from CRSP. We compute the real interest rate and the real stock return by substracting the inflation rate, where inflation is measured from the GDP deflator.

TFP is measured by Solow residuals using the production function

$$SR_t = \ln Y_t - \alpha \ln K_t - (1 - \alpha) \ln N_t.$$

Constructing this series requires an empirical measure of the capital stock. In practice, this is hard to measure and most existing capital stock series are only available at an annual frequency. For example, BEA contains tables of annual fixed assets. Typically researchers use the perpetual inventory method to measure the capital stock. This method essentially takes data on investment, an initial capital

Table 14.1
Business cycle statistics

	Standard deviation (%)	Relative standard deviation	First order auto correlation	Contemporaneous correlation with Y
Y	1.52 (1.85)	1.00 (1.00)	0.72 (0.85)	1 (1)
C	0.74 (1.17)	0.45 (0.63)	0.76 (0.86)	0.97 (0.80)
I	4.19 (4.41)	2.75 (2.38)	0.71 (0.84)	0.99 (0.62)
N	0.55 (1.95)	0.36 (1.05)	0.71 (0.90)	0.98 (0.82)
Y/N	0.99 (1.12)	0.65 (0.60)	0.74 (0.72)	0.99 (0.26)
w	0.99 (0.87)	0.65 (0.47)	0.74 (0.72)	0.99 (−0.06)
TFP	0.89 (1.10)	0.54 (0.60)	0.99 (0.80)	1.00 (0.68)
Price	NA (0.94)	NA (0.51)	NA (0.91)	NA (0.00)
$\ln R^f$	0.05 (0.70)	0.04 (0.38)	0.71 (0.71)	0.95 (0.02)
$\ln R^s$	0.05 (8.40)	0.03 (4.51)	0.71 (0.09)	0.96 (−0.23)

Note: All variables are in logarithms. Numbers in the brackets are computed from the US quarterly data from 1948Q1–2010Q4. Other numbers are computed from the basic RBC model.

stock, and an estimate of the rate of depreciation and constructs a series using the accumulation equation for capital:

$$K_{t+1} = (1 - \delta) K_t + I_t.$$

After constructing Solow residuals $\{SR_t\}$, we can then use equations (14.29) and (14.30) to estimate the TFP shock.

The selected moments from the model and from the data (in brackets) are shown in table 14.1. This table discloses the following stylized facts:

- Consumption is less volatile than output.
- Investment is about two times more volatile than output.
- Total hours worked have about the same volatility as output.
- Labor productivity is less volatile than output.
- The real wage is less volatile than output.
- All macroeconomic series are highly persistent.
- Most macroeconomic series are procyclical. Hours are strongly procyclical, but labor productivity and output are weakly correlated. The real wage is essentially acyclical.

Table 14.1 also shows that the basic RBC model explains the US business cycles reasonably well.[4] However, the basic RBC model fails in many dimensions.

---

4. The Dynare code is rbc1.mod.

First, consumption and hours are too smooth. Second, the real wage rate and labor productivity are too strongly procyclical. Finally, statistics related to the real interest rate and stock returns are far off from the data.

Because the TFP shock is the driving force of business cycles, we next examine the impact of the TFP shock more extensively below.

14.2.5   Impact of a Permanent TFP Shock

Suppose that there is an unexpected permanent increase in total factor productivity. In this case both isoclines $\Delta \hat{C}_t = 0$ and $\Delta \hat{K}_t = 0$ shift up. Figure 14.3 plots this effect. After the permanent shock, the economy moves to a new nonstochastic steady state. Figure 14.3 also plots the new saddle path. Initial consumption must jump to this path. Since this path may be above or below the original steady state, the impact of initial consumption is ambiguous. An initial fall of consumption may seem counterintuitive. This is possible if the initial rise in investment exceeds the increase in output. In the figure we suppose that initial consumption jumps up. This rise is due to the wealth effect and is consistent with the permanent income hypothesis.

Turn to the labor market as illustrated in figure 14.4. Higher TFP shifts the labor demand curve out. High consumption shifts the labor supply curve in. The net

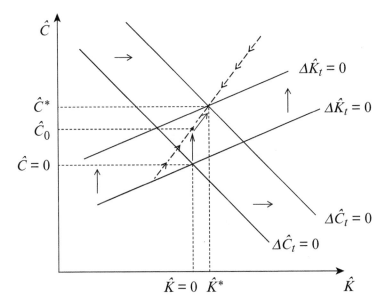

Figure 14.3
Phase diagram after a permanent TFP shock for the log-linearized basic RBC model

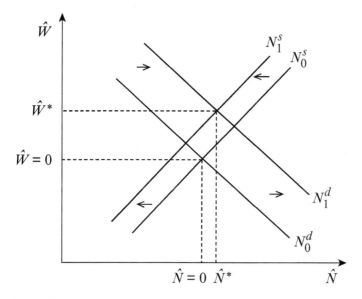

Figure 14.4
Labor market responses following a permanent TFP shock for the log-linearized basic RBC model

effect is to cause the wage rate to rise, but the impact on hours is ambiguous. In the figure we suppose that hours rise.

The interest rate must go up because consumption rises along the saddle path. Since capital also rises along the saddle path, investment must rise too.

14.2.6   Impact of a Temporary TFP Shock

Say that there is an unexpected, purely temporary TFP shock in that $\hat{z}_t$ only increases today and then remains zero in the future. Because the changes in the isoclines last for only one period, the initial impact on consumption is very small. Consumption rises initially and then falls back to original steady state along the saddle path. Thus the labor supply curve has a very small change initially. But the labor demand curve goes up for one period, causing the wage rate and hours to rise. The impact on hours is larger in the temporary shock case than in the permanent shock case. Hence the initial impact on output is also larger in the temporary shock case than in the permanent shock case. Since initial output goes up, but consumption does not change much, initial investment must rise. This rise is also higher than that in the permanent shock case. The interest rate must fall on impact because consumption is expected to fall. It then rises to the steady-state level.

14.2.7 Effects of Persistence and Critiques of the RBC Model

As was shown above, the persistence of the TFP shock plays an important role. In figures 14.5 and 14.6 we consider the impulse response functions for different values of persistence of the TFP shock.[5] These figures show that when the TFP shock is more persistent, consumption and real wages rise more on impact but hours, investment, and output rise less on impact. Notice in the figures that the RBC model lacks an amplification and propagation mechanism as the impact effect on output is small, and output does not exhibit a hump-shaped response (Cogley and Nason 1995). The response of output essentially follows the same shape as the TFP shock. Much of the recent business cycle research has tried to extend the basic RBC model by introducing various new elements in order to provide an

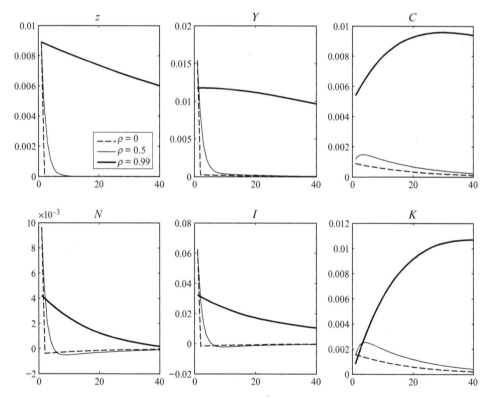

Figure 14.5
Comparison of impulse responses to a TFP shock with different levels of persistence

---

5. The Matlab and Dynare codes are RBCrho.m and rbc2.mod.

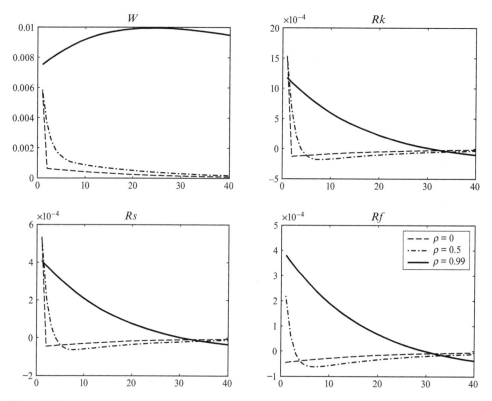

Figure 14.6
Comparison of impulse responses to a TFP shock with different levels of persistence

amplification and propagation mechanism. These extensions can overcome some limitations pointed out earlier.

14.3   Extensions of the Basic RBC Model

The basic RBC model has been extended in many ways. Because this model has an explicit microfoundation, the model can be extended from either the preference side or the technology side. We now discuss some extensions along these two dimensions.

14.3.1   Various Utility Functions

In the basic RBC model we have adopted a utility specification within the class of models in King, Plosser, and Rebelo (1988). We now consider other utility specifications within this class. We also consider other utility models outside the KPR class.

KPR Utility The following specification of KPR utility functions in (14.5) and (14.6) are widely adopted in the literature:

$$u\left(c,n\right) = \frac{\left(c\left(1-n\right)^{\chi}\right)^{1-\gamma}}{1-\gamma} \tag{14.38}$$

and

$$u\left(c,n\right) = \ln c - \chi\frac{n^{1+\nu}}{1+\nu}, \tag{14.39}$$

where χ, γ, and $1/\nu$ represents the utility weight on leisure, relative risk aversion, and Frisch elasticity of labor supply. When $\gamma = 1$, (14.38) reduces to (14.22). When $\nu = 0$, (14.39) is the indivisible labor model studied by Hansen (1985) and Rogerson (1988).

Using the previous calibration strategy, we still obtain $\chi = 1.75$ in (14.38). Figure 14.7 plots the impulse responses for different values of γ in (14.38).[6] This figure shows that the impact effect on consumption is increasing in γ because households want smoother consumption. This means that the initial jump in labor is decreasing in γ. The intuition is as follows. When TFP increases, labor demand shifts right, which is independent of γ. When consumption increases, labor supply shifts left. The larger the consumption increase, the larger is the inward shift in labor supply, and therefore the smaller is the hours response in equilibrium and the larger is the wage response. As a result the initial jump in output is smaller. Moreover when γ is larger, the initial jump in the stock return, the risk-free rate, and the capital rental rate are also smaller. This figure suggests that a smaller value of γ fits the data better. However, microeconomic evidence suggests that γ is around 2.

Figure 14.8 plots the impulse responses for different values of ν in (14.39).[7] Notice that when we change ν, we have to recalibrate the model to pin down ν because the steady state changes with ν. Figure 14.8 shows that the indivisible labor model ($\nu = 0$) delivers much larger impact effects on output, hours, and investment. Also the initial jump in wage is smaller. Thus the indivisible labor model is very useful in improving the model performance.

GHH Utility Greenwood, Hercowitz, and Huffman (1988) propose the following utility specification:

$$u\left(c,n\right) = U\left(c - G\left(n\right)\right), \tag{14.40}$$

---

6. The Matlab and Dynare codes are RBCgamma.m and rbc3.mod.
7. The Matlab and Dynare codes are calibration2.m, RBCnu.m and rbc4.mod.

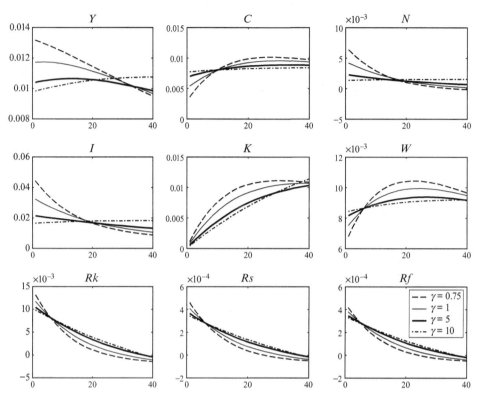

Figure 14.7
Comparison of impulse responses to a TFP shock for different values of the risk aversion parameter

where U and G satisfy the usual assumption. This utility function implies that the labor supply decision is determined by

$$G'(n) = w.$$

Unlike King, Plosser, and Rebelo (1988) utility, consumption does not affect labor supply. Thus there is no wealth effect or intertemporal substitution effect in determining labor supply. The shift in labor demand determines the change in hours and wage.

Habit Formation   The idea of the habit formation model is that people get utility from current consumption relative to past consumption. Habit formation can help resolve some empirical failings of the permanent income hypothesis.

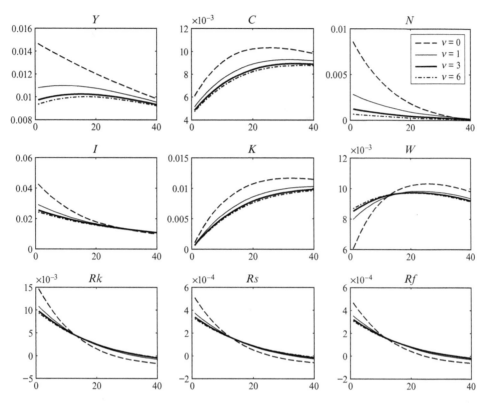

Figure 14.8
Comparison of impulse responses to a TFP shock for different values of the Frisch elasticity of labor supply

For example, habit formation can help resolve the "excess smoothness" puzzle because, as habit formation gets larger, the less consumption will jump in response to news about permanent income. Habit formation is also useful in resolving the equity premium puzzle. A high level of habit formation makes people behave as if they are extremely risk averse, and can thereby help explain a large equity premium without necessarily resorting to extremely large coefficients of relative risk aversion.

There are several different habit formation types. Here we consider the internal habit model widely used in macroeconomics:

$$E \sum_{t=0}^{\infty} \beta^t \left[\ln \left(C_t - bC_{t-1} \right) + \chi \ln \left(1 - N_t \right) \right],$$

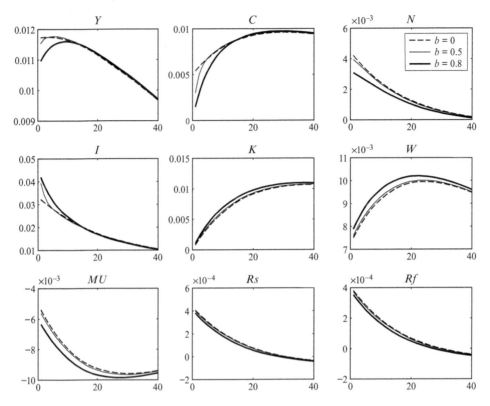

Figure 14.9
Comparison of impulse responses to a TFP shock for different values of the habit formation
parameter

where b is the habit parameter. In this case marginal utility of consumption is
given by

$$\Lambda_t = \frac{1}{C_t - bC_{t-1}} - \beta b E_t \frac{1}{C_{t+1} - bC_t}.$$

To study the impact of habit formation, we recalibrate the model and present
impulse response functions for different values of b in figure 14.9.[8]

   As this figure shows, a high degree of habit formation makes the initial
responses of output, consumption, and hours small but makes the initial response
of investment large. The intuition is that the household cares about past consumption. The initial adjustment of consumption is more sluggish, but the fall in
marginal utility is larger, when the degree of habit formation is larger. Hence the

_____

8. The Matlab and Dynare codes are calibration3.m, RBChabit.m, and rbc5.mod.

negative wealth effect of labor supply is larger when b is larger. Habit formation is not useful for amplification. However, habit formation helps generate propagation. For example, for $b = 0.8$ both consumption and output follow hump-shaped responses. Figure 14.9 also shows that habit formation alone will not help generate a large equity premium because the impulse responses of the stock return and the interest rate are similar for $b = 0$, 0.5, and 0.8. We will see below that introducing adjustment costs is important.

14.3.2   Capacity Utilization

The basic RBC model has weak amplification. Output can jump initially because TFP and labor jump since capital is predetermined. The idea of capacity utilization is to allow the intensity of the use of capital to vary in response to TFP shocks. The cost of high capacity utilization is to make capital depreciate faster. Assume that the dependence of capital depreciation on capacity utilization is modeled as

$$\delta\left(u_t\right) = \delta_0 u_t^{\delta_1}, \quad \delta_0 > 0, \delta_1 > 1,$$

where $u_t > 0$ represents the capacity utilization rate and the curvature parameter δ_1 determines the intensity of capacity utilization. The capital accumulation equation becomes

$$K_{t+1} = \left(1 - \delta\left(u_t\right)\right) K_t + I_t.$$

Let the production function be

$$Y_t = z_t \left(K_t u_t\right)^\alpha N_t^{1-\alpha}.$$

From the social planner's problem, we can derive first-order conditions

$$u'\left(C_t\right) = \beta E_t u'\left(C_{t+1}\right) \left(1 - \delta\left(u_{t+1}\right) + \frac{\alpha Y_{t+1}}{K_{t+1}}\right),$$

$$\delta'\left(u_t\right) = \frac{\alpha Y_t}{\left(K_t u_t\right)}.$$

In a decentralized equilibrium when households own capital, we assume that households rent capital $u_t K_t$ to the firm at the rental rate R_{kt}. The firm demands capital and labor by solving the problem

$$\max_{k_t, n_t} z_t k_t^\alpha n_t^{1-\alpha} - R_{kt} k_t - w_t n_t.$$

In equilibrium, $k_t = K_t u_t$ and $n_t = N_t$. We then obtain

$$R_{kt} = \frac{\alpha Y_t}{K_t u_t}.$$

Households choose optimal capacity utilization so that

$$\delta'(u_t) = R_{kt}. \tag{14.41}$$

The marginal benefit of an additional unit of capital utilization is the rental rate R_{kt} and the marginal cost is $\delta'(u_t)$. To calibrate this model, we can assume that the steady-state capacity utilization rate is equal to one. We can use (14.41) to pin down $\delta_0 \delta_1$. We set $\delta_0 = 0.025$. We can then determine δ_1.

14.3.3   Capital or Investment Adjustment Costs

Without investment frictions, investment would respond too much to profitability shocks compared to the firm-level empirical evidence. A natural way to improve model performance is to introduce convex adjustment costs. These costs are important to generate movements of asset prices and hence are useful for understanding asset pricing phenomena. Changes in asset prices also provide a propagation mechanism in models with financial frictions. We now introduce convex adjustment costs in the basic RBC model.

There are two general ways to model convex adjustment costs. First, changes in capital stock incur costs. These adjustment costs can be modeled as a nonlinear function of investment. Capital stock is often introduced in this function too. We have presented this modeling in partial equilibrium in section 8.6.2. Second, changes in investment incur costs. These adjustment costs can be modeled as a nonlinear function of the change in investment. For both modeling approaches, we can introduce adjustment costs in two ways. In the first way, adjustment costs reduce profits directly and hence represent a loss of output in general equilibrium. In the second way, adjustment costs enter the capital accumulation equation, meaning that one unit of investment does not necessarily increase capital stock by one unit.

We start by the usual case where adjustment costs are a function of investment and capital. We will extend the Q-theory of Hayashi (1982) to general equilibrium. Assume that adjustment costs change the capital accumulation equation,

$$K_{t+1} = (1 - \delta) K_t + \Phi(I_t, K_t), \tag{14.42}$$

where Φ is the adjustment cost function satisfying $\Phi_I > 0$ and $\Phi_{II} < 0$. In applications the following form is often used:

$$\Phi(I, K) = \varphi\left(\frac{I}{K}\right) K, \tag{14.43}$$

where $\varphi'' < 0$, $\varphi(\delta) = \delta$, $\varphi'(\delta) = 1$, and $\varphi''(\delta) = \kappa$. This assumption ensures that the investment rate is $I/K = \delta$ and $Q = 1$ in the nonstochastic steady state, and that the parameter κ controls the dynamic responses of investment to shocks. In the log-linearized solution, the parameter κ does not affect nonstochastic steady state and no specific functional form is required.

We first solve the social planner's problem:

$$\max_{\{C_t, N_t, I_t, K_{t+1}\}} E \sum_{t=0}^{\infty} \beta^t u\left(C_t, N_t\right)$$

subject to (14.42) and the resource constraint

$$C_t + I_t = z_t F\left(K_t, N_t\right), \tag{14.44}$$

where the utility function u and the production function F satisfy the usual smoothness and concavity assumptions. First-order conditions are given by

$$C_t : u_C\left(C_t, N_t\right) = \Lambda_t,$$

$$N_t : -u_N\left(C_t, N_t\right) = \Lambda_t z_t F_N\left(K_t, N_t\right),$$

$$I_t : Q_t \Phi_I\left(I_t, K_t\right) = 1, \tag{14.45}$$

$$K_{t+1} : \Lambda_t Q_t = \beta E_t \Lambda_{t+1}\left(z_{t+1} F_K\left(K_{t+1}, N_{t+1}\right) + Q_{t+1}\left(1 - \delta + \Phi_K\left(I_{t+1}, K_{t+1}\right)\right)\right),$$

where $\beta^t \Lambda_t Q_t$ and $\beta^t \Lambda_t$ are the Lagrange multipliers associated with (14.42) and (14.44), respectively.

In turning to the decentralized market equilibrium, we consider three types of decentralized equilibria. First, when households own capital and make investment, the representative household's problem is as follows:

$$\max_{\{C_t, N_t, I_t, K_{t+1}\}} E \sum_{t=0}^{\infty} \beta^t u\left(C_t, N_t\right)$$

subject to (14.42) and

$$C_t + I_t = R_{kt} K_t + w_t N_t. \tag{14.46}$$

First-order conditions are given by

$$C_t : u_C\left(C_t, N_t\right) = \Lambda_t,$$

$$N_t : -u_N\left(C_t, N_t\right) = \Lambda_t w_t,$$

$$I_t : Q_t \Phi_I\left(I_t, K_t\right) = 1,$$

$$K_{t+1} : \Lambda_t Q_t = \beta E_t \Lambda_{t+1}\left[R_{k,t+1} + Q_{t+1}\left(1 - \delta + \Phi_K\left(I_{t+1}, K_{t+1}\right)\right)\right],$$

where $\beta^t \Lambda_t Q_t$ and $\beta^t \Lambda_t$ are the Lagrange multipliers associated with (14.42) and (14.46), respectively.

The firm's problem is given by

$$\max_{K_t, N_t} z_t F\left(K_t, N_t\right) - R_{kt} K_t - w_t N_t. \tag{14.47}$$

First-order conditions are given by

$$R_{kt} = z_t F_K(K_t, N_t), \quad w_t = z_t F_N(K_t, N_t).$$

Second, we introduce a stock market for trading of firm shares. Firms own capital and make investment decisions. The household's problem is given by

$$\max_{\{C_t, N_t, I_t, K_{t+1}\}} E \sum_{t=0}^{\infty} \beta^t u(C_t, N_t)$$

subject to

$$C_t + \psi_{t+1}(V_t - D_t) + B_{t+1} = \psi_t V_t + B_t R_{ft} + w_t N_t,$$

where V_t represents the cum-dividends equity value, D_t represents dividends, R_{ft} represents risk-free rate between periods $t-1$ and t, and ψ_t and B_t represent share and bond holdings, respectively. First-order conditions are given by

$$C_t : u_C(C_t, N_t) = \Lambda_t,$$
$$N_t : -u_N(C_t, N_t) = \Lambda_t w_t,$$
$$\psi_{t+1} : \Lambda_t(V_t - D_t) = \beta E_t \Lambda_{t+1} V_{t+1},$$
$$B_{t+1} : \Lambda_t = \beta E_t \Lambda_{t+1} R_{ft+1}.$$

The firm's optimization problem is given by

$$V_0 = \max_{\{I_t\}} E \sum_{t=0}^{\infty} \frac{\beta^t \Lambda_t}{\Lambda_0} D_t$$

subject to (14.42) and

$$D_t = z_t F(K_t, N_t) - w_t N_t - I_t.$$

First-order conditions are given by

$$I_t : Q_t \Phi_I(I_t, K_t) = 1, \tag{14.48}$$

$$K_{t+1} : \Lambda_t Q_t = \beta E_t \Lambda_{t+1} [z_{t+1} F_K(K_{t+1}, N_{t+1}) + Q_{t+1}(1 - \delta + \Phi_K(I_{t+1}, K_{t+1}))], \tag{14.49}$$

where $Q_t \beta^t \Lambda_t / \Lambda_0$ is the Lagrange multiplier associated with (14.42). Equation (14.48) combined with equation (14.42) can be interpreted as the capital supply equation, whereas (14.49) can be interpreted as the capital demand equation. In the case without capital adjustment costs (i.e., $\Phi(I, K) = I$), $Q_t = 1$, and hence capital supply is flat. Changes in capital demand changes quantity but not its shadow price.

As in the partial equilibrium model studied in section 8.6.2, Q_t is Tobin's marginal Q, which is unobservable. We want to link Q_t to some observable variable such as Tobin's average Q. The following result is a generalization of that in Hayashi (1982). Its proof is left as an exercise.

Proposition 14.3.1 *If F and Φ are linearly homogeneous, then*

$$Q_t = \frac{P_t}{K_{t+1}} = \frac{\partial P_t}{\partial K_{t+1}},$$

where P_t is ex-dividend equity value defined as

$$P_t = E_t \frac{\beta \Lambda_{t+1}}{\Lambda_t} V_{t+1}.$$

Now define the investment return as

$$R_{I,t+1} = \frac{Q_{t+1}\left[1 - \delta + \Phi_K\left(I_{t+1}, K_{t+1}\right)\right] + R_{k,t+1}}{Q_t}.$$

Using the result above, we can prove that the stock return is equal to the investment return

$$R_{s,t+1} = \frac{P_{t+1} + D_{t+1}}{P_t} = R_{I,t+1}.$$

The proof is simple. First, we write dividends as

$$D_{t+1} = R_{k,t+1}K_{t+1} - I_{t+1}.$$

Since Φ is linearly homogeneous,

$$\Phi\left(I, K\right) = \Phi_I I + \Phi_K K.$$

Using these equations, equation (14.45), and proposition 14.3.1, we can show that

$$\begin{aligned}
R_{s,t+1} &= \frac{P_{t+1} + D_{t+1}}{P_t} = \frac{Q_{t+1}K_{t+2} + R_{k,t+1}K_{t+1} - I_{t+1}}{Q_t K_{t+1}} \\
&= \frac{Q_{t+1}\left(1 - \delta\right)K_{t+1} + Q_{t+1}\Phi\left(I_{t+1}, K_{t+1}\right) + R_{k,t+1} - I_{t+1}}{Q_t K_{t+1}} \\
&= \frac{Q_{t+1}\left(1 - \delta\right)K_{t+1} + Q_{t+1}\Phi_K\left(I_{t+1}, K_{t+1}\right)K_{t+1} + R_{k,t+1}K_{t+1}}{Q_t K_{t+1}} \\
&= \frac{Q_{t+1}\left[1 - \delta + \Phi_K\left(I_{t+1}, K_{t+1}\right)\right] + R_{k,t+1}}{Q_t} = R_{I,t+1}.
\end{aligned}$$

This result is useful for asset pricing.

In the third type of decentralization, we introduce capital goods producers and a market for capital goods. In this setup we can price the capital stock. Capital producers purchase undepreciated capital $(1 - \delta)K_t$ from households and sell them new capital K_{t+1} at the price Q_t at time t. New capital is produced by making investment I_t. Capital goods producers' problem is given by

$$\max_{I_t} \ Q_t K_{t+1} - Q_t (1 - \delta) K_t - I_t,$$

subject to (14.42). Note that the profits from capital goods producers are redistributed to households. Final goods firms rent capital, hire labor from households, and solve the static profit maximization problem (14.47). Households trade capital goods, rent capital, and supply labor. They solve the following problem:

$$\max_{\{C_t, N_t, K_{t+1}\}} \ E \sum_{t=0}^{\infty} \beta^t u \left(C_t, N_t \right)$$

subject to

$$C_t + Q_t K_{t+1} = Q_t (1 - \delta) K_t + R_{kt} K_t + w_t N_t + \Pi_t,$$

where Π_t represents the profits from capital producers.

   Finally, we consider the case where changes in investment incur adjustment costs. Following Christiano, Eichenbaum, and Evans (2005), we assume that capital evolves according to

$$K_{t+1} = (1 - \delta) K_t + G \left(I_t, I_{t-1} \right),$$

where G represents investment adjustment costs satisfying $G_1 > 0$ and $G_{11} < 0$. The firm's first-order conditions are given by

$$I_t : Q_t G_1 \left(I_t, I_{t-1} \right) + E_t \frac{\beta \Lambda_{t+1}}{\Lambda_t} Q_{t+1} G_2 \left(I_{t+1}, I_t \right) = 1, \tag{14.50}$$

$$K_{t+1} : \Lambda_t Q_t = \beta E_t \Lambda_{t+1} \left[z_{t+1} F_K \left(K_{t+1}, N_{t+1} \right) + Q_{t+1} (1 - \delta) \right]. \tag{14.51}$$

What is the relationship between Q_t and P_t? Q_t may not be equal to Tobin's average Q. Eberly, Rebelo, and Vincent (2011) show that in a log-linearized system, one can replace marginal Q by average Q and hence current investment is related to past investment and Tobin's average Q.

   In applications the following specification is often used:

$$G \left(I_t, I_{t-1} \right) = \left[1 - S \left(\frac{I_t}{I_{t-1}} \right) \right] I_t, \tag{14.52}$$

where S satisfies $S'' > 0$, $S (1) = S' (1) = 0$, and $S'' (1) = \kappa > 0$. These assumptions ensure that the steady-state investment rate I/K is equal to δ and $Q = 1$ and that the parameter κ controls the dynamic responses of investment to shocks. In the log-linearized solution the parameter κ does not affect nonstochastic steady state, and no specific functional form is required.

14.3.4 Stochastic Trends

So far we have assumed that the data and the model are trend stationary. To incorporate deterministic trend, we can assume that output satisfies

$$Y_t = z_t K_t^\alpha \left(A_t N_t\right)^{1-\alpha},$$

where $A_t = g_a^t A_0$. King et al. (1991) show that many macro data exhibit common stochastic trends. To capture this fact, we assume that TFP shocks follow a stochastic trend in the basic RBC model:

$$\ln z_t = \mu_z + \ln z_{t-1} + \sigma \varepsilon_t, \quad z_{-1} = 1.$$

where μ_z represents the trend growth and ε_t is IID standard normal. In this case we need to detrend variables. Define detrended variables $\tilde{X}_t = X_t / z_t^{1/(1-\alpha)}$ for $X_t = C_t$, I_t, Y_t, and w_t. Since K_{t+1} is chosen in period t, we define $\tilde{K}_{t+1} = K_{t+1} / z_t^{1/(1-\alpha)}$. We then obtain the detrended system:

$$\frac{1}{\tilde{C}_t} = E_t \frac{\beta}{\tilde{C}_{t+1}} \exp\left(\frac{1}{\alpha-1}\left(\mu_z + \sigma\varepsilon_{t+1}\right)\right)\left(R_{k,t+1} + 1 - \delta\right),$$

$$\frac{\chi \tilde{C}_t}{1 - N_t} = \tilde{w}_t,$$

$$\tilde{C}_t + \tilde{I}_t = \tilde{Y}_t = \exp\left(\frac{\alpha}{\alpha-1}\left(\mu_z + \sigma\varepsilon_t\right)\right)\tilde{K}_t^\alpha N_t^{1-\alpha},$$

$$\tilde{K}_{t+1} = \exp\left(\frac{1}{\alpha-1}\left(\mu_z + \sigma\varepsilon_t\right)\right)(1-\delta)\tilde{K}_t + \tilde{I}_t,$$

$$R_{kt} = \frac{\alpha \tilde{Y}_t}{\tilde{K}_t}\exp\left(\frac{1}{1-\alpha}\left(\mu_z + \sigma\varepsilon_t\right)\right),$$

$$\tilde{w}_t = (1-\alpha)\exp\left(\frac{\alpha}{\alpha-1}\left(\mu_z + \sigma\varepsilon_t\right)\right)\tilde{K}_t^\alpha N_t^{-\alpha}.$$

We can solve the model using calibrated parameter values.[9] Dynare will produce impulse responses of the detrended variables. To construct impulse responses of the original variables, we need to transform back, namely $\ln x_t = \ln \tilde{x}_t + (\ln z_t)/(1 - \alpha)$ for any variable x_t. Figure 14.10 presents the results for

$$\ln x_t - \ln \tilde{x}^{ss} = \ln \tilde{x}_t - \ln \tilde{x}^{ss} + \frac{\ln z_t}{1 - \alpha},$$

---

9. The Matlab and Dynare codes are calibtrend.m and stochtrend2.mod.

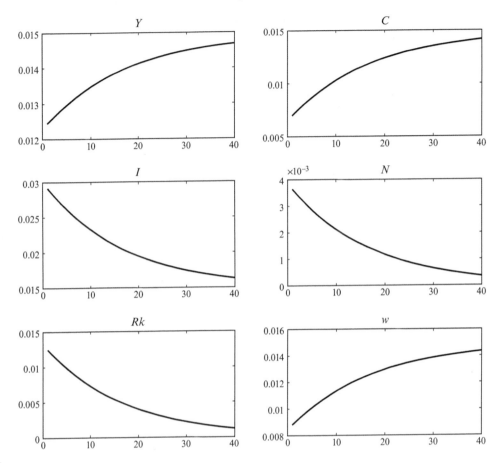

Figure 14.10
Impulse responses to a permanent TFP shock

in response to a 1 percent increase in ε_0, where $\tilde{x}^{ss}$ is the steady state for the detrended system.

As this figure shows, the model with stochastic trend generates much less volatility in hours than do transitory TFP shocks. The intuition for this result is based on the permanent income hypothesis and our graphical analysis of the basic RBC model. If the TFP shock is permanent, consumption will jump up by more. Consumption jumping up by more means that labor supply shifts in by more. Hence hours rise by less and the real wage rises by more. Since hours rise by less, output rises by less. Given a larger increase in consumption, investment would also rise by less on impact.

14.3.5 Other Sources of Shocks

The main finding of the RBC theory is that technology shocks are the driving force of business cycles. Recently researchers have found that other shocks also play important roles. We now examine some widely studied shocks.

Investment-Specific Technology Shocks Greenwood, Hercowitz, and Krusell (1997) find that investment-specific technical change is the major source of economic growth. This suggests that it could be important for short-run fluctuations as well. Fisher (2006) finds that combining investment-specific technology shock with the TFP shock accounts for about 40 to 60 percent of the fluctuations in output and hours at business cycle frequencies. We now introduce an investment-specific technology shock into the basic RBC model. We replace the law of motion for capital (14.24) by

$$K_{t+1} = (1 - \delta) K_t + v_t I_t,$$

where v_t follows the process

$$\ln v_t = (1 - \rho_v) \ln \bar{v} + \rho_v \ln v_{t-1} + \sigma_v \varepsilon_{vt}.$$

Consider the decentralization where households own capital and make investment decisions. Then we have

$$I_t : Q_t = \frac{1}{v_t},$$

$$K_{t+1} : Q_t \Lambda_t = \beta E_t \Lambda_{t+1} [R_{k,t+1} + (1 - \delta) Q_{t+1}].$$

The other equations are identical. Here the capital price is equal to $1/v_t$. Set $v = 1$, $\rho_v = 0.90, \sigma_v = 0.01, \rho = 0.95,$ and $\sigma = 0.01$. The other parameter values are the same as those in the basic RBC model. Figure 14.11 presents the impulse responses to both the TFP shock and the investment-specific shock.[10]

As this figure shows, in response to an investment-specific technology shock, consumption, wage, labor productivity, and the capital price fall on impact. The intuition is that a positive shock to the investment-specific technology reduces the price of investment goods and raises the relative price of consumption goods. Hence consumption falls and investment rises on impact. Because of the fall in consumption, labor supply rises on impact. But labor demand does not change. Thus hours rise and the wage rate falls on impact. This causes labor productivity to fall on impact. Consequently combining the investment-specific shock with the TFP shock will help the model match the cyclicality of labor productivity and the real wage rate in the data.

---

10. The Matlab and Dynare codes are RBCINshock.m, calibration.m and rbc6.mod.

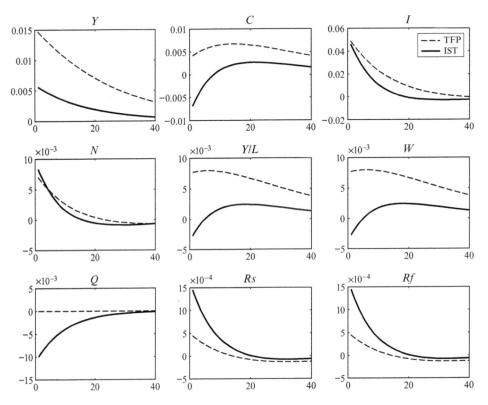

Figure 14.11
Impulse responses to a TFP shock and an investment-specific technology (IST) shock

Government-Spending Shocks   We now introduce a government in the basic
RBC model. Suppose that government spending G_t is financed by lump-sum taxes.
The resource constraint becomes

$$C_t + I_t + G_t = z_t K_t^\alpha N_t^{1-\alpha},$$

where G_t follows the process

$$\ln G_t = \left(1 - \rho_g\right) \ln \bar{G} + \rho_g \ln G_{t-1} + \sigma_g \varepsilon_{gt}.$$

We recalibrate the model so that government spending accounts for 20 percent
of output in the nonstochastic steady state. Figure 14.12 presents the impulse
responses to a 1 percent increase in government spending for different levels of
persistence ρ_g.[11]

---

11. The Matlab and Dynare codes are RBCrhog.m, calibgov.m and rbc7.mod.

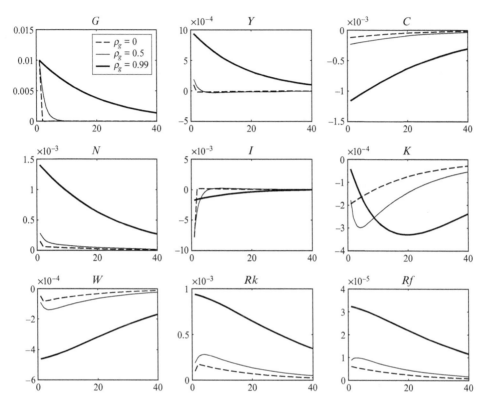

Figure 14.12
Impulse responses to a government-spending shock at different levels of persistence

As this figure shows, consumption and investment fall on impact due the wealth effect. But hours rise on impact because of the rise in labor supply. Thus output also rises on impact. The larger the persistence, the larger is the impact on output, consumption, and hours but the smaller is the impact on investment.

Preference Shocks   Last we introduce a preference shock so that the utility function is given by

$$E \sum_{t=0}^{\infty} \beta^t \varphi_t \left(\ln C_t + \chi \ln (1 - N_t) \right),$$

where the preference shock φ_t follows the process

$$\ln \varphi_t = \rho_p \ln \varphi_{t-1} + \sigma_p \varepsilon_{pt}.$$

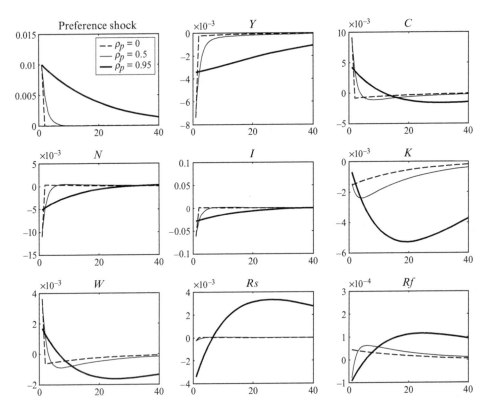

Figure 14.13
Impulse responses to a preference shock at different levels of persistence

Figure 14.13 presents the impulse responses to a positive 1 percent shock to preferences for different levels of persistence.[12] It shows that when the preference shock is more persistent, the initial rise in consumption is less, but the initial drop in hours, investment, and output is larger. The intuition is that a more persistent preference shock gives a smoother consumption path. Thus the wealth effect on labor supply is smaller on impact.

14.4   Exercises

1. Formulate the model in section 14.1.2 using the Arrow–Debreu setup. Do it again using the market arrangements in which households own capital and

---

12. The Matlab and Dynare codes are RBCpref.m, calibration.m and rbc8.mod.

make investment decisions. Show that these two formulations and the one in section 14.1.2 yield identical allocation.

2. Derive the steady-state equilibrium for the model in section 14.1.2.

3. Calibrate the capacity utilization model and use Dynare to solve it. Plot impulse responses to a positive 1 percent TFP shock for different parameter values of δ_0 and δ_1.

4. Prove proposition 14.3.1.

5. Show that the three types of decentralization for the model with capital adjustment costs yield the same allocation.

6. Assume risk neutral preferences. Derive the log-linearized system for the investment dynamics for the model with capital adjustment costs in (14.43) and investment adjustment costs (14.52). Discuss the differences.

7. Calibrate two RBC models with capital adjustment costs (14.43) and with investment adjustment costs (14.52). Use Dynare to solve these two models, and plot impulse responses to a positive 1 percent TFP shock for different curvature parameter values κ.

15   Bayesian Estimation of DSGE Models Using Dynare

There are several different formal and informal econometric procedures to evaluate DSGE models quantitatively. Kydland and Prescott (1982) advocate a calibration procedure. This procedure is dominant in the early literature on real business cycles. Christiano and Eichenbaum (1992) use the generalized method of moments (GMM) to estimate equilibrium relationships. Rotemberg and Woodford (1997) and Christiano, Eichenbaum, and Evans (2005) use the minimum distance estimation method based on the discrepancy between VAR and DSGE model impulse response functions. Altug (1989), McGrattan (1994), Leeper and Sims (1994), and Kim (2000) adopt the full-information likelihood-based estimation method. Ireland (2004) develops a hybrid method that combines DSGE models and VAR methods. The reader is referred to Kydland and Prescott (1996), Hansen and Heckman (1996), and Sims (1996) for discussions of methodological issues.

In this chapter we focus on the Bayesian estimation of DSGE models. This method has several advantages over other methods. First, unlike the GMM estimation based on equilibrium relationships such as the consumption Euler equation, the Bayesian analysis is system based and fits the solved DSGE model to a vector of aggregate time series. Second, the estimation is based on the likelihood function generated by the DSGE model rather than, for instance, the discrepancy between DSGE model responses and VAR impulse responses. Third, maximizing the likelihood function in the maximum likelihood method is challenging. By contrast, computing posteriors in the Bayesian method is much easier. Fourth, prior distributions can be used to incorporate additional information into the parameter estimation.

We refer the reader to An and Schorfheide (2007), DeJong and Dave (2007), and Fernández-Villaverde (2010) for an introduction to Bayesian estimation of DSGE models.

15.1   Principles of Bayesian Estimation

Suppose that we want to estimate a vector of parameters θ in some set Θ. Let the prior density be $p(\theta)$. The econometrician observes the data $Y^T = \{y_1, y_2, \ldots, y_T\}$. The likelihood density is the density of data Y^T given the parameter θ:

$$p\left(Y^T|\theta\right) = p\left(y_1|\theta\right) \prod_{t=2}^{T} p\left(y_t|Y^{t-1}, \theta\right).$$

The likelihood function of the parameter is given by

$$L\left(\theta; Y^T\right) \equiv p\left(Y^T|\theta\right).$$

The maximum likelihood method of estimation is to search for a parameter value that will maximize the likelihood function $L\left(\theta; Y^T\right)$.

Using the Bayesian rule, we can compute the posterior as

$$p\left(\theta|Y^T\right) = \frac{p\left(Y^T, \theta\right)}{p\left(Y^T\right)} = \frac{p\left(Y^T|\theta\right) p\left(\theta\right)}{\int p\left(Y^T|\theta\right) p\left(\theta\right) d\theta}.$$

Define the **posterior kernel** $\mathcal{K}\left(\theta|Y^T\right)$ as

$$p\left(\theta|Y^T\right) \propto p\left(Y^T|\theta\right) p\left(\theta\right) \equiv \mathcal{K}\left(\theta|Y^T\right).$$

The Bayesian method is to choose a parameter value so as to maximize the posterior density $p\left(\theta|Y^T\right)$ or the posterior kernel $\mathcal{K}\left(\theta|Y^T\right)$.

The difficulty of using the maximum likelihood method or the Bayesian method is that the likelihood function typically has no analytical solution. Also Bayesian analysis involves the computation of the conditional distribution of a function of the parameters $h(\theta)$:

$$E\left[h\left(\theta\right)|Y^T\right] = \int h\left(\theta\right) p\left(\theta|Y^T\right) d\theta. \tag{15.1}$$

Numerical integration is often needed. To implement the Bayesian method, we use a filtering procedure to evaluate the likelihood function. We then simulate the posterior kernel using a Markov chain Monte Carlo (MCMC) method such as the Metropolis–Hastings algorithm.

We now use an example to illustrate Bayesian estimation. This example illustrates that Bayesian estimation is essentially between calibration and maximum likelihood estimation. Suppose that the data-generating process is given by

$$y_t = \mu + \varepsilon_t,$$

where $\varepsilon_t \sim N(0,1)$ is Gaussian white noise. We want to estimate the parameter μ from a sample of data Y^T. We can compute the likelihood density

$$p\left(Y^T|\mu\right) = (2\pi)^{-T/2} \exp\left(-\frac{1}{2}\sum_{t=1}^{T}(y_t - \mu)^2\right).$$

We then obtain the maximum likelihood estimate

$$\hat{\mu}_{ML} = \frac{1}{T}\sum_{t=1}^{T} y_t,$$

which is the sample average.

Suppose that the prior is Gaussian with mean μ_0 and variance σ_μ^2. Then the posterior kernel is given by

$$\left(2\pi\sigma_\mu^2\right)^{-T/2} \exp\left(-\frac{1}{2\sigma_\mu^2}(\mu - \mu_0)^2\right)(2\pi)^{-T/2}\exp\left(-\frac{1}{2}\sum_{t=1}^{T}(y_t - \mu)^2\right).$$

Thus the Bayesian estimate is given by

$$\hat{\mu}_{BE} = \frac{T\hat{\mu}_{ML} + \sigma_\mu^{-2}\mu_0}{T + \sigma_\mu^{-2}},$$

which is a linear combination of the prior mean and the maximum likelihood estimate. When we have no prior information (i.e., $\sigma_\mu^2 \to \infty$), the Bayesian estimate converges to the maximum likelihood estimate. When we are sure that the prior calibrated value is true (i.e., $\sigma_\mu^2 \to 0$), then $\hat{\mu}_{BE} \to \mu_0$.

15.2 Bayesian Estimation of DSGE Models

As discussed in section 2.5, the equilibrium system for a DSGE model can often be summarized by the nonlinear system (2.34). If we use M^+ and M^- to denote the matrices that extract variables $y_t^+ = M^+ y_t$ and $y_t^- = M^- y_t$, then we can rewrite this system as

$$E_t f(y_{t-1}, y_t, y_{t+1}, \varepsilon_t) = 0 \tag{15.2}$$

and write the solution as

$$y_t = g(y_{t-1}, \varepsilon_t);$$

here we still use the notations f and g without risk of confusion. In these equations, ε_t is a vector of exogenous IID shocks with zero mean and constant variance, and y_t is a vector of equilibrium variables and exogenous states. Our objective is to estimate the vector of structural parameters θ of the model. Bayesian estimation typically consists of the following steps.

15.2.1   Numerical Solution and State-Space Representation

The first step is to solve for the decision rule numerically given a parameter value θ:

$$y_t = g\left(y_{t-1}, \varepsilon_t; \theta\right). \tag{15.3}$$

This equation is also called the transition equation. We can use many numerical methods to solve the model. For estimation, we need to balance speed and accuracy. Linearization or log-linearization is the most widely used method. The perturbation method is often used to derive nonlinear solutions.

Not all variables in y_t are observable. The observable vector y_t^* is a subset of y_t. We write its relation to y_t as a measurement equation

$$y_t^* = h\left(y_t, v_t; \theta\right), \tag{15.4}$$

where v_t is a vector of IID shocks to the observables, like the measurement error. We assume that v_t and ε_t are independent.

While the transition equation is typically unique, the measurement equation depends on the selected observable variables, which allow for many degrees of freedom. For example, we can assume that we observe wages or that we observe hours (or even that we have access to both series), since the model has predictions regarding both variables. The only restriction is that we can only select a number of series less than or equal to the number of shocks in the model (ε_t and v_t). Otherwise, the model would be up to first-order, stochastically singular. That is, the extra observables would be a deterministic function of the other observables and the likelihood would be $-\infty$ with probability 1.

In general, researchers should focus on the time series that they find particularly informative for their models. For instance, to study the impact of monetary policy on output and investment, the federal funds rate, output, and investment should be included, but data on unemployment may not be useful unless the focus is on the labor market.

Given (15.3), we can compute the density $p\left(y_t | y_{t-1}, \theta\right)$. Given (15.4), we can compute the density $p\left(y_t^* | y_t, \theta\right)$. Moreover we can derive

$$y_t^* = h\left(y_t, v_t; \theta\right) = h\left(g\left(y_{t-1}, \varepsilon_t; \theta\right), v_t; \theta\right).$$

Thus we can compute the density $p\left(y_t^* | y_{t-1}, \theta\right)$.

15.2.2 Evaluating the Likelihood Function

The next step is to compute the likelihood density:

$$p\left(Y^{*T}|\theta\right) = p\left(y_1^*|\theta\right) \prod_{t=2}^{T} p\left(y_t^*|Y^{*t-1},\theta\right)$$

$$= \int p\left(y_1^*|y_1\theta\right) p\left(y_1|\theta\right) dy_1$$

$$\times \prod_{t=2}^{T} \int p\left(y_t^*|Y^{*t-1},y_t,\theta\right) p\left(y_t|Y^{*t-1},\theta\right) dy_t.$$

Note that $p\left(y_t^*|Y^{*t-1},y_t,\theta\right) = p\left(y_t^*|y_t,\theta\right)$. Assume that $p\left(y_1|\theta\right)$ is exogenously given. Thus we only need to compute $\{p\left(y_t|Y^{*t-1},\theta\right)\}_{t=1}^{T}$.

Filtering theory gives a procedure to compute this conditional density. First, we use the Chapman–Kolmogorov equation:

$$p\left(y_{t+1}|Y^{*t},\theta\right) = \int p\left(y_{t+1}|y_t,\theta\right) p\left(y_t|Y^{*t},\theta\right) dy_t.$$

Second, use the Bayesian theorem to derive

$$p\left(y_t|Y^{*t},\theta\right) = \frac{p\left(y_t^*|y_t,\theta\right) p\left(y_t|Y^{*t-1},\theta\right)}{p\left(y_t^*|Y^{*t-1},\theta\right)},$$

where

$$p\left(y_t^*|Y^{*t-1},\theta\right) = \int p\left(y_t^*|y_t,\theta\right) p\left(y_t|Y^{*t-1},\theta\right) dy_t$$

is the conditional likelihood.

The Chapman–Kolmogorov equation says that the distribution of states tomorrow given an observation until today, $p\left(y_{t+1}|Y^{*t},\theta\right)$, is equal to the distribution today of $p\left(y_t|Y^{*t},\theta\right)$ times the transition probabilities $p\left(y_{t+1}|y_t,\theta\right)$ integrated over all possible states. Therefore the Chapman–Kolmogorov equation just gives us a forecasting rule for the evolution of states. The Bayesian theorem updates the distribution of states $p\left(y_t|Y^{*t-1},\theta\right)$ when a new observation y_t^* arrives given its probability $p\left(y_t^*|y_t,\theta\right)$. By a recursive application of forecasting and updating, we can generate the complete sequence $\{p\left(y_t|Y^{*t-1},\theta\right)\}_{t=1}^{T}$ given an initial condition $p\left(y_1|\theta\right)$.

Numerical computation of this equation is nontrivial because it involves computing numerical integration. The simplest case is the linear Gaussian case. We can then use the Kalman filter discussed in section 10.1.1. We first use the linear or log-linear approximation method to solve the DSGE model. We then obtain a linear state space representation

$$\tilde{y}_t = A(\theta)\tilde{y}_{t-1} + C(\theta)\varepsilon_t,$$
$$y_t^* = G\bar{y}(\theta) + G\tilde{y}_t + v_t,$$

where

$$E\varepsilon_t = Ev_t = 0,$$
$$E\varepsilon_t\varepsilon_t' = Q(\theta),$$
$$Ev_tv_t' = V(\theta),$$

and $\tilde{y}_t$ represents the deviation from the steady state $\bar{y}(\theta)$ for the variable y_t.[1] Note that the coefficients in the decision rules or the transition equation and the steady-state values depend on the structural parameter θ to be estimated. The matrix G extracts the vector of observable variables from the vector of all equilibrium variables y_t. The error term v_t may contain measurement errors if the dimension of ε_t is less than that of y_t^*.

Define

$$\hat{y}_{t|t-1} = E_t\left[\tilde{y}_t | Y^{*t-1}\right], \quad P_t = E\left[(\tilde{y}_t - \hat{y}_{t|t-1})(\tilde{y}_t - \hat{y}_{t|t-1})' | Y^{*t-1}\right].$$

For $t = 1, 2, ..., T$ and with initial values $\hat{y}_{1|0}$ and P_1 given, the Kalman filter discussed in section 10.1.1 gives the following recursion:

$$a_t = y_t^* - \hat{y}_{t|t-1}^* = y_t^* - G\bar{y}(\theta) - G\hat{y}_{t|t-1},$$

$$\Omega_{t|t-1} \equiv E\left[\left(y_t^* - \hat{y}_{t|t-1}^*\right)\left(y_t^* - \hat{y}_{t|t-1}^*\right)' | y^{*t-1}\right] = GP_tG' + V(\theta),$$

$$K_t = A(\theta)P_tG'\Omega_{t|t-1}^{-1},$$

$$P_{t+1} = A(\theta)P_t(A(\theta) - K_tG)' + C(\theta)Q(\theta)C(\theta)',$$

$$\hat{y}_{t+1|t} = A(\theta)\hat{y}_{t|t-1} + K_ta_t.$$

From the Kalman filter we can compute the log likelihood density

$$\ln p\left(Y^{*T}|\theta\right) = \sum_{t=1}^{T} \ln p\left(y_t^*|Y^{*t-1}, \theta\right)$$

$$= -\frac{n^*T}{2}\ln(2\pi) - \sum_{t=1}^{T}\frac{1}{2}\ln\left|\Omega_{t|t-1}\right| - \frac{1}{2}\sum_{t=1}^{T}a_t'\Omega_{t|t-1}^{-1}a_t,$$

---

1. The variable y_t could be in levels or in logs.

where n^* is the number of observables, $a_t = y_t^* - \hat{y}_{t|t-1}^*$ is the innovation, and $\Omega_{t|t-1}$ is given above.

Linear approximations are inadequate to address some economic problems such as precautionary savings, risk premium, and asymmetric effects. For these problems one has to use nonlinear solution methods to capture the impact of higher order moments. In this case the Kalman filter cannot be used and a nonlinear filter is needed. Fernández-Villaverde and Rubio-Ramírez (2005, 2007) introduce particle filter to the analysis of DSGE models. The reader is referred to DeJong and Dave (2007) for an introduction.

15.2.3 Computing the Posterior

The final step is to compute the posterior $p\left(\theta|Y^{*T}\right)$ or the posterior kernel $\mathcal{K}\left(\theta|Y^{*T}\right)$. Because there is no analytical expression for $p\left(\theta|Y^{*T}\right)$, implementing Bayesian estimation is challenging. We first derive a Bayesian estimate. Given a parameter value for θ, we can use the previous step to compute $p\left(\theta|Y^{*T}\right)$ or $\mathcal{K}\left(\theta|Y^{*T}\right)$. We can then find the posterior mode θ^m by a numerical optimization method. We may use this posterior mode as the Bayesian estimate for the parameter. We can estimate the covariance matrix by the negative inverse Hessian matrix evaluated at the posterior mode:

$$
\Sigma_m = \left(-\frac{\partial^2 \ln\left(\mathcal{K}\left(\theta|Y^{*T}\right)\right)}{\partial\theta\partial\theta'}\bigg|_{\theta=\theta^m} \right)^{-1}. \tag{15.5}
$$

The more difficult part is to find the posterior $p\left(\theta|Y^{*T}\right)$ for inference and for computing integration of functions of the parameter. We can use the Markov chain Monte Carlo (MCMC) method to produce a Markov chain (or a sequence of samples) whose ergodic distribution is given by $p\left(\theta|Y^{*T}\right)$. We then simulate from this chain and approximate $p\left(\theta|Y^{*T}\right)$ by the empirical distribution generated by the chain. One efficient algorithm to generate the Markov chain is the **Metropolis–Hastings algorithm**. This algorithm is quite general and can be implemented in several ways. We will focus on the **Random Walk Metropolis–Hastings (RWMH) algorithm**. This algorithm builds on the fact that under general conditions the distribution of the structural parameters will be asymptotically normal. The algorithm constructs a Gaussian approximation around the posterior mode and uses a scaled version of the asymptotic covariance matrix as the covariance matrix for the proposal distribution. This allows for an efficient exploration of the posterior distribution at least in the neighborhood of the mode. More precisely, the RWMH algorithm implements the following steps:

Step 1. Choose a starting point θ^0, which is typically the posterior mode, and run a loop over steps 2, 3, and 4.

Step 2. Draw a proposal θ^* from a jumping distribution

$$J\left(\theta^*|\theta^{t-1}\right) = N\left(\theta^{t-1}, c\Sigma_m\right),$$

where Σ_m is given by (15.5) and c is a scaling factor.

Step 3. Solve the model numerically given θ^* and compute $p\left(\theta^*|Y^{*T}\right)$ by the Kalman filter. Compute the acceptance ratio

$$r = \frac{p\left(\theta^*|Y^{*T}\right)}{p\left(\theta^{t-1}|Y^{*T}\right)} = \frac{\mathcal{K}\left(\theta^*|Y^{*T}\right)}{\mathcal{K}\left(\theta^{t-1}|Y^{*T}\right)}.$$

Step 4. Jump from θ^{t-1} to the proposal θ^* with probability $\min\left(r, 1\right)$ and reject the proposal (i.e., $\theta^t = \theta^{t-1}$) with the remaining probability. Update the jumping distribution and go to step 2.

The algorithm above can be intuitively explained as follows. After initializing in step 1, in step 2, draw a candidate parameter θ^* from a normal distribution, whose mean has been set to θ^{t-1}. The scalar c is a scale factor for the variance that plays an important role as will be explained below. In step 3, after solving the model numerically given θ^*, compute the acceptance ratio r as the ratio of the posterior kernel evaluated at θ^*, $\mathcal{K}\left(\theta^*|Y^{*t}\right)$, to the posterior kernel evaluated at the mean of the drawing distribution, $\mathcal{K}\left(\theta^{t-1}|Y^{*t}\right)$. In step 4, decide whether or not to hold on to your candidate parameter θ^*. If the acceptance ratio r is greater than one, then definitely keep your candidate θ^*. Otherwise, go back to the previous candidate θ^{t-1} with probability $1 - r$. Then update the jumping distribution and go to step 2.

After having repeated these steps to generate sufficiently many draws $\theta^0, \theta^1, ..., \theta^n$, we can build a histogram of these draws and construct empirical distribution. Additionally, we can approximate the expectation in (15.1) by

$$E\left[h\left(\theta\right)|Y^{*T}\right] = \frac{1}{n}\sum_{i=1}^{n} h\left(\theta^i\right).$$

Why should one adopt the acceptance rule in step 4? The reason is that this rule ensures that the entire domain of the posterior distribution can be visited. One should not be too quick to throw out the candidate giving a lower value of the posterior kernel. If the jump is "uphill," one always accepts. But if the jump is "downhill," one should reject with some probability. Of course, an important parameter in this procedure is the variance of the jumping distribution and, in particular, the scale factor c. If, on the one hand, the scale factor is too small, the acceptance rate (the fraction of candidate parameters that are accepted in a window of time) will be too high and the Markov chain of candidate parameters will "mix slowly," meaning that the distribution will take a long time to converge to the posterior distribution since the chain is likely to get stuck around a local maximum. If, on the other hand, the scale factor is too large, the acceptance rate will be very low (as the candidates are likely to land in regions of low probability density) and the chain will spend too much time in the tails of the posterior distribution.

Several questions arise in implementing the RWMH algorithm in practice: How should we choose the scale factor c? What is a satisfactory acceptance rate? How many draws are ideal? How is convergence of the Metropolis–Hastings iterations assessed? These are all important questions that will come up in your usage of Dynare.

15.3 An Example

We use our basic RBC model studied in the previous chapter as an example to illustrate how to use Dynare to conduct Bayesian estimation. We set the parameter values of the model as

$$\alpha = 0.33, \quad \beta = 0.99, \quad \delta = 0.025, \quad \chi = 1.75, \quad \rho = 0.95, \quad \sigma = 0.01. \tag{15.6}$$

Note that these parameter values imply that the steady-state hours $N = 0.33$. We then solve the model using Dynare by log-linearization and obtain simulated data in the file simuldataRBC.m.[2] Suppose that we only observe the data of output in percentage deviations. The parameters of the model are unknown. Our objective is to use these data to estimate the parameters of the model by the Bayesian method.

15.3.1 Dynare Codes
A Dynare code consists of the following blocks.[3] In the first block, one defines endogenous variables, exogenous shocks, and parameters:

```
%-------------------------------------
% 1. Defining variables
%-------------------------------------
var ly lc lk li lh lw Rk z;
varexo e;
parameters beta delta chi alpha rho;
```

In the second block, one defines the observable variables:

```
%-------------------------------------
% 2. Declaring observable variables
%-------------------------------------
varobs ly;
```

2. The Dynare code to generate the data is rbcdata.mod.
3. The Dynare estimation codes are rbcEST.mod and rbcEST2.mod.

In the third block, one inputs model equations:

```
%---------------------------------------
% 3. Model
%---------------------------------------
model;
//Consumption Euler equation
(1/exp(lc)) = beta*(1/exp(lc(+1)))*(1+alpha...
*(exp(lk)^(alpha-1))*exp(z(+1))*exp(lh(+1))^(1-alpha)-delta);
// Labor supply
chi*exp(lc)/(1-exp(lh)) = exp(lw);
// Labor demand
exp(lw) = exp(z)*(1-alpha)*exp(lk(-1))^alpha*exp(lh)^(-alpha);
//Resource constraint
exp(lc)+exp(li) = exp(ly);
//Production function
exp(ly) = exp(z)*(exp(lk(-1))^alpha)*(exp(lh))^(1-alpha);
//Capital accumulation equation
exp(li) = exp(lk)-(1-delta)*exp(lk(-1));
//Capital rental rate
exp(Rk) = alpha*exp(ly)/exp(lk(-1));
//TFP shock
z = rho*z(-1)+e;
end;
```

In the fourth block, one specifies the steady state. During estimation, Dynare recalculates the steady state of the model at each iteration of optimization when parameter values are updated. This step typically takes a significant amount of time. It will be much more efficient if one can solve for the steady state separately either by hand or using a Matlab program. If one asks Dynare to solve for the steady state, then the fourth block reads:

```
%---------------------------------------
% 4. Specifying Steady State
%---------------------------------------
initval;
 lk = 2.2;
 lc = -0.26;
 lh = -1.098;
```

```
    li = -1.44;
    ly = 0.005;
    lw = 0.7;
    Rk = -3.3;
     z = 0;
end;
```

If one solves for the steady state by hand as we described in the last chapter, the fourth block can then be written as follows:

```
steady_state_model;
    N = 1/3;
    KoverN = (alpha/(1/beta-1+delta))^(1/(1-alpha));
    Y = (KoverN)^alpha*N;
    I = delta*KoverN*N;
    K = KoverN*N;
    C = Y-I;
    w = (1-alpha)*K^alpha*N^(-alpha);
    Rk1 = alpha*Y/K;
    chi = (1-alpha)*(KoverN)^alpha*(1-N)/C; %for
            KPR0 and KPR3
    ly = log(Y); lc = log(C); lk = log(K);
    lh = log(N); li = log(I); lw = log(w);
    Rk = log(Rk1); z = 0;
end;
```

Note that we essentially calibrate the parameter χ to target the steady-state hours $N = 1/3$. In this case, the parameter χ must be excluded from the list of parameters to be estimated. The key Dynare command in this block is steady_state_model. When the analytical solution of the model is known, this command can be used to help Dynare find the steady state in a more efficient and reliable way, especially during estimation where the steady state has to be recomputed repeatedly when updating parameter values. Each line of this block consists of a variable (which can be an endogenous variable, a temporary variable, or a parameter) that is assigned an expression (which can contain parameters, exogenous at the steady state, or any endogenous or temporary variable already declared above). Each line therefore looks like:

```
VARIABLE_NAME = EXPRESSION;
```

Note that it is also possible to assign several variables at the same time if the main function on the right-hand side is a Matlab function returning several arguments:

```
[VARIABLE_NAME, VARIABLE_NAME... ] = FUNCTION_NAME;
```

Dynare will automatically generate a steady-state file using the information provided in this block.

In the fifth block, one declares priors. The general syntax to introduce priors in Dynare is the following:

```
estimated_params;
Parameter Name, PRIOR_SHAPE, PRIOR_MEAN, PRIOR_STANDARD_ERROR
[,PRIOR THIRD PARMAETER] [,PRIOR FOURTH PARAMETER];
```

Table 15.1 defines each term. In the table, μ is the PRIOR_MEAN, σ is the PRIOR_STANDARD_ERROR, p_3 is the PRIOR THIRD PARAMETER (default is 0), and p_4 is the PRIOR FOURTH PARAMETER (default is 1). Note that when specifying a uniform distribution between 0 and 1 as a prior for a parameter, say α, one has to put two empty spaces for μ and σ. For example, alpha, uniform_pdf, , , 0, 1;. This block for our model is given as follows:

```
%----------------------------------------
% 5. Declaring priors
%----------------------------------------
estimated_params;
    alpha, beta_pdf, 0.35, 0.02;
    beta, beta_pdf, 0.99, 0.002;
    delta, beta_pdf, 0.025, 0.003;
    chi, gamma_pdf, 1.65, 0.02;
    rho, beta_pdf, 0.9, 0.05;
    stderr e, inv_gamma_pdf, 0.01, inf;
end;
```

Table 15.1
Prior distributions

PRIOR_SHAPE	DISTRIBUTION	RANGE
NORMAL_PDF	$N(\mu, \sigma)$	$\mathbb{R}$
GAMMA_PDF	$G_2(\mu, \sigma, p_3)$	$[p_3, +\infty)$
BETA_PDF	$B(\mu, \sigma, p_3, p_4)$	$[p_3, p_4]$
INV_GAMMA_PDF	$IG_1(\mu, \sigma)$	$\mathbb{R}^+$
UNIFORM_PDF	$U(p_3, p_4)$	$[p_3, p_4]$

As mentioned before, the parameter χ need not be estimated when we use the steady_state_model command. In this case the line starting chi must be deleted in the estimation block.

In the final block, one launches the estimation. The Dynare command is estimation. It has many options. The reader is referred to the *Dynare Reference Manual* or the *Dynare User Guide*.

```
estimation(datafile = simuldataRBC, nobs = 200, order = 1,
first_obs = 500, mh_replic = 2000, mh_nblocks = 2, mh_drop = 0.45,
mh_jscale = 0.8, mode_compute = 6) ly;
```

15.3.2   Dynare Output

Dynare output consists of tables and graphs. There are two main tables. The first table displays results from posterior maximization generated before the MCMC part. When all parameters are estimated, this table appears as shown in table 15.2. In this table, "pstdev" represents prior standard deviation. When χ is calibrated to target the steady state $N = 1/3$, the table becomes as shown in table 15.3.

Given other estimated parameter values in the table, the calibrated χ is equal to 1.757. Comparing the above two tables, we can see that the method of calibrating χ to target the steady state $N = 1/3$ gives better estimates of parameters.

Table 15.2
Priors and posteriors of all estimated parameters

	prior mean	posterior mode	std	t-stat	prior	pstdev
α	0.350	0.3283	0.0038	85.347	Beta	0.020
β	0.990	0.9896	0.0003	3056.29	Beta	0.002
δ	0.025	0.0258	0.0006	43.846	Beta	0.003
χ	1.650	1.6513	0.0050	328.398	Gamma	0.020
ρ	0.900	0.9481	0.0095	100.218	Beta	0.050
σ	0.010	0.0096	0.0005	20.590	invGamma	*Inf*

Table 15.3
Priors and posteriors at steady state $N = 1/3$

	prior mean	posterior mode	std	t-stat	prior	pstdev
α	0.350	0.3287	0.0037	88.8908	Beta	0.020
β	0.990	0.9899	0.0004	2212.18	Beta	0.002
δ	0.025	0.0259	0.0007	38.445	Beta	0.003
ρ	0.900	0.9573	0.0141	67.821	Beta	0.050
σ	0.010	0.01	0.0004	22.417	invGamma	*Inf*

Dynare also presents a second table that displays estimation results based on MCMC. We will not show the table here. Dynare output shows the following graphs:

- Priors
- MCMC univariate diagnostics
- Multivariate diagnostic
- Priors and posteriors
- Shocks implied at the posterior mode
- Observables and corresponding implied values

Here we only show the figure for priors and posteriors (figure 15.1).

15.3.3   Stochastic Trends

Many DSGE models feature stochastic trends. In this case one has to detrend the model as discussed in the last chapter. For example, suppose that the technology shock follows a unit root process:

$$\ln z_t = \mu_z + \ln z_{t-1} + \sigma \varepsilon_t, \; z_{-1} = 1.$$

After detrending, Dynare solves the detrended system. We then have to link detrended variables to observables. There are two ways to do this. First, we can

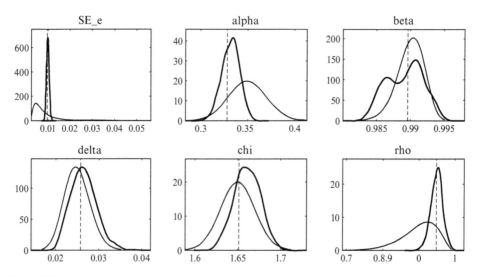

Figure 15.1
Priors and posteriors

transform the data in terms of growth rates. Second, we can directly work with the data in levels. We will focus on the first approach and refer the reader to the *User Guide* for an introduction of the second approach. Say that in the first approach we observe output Y_t. We then transform the data to the observable $\ln(Y_t/Y_{t-1})$, denoted by *gy_obs*. We want to link this observable to the Dynare solution, the detrended output $\tilde{Y}_t = Y_t/z_t^{1/(1-\alpha)}$. So we add the following code to the Dynare model block:

```
dz = muz + e;
gy_obs = ly-ly(-1)- (1/(1-alpha))*dz;
```

The rest of the codes are similar and are omitted here.

15.4   Exercises

1. Derive the Kalman filter in section 15.2.2 using the result in section 10.1.1.

2. Consider the example in section 15.3. Use the parameter values in (15.6) to solve the model by linear approximations in levels. First generate artificial data for consumption. Then use these consumption data to estimate the model by the Bayesian method.

3. Use the basic RBC model with a stochastic trend to generate artificial data. Suppose that the observable data are output. Use Dynare to estimate this model.

16 Overlapping Generations Models

An overlapping generations (OLG) model is a type of economic model in which agents live a finite length of time and people from different generations coexist at any point in time. In each period some old generations die and a new generation is born. This induces a natural heterogeneity across individuals at a point in time, as well as nontrivial life-cycle considerations for a given individual across time. These features of the model generate different implications from models with infinitely lived agents studied in chapters 13 and 14. In particular, competitive equilibria in the OLG model may not to be Pareto optimal. A natural question is how to remedy this inefficiency. One solution is to rely on a government. Thus the OLG model is a workhorse in public finance. The other solution is to use a market mechanism. If agents accept an intrinsically useless asset, such as fiat money, to transfer resources across generations, then welfare can be improved. Thus the OLG model has a role for fiat money and can be used to address a variety of substantive issues in monetary economics. Because an intrinsically useless asset can be valued in an OLG model, it is also a workhorse model for studying asset bubbles.

Samuelson (1958) introduces the OLG model in a pure-exchange economy. Building on this model, Diamond (1965) introduces production and studies the role of national debt. Tirole (1985) uses the Diamond (1965) model to study asset bubbles. Weil (1987) introduces stochastic bubbles in the Samuelson–Diamond–Tirole model. In this chapter we study these models.

16.1 Exchange Economies

Time starts at date 1, lasts forever, and is denoted by $t = 1, 2, \ldots$. There is no uncertainty. The economy consists of overlapping generations of identical, two-period lived agents. At any date $t \geq 1$, the population consists of N_t young agents and N_{t-1} old agents, where $N_t = g_n N_{t-1}$, $g_n > 0$. Output is nonproduced and perishable. Each young and each old agent is endowed with e_1 and e_2 units of output, respectively.

An agent of generation $t \geq 1$ consumes c_t^t when young, and c_{t+1}^t when old. His preferences are represented by the utility function

$$u\left(c_t^t\right) + \beta u\left(c_{t+1}^t\right),$$

where $\beta \in (0,1]$, $u' > 0$, $u'' < 0$, and $\lim_{c \to 0} u'(c) = \infty$. An initial old agent at time 1 consumes c_1^0 and derives utility according to $u\left(c_1^0\right)$. He is also endowed with m_0^0 units of an intrinsically useless and unbacked asset, called fiat money. Money is the only asset used by agents to smooth consumption.

The aggregate nominal money balances in the initial period 1 are $M_0 = N_0 m_0^0$. A monetary authority supplies money by lump-sum transfers. For all $t \geq 1$, the post-transfer time t stock of money M_t satisfies $M_t = g_m M_{t-1}$, $g_m > 0$. The time t transfer (or tax), which is $(g_m - 1) M_{t-1}$, is divided equally among the N_{t-1} members of the current old generation. The transfer (or tax) is taken as given and does not affect each agent's consumption-saving decision.

By buying m_t^t units of money at the price $1/p_t$, a young agent acquires a claim to m_t^t/p_{t+1} units of the consumption good next period. A young agent will buy money only if he believes that he will be able to resell it at a positive price to the yet unborn young of the coming generation. The purchase of money in this model is thus purely speculative. The budget constraints of a young agent of generation $t \geq 1$ are given by

$$c_t^t + \frac{m_t^t}{p_t} \leq e_1, \tag{16.1}$$

$$c_{t+1}^t \leq e_2 + \frac{m_t^t}{p_{t+1}} + \frac{(g_m - 1)}{N_t} \frac{M_t}{p_{t+1}}, \tag{16.2}$$

where $m_t^t \geq 0$, and $p_t > 0$ is the time t price level. The budget constraint of an initial old agent at date 1 is given by

$$c_1^0 \leq e_2 + \frac{m_0^0}{p_1} + \frac{(g_m - 1)}{N_0} \frac{M_0}{p_1}.$$

A **monetary equilibrium** consists of sequences of finite and positive prices $\{p_t\}$ and allocations $\left\{c_1^0, \left(c_t^t, c_{t+1}^t, m_t^t\right), t \geq 1\right\}$ such that given the price sequence, $\left\{c_1^0, \left(c_t^t, c_{t+1}^t, m_t^t\right), t \geq 1\right\}$ maximize the utility of agents in each generation and markets clear so that $M_t = N_t m_t^t$, and

$$N_t c_t^t + N_{t-1} c_t^{t-1} = N_t e_1 + N_{t-1} e_2, \quad t \geq 1. \tag{16.3}$$

If $p_t = \infty$, then the real value of money is zero. No one will hold money except for the initial old, $m_t^t = 0$. It follows that autarky is an equilibrium. We call this equilibrium a **nonmonetary equilibrium**.

In a monetary equilibrium, the consumption Euler equation gives

$$\frac{u'\left(c_t^t\right)}{\beta u'\left(c_{t+1}^t\right)} = \frac{p_t}{p_{t+1}} = R_{t+1},$$
(16.4)

where R_{t+1} is the gross interest rate or the return on money. We can also define an implicit interest rate in the nonmonetary equilibrium as

$$\frac{u'\left(e_1\right)}{\beta u'\left(e_2\right)} = R_{aut}.$$
(16.5)

Let $\hat{m}_t = M_t / (N_t p_t)$ denote the equilibrium real money balances of a young agent at time t. Imposing market-clearing conditions in (16.1) and (16.2) yields $c_t^t = e_1 - \hat{m}_t$ and $c_{t+1}^t = e_2 + g_n \hat{m}_{t+1}$. In a monetary equilibrium $\hat{m}_t > 0$. It follows from (16.4) and (16.5) that

$$\frac{u'\left(e_1 - \hat{m}_t\right)}{\beta u'\left(e_2 + g_n \hat{m}_{t+1}\right)} = R_{t+1} > R_{aut}.$$
(16.6)

16.1.1   A Special Case and Multiple Equilibria

Consider the special case where there is no population and money supply growth. We use the special case to illustrate some peculiar features of the OLG model. Suppose a unit measure of identical agents is born each period. The money supply is constant M.

Define the excess supply of goods (saving or real balances) when young as

$$m_t \equiv \frac{m_t^t}{p_t} = e_1 - c_t^t$$

and the excess demand of goods when old as

$$z_t \equiv \frac{m_t^t}{p_{t+1}} = c_{t+1}^t - e_2.$$

Note that saving m_t is a function of the relative prices or the interest rate $p_t / p_{t+1} = R_{t+1}$. Since

$$z_t = \frac{M_t^t}{p_{t+1}} = \frac{M_t^t}{p_t} \frac{p_t}{p_{t+1}} = m_t \frac{p_t}{p_{t+1}},$$

we then obtain a relationship between z_t and m_t as p_t / p_{t+1} varies. Figure 16.1 plots this relationship, which is called the **offer curve**. The slope of the line from the origin to any point on the offer curve is equal to p_t / p_{t+1}. Offer curves must lie to the left of the vertical line at e_1.

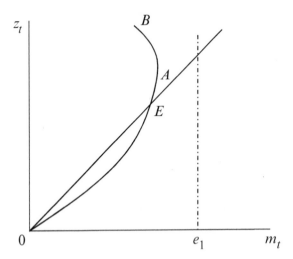

Figure 16.1
Offer curve

The slope of the offer curve is important for the analysis. To derive the slope, we use the Euler equation

$$u'\left(e_1 - m_t\right) = \beta u'\left(m_t R_{t+1} + e_2\right) R_{t+1}$$

to derive

$$\frac{dm_t}{dR_{t+1}} = \frac{-\left[R_{t+1} m_t \beta u''\left(c_{t+1}^t\right) + \beta u'\left(c_{t+1}^t\right)\right]}{u''\left(c_t^t\right) + \beta R_{t+1}^2 u''\left(c_{t+1}^t\right)}.$$

Using $z_t = m_t R_{t+1}$ obtains

$$\frac{dz_t}{dR_{t+1}} = \frac{m_t u''\left(c_t^t\right) - \beta u'\left(c_{t+1}^t\right) R_{t+1}}{u''\left(c_t^t\right) + \beta R_{t+1}^2 u''\left(c_{t+1}^t\right)} > 0.$$

Thus the shape of the offer curve depends on the sign of dm_t/dR_{t+1}.

An increase in the interest rate decreases the price of second-period consumption, leading agents to save consumption from the first period to the second period; this is the substitution effect. But it also increases the feasible consumption set, making it possible to increase consumption in both periods; this is the income effect. The net effect of these substitution and income effects is ambiguous.

More formally, since $u''\left(c_t^t\right) + \beta R_{t+1}^2 u''\left(c_{t+1}^t\right) < 0$, $dm_t/dR_{t+1} < 0$ if and only if

$$0 < -\left[R_{t+1} m_t \beta u''\left(c_{t+1}^t\right) + \beta u'\left(c_{t+1}^t\right)\right] = \beta u'\left(c_{t+1}^t\right)\left[\frac{z_t}{c_{t+1}^t}\gamma\left(c_{t+1}^t\right) - 1\right],$$

where $\gamma(c) = -cu''(c)/u'(c)$ is the coefficient of relative risk aversion at c. It is also equal to the inverse elasticity of substitution. Since $z_t < c^t_{t+1}$, a necessary condition for the offer curve to be backward bending is that $\gamma(c^t_{t+1}) > 1$. That is, the substitution effect must be sufficiently small. If $\gamma(c^t_{t+1}) \leq 1$, the offer curve is always upward sloping.

In equilibrium the demand for money is equal to the supply of money so that $z_t = m_{t+1}$. We then obtain the equilibrium system represented by the dynamic relation between m_{t+1} and m_t, as illustrated in figure 16.2. The steady state of the economy is at the intersection of the offer curve and the 45-degree line. Figure 16.2 shows that there are two steady states, one nonmonetary at the origin and one monetary.

Whether there is a monetary equilibrium depends on the slope of the offer curve at the origin. If the slope is less than one, a monetary equilibrium exists. Proposition 16.1.1 below shows that this condition is necessary and sufficient for a more general setup. A monetary steady state is unstable if and only if $|dm_{t+1}/dm_t| > 1$. Figure 16.2 shows that at the monetary steady state m^*, $dm_{t+1}/dm_t > 1$. Paths starting to the right of m^* increase until eventually m_t becomes larger than e_1, which is impossible. We can rule out this solution. Paths starting to the left have steadily decreasing real money balances, and all converge asymptotically to the nonmonetary steady state. The rate of inflation increases and tends asymptotically to the inverse of the slope of the offer curve at the origin minus one.

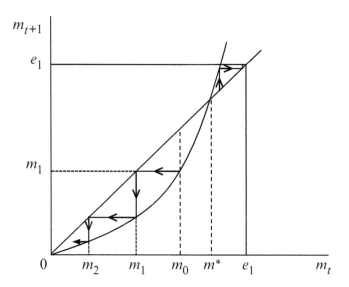

Figure 16.2
One stable nonmonetary steady state and one unstable monetary steady state

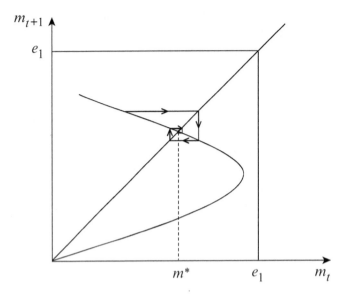

Figure 16.3
Locally stable monetary steady state

When the offer curve is sufficiently backward bending, we have $|dm_{t+1}/dm_t| < 1$ and the monetary equilibrium is locally stable, as shown in figure 16.3. In this case the economy eventually converges to the monetary steady state starting from any price level in a neighborhood of m^*. The equilibrium is indeterminate since m_t is a non-predetermined variable. As analyzed earlier, this case happens when the substitution effect is sufficiently small and the income effect is sufficiently large.

When the monetary steady state is locally stable, cyclical solutions can exist. Figure 16.4 plots the offer curve from figure 16.3 and its mirror image around the 45-degree line. The two curves intersect at the steady state on the diagonal. Given that the slope of the offer curve at the steady state is less than one in absolute value, they also intersect at two other points, A and B.

We show that the economy may have a two-period cycle. Suppose that real balances are equal to m_a in period 1. Then real balances are equal to m_b in period 2. But in period 3 real balances are equal to m_a. The economy then repeats itself as if it is in period 1.

Example 16.1.1   *Let $u(c) = \ln c$ and $\beta = 1$. Assume that $e_1 > e_2$. From the consumption Euler equation, we obtain the difference equation*

$$p_t e_1 - M = p_{t+1} e_2 + M.$$

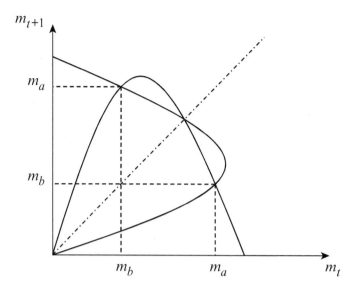

Figure 16.4
Two-period cycle equilibrium

The general solution to this difference equation is given by

$$p_t = \frac{2M}{e_1 - e_2} + c \left(\frac{e_1}{e_2} \right)^t,$$

where c is a constant to be determined. If $c = 0$, we obtain a stationary monetary equilibrium with a sequence of positive constant prices. For any $c > 0$, the price level goes to infinity, and hence money has no value in the long run. The economy approaches the autarky steady state. We cannot rule out this explosive solution because there is no transversality condition for the finitely lived agents.

Example 16.1.2   *Let $\beta = 1$, $e_1 = 1 - \varepsilon$, and $e_2 = \varepsilon \in (0, 0.5)$. Assume that the initial old agent has no endowment of any asset or money. The monetary authority supplies money $M = 0.5 - \varepsilon$, $t \geq 1$. We construct two stationary equilibria using a guess-and-verify method.*

- *A high-interest-rate equilibrium   Set $p_t = 1$, $c_t^t = c_{t+1}^t = 0.5$, $m_t^t = 0.5 - \varepsilon$ for all $t \geq 1$ and $c_1^0 = 0.5$. This is a monetary equilibrium. The interest rate is $R_{t+1} = 1$.*

- *A low-interest-rate equilibrium   Let $p_1 = 1$ and $p_t / p_{t+1} = u'(1 - \varepsilon) / u'(\varepsilon)$. The price will approach infinity and hence money is worthless in the limit. Based on this belief, no one will hold money. Given this price system, autarky is an equilibrium. In this equilibrium the present value of aggregate endowment is infinity because the interest* rate $R_{aut} = p_t/p_{t+1} < 1$. Thus the assumption of the first fundamental theorem of welfare economics is violated. The autarky equilibrium is not Pareto optimal.

16.1.2 Existence and Efficiency

Now we study two related theoretical questions in the general setup. Under what conditions does a monetary equilibrium exist? When it exists, under what conditions does it improve welfare? The exposition below follows from Wallace (1980) and Ljungqvist and Sargent (2004).

Proposition 16.1.1 *The condition $R_{aut}g_m < g_n$ is necessary and sufficient for the existence of at least one monetary equilibrium.*

Proof We first prove necessity. Suppose, to the contrary, that there is a monetary equilibrium with $R_{aut}g_m \geq g_n$. By definition,

$$R_{t+1} = \frac{p_t}{p_{t+1}} = \frac{M_{t+1}}{g_m M_t} \frac{p_t}{p_{t+1}} = \frac{N_{t+1}}{g_m N_t} \frac{\hat{m}_{t+1}}{\hat{m}_t} = \frac{g_n}{g_m} \frac{\hat{m}_{t+1}}{\hat{m}_t}. \tag{16.7}$$

Since $R_{t+1} > R_{aut}$,

$$\frac{\hat{m}_{t+1}}{\hat{m}_t} = R_{t+1}\frac{g_m}{g_n} > R_{aut}\frac{g_m}{g_n} \geq 1. \tag{16.8}$$

If $R_{aut}g_m/g_n > 1$, the growth rate of $\hat{m}_t$ is bounded uniformly above one. Hence, the sequence $\{\hat{m}_t\}$ is unbounded, which is inconsistent with an equilibrium because real money balances per capita cannot exceed the endowment e_1 of a young agent.

If $R_{aut}g_m/g_n = 1$, the strictly increasing sequence $\{\hat{m}_t\}$ converges to some limit $\hat{m}_\infty$. If this limit is finite, then taking limits in (16.6) and (16.7) yields

$$\frac{u'(e_1 - \hat{m}_\infty)}{\beta u'(e_2 + g_n\hat{m}_\infty)} = R_\infty = \frac{g_n}{g_m} = R_{aut}.$$

Thus $\hat{m}_\infty = 0$, contradicting the existence of a strictly increasing sequence of positive real balances in (16.8).

To show sufficiency, we prove the existence of a unique equilibrium with constant per capita real money balances when $R_{aut}g_m < g_n$. Substituting the candidate equilibrium, $\hat{m}_{t+1} = \hat{m}_t = \hat{m}$, into (16.6) and (16.7) yields

$$\frac{u'(e_1 - \hat{m})}{\beta u'(e_2 + g_n\hat{m})} = \frac{g_n}{g_m} > R_{aut} = \frac{u'(e_1)}{\beta u'(e_2)}.$$

Thus there exists a unique solution $\hat{m} > 0$ such that the first equality holds. ∎

Next we turn to Pareto optimality.

Definition 16.1.1 *An allocation* $C = \{c_1^0, (c_t^t, c_{t+1}^t), t \geq 1\}$ *for the OLG model is* **feasible** *if (16.3) holds or, equivalently, if*

$$g_n c_t^t + c_t^{t-1} = g_n e_1 + e_2, \quad t \geq 1. \tag{16.9}$$

Definition 16.1.2 *A feasible allocation C for the OLG model is* **Pareto optimal** *if there is no other feasible allocation* $\tilde{C}$ *such that*

$$\tilde{c}_1^0 \geq c_1^0,$$
$$u(\tilde{c}_t^t) + \beta u(\tilde{c}_{t+1}^t) \geq u(c_t^t) + \beta u(c_{t+1}^t),$$

and at least one of the weak inequalities holds with strict inequality.

Definition 16.1.3 *An allocation* $\{c_1^0, (c_t^t, c_{t+1}^t), t \geq 1\}$ *for the OLG model is* **stationary** *if* $c_t^t = c_y$ *and* $c_{t+1}^t = c_o$ *for all* $t \geq 1$.

Note that we do not require that $c_1^0 = c_o$. We call an equilibrium with a stationary allocation a **stationary equilibrium**.

Proposition 16.1.2 $R_{aut} \geq g_n$ *is necessary and sufficient for the optimality of the non-monetary equilibrium (autarky).*

Proof To prove sufficiency, suppose to the contrary that there exists another feasible allocation $\tilde{C}$ that is Pareto superior to autarky and $R_{aut} \geq g_n$. Let t be the first period when this alternative allocation $\tilde{C}$ differs from the autarkic allocation. The requirement that the old generation in this period is not made worse off, $\tilde{c}_t^{t-1} \geq e_2$, implies that the first perturbation from the autarkic allocation must be $\tilde{c}_t^t < e_1$, with the subsequent implication that $\tilde{c}_{t+1}^t > e_2$. It follows from feasibility that the consumption of young agents at time $t+1$ must also fall below e_1 so that

$$\varepsilon_{t+1} \equiv e_1 - \tilde{c}_{t+1}^{t+1} > 0. \tag{16.10}$$

Now, given $\tilde{c}_{t+1}^{t+1}$, define $\bar{c}_{t+2}^{t+1}$ as the solution for c_{t+2}^{t+1} to the equation

$$u\left(\tilde{c}_{t+1}^{t+1}\right) + \beta u\left(c_{t+2}^{t+1}\right) = u(e_1) + \beta u(e_2).$$

Clearly, $\bar{c}_{t+2}^{t+1} > e_2$. Since the allocation $\tilde{C}$ is Pareto superior to autarky, we have $\tilde{c}_{t+2}^{t+1} \geq \bar{c}_{t+2}^{t+1}$.

We now derive an expression for $\bar{c}_{t+2}^{t+1}$. Consider the indifference curve of $u(c_1) + \beta u(c_2)$ that yields a fixed utility equal to $u(e_1) + \beta u(e_2)$. Along an indifference curve, $c_2 = h(c_1)$, where $h' = -u'(c_1)/(\beta u'(c_2)) = -R < 0$ and $h'' > 0$. Thus, applying the intermediate value theorem to h, we have

$$h(c_1) = h(e_1) + (e_1 - c_1)\left[-h'(e_1) + f(e_1 - c_1)\right], \tag{16.11}$$

where the function f is strictly increasing on $[0, e_1]$ with $f(0) = 0$.

Now since $\left(\tilde{c}_{t+1}^{t+1}, \tilde{c}_{t+2}^{t+1}\right)$ and (e_1, e_2) are on the same indifference curve, we can use (16.10) and (16.11) to write

$$\bar{c}_{t+2}^{t+1} = e_2 + \varepsilon_{t+1}\left[R_{aut} + f(\varepsilon_{t+1})\right],$$

and after invoking $\tilde{c}_{t+2}^{t+1} \geq \bar{c}_{t+2}^{t+1}$, we have

$$\tilde{c}_{t+2}^{t+1} - e_2 \geq \varepsilon_{t+1}\left[R_{aut} + f(\varepsilon_{t+1})\right].$$

Since $\tilde{C}$ is feasible,

$$\varepsilon_{t+2} \equiv e_1 - \tilde{c}_{t+2}^{t+2} = \frac{\tilde{c}_{t+2}^{t+1} - e_2}{g_n}.$$

It follows that

$$\varepsilon_{t+2} \geq \varepsilon_{t+1}\frac{R_{aut} + f(\varepsilon_{t+1})}{g_n} > \varepsilon_{t+1},$$

where the last inequality follows from the assumption and $f(\varepsilon_{t+1}) > 0$ for $\varepsilon_{t+1} > 0$. Continuing in this fashion yields

$$\varepsilon_{t+k} \equiv e_1 - \tilde{c}_{t+k}^{t+k} \geq \varepsilon_{t+1}\prod_{j=1}^{k-1}\frac{R_{aut} + f(\varepsilon_{t+j})}{g_n} > \varepsilon_{t+1}\left[\frac{R_{aut} + f(\varepsilon_{t+1})}{g_n}\right]^{k-1}$$

for $k > 2$, where the last inequality follows from the fact that $\{\varepsilon_{t+j}\}$ is a strictly increasing sequence. Thus $\{\varepsilon_{t+k}\}$ is unbounded, contradicting the fact that $\varepsilon_{t+k} < e_1$.

To prove necessity, we show the existence of an alternative feasible allocation that is Pareto superior to autarky when $R_{aut} < g_n$. Imagine that a social planner transfers $\varepsilon > 0$ units of each young agent's consumption to the old in the same period. Because there are $N_t = g_n N_{t-1}$ young agents and N_{t-1} old agents in period t, old agents will receive transfers $g_n \varepsilon$. Suppose that the social planner keeps doing this for each period. Then the initial old agents are better off. Consider the utility of an agent in generation t, $f(\varepsilon) \equiv u(e_1 - \varepsilon) + \beta u(e_2 + g_n \varepsilon)$. Clearly, $f(0) = u(e_1) + \beta u(e_2)$. But $f'(0) = -u'(e_1) + \beta g_n u'(e_2) > 0$ as long as $g_n > R_{aut}$. Thus each agent in generation t is better off when small $\varepsilon > 0$. ∎

What is the intuition behind the condition $R_{aut} \geq g_n$? If $R_{aut} < g_n$, then the interest rate is less than the growth rate of the economy, and hence the present value of endowments is infinite. This violates the assumption of the First Welfare Theorem. Note that in the proof of the necessity part given above, the construction of a Pareto-improving allocation relies on the fact that a planner can continually transfer resources from the young to the old indefinitely. Because this inefficiency comes from the intertemporal structure of the economy, it is often called **dynamic inefficiency**.

With a constant nominal money supply, $g_m = 1$, the previous two propositions show that a monetary equilibrium exists if and only if the nonmonetary equilibrium is Pareto inefficient. The following proposition shows that the stationary monetary equilibrium is then Pareto optimal.

Proposition 16.1.3   *Given $R_{aut}g_m < g_n$, then $g_m \leq 1$ is necessary and sufficient for the optimality of the stationary monetary equilibrium.*

Proof   The class of feasible stationary allocations with $\left(c_t^t, c_{t+1}^t\right) = (c_1, c_2)$ for all $t \geq 1$ is given by

$$c_1 + \frac{c_2}{g_n} = e_1 + \frac{e_2}{g_n}. \tag{16.12}$$

Consider the stationary monetary equilibrium with allocation $(\hat{c}_1, \hat{c}_2)$ and constant per capital real balances $\hat{m}$. We can rewrite the budget constraints (16.1) and (16.2) as

$$c_1 + \frac{g_m}{g_n}c_2 \leq e_1 + \frac{g_m}{g_n}e_2 + \frac{g_m}{g_n}\frac{(g_m - 1)}{N_t}\frac{M_t}{p_{t+1}},$$

where we have used the fact that $p_t/p_{t+1} = g_n/g_m$. It follows that

$$c_1 + \frac{g_m}{g_n}c_2 \leq e_1 + \frac{g_m}{g_n}e_2 + (g_m - 1)\hat{m}. \tag{16.13}$$

To prove necessity, we plot the two curves (16.12) and (16.13), shown in figure 16.5, when condition $g_m \leq 1$ fails to hold, that is, when $g_m > 1$. The point that maximizes utility subject to (16.12) is denoted $(\bar{c}_1, \bar{c}_2)$. Transitivity of preferences and the fact that the slope of budget line (16.13) is flatter than that of (16.12) imply that $(\hat{c}_1, \hat{c}_2)$ lies southeast of $(\bar{c}_1, \bar{c}_2)$. By revealed preference, $(\bar{c}_1, \bar{c}_2)$ is preferred to $(\hat{c}_1, \hat{c}_2)$, and all generations born in period $t \geq 1$ are better off under the allocation $\bar{C}$. The initial old generation can also be made better off under this alternative allocation since it is feasible to strictly increase their consumption,

$$\bar{c}_1^0 = e_2 + g_n\left(e_1 - \bar{c}_1^1\right) > e_2 + g_n\left(e_1 - \hat{c}_1^1\right) = \hat{c}_1^0.$$

This proves necessity.

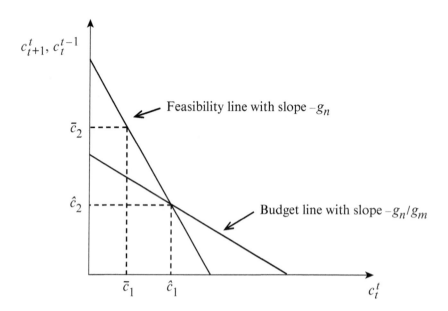

Figure 16.5
Feasibility and budget lines

To prove sufficiency, note that the consumption Euler equation, (16.7) and $g_m \leq 1$ imply that

$$\frac{u'(c_1)}{\beta u'(c_2)} = R_{t+1} = \frac{g_n}{g_m} \geq g_n.$$

We can then use the same argument as that in the proof of the previous proposition. ∎

For the case of constant population, Balasko and Shell (1980) establish a convenient general criterion for testing whether allocations are optimal. Define the interest rate $R_{t+1} = u'\left(c_t^t\right) / \left[\beta u'\left(c_{t+1}^t\right)\right]$. Balasko and Shell show that an allocation $\left\{c_1^0, \left(c_t^t, c_{t+1}^t\right), t \geq 1\right\}$ is Pareto optimal if and only if

$$\sum_{t=1}^{\infty} \prod_{s=1}^{t} R_{s+1} = +\infty.$$

Normalize $p_1 = 1$. It follows from $R_{t+1} = p_t / p_{t+1}$ that the condition above is equivalent to

$$\sum_{t=1}^{\infty} \frac{1}{p_t} = +\infty.$$

The Balasko–Shell criterion for optimality shows that low-interest-rate economies are typically not optimal.

The proof of the Balasko and Shell (1980) result is quite involved. Here we develop some intuition informally. Take the autarkic allocation e_1^0, $\{e_t^t, e_{t+1}^t\}$, $t \geq 1$, and try to construct a Pareto improvement. In particular, take $\delta_0 > 0$ units of consumption from generation 1 to the initial old generation. This obviously improves the initial old's utility. For agents in generation 1 not to be worse off, they have to receive δ_1 in additional consumption in their second period of life, with δ_1 satisfying

$$\delta_0 u' \left(e_1^1\right) = \delta_1 \beta u' \left(e_2^1\right),$$

or

$$\delta_1 = \frac{\delta_0 u' \left(e_1^1\right)}{\beta u' \left(e_2^1\right)} = \delta_0 R_2 > 0.$$

In general, the amount

$$\delta_t = \delta_0 \prod_{s=1}^{t} R_{s+1}$$

is the required transfers to an agent in generation t when old to compensate for the reduction of his consumption when young. Obviously such a scheme does not work if the economy ends at a finite time T since the last generation (which lives only through youth) is worse off. But since our economy has an infinite horizon, such an intergenerational transfer scheme is feasible provided that the δ_t's do not grow too fast, that is, provided that interest rates are sufficiently small. If such a transfer scheme is feasible, then we have found a Pareto improvement over the original autarkic allocation, and hence the autarkic equilibrium allocation is not Pareto efficient.

The Balasko and Shell (1980) result can be generalized to the case with production and with population growth, as will be seen in the next section.

16.2   Production Economies

We now introduce production to the economy studied in the previous section. This is the model analyzed by Diamond (1965). The production technology is represented by a constant-returns-to-scale aggregate production function, $F(K, N)$. Assume that F satisfies the assumptions given in section 14.1.1. Define $f(k) = F(K/N, 1)$, where $k = K/N$. Then f satisfies $f' > 0, f'' < 0, f(0) = 0, f'(0) = \infty$, and $f'(\infty) = 0$.

The initial old agents are endowed with K_1 units of capital. Agents in other generations do not have any endowment and work only when young, supplying inelastically one unit of labor and earning a real wage of w_t. They consume part of their wage income and save the rest to finance their retirement consumption when old. The saving of the young in period t generates the capital stock that is used to produce output in period $t+1$ in combination with the labor supplied by the young generation of period $t+1$. Assume that there is no capital depreciation.

A young agent at date t solves the following problem:

$$\max u\left(c_t^t\right) + \beta u\left(c_{t+1}^t\right)$$

subject to

$$c_t^t + s_t = w_t,$$
$$c_{t+1}^t = R_{t+1}s_t,$$

where s_t is saving in period t and R_{t+1} is the gross interest rate paid on saving held from period t to period $t+1$. The consumption Euler equation gives

$$u'\left(w_t - s_t\right) = \beta u'\left(R_{t+1}s_t\right) R_{t+1}.$$

Solving yields a saving function:

$$s_t = s\left(w_t, R_{t+1}\right), \quad 0 < s_w < 1.$$

Saving is an increasing function of the wage rate by the concavity of u. The effect of an increase in the interest rate is ambiguous depending on the income and substitution effects. As we showed in section 16.1, if the coefficient of relative risk aversion is less than one, then the substitution effect dominates, and an increase in interest rates leads to an increase in saving.

Firms act competitively, hiring labor and renting capital according to the following conditions:

$$f\left(k_t\right) - k_t f'\left(k_t\right) = w_t, \tag{16.14}$$
$$1 + f'\left(k_t\right) = R_t, \tag{16.15}$$

where k_t is the capital–labor ratio, $t \geq 1$.

Capital market equilibrium implies that

$$K_{t+1} = N_t s\left(w_t, R_{t+1}\right).$$

Factor market equilibrium implies that $K_t = k_t N_t$. We then obtain

$$g_n k_{t+1} = s\left(w_t, R_{t+1}\right).$$

Substituting (16.14) and (16.15) into the equation above yields

$$k_{t+1} = \frac{s\left(f\left(k_t\right) - k_t f'\left(k_t\right), f'\left(k_{t+1}\right) + 1\right)}{g_n}, \quad k_1 \text{ given.} \tag{16.16}$$

This equation characterizes the equilibrium of the Diamond model.

16.2.1   Multiple Equilibria
The dynamics of k_t depend on the slope:

$$\frac{dk_{t+1}}{dk_t} = \frac{-s_w k_t f''\left(k_t\right)}{g_n - s_R f''\left(k_{t+1}\right)}.$$

Note that the numerator of this expression is positive because an increase in the capital stock in period t increases the wage, which increases saving. The sign of the denominator is ambiguous because the effects of an increase in the interest rate on saving are ambiguous.

If $s_R > 0$, then the denominator is positive. We can apply the implicit function theorem to solve for k_{t+1} as a function of k_t, $k_{t+1} = G\left(k_t\right)$, where G is an increasing function. We can show that $G\left(0\right) = 0$ and

$$\lim_{k \to \infty} \frac{G\left(k\right)}{k} = 0.$$

The limit follows from the fact that

$$\frac{g_n k_{t+1}}{k_t} \leq \frac{w_t}{k_t} \Rightarrow \lim_{k \to \infty} \frac{g_n G\left(k\right)}{k} \leq \lim_{k_t \to \infty} \frac{f\left(k_t\right)}{k_t} - f'\left(k_t\right) = 0.$$

As a result $k_{t+1}/k_t = G\left(k_t\right)/k_t < 1$ for k_t sufficiently large, implying that the graph of G eventually falls below the diagonal.

The function G passes through the origin and lies below the 45-degree line for large k. Whether additional steady states with $k > 0$ exist depends on the slope of G at the origin. If $G'\left(0\right) > 1$, then an odd number of positive steady states exist, as illustrated in figure 16.6. If $G'\left(0\right) < 1$, then an even number of positive steady states exist, possibly zero, as illustrated in figures 16.7 and 16.8.

If $s_R < 0$, then (16.16) may not give a unique solution for k_{t+1} given k_t. Figure 16.9 plots an example in which k_{t+1} is not uniquely determined by k_t when k_t is between k_a and k_b. The intuition is the following: If on the one hand, agents believe that k_{t+1} is high, then the interest rate is low and hence saving is high. This can support the agents' belief about high k_{t+1}. If, on the other hand, agents believe that k_{t+1} is low, then the interest rate is high and hence saving is low. This can also support the agents' belief about low k_{t+1}. Thus both paths can be at equilibrium. This is an example of **self-fulfilling prophecies**. The economy can exhibit fluctuations

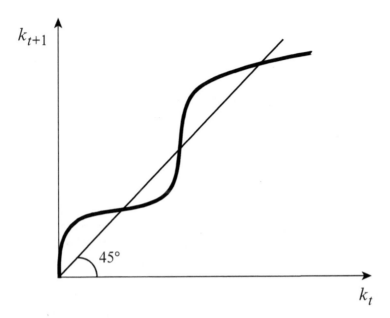

Figure 16.6
Three positive steady states and $G'(0) > 1$

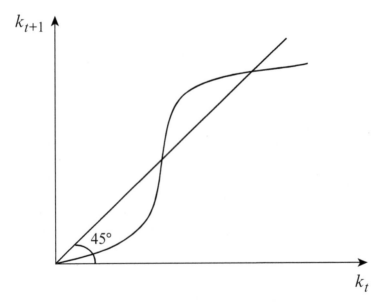

Figure 16.7
Two positive steady states and $G'(0) < 1$

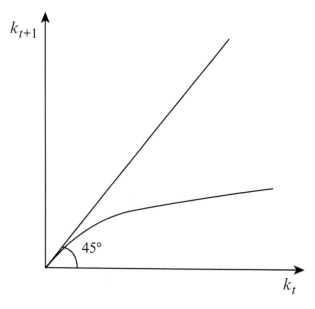

Figure 16.8
Zero positive steady state and $G'(0) < 1$

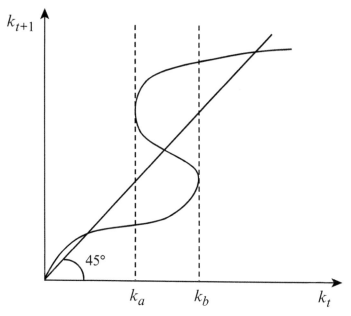

Figure 16.9
Indeterminancy

even though there are no exogenous shocks. Depending on agents' beliefs, various dynamics are possible.

The condition for the stability of a positive steady state $k_{t+1} = k_t = k^* > 0$ is given by

$$G'(k^*) = \left| \frac{-s_w k^* f''(k^*)}{g_n - s_R f''(k^*)} \right| < 1.$$

We call the following conditions the Diamond conditions: (1) $s_w \in (0,1)$, (2) $g_n - s_R f'' > 0$, (3) $G'(0) > 1$, and (4) at a steady state $k^* > 0$,

$$0 < G'(k^*) = \frac{-s_w k^* f''(k^*)}{g_n - s_R f''(k^*)} < 1.$$

Condition 4 is a stability condition. Conditions 1 and 2 ensure that savings increase with the wage, but the interest rate decrease with the wage. Formally, from equations $s_t = s(w_t, R_{t+1})$ and $R_{t+1} = f'(k_{t+1}) + 1 = f'\left(\frac{s(w_t, R_{t+1})}{g_n}\right) + 1$, we can solve for R_{t+1} and s_t as functions of w_t. We can then check the previous claim by differentiation.

Figure 16.10 plots the dynamics under these conditions. In this case there is only one steady state k_D with positive capital, which will be called the Diamond steady state.

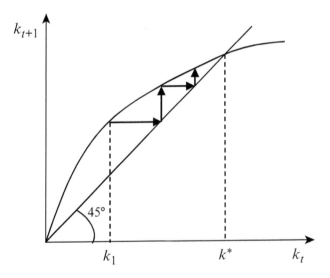

Figure 16.10
Unique positive and stable steady state

16.2.2 Dynamic Efficiency

Is the decentralized market equilibrium efficient? To answer this question, we write down the aggregate resource constraint

$$K_t + F(K_t, N_t) = K_{t+1} + N_t c_t^t + N_{t-1} c_t^{t-1}, \quad t \geq 1.$$

An allocation $(c_1^0, \{c_t^t, c_{t+1}^t, k_{t+1}\}, t \geq 1)$ is feasible if it satisfies the resource constraint above. Dividing the resource constraint by the number of workers N_t yields

$$k_t + f(k_t) = g_n k_{t+1} + c_t^t + g_n^{-1} c_t^{t-1}.$$

In the steady state, $k_t = k$, $c_t^t = c_y$ and $c_{t+1}^t = c_o$ for all $t \geq 2$. We then rewrite the resource constraint as

$$c_y + g_n^{-1} c_0 = f(k) - (g_n - 1) k. \tag{16.17}$$

Consider a social planner that solves the problem in the steady state:

$$\max_{c_y, c_o, k} \lambda_0 u(c_1^0) + \lambda_1 [u(c_y) + \beta u(c_o)],$$

subject to (16.17) and

$$c_y + g_n^{-1} c_1^0 = f(k_1) + k_1 - g_n k,$$

where λ_0 is the weight on the initial old and λ_1 is the weight on the other generations. Let μ and θ be the Lagrange multiplier associated with the two constraints, respectively. We may replace these two constraints with inequality constraints. The first-order conditions are given by

$$\frac{u'(c_y)}{\beta u'(c_o)} = g_n,$$

$$\lambda_0 u'(c_1^0) = \theta g_n^{-1},$$

$$f'(k) = g_n - 1 + \frac{\theta}{\mu} \geq g_n - 1.$$

When the planner does not consider the initial old, $\lambda_0 = 0$, so that $\theta = 0$. We then obtain the **Golden Rule** level of capital stock k_G such that $f'(k_G) = g_n - 1$. At this level, consumption per worker $c_y + g_n^{-1} c_0$ is maximized and the marginal product of capital or the (net) interest rate is equal to the (net) population growth rate. When the marginal product of capital is smaller than the population growth rate, the economy accumulates too much capital such that $k^* > k_G$, and hence it is dynamically inefficient. A planner can reduce saving from k^* to k_G and makes everyone better off.

We have shown that the steady-state capital stock $k^* \leq k_G$ is necessary for the allocation to be dynamically efficient. Is it a sufficient condition? Cass (1972) and

Balasko and Shell (1980) show that a feasible allocation is Pareto optimal (or dynamically efficient) if and only if

$$\sum_{t=1}^{\infty} (g_n)^{-t} \prod_{s=1}^{t} R_{s+1} = +\infty,$$

where $R_t = 1 + f'(k_t)$. An immediate corollary is that a steady-state equilibrium is Pareto optimal (or dynamically efficient) if and only if $k^* \leq k_G$ or $f'(k^*) \geq g_n - 1$.

16.3   Asset Price Bubbles

We now introduce an intrinsically useless asset into the Diamond model studied in the previous section. Suppose that the total supply of this asset is one unit and that the initial old holds this unit. The fundamental value of the asset is zero. We will show that this asset may have a positive value in equilibrium depending on self-fulfilling beliefs. Tirole (1985) studies this issue and our presentation follows his study closely.

Suppose that the Diamond conditions hold. Since a young agent can use saving to buy the bubble asset or to accumulate capital, the capital market-clearing condition becomes

$$N_t s_t = B_t + K_{t+1},$$

where B_t denotes the price of the intrinsically useless asset. If it is positive, we call the price a bubble. Let $b_t = B_t/N_t$ denote the per capita bubble. Then the condition above becomes

$$g_n k_{t+1} + b_t = s(w_t, R_{t+1}). \tag{16.18}$$

By no arbitrage, the return on the bubble asset must be equal to the interest rate,

$$B_{t+1} = R_{t+1} B_t.$$

We require that $B_t \geq 0$ for all $t \geq 1$. In per capita terms,

$$g_n b_{t+1} = R_{t+1} b_t. \tag{16.19}$$

Substituting (16.14) and (16.15) into equations (16.18) and (16.19) yields a system of two difference equations for two unknowns k_t and b_t :

$$b_{t+1} = \frac{1 + f'(k_{t+1})}{g_n} b_t, \tag{16.20}$$

$$g_n k_{t+1} + b_t = s(f(k_t) - k_t f'(k_t), f'(k_{t+1}) + 1). \tag{16.21}$$

Clearly, if $b_t = 0$ for all t, then (16.20) is redundant and (16.21) reduces to (16.16). We then obtain the Diamond equilibrium studied earlier. We are interested in the **bubbly equilibrium** in which $b_t > 0$ for all t. In the bubbly steady state we have

$$g_n = f'(k) + 1,$$
$$g_n k + b = s\left(f(k) - kf'(k), f'(k) + 1\right),$$

Thus the bubbly steady-state capital stock is equal to the Golden Rule capital stock k_G. The steady-state bubble b^* is then determined by the second equation given above. To study the stability of this steady state (k_G, b^*), we use the phase diagram.

Let $k_{t+1} = G(k_t, b_t)$ denote the solution to (16.21). Substituting this solution into (16.20) yields

$$b_{t+1} = \frac{1 + f'\left(G\left(k_t, b_t\right)\right)}{g_n} b_t.$$

Differentiating with respect to b_t and k_t in equation (16.21) yields

$$G_k\left(k_t, b_t\right) = \frac{-s_w k_t f''\left(k_t\right)}{g_n - s_R f''\left(k_t\right)} > 0, \quad G_b\left(k_t, b_t\right) = \frac{-1}{g_n - s_R f''\left(k_t\right)} < 0,$$

where the signs follow from Diamond conditions 1 and 2.

Figure 16.11 plots the locus where

$$\Delta k_t \equiv k_{t+1} - k_t = G\left(k_t, b_t\right) - k_t = 0.$$

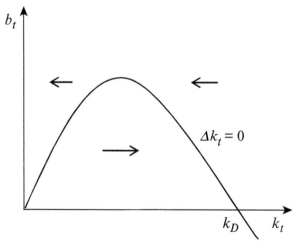

Figure 16.11
Locus $\Delta k_t = k_{t+1} - k_t = 0$ and vector fields

This curve crosses the horizontal axis at the origin and the Diamond steady state k_D. Differentiation yields

$$\frac{db_t}{dk_t} = \frac{1 - G_k(k_t, b_t)}{G_b(k_t, b_t)}.$$

Under Diamond conditions 3 and 4, we can check that

$$\frac{db_t}{dk_t}(0,0) > 0 \quad \text{and} \quad \frac{db_t}{dk_t}(k_D, 0) < 0.$$

Thus the locus $\Delta k_t = 0$ has a positive slope at the origin and a negative slope at the Diamond steady state. Since $G_b < 0$ and

$$k_{t+1} > k_t \iff G(k_t, b_t) - k_t > 0,$$

we can derive the vector fields as in figure 16.11.

Next figure 16.12 plots the locus for

$$\Delta b_t \equiv b_{t+1} - b_t = \frac{1 + f'(G(k_t, b_t))}{g_n} b_t - b_t = 0.$$

Differentiation yields

$$\frac{db_t}{dk_t} = -\frac{G_k(k_t, b_t)}{G_b(k_t, b_t)} > 0.$$

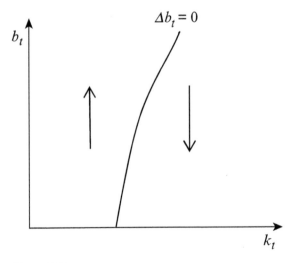

Figure 16.12
Locus $\Delta b_t = b_{t+1} - b_t = 0$ and vector fields

Thus this locus always slopes up. It crosses the locus $\Delta k_t = 0$ at the bubbly steady state (k_G, b^*). We can show that

$$b_{t+1} > b_t \iff \frac{1 + f'\left(G\left(k_t, b_t\right)\right)}{g_n} b_t - b_t > 0 \iff G\left(k_t, b_t\right) < k_G.$$

Since $G_b < 0$, we obtain the vector fields shown in figure 16.12.

Now, we combine Figures 16.11 and 16.12 together to plot Figure 16.13. This figure shows that for a bubbly steady state to exist, we must have $k_G < k_D$ or $R_D < g_n$. That is, the bubbleless equilibrium must be dynamically inefficient. In this case the bubbly steady state (k_G, b^*) is at the intersection of the loci $k_{t+1} = k_t$ and $b_{t+1} = b_t$. Figure 16.13 shows that this steady state is a saddle point. For any given initial value k_1, there is a unique $b_1 = b(k_1)$ on the saddle path such that (k_t, b_t) moves along the saddle path and converges to the bubbly steady state. However, if we start from any $b_1 < b(k_1)$, then (k_t, b_t) will converge to the Diamond steady state without a bubble.

Tirole (1985) introduces other assets with exogenously given dividends or rents in the model above in order to study when a bubble can emerge in these assets.

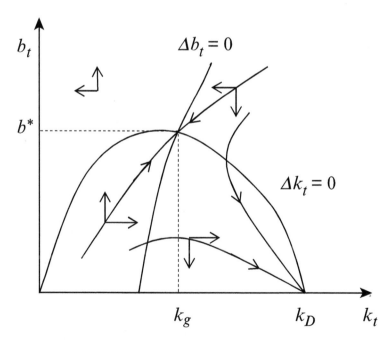

Figure 16.13
Phase diagram. The bubbly steady state is (k_g, b^*). It is a saddle point. The Diamond bubbleless steady state is $(k_D, 0)$. There are infinitely many equilibria converging to the Diamond steady state.

Weil (1987) introduces a randomizing device in the Tirole (1985) analysis. A bubble exists initially and agents believe that the bubble may collapse with some probability each period. Weil (1987) shows that when this probability is sufficiently small, an equilibrium with stochastic bubble can exist. Santos and Woodford (1997) study conditions for the existence of rational bubbles in a general framework. Kocherlakota (1992, 2009) study rational bubbles in models with infinitely lived agents. These studies analyze bubbles on assets with exogenously given payoffs. Miao and Wang (2011b,c, 2012a, b) study credit-driven stock market bubbles when dividends are endogenously generated by production. They show that bubbles can help relax collateral constraints and allow firms to borrow more and make more investments, generating a high firm value.

16.4   Exercises

1. Consider the Samuelson (1958) model in section 16.1. Suppose that utility is $\ln\left(c_t^t\right) + \ln\left(c_{t+1}^t\right)$. Population is given by $N_t = g_n N_{t-1}$. Let $e_1 > e_2$. Each initial old agent is endowed with one unit of intrinsically worthless fiat money. The stock of money is constant over time.
   a. Compute the nonmonetary equilibrium.
   b. Compute all stationary monetary equilibria. Can you rank these equilibria according to the Pareto criterion?
   c. Find the limiting rates of return on money as $t \to \infty$ for all monetary equilibria.

2. Consider the model in exercise 1. Endow the initial old agent with a tree that yields a constant dividend of $d > 0$ units of the consumption good for each $t \geq 1$.
   a. Compute all the equilibria with valued fiat money.
   b Compute all nonmonetary equilibria.

3. Consider the Diamond (1965) model with $u(c) = c^{1-\gamma}/(1-\gamma)$ and $f(k) = k^\alpha$. Solve for the saving function $s(R)$. Characterize the properties of $s(R)$ for different values of γ. Derive the equilibrium law of motion for capital.

4. Consider the Diamond (1965) model with $u(c) = \ln c$ and $f(k) = k^\alpha$. Derive the equilibrium law of motion for capital and the steady-state capital stock.

5. Consider the Diamond (1965) model with $u(c) = \ln c$ and

$$f(k) = A \left[ak^{\sigma-1/\sigma} + 1 - a \right]^{\sigma/\sigma-1},$$

where σ is the elasticity of substitution. Note that $\sigma = 1$ corresponds to the Cobb–Douglas production function.
   a. Prove that if $\sigma \geq 1$, then a positive steady state exists.

b. Suppose $\sigma < 1$. Derive the equilibrium law of motion for capital. Analyze the existence, uniqueness and stability properties of the steady state. In particular, prove that for a sufficiently small, there is no positive steady state.

6. In section 16.2 we have assumed zero depreciation. Suppose that the depreciation rate is δ. Derive the equilibrium law of motion for capital. What is this law for $\delta = 1$.

7. (Government in the Diamond 1965 model) Consider the model in section 16.2. Let G_t denote the per capita government spending. Suppose that government spending is financed by lump-sum taxes levied on the young. Let $u(c) = \ln c$ and $f(k) = k^\alpha$.
   a. Derive the equilibrium law of motion for capital.
   b. Analyze the impact of a permanent increase of government spending from G_L to G_H. Draw the path of the capital stock.
   c. Analyze the impact of a temporary increase of government spending from G_L to G_H. Draw the path of the capital stock.

8. (Social security in the Diamond 1965 model) Let $u(c) = \ln c$ and $f(k) = k^\alpha$.
   a. *Pay-as-you-go social security*   Suppose that the government taxes each young individual an amount d_t and uses the proceeds to pay benefits to the current old individuals. Thus each old individual receives $g_n d_t$.
      i. Derive the equilibrium law of motion for capital.
      ii. What is the impact of introducing social security tax on the equilibrium capital stock?
      iii. If the economy is initially on a balanced growth path that is dynamically efficient, how does a marginal increase in d_t affect the welfare of current and future generations? What happens if the initial balanced growth path is dynamically inefficient?
   b. *Fully funded social security*   Suppose that the young contributes d_t. This amount is invested and returned with interest at time $t+1$ to the then old, $R_{t+1} d_t$.
      i. Derive the equilibrium law of motion for capital.
      ii. What is the impact on capital and welfare? Explain the intuition behind the result.

9. Linearize the equilibrium system for the model of section 16.3. Use this system to analyze the stability of the bubbly steady state.

17 Incomplete Markets Models

In chapter 13 we showed that the optimal consumption allocation is not history dependent in complete markets exchange economies when the aggregate endowment is determined by an exogenous Markov state variable. This chapter and chapter 22 introduce models in which there are frictions in exchanging risks. In this case the consumption allocation will be history dependent. In the incomplete markets models of this chapter, the history dependence is encoded in the dependence of a household's consumption on its current asset holdings. In chapter 22 history dependence is encoded in the dependence of the consumption allocation on a continuation value promised by a principal.

In this chapter we introduce a particular type of incomplete markets models—the Aiyagari–Bewley–Huggett model. In this type of model there is a continuum of ex ante identical agents. These agents face idiosyncratic shocks and hence are heterogeneous ex post. Markets are incomplete and hence idiosyncratic risks cannot be diversified or hedged away. These models are built on the income fluctuation problem studied in section 8.3. The models are closed by introducing an asset market, and equilibrium is obtained from the market-clearing conditions. In section 17.1 we study production economies in which the asset is productive. In section 17.2 we study exchange economies in which the asset is either a riskless bond or fiat money. In section 17.3 we introduce aggregate shocks and study business cycle implications. For other excellent exposition of the Aiyagari–Bewley–Huggett model, we refer the reader to Ljungqvist and Sargent (2004).

17.1 Production Economies

In this section we introduce the model of Aiyagari (1994). We begin with an income fluctuation problem. We then introduce production and define the equilibrium. We finally discuss computation methods.

17.1.1   Income Fluctuation Problem

Consider an agent's consumption/saving problem. Let $c_t \geq 0$ denote consumption, $a_t \geq -b$ denote asset holdings (or borrowing if $a_t < 0$), and l_t denote labor endowment shock. The agent takes the interest rate r and the wage rate w as given and solves the following problem:

$$\max_{\{c_t, a_{t+1}\}} E \sum_{t=0}^{\infty} \beta^t u\left(c_t\right) \tag{17.1}$$

subject to

$$c_t + a_{t+1} = (1+r)\, a_t + w l_t, \quad a_t \geq -b. \tag{17.2}$$

Assume that l_t takes values on $[l_{\min}, l_{\max}]$ and follows a Markov process with transition function Q. By theorem 8.3.1, the no-Ponzi-scheme condition $\lim_{t \to \infty} a_t / (1+r)^t \geq 0$ for $r > 0$ and nonnegative consumption imply that $a_t \geq -w l_{\min}/r$. This borrowing constraint is called the natural borrowing constraint. Thus we can impose the following borrowing constraint:

$$a_t \geq -\phi, \tag{17.3a}$$

$$\phi = \min\{b, w l_{\min}/r\} \quad \text{for } r > 0; \phi = b \text{ for } r < 0. \tag{17.3b}$$

Define the cash on hand or total resource x_t as

$$x_t \equiv (1+r)\, a_t + w l_t + \phi.$$

Let $\hat{a}_t = a_t + \phi$. The agent solves the following dynamic programming problem:

$$V\left(x_t, l_t\right) = \max_{\hat{a}_{t+1} \in [0, x_t]} u\left(x_t - \hat{a}_{t+1}\right) + \beta \int V\left(x_{t+1}, l_{t+1}\right) Q\left(dl_{t+1}, l_t\right)$$

subject to

$$x_{t+1} = (1+r)\, \hat{a}_{t+1} + w l_{t+1} - r\phi.$$

Let the policy function be

$$\hat{a}_{t+1} = A\left(x_t, l_t\right).$$

Clearly, if l_t is IID, then we can remove l_t as a state variable. In this case the process (x_t) defined by

$$x_{t+1} = (1+r)\, A\left(x_t, l_t\right) + w l_{t+1} - r\phi$$

is a Markov process. In section 8.3.3 we showed that if $\beta(1+r) \geq 1$, x_t, and a_t converge to infinity. But, if $\beta(1+r) < 1$, $\{x_t\}$ has a unique invariant measure λ^*.

Given this measure, we can compute the long-run average assets $Ea(r,w) = E_{\lambda^*}[A(x_t)] - \phi$.

Huggett (1993) generalizes these results to the case of Markov processes with two states. The results for general Markov processes are unknown. In applications researchers typically use numerical methods. In this case the following dynamic programming formulation is more convenient:

$$V(a_t, l_t) = \max_{a_{t+1} \geq -\phi} u(c_t) + \beta \int V(a_{t+1}, l_{t+1}) Q(dl_{t+1}, l_t) \tag{17.4}$$

subject to (17.2) and (17.3). This problem delivers a policy function

$$a' = g(a, l),$$

where we have remove time subscripts and used a variable with a prime to denote its next-period value. Let the state space of (a, l) be S. The joint process $(a_t, l_t)_{t \geq 0}$ follows a Markov process with a transition function given by

$$P(A \times B, (a, l)) = 1_{g(a, l) \in A} Q(B, l),$$

where $A \times B$ is a Borel set for S. This transition function induces a sequence of distributions on the state space for (a, l):

$$\lambda_{t+1}(A \times B) = \int P(A \times B, (a, l)) d\lambda_t(a, l).$$

Suppose that it converges weakly to an invariant distribution, denoted by $\lambda^*(a, l)$ without risk of confusion. Given this distribution, we can compute the long-run average assets $Ea(r, w) = \int g(a, l) d\lambda^*(a, l)$.

17.1.2 Production

There is a representative firm using capital and labor to produce output. The production function is given by

$$Y_t = F(K_t, L_t),$$

where F has constant returns to scale. Static profit maximization implies the first-order conditions

$$F_K(K, L) = r + \delta, \tag{17.5}$$

$$F_L(K, L) = w, \tag{17.6}$$

where δ denotes the depreciation rate of capital.

17.1.3 Stationary Recursive Equilibrium

Suppose that there is no aggregate shock. There is a continuum of ex ante agents subject to idiosyncratic labor endowment shocks or earnings shocks. We can reinterpret the distribution $\lambda^*(a, l)$ as the cross-sectional asset-employment distribution. We will focus on a stationary recursive equilibrium in which all aggregate variables and factor prices r and w are constant over time.

Definition 17.1.1 *A stationary recursive competitive equilibrium is a value function* $V : S \to \mathbb{R}$, *policy functions for the household* $g : S \to \mathbb{R}$ *and* $c : S \to \mathbb{R}_+$, *firm's choices* L *and* K, *prices* r *and* w, *and a stationary measure* λ^* *on* S *such that:*

a. *given prices* r *and* w, *the policy functions* g *and* c *solve the household's problem and* V *is the associated value function.*

b. *given* r *and* w, *the firm chooses optimally its capital* K *and its labor* L, *meaning (17.5) and (17.6) hold.*

c. *The labor market clears:* $L = \int l d\lambda^*(a, l)$.

d. *The asset market clears:* $K = \int g(a, l) d\lambda^*(a, l)$.

e. *The resource constraint holds:*

$$\int c(a, l) d\lambda^*(a, l) + \delta K = F(K, L).$$

f. λ^* *is a stationary distribution:*

$$\lambda^*(A \times B) = \int \mathbf{1}_{g(a,l) \in A} Q(B, l) d\lambda^*(a, l) \tag{17.7}$$

for all Borel sets $A \times B$ *on* S.

Note that the resource constraint is redundant given the other equilibrium conditions. Moreover aggregate labor is L exogenously given and determined by the mean of l_t, typically normalized to 1.

There is no general theoretical results for the existence and uniqueness of a stationary recursive equilibrium.[1] A typical argument to establish existence is nicely discussed by Aiyagari (1994). The argument can be illustrated by figure 17.1. The downward sloping curve in figure 17.1 represents the aggregate capital demand function $K^d(r)$ that is derived from (17.5). The upward sloping curve represents the capital supply function $Ea(r)$, which is derived from the long-run average assets $\int g(a, l) d\lambda^*(a, l)$. Specifically, given (17.5) and (17.6), we can show that w is a continuous function of r. Thus we can show that the policy function g and

---

1. See Aiyagari (1994), Huggett (1993), Acemoglu and Jensen (2012), and Miao (2006) for some theoretical results.

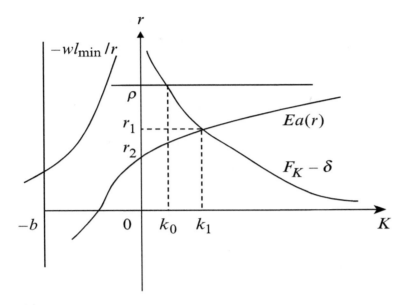

Figure 17.1
Determination of equilibrium in Aiyagari's (1994) model. The intersection of the $Ea(r)$ curve and the $F_K - \delta$ curve gives the equilibrium interest rate and the capital stock

the stationary distribution λ^* are also continuous functions of r. This implies that $\int g(a,l) d\lambda^*(a,l)$ is also a continuous function of r, which is equal to $Ea(r)$.

As $(1+r)\beta$ approaches 1 from below, $Ea(r)$ approaches infinity since a_t approaches infinity. When $r < 0$, $Ea(r)$ approaches $-b$. Therefore there is a point such that the capital demand curve $K^d(r)$ crosses the capital supply curve $Ea(r)$ by the Intermediate Value Theorem. Since there is no guarantee that $Ea(r)$ is monotonic, there may exist multiple crossing points. Thus there may exist multiple equilibria for the Aiyagari model. However, in applications this case seldom happens.

Figure 17.1 shows clearly that the equilibrium interest rate is less than $\rho \equiv 1/\beta - 1$, which is the equilibrium interest rate under complete markets. This implies that the capital stock under incomplete markets is higher than that under complete markets. The intuition is that households hold extra assets for precautionary motives. To see the quantitative importance, one needs to calibrate the model and solve it numerically.

17.1.4   Computation and Implications
There are several ways to solve the Aiyagari (1994) model. The following algorithm is one of them:

Step 1. Fix an initial guess for the interest rate $r^0 \in (-\delta, 1/\beta - 1)$, where these bounds follow from our previous discussion. The interest rate r^0 is our first candidate for the equilibrium (the superscript denotes the iteration number).

Step 2. Given the interest rate r^0, derive the wage rate $w(r^0)$ using (17.6).

Step 3. Given prices $(r^0, w(r^0))$, solve the dynamic programming problem (17.4) to obtain decision rules $a' = g(a, l; r)$ and $c = c(a, l; r^0)$. We described several solution methods in chapter 11. For each method we typically have to discretize the state space for a and l. We can use the methods discussed in section 11.2 to discretize a continuous Markov process as a discrete Markov chain.

Step 4. Given the policy function $a' = g(a, l; r^0)$ and the transition function Q for (l_t), we use (17.7) to solve for a stationary distribution $\lambda^*(r^0)$. Compute the aggregate supply of capital:

$$Ea(r^0) = \int g(a, l; r^0) \, d\lambda^*(a, l; r^0).$$

Step 5. Compute the aggregate demand of capital $K(r^0) = F_K^{-1}(r^0 + \delta)$ using (17.5).

Step 6. Search r such that the asset market clears. Specifically, if $Ea(r^0) > (<) K(r^0)$, set $r^1 < (>) r^0$. To obtain the new candidate r^1, a good choice is the bisection method:

$$r^1 = \frac{1}{2} \left[r^0 + F_K \left(Ea(r^0), 1 \right) - \delta \right].$$

Step 7. Update the initial guess to r^1 and go back to step 1. Keep iterating until the interest rate converges, meaning until $|r^{n+1} - r^n| < \varepsilon$ for small $\varepsilon > 0$.

There are several methods that can be used to implement step 4. Here we discuss only two methods. First, one could discretize the state space for (a, l). This also requires the Markov process $\{l_t\}$ to be discretized as a Markov chain with transition matrix $\pi(l, l')$. We can use methods presented in section 11.2. We then iterate the equation

$$\lambda_{t+1}(a', l') = \sum_l \sum_{\{a: a' = g(a, l)\}} \lambda_t(a, l) \, \pi(l, l')$$

until convergence to λ^*, where (a, l) and (a', l') are all on the grid. We can then compute

$$Ea(r^0) = \sum_{(a, l)} g(a, l; r^0) \, \lambda^*(a, l; r^0).$$

The second method is to use simulations: (1) We simulate a large number of households (e.g., 100,000) and track them over time, like survey data do. We then initialize each individual in the sample with a pair (a_0, l_0) and use the decision rule $a' = g(a, l)$ and a random number generator that replicates the Markov shock $\{l_t\}$ to generate a joint Markov process $\{a_t, l_t\}$. (2) For every t, we can compute a set of cross-sectional moments m_t that summarize the distribution of assets (e.g., mean, variance, and various percentiles). We stop when m_t and m_{t+1} are close enough. In this case the cross-sectional distribution has converged for a given r. (3) $Ea(r^0)$ is the cross-sectional mean.

An alternative algorithm discussed by Ljungqvist and Sargent (2004) is to iterate on capital instead of on the interest rate. Start with a guess of K^0. Solve for r and w using (17.5) and (17.6). Solve for the decision rule $g(a, s; K^0)$ and stationary distribution $\lambda^*(K^0)$. Compute an updated capital stock

$$K^1 = \sum_{(a, l)} g(a, l; K^0) \lambda^*(a, l).$$

Set

$$K^2 = \xi K^1 + (1 - \xi) K^0, \quad \xi \in (0, 1).$$

Replace K^0 with K^2 and iterate on the procedure above until convergence.

Aiyagari (1994) solves a calibrated model and studies how much uninsured idiosyncratic risk contributes to aggregate saving. He finds that for reasonably calibrated parameter values, the aggregate saving rate in the incomplete markets model is higher than in the complete markets model by no more than 3 percent.[2] He also finds that the income and wealth distributions are positively skewed (median less than mean), the wealth distribution is much more dispersed than the income distribution, and inequality as measured by the Gini coefficient is significantly higher for wealth than for income.

The Gini coefficient is associated with the Lorenz curve. To derive the Lorenz curve, suppose that we observe data of income for n individuals $\{x_1, x_2, ..., x_n\}$. We order $\{x_1, x_2, ..., x_n\}$ by size in an ascending order, yielding $\{y_1, y_2..., y_n\}$. The Lorenz curve plots i/n against $z_i = \sum_{j=1}^{i} y_j / \sum_{j=1}^{n} y_j$ for $i = 1, ..., n$. In other words, it plots the percentile of households against the fraction of total income that this percentile of households holds. For example, if $n = 100$, then $i = 10$ corresponds to the 10 percentile of households. Note that since the $\{y_i\}$ are ordered ascendingly, $\{z_i\}$ is an increasing sequence with $z_n = 1$. The closer the Lorenz curve is to the 45-degree line, the more equal is $\{x_i\}$ distributed. The Gini coefficient (or Gini index) is twice the area between the Lorenz curve and the 45-degree line. If $x_i \geq 0$ for all i, then the Gini coefficient is between zero and one, with a higher Gini coefficient indicating bigger concentration of $\{x_i\}$. As extremes, for complete equality of income, the

---

2. The aggregate saving rate is defined as $\delta K / (AF(K, L)) = \delta \alpha / (r + \delta)$ for the production function $F(K, L) = AK^\alpha L^{1-\alpha}$.

Gini coefficient is zero, and for complete concentration (the richest person has all income), the Gini coefficient is 1.

Example 17.1.1 *We use Matlab codes to compute some numerical examples.*[3] *The utility function is* $u(c) = c^{1-\gamma}/(1-\gamma)$ *with* $\gamma = 3$. *The production function is* $F(k,l) = k^\alpha l^{1-\alpha}$. *We set* $\beta = 0.96$, $\delta = 0.08$, *and* $\alpha = 0.36$. *The earnings shock follow the process*

$$\ln l_t = \rho \ln l_{t-1} + \varepsilon_t,$$

where ε_t *is IID normal with mean 0 and variance* σ^2. *We set* $\rho = 0.2$ *and* $\sigma = 0.4\sqrt{1-\rho^2}$. *We use Tauchen's (1986) method with 7 grid points to discretize the AR(1) process as a Markov chain. The mean of l is 1.0904.*

Figure 17.2 plots the asset supply curve $Ea(r)$ *and asset demand curve* $K^d(r)$ *for* $b = 3$ *and* 5. *The* $Ea(r)$ *curve for* $b = 5$ *shifts to the left, implying that the equilibrium interest rate is higher, but the equilibrium capital stock is lower than*

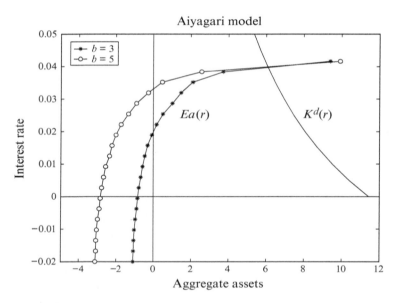

Figure 17.2
Determination of equilibrium in Aiyagari's model in example 17.1.1

---

3. The codes are `Bewley99.m` and `Aiyagari2.m`, which are slight modifications of the codes accompanying Ljungqvist and Sargent (2004). The code `markovappr.m` implements Tauchen's (1986) method for approximating a continuous AR(1) process with a Markov chain. The program `markovsimul.m` simulates a Markov chain.

in the case for b = 3. The intuition is that households have a stronger precautionary saving motive when the borrowing constraint is tighter, inducing them to save more.

17.2   Endowment Economies

In this section we focus on endowment economies. We first introduce the Huggett (1993) model and then introduce the models of Bewley (1980, 1983, 1986).

17.2.1   Risk-Free Rate

Huggett (1993) builds an incomplete markets model with borrowing constraints to explain why the risk-free rate is so low in the data. The model is also based on the income fluctuation problem studied in sections 8.3 and 17.1.1. Unlike the Aiyagari model, there is no production. A household receives idiosyncratic endowments $e_t = w l_t$ each period. The endowment stream $\{e_t\}$ follows a Markov process with transition function Q and is independent across households. The model is closed by imposing the market-clearing condition that the aggregate assets are equal to zero. This means that there are no outside assets. Setting $w = 1$, we can use e_t and l_t interchangeably. Let the state space for assets and endowments (a, e) be S. We formally define a stationary recursive equilibrium as follows:

Definition 17.2.1 *A stationary recursive competitive equilibrium is a value function $V : S \rightarrow \mathbb{R}$, an asset accumulation policy function for the household $g : S \rightarrow \mathbb{R}$, a risk-free rate r, and a stationary measure λ^* on S such that:*

a. given r, the policy function g solves the household's problem (17.4) and V is the associated value function.

b. the asset market clears: $\int g(a, e) \, d\lambda^*(a, e) = 0$.

c. λ^* is a stationary distribution:

$$\lambda^*(A \times B) = \int \mathbf{1}_A(g(a, e)) Q(B, e) \, d\lambda^*(a, e) \tag{17.8}$$

for all Borel sets $A \times B$ on S.

How will the debt limit b and market incompleteness affect the equilibrium risk-free rate? Figure 17.3 illustrates the equilibrium determination for two values of b. The parameter values are given in example 17.1.1. The equilibrium interest rate is given by the intersection of the $Ea(r)$ curve with the vertical axis. The $Ea(r)$ curve shifts to the left when b becomes larger. This means that the interest rate is lower for a smaller value of b. The intuition is that when the borrowing constraint is tighter, households have higher incentives to hold more assets for precautionary

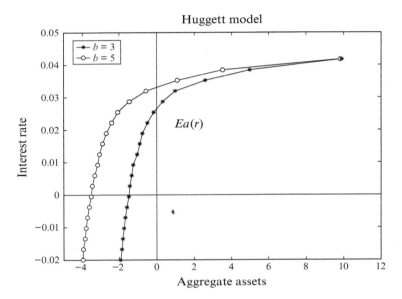

Figure 17.3
Determination of equilibrium in Huggett's (1993) model

motives. Since households are not restricted from holding large assets, a lower risk-free rate is needed to persuade them not to accumulate large credit balances so that the credit market can clear. When b is sufficiently large, the borrowing constraint reduces to the natural borrowing constraint. In this case the interest rate is the highest. However, it is still lower than $1/\beta - 1$, the equilibrium interest rate under complete markets.

Proposition 17.2.1   *When $r = 0$, $Ea(0;b) = Ea(0;0) - b$.*

Proof   Let $\hat{a}_t = a_t + b$. Equation (17.2) becomes

$$c_t + \hat{a}_{t+1} = \hat{a}_t + wl_t, \quad \hat{a}_t \geq 0.$$

Thus optimal policy $\hat{a}_{t+1} = A(a_t, l_t)$ is independent of b. This implies that $A(a_t, l_t; b) = a_{t+1} + b = A(a_t, l_t; 0)$. Hence $Ea(0;b) = Ea(0;b) - b$.   ∎

Huggett's model can be viewed as a model of pure "inside money," or of circulating private IOUs. Every household is a "banker" in his model, entitled to issue "notes" subject to the credit limit $a_{t+1} \geq -\phi$. A household issues notes whenever $a_{t+1} < 0$. Under the natural borrowing limit we can think of this pure consumption loan or insider money model as a model of free banking. In the model each household's ability to issue an IOU is restricted only by the requirement that all loans be one period and risk free. In subsequent subsections we will use the equilibrium allocation of this free banking model as a benchmark against which to judge the celebrated Friedman rule in a model with outside money and a severe borrowing limit.

17.2.2 Fiat Money

Suppose that a government supplies a fixed nominal amount of money. Money is intrinsically useless. Why should households hold it? Bewley (1980, 1983) proposes a model in which households hold money because money is an asset used by households to insure against idiosyncratic risks. Households can hold money but not issue it. To map a household's problem into problem (17.1) subject to (17.2), we set $m_{t+1}/p = a_{t+1}$, $w = 1$, $b = 0$, and $r = 0$, where m_{t+1} be the money holdings from t to $t+1$ and p is a constant price level. The fixed money supply is M. The market-clearing condition for a stationary equilibrium is given by

$$Ea(0) = \frac{M}{p}.$$

This condition determines the equilibrium price level p, which is a version of the quantity theory of money.

If we relax the borrowing constraint from $b = 0$ to permit some borrowing ($b > 0$), the $Ea(r)$ curve shifts to the left, causing $Ea(0)$ to fall and the equilibrium price level p to rise. Borrowing means that households can issue private IOUs or "inside money." Thus expanding the amount of "inside money" by substituting outside money causes the value of outside money to fall. When b is sufficiently large, e.g., $b > Ea(0;0)$, then $Ea(0;b) < 0$ by proposition 17.2.1. The interest rate on inside money must rise to clear the market. In this case inside money dominates fiat money in rate of return and drives it out of the market. One way to get fiat money back into the model is to pay interest on it.

17.2.3 Interest on Currency

Bewley (1980, 1983) shows that paying interest on currency could improve welfare in a stationary equilibrium, but the interest payment could not implement an optimal allocation. We now formalize his argument. Suppose that households cannot borrow ($b = 0$). The budget constraint is given by

$$\frac{m_{t+1}}{p_t} + c_t \leq \frac{(1+\tilde{r})\, m_t}{p_t} + wl_t - \tau,$$

where $m_{t+1} \geq 0$ is currency carried over from t to $t+1$, p_t is the price level at t, $\tilde{r}$ is nominal interest on currency paid by the government, and τ is a real lump-sum tax. This tax is used to finance the interest payments on currency. The government budget constraint is given by

$$\tau p_t + M_{t+1} = M_t + \tilde{r} M_t, \tag{17.9}$$

where M_t is the money supply.

There are two settings of the model: one where the government pays explicit interest while keeping the nominal stock of currency fixed; another where the government pays no explicit interest but decreases money supply to pay interest through deflation. For each setting, we can show that paying interest on money with the nonnegativity constraint on money holdings can be viewed as a device for weakening the impact of this constraint. Relaxing borrowing constraint improves welfare. We establish this point for each setting by showing that the household's problem is isomorphic with problem (17.1) subject to (17.2) and (17.3).

Explicit Interest   In the first setting, the government sets fixed money supply $M_t = M_{t+1}$ for all t and tries to support a constant price level. There is no government spending or other taxes. This makes the government budget constraint become

$$\tau = \frac{\tilde{r} M}{p}. \tag{17.10}$$

Substituting (17.10) into the household's budget constraint and rearranging gives

$$\frac{m_{t+1}}{p} + c_t \leq \frac{(1 + \tilde{r}) m_t}{p} + w l_t - \frac{\tilde{r} M}{p}, \quad m_{t+1} \geq 0.$$

The market-clearing condition is given by

$$E \frac{m_{t+1}}{p} = \frac{M}{p}, \tag{17.11}$$

which determines the equilibrium price level p. The lump-sum taxes τ in equation (17.10) determines the interest rate $\tilde{r}$.

To map the household's problem into problem (17.1) subject to (17.2), we set $m_{t+1}/p = \hat{a}_{t+1} \geq 0$, $\phi = M/p$, and $r = \tilde{r}$. Given this mapping, the solution of the household problem in an economy with aggregate real balances of M/p and with nominal interest $\tilde{r}$ on currency can be read from the solution of the household problem in an economy with the real interest rate $\tilde{r}$ and a borrowing constraint parameter $\phi = M/p$. Let the solution of the latter problem be given by the policy function $a_{t+1} = g(a_t, l_t; \tilde{r}, \phi)$. Because we have set $m_{t+1}/p = \hat{a}_{t+1} = a_{t+1} + \phi$, the market-clearing condition in the Bewley model (17.11) is equivalent to $Ea(\tilde{r}) = 0$, which is the market-clearing condition in the Huggett model. We then have the following result:

Proposition 17.2.2   *A stationary equilibrium for the Bewley model with interest on currency financed by lump-sum taxes has the same allocation and interest rate as an equilibrium of Huggett's model for debt limit ϕ equaling the equilibrium real balances in the Bewley model.*

We can use a "back-solving" method to compute an equilibrium with interest on currency.[4] This method consists of the following steps:

Step 1.   Set ϕ to satisfy $0 \leq \phi \leq wl_{\min}/\tilde{r}$. Solve for $p = M/\phi$.
Step 2.   Find $\tilde{r}$ such that $Ea(\tilde{r}) = 0$.
Step 3.   Compute taxes $\tau = \tilde{r}M/p$.

Instead of taking τ as exogenous and M/p as endogenous, the method above takes $\phi = M/p$ as exogenous but τ as endogenous.

The largest level of real balances M/p that can be supported in a stationary equilibrium is equal to $wl_{\min}/\tilde{r}$, which is the natural borrowing limit in the Huggett model. The equilibrium interest rate $\tilde{r}$ can be read from the intersection of the $Ea(r)$ curve and the vertical axis in figure 17.3. As b increases, the $Ea(r)$ curve shifts to the left. The highest interest rate in the Bewley model is determined by the point where $Ea(r)$ curve for the natural borrowing limit passes through the vertical axis. This is higher than the equilibrium interest rate associated with any of the ad hoc borrowing limits, but it must be below $1/\beta - 1$. Note that $1/\beta - 1$ is the interest rate associated with the optimal quantity of money proposed by the Friedman rule. We then have the following result:

Proposition 17.2.3   *The highest interest rate that can be supported by paying interest on currency equals that associated with the Huggett model with the natural borrowing limit. This interest rate is less than the rate of time preference.*

Implicit Interest   In the second setting, there is no explicit interest on currency, but the government can pay interest implicitly through deflation. The government can change money supply according to

$$M_{t+1} = M_t(1+g).$$

---

4. See Sims (1989) and Díaz-Giménez et al. (1992) for applications of this method.

This is equivalent to

$$\frac{M_{t+1}}{p_t} = \frac{M_t}{p_{t-1}} \frac{p_{t-1}}{p_t} (1+g).$$

We seek a steady state with constant real balances $M_{t+1}/p_t = M_t/p_{t-1}$ and constant inflation rate $p_t/p_{t-1} = 1/(1+r)$. Such a steady state and the equation above imply that $1+r = 1/(1+g)$. By (17.9) with $\tilde{r} = 0$, the implied lump-sum tax is equal to

$$\tau = -\frac{gM_t}{p_t} = -\frac{gM_t}{p_{t-1}} \frac{p_{t-1}}{p_t} = \frac{M_t}{p_{t-1}} r.$$

The household's budget constraint with taxes set in this way becomes

$$\frac{m_{t+1}}{p_t} + c_t \leq \frac{m_t}{p_t} + wl_t - \frac{M_t}{p_{t-1}} r.$$

This matches the Huggett model with $\phi = M_t/p_{t-1}$. Given this formulation, the steady-state equilibrium is just as though explicit interest were paid on currency. The intersection of the $Ea(r)$ curve with the vertical axis determines the real interest rate. Given the parameter ϕ setting the borrowing limit, the interest rate equals that for the economy with explicit interest on currency. For the equilibrium interest rate $r > 0$ to be positive, the government must retire money at the rate $r/(1+r)$ so that deflation occurs.

17.2.4   Seigniorage

Suppose that there is no tax, but the government can issue money to finance a fixed aggregate flow of real purchases G. Suppose that households cannot borrow so that $\phi = b = 0$. The government budget constraint becomes

$$\frac{M_{t+1}}{p_t} = \frac{M_t}{p_t} + G,$$

which can be expressed as

$$\frac{M_{t+1}}{p_t} = \frac{M_t}{p_{t-1}} \frac{p_{t-1}}{p_t} + G.$$

We want to find a stationary equilibrium with $p_{t-1}/p_t = 1+r$ for $t \geq 1$ and $M_{t+1}/p_t = \bar{m}$ for $t \geq 0$. For this equilibrium

$$\bar{m} = -\frac{G}{r}.$$

For $G > 0$ this is a rectangular hyperbola in the southeast quadrant as illustrated in figure 17.4. A stationary equilibrium value of r is determined at the intersection of this curve with the $Ea(r)$ curve. Clearly, when $G > 0$, the equilibrium net interest

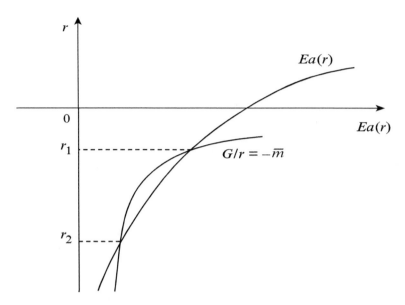

Figure 17.4
Two stationary equilibrium rates of return on currency that finance the constant government deficit G

rate $r < 0$; $-r$ can be regarded as an inflation tax. Notice that there may be multiple stationary equilibria as revealed by figure 17.4.

After r is determined, the initial price level is determined by the initial government budget constraint:

$$\bar{m} = \frac{M_0}{p_0} + G,$$

provided that M_0 is exogenously given. This is a version of the quantity theory of money. An increase in M_0 increases p_0 and all subsequent prices proportionately.

Which one should we select from multiple equilibria? Ljungqvist and Sargent (2004) recommend choosing the one with the highest rate of return on currency or with the lowest inflation tax. This selection gives the standard comparative statics: increasing G causes r to fall and inflation to rise. This selection can be justified by a learning procedure in related settings studied by Marcet and Sargent (1989) and Bruno and Fischer (1990).

Note that if we allow borrowing by setting $b > 0$, then raising b causes the $Ea(r)$ curve to shift to the left, and lowers r. It is even possible for such an increase in b to cause all stationary equilibria to vanish. This result explains why governments intent on raising seigniorage might want to restrict private borrowing.

17.3   Aggregate Shocks

The models in the previous sections focus on stationary equilibrium, which are useful to study the steady-state properties of cross-sectional objects such as the wealth distribution. However, these models are not useful for understanding business cycles. In this section we introduce aggregate shocks into these models following Krusell and Smith (1998). Models with both aggregate and idiosyncratic shocks with a continuum of agents are hard to compute numerically because the cross-sectional distribution is an infinite-dimensional state variable. We will present an algorithm proposed by Krusell and Smith (1998).

17.3.1   Recursive Equilibrium

We want to introduce aggregate productivity shocks z_t into the Aiyagari (1994) model studied in section 17.1. Let the production function be

$$Y_t = z_t F(K_t, L_t),$$

where the joint process $(z_t, l_t)_{t \geq 0}$ follows a (discrete) Markov process with transition function $Q(\cdot, \cdot; z, l)$. The aggregate shock (z_t) and the idiosyncratic shock (l_t) may be correlated. Let the state space for the individual states (a, l) be S.

Definition 17.3.1 *A recursive (competitive) equilibrium consists of a value function $V(k, l; \lambda, z)$, a policy function $g(a, l; \lambda, z)$, a law of motion $G(\lambda, z; z')$, and pricing functions $r(\lambda, z)$ and $w(\lambda, z)$, such that:*

a. given $G(\lambda, z; z')$, $r(\lambda, z)$ and $w(\lambda, z)$, g and V solve the Bellman equation:

$$V(a, l; \lambda, z) = \max_{a'} u(c) + \beta \int V(a', l'; \lambda', z') Q(dz', dl'; z, l)$$

subject to

$$c + a' = (1 + r(\lambda, z)) a + w(\lambda, z) l, \quad a' \geq 0,$$

$$\lambda' = G(\lambda, z; z').$$

b. firms maximize profits so that

$$z F_K(K, L) = r(\lambda, z) + \delta,$$

$$z F_L(K, L) = w(\lambda, z).$$

c. markets clear,

$$K = \int a \lambda(da, dl),$$

$$L = \int l \lambda(da, dl).$$

d. *the law of motion for the aggregate distribution G is generated by the individual optimal policy g, that is, for all Borel sets $A \times B$ on S,*

$$G(\lambda, z; z')(A \times B) = \int 1_A(g(a,l; \lambda, z)) Q(z', B, z, l) \lambda(da, dl).$$

Note that if the aggregate shock and the individual shock are independent, then we can write the transition function for the joint process (z_t, l_t) as

$$Q(\cdot, \cdot, z, l) = Q_l(\cdot, l) Q_z(\cdot, z),$$

where Q_l and Q_z are the transition functions for (l_t) and (z_t), respectively. In this case the law of motion $G(\lambda, z; z')$ does not depend on z'.

A recursive equilibrium induces a sequential competitive equilibrium as follows:

$$a_{t+1} = g(a_t, l_t; \lambda_t, z_t),$$

$$w_t = w(\lambda_t, z_t) = z_t F_L(K_t, L_t),$$

$$r_t = r(\lambda_t, z_t) = z_t F_K(K_t, L_t) - \delta,$$

$$K_t = \int a_t \lambda_t(da_t, dl_t),$$

$$L_t = \int l_t \lambda_t(da_t, dl_t),$$

$$\lambda_{t+1} = G(\lambda_t, z_t; z_{t+1}),$$

for all $t \geq 0$. The initial values $(a_0, l_0, \lambda_0, z_0)$ are given. The existence of a recursive equilibrium is an open question. Miao (2006) proves the existence of a sequential competitive equilibrium. Inspired by Duffie et al. (1994), he also provides a recursive characterization, which includes an addition state variable—the distribution of continuation values. Kubler and Schmedders (2002) construct an example of an incomplete markets model with a finite number of agents, which does not have a recursive equilibrium with the natural state space as defined in 17.3.1.

17.3.2   Krusell–Smith Method

Since the aggregate distribution is an infinite-dimensional state variable, one has to find an efficient way to approximate this distribution in the dynamic programming problem. Krusell and Smith (1998) propose to approximate the distribution by a set of moments, which are finite-dimensional objects.

Let $\mathbf{m}$ be an I-dimensional vector of the first I moments (mean, variance, skewness, kurtosis, etc.) of the wealth distribution, namely the marginal of λ with respect to a. Replace λ with the vector $\mathbf{m} = \{m_1, ..., m_I\}$ whose law of motion is given by

$$\mathbf{m}' = H_I(\mathbf{m}, z).$$

To make this method operational, we need to choose the number I and specify a functional form for H_I. Krusell and Smith (1998) show that one obtains an accurate solution by simply setting $I = 1$ and by specifying a law of motion of the form

$$\ln K' = b_z^0 + b_z^1 \ln K, \tag{17.12}$$

where only the first moment $m_1 = K$ matters to predict the first moment next period. Moreover the law of motion does not depend on z' since capital is predetermined.

The agent's decision problem becomes

$$V(a, l; K, z) = \max_{a'} u(c) + \beta E\left[V(a', l'; K', z') \,|\, z, l\right] \tag{17.13}$$

subject to (17.12) and

$$c + a' = (1 + r(K, L, z))\, a + w(K, L, z)\, l, \quad a' \geq 0,$$

where r and w satisfy

$$z F_K(K, L) = r(K, L, z) + \delta,$$
$$z F_L(K, L) = w(K, L, z).$$

Now we describe the Krusell and Smith algorithm.

Step 1. Guess the coefficients of the law of motion $\{b_z^0, b_z^1\}$ for each z.
Step 2. Solve the household's dynamic programming problem (17.13) and obtain the decision rule $a' = g(a, l; K, z)$.
Step 3. Simulate the economy for N individuals and T periods. For example, $N = 100,000$ and $T = 2,000$. Draw a random sequence for the aggregate shocks $\{z_t\}$ and a random sequence for the individual productivity shocks $\{l_t^i\}$ for each $i = 1, 2, ..., N$ conditional on the path for the aggregate shocks. Use the decision rule g to recursively generate sequences of asset holdings $\{a_t^i\}_{i=1}^N$, $t = 1, 2, ..., T$, and in each period compute the average capital stock

$$\bar{K}_t = \frac{1}{N} \sum_{i=1}^N a_t^i.$$

Step 4. Discard the first T_0 periods (e.g., $T_0 = 500$) to avoid dependence from the initial conditions. Using the remaining sequence, run the regression

$$\ln \bar{K}_{t+1} = \beta_z^0 + \beta_z^1 \ln \bar{K}_t$$

to estimate $\left(\beta_z^0, \beta_z^1\right)$ for each z.

Step 5. If $\left(\beta_z^0, \beta_z^1\right) \neq \left(b_z^0, b_z^1\right)$, then try a new guess and go back to step 1. If the two pairs are sufficiently close for each z, then it means that the approximate law of motion used by the agents is consistent with the one generated in equilibrium by aggregating individual choices.

Step 6. To verify whether this approximation is accurate, compute a measure of the fit of the regression in step 4, for example, by using R^2. Next try augmenting the state space with another moment, for example, using the sample second moments m_{2t} of $\{a_t^i\}$ from step 3. Repeat steps 1 to 5 until convergence. If the R^2 of the regression above has improved significantly, keep adding moments until R^2 is large enough and does not respond to addition of new explanatory moments.

An important finding of Krusell and Smith (1998) is the approximate aggregation result that the behavior of the macroeconomic aggregates can be almost perfectly described using the mean of the wealth distribution. Why do we get near-aggregation in practice? There are three reasons. First, the asset-holdings policy functions for this class of problems usually display lots of curvature for low levels of individual shocks and low levels of assets, but beyond this region they are almost linear. Second, the agents with this high curvature are few and have low wealth, so they matter very little in determining aggregate wealth. What matters for the determination of the aggregate capital stock are the ones who hold large capital, meaning the rich, not the poor! Third, aggregate productivity shocks move the wealth distribution only very slightly, and the mass of the distribution is always where the asset holdings functions are linear.

There are several other methods to solve the Krusell and Smith type models. We refer the reader to the special issue edited by den Haan, Judd, and Juillard (2009) in *Journal of Economic Dynamics and Control*.

17.4 Exercises

1. Write a computer code to solve the Aiyagari (1994) model. Try to replicate the results in his paper.

2. Write a computer code to solve the Huggett (1993) model. Try to replicate the results in his paper.

3. Write a computer code to solve the Krusell and Smith (1998) model. Try to replicate the results in their paper.

4. Introduce endogenous leisure in the Aiyagari (1994) model and define a stationary equilibrium.

5. Introduce endogenous leisure in the Krusell and Smith (1998) model and define a recursive equilibrium.

6. (Imrohoroglu 1992) There is a continuum of households. Each household has a utility function given by

$$
E \sum_{t=0}^{\infty} \beta^t \frac{c_t^{1-\gamma}}{1-\gamma}.
$$

Agents are endowed with one indivisible unit of time in each period and face an employment opportunity that is independent across agents. The employment state, l, is assumed to follow a first-order Markov process with two possible states, $l = u$ and $l = e$, that stand for unemployed and employed, respectively. Transition probabilities for this process are given by $\pi_{ll'}$. If the employed state $l = e$ occurs, an agent produces $y_t = y$ units of the consumption good using the time allocation. In the unemployed state $l = u$, an agent produces $y_t = \theta y$ units of consumption good through household production, where $0 < \theta < 1$. Individuals enter each period with individual nominal money balances equal to m_t that are carried over from the previous period. These balances are augmented with a lump-sum transfer equal to gM_t, where M_t is the per capita nominal money supply at time t and g is the constant growth rate of money supply. The money supply follows the law of motion

$$
M_{t+1} = (1+g)M_t.
$$

The household budget constraint is given by

$$
c_t + \frac{m_{t+1}}{p_t} = \frac{m_t}{p_t} + \frac{gM_t}{p_t} + y_t, \quad m_{t+1} \geq 0.
$$

a. Write down the household's dynamic programming problem.

b. Define a stationary equilibrium.

c. Write down a computer code to solve the model numerically. Try to replicate the results in Imrohoroglu (1992). Estimate the welfare cost of inflation.

18   Search and Matching Models of Unemployment

So far we have focused on the neoclassical theory of the labor market. This means that the labor supply is determined by a household's utility maximization problem and the labor demand is determined by a firm's profit maximization problem. In both problems the wage rate is taken as given in a competitive labor market and the equilibrium wage is determined by the market-clearing condition: the labor supply is equal to the labor demand. This approach suffers from two major limitations. First, it cannot explain the magnitude of the observed fluctuations in hours worked. By neoclassical theory, the marginal rate of substitution between leisure and consumption is equal to the marginal product of labor, after adjusting for labor and consumption taxes. However, this relationship does not hold in the data (e.g., see Rotemberg and Woodford 1991, 1999; Hall 1997; Chari, Kehoe, and McGrattan 2007). In particular, there is a labor wedge between the marginal rate of substitution and the marginal product of labor. Second, the neoclassical approach delivers predictions of hours worked but not unemployment. Thus this approach cannot explain the empirical fact that most cyclical movements in the aggregate amount of hours worked are accounted for by movements between employment and unemployment, not by movements in hours worked by employed workers.

In this chapter we introduce the search and matching theory developed by Diamond (1982), Mortensen (1982), and Pissarides (1985) (henceforth, DMP). This theory can potentially overcome the two limitations mentioned above. Its key idea is that it takes time for an unemployed worker to find a job and for a vacancy to be filled by a worker. Moreover the wage rate is not determined in a centralized market. Rather, it is determined by bilateral bargaining. This theory can be used to account for unemployment. However, it still faces several difficulties in accounting for some labor market facts quantitatively. For example, the standard DMP model assumes that job destruction is exogenous. But empirical evidence shows that both job creation and job destruction respond to exogenous shocks. Mortensen and Pissarides (1994) introduce endogenous job destruction in the DMP framework.

In addition the standard DMP model cannot explain the large cyclical movements of the labor wedge, unemployment, and vacancies observed in the data (Shimer 2005; Hall 2005). Thus modification of this model is needed. As Shimer (2005) and Hall (2005) argue, introducing wage rigidity is important. We refer the reader to Shimer (2010) for a thorough treatment of this issue and to Pissarides (2000) for a textbook treatment of the search and matching theory of unemployment.

18.1   A Basic DMP Model

We start with a basic search and matching model with exogenous separation based on Pissarides (1985, 2000). Consider an infinite-horizon setup without aggregate uncertainty. There is a continuum of identical workers of unit measure. Each worker is infinitely lived and derive utility from consumption $\{C_t\}$ according to the function $\sum_{t=0}^{\infty} \beta^t C_t$, where $\beta \in (0,1)$.

The production technology has constant returns to scale, with labor as the only input. The marginal productivity of labor is denoted by A. Suppose that each firm employs at most one worker. A firm can enter the economy by posting a vacancy at the cost κ. Once a worker finds a match with a firm, the firm and the worker negotiate a wage w_t and the firm generates profits $A - w_t$. All matches resolve in the end of the period with an exogenously given probability ρ.

The measure of total successful matches in period t is given by a matching function $m_t = M(u_t, v_t)$, where u_t and v_t are the aggregate measures of unemployed workers and vacancies. Assume that the matching function is increasing in both arguments, concave, and linearly homogeneous. Then the probability that an unemployed worker finds a job (the job-finding rate) is given by $q_t^u = m_t/u_t$ and the probability that an open vacancy is filled (the job-filling rate) is given by $q_t^v = m_t/v_t$. Assume that the matched relationship starts to produce in the next period.

Define the market tightness by $\theta_t = v_t/u_t$. Then by the linear homogeneity property,

$$q_t^v = \frac{M(u_t, v_t)}{v_t} \equiv q(\theta_t), \quad q_t^u = \frac{M(u_t, v_t)}{u_t} \equiv q(\theta_t)\,\theta_t, \tag{18.1}$$

where it follows from the properties of the matching function M that $q'(\theta) < 0$ and $d\ln q(\theta)/d\ln\theta \in (-1,0)$. Intuitively, when the labor market is tighter, it is harder for a firm to meet a worker and it is easier for a worker to find a job. Denote by N_t the aggregate employment rate. Then N_t takes the following dynamics:

$$N_{t+1} = (1 - \rho)N_t + M(u_t, v_t), \quad N_0 \text{ given.} \tag{18.2}$$

Define the unemployment rate as

$$u_t = 1 - N_t. \tag{18.3}$$

Suppose that the wage rate w_t is determined in a Nash bargain between a matched firm and worker. To describe this bargaining problem, we need to derive the surplus to the worker and the firm. Let J_t^F be the value to a filled job and V_t be the value to a vacancy. Then J_t^F and V_t satisfy the asset-pricing equations

$$J_t^F = A - w_t + \beta \left(\rho V_{t+1} + (1 - \rho) J_{t+1}^F \right), \tag{18.4}$$

$$V_t = -\kappa + \beta \left[q_t^v J_{t+1}^F + (1 - q_t^v) V_{t+1} \right]. \tag{18.5}$$

Competition drives the value to a vacancy to zero so that $V_t = 0$ for all t. It follows from (18.5) that

$$J_{t+1}^F = \frac{\kappa}{\beta q_t^v}. \tag{18.6}$$

Substituting into (18.4) yields

$$J_t^F = A - w_t + \frac{(1 - \rho) \kappa}{q_t^v}. \tag{18.7}$$

Combining the preceding two equations yields

$$\frac{\kappa}{q_t^v} = \beta \left(A - w_{t+1} + \frac{(1 - \rho) \kappa}{q_{t+1}^v} \right). \tag{18.8}$$

Let J_t^W and J_t^U denote the values to an employed and an unemployed worker, respectively. Then they satisfy the following asset pricing equations:

$$J_t^W = w_t + \beta \left(\rho J_{t+1}^U + (1 - \rho) J_{t+1}^W \right), \tag{18.9}$$

$$J_t^U = b + \beta \left[q_t^u J_{t+1}^W + (1 - q_t^u) J_{t+1}^U \right], \tag{18.10}$$

where b denotes unemployment insurance benefits, which are financed by lump-sum taxes. One may interpret b broadly as nonmarket income.

The Nash bargaining problem is given by

$$\max_{w_t} \left(J_t^W - J_t^U \right)^\eta \left(J_t^F - V_t \right)^{1-\eta} \tag{18.11}$$

subject to $J_t^W \geq J_t^U$ and $J_t^F \geq V_t = 0$, where $\eta \in (0, 1)$ denotes the worker's bargain power. The first-order condition gives

$$\eta J_t^F = (1 - \eta) \left(J_t^W - J_t^U \right).$$

Define total surplus by

$$S_t = J_t^F + J_t^W - J_t^U.$$

It follows that

$$\eta S_t = J_t^W - J_t^U, \tag{18.12}$$

$$(1 - \eta) S_t = J_t^F = \frac{\kappa}{\beta q_{t-1}^v}, \tag{18.13}$$

where the last equality in (18.13) follows from the free entry condition (18.6).

By (18.4), (18.9), and (18.10), S_t satisfies the asset-pricing equation

$$\begin{aligned}
S_t &= A - b + \beta (1 - \rho) S_{t+1} - \beta q_t^u \left(J_{t+1}^W - J_{t+1}^U \right) \\
&= A - b + \beta (1 - \rho - \eta q_t^u) S_{t+1} \\
&= A - b + \frac{\kappa (1 - \rho - \eta q_t^u)}{(1 - \eta) q_t^v},
\end{aligned} \tag{18.14}$$

where the second equality follows from (18.12) and the last equality follows from (18.13). Thus

$$\begin{aligned}
\eta S_t = J_t^W - J_t^U &= w_t - b + \beta (1 - \rho - q_t^u) \left(J_{t+1}^W - J_{t+1}^U \right) \\
&= w_t - b + \beta (1 - \rho - q_t^u) \eta S_{t+1},
\end{aligned}$$

where the second equality follows from (18.9) and (18.10) and the last equality follows from (18.12). Substituting (18.14) for S_t and (18.13) for S_{t+1} into the equation above and solving for w_t yield

$$w_t = \eta (A + \kappa \theta_t) + (1 - \eta) b. \tag{18.15}$$

Note that this solution implies that any firm and worker match offers the same wage w_t because it depends only on the aggregate variables.

A search equilibrium consists of sequences of allocations $\{N_t, u_t, v_t, \theta_t\}$, wage $\{w_t\}$, and the job filling rate $\{q_t^v\}$ such that equations (18.1), (18.2), (18.3), (18.8), and (18.15) are satisfied.

18.1.1   Steady State

Consider the steady state in which all variables are constant over time. We write the steady-state version of equation (18.8) as

$$\frac{\kappa}{q(\theta)} (1 - \beta (1 - \rho)) = \beta (A - w). \tag{18.16}$$

This equation gives a relationship between θ and w. We plot this relation in figure 18.1 and call it the job creation curve. In the (θ, w) space it slopes down: higher wage rate makes job creation less profitable and thus leads to a lower equilibrium ratio of new hires to unemployed workers. It replaces the demand curve of Walrasian economics.

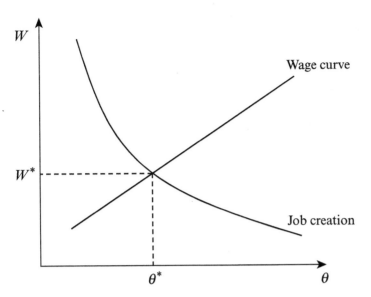

Figure 18.1
Steady-state equilibrium market tightness and wage

We can write the steady-state version of equation (18.15) as

$$w = \eta \left(A + \kappa\theta \right) + \left(1 - \eta \right) b. \tag{18.17}$$

This equation also gives a relationship between θ and w. We plot this relation in figure 18.1 and call it the wage curve. This curve slopes up: at higher market tightness the relative bargaining strength of market participants shifts in favor of workers. It replaces the supply curve of Walrasian economics.

The intersection of the wage and job creation curves gives the steady-state equilibrium (θ^*, w^*). In particular, if we eliminate w, we can show that θ^* is the unique solution to the following equation:

$$\frac{\kappa}{q\left(\theta\right)} \left(1 - \beta\left(1 - \rho\right) \right) + \beta\eta\kappa\theta = \beta\left(1 - \eta\right)\left(A - b\right). \tag{18.18}$$

Given the solution θ, we plot the job creation curve $v = u\theta$ in figure 18.2. We write the steady-state version of the employment dynamics (18.2) as

$$\rho\left(1 - u\right) = M\left(u, v\right), \tag{18.19}$$

which gives the so-called **Beveridge curve** for (u, v) in figure 18.2. By the property of the matching function, it is downward sloping and convex. The intersection of the job creation curve and the Beveridge curve determines the steady-state equilibrium vacancy and unemployment rates.

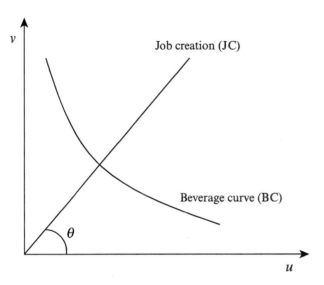

Figure 18.2
Steady-state equilibrium vacancies and unemployment

These two figures are useful for understanding comparative statics properties of the model. First, consider the impact of an increase in productivity A. It shifts the job creation curve in figure 18.1 to the right and shifts the wage curve up. Since $0 < \eta < 1$, the job creation curve shifts by more, so both wages and market tightness increase. In figure 18.2 this rotates the job creation line anticlockwise, increasing vacancies and reducing unemployment. Next consider the impact of an increase in the unemployment benefit b. It shifts the wage curve up but does not change the job creation curve in figure 18.1. Thus it raises the wage and lowers market tightness. In addition it rotates the job creation curve in figure 18.2 down, thereby increasing the unemployment rate and reducing the vacancy rate. The effect of an increase in the worker bargaining power η has a similar result.

18.1.2   Transitional Dynamics
Now we turn to transitional dynamics. Substituting equation (18.15) into equation (18.8) yields the dynamic job creation equation

$$\frac{\kappa}{q\left(\theta_t\right)} = \beta \left((1-\eta)\left(A-b\right) - \eta\kappa\theta_{t+1} + \frac{(1-\rho)\,\kappa}{q\left(\theta_{t+1}\right)} \right). \tag{18.20}$$

We next rewrite the employment dynamics equation (18.2) as

$$u_{t+1} = \left(1 - \rho - q\left(\theta_t\right)\theta_t\right)u_t + \rho, \quad u_0 \text{ given.} \tag{18.21}$$

We then obtain a system of two differential equations for two unknowns (u_t, θ_t). To analyze the stability of the system, we linearize it around the steady state (u^*, θ^*):

$$\begin{bmatrix} d\theta_{t+1} \\ du_{t+1} \end{bmatrix} = \begin{bmatrix} a_{11} & 0 \\ a_{21} & a_{22} \end{bmatrix} \begin{bmatrix} d\theta_t \\ du_t \end{bmatrix},$$

where

$$a_{11} = \frac{q'(\theta^*)/q^2(\theta^*)}{\beta(1-\rho)q'(\theta^*)/q^2(\theta^*) + \beta\eta},$$
$$a_{21} = uq(\theta^*)[1 - \xi(\theta^*)],$$
$$a_{22} = 1 - \rho - q(\theta^*)\theta^*,$$

where we define the elasticity of $q(\theta)$ as $\xi(\theta) = -\theta q'(\theta)/q(\theta)$. We can check that $\xi(\theta) \in (0,1)$. Note that u_t is predetermined, but θ_t is non-predetermined. Suppose that $1 - \rho - \eta q(\theta^*)\theta^*/\xi(\theta^*) > 0$. Then $a_{11} > 1$. We can also check that $a_{22} \in (-1,1)$ and $a_{21} > 0$. Thus the steady state is a local saddle point. Because the equation for θ_t does not depend on N_t, the solution for θ_t is constant over time.

Figure 18.3 gives the phase diagram for (u_t, θ_t). Clearly, the locus $\Delta u_t = u_{t+1} - u_t = 0$ is downward sloping and the locus $\Delta\theta_t = 0$ is a horizontal line. If the initial unemployment rate is u_0, then the market tightness immediately jumps to the saddle path on the locus $\Delta\theta_t = \theta_{t+1} - \theta_t = 0$. During the transition path, θ_t is constant,

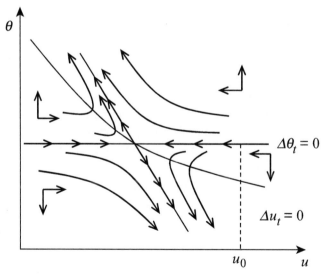

Figure 18.3
Phase diagram

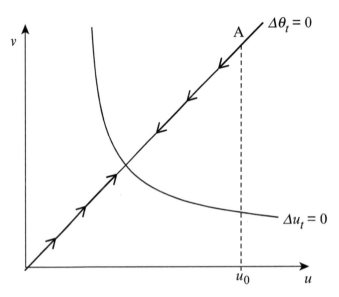

Figure 18.4
Adjustments of vacancies and unemployment

but u_t falls until reaching the steady state. Figure 18.4 shows the adjustment of vacancies. Vacancy initial jumps higher than its steady-state value and then gradually falls by keeping the market tightness constant over time.

18.1.3 Large Firms

So far we have assumed that each firm has only one worker. Now we assume that each firm has many workers. There is a continuum of firms of measure unity. The timing is as follows: At the beginning of period t, there are N_t^j workers in firm j. The firm produces output AN_t^j and engages in Nash bargaining with each employee separately, by taking the wages of all other employees as given. After production and paying the wage rate w_t, the job separation occurs whereby the firm loses a fraction ρ of workers. After separation, the firm posts v_t^j vacancies. These vacancies are filled with probability q_t^v so that at the end of period t, the firm has workers N_{t+1}^j given by

$$N_{t+1}^j = (1 - \rho)\, N_t^j + q_t^v v_t^j. \tag{18.22}$$

Define aggregate employment and aggregate vacancies as $N_t = \int N_t^j dj$ and $v_t = \int v_t^j dj$. The job-filling rate q_t^v and the job-finding rate q_t^u are defined in (18.1). The aggregate law of motion for N_t is given by (18.2).

Firm j's problem is given by

$$\max_{\left\{N_t^j, v_t^j\right\}} \sum_{t=0}^{\infty} \beta^t \left(AN_t^j - w_t N_t^j - v_t^j \kappa \right)$$

subject to (18.22). The first-order conditions are given by

$$v_t^j : -\kappa + \mu_t q_t^v = 0, \tag{18.23}$$

$$N_t^j : (A - w_t) + \mu_t (1 - \rho) - \beta^{-1} \mu_{t-1} = 0,$$

where $\beta^t \mu_t$ is the Lagrange multiplier associated with (18.22). Combining the two equations yields

$$\frac{\kappa}{q_t^v} = \beta \left(A - w_{t+1} + \frac{(1 - \rho) \kappa}{q_{t+1}^v} \right).$$

This equation is identical to (18.8). Note that equation (18.23) plays the same role as the free-entry condition (18.6), which determines the equilibrium number of vacancies. Moreover the firm takes $q_t^v = q(\theta_t)$ or the market tightness θ_t as given when solving an individual firm problem. This causes an externality to other firms.

We can write a firm's problem by dynamic programming:

$$J_t \left(N_t^j \right) = \max_{v_t^j} AN_t^j - w_t N_t^j - v_t^j \kappa + \beta J_{t+1} \left(N_{t+1}^j \right)$$

subject to (18.22). By the envelope condition,

$$\frac{\partial J_t \left(N_t^j \right)}{\partial N_t^j} = A - w_t + (1 - \rho) \mu_t = A - w_t + \frac{(1 - \rho) \kappa}{q_t^v} = J_t^F, \tag{18.24}$$

where the last equality follows from (18.7). Consider the firm's marginal value if it has additional ε workers at the end of period $t - 1$ before separation occurs. Let w be the wage rate bargained between the firm and the additional workers. The Bellman equation is given by

$$J_t \left(N_t^j + \varepsilon \right) = \max_{v_t^j} A \left(N_t^j + \varepsilon \right) - w_t N_t^j - w\varepsilon - v_t^j \kappa + \beta J_{t+1} \left(N_{t+1}^j \right)$$

subject to

$$N_{t+1}^j = (1 - \rho) \left(N_t^j + \varepsilon \right) + q_t^v v_t^j. \tag{18.25}$$

By the envelope condition,

$$\frac{\partial J_t \left(N_t^j \right)}{\partial \varepsilon} \Big|_{\varepsilon=0} = A - w + (1 - \rho) \beta \frac{\partial J_{t+1} \left(N_{t+1}^j \right)}{\partial N_{t+1}^j}.$$

The first-order condition with respect to v_t^j is given by

$$\kappa = \beta \frac{\partial J_{t+1}\left(N_{t+1}^j\right)}{\partial N_{t+1}^j} q_t^v.$$

Using the preceding two equations and (18.24) yields

$$\frac{\partial J_t\left(N_t^j\right)}{\partial \varepsilon}\Big|_{\varepsilon=0} = (w_t - w) + \frac{\partial J_t\left(N_t^j\right)}{\partial N_t^j} \equiv J_n\left(w, t\right).$$

The values of an employed worker $J_t^W\left(w\right)$ and an unemployed worker $J_t^U\left(w\right)$ are the same as before except that we replace w_t by w. The wage rate w_t is determined by the Nash bargaining problem

$$w_t = \arg\max_w \; \left(J_t^W\left(w\right) - J_t^U\left(w\right)\right)^\eta J_n\left(w, t\right)^{1-\eta}. \tag{18.26}$$

This problem is equivalent to (18.11). As a result the large firm formulation and the previous formulation give an identical equilibrium outcome. Note that one can also directly derive the wage rate w_t by solving the following simpler problem:

$$\max_{w_t} \; \left(J_t^W - J_t^U\right)^\eta \left(\frac{\partial J_t\left(N_t^j\right)}{\partial N_t^j}\right)^{1-\eta}. \tag{18.27}$$

18.1.4   Efficiency

Is the decentralized search equilibrium efficient? The search equilibrium suffers from trading externalities. The externalities are shown by the dependence of the transition probabilities of unemployed workers and vacant firms on the tightness of the labor market. Imagine that there is a social planner that maximizes the social welfare subject to the same search and matching frictions as firms and workers. His problem is given by

$$\max_{\{N_t, v_t\}} \; \sum_{t=0}^{\infty} \beta^t \left(AN_t + bu_t - v_t\kappa\right),$$

subject to (18.21), (18.3), and $\theta_t = v_t/u_t$. The social planner can internalize externalities by adjusting market tightness θ_t via the choice of v_t and u_t (or N_t). The first-order conditions are given by

$$v_t : -\kappa + \mu_t \left(q\left(\theta_t\right)\theta_t\right)' = 0,$$

$$N_t : 0 = (A - b) - \beta^{-1}\mu_{t-1}$$
$$+ \mu_t \left[1 - \rho - q\left(\theta_t\right)\theta_t + \left(q\left(\theta_t\right)\theta_t\right)'\theta_t\right],$$

where $\beta^t \mu_t$ is the Lagrange multiplier associated with (18.21). We can combine the two preceding conditions and write the resulting steady-state equation as

$$\frac{\kappa}{q(\theta)}\left(1 - \beta\left(1 - \rho\right)\right) + \beta\xi\left(\theta\right)\kappa\theta = \beta\left(1 - \xi\left(\theta\right)\right)\left(A - b\right). \tag{18.28}$$

Comparing with equation (18.18), we deduce that when $\xi(\theta) = \eta$, the steady-state search equilibrium is socially efficient.

To understand the intuition behind this result, notice that $\xi(\theta)$ is the elasticity of the expected duration of a job vacancy with respect to the number of job vacancies and $1 - \xi(\theta)$ is the elasticity of the expected duration of unemployment with respect to unemployment. If $\xi(\theta)$ is high, then it means that at the margin firms are causing more congestion to other firms than workers are causing to other workers. Firms must be "taxed" by the social planner by giving workers a higher share in the wage bargain. If and only if $\xi(\theta) = \eta$, the two congestion effects offset each other.

18.2   Endogenous Job Destruction

So far we have assumed that separation is exogenous. In this section we introduce endogenous separation as in Mortensen and Pissarides (1994). Suppose that exogenous separation occurs at the end of each period with probability ρ^x. After exogenous separation at the end of period $t - 1$, each firm is subject to an idiosyncratic productivity shock z_t at the beginning of period t, which is drawn independently and identically over time and across firms from the fixed distribution $G(z)$ over $(0, \infty)$. Let the mean of z_t be 1. After observing z_t, the firm decides whether to stay with the hired worker or to separate. If it separates from the worker, the job becomes vacant and the firm obtains value V_t. It can pay a cost κ to post a vacancy and start producing in the next period. The new job's idiosyncratic productivity is also drawn from the distribution G. But if the employer stays with the worker, it produces output Az_t and bargains the wage w_t. Then we move to period $t + 1$.

Let $J_t^F(z_t)$ be the value of a filled job for the firm with idiosyncratic shock z_t. It satisfies the following Bellman equation:

$$J_t^F(z_t) = Az_t - w_t + \beta E_t\left[\left(1 - \rho^x\right)\max\left\{J_{t+1}^F(z_{t+1}), V_{t+1}\right\} + \rho^x V_{t+1}\right].$$

Clearly, there is a cutoff value z_t^* such that when $z_t \le z_t^*$, the firm and the worker separate. Thus the endogenous separation rate is given by $\rho_t^n = G(z_t^*)$ and the total separation rate is given by

$$\rho_t = \rho^x + \left(1 - \rho^x\right)\rho_t^n.$$

Aggregate employment follows dynamics

$$N_{t+1} = (1 - \rho_t) N_t + q_t^v v_t, \quad N_0 \text{ given,} \tag{18.29}$$

where $q_t^v = q(\theta_t)$ is the job-filling rate and $\theta_t = v_t/u_t$ is the market tightness. The unemployment rate is defined as $u_t = 1 - N_t$.

We can rewrite the value of a filled job as

$$J_t^F (z_t) = Az_t - w_t + \beta \left[(1 - \rho^x) \int_{z_{t+1}^*}^{\infty} \left(J_{t+1}^F (z_{t+1}) - V_{t+1} \right) dG (z_{t+1}) + V_{t+1} \right].$$

The value of a vacancy V_t satisfies

$$V_t = -\kappa + \beta \left[q_t^v \int_{z_{t+1}^*}^{\infty} \left(J_{t+1}^F (z_{t+1}) - V_{t+1} \right) dG (z_{t+1}) + V_{t+1} \right], \tag{18.30}$$

where the vacancy is filled with probability q_t^v. Free entry implies that $V_t = 0$ for all t. Thus we obtain

$$\beta \int_{z_{t+1}^*}^{\infty} J_{t+1}^F (z_{t+1}) dG (z_{t+1}) = \frac{\kappa}{q_t^v} \tag{18.31}$$

and

$$J_t^F (z_t) = Az_t - w_t + \frac{(1 - \rho^x) \kappa}{q_t^v}. \tag{18.32}$$

Moreover

$$\frac{\kappa}{q_t^v} = \beta \int_{z_{t+1}^*}^{\infty} \left(Az_{t+1} - w_{t+1} + \frac{(1 - \rho^x) \kappa}{q_{t+1}^v} \right) dG (z_{t+1}). \tag{18.33}$$

The reservation productivity z_t^* is determined by the condition $J_t^F (z_t^*) = 0$, which implies that

$$Az_t^* - w_t + \frac{(1 - \rho^x) \kappa}{q_t^v} = 0. \tag{18.34}$$

The values of an employed and an unemployed worker, respectively, satisfy the Bellman equations:

$$J_t^W (z_t) = w_t (z_t) + \beta \left[(1 - \rho^x) \int_{z_{t+1}^*}^{\infty} \left(J_{t+1}^W (z_{t+1}) - J_{t+1}^U \right) dG (z_{t+1}) + J_{t+1}^U \right], \tag{18.35}$$

$$J_t^U = b + \beta E_t \left[q_t^u \int_{z_{t+1}^*}^{\infty} \left(J_{t+1}^w (z_{t+1}) - J_{t+1}^U \right) dG (z_{t+1}) + J_{t+1}^U \right]. \tag{18.36}$$

The wage rate is determined by Nash bargaining:

$$\max_{w_t} \; \left(J_t^W\left(z_t\right) - J_t^U\right)^{\eta} \left(J_t^F\left(z_t\right)\right)^{1-\eta}.$$

The first-order condition gives

$$\eta S_t\left(z_t\right) = J_t^w\left(z_t\right) - J_t^U, \tag{18.37}$$

$$(1-\eta)\, S_t\left(z_t\right) = J_t^F\left(z_t\right) = A z_t - w_t + \frac{\left(1-\rho^x\right)\kappa}{q_t^v}, \tag{18.38}$$

where the matching surplus $S_t\left(z_t\right) = J_t^F\left(z_t\right) + J_t^W\left(z_t\right) - J_t^U$. Using (18.37), (18.35), and (18.36), we can derive

$$\eta S_t\left(z_t\right) = J_t^W\left(z_t\right) - J_t^U = w_t\left(z_t\right) - b$$
$$+ \beta\left(1-\rho^x-q_t^u\right) \int_{z_{t+1}^*}^{\infty} \left(J_{t+1}^W\left(z_{t+1}\right) - J_{t+1}^U\right) dG\left(z_{t+1}\right)$$
$$= w_t\left(z_t\right) - b + \beta\left(1-\rho^x-q_t^u\right)\eta \int_{z_{t+1}^*}^{\infty} S_{t+1}\left(z_{t+1}\right) dG\left(z_{t+1}\right).$$

Substituting (18.38) into the equation above yields

$$w_t\left(z_t\right) = (1-\eta)\,b + \eta\left(A z_t + \frac{\left(1-\rho^x\right)\kappa}{q_t^v}\right)$$
$$- \eta\beta\left(1-\rho^x-q_t^u\right) \int_{z_{t+1}^*}^{\infty} \left(A z_{t+1} - w_{t+1} + \frac{\left(1-\rho^x\right)\kappa}{q_{t+1}^v}\right) dG\left(z_{t+1}\right).$$

Plugging equation (18.33) yields the wage equation

$$w_t\left(z_t\right) = \eta\left(A z_t + \theta_t \kappa\right) + (1-\eta)\,b. \tag{18.39}$$

Note that the Nash bargained wage depends on the specific firm–worker match because it depends on z_t.

A search equilibrium consists of $\left(N_t, u_t, v_t, z_t^*, w_t\left(z_t\right)\right)$ such that equations (18.29), (18.3), (18.33), (18.34), and (18.39) hold. To solve for the equilibrium, we substitute the wage equation (18.39) into (18.32) to derive

$$J_t^F\left(z_t\right) = (1-\eta)\left(A z_t - b\right) - \eta\theta_t \kappa + \frac{\left(1-\rho^x\right)\kappa}{q_t^v}.$$

At the reservation productivity z_t^*,

$$0 = J_t^F\left(z_t^*\right) = (1-\eta)\left(A z_t^* - b\right) - \eta\theta_t \kappa + \frac{\left(1-\rho^x\right)\kappa}{q_t^v}. \tag{18.40}$$

Taking the difference between the two equations above yields

$$J_t^F(z_t) = (1 - \eta) A (z_t - z_t^*).$$

Substituting this equation into (18.31) yields

$$\frac{\kappa}{q(\theta_t)} = \beta (1 - \eta) A \int_{z_t^*}^{\infty} (z_{t+1} - z_t^*) dG(z_{t+1}), \qquad (18.41)$$

where we have used the fact that $q_t^v = q(\theta_t)$. This equation gives the job creation condition.

Substituting the preceding equation into (18.40) yields

$$\eta \theta_t \kappa = (1 - \eta)(A z_t^* - b) + \beta (1 - \rho^x)(1 - \eta) A \int_{z_t^*}^{\infty} (z_{t+1} - z_t^*) dG(z_{t+1}). \qquad (18.42)$$

We call this equation the job destruction condition. The job creation and destruction conditions (18.41) and (18.42) determine the equilibrium reservation productivity z_t^* and market tightness θ_t. These equilibrium values are constant over time. The equilibrium unemployment rate u_t is then determined by equation (18.29), which can be rewritten as

$$u_{t+1} = (1 - \rho_t - q(\theta_t) \theta_t) u_t + \rho_t, \quad u_0 \text{ given.} \qquad (18.43)$$

We introduce two new variables useful for empirical analysis. First, the job destruction rate is defined as the ratio of total job destruction to employment:

$$jd_t = \rho^x + (1 - \rho^x) G(z_t^*).$$

Second, the job creation rate is defined as the ratio of total new matches to employment:

$$jc_t = \frac{M(u_t, v_t)}{1 - u_t} = \frac{q(\theta_t) \theta_t u_t}{1 - u_t}.$$

18.2.1   Steady State

In the steady state all variables are constant over time. We can then write the steady-state job creation equation as

$$\frac{\kappa}{q(\theta)} = \beta (1 - \eta) A \int_{z^*}^{\infty} (z - z^*) dG(z). \qquad (18.44)$$

It is downward sloping. The intuition is that a higher reservation productivity implies that the match is more likely to separate. This reduces the expected present value of the job. Thus the firm posts fewer vacancies. We can also write the steady-state job destruction equation as

$$\eta\theta\kappa = (1-\eta)\,(Az^* - b) + \beta\,(1-\rho^x)\,(1-\eta)\,A\int_{z^*}^{\infty}(z-z^*)\,dG\,(z), \qquad (18.45)$$

which is upward sloping. The intuition is that at higher θ, the worker's outside opportunities are better (and wages are higher), and so more marginal jobs are destroyed. The intersection of these two curves gives the steady-state reservation productivity $\bar{z}^*$ and the market tightness θ^* as illustrated in figure 18.5.

After we determine $(\theta^*, \bar{z}^*)$, we use the Beveridge diagram to determine the steady state (u^*, v^*). The Beveridge curve is still described by equation (18.19), except that the separation rate is given by

$$\rho = \rho^x + (1-\rho^x)\,G\,(\bar{z}^*).$$

It is downward sloping and convex. Figure 18.6 plots the Beveridge curve and the job creation curve $v = \theta u$. The intersection of these two curves gives (u^*, v^*).

We now use the previous two curves to conduct a comparative statics analysis. Consider a permanent increase in productivity A. An increase in A shifts the job destruction curve in figure 18.5 down and to the right. For a given market tightness, a higher productivity raises the value of a job and makes the job less likely to be destructed. It also shifts the job creation curve to the right. A higher productivity induces the firm to post more vacancies, holding the reservation productivity

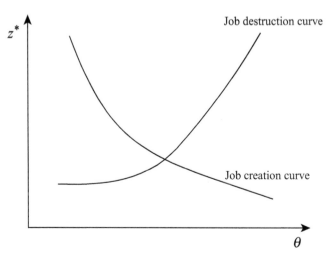

Figure 18.5
Equilibrium reservation productivity and market tightness

fixed. The net effect is to raise the market tightness. But the effect on the reservation productivity is ambiguous.

We can assume that the vacancy posting cost is proportional to the productivity, so we can replace κ with κA. This assumption is reasonable. It is intuitive that hiring a more productivity worker is more costly. In addition, if there is growth in A, this assumption ensures the existence of a balanced growth path. We will maintain this assumption in the analysis below. As a result A is canceled out on the two sides of the job creation equation (18.41). We can then deduce that an increase in A reduces the reservation productivity. At a given level of unemployment, the job destruction rate decreases, and the job creation rate increases (since market tightness ensues). Unemployment must decrease until the job creation rate falls to the level of the lower job destruction rate. Thus the steady-state effect of a higher productivity is to reduce the job creation and job destruction rates and unemployment.

Figure 18.6 shows that an increase in A rotates the job creation line counterclockwise. Additionally it shifts the Beveridge curve down. Thus it reduces unemployment, but the effect on vacancies is ambiguous. When the effect on the job creation condition is larger, an increase in A raises vacancies.

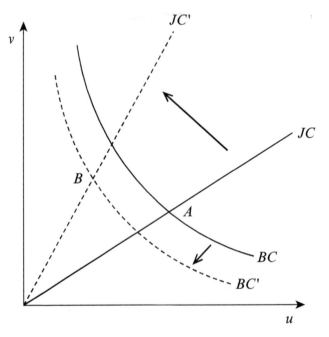

Figure 18.6
Effect of higher productivity on equilibrium vacancies and unemployment

18.2.2 Transitional Dynamics

Consider the transitional dynamics of a permanent increase in aggregate productivity A. The equilibrium system consists of three equations (18.41), (18.42), and (18.43) for three variables (θ_t, z_t^*, u_t). Note that θ_t and z_t^* are jump variables and u_t is the predetermined state variable. The steady state is a saddle point. In the absence of expected parameter changes, all three variables, z_t^*, θ_t, and u_t must be at their steady state at all times. Following a permanent increase in the aggregate productivity, the job creation rate jumps up and the job destruction rate jumps down. The job destruction rate remains at this constant lower level at all times. The unemployment rate falls until the job creation rate falls down to the level of the job destruction rate when the economy reaches a new steady state.

18.3 Unemployment and Business Cycles

In this section we embed the basic DMP model in a real business cycle framework. In particular, we incorporate risk aversion, capital accumulation, and aggregate productivity shocks. Important early contributions in this literature include Merz (1995), Andolfatto (1996), and den Haan, Ramey, and Watson (2000).

18.3.1 Households

There is a continuum of identical households of measure unity. Each household has a continuum of members of measure unity. Each member can be either employed or unemployed. An unemployed member earns nonmarket income b, and each employed member earns wage w_t. The representative household accumulates capital and rents to firms at the rental rate R_{kt}. It also owns firms and receive aggregate dividends D_t. Let N_t denote the number of employed household members. Household members pool income together and get full risk sharing within the family. Thus each member consumes the same level of consumption, denoted by C_t. The budget constraint for a representative household is given by

$$C_t + I_t = D_t + R_{kt}K_t + w_t N_t + b(1 - N_t) - T_t, \tag{18.46}$$

where T_t represents lump-sum taxes and I_t represents investment. We interpret b as unemployment benefits financed by lump-sum taxes. Capital evolves according to

$$K_{t+1} = (1 - \delta)K_t + I_t, \quad K_0 \text{ given.} \tag{18.47}$$

The household derives utility according to

$$E \sum_{t=0}^{\infty} \beta^t \left(\frac{C_t^{1-\gamma} - 1}{1 - \gamma} - \frac{\chi N_t^{1+\phi}}{1 + \phi} \right), \quad \gamma, \chi, \phi > 0.$$

We may give a microfoundation of the disutility function of work by assuming that an employed household member $j \in [0, N_t]$ derives disutility of work χj^ϕ. Then the total disutility of work is given by

$$\int_0^{N_t} \chi j^\phi dj = \frac{\chi N_t^{1+\phi}}{1+\phi}.$$

The employment rate N_t within the representative household follows dynamics

$$N_{t+1} = (1 - \rho) N_t + q_t^u u_t, \tag{18.48}$$

where $u_t = 1 - N_t$ and q_t^u represents the job-finding rate. By the matching technology in section 18.1, we obtain $q_t^u = q(\theta_t) \theta_t$, where θ_t represents market tightness. In equilibrium, since households are identical, N_t and u_t also represent aggregate employment and unemployment rates. Moreover $\theta_t = v_t / u_t$, where v_t represents aggregate vacancies.

We can write the representative household's problem by dynamic programming:

$$V_t (K_t, N_t) = \max_{C_t, I_t} \frac{C_t^{1-\gamma}}{1-\gamma} - \frac{\chi N_t^{1+\phi}}{1+\phi} + \beta E_t V_{t+1} (K_{t+1}, N_{t+1})$$

subject to (18.46) and (18.47). Note that we have suppressed the aggregate state variables in the household value function $V_t (K_t, N_t)$. We can derive the Euler equation

$$C_t^{-\gamma} = \beta E_t C_{t+1}^{-\gamma} (R_{k,t+1} + 1 - \delta). \tag{18.49}$$

By the envelope condition,

$$\frac{\partial V_t (K_t, N_t)}{\partial N_t} = \Lambda_t (w_t - b) - \chi N_t^\phi + \frac{\partial N_{t+1}}{\partial N_t} \beta E_t \frac{\partial V_{t+1} (K_{t+1}, N_{t+1})}{\partial N_{t+1}}$$

$$= \Lambda_t (w_t - b) - \chi N_t^\phi + (1 - \rho - q(\theta_t) \theta_t) \beta E_t \frac{\partial V_{t+1} (K_{t+1}, N_{t+1})}{\partial N_{t+1}},$$

where $\Lambda_t = C_t^{-\gamma}$. Note that when computing $\partial N_{t+1}/\partial N_t$, we have used equation (18.48) and taken $q_t^u = q(\theta_t) \theta_t$ as given.

Define the marginal household surplus (measured in consumption units) of getting one more household member hired as

$$S_t^H = \frac{1}{\Lambda_t} \frac{\partial V_t (K_t, N_t)}{\partial N_t}.$$

In this definition we have assumed the new employed member and all other employed members earn the same wage w_t. We then have

$$S_t^H = w_t - b - \frac{\chi N_t^\phi}{\Lambda_t} + (1 - \rho - q\left(\theta_t\right)\theta_t) E_t \frac{\beta \Lambda_{t+1}}{\Lambda_t} S_{t+1}^H. \tag{18.50}$$

We may assume that the newly employed member earns a possibly different wage w. We now derive the marginal household surplus. Consider the dynamic programming problem

$$V_t\left(K_t, N_t + \varepsilon\right) = \max_{C_t, I_t} \frac{C_t^{1-\gamma}}{1-\gamma} - \frac{\chi\left(N_t + \varepsilon\right)^{1+\phi}}{1+\phi} + \beta E_t V_{t+1}\left(K_{t+1}, N_{t+1}\right)$$

subject to (18.47) and

$$C_t + I_t = D_t + R_{kt}K_t + w_t N_t + w\varepsilon + b\left(1 - N_t\right) - T_t,$$

$$N_{t+1} = \left(1 - \rho\right)\left(N_t + \varepsilon\right) + q\left(\theta_t\right)\theta_t\left(1 - \left(N_t + \varepsilon\right)\right).$$

By the envelope condition,

$$\frac{\partial V_t\left(K_t, N_t + \varepsilon\right)}{\partial \varepsilon}\bigg|_{\varepsilon=0}$$

$$= -\chi N_t^\phi + \Lambda_t w + \left(1 - \rho - q\left(\theta_t\right)\theta_t\right) E_t \beta \frac{\partial V_{t+1}\left(K_{t+1}, N_{t+1}\right)}{\partial N_{t+1}}$$

$$= \Lambda_t\left(w - w_t\right) + \frac{\partial V_t\left(K_t, N_t\right)}{\partial N_t}$$

$$\equiv V_n\left(w, t\right).$$

Here $V_n\left(w, t\right)$ denotes the marginal surplus to the household when an additional household member is hired at the wage rate w.

18.3.2   Firms

There is a continuum of firms of measure unity. Each firm rents capital K_t^j and hires labor N_t^j to produce output according to an identical constant-returns-to-scale production function F. Production is subject to an aggregate labor-augmenting productivity shock A_t, which follows a Markov process. Each firm j chooses capital K_t^j and vacancies v_t^j to solve the following problem:

$$\max_{\left\{K_t^j, v_t^j\right\}} E \sum_{t=0}^{\infty} \frac{\beta^t \Lambda_t}{\Lambda_0} \left[F\left(K_t^j, A_t N_t^j\right) - w_t N_t^j - R_t K_t^j - v_t^j \kappa\right]$$

subject to (18.22), where $q_t^v = q\left(\theta_t\right)$ is the job-filling rate. Note that since households own the firm, we use the household pricing kernel to compute firm value.

We can write down firm j's problem by dynamic programming:

$$J_t\left(N_t^j\right) = \max_{K_t^j, v_t^j} F\left(K_t^j, A_t N_t^j\right) - w_t N_t^j - R_{kt} K_t^j - v_t^j \kappa + E_t \frac{\beta \Lambda_{t+1}}{\Lambda_t} J_{t+1}\left(N_{t+1}^j\right)$$

subject to (18.22), where we have suppressed aggregate state variables in the value function $J_t\left(N_t^j\right)$. The first-order conditions are given by

$$F_1\left(K_t^j, A N_t^j\right) = R_{kt}, \tag{18.51}$$

$$\kappa = E_t \frac{\beta \Lambda_{t+1}}{\Lambda_t} \frac{\partial J_{t+1}\left(N_{t+1}^j\right)}{\partial N_{t+1}^j} q_t^v. \tag{18.52}$$

Equation (18.51) implies that K_t^j / N_t^j does not depend on firm identity j. By the envelope condition,

$$\frac{\partial J_t\left(N_t^j\right)}{\partial N_t^j} = A_t F_2\left(K_t^j, A_t N_t^j\right) - w_t + (1 - \rho) E_t \frac{\beta \Lambda_{t+1}}{\Lambda_t} \frac{\partial J_{t+1}\left(N_{t+1}^j\right)}{\partial N_{t+1}^j}. \tag{18.53}$$

Define marginal firm surplus as

$$S_t^F = \frac{\partial J_t\left(N_t^j\right)}{\partial N_t^j}.$$

Using this definition and equations (18.52) and (18.53), we derive

$$S_t^F = A_t F_2\left(K_t^j, A_t N_t^j\right) - w_t + \frac{(1 - \rho) \kappa}{q_t^v}. \tag{18.54}$$

Substituting back into equation (18.52) yields

$$\frac{\kappa}{q(\theta_t)} = E_t \frac{\beta \Lambda_{t+1}}{\Lambda_t} \left\{ A_{t+1} F_2\left(K_{t+1}^j, A_{t+1} N_{t+1}^j\right) - w_{t+1} + \frac{(1 - \rho) \kappa}{q(\theta_{t+1})} \right\}. \tag{18.55}$$

Next we compute its value when firm j hires an additional ε of workers in the beginning of period t. The firm pays these workers the wage rate w. It solves the following problem:

$$J_t\left(N_t^j + \varepsilon\right) = \max_{K_t^j, v_t^j} F\left(K_t^j, A_t(N_t^j + \varepsilon)\right) - w_t N_t^j - w\varepsilon - R_t K_t^j - v_t^j \kappa$$

$$+ E_t \frac{\beta \Lambda_{t+1}}{\Lambda_t} J_{t+1}\left(N_{t+1}^j\right)$$

subject to

$$N_{t+1}^j = (1 - \rho)\left(N_t^j + \varepsilon\right) + q_t^v v_t^j.$$

By the envelope condition,

$$\frac{\partial J_t\left(N_t^j+\varepsilon\right)}{\partial \varepsilon}\bigg|_{\varepsilon=0} = A_t F_2\left(K_t^j, A_t N_t^j\right) - w + (1-\rho) E_t \frac{\beta \Lambda_{t+1}}{\Lambda_t} \frac{\partial J_{t+1}\left(N_{t+1}^j\right)}{\partial N_{t+1}^j}$$

$$= w_t - w + \frac{\partial J_t\left(N_t^j\right)}{\partial N_t^j}$$

$$\equiv J_n(w,t),$$

where the second equality follows from (18.53). The value $J_n(w,t)$ denotes the marginal surplus to the firm when it hires an additional unit of worker at the wage rate w.

18.3.3   Nash Bargained Wages
The firm and the newly hired household member bargains over the wage rate w using the Nash bargaining solution. The Nash bargaining problem is given by

$$w_t = \arg\max_{w}\ V_n(w,t)^\eta J_n(w,t)^{1-\eta},$$

where we impose that the Nash solution gives the same wage w_t as that offered to the previously hired workers. By the first-order condition,

$$\eta \frac{\partial V_n(w,t)}{\partial w} J_n(w,t) + (1-\eta) \frac{\partial J_n(w,t)}{\partial w} V_n(w,t) = 0.$$

Setting $w = w_t$ and using the definitions of $J_n(w,t)$ and $V_n(w,t)$, we obtain

$$\eta \frac{\partial J_t\left(N_t^j\right)}{\partial N_t^j} = (1-\eta) \frac{1}{\Lambda_t} \frac{\partial V_t(N_t)}{\partial N_t}.$$

This condition can be equivalently derived from the following Nash bargaining problem:

$$\max_{w_t}\ \left(S_t^H\right)^\eta \left(S_t^F\right)^{1-\eta}.$$

The first-order condition is given by

$$(1-\eta) S_t^H = \eta S_t^F.$$

Using this condition, we can rewrite equation (18.50) as

$$\frac{\eta}{1-\eta} S_t^F = w_t - b - \frac{\chi N_t^\phi}{\Lambda_t} + (1-\rho - q(\theta_t)\theta_t) E_t \frac{\beta \Lambda_{t+1}}{\Lambda_t} \frac{\eta}{1-\eta} S_{t+1}^F.$$

Substituting equations (18.54) and (18.52) yields:

$$\frac{\eta}{1-\eta}\left(A_t F_2\left(K_t^j, A_t N_t^j \right) - w_t + \frac{(1-\rho)\kappa}{q_t^v} \right)$$

$$= w_t - b - \frac{\chi N_t^\phi}{\Lambda_t} + (1 - \rho - q\left(\theta_t\right)\theta_t)\frac{\eta}{1-\eta}\frac{\kappa}{q_t^v}.$$

Solving for w_t yields

$$w_t = (1-\eta)\left(b + \frac{\chi N_t^\phi}{\Lambda_t} \right) + \eta\left[A_t F_2\left(K_t^j, A_t N_t^j \right) + \kappa\theta_t \right]. \qquad (18.56)$$

Since K_t^j / N_t^j is identical for all firm j, we deduce that the wage rate w_t does not depend on j.

18.3.4   Equilibrium

Define aggregate output, aggregate capital, aggregate employment, and aggregate vacancies as $Y_t = \int F(K_t^j, A_t N_t^j) dj$, $K_t = \int K_t^j dj$, $N_t = \int N_t^j dj$, and $v_t = \int v_t^j dj$. A search equilibrium consists of stochastic processes $\{Y_t, C_t, K_t, N_t, u_t, v_t, \theta_t, w_t, R_{kt}\}$ such that equations $Y_t = F(K_t, A_t N_t)$, (18.49), (18.51), (18.48), $u_t = 1 - N_t$, $v_t = u_t\theta_t$, (18.55), (18.56) and the following resource constraint hold:

$$C_t + K_{t+1} - (1 - \delta) K_t = F(K_t, A_t N_t) - \kappa v_t.$$

18.4   Exercises

1. For the model in section 18.1 suppose that firms own capital and make investment decisions. Households trade firm shares. Formulate this market arrangement and define a search equilibrium. Analyze this equilibrium.

2. Following a similar analysis in section 18.1, derive the social planner's problem for the model in section 18.2. Study efficiency properties of the decentralized search equilibrium.

3. Suppose that there is a mean-preserving spread change in the distribution G. Study the steady-state effect on the reservation productivity and the unemployment rate.

4. Following a similar analysis in section 18.1, derive the social planner's problem for the model in section 18.3. Study efficiency properties of the decentralized search equilibrium.

5. Calibrate the model in section 18.3 to match the US data. Solve the model numerically.

19 Dynamic New Keynesian Models

Since the late 1980s many researchers have documented empirical evidence that monetary policy influences short-run economic fluctuations.[1] This evidence suggests that models incorporating monetary policy should be useful for understanding business cycles. Beginning from the late 1990s, a number of researchers have made important contributions in combining New Keynesian theory and real business cycle theory.[2] New Keynesian theory arose in the 1980s as an attempt to provide microfoundations to the traditional Keynesian ideas such as price rigidities and nonneutrality of money (see Mankiw and Romer 1991). This literature typically focuses on static models that are designed for qualitative analysis but not quantitative analysis. Real business cycle theory uses the dynamic stochastic general equilibrium framework but does not consider monetary and financial factors. It was natural to provide a synthesis of these two theories. Such an approach resulted in what is called the "new neoclassical synthesis" by Goodfriend and King (1997) and the "Neo-Wicksellian" approach by Woodford (2003). Here we use the seemingly more common term, "dynamic New Keynesian (DNK)" approach. A typical DNK model contains three key elements: (1) monopolistic competition, (2) sticky prices or wages, and (3) dynamic stochastic general equilibrium. Standard references for this literature include Woodford (2003), Gali (2008), and Walsh (2010).

In this chapter we first present a basic DNK model in which there is no capital. We then use this basic model to study monetary and fiscal policy. We finally introduce capital and study a medium-scale DNK model.

---

1. See, example Romer and Romer (1989), Bernanke and Blinder (1992), Gali (1992), Bernanke and Mihov (1997), Christiano, Eichenbaum and Evans (1996, 1998), and Leeper, Sims, and Zha (1996).
2. See, example Goodfriend and King (1997), Walsh (1998), and Woodford (2003).

19.1   A Basic DNK Model

Consider an economy consisting of a representative household, a continuum of identical final goods firms, a continuum of intermediate goods firms, and a central bank. To have money play a role, one has to introduce a demand for money. There are three general approaches in the literature: (1) the money-in-the-utility function (MIU) approach assumes that money yields direct utility (Sidrauski 1967); (2) the cash-in-advance (CIA) approach assumes that money is needed for certain types of transactions (Clower 1967); (3) the overlapping generations approach assumes that money is an asset to transfer resources intertemporally (Samuelson 1958). There are also other related approaches such as the shopping-time approach (Brock 1974; McCallum and Goodfriend 1988), the transaction-costs approach (Baumol 1952; Tobin 1956), and the search approach (Kiyotaki and Wright 1989). In this chapter we will adopt the MIU approach.

19.1.1   Households

The representative household derives utility from stochastic processes of consumption $\{C_t\}$ of final goods, labor $\{N_t\}$, and real money balances $\{m_t\}$, according to the following expected utility function:

$$E \sum_{t=0}^{\infty} \beta^t u\left(C_t, N_t, m_t\right),$$

where $\beta \in (0,1)$ is the subjective discount factor, and u satisfies $u_1 > 0$, $u_2 < 0$, $u_3 > 0$, $u_{11} < 0$, $u_{22} < 0$, and $u_{33} < 0$, and the usual Inada condition. To ensure that a monetary equilibrium exists, it is often assumed that there exists a finite $m^* > 0$ such that $u_3\left(\cdot, \cdot, m\right) \leq 0$ for all $m > m^*$. For simplicity, we consider the following separable specification:

$$u\left(C, N, m\right) = \frac{C^{1-\gamma}}{1-\gamma} - \frac{\chi N^{1+\nu}}{1+\nu} + \frac{m^{1-\varphi}}{1-\varphi}, \tag{19.1}$$

where $\gamma, \nu, \varphi > 0$. The household chooses stochastic processes of consumption $\{C_t\}$, money holdings $\{M_t\}$, and bond holdings $\{B_t\}$ to maximize utility subject to the following budget constraint:

$$C_t + \frac{M_{t+1}}{P_t} + \frac{B_{t+1}}{P_t\left(1+i_t\right)} = \frac{M_t}{P_t} + \frac{B_t}{P_t} + \frac{W_t}{P_t} N_t + \Upsilon_t + T_t,$$

where B_0 and M_0 are exogenously given, P_t represents the price of the final good, W_t represents the nominal wage rate, i_t represents the nominal interest rate on the risk-free bond between period t to $t+1$, and Υ_t represents real profits from firms, and T_t represents the real transfers or taxes from the government. Define the real balance m_t as the end-of-period holdings after having purchased consumption goods, where $m_t = M_{t+1}/P_t$.[3] Bonds are risk free, nominal, and in zero supply.

First-order conditions are given by

$$C_t : C_t^{-\gamma} = \Lambda_t,$$

$$N_t : \chi N_t^{\nu} = \Lambda_t \frac{W_t}{P_t},$$

$$B_{t+1} : \frac{\Lambda_t}{P_t(1+i_t)} = E_t \frac{\beta \Lambda_{t+1}}{P_{t+1}},$$

$$M_{t+1} : \left(\frac{M_{t+1}}{P_t}\right)^{-\varphi} \frac{1}{P_t} - \frac{\Lambda_t}{P_t} + E_t \frac{\beta \Lambda_{t+1}}{P_{t+1}} = 0,$$

where Λ_t denotes marginal utility of consumption. The transversality condition must hold:

$$\lim_{t \to \infty} E\beta^t \Lambda_t \frac{B_{t+1}}{P_t} = 0, \quad \lim_{t \to \infty} E\beta^t \Lambda_t \frac{M_{t+1}}{P_t} = 0.$$

By the first-order conditions above,

$$\frac{\chi N_t^{\nu}}{C_t^{-\gamma}} = \frac{W_t}{P_t}, \tag{19.2}$$

$$1 = \beta (1 + i_t) E_t \left[\left(\frac{C_{t+1}}{C_t}\right)^{-\gamma} \frac{P_t}{P_{t+1}}\right], \tag{19.3}$$

$$\frac{(M_{t+1}/P_t)^{-\varphi}}{C_t^{-\gamma}} = \frac{i_t}{1+i_t}. \tag{19.4}$$

Equation (19.2) indicates that the marginal rate of substitution between labor and consumption is equal to the real wage. Equation (19.3) is the consumption Euler equation. Equation (19.4) is the money demand equation.

19.1.2 Final Goods Firms

Let Y_t be the output of the final good that is produced using inputs of the intermediate goods according to

$$Y_t = \left[\int_0^1 \left(Y_t^j\right)^{(\varepsilon-1)/\varepsilon} dj\right]^{\varepsilon/(\varepsilon-1)}, \tag{19.5}$$

---

3. An alternative approach is to assume that the beginning-of-the-period money enters utility, $m_t = M_t/P_t$ (Carlstrom and Fuerst 2001).

where $\varepsilon > 1$ is the elasticity of substitution among differentiated goods and Y_t^j is the input of intermediate good $j \in [0, 1]$.[4] Final goods firms are competitive and maximize profits

$$\max_{Y_t^j} P_t Y_t - \int_0^1 P_t^j Y_t^j dj.$$

Solving yields the demand for good j:

$$Y_t^j = \left(\frac{P_t^j}{P_t} \right)^{-\varepsilon} Y_t. \tag{19.6}$$

The zero profit condition implies that

$$P_t = \left[\int_0^1 \left(P_t^j \right)^{1-\varepsilon} dj \right]^{1/(1-\varepsilon)}. \tag{19.7}$$

19.1.3   Intermediate Goods Firms

Intermediate goods firms produce and sell differentiated products to final goods firms in monopolistically competitive goods markets. A firm producing intermediate good j has a decreasing-returns-to-scale production function given by

$$Y_t^j = A_t \left(N_t^j \right)^{1-\alpha}, \quad \alpha \in [0, 1), \tag{19.8}$$

where A_t represents an aggregate productivity shock and N_t^j represents labor input. When $\alpha = 0$, the technology exhibits constant returns to scale. The firm faces a downward-sloping demand curve given by (19.6) and makes the pricing decision. Before analyzing this decision, we first study the cost minimization problem:

$$TC_t^j \left(Y_t^j \right) = \min_{N_t^j} \frac{W_t N_t^j}{P_t} \quad \text{subject to (19.8),}$$

where $TC_t^j \left(Y_t^j \right)$ denotes the real total cost of firm j as a function of output Y_t^j. Let MC_t^j denote the real marginal cost of firm j. It is equal to the Lagrange multiplier associated with constraint (19.8):

$$MC_t^j = \frac{W_t/P_t}{A_t (1-\alpha) \left(N_t^j \right)^{-\alpha}} = \frac{W_t/P_t}{A_t (1-\alpha) \left(Y_t^j/A_t \right)^{-\alpha/(1-\alpha)}}.$$

---

4. See chapter 19.3 for an alternative way to introduce monopolistic competition.

Define the economy-wide average real marginal cost as

$$MC_t = \frac{W_t/P_t}{A_t \left(1-\alpha\right)\left(Y_t/A_t\right)^{-\alpha/(1-\alpha)}}.$$ (19.9)

From the preceding two equations, we can derive the relation between firm j's marginal cost and the economywide average marginal cost:

$$MC_t^j = MC_t \left(\frac{Y_t}{Y_t^j}\right)^{-\alpha/(1-\alpha)} = MC_t \left(\frac{P_t^j}{P_t}\right)^{\varepsilon\alpha/(\alpha-1)}.$$ (19.10)

This equation reveals that firms with relatively high prices have relatively low real marginal costs.

Turn to the pricing decision. Following Calvo (1983), assume that each period a firm adjusts its price with probability $1 - \theta$ and does not adjust its price with probability θ. The event of whether to make adjustment arrives independently across firms and over time. By using a law of large numbers, we can interpret θ as the fraction of firms that do not adjust their prices each period. Let P_t^* be the price chosen by firm j in period t. Firm j's objective is to maximize the discounted present value of real profits:

$$\max_{P_t^*} E_t \sum_{k=0}^{\infty} \theta^k \frac{\beta^k \Lambda_{t+k}}{\Lambda_t} \left(\frac{P_t^* Y_{t+k|t}^j}{P_{t+k}} - TC_{t+k|t}^j \left(Y_{t+k|t}^j\right)\right)$$

subject to

$$Y_{t+k|t}^j = \left(\frac{P_t^*}{P_{t+k}}\right)^{-\varepsilon} Y_{t+k},$$

where $Y_{t+k|t}^j$ and $TC_{t+k|t}^j$ denote the real output and the real total cost in period $t + k$ of firm j that last set its price at P_t^* in period t. The first-order condition is given by

$$E_t \sum_{k=0}^{\infty} \theta^k \frac{\beta^k \Lambda_{t+k}}{\Lambda_t} \frac{Y_{t+k}}{P_{t+k}^{1-\varepsilon}} \left(P_t^* - \mu MC_{t+k|t}^j P_{t+k}\right) = 0,$$

where $MC_{t+k|t}^j$ denotes the real marginal cost in period $t + k$ of firm j that last set its price at P_t^* in period t and $\mu \equiv \varepsilon/\left(\varepsilon - 1\right)$ denotes the desired markup in the case of the frictionless price adjustment. Solving yields

$$P_t^* = \frac{\varepsilon}{\varepsilon - 1} \frac{E_t \sum_{k=0}^{\infty} \theta^k \beta^k \Lambda_{t+k} P_{t+k}^{\varepsilon} Y_{t+k} MC_{t+k|t}^j}{E_t \sum_{k=0}^{\infty} \theta^k \beta^k \Lambda_{t+k} P_{t+k}^{\varepsilon-1} Y_{t+k}},$$ (19.11)

where it follows from (19.10) that

$$MC^j_{t+k|t} = MC_{t+k} \left(\frac{P^*_t}{P_{t+k}} \right)^{\varepsilon \alpha/(\alpha-1)}. \tag{19.12}$$

By the law of large numbers, we can rewrite (19.7) as

$$P^{1-\varepsilon}_t = \theta P^{1-\varepsilon}_{t-1} + (1-\theta)(P^*_t)^{1-\varepsilon}. \tag{19.13}$$

This means that a fraction θ of firms does not adjust prices and keeps prices at the previous period level and the remaining fraction adjusts to the new level P^*_t.

19.1.4   Central Bank

There is a central bank that conducts monetary policy. Suppose that the nominal interest rate is the monetary policy instrument. The central bank implements the following Taylor (1993) rule:

$$\ln \frac{1+i_t}{1+i} = \phi_\pi \ln \frac{P_t}{P_{t-1}} + \phi_y \ln \left(\frac{Y_t}{Y^f_t} \right) + v_t, \tag{19.14}$$

where $i = 1/\beta - 1$ is the nominal interest rate in the deterministic steady state with zero inflation, Y^f_t is the output in the flexible-price equilibrium (also called **natural or potential output**), and v_t is IID normally distributed with mean zero and variance σ^2_v. We then use the money demand equation (19.4) to determine money supply. The Taylor rule indicates that the central bank raises the nominal interest rate whenever actual output exceeds natural output or inflation rate exceeds the target zero inflation rate. Alternatively, if the central bank implements monetary policy by setting a path for the nominal supply of money, then we can use the money demand equation (19.4) to determine the nominal interest rate. Finally, the interest rate can be determined from a Ramsey problem in which the central bank maximizes the representative agent's utility.

19.1.5   Sticky-Price Equilibrium

Before defining equilibrium, we conduct aggregation. Define aggregate labor as $N_t = \int_0^1 N^j_t dj$. It follows from (19.6) and (19.8) that

$$N_t = \int_0^1 \left(\frac{Y^j_t}{A_t} \right)^{1/(1-\alpha)} dj = \int_0^1 \left(\frac{\left(P^j_t/P_t \right)^{-\varepsilon} Y_t}{A_t} \right)^{1/(1-\alpha)} dj. \tag{19.15}$$

Solving for Y_t yields

$$Y_t = A_t N_t^{1-\alpha} \left[\int_0^1 \left(\frac{P_t^j}{P_t} \right)^{-\varepsilon/(1-\alpha)} dj \right]^{\alpha-1}. \tag{19.16}$$

This equation shows that aggregate output differs from the aggregate production function $A_t N_t^{1-\alpha}$ up to a price dispersion term $\Delta_t^{\alpha-1}$, where

$$\Delta_t \equiv \int_0^1 \left(\frac{P_t^j}{P_t} \right)^{-\varepsilon/(1-\alpha)} dj$$

By the property of Calvo pricing,

$$\Delta_t = \theta \int_0^1 \left(\frac{P_{t-1}^j}{P_t} \right)^{-\varepsilon/(1-\alpha)} dj + (1-\theta) \left(\frac{P_t^*}{P_t} \right)^{-\varepsilon/(1-\alpha)}$$

$$= \theta \Pi_t^{\varepsilon/(1-\alpha)} \Delta_{t-1} + (1-\theta) \left(\frac{P_t^*}{P_t} \right)^{-\varepsilon/(1-\alpha)}, \tag{19.17}$$

where $\Pi_t \equiv P_t/P_{t-1}$.

An equilibrium consists of 9 stochastic processes, $\{C_t\}$, $\{N_t\}$, $\{Y_t\}$, $\{W_t\}$, $\{i_t\}$, $\{M_t\}$, $\{\Delta_t\}$, $\{\Pi_t\}$, and $\{P_t^*/P_t\}$ such that a system of nine equations (19.2), (19.3), (19.4), (19.11), (19.13), (19.14), (19.16), (19.17), and $C_t = Y_t$ hold.

19.1.6 Flexible-Price Equilibrium

When $\theta \to 0$, the model reduces to the one with flexible prices. It follows (19.11) that

$$\frac{P_t^*}{P_t} = \mu MC_t^j.$$

This equation shows that each firm sets its price P_t^* equal to a markup $\mu > 1$ over its nominal marginal cost $\mu P_t MC_t^j$. Because prices exceed marginal costs, output is inefficiently low. When prices are flexible, all firms are symmetric and charge the same price. Thus $P_t^* = P_t$, $MC_t^j = 1/\mu$, $Y_t^j = Y_t$, and $N_t^j = N_t$ for all j. We can then use (19.9) to solve for

$$\frac{W_t}{P_t} = \frac{1}{\mu} (1-\alpha) A_t N_t^{-\alpha}.$$

By (19.2),

$$\frac{\chi N_t^{\nu}}{C_t^{-\gamma}} = \frac{W_t}{P_t} = \frac{1}{\mu} (1-\alpha) A_t N_t^{-\alpha}.$$

By the resource constraint,

$$C_t = Y_t = A_t N_t^{1-\alpha}.$$

Using these three equations, we can solve for the flexible-price equilibrium output:

$$Y_t^f = \left(\frac{1-\alpha}{\mu\chi}\right)^{(1-\alpha)/(\gamma(1-\alpha)+\alpha+\nu)} A_t^{(1+\nu)/(\gamma(1-\alpha)+\alpha+\nu)}. \tag{19.18}$$

This equation shows that flexible-price output is determined by aggregate productivity.

19.1.7   Log-Linearized System

We shall derive a log-linearized system for the sticky price equilibrium around the deterministic steady state with zero inflation in which $P_t = P^* = P$ and $MC_t^j = MC_t = 1/\mu$ for all t. Define the inflation rate as $\Pi_t = P_t/P_{t-1}$ and $\pi_t = \ln \Pi_t$. Let $\hat{X}_t = \ln X_t - \ln X$, where X denote the zero inflation deterministic steady-state value of any variable X_t. Define $q_t = \hat{P}_t^* - \hat{P}_t$. Note that $d \ln \Pi_t \simeq d\Pi_t/\Pi \simeq \pi_t$ since the steady-state inflation rate is zero. Log-linearizing (19.13) yields

$$q_t = \frac{\theta}{1-\theta}\pi_t. \tag{19.19}$$

By (19.11),

$$P_t^* E_t \sum_{k=0}^{\infty} \theta^k \beta^k Y_{t+k}^{1-\gamma} P_{t+k}^{\varepsilon-1} = \mu E_t \sum_{k=0}^{\infty} \theta^k \beta^k Y_{t+k}^{1-\gamma} P_{t+k}^{\varepsilon} MC_{t+k|t}^j.$$

Log-linearizing this equation yields

$$P^* \sum_{k=0}^{\infty} \theta^k \beta^k Y^{1-\gamma} P^{\varepsilon-1} \hat{P}_t^* + E_t \sum_{k=0}^{\infty} \theta^k \beta^k P^* Y^{1-\gamma} P^{\varepsilon-1} (1-\gamma) \hat{Y}_{t+k}$$

$$+ E_t \sum_{k=0}^{\infty} \theta^k \beta^k P^* Y^{1-\gamma} P^{\varepsilon-1} (\varepsilon-1) \hat{P}_{t+k}$$

$$= \mu E_t \sum_{k=0}^{\infty} \theta^k \beta^k Y^{1-\gamma} P^{\varepsilon} MC^j \left[(1-\gamma)\hat{Y}_{t+k} + \varepsilon\hat{P}_{t+k} + \widehat{MC}_{t+k|t}^j \right].$$

Simplifying yields

$$\frac{\hat{P}_t^*}{1-\beta\theta} = E_t \sum_{k=0}^{\infty} \theta^k \beta^k \left[\hat{P}_{t+k} + \widehat{MC}_{t+k|t}^j \right]. \tag{19.20}$$

Log-linearizing (19.12) yields

$$\widehat{MC}^j_{t+k|t} = \widehat{MC}_{t+k} - b\left(\hat{P}^*_t - \hat{P}_{t+k}\right),\tag{19.21}$$

where we define

$$b \equiv \frac{\varepsilon\alpha}{1-\alpha}.\tag{19.22}$$

Plugging (19.21) into (19.20) and simplifying, we obtain

$$\frac{\hat{P}^*_t(1+b)}{1-\beta\theta} = E_t\sum_{k=0}^{\infty}\theta^k\beta^k\left[(1+b)\,\hat{P}_{t+k} + \widehat{MC}_{t+k}\right].$$

Rewriting it in a recursive form yields

$$\hat{P}^*_t = (1-\beta\theta)\left(\frac{\widehat{MC}_t}{1+b} + \hat{P}_t\right) + \beta\theta E_t\left[\hat{P}^*_{t+1}\right].$$

By definition of $q_t = \hat{P}^*_t - \hat{P}_t$,

$$q_t = \frac{1-\beta\theta}{1+b}\widehat{MC}_t + \beta\theta E_t\left[q_{t+1} + \hat{P}_{t+1} - \hat{P}_t\right].$$

Using (19.19) yields

$$\pi_t = \beta E_t\pi_{t+1} + \frac{(1-\beta\theta)\,(1-\theta)}{\theta\,(1+b)}\widehat{MC}_t.$$

Solving this equation forward and imposing a transversality condition, we deduce that the inflation rate is determined by the present value of the marginal cost discounted by β. We can use (19.9) to compute the percentage change in marginal cost as

$$\widehat{MC}_t = \hat{W}_t - \hat{P}_t + \frac{\alpha}{1-\alpha}\hat{Y}_t - \frac{1}{1-\alpha}\hat{A}_t.$$

Using the log-linearized equation (19.2) to replace $\hat{W}_t - \hat{P}_t$ in the equation above yields

$$\widehat{MC}_t = \nu\hat{N}_t + \gamma\hat{Y}_t + \frac{\alpha}{1-\alpha}\hat{Y}_t - \frac{1}{1-\alpha}\hat{A}_t.\tag{19.23}$$

Total differentiatiation of (19.16) yields:

$$dY_t = (1-\alpha)\,AN^{-\alpha}dN_t + N^{1-\alpha}dA_t$$
$$- \varepsilon AN^{1-\alpha}[-\theta dP_{t-1} + \theta dP_t - (1-\theta)\,dP^*_t + (1-\theta)\,dP_t].$$

It follows from (19.19) that

$$\hat{Y}_t = \hat{A}_t + (1 - \alpha)\hat{N}_t.$$

This equation reveals that the price dispersion term does not matter for aggregate output up to first-order approximation. Using it to eliminate $\hat{N}_t$ in (19.23) yields

$$\widehat{MC}_t = \frac{\nu + \alpha + \gamma(1 - \alpha)}{1 - \alpha}\hat{Y}_t - \frac{\nu + 1}{1 - \alpha}\hat{A}_t$$

$$= \frac{\nu + \alpha + \gamma(1 - \alpha)}{1 - \alpha}\left(\hat{Y}_t - \hat{Y}_t^f\right),$$

where we have used the log-linearized equation for (19.18) in the second equality. Define the **output gap** as the difference between actual output and flexible price output, $x_t = \hat{Y}_t - \hat{Y}_t^f$. Since we log-linearize around the same steady state, $x_t = \ln Y_t - \ln Y_t^f$. We then obtain the New Keynesian Phillips curve equation:

$$\pi_t = \beta E_t \pi_{t+1} + \kappa x_t. \tag{19.24}$$

where

$$\kappa \equiv \frac{(1 - \beta\theta)(1 - \theta)}{\theta(1 + b)}\frac{\nu + \alpha + \gamma(1 - \alpha)}{1 - \alpha}$$

$$= \frac{(1 - \beta\theta)(1 - \theta)(\nu + \alpha + \gamma(1 - \alpha))}{\theta(1 - \alpha + \varepsilon\alpha)}. \tag{19.25}$$

Note that in the last equality we have substituted the expression for b in (19.22).

Log-linearizing the consumption Euler equation (19.3) and using the resource constraint, we obtain

$$\hat{Y}_t = E_t\hat{Y}_{t+1} - \frac{1}{\gamma}(i_t + \ln\beta - E_t\pi_{t+1}), \tag{19.26}$$

where we have used the approximation that

$$\hat{i}_t = \frac{d(1 + i_t)}{1 + i} = d\ln(1 + i_t) = i_t + \ln\beta.$$

This equation also holds for natural output:

$$\hat{Y}_t^f = E_t\hat{Y}_{t+1}^f - \frac{1}{\gamma}(r_t^n + \ln\beta), \tag{19.27}$$

where r_t^n is the **natural rate of interest,** which is defined as the real interest rate that keeps output equal to its natural rate (flexible price output) at all times, that is,

$$1 = \beta(1 + r_t^n)E_t\left(\frac{Y_{t+1}^f}{Y_t^f}\right)^{-\gamma}.$$

In log-linear form

$$r_t^n = -\ln \beta + \gamma \left(E_t \hat{Y}_{t+1}^f - \hat{Y}_t^f \right).$$

We can define $\hat{r}_t^n = r_t^n + \ln \beta$. By equation (19.18), r_t^n depends only on the productivity shock. Combining equations (19.26) and (19.27) yields the intertemporal IS curve equation:

$$x_t = E_t x_{t+1} - \frac{1}{\gamma} (i_t - E_t \pi_{t+1} - r_t^n). \tag{19.28}$$

Finally, log-linearizing the Taylor rule (19.14) yields

$$i_t = -\ln \beta + \phi_\pi \pi_t + \phi_y x_t + v_t. \tag{19.29}$$

Equations (19.24), (19.28), and (19.29) constitute a linear system of three equations for three variables x_t, π_t, and i_t.

Figure 19.1 illustrates the impact of a monetary policy shock (an increase in the nominal interest rate).[5] The parameter values are $\beta = 0.99, \gamma = \nu = 1, \phi_\pi = 1.5$, $\phi_y = 0.25$, and $\theta = 0.8$. The shock follows an AR(1) process given by $v_t = \rho_v v_{t-1} + \varepsilon_{vt}$, with $\rho_v = 0.5$. In response to a positive 1 percent monetary policy shock, the

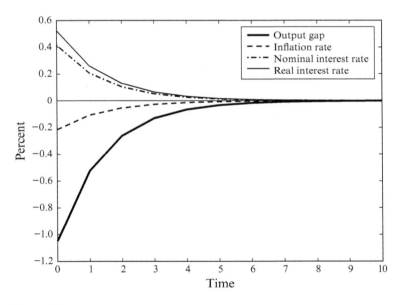

Figure 19.1
Impulse responses to a positive 1 percent shock to monetary policy

5. The Dynare code for producing figures 19.1 and 19.2 is Chapter19_1.mod.

rise in the nominal rate causes inflation and the output gap to fall immediately. This reflects the forward-looking nature of both variables. The real interest rate rises more than the nominal rate due to the fall of the expected inflation rate. Here we define the real interest rate as $r_t = i_t - E_t\pi_{t+1}$.

Figure 19.2 plots the impulse responses to a positive 1 percent shock to the natural rate. Let $\hat{r}_t^n = \rho_r \hat{r}_{t-1}^n + \varepsilon_{rt}$ with $\rho_r = 0.5$. The output gap rises on impact because the interest rate gap $\hat{r}_t - \hat{r}_t^n$ falls. As a result the inflation rate rises along the New Keynesian Phillips curve, and the nominal interest rate also rises by the Taylor rule. The real interest rate rises too, but by less than 1 percent.

In the basic DNK model the impact of monetary policy on output and inflation operates through the real interest rate. As long as the central bank is able to affect the real interest rate through its control of the nominal interest rate, monetary policy can affect real output. Changes in the real interest rate alter the optimal time path of consumption. An increase in the real rate of interest induces households to reduce current consumption relative to future consumption. The interest rate channel also applies to the case with capital (Christiano, Eichenbaum, and Evans 2005; Dotsey and King 2001). Increases in the real interest rate will reduce the demand for capital and lead to a fall in investment spending.

In addition to the interest-rate channel, monetary policy may affect the economy, either indirectly through credit channels or directly through the quantity of money.

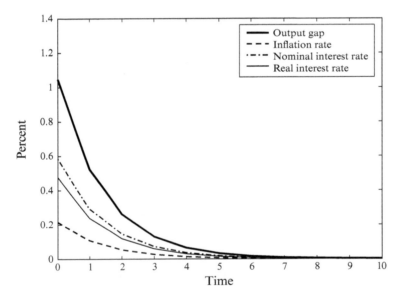

Figure 19.2
Impulse responses to a positive 1 percent shock to the natural rate

Real money holdings represent part of household wealth; an increase in real balances should increase consumption spending through the wealth effect. This channel is often called the Pigou effect, and it is viewed as generating a channel through which declines in price level during a depression will eventually increase real balances and household wealth sufficiently to restore consumption spending.

Direct effects of the quantity of money are not present in the model because we have assumed a separable utility function in an MIU framework. When money is not separable from consumption or leisure in the utility function, money holdings affect the intertemporal IS curve or the New Keynesian Phillips curve. However, McCallum and Nelson (1999) and Woodford (2001) find that the effects arising with nonseparable utility are quite small, so that little is lost by assuming separability. Ireland (2001) finds little evidence for nonseparable preferences in a model estimated on US data.

In this book we will not study the role of credit channels in the monetary transmission process. We refer the reader to Bernanke, Gertler, and Gilchrist (1999) for a model of such a channel and to Walsh (2010, ch. 10) for a textbook treatment.

19.2   Monetary Policy Design

We first study efficient allocation and then introduce a microfounded linear-quadratic approach to monetary policy analysis (see Woodford 2003; Benigno and Woodford 2005).

19.2.1   Efficient Allocation

The efficient allocation is obtained by solving the following social planner's problem:

$$\max_{\left\{C_t, N_t, Y_t^j, N_t^j\right\}} \quad E \sum_{t=0}^{\infty} \beta^t u\left(C_t, N_t\right)$$

subject to

$$C_t = Y_t,$$

$$Y_t = \left[\int_0^1 \left(Y_t^j\right)^{(\varepsilon-1)/\varepsilon} dj\right]^{\varepsilon/(\varepsilon-1)},$$

$$Y_t^j = A_t \left(N_t^j\right)^{1-\alpha},$$

$$N_t = \int_0^1 N_t^j dj.$$

It is easy to show that

$$Y_t^j = Y_t = C_t, \quad N_t^j = N_t \quad \text{for all } j.$$

Moreover

$$\frac{-u_N(C_t, N_t)}{u_C(C_t, N_t)} = (1 - \alpha) A_t N_t^{-\alpha} \equiv MPN_t.$$

Thus an efficient allocation must ensure that the marginal rate of substitution between leisure and consumption is equal to the marginal product of labor. We can show that the efficient output Y_t^e is given by (19.18) for $\mu = 1$.

There are two sources of distortions in the basic DNK model. First, monopolistic competition generates low employment and low output. This distortion can be corrected by providing employment subsidy $\tau = 1/\varepsilon$ to firms.[6] This subsidy is financed by lump-sum taxes. In this case the firm's first-order condition becomes

$$\frac{(1 - \tau) W_t}{P_t} = \frac{1}{\mu} (1 - \alpha) A_t N_t^{-\alpha},$$

so that the real wage is equal to the marginal product of labor or the price is equal to the nominal marginal cost.

The second source of distortions comes from the staggered price setting. As a result of the lack of synchronization in price adjustments, relative prices of different goods will vary in a way unwarranted by changes in preferences or technologies. Thus, whenever $P_t^i \neq P_t^j$, the price is not equal to the nominal marginal cost. The goal of monetary policy is to ensure that the relative price of all firms to be equal.

19.2.2   Quadratic Approximation to Utility

Suppose that the central bank's objective is to maximize the representative agent's utility. Following Rotemberg and Woodford (1999), Woodford (2003), and Benigno and Woodford (2005), we will derive a second-order approximation to the agent's utility. The approximation is around the zero inflation nonstochastic steady state. We study the general case where the steady state is inefficient due to monopolistic competition. The efficient steady state with employment subsidy is a special case.

For any variable we use its lowercase letter to denote its log value. We use a variable without time subscript to denote its steady-state value. Let $\hat{z}_t = z_t - z$ denote the log deviation from steady state for a generic variable z_t. Let $u_t = u(C_t, N_t)$ and

---

6. If employment subsidy is given to the household, then it must be equal to $1/(\varepsilon - 1)$ to achieve an efficient allocation.

$u = u(C, N)$. The following Taylor approximation will be repeatedly used:

$$\frac{C_t - C}{C} = \frac{e^{c_t} - C}{C} \simeq \frac{e^c - C}{C} + \frac{e^c(c_t - c)}{C} + \frac{1}{2}\frac{e^c}{C}(c_t - c)^2$$

$$= c_t - c + \frac{1}{2}(c_t - c)^2 = \hat{c}_t + \frac{1}{2}\hat{c}_t^2.$$

Similarly

$$\frac{N_t - N}{N} \simeq \hat{n}_t + \frac{1}{2}\hat{n}_t^2.$$

We adopt utility given in (19.1) and ignore money. Applying Taylor expansion yields

$$u_t - u \simeq u_C C\frac{C_t - C}{C} + u_N N\frac{N_t - N}{N} + \frac{1}{2}u_{CC}C^2\left(\frac{C_t - C}{C}\right)^2$$

$$+ \frac{1}{2}u_{NN}N^2\left(\frac{N_t - N}{N}\right)^2$$

$$\simeq u_C C\left(\hat{c}_t + \frac{1}{2}\hat{c}_t^2\right) + u_N N\left(\hat{n}_t + \frac{1}{2}\hat{n}_t^2\right) + \frac{1}{2}u_{CC}C^2\left(\hat{c}_t + \frac{1}{2}\hat{c}_t^2\right)^2$$

$$+ \frac{1}{2}u_{NN}N^2\left(\hat{n}_t + \frac{1}{2}\hat{n}_t^2\right)^2.$$

Keeping terms up to second order and use (19.1), it follows that

$$\frac{u_t - u}{u_C C} = \hat{c}_t + \frac{1-\gamma}{2}\hat{c}_t^2 + \frac{u_N N}{u_C C}\left(\hat{n}_t + \frac{1+\nu}{2}\hat{n}_t^2\right). \tag{19.30}$$

Our goal is to represent the expression above in terms of steady-state deviations, namely in terms of the gap in actual output from natural output and the gap in inflation from zero inflation. This involves several steps.

Step 1. Taking log on the two sides of equation (19.16) yields

$$n_t = \frac{1}{1-\alpha}(y_t - a_t) + \ln\Delta_t.$$

Thus, in terms of deviation from steady state,

$$\hat{n}_t = \frac{1}{1-\alpha}(\hat{y}_t - a_t) + \hat{\Delta}_t.$$

We have shown before that $\hat{\Delta}_t = 0$ up to first-order approximation. Now we want to derive a second-order approximation.

By (19.13) and (19.17),

$$\Delta_t = \theta \Pi_t^{\varepsilon/(1-\alpha)} \Delta_{t-1} + (1-\theta) \left[\frac{1 - \theta \Pi_t^{\varepsilon-1}}{1-\theta} \right]^{-\varepsilon/((1-\alpha)(1-\varepsilon))}.$$

A second-order Taylor expansion yields

$$\hat{\Delta}_t = \theta \hat{\Delta}_{t-1} + \frac{(1-\alpha+\alpha\varepsilon)\,\varepsilon\theta}{2\,(1-\alpha)^2\,(1-\theta)} \pi_t^2.$$

Thus

$$\sum_{t=0}^{\infty} \beta^t \hat{\Delta}_t = \frac{\varepsilon\theta}{2\,(1-\alpha)\,\Theta\,(1-\theta)\,(1-\theta\beta)} \sum_{t=0}^{\infty} \beta^t \pi_t^2,$$

where we have supposed that $\hat{\Delta}_{-1} = 0$ and defined

$$\Theta \equiv \frac{1-\alpha}{1-\alpha+\alpha\varepsilon}.$$

Step 2. Applying step 1 to (19.30) yields

$$\frac{u_t - u}{u_C C} = \left(\hat{y}_t + \frac{1-\gamma}{2} \hat{y}_t^2 \right)$$
$$+ \frac{u_N N}{(1-\alpha)\,u_C C} \left(\hat{y}_t + (1-\alpha)\,\hat{\Delta}_t + \frac{1+\nu}{2\,(1-\alpha)}\,(\hat{y}_t - a_t)^2 \right) + \text{t.i.p.}$$

where t.i.p. stands for terms independent of policy.
Let Φ denote the size of the steady-state distortion, implicitly defined by

$$\frac{-u_N}{u_C} = MPN\,(1-\Phi).$$

With employment subsidy τ,

$$\Phi = 1 - \frac{1}{(1-\tau)\,\mu}.$$

Using the fact that $MPN = (1-\alpha)\,Y/N$ and $Y = C$ yields

$$\frac{u_t - u}{u_C C} = \left(\hat{y}_t + \frac{1-\gamma}{2} \hat{y}_t^2 \right)$$
$$- (1-\Phi) \left(\hat{y}_t + (1-\alpha)\,\hat{\Delta}_t + \frac{1+\nu}{2\,(1-\alpha)}\,(\hat{y}_t - a_t)^2 \right) + \text{t.i.p.}$$

Under the small distortion assumption so that the product of Φ with a second-order term can be ignored as negligible, we can derive

$$\frac{u_t - u}{u_C C} = \Phi \hat{y}_t - (1 - \alpha) \hat{\Delta}_t - \frac{1}{2} \left(\frac{1+\nu}{1-\alpha} \left(\hat{y}_t - a_t \right)^2 - (1 - \gamma) \hat{y}_t^2 \right) + \text{t.i.p.}$$

$$= \Phi \hat{y}_t - (1 - \alpha) \hat{\Delta}_t - \frac{1}{2} \left[\left(\gamma + \frac{\nu + \alpha}{1 - \alpha} \right) \hat{y}_t^2 - 2 \left(\frac{1+\nu}{1-\alpha} \right) \hat{y}_t a_t \right] + \text{t.i.p.}$$

$$= -\frac{1}{2} \left(\gamma + \frac{\nu + \alpha}{1 - \alpha} \right) \left[\hat{y}_t^2 - 2 \left(x^* + \hat{y}_t^f \right) \hat{y}_t \right] - (1 - \alpha) \hat{\Delta}_t + \text{t.i.p.}$$

$$= -\frac{1}{2} \left(\gamma + \frac{\nu + \alpha}{1 - \alpha} \right) (x_t - x^*)^2 - (1 - \alpha) \hat{\Delta}_t + \text{t.i.p.}$$

where $x_t = \hat{y}_t - \hat{y}_t^f = y_t - y_t^f$ is the output gap and where we have defined

$$x^* \equiv \frac{\Phi (1 - \alpha)}{\gamma (1 - \alpha) + \nu + \alpha}$$

and used the fact that

$$\hat{y}_t^f = \frac{1+\nu}{\gamma (1 - \alpha) + \nu + \alpha} a_t.$$

Note that up to the first-order approximation, x^* is equal to the log of the ratio of the efficient steady-state output level to the steady-state natural output level, $\ln \left(Y^e / Y^f \right)$, and is a measure of the distortion created by the presence of monopolistic competition.

Step 3. We can now compute a second-order approximation to the household's welfare losses, which are expressed as a fraction of steady-state consumption:

$$\mathbb{W} = E \sum_{t=0}^{\infty} \beta^t \frac{u_t - u}{u_C C}$$

$$= E \sum_{t=0}^{\infty} \beta^t \left\{ -\frac{1}{2} \left(\gamma + \frac{\nu + \alpha}{1 - \alpha} \right) (x_t - x^*)^2 - (1 - \alpha) \hat{\Delta}_t + \text{t.i.p.} \right\}$$

$$= -\frac{\Omega}{2} E \sum_{t=0}^{\infty} \beta^t \left\{ \lambda (x_t - x^*)^2 + \pi_t^2 \right\} + \text{t.i.p.},$$

where

$$\Omega \equiv \frac{\varepsilon \theta}{\Theta (1 - \theta) (1 - \theta \beta)}, \quad \lambda \equiv \left(\gamma + \frac{\nu + \alpha}{1 - \alpha} \right) \frac{1}{\Omega}.$$

When there is no economic distortion, $\Phi = 0$ so that $x^* = 0$. Economic distortions affect x^* only and do not affect λ. The approximate welfare computed above provides a microfoundation for the use of the quadratic objective function for the central bank.

19.2.3   Commitment versus Discretion

For the log-linearized basic DNK model in section 19.1, the optimal monetary policy is to maintain price stability in the sense that $\pi_t = 0$ for all t. In this case the output gap $x_t = 0$ for all t. Hence $i_t = r_t^n$ and the flexible price equilibrium allocation can be achieved. In this case the relative price distortion is removed and the monopoly distortion can be offset by employment subsidy. This monetary policy is called **strict inflation targeting**. It can be implemented by assuming a Taylor rule as in (19.29), where the monetary policy shock v_t is removed when the following condition holds:

$$\kappa\left(\phi_\pi - 1\right) + \left(1 - \beta\right)\phi_y > 0. \tag{19.31}$$

For the microfounded DNK model in section 19.1, Yun (2005) shows that if there is no inherited relative price distortion, namely $P_{-1}^j = P_{-1}$ for all $j \in [0, 1]$, the strict inflation targeting policy is also optimal. In the case of a nondegenerate initial distribution of prices, the optimal monetary policy converges to the policy above after a transition period.

In practice, central banks often face short-run trade-offs. One way to introduce a trade-off is to add a cost-push shock u_t in the New Keynesian Phillips curve (19.24):

$$\pi_t = \kappa x_t + \beta E_t \pi_{t+1} + u_t. \tag{19.32}$$

In the presence of this shock, $\pi_t = 0$ for all t does not imply that the output gap $x_t = 0$. This shock can be microfounded by the introduction of markup shocks or variations in labor income taxes.

We now use a quadratic function to describe a central bank's objective function and consider the following optimal monetary policy problem under commitment:

$$\max_{\{\pi_t, x_t\}} \quad -\frac{1}{2}E\sum_{t=0}^{\infty}\beta^t\left[\pi_t^2 + \lambda\left(x_t - x^*\right)^2\right]$$

subject to (19.32) and

$$u_t = \rho_u u_{t-1} + \sigma_u \varepsilon_t.$$

Let $\beta^{t+1}\mu_{xt+1}$ be the Lagrange multiplier associated with constraint (19.32). We then have the first-order conditions

$$\pi_t: \ \pi_t + \beta\mu_{xt+1} - \beta\mu_{xt} = 0, \quad t \geq 1, \tag{19.33}$$

$$x_t: \ \lambda(x_t - x^*) - \beta\kappa\mu_{xt+1} = 0, \quad t \geq 0. \tag{19.34}$$

The first-order condition for π_0 gives $\mu_{x0} = 0$. As in chapter 9.4, we can solve for

$$\mu_{xt+1} = a\mu_{xt} - \frac{a}{\beta}\left(\frac{\kappa x^*}{1 - \beta a} + \frac{u_t}{1 - \beta a\rho_u}\right),$$

where a is the smaller root of equation (9.29). It follows from these two first-order conditions that

$$x_t = ax_{t-1} - \frac{a\kappa}{\lambda}\frac{u_t}{1 - \beta a\rho_u},$$

$$\pi_t = a\pi_{t-1} + \frac{a}{1 - \beta a\rho_u}(u_t - u_{t-1}),$$

where the initial values are given by

$$x_0 = \frac{\beta\kappa}{\lambda}\mu_{x1} + x^* = x^* - \frac{a\kappa}{\lambda}\left(\frac{\kappa x^*}{1 - \beta a} + \frac{u_0}{1 - \beta a\rho_u}\right),$$

$$\pi_0 = -\beta\mu_{x1} = a\left(\frac{\kappa x^*}{1 - \beta a} + \frac{u_0}{1 - \beta a\rho_u}\right).$$

Since $\pi_t = p_t - p_{t-1}$, it follows that the price level is stationary:

$$p_t = ap_{t-1} + \frac{a}{1 - \beta a\rho_u}u_t.$$

An alternative approach to optimal policy under commitment is to assume that (19.33) and (19.34) hold for all time $t \geq -1$. This approach is called the **timeless perspective approach**, which is proposed by Woodford (1999). The idea of this approach is to eliminate the Lagrange multipliers associated with the forward-looking equations and express the equilibrium system in terms of endogenous variables only. Specifically, eliminating μ_{xt} from (19.33) and (19.34) yields

$$\pi_t = -\frac{\lambda}{\kappa}(x_t - x_{t-1}) \quad \text{for all } t \geq 0. \tag{19.35}$$

Substituting this equation into (19.32) yields

$$\left(1 + \beta + \frac{\kappa^2}{\lambda}\right)x_t = \beta E_t x_{t+1} + x_{t-1} - \frac{\kappa}{\lambda}u_t.$$

Solving yields

$$x_t = a x_{t-1} - \frac{\kappa}{\lambda \left(1 + \beta \left(1 - \rho - a\right)\right) + \kappa^2} u_t.$$

Note that this equation is the same as that under optimal commitment using equation (9.29). Substituting it into (19.35) yields

$$\pi_t = \frac{\lambda}{\kappa} \left(1 - a\right) x_{t-1} + \frac{\lambda}{\lambda \left(1 + \beta \left(1 - \rho_u - a\right)\right) + \kappa^2} u_t.$$

We need an initial condition x_{-1} to determine the whole paths of x_t and π_t. Note that under optimal precommitment, $\mu_{x0} = 0$ so that

$$\pi_0 = -\frac{\lambda}{\kappa} \left(x_0 - x^*\right),$$

which is different from (19.35). If $x_{-1} = x^*$, then the solution from the timeless perspective is the same as the optimal commitment solution.

Because the timeless perspective commitment policy is generally not the solution to the policy problem under optimal commitment, the policy rule given by (19.35) may be dominated by other policy rules. For instance, it may be dominated by the optimal discretion policy for some initial condition x_{-1} (see Dennis 2010).

Let us turn to discretionary policy. In chapter 9.5 we derived the discretionary inflation rate and showed that it is given by

$$\pi_t = \frac{\lambda}{\kappa^2 + \lambda} \sum_{j=0}^{\infty} \beta^j \left(\frac{\lambda}{\kappa^2 + \lambda}\right)^j \left[\kappa x^* + E_t u_{t+j}\right]$$

$$= \frac{\lambda \kappa x^*}{\kappa^2 + \lambda - \beta \lambda} + \frac{\lambda \kappa}{\kappa^2 + \lambda - \beta \lambda \rho_u} u_t.$$

Because $x^* > 0$, there is inflation bias in the long run. The discretionary policy maker does not taken into account the consequences of choosing a higher inflation rate in the current period on expected inflation, and hence upon the location of the Phillips curve trade-off in the previous period. Because the neglected effect of higher inflation on previous expected inflation is an adverse one, in the case where $x^* > 0$ (so that the policy maker would wish to shift the Phillips curve down if possible), neglecting this effect leads the discretionary policy maker to choose a higher inflation rate at all times than would be chosen under optimal commitment. And because this neglected effect is especially strong immediately following a positive cost-push shock, the gap between the inflation rate chosen under discretion and the one that would be chosen under an optimal policy is even larger than average at such a time.

Figure 19.3 illustrates the impulse responses of inflation and output gap to a one standard deviation cost-push shock under optimal commitment and discretionary

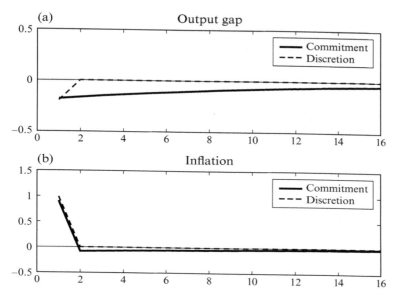

Figure 19.3
Impulse responses under optimal commitment and discretionary policies

policies.[7] We set parameter values as $\beta = 0.99, \kappa = 0.05, \gamma = 1, x^* = 0, \lambda = 0.25,$ $\rho_u = 0$, and $\sigma_u = 1$. This figure shows that for both types of policy, inflation rises on impact, and the output gap falls. The discretionary policy inherits the persistence property of the predetermined state variables—the cost-push shock. Since the cost-push shock is temporary, both the inflation and the output gap return to the long-run steady-state levels starting at period 2n. By contrast, the optimal commitment policy is history dependent. The output gap displays strong positive serial correlation. By keeping output below the natural rate level (a negative output gap) for several periods into the future after a positive cost shock, the central bank is able to lower expectations of future inflation. A fall in $E_t\pi_{t+1}$ at the time of the positive cost-push shock improves the trade-off between inflation and output gap stabilization faced by the central bank.

19.3 Fiscal Stimulus

What is the impact of government spending on aggregate economic activity? This question is important especially during the recent Great Recession when the

---

7. The Matlab code for producing figure 19.3 is Chapter19_2.m. This code applies Paul Söderlind's code on the website: http://home.datacomm.ch/paulsoderlind/.

short-term nominal interest rate was close to zero. In this case monetary policy in the form of interest rate cuts has been a less effective alternative. In this section we follow Woodford's (2011) analysis closely to understand the role of government expenditure in a series of models.

19.3.1   A Neoclassical Model

We start with a neoclassical benchmark with perfect competition. Consider a deterministic model. There is a representative household with the utility function

$$\sum_{t=0}^{\infty} \beta^t \left[u\left(C_t\right) - v\left(N_t\right)\right],$$ (19.36)

where C_t represents consumption, N_t represents hours, $\beta \in (0,1)$, $u' > 0$, $u'' < 0$, $v' > 0$, and $v'' < 0$. There is a representative firm using labor to produce output with the aggregate production function:

$$Y_t = f\left(N_t\right),$$ (19.37)

where $f' > 0$ and $f'' < 0$. There is a government with expenditure G_t financed by lump-sum taxes. The resource constraint is given by

$$C_t + G_t = Y_t.$$ (19.38)

In a competitive equilibrium,

$$\frac{v'\left(N_t\right)}{u'\left(C_t\right)} = \frac{W_t}{P_t},$$ (19.39)

$$f'\left(N_t\right) = \frac{W_t}{P_t},$$

where W_t and P_t represent the nominal wage and the price level, respectively. Using (19.37) and (19.38), we obtain

$$u'\left(Y_t - G_t\right) = \frac{v'\left(f^{-1}\left(Y_t\right)\right)}{f'\left(f^{-1}\left(Y_t\right)\right)} = \tilde{v}'\left(Y_t\right),$$ (19.40)

where $\tilde{v}\left(Y_t\right) \equiv v\left(f^{-1}\left(Y_t\right)\right)$. We can then compute the steady-state **fiscal multiplier**

$$\frac{dY}{dG} = \frac{\eta_u}{\eta_u + \eta_v},$$ (19.41)

where

$$\eta_u = -\bar{Y}\frac{u''\left(\bar{Y} - \bar{G}\right)}{u'\left(\bar{Y} - \bar{G}\right)} > 0, \quad \eta_v = \bar{Y}\frac{\tilde{v}''\left(\bar{Y}\right)}{\tilde{v}'\left(\bar{Y}\right)} > 0.$$

Here a variable with a bar denotes its steady-state value. It follows that the fiscal multiplier is positive but less than one. This means that private expenditure (here entirely modeled as nondurable consumer expenditure) is necessarily crowded out, at least partially, by government purchases. The intuition is as follows: An increase in government purchases must be financed by taxes, which lower household wealth. The negative wealth effect reduces private consumption and leisure. Households then work harder, thereby raising output.

19.3.2 Monopolistic Competition

The mere existence of some degree of market power in either product or labor market does not change this result much. Suppose, for example, that instead of a single good there is a large number of differentiated goods, each with a single monopoly producer. As in the familiar Dixit–Stiglitz model of monopolistic competition, suppose that the representative household's preferences are again of the form (19.36), but that C_t is now a constant-elasticity-of-substitution aggregate of the household's purchases of each of the differentiated goods,

$$C_t = \left[\int_0^1 \left(C_t^j \right)^{(\varepsilon-1)/\varepsilon} dj \right]^{\varepsilon/(\varepsilon-1)},$$

where C_t^j is the quantity purchased of good j, and $\varepsilon > 1$ is the elasticity of substitution among differentiated goods. The budget constraint is given by

$$\int_0^1 P_t^j C_t^j dj + \frac{B_{t+1}}{1+i_t} = B_t + W_t N_t + T_t,$$

where B_t denotes bond holdings, i_t denotes the nominal interest rate, and T_t denotes income including profits from ownership of firms and lump-sum taxes (or transfers). We can then derive a price index P_t given by (19.7) such that

$$\int_0^1 P_t^j C_t^j dj = P_t C_t.$$

Suppose, for simplicity, that each good is produced using a common production function of the form (19.37), with a single homogeneous labor input used in producing all goods. Each firm faces a downward-sloping demand curve for its product, with elasticity ε. Firms can adjust prices frictionlessly as in chapter 19.1.6. Profit maximization implies that the real price is equal to a markup $\mu = \varepsilon/(\varepsilon-1)$ over the real marginal cost. This implies that the real marginal cost is equal to $1/\mu$ in a symmetric equilibrium so that

$$\frac{W_t}{P_t f'(N_t)} = \frac{1}{\mu} \quad \text{or} \quad P_t = \mu \frac{W_t}{f'(N_t)}. \tag{19.42}$$

By (19.38) and (19.39), we can show that

$$u'(Y_t - G_t) = \mu \tilde{v}'(Y_t). \tag{19.43}$$

In this case the fiscal multiplier is still given by (19.41). A similar conclusion is obtained in the case of a constant markup of wages relative to households' marginal rate of substitution: aggregate output is again determined by (19.43), where μ is now an "efficiency wedge" that depends on the degree of market power in both product and labor markets, and so the multiplier calculation remains the same.

A different result can be obtained, however, if the size of the efficiency wedge is endogenous. One of the most obvious sources of such endogeneity is stickiness in the adjustment of wages or prices to changing market conditions. If prices are not immediately adjusted in full proportion to the increase in marginal cost resulting from an increase in government purchases, the right-hand side of (19.42) will increase more than does the left-hand side. As a consequence the right-hand side of (19.43) will increase more than does the left-hand side of that expression. This implies an increase in Y_t greater than the one implied by (19.43). A similar argument applies to the case where there is friction in wage adjustment.

19.3.3   A DNK Model

Let us introduce sticky prices and monetary policy to the model. Suppose that prices are determined by the model of Calvo (1983) but wages are flexible. It is important to consider how fiscal and monetary policies are coordinated. As a benchmark, we want to first consider a policy experiment in which the central bank maintains an unchanged path for the real interest rate, regardless of the path of government purchases. Again, we consider a deterministic economy, and let the path of government purchases be given by a sequence $\{G_t\}$, such that $G_t \to \bar{G}$ in the limit. We let the inflation rate be zero in the long run.

From the consumption Euler equation,

$$\frac{u'(C_t)}{\beta u'(C_{t+1})} = \exp(r_t), \tag{19.44}$$

where r_t is the (continuously compounded) real interest rate between t and $t + 1$. It follows that in the long-run steady state, $\bar{r} = -\ln \beta > 0$. Since we wish to consider a monetary policy that maintains a constant real rate of interest, regardless of the temporary variation in government purchases, it is necessary to assume that monetary policy maintains $r_t = \bar{r}$ for all t. In this case $C_t = \bar{C}$ for all t. It follows from $\bar{C} + G_t = Y_t$ that the fiscal multiplier is equal to one.

Now we consider alternative assumptions about the degree of monetary accommodation of the fiscal stimulus. Unlike in the model of section 19.1, suppose that each differentiated good j is produced using a constant-returns-to-scale technology of the form

$$Y_t^j = K_t^j f\left(\frac{N_t^j}{K_t^j}\right), \tag{19.45}$$

where K_t^j is the quantity of capital goods used in production by firm j, N_t^j are the hours of labor hired by the firm, and f is the same increasing, concave function as before. We will assume, for simplicity, that the total supply of capital goods is exogenously given (and can be normalized to equal one) but that capital goods are allocated to firms each period through a competitive rental market. In this case the cost minimization problem is given by

$$\min_{K_t^j, N_t^j} \frac{R_t^k}{P_t} K_t^j + \frac{W_t}{P_t} N_t^j$$

subject to (19.45), where R_t^k represents the nominal rental rate of capital. First-order conditions are given by

$$\frac{R_t^k}{P_t} = MC_t^j \left(f\left(\frac{N_t^j}{K_t^j}\right) - f'\left(\frac{N_t^j}{K_t^j}\right)\frac{N_t^j}{K_t^j}\right),$$

$$\frac{W_t}{P_t} = MC_t^j f'\left(\frac{N_t^j}{K_t^j}\right),$$

where MC_t^j is the Lagrange multiplier associated with (19.45), which also represents firm j's real marginal cost. Eliminating MC_t^j from these two equations gives an implicit function of N_t^j/K_t^j in terms of R_t^k/P_t and W_t/P_t. Thus each firm chooses the same labor–capital ratio, regardless of its scale of production, and in equilibrium this common labor–capital ratio will equal N_t, the aggregate labor supply (recalling that aggregate capital is equal to one). Moreover each firm will have a common marginal cost of production, MC_t, which is independent of the firm's chosen scale of production,

$$MC_t = \frac{W_t}{P_t f'(N_t)}. \tag{19.46}$$

Using the first-order condition for the consumption-leisure choice and the resource constraint yields

$$\frac{v'(N_t)}{u'(Y_t - G_t)} = \frac{W_t}{P_t} = MC_t f'(N_t),$$

or

$$\frac{\tilde{v}'(Y_t)}{u'(Y_t - G_t)} = MC_t,$$

(19.47)

where $\tilde{v}(Y_t)$ is defined as in (19.40).

As in section 19.1 the optimal price is determined by (19.11), where $MC^j_{t+k|t} = MC_{t+k}$. Log-linearizing this equation yields[8]

$$\hat{P}^*_t = (1 - \beta\theta) E_t \sum_{k=0}^{\infty} \theta^k \beta^k \left[\hat{P}_{t+k} + \widehat{MC}_{t+k}\right].$$

Rewriting it in a recursive form yields

$$\hat{P}^*_t = (1 - \beta\theta) \left(\widehat{MC}_t + \hat{P}_t\right) + \beta\theta E_t \left[\hat{P}^*_{t+1}\right].$$

By definition of q_t,

$$q_t = (1 - \beta\theta) \widehat{MC}_t + \beta\theta E_t \left[q_{t+1} + \hat{P}_{t+1} - \hat{P}_t\right].$$

Using (19.19) yields

$$\pi_t = \beta E_t \pi_{t+1} + \frac{(1 - \beta\theta)(1 - \theta)}{\theta} \widehat{MC}_t.$$

Log-linearizing (19.47) yields

$$\widehat{MC}_t = \eta_v \hat{Y}_t + \eta_u \left(\hat{Y}_t - \hat{G}_t\right) = (\eta_u + \eta_v) \left(\hat{Y}_t - \Gamma\hat{G}_t\right),$$

where Γ is the multiplier defined in (19.41), $\hat{Y}_t = \ln\left(Y_t/\bar{Y}\right) \simeq (Y_t - \bar{Y})/\bar{Y}$, and $\hat{G}_t = (G_t - \bar{G})/\bar{Y}$. From the preceding two equations we deduce that

$$\pi_t = \kappa \sum_{j=0}^{\infty} \beta^j E_t \left(\hat{Y}_{t+j} - \Gamma\hat{G}_{t+j}\right),$$

(19.48)

where $\kappa = (1 - \beta\theta)(1 - \theta)(\eta_u + \eta_v)/\theta > 0$.

Suppose that the central bank follows a Taylor rule of the form

$$i_t = \bar{r} + \phi_\pi \pi_t + \phi_y \hat{Y}_t,$$

(19.49)

where $\phi_\pi > 1$ and $\phi_y > 0$. Log-linearizing the consumption Euler equation yields

$$\hat{Y}_t - \hat{G}_t = E_t \left(\hat{Y}_{t+1} - \hat{G}_{t+1}\right) - \sigma(i_t - E_t \pi_{t+1} - \bar{r}),$$

(19.50)

---

8. We have added conditional expectation in the equation to anticipate that we will introduce shocks in the model later.

where $\sigma \equiv 1/\eta_u$ represents the elasticity of intertemporal substitution. An equilibrium $\left\{\hat{Y}_t, \pi_t, i_t\right\}$ is characterized by equations (19.48), (19.49), and (19.50).

Let $\hat{G}_t = \rho^t \hat{G}_0$. Conjecture an equilibrium of the form

$$\hat{Y}_t = \gamma_y \hat{G}_t, \tag{19.51a}$$

$$\pi_t = \gamma_\pi \hat{G}_t, \tag{19.51b}$$

$$i_t = \bar{r} + \gamma_i \hat{G}_t, \tag{19.51c}$$

for some coefficients γ_y, γ_π, and γ_i to be determined. It is straightforward to show that the multiplier is given by

$$\gamma_y = \frac{1 - \rho + (\psi - \sigma\phi_y)\,\Gamma}{1 - \rho + \psi}, \tag{19.52}$$

where

$$\psi \equiv \sigma \left[\phi_y + \frac{\kappa}{1 - \beta\rho} (\phi_\pi - \rho) \right] > 0.$$

One can check that $\gamma_y < 1$. Thus the multiplier is smaller than under the constant-real-interest-rate policy because the real interest rate is increased in response to the increases in inflation and in the output gap. Note that for a Taylor rule, the size of the multiplier depends on the degree of stickiness of prices (through the dependence of ψ on the value of κ).

The multiplier under Taylor rule (19.49) may be smaller than the one predicted by the neoclassical model in the case of any large enough value of ϕ_y. In such a case price stickiness results in even less output increase than would occur with flexible prices, since the central bank's reaction function raises real interest rates more than would occur with flexible prices (and more than is required to maintain zero inflation). Hence, while larger multipliers are possible according to a New Keynesian model, they are predicted to occur only in the case of a sufficient degree of monetary accommodation of the increase in real activity. In general, this will also require the central bank to accommodate an increase in the rate of inflation. This case can occur when the nominal interest rate is constrained by the zero lower bound.

19.3.4   Zero-Interest-Rate Lower Bound

When the zero lower bound on the short-term nominal interest rate is binding, the central bank will not tighten policy in response to an increase in government purchases. To the extent that the fiscal stimulus is associated with increased inflation expectations, the real interest rate will fall in response to fiscal stimulus. Hence government purchases should have an especially strong effect on aggregate output when the central bank's policy rate is at the zero lower bound. In this case fiscal stimulus becomes more urgent because there is no room for interest rate cuts.

In practice, the zero lower bound is most likely to become a binding constraint on monetary policy when financial intermediation is severely disrupted, as during the Great Depression or the recent financial crisis. We now extend the model above to include zero-interest-rate lower bound. Suppose that the interest rate that is relevant in the consumption Euler equation (19.44) is not the same as the central bank's policy rate and furthermore that the spread between the two interest rates varies over time, due to changes in the efficiency of financial intermediation. If we let i_t denote the policy rate and $i_t + \Delta_t$ the interest rate that is relevant for the intertemporal allocation of consumption, then (19.50) takes the more general form

$$\hat{Y}_t - \hat{G}_t = E_t\left(\hat{Y}_{t+1} - \hat{G}_{t+1}\right) - \sigma\left(i_t - E_t\pi_{t+1} - r_t^{net}\right), \tag{19.53}$$

where $r_t^{net} \equiv -\ln\beta - \Delta_t$ is the real policy rate required to maintain a constant path for private consumption at the steady-state level. If the spread Δ_t becomes large enough for a period of time, as a result of a disturbance to the financial sector, then the value of r_t^{net} may temporarily be negative. In such a case the zero lower bound on i_t will make (19.53) incompatible with achievement of the zero-inflation steady state with government purchases equal to $\bar{G}$ in all periods.

As a simple example (based on Eggertsson 2009), suppose that under normal conditions, $r_t^{net} = -\ln\beta = \bar{r} > 0$, but that as a result of a financial disturbance at date 0, credit spreads increase, and r_t^{net} falls to a value $r_L < 0$.[9] Suppose that each period thereafter, there is a probability $\mu \in (0,1)$ that the elevated credit spreads persist in period t and that r_t^{net} continues to equal r_L if credit spreads were elevated in period $t-1$, but with probability $1-\mu$ credit spreads return to their normal level and $r_t^{net} = \bar{r}$. Once credit spreads return to normal, they remain at the normal level thereafter. This exogenous evolution of the credit spread is assumed to be unaffected by either monetary or fiscal policy choices. Suppose further that monetary policy is described by a Taylor rule, except that the interest rate target is set to zero if the linear rule would call for a negative rate. Specifically, let

$$i_t = \max\left\{\bar{r} + \phi_\pi\pi_t + \phi_y\hat{Y}_t, 0\right\} \tag{19.54}$$

so that the rule is consistent with the zero-inflation steady state if $r_t^{net} = \bar{r}$ at all times. We will again suppose that $\phi_\pi > 1$ and $\phi_y > 0$.

---

9. See Christiano, Eichenbaum, and Rebelo (2011) for a quantitative DSGE model with capital and a zero-interest-rate lower bond.

Consider fiscal policies under which government purchases are equal to some level G_L for all $0 \leq t < T$, where T is the random date at which credit spreads return to their normal level, and equal to $\bar{G}$ for all $t \geq T$. The question we wish to study is the effect of choosing a higher level of government purchases G_L during the crisis, taking as given the monetary policy rule (19.54).

We solve the equilibrium by backward induction. After date T, the equilibrium should be the zero inflation steady state; hence the equilibrium values will be $\pi_t = \hat{Y}_t = 0$, $i_t = \bar{r} > 0$ for all $t \geq T$. Turn to the equilibrium prior to date T. Equilibrium conditions (19.48), (19.53), and (19.54) can be solved forward to obtain a unique bounded solution if and only if the model parameters satisfy

$$\kappa \sigma \mu < (1 - \mu)(1 - \beta\mu). \tag{19.55}$$

Note that this condition holds for all $0 \leq \mu \leq \bar{\mu}$, where the upper bound $\bar{\mu} < 1$ depends on the model parameters (β, κ, σ). We solve for an equilibrium such that $\pi_t = \pi_L$, $Y_t = Y_L$ and $i_t = i_L$ for each $t < T$. These constant values can be obtained by observing that (19.48) requires that

$$\pi_L = \frac{\kappa}{1 - \beta\mu}\left(\hat{Y}_L - \Gamma\hat{G}_L\right) \tag{19.56}$$

and that (19.53) requires that

$$(1 - \mu)\left(\hat{Y}_L - \hat{G}_L\right) = \sigma\left(-i_L + \mu\pi_L + r_L\right). \tag{19.57}$$

Using (19.56) to substitute for π_L in (19.57), we can derive

$$\hat{Y}_L = \vartheta_r\left(r_L - i_L\right) + \vartheta_G\hat{G}_L, \tag{19.58}$$

where

$$\vartheta_r \equiv \frac{\sigma(1 - \beta\mu)}{(1 - \mu)(1 - \beta\mu) - \kappa\sigma\mu} > 0, \tag{19.59}$$

$$\vartheta_G \equiv \frac{(1 - \mu)(1 - \beta\mu) - \kappa\sigma\mu\Gamma}{(1 - \mu)(1 - \beta\mu) - \kappa\sigma\mu} > 1.$$

Here these bounds follow from (19.55) and $0 < \Gamma < 1$.

We substitute (19.58) and the associated solution for the inflation rate into (19.54) and solve the resulting equation for i_L. The solution lies on the branch of (19.54), where $i_L = 0$ if and only if $\hat{G}_L < \hat{G}^c$, with

$$\hat{G}^c \equiv \frac{-\left(\frac{\kappa\phi_\pi}{1 - \beta\mu} + \phi_y\right)\vartheta_r r_L - \bar{r}}{\frac{\kappa\phi_\pi}{1 - \beta\mu}(\vartheta_G - \Gamma) + \phi_y\vartheta_G} > 0.$$

This condition can hold when r_L is sufficiently negative. For any level of government purchases below this critical level, equilibrium output will be given by

$$\hat{Y}_L = \vartheta_r r_L + \vartheta_G \hat{G}_L \tag{19.60}$$

for all $t < T$, and the inflation rate will equal the value π_L given by (19.56). In this equilibrium there will be both deflation and a negative output gap (output below its level with flexible wages and prices). The deflation and economic contraction can be quite severe, for even a modestly negative value of r_L, in the case that μ is large. Under such circumstances it can be highly desirable to stimulate aggregate demand by increasing the level of government purchases.

When $\hat{G}_L > \hat{G}^c$, the zero lower bound does not bind. Then the three equations (19.56), (19.58), and

$$i_L = \bar{r} + \phi_\pi \pi_L + \phi_y \hat{Y}_L > 0$$

can be used to solve for i_L, π_L and $\hat{Y}_L$. The solution is left as an exercise for the reader.

Figure 19.4 plots $\hat{Y}_L$ as a function of $\hat{G}_L$. The parameter values are given by $\beta = 0.997$, $\kappa = 0.00859$, $\sigma = 0.862$, $\Gamma = 0.425$, $\phi_\pi = 1.5$, $\phi_y = 0.25$, $r_L = -0.0104$, and

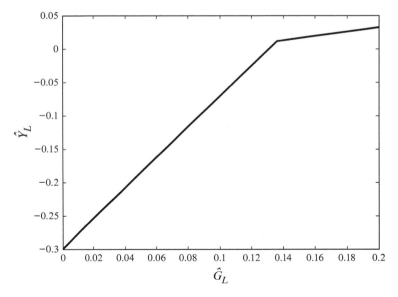

Figure 19.4
$\hat{Y}_L$ as a function of $\hat{G}_L$

$\mu = 0.903$. The kink appears at $\hat{G}^c = 0.136$.[10] For levels of government purchases up to G^c, (19.60) implies that each additional dollar spent by the government increases gross domestic product (GDP) by ϑ_G dollars. Increases in government purchases beyond that level result in even higher levels of GDP, though the increase per dollar of additional government purchases is smaller, as shown in figure 19.4, owing to the central bank's increase in interest rates in accordance with the Taylor rule. In figure 19.4, G^c is reached when government purchases exceed their steady-state value by 13.6 percent of steady-state GDP. For values $G_L > G^c$, the multiplier is no longer ϑ_G, but instead the coefficient $\gamma_y = 0.324$ defined in (19.52), where the persistence parameter ρ is now replaced by μ.

It follows from (19.59) that the multiplier $dY_L/dG_L = \vartheta_G$ for government purchases up to the level G^c is necessarily greater than one (for any $\mu > 0$). The reason is that given that the nominal interest rate remains at zero in periods $t < T$, an increase in G_L, which increases π_L, accordingly increases expected inflation (given some positive probability of elevated credit spreads continuing for another period), and hence lowers the real rate of interest.[11] Hence monetary policy is even more accommodative than is assumed in the benchmark analysis, and the increase in aggregate output is correspondingly higher.

When the policy rate remains at the zero bound, the multiplier can be unboundedly large, for a sufficiently large value of the persistence parameter μ. Figure 19.5 plots the multiplier as a function of μ, holding the other model parameters fixed at the values used by Eggertsson (2009). The figure illustrates that the multiplier is monotonically increasing in μ, and increases without bound as μ approaches $\bar{\mu}$. The figure also indicates that the multiplier is, in general, not too much greater than 1, except if μ is fairly large. However, it is important to note that the case where μ is large (in particular, a large fraction of $\bar{\mu}$) is precisely the case where the multiplier dY_L/dr_L is also large, which is to say, the case where a moderate increase in the size of credit spreads can cause a severe output collapse. Thus increased government purchases when interest rates are at the zero bound should be a powerful means through which to stave off an economic crisis precisely in those cases where the constraint of the zero lower bound would otherwise be most crippling—namely those cases where there is insufficient confidence that the disruption of credit markets will be short-lived.

19.3.5   Duration of Fiscal Stimulus

In our simple model the increase in output will be much smaller if a substantial part of the increased government purchases are expected to occur after the zero

---

10. The Matlab code Chapter19_3.m produces figures 19.4 through 19.7.
11. Note that the increase in expected inflation referred to here is actually a reduction in the expected rate of deflation.

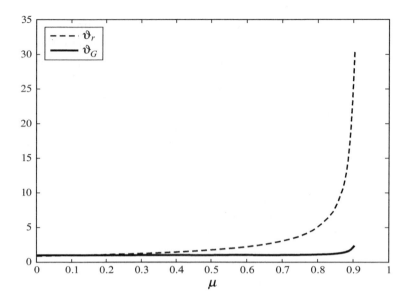

Figure 19.5
Derivatives of Y_L with respect to the values of r_L and G_L, for alternate degrees of persistence μ of the financial disturbance

lower bound ceases to bind. Once interest rates are determined by a Taylor rule, a higher level of government purchases should crowd out private spending (raising the marginal utility of private expenditure) and may cause lower inflation as well. But the expectation of a higher marginal utility of expenditure and of lower inflation in the event that credit spreads normalize in the following period both act as disincentives to private expenditure while the nominal interest rate remains at zero. Hence, while there is a positive effect on output during the crisis of increased government purchases at dates $t < T$, an anticipation of increased government purchases at dates $t > T$ has a negative effect on output prior to date T.

We use a simple example to illustrate this. Suppose that instead of the two-state Markov chain considered above, there are three states: after the "crisis" state (in which $r_t^{net} = r_L$ and $\hat{G}_t = \hat{G}_L$) ends, there is a probability $\lambda \in (0,1)$ each period that government purchases will remain at their elevated level ($\hat{G}_t = \hat{G}_L$), even though $r_t^{net} = \bar{r}$, yet with probability $1 - \lambda$ each period the economy returns to the "normal" state (in which $r_t^{net} = \bar{r}$ and $G_t = \bar{G}$) and remains there forever. If we let $\left(\pi_S, \hat{Y}_S, i_S\right)$ be the constant values for $\left(\pi_t, \hat{Y}_t, i_t\right)$ in the transitional state (i.e., for all $T \geq t < T'$, where T' is the random date at which government purchases return to their "normal" level), then the value of $E_t\hat{Y}_{t+1}$ during the "crisis" period is not $\mu\hat{Y}_L$, but $\mu \hat{Y}_L + (1 - \mu) \lambda \hat{Y}_S$, and similarly for expected future government purchases and expected future inflation. We can repeat the previous derivation, obtaining instead of (19.60) the more general form

$$\hat{Y}_L = \vartheta_r r_L + \vartheta_G \hat{G}_L + \vartheta_\pi \pi_S + \vartheta_C \left(\hat{Y}_S - \hat{G}_L \right),$$

where

$$\vartheta_\pi \equiv (1 - \mu) \lambda \vartheta_r > 0,$$
$$\vartheta_C \equiv \sigma^{-1} \vartheta_\pi > 0.$$

The fact that $\vartheta_\pi, \vartheta_C > 0$ indicates that an expectation of either lower private expenditure or lower inflation in the transitional state will lower output during the crisis.

Using the same analysis as before, we can show that the levels of output and inflation during the transitional state, when the interest rate is determined by the Taylor rule but government purchases remain high, are given by $\hat{Y}_S = \gamma_y \hat{G}_L, \pi_S = \gamma_\pi \hat{G}_L$ where γ_y is the coefficient defined in (19.52) (but with the persistence coefficient ρ equal to λ) and $\gamma_\pi = \kappa \left(\gamma_y - \Gamma \right) / (1 - \beta \lambda)$.

We thus obtain a multiplier

$$\frac{dY_L}{dG_L} = \vartheta_G + \vartheta_\pi \gamma_\pi + \vartheta_C \left(\gamma_y - 1 \right), \tag{19.61}$$

for government purchases below the critical level that causes the zero bound to no longer bind even in the crisis state. Since $\gamma_y < 1$ as explained earlier, the contribution of the final term is necessarily negative. In the case where either of the response coefficients (ϕ_y, ϕ_π) is sufficiently large, the Taylor rule will not allow a large increase in inflation during the transitional phase, and one obtains a multiplier smaller than ϑ_G when $\lambda > 0$. Figure 19.6 plots the value of the multiplier (19.61) as a function of λ, in the case where the other parameters are set as before. When $\lambda = 0$, the multiplier is nearly 2.3, but it steadily falls as λ is increased. For values of λ equal to 0.8 or higher (an expected duration of the fiscal stimulus for four quarters or more after the end of the financial disturbance), the multiplier falls below one. For values of λ equal to 0.91 or higher (an expected duration of ten quarters or more), the multiplier is negative. Hence a finding that a long-lasting fiscal stimulus is predicted to increase output only modestly, as in the simulations of Cogan et al. (2010), does not mean that a better-targeted fiscal stimulus cannot be much more effective.

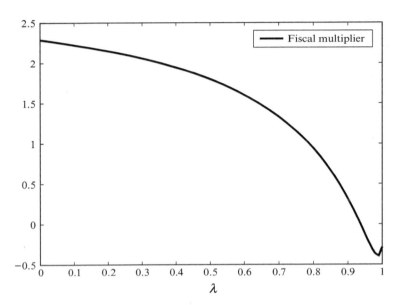

Figure 19.6
Fiscal multiplier as a function of λ

19.3.6   Government Purchases and Welfare

In the neoclassical model the optimal government purchases should be zero if they do not have intrinsic value. We thus suppose that the household has utility

$$\sum_{t=0}^{\infty} \beta^t \left[u\left(C_t\right) + g\left(G_t\right) - v\left(N_t\right) \right],\tag{19.62}$$

where $g' > 0$ and $g'' < 0$. The optimal path of government purchases should satisfy the first-order condition

$$u'\left(Y_t - G_t\right) = g'\left(G_t\right).\tag{19.63}$$

Because an increase in G_t can raise output Y_t, utility will be increased if

$$(u' - \tilde{v}')\frac{dY_t}{dG_t} + g' - u' > 0.$$

In the neoclassical model the first term in the expression above is zero.

Let us turn to the DNK model. If there is employment subsidy to offset distortions due to monopolistic competition, then a monetary policy that maintains price stability at all times achieves the flexible price equilibrium (efficient) allocation, regardless of the path of government purchases. The optimal-level government purchases is the same as that in the neoclassical model.

In the presence of the zero interest rate lower bound, substantial distortions due to deflation and a large negative output gap can exist in equilibrium. It can then be desirable to use government purchases to "fill the output gap," at least partially, even at the price of distorting, to some extent, the composition of expenditure in the economy.

As an example, consider the welfare effects of fiscal stimulus in the two-state example analyzed before. Suppose that the central bank maintains a strict zero inflation target whenever this is possible, and a nominal interest rate of zero whenever deflation is unavoidable. Let us consider only fiscal policies under which G_t is equal to some constant G_L for all $t < T$, and equal to $\bar{G}$ for all $t \geq T$, where $\bar{G}$ is the optimal level of government purchases under "normal" conditions; that is, the value that satisfies (19.63) when $Y_t = \bar{Y}$. Assume that there exists a subsidy such that the flexible price equilibrium allocation is optimal. In this case the steady state with $Y_t = \bar{Y}$ and $G_t = \bar{G}$ represents an optimal allocation of resources, and the assumed monetary policy would be optimal in the event that credit spreads were to remain always modest in size, so that the zero bound were never a binding constraint.

We want to consider the welfare effects of increasing G_L above the normal level $\bar{G}$, and the way in which the optimal choice of G_L depends on the size and expected duration of the financial disturbance. We can show that a quadratic approximation to the expected value of (19.62) varies inversely with

$$E \sum_{t=0}^{\infty} \beta^t \left[\pi_t^2 + \lambda_y \left(\hat{Y}_t - \Gamma \hat{G}_t \right)^2 + \lambda_g \hat{G}_t^2 \right], \qquad (19.64)$$

where

$$\lambda_y \equiv \frac{\kappa}{\theta} > 0,$$

$$\lambda_g \equiv \left[\frac{\eta_g}{\eta_u} + 1 - \Gamma \right] \Gamma \lambda_y > 0,$$

and $\eta_g \geq 0$ is (the negative of) the elasticity of g' with respect to G, a measure of the degree to which there are diminishing returns to additional government expenditure. Here the final two terms inside the square brackets represent a quadratic approximation to $u(Y_t - G_t) + g(G_t) - \tilde{v}(Y_t)$, which would be the period contribution to utility if the prices of all goods were the same, as would occur with flexible prices or in an environment with complete price stability. The additional π_t^2 term represents the additional welfare loss due to an inefficient composition of the economy's aggregate product as a result of price dispersion.

If the zero bound were never a binding constraint on monetary policy, the only constraint on feasible paths for the inflation rate and the output gap $\hat{Y}_t - \Gamma \hat{G}_t$ would be (19.48) regardless of the path of $\hat{G}_t$. Hence optimal monetary policy would maintain a zero inflation rate and output gap at all times, reducing each of the first two terms inside the square brackets in (19.64) to their minimum possible values each period. Such a policy can be implemented by a Taylor rule in (19.49). The optimal path of government purchases would then be chosen simply to minimize the remaining term, by setting $\hat{G}_t$ each period. (This would achieve an optimal composition of expenditure, as it would result in $Y_t = \bar{Y}$, $G_t = \bar{G}$ each period.)

However, the zero lower bound on interest rates precludes this first-best outcome. Under the policy in (19.54), the equilibrium is of the kind characterized before. In any equilibrium of this kind, the objective (19.64) takes the value

$$\frac{1}{1 - \beta\mu} \left[\pi_L^2 + \lambda_y \left(\hat{Y}_L - \Gamma\hat{G}_L \right)^2 + \lambda_g \hat{G}_L^2 \right]. \tag{19.65}$$

The optimal policy within this family is therefore obtained by minimizing (19.65) with respect to $\hat{G}_L$, taking into account the dependence of $(\pi_L, \hat{Y}_L)$ on $\hat{G}_L$ implied by (19.56) and (19.60). The first-order conditions for the minimization of this quadratic objective subject to the two linear constraints can be uniquely solved for a linear solution

$$\hat{G}_L = -\frac{\xi \left(\vartheta_G - \Gamma \right) \vartheta_r}{\xi \left(\vartheta_G - \Gamma \right)^2 + \lambda_g} r_L > 0,$$

where

$$\xi \equiv \left(\frac{\kappa}{1 - \beta\mu} \right)^2 + \gamma_y > 0.$$

Figure 19.7 plots the optimal value of $\hat{G}_L / |r_L|$ defined above for alternative values of μ, given $\theta = 12.77$ and other parameter values set as before. The optimal value is plotted under two different assumptions about the degree of diminishing returns to additional government expenditure. In case A, it is assumed that utility is linear in government purchases ($\eta_g = 0$); this provides an upper bound for the degree to which it can be cost effective to increase government purchases. In case B, it is instead assumed that $\eta_g = 4\eta_u$; this corresponds to the case where the marginal utility of government purchases decreases at the same rate (per percentage point increase in spending) as the marginal utility of private purchases, and private expenditure is four times as large as government purchases in the steady state. In this case, because of the diminishing returns to additional government purchases, the optimal increase in government spending is less for any given financial disturbance.

For the purpose of comparison, the solid line in figure 19.7 also plots the level of government purchases, $\hat{G}_L / |r_L| = \vartheta_r / \vartheta_G$, that would be required to fully eliminate the output gap (i.e., keep output at the flexible price equilibrium level) and prevent any decline in inflation as a result of the financial disturbance. This line also

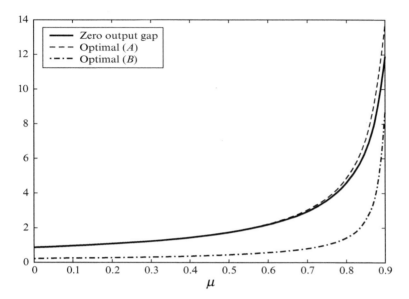

Figure 19.7
Optimal value of $\hat{G}_L/|r_L|$ for alternate values of μ. Case A: $\eta_g = 0$. Case B: $\eta_g = 4\eta_u$. The solid line shows the value of $\hat{G}_L/|r_L|$ required to maintain a zero output gap.

indicates the critical level of government purchases at which the zero lower bound ceases to bind.

Figure 19.7 shows that when the financial disturbance is not too persistent (small values of μ), the optimal increase in government purchases is only a small fraction of the increase that would be required to eliminate the output gap, if we assume diminishing returns to additional public expenditure. The optimal fiscal stimulus would be even smaller if one were to assume even more sharply diminishing returns to public expenditure. The optimal size of fiscal stimulus can be quite substantial in the case where μ is large. In this case, when there is a substantial probability that the financial disruption will persist for years, and when a serious depression could result in the absence of fiscal stimulus, welfare is maximized by an aggressive increase in government purchases of nearly the size required to fully stabilize inflation and the output gap.

19.4 A Medium-Scale DSGE Model

In this section we introduce a few new elements into the basic DNK model: (1) habit formation preferences, (2) capital and investment adjustment costs, (3) capacity utilization, (4) sticky wages, (5) partial indexation, (6) long-run growth, and (7) multiple shocks. Such a model is considered the current standard of New Keynesian macroeconomics (see Christiano, Eichenbaum, and Evans 2005; Smets and Wouters 2007), and it is close to the models employed by several central banks as inputs for policy analysis.

19.4.1   Households

There is a continuum of households in the economy indexed by $i \in [0,1]$. Household i maximizes the following lifetime utility function, which is separable in consumption, C_{it}, real money balances, M_{it+1}/P_t, and hours worked, N_{it}:

$$E \sum_{t=0}^{\infty} \beta^t \left[\ln\left(C_{it} - bC_{it-1}\right) + \chi_m \ln\left(\frac{M_{it+1}}{P_t}\right) - \frac{\chi N_{it}^{1+\nu}}{1+\nu} \right].$$

The budget constraint is given by

$$C_{it} + I_{it} + \frac{M_{it+1}}{P_t} + \frac{B_{it+1}}{(1+i_t)P_t}$$

$$= \frac{W_{it}}{P_t} N_{it} + \left(\frac{R_t^k}{P_t} u_t - Z_t^{-1} a\left(u_{it}\right) \right) K_{it} + \frac{M_{it}}{P_t} + \frac{B_{it}}{P_t} + T_t,$$

where W_{it} is the nominal wage rate, R_t^k is nominal rental rate of capital, I_{it} represents investment, $u_{it} > 0$ is the intensity of use of capital, $Z_t^{-1} a\left(u_{it}\right)$ is the physical cost of use of capital in resource terms, Z_t is an investment-specific technological shock to be described momentarily, and T_t includes lump-sum transfers and the profits of the firms in the economy. Normalizing the capacity utilization cost by Z_t^{-1} preserves balanced growth. Assume that $a\left(1\right) = 0$ and $a', a'' > 0$.

Investment I_{it} induces a law of motion for capital,

$$K_{it+1} = (1-\delta) K_{it} + Z_t \left(1 - S\left(\frac{I_{it}}{I_{it-1}} \right) \right) I_{it},$$

where δ is the depreciation rate and S is an adjustment cost function such that $S\left(g_I\right) = 0$, $S'\left(g_I\right) = 0$, $S'' > 0$ where g_I is the gross growth rate of investment along the balance growth path, which will be equal to the long-run economic growth rate. We will determine that growth rate later. Suppose that

$$Z_t = Z_{t-1} \exp\left(g_z + \sigma_z \varepsilon_{zt}\right), \quad \varepsilon_{It} \sim N\left(0,1\right).$$

First-order conditions are given by

$$\Lambda_{it} = \left(C_{it} - bC_{it-1}\right)^{-1} - b\beta E_t \left(C_{it+1} - bC_{it}\right)^{-1},$$

$$\Lambda_{it} = \beta E_t \Lambda_{it+1} \frac{(1+i_t) P_t}{P_{t+1}},$$

$$\frac{R_t^k}{P_t} = Z_t^{-1} a'(u_{it}),$$

$$Q_{it} = \beta E_t \left\{ \frac{\Lambda_{it+1}}{\Lambda_{it}} \left((1-\delta) Q_{it+1} + \frac{R_{t+1}^k}{P_{t+1}} u_{it+1} - Z_{t+1}^{-1} a(u_{it+1}) \right) \right\},$$

$$1 = Q_{it} Z_t \left(1 - S \left(\frac{I_{it}}{I_{it-1}} \right) - S' \left(\frac{I_{it}}{I_{it-1}} \right) \frac{I_{it}}{I_{it-1}} \right)$$

$$+ \beta E_t Q_{it+1} Z_{t+1} \frac{\Lambda_{it+1}}{\Lambda_{it}} S' \left(\frac{I_{it+1}}{I_{it}} \right) \left(\frac{I_{it+1}}{I_{it}} \right)^2,$$

where Q_{it} represents Tobin's marginal Q and Λ_{it} is the Lagrange multiplier associated with household i's budget constraint. If $S = 0$ (i.e., there are no adjustment costs), then $Q_{it} = 1/Z_t$; that is, the marginal Q is equal to the replacement cost of capital (the relative price of capital). Furthermore, if $Z_t = 1$, as in the standard neoclassical growth model, $Q_{it} = 1$.

Each household supplies differentiated labor services that are aggregated by a labor "packer" into a homogeneous labor unit according to the function

$$N_t^d = \left(\int_0^1 N_{it}^{(\eta-1)/\eta} di \right)^{\eta/(\eta-1)}, \tag{19.66}$$

where $\eta \geq 0$ is the elasticity of substitution among different types of labor. The labor "packer" takes all wages W_{it} of the differentiated labor and the wage of the homogeneous labor unit W_t as given and maximizes real profits

$$\frac{W_t}{P_t} N_t^d - \int_0^1 \frac{W_{it}}{P_t} N_{it} di$$

subject to the production function (19.66). The first-order condition of the labor "packer" implies that

$$N_{it} = \left(\frac{W_{it}}{W_t} \right)^{-\eta} N_t^d.$$

The zero profit condition implies that the aggregate wage index W_t satisfies

$$W_t = \left(\int_0^1 W_{it}^{1-\eta} di \right)^{1/(1-\eta)}.$$

Because households have monopoly power over labor supply, they can set wages. Wages are sticky as in the Calvo (1983) model. In each period household i has a probability $1 - \theta_w$ of being able to change its wages. Otherwise, it can only partially index its wages by a fraction $\chi_w \in [0,1]$ of past inflation. Therefore, if a household has not been able to change its wage for τ periods, its real wage after τ periods is equal to

$$\prod_{s=1}^{\tau} \frac{\Pi_{t+s-1}^{\chi_w} W_{it}}{P_{t+\tau}} = \prod_{s=1}^{\tau} \frac{\Pi_{t+s-1}^{\chi_w}}{\Pi_{t+s}} w_{it},$$

which is the original nominal wage times the indexation divided by the price level at time $t + \tau$. Here $w_{it} \equiv W_{it}/P_t$ represents the real wage rate for household i's labor. Let $w_t \equiv W_t/P_t$ denote the aggregate real wage index.

Household i sets wages according to the following problem:

$$\max_{w_{it}} E_t \sum_{\tau=0}^{\infty} (\beta\theta_w)^{\tau} \left\{ -\chi \frac{N_{i\tau}^{1+\nu}}{1+\nu} + \Lambda_{i\tau} \prod_{s=1}^{\tau} \frac{\Pi_{t+s-1}^{\chi_w}}{\Pi_{t+s}} w_{it} N_{it} \right\}$$

subject to

$$N_{it+\tau} = \left(\prod_{s=1}^{\tau} \frac{\Pi_{t+s-1}^{\chi_w}}{\Pi_{t+s}} \frac{w_{it}}{w_{t+\tau}} \right)^{-\eta} N_{t+\tau}^d.$$

The first-order condition implies that the optimal real wage w_t^* satisfies

$$\frac{\eta-1}{\eta} w_t^* E_t \sum_{\tau=0}^{\infty} (\beta\theta_w)^{\tau} \Lambda_{t+\tau} \left(\prod_{s=1}^{\tau} \frac{\Pi_{t+s-1}^{\chi_w}}{\Pi_{t+s}} \right)^{1-\eta} \left(\frac{w_t^*}{w_{t+\tau}} \right)^{-\eta} N_{t+\tau}^d$$

$$= E_t \sum_{\tau=0}^{\infty} (\beta\theta_w)^{\tau} \chi \left(\prod_{s=1}^{\tau} \frac{\Pi_{t+s-1}^{\chi_w}}{\Pi_{t+s}} \frac{w_t^*}{w_{t+\tau}} \right)^{-\eta(1+\nu)} \left(N_{t+\tau}^d \right)^{1+\nu},$$

where we have suppressed the household index i since we will focus on a symmetric equilibrium in which all households set the same wage and make the same decisions. Define f_t as the value in the equation above. It satisfies the recursion

$$f_t = \frac{\eta-1}{\eta} (w_t^*)^{1-\eta} \Lambda_t w_t^{\eta} N_t^d + \beta\theta_w E_t \left(\frac{\Pi_t^{\chi_w}}{\Pi_{t+1}} \right)^{1-\eta} \left(\frac{w_{t+1}^*}{w_t^*} \right)^{\eta-1} f_{t+1},$$

$$f_t = \chi \left(\frac{w_t^*}{w_t} \right)^{-\eta(1+\nu)} \left(N_t^d \right)^{1+\nu} + \beta\theta_w E_t \left(\frac{\Pi_t^{\chi_w}}{\Pi_{t+1}} \right)^{-\eta(1+\nu)} \left(\frac{w_{t+1}^*}{w_t^*} \right)^{\eta(1+\nu)} f_{t+1}.$$

These two equations determine f_t and w_t^* jointly.

In a symmetric equilibrium, in every period, a fraction $1 - \theta_w$ of households set w_t^* as their wage, while the remaining fraction θ_w partially index their wages by past inflation. Consequently the real wage index evolves according to

$$w_t^{1-\eta} = \theta_w \left(\frac{\Pi_{t-1}^{\chi_w}}{\Pi_t} \right)^{1-\eta} w_{t-1}^{1-\eta} + (1 - \theta_w) (w_t^*)^{1-\eta}.$$

19.4.2   Firms

Let us turn to the firms' problem. The final goods producers' problem is the same as that in section 19.1. There is a continuum of intermediate goods producers $j \in [0, 1]$. Each intermediate goods producer j has access to a technology described by a production function of the form

$$Y_t^j = A_t \left(K_t^j \right)^\alpha \left(N_t^{jd} \right)^{1-\alpha} - \phi \xi_t,$$

where ϕ represents fixed costs of production and A_t satisfies

$$A_t = A_{t-1} \exp \left(g_a + \sigma_a \varepsilon_{at} \right), \quad \varepsilon_{at} \sim N(0, 1).$$

Fixed costs are scaled by $\xi_t \equiv A_t^{1/(1-\alpha)} Z_t^{\alpha/(1-\alpha)}$ to guarantee that economic profits are roughly zero. It can be shown that the long-run economic growth rate is equal to

$$g_e = \frac{g_a + \alpha g_z}{1 - \alpha}.$$

Intermediate good producers solve a two-stage problem. First, given the real wage w_t and the real rental rate $r_t^k = R_t^k / P_t$, they rent N_t^{jd} and K_t^j to minimize real costs of production:

$$\min_{N_t^{jd}, K_t^j} w_t N_t^{jd} + r_t^k K_t^j$$

subject to

$$Y_t^j = \begin{cases} A_t \left(K_t^j \right)^\alpha \left(N_t^{jd} \right)^{1-\alpha} - \phi \xi_t & \text{if } Y_t^j > 0, \\ 0 & \text{otherwise.} \end{cases}$$

We assume an interior solution so that the real marginal cost is the Lagrange multiplier associated with the production function,

$$MC_t = \frac{1}{A_t} \left(\frac{1}{1 - \alpha} \right)^{1-\alpha} \left(\frac{1}{\alpha} \right)^\alpha w_t^{1-\alpha} r_t^\alpha.$$

The first-order condition implies that

$$\frac{K_t^j}{N_t^{jd}} = \frac{\alpha}{1 - \alpha} \frac{w_t}{r_t^k}.$$

Thus the capital–labor ratio is identical for all firms. It follows that the equation above holds in the aggregate:

$$\frac{\int K_t^j dj}{N_t^d} = \frac{\alpha}{1-\alpha} \frac{w_t}{r_t^k},$$

where $\int_0^1 N_t^{dj} dj = N_t^d$.

In the second stage, intermediate goods producers choose the price that maximizes discounted real profits. In each period a fraction $1 - \theta_p$ of firms can change their prices. All other firms can only index their prices by past inflation. Indexation is controlled by the parameter $\chi_p \in [0,1]$, where $\chi_p = 0$ represents no indexation and $\chi_p = 1$ represents full indexation. Firm j's pricing problem is given by

$$\max_{P_t^j} \ E_t \sum_{\tau=0}^{\infty} (\beta \theta_w)^\tau \frac{\Lambda_{t+\tau}}{\Lambda_t} \left\{ \left(\prod_{s=1}^{\tau} \Pi_{t+s-1}^{\chi_p} \frac{P_t^j}{P_{t+\tau}} - MC_{t+\tau} \right) Y_{t+\tau} \right\}$$

subject to

$$Y_{t+\tau}^j = \left(\prod_{s=1}^{\tau} \Pi_{t+s-1}^{\chi_p} \frac{P_t^j}{P_{t+\tau}} \right)^{-\varepsilon} Y_{t+\tau},$$

where $Y_{t+\tau}$ is given by (19.5).

In a symmetric equilibrium the first-order condition implies that

$$E_t \sum_{\tau=0}^{\infty} (\beta \theta_p)^\tau \frac{\Lambda_{t+\tau}}{\Lambda_t} Y_{t+\tau} \left(\begin{array}{c} \left(\prod_{s=1}^{\tau} \frac{\Pi_{t+s-1}^{\chi_p}}{\Pi_{t+s}} \right)^{1-\varepsilon} \frac{P_t^*}{P_t} \\ -\frac{\varepsilon}{\varepsilon-1} \left(\prod_{s=1}^{\tau} \frac{\Pi_{t+s-1}^{\chi_p}}{\Pi_{t+s}} \right)^{1-\varepsilon} MC_{t+\tau} \end{array} \right) = 0.$$

We can write it in a recursive form:

$$g_t = \frac{\varepsilon}{\varepsilon-1} MC_t Y_t + \beta \theta_p E_t \frac{\Lambda_{t+1}}{\Lambda_t} \left(\frac{\Pi_t^{\chi_p}}{\Pi_{t+1}} \right)^{-\varepsilon} g_{t+1},$$

$$g_t = \Pi_t^* Y_t + \beta \theta_p E_t \frac{\Lambda_{t+1}}{\Lambda_t} \left(\frac{\Pi_t^{\chi_p}}{\Pi_{t+1}} \right)^{1-\varepsilon} \left(\frac{\Pi_t^*}{\Pi_{t+1}^*} \right) g_{t+1},$$

where $\Pi_t^* = P_t^*/P_t$.

The price index evolves as

$$1 = \theta_p \left(\frac{\Pi_{t-1}^{\chi_p}}{\Pi_t} \right)^{1-\varepsilon} + (1 - \theta_p) \Pi_t^{*1-\varepsilon}.$$

19.4.3   Monetary and Fiscal Policies

The central bank sets the nominal interest rate according to a Taylor rule through open market operations,

$$\ln\left(\frac{1+i_t}{1+i}\right) = \phi_R \ln\left(\frac{1+i_{t-1}}{1+i}\right) + (1-\phi_R)$$
$$\times \left(\phi_\pi \ln\left(\frac{\Pi_t}{\Pi}\right) + \phi_y \ln\left(\frac{Y_t/Y_{t-1}}{g_e}\right)\right) + \sigma\varepsilon_{mt},$$

where ε_{mt} is IID standard normal, $\phi_R \in (0,1)$ and a variable without a time subscript denotes its steady-state value. Here g_e denotes the long-run growth rate of the economy. In this Taylor rule the interest rate responds to the past interest rate and growth gap instead of the output gap.

The government spends G_t, which is financed by lump-sum taxes, government debt, and seigniorage. To have balanced growth, assume that G_t is a constant fraction of aggregate output.

19.4.4   Aggregation and Equilibrium

The market-clearing conditions for the labor and capital are given by

$$\int_0^1 K_t^j dj = \int_0^1 u_{it} K_{it} di = u_t K_t$$

and

$$N_t \equiv \int_0^1 N_{it} di = \int_0^1 \left(\frac{w_{it}}{w_t}\right)^{-\eta} N_t^d di = \Delta_t^w N_t^d,$$

where

$$\Delta_t^w = \int_0^1 \left(\frac{w_{it}}{w_t}\right)^{-\eta} di$$

represents a measure of wage dispersion. It follows dynamics

$$\Delta_t^w = \theta_w \left(\frac{w_{t-1}}{w_t} \frac{\Pi_{t-1}^{\chi_w}}{\Pi_t}\right)^{-\eta} \Delta_{t-1}^w + (1-\theta_w) \left(\frac{w_t^*}{w_t}\right)^{-\eta}.$$

Since all the intermediate goods firms will have the same capital–labor ratio, we can find aggregate output supply:

$$Y_t = \frac{1}{\Delta_t^p} \left[A_t \left(u_t K_t\right)^\alpha \left(N_t^d\right)^{1-\alpha} - \phi\xi_t \right],$$

where

$$\Delta_t^p = \int_0^1 \left(\frac{P_t^j}{P_t} \right)^{-\varepsilon} dj$$

represents price dispersion. It satisfies dynamics

$$\Delta_t^p = \theta_p \left(\frac{\Pi_{t-1}^{\chi_p}}{\Pi_t} \right)^{-\varepsilon} \Delta_{t-1}^p + (1 - \theta_p) \left(\Pi_t^* \right)^{-\varepsilon}.$$

Equating the aggregate demand and the aggregate supply delivers the resource constraint:

$$C_t + I_t + Z_t^{-1} a(u_t) K_t + G_t = Y_t.$$

A competitive equilibrium consists of twenty variables C_t, I_t, K_t, N_t, N_t^d, Y_t, u_t, Λ_t, Q_t, w_t, r_t^k, Π_t, Π_t^*, w_t^*, MC_t, Δ_t^p, Δ_t^w, i_t, f_t, g_t such that twenty equations holds. The predetermined variables are two exogenous shocks and endogenous variables Δ_t^p, Δ_t^w, Π_t, i_t, K_t, and C_t. One can easily introduce more exogenous shocks in this model and then estimate it by the Bayesian method (see Fernández-Villaverde, Guerrón-Quintana and Rubio-Ramírez 2010).

19.5 Exercises

1. (Bullard and Mitra 2002) For the model in section 19.1 prove that the necessary and sufficient condition for the existence of a unique stable equilibrium solution is given by (19.31).

2. Consider the log-linearized basic DNK model. Prove that the Taylor rule in (19.29), where the monetary policy shock v_t is removed, implements the optimal monetary policy if and only if condition (19.31) holds.

3. Consider the model in section 19.3. Prove that the equilibrium conditions (19.48) and (19.53), where $i_t = 0$, can be solved forward to obtain a unique bounded solution for $\left\{ \hat{Y}_t, \pi_t \right\}$ if and only if the model parameters satisfy (19.55).

4. Consider the model in Section 19.3. Prove that $\hat{Y}_S = \gamma_y \hat{G}_L$, $\pi_S = \gamma_\pi \hat{G}_L$, and derive the coefficients γ_y and γ_π. Show that the fiscal multiplier is given by (19.61).

5. Derive (19.64) by second-order approximations.

6. Derive the steady-state conditions and the log-linearized equilibrium conditions for the model in section 19.4.

IV Further Topics

In this part we introduce further topics, including recursive utility, dynamic games, and recursive contracts. These topics require us to extend the previous dynamic programming methods. In particular, we will study how the standard dynamic programming approach can be applied to recursive utility and how the method of "dynamic programming squared" can be used to solve dynamic games and contracting problems.[12] The idea of dynamic programming squared is to use continuation values as state variables in terms of which a Bellman equation is cast. The term "squared" comes from the fact that the continuation values themselves satisfy annother Bellman equation.

---

12. The term "dynamic programming squared" is borrowed from Ljungqvist and Sargent (2004).

20 Recursive Utility

Dynamic utility models must deal with how future utilities are aggregated and discounted to the present, how uncertainty is resolved over time, and how a decision maker reacts to the uncertainty. The standard approach is to adopt the time-additive expected utility model. This utility has some shortcomings.

First, this utility implies some undesirable properties of the marginal rate of substitution between consumption in different periods. Consider the case where consumption is constant over time. Then the marginal rate of substitution between consumption today and consumption tomorrow is the inverse of the subjective discount factor. It is unaffected by the level of consumption. This constant marginal rate of substitution severely constrains the long-run behavior of economic models. For example, a consumer facing a fixed interest rate will try either to save without limit or to borrow without limit, except in the knife-edge case where the subjective discount rate equals the interest rate. This problem is especially severe when there are heterogeneous households. Unless all of the households have the same subjective discount rate, the most patient household ends up with all the capital in the long run, while all other households consume nothing, using their labor income to service their debt (Becker 1980).

Second, the time-additive expected utility model implies that the **elasticity of intertemporal substitution (EIS)** is equal to the inverse of the relative risk aversion coefficient. This restriction severely limits the application of the model, especially in the asset market. For example, this model does not explain the equity premium puzzle and the risk-free rate puzzle (Mehra and Prescott 1980; Epstein and Zin 1989; Weil 1989). In particular, a high coefficient of relative risk aversion is needed to match the high equity premium in the data. However, this implies that the EIS is low and hence the risk-free rate is high, which contradicts the low risk-free rate in the data.

Third, the time-additive expected utility model implies that the agent is indifferent to the timing of resolution of uncertainty. To illustrate this point, consider a simple two-period example with the utility function given by $E\left[u\left(c_0\right) + \beta u\left(c_1\right)\right]$.

Say we flip a fair coin at time zero. If it comes up heads, the consumption levels at time 0 and time 1 are c_0 and c_1^1, respectively. But if it comes up tails, they are c_0 and $c_1^2 \neq c_1^1$. Now suppose that the consumption level at time zero is still c_0, but we flip a coin at date 1 with the same outcome of c_1^1 or c_1^2. Then the expected utility from these two experiments is identical. Is the timing of the resolution of uncertainty relevant for economics? It matters for asset pricing as shown by Bansal and Yaron (2004) in a model with long-run risks. They show that aversion to long-run risks can help explain the equity premium puzzle. Epstein, Farhi, and Strzalecki (2012) define a concept of timing premium and show that it pays to resolve long-run risk in a class of recursive utility.

Finally, the expected utility model cannot explain some experimental evidence, such as the Ellsberg paradox and the Allais paradox. Researchers in decision theory have developed many static nonexpected utility models to deal with these paradoxes. To study questions in macroeconomics and finance using these models, one has to embed them in dynamic settings.

Motivated by the considerations above, this chapter introduces a few classes of recursive utility models developed recently in the literature. These models explain many puzzling phenomena in financial markets and the real economy and also deliver some new theoretical insights and testable implications. We refer the reader to Epstein (1992), Backus, Routledge, and Zin (2004), and Epstein and Schneider (2010) for surveys of the related literature. Also see Skiadas (2009) for a textbook treatment of recursive utility.

20.1   Deterministic Case

We start with the deterministic case. Fisher (1906) introduces the concept of impatience to capture a preference for advanced timing of satisfaction. This notion was formalized and axiomatized by Koopmans and his collaborators in the 1960s and early 1970s (Koopmans 1960, 1972a, b; Koopmans, Diamond, and Williamson 1964). They proposed a deterministic recursive utility model. To introduce this model, we consider an infinite-horizon setup.

20.1.1   Koopmans's Utility

Time is indexed by $t = 0, 1, \ldots.$ Let $c = (c_0, c_1, c_2, \ldots)$ be a sequence of consumption bundles $c_t \in \mathbb{R}_+^l$ in each time period t. Let L be the space of sequences c that are bounded in the norm

$$\|c\|_L = \sup_t \ \|c_t\|_E,$$

where $\|\cdot\|_E$ is the Euclidean norm on $\mathbb{R}^l$. For any $c = (c_0, c_1, \ldots) \in L$, define $_tc = (c_t, c_{t+1}, \ldots) \in L$.

Suppose that we have a continuous preference relation $\succeq$ defined on L. We say this preference relation has a **recursive utility** representation if there is a utility function U, a function W (called the **time aggregator**) and a period utility function $u : \mathbb{R}^l_+ \to \mathbb{R}$, satisfying

$$U(c) = W(u(c_0), U({}_1c)), \quad c \in L. \tag{20.1}$$

An example is the time-additive utility, $U(c) = \sum_{t=0}^{\infty} \beta^t u(c_t)$.

Koopmans introduces the following axioms:

(K1) $\succeq$ is a stationary relation: $(c_0, {}_1c) \succeq (c_0, {}_1c')$ for all $c_0 \in \mathbb{R}^l_+$ if and only if ${}_1c \succeq {}_1c'$.

(K2) $\succeq$ exhibits limited independence: for all $c_0, c'_0 \in \mathbb{R}^l_+$ and ${}_1c, {}_1c' \in L$, $(c_0, {}_1c) \succeq (c'_0, {}_1c)$ if and only if $(c_0, {}_1c') \succeq (c'_0, {}_1c')$.

(K3) $\succeq$ is a sensitive relation: there is a ${}_1c \in L$ and $c_0, c'_0 \in \mathbb{R}^l_+$ such that $(c_0, {}_1c) \succ (c'_0, {}_1c)$.

Axiom (K1) ensures dynamic consistency. Dynamic consistency rules out the situation where a decision maker chooses a consumption plan c_0 at time 0, but he prefers another plan in the future. Formally, we define the following:

Definition 20.1.1 *The utility function $U : L \to \mathbb{R}$ is **dynamically consistent** if for any c, c' with $c_s = c'_s$, $0 \le s < t$, for any t, we have that $U_0(c) > U_0(c')$ if $U_t(c) > U_t(c')$.*

It is easy to show that any preference order with a recursive representation satisfies Koopmans's axioms. Koopmans (1960) shows that if a preference relation satisfies (K1) to (K3) and has a utility representation U, then U satisfies (20.1). The representation is unique in the sense of ordinal utility.

For differentiable utility we can define the subjective discount factor associated with a constant consumption stream $(x, x, ...) \in L$ by

$$\beta(x) = \left. \frac{\partial W(u, U)}{\partial U} \right|_{(x,x,...)}.$$

In general, $\beta(x)$ depends on the consumption level.

We now define the **elasticity of intertemporal substitution (EIS)** between date s and date t consumption:

$$\mathrm{EIS} = \left| \frac{d \ln(c_s/c_t)}{d \ln MRS_{s,t}} \right| = \left| \frac{d \ln\left(\frac{c_s}{c_t}\right)}{d \ln\left(\frac{\partial U/\partial c_s}{\partial U/\partial c_t}\right)} \right|.$$

The interpretation is that EIS measures the percentage change in date s consumption relative to date t consumption when their relative price changes by 1 percent. In general, EIS depends on consumption level. But for homothetic utility, it is constant.

Example 20.1.1   *Uzawa (1968) studies a utility function of the following form:*

$$U(c) = u(c_0) + \beta(u(c_0)) U({}_1c).$$

The subjective discount factor is given by $\beta(u(c_0))$. Epstein and Hynes (1983) introduce the following utility function:

$$U(c) = u(c_0) + \beta(c_0) U({}_1c).$$

The subjective discount factor is given by $\beta(c_0)$.

Example 20.1.2   *Consider the following recursive utility with constant elasticity of substitution (CES) time aggregator:*

$$U(c) = \left[(1 - \beta) c_0^{1-\rho} + \beta U({}_1c)^{1-\rho}\right]^{1/(1-\rho)}, \quad \rho > 0.$$

One can compute that EIS is equal to $1/\rho$ and the subjective discount factor is equal to β.

20.1.2   Construction

Koopmans's utility function satisfies a recursive equation (20.1), which does not ensure existence. Lucas and Stokey (1984) first use the Contraction Mapping Theorem to construct recursive utility. To apply this theorem, let $C(L)$ denote the Banach space of all bounded continuous functions $U : L \to \mathbb{R}$ with the norm $\|U\| = \sup_{c \in L} |U(c)|$. Let $W : \mathbb{R}_+^l \times \mathbb{R} \to \mathbb{R}$ be a continuous function with the following properties:

(W1) for any $z \in \mathbb{R}_+$, $W(\cdot, z) : \mathbb{R}_+^l \to \mathbb{R}$ is bounded.

(W2) for some $\beta \in (0, 1)$,

$$|W(x, z) - W(x, z')| \le \beta |z - z'|, \quad \text{all } x \in \mathbb{R}_+^l \text{ and } z, z' \in \mathbb{R}.$$

(W3) W is increasing.

(W4) W is concave.

Define the operator $T_W : C(L) \to C(L)$ by $T_W f(c) = W(c_0, f({}_1c))$. It is straightforward to prove the following:

Theorem 20.1.1 *Let W satisfy (W1) and (W2). Then T_W has a unique fixed point U that is the unique solution to*

$$U(c) = W(c_0, U({}_1c)).$$

If W satisfies (W3), then U is increasing. If (W3)–(W4) hold, then U is concave.

A restrictive assumption of this theorem is that W is bounded. This rules out many commonly used utility functions. For example, the aggregator $W(x,y) = x^{1-\gamma}/(1-\gamma) + \beta y$, which leads to the utility function $U(c) = \sum_{t=0}^{\infty} \beta^t c_t^{1-\gamma}/(1-\gamma)$, does not fit into Lucas and Stokey's framework. Many researchers have proposed solutions to this problem. The most notable are the weighted contraction method (Boyd 1990), the "partial sum" method (Boyd 1990), Streufert's (1990) biconvergence condition, and the k-local contraction method recently used by Rincon-Zapatero and Rodringuez-Palmero (2003).

Here we introduce the weighted contraction mapping approach only. We weaken assumptions (W2) and (W4) as follows:

(W5) W satisfies a Lipschitz condition of order one: there exists $\delta > 0$ such that $|W(x,y) - W(x,y_0)| < \delta |y - y_0|$ for all $x \in \mathbb{R}^l_+$, and $y, y_0 \in \mathbb{R}^l_+$.

(W6) $T_W^n y(c)$ is concave in c for all n and all constant functions $y \in L$.

In (W5), δ can be greater than 1. The purpose of condition (W6) is to ensure concavity of the utility function. It is not required for the existence results. Joint concavity of W is not required for the associated recursive utility function to be concave.

For $\theta \geq 1$ define the θ-norm by $|c|_\theta = \sup_t \|c_t\|_E / \theta^t$ for any $c \in \mathbb{R}^{l\infty}_+$, where $\|\cdot\|_E$ is the Euclidean norm on $\mathbb{R}^l$. Then define the θ-weighted ℓ^∞ space by $\ell_\theta^\infty = \{c \in \mathbb{R}^{l\infty}_+ : |c|_\theta < \infty\}$. The space ℓ_θ^∞ is a Banach space under the norm $|c|_\theta$. Let $C(\ell_\theta^\infty)$ be the space of continuous functions on ℓ_θ^∞. Let $\varphi \in C(\ell_\theta^\infty)$ with $\varphi > 0$. Define the φ-weighted norm by $\|f\|_\varphi = \sup_{x \in \ell_\theta^\infty} |f(x)/\varphi(x)|$. The space $C_\varphi(\ell_\theta^\infty) = \{f \in C(\ell_\theta^\infty) : \|f\|_\varphi < \infty\}$ is then a Banach space under the φ-norm $\|f\|_\varphi$.

Theorem 20.1.2 *Suppose that the continuous function $W : \mathbb{R}^l_+ \times \mathbb{R} \to \mathbb{R}$ satisfies (W2) and (W5) and $\varphi > 0$ is continuous on ℓ_θ^∞. Suppose further that $W(c_0, 0)$ is bounded under the φ-weighted norm and*

$$\delta \sup_{c \in \ell_\theta^\infty} \frac{\varphi({}_1c)}{\varphi(c)} < 1.$$

Then there exists a unique $U \in C_\varphi(\ell_\theta^\infty)$ such that $W(c_0, U({}_1c)) = U(c)$. Moreover $T_W^n 0(c) \to U(c)$ in $C_\varphi(\ell_\theta^\infty)$. If (W6) holds, then U is concave. If, in addition, $W(x,y)$ is strictly concave in x and strictly increasing in y, then U is strictly concave.

Proof   Since W is increasing in y, the operator T_W is increasing. Since $W(c_0, 0)$ is bounded under the φ-weighted norm,

$$\frac{|T_W 0|}{\varphi(c)} = \frac{|W(c_0, 0)|}{\varphi(c)} < \infty.$$

Thus $T_W 0 \in C_\varphi(\ell_\theta^\infty)$. Moreover, by (W5), for any $a > 0$ and $f \in C_\varphi(\ell_\theta^\infty)$,

$$
\begin{aligned}
T_W(f + a\varphi)(c) &= W(c_0, (f + a\varphi)(_1c)) \\
&\le W(c_0, f(_1c)) + a\delta\varphi(_1c) \\
&\le T_W f(c) + a\varphi(c)\,\delta \sup_{c \in \ell_\theta^\infty} \frac{\varphi(_1c)}{\varphi(c)}.
\end{aligned}
$$

Applying the Weighted Contraction Mapping Theorem 7.3.6 with $\delta \sup_{c \in \ell_\theta^\infty} \frac{\varphi(_1c)}{\varphi(c)} < 1$ shows that T_W has a unique fixed point U. Now consider

$$
\begin{aligned}
\|U(c) - T_W^n 0\|_\varphi &\le \delta^n \|U(_nc)\|_\varphi = \delta^n \sup_c \frac{U(_nc)}{\varphi(_nc)} \frac{\varphi(_nc)}{\varphi(_{n-1}c)} \cdots \frac{\varphi(_1c)}{\varphi(c)} \\
&\le \|U\|_\varphi \left(\delta \sup_c \frac{\varphi(_1c)}{\varphi(c)}\right)^n \to 0.
\end{aligned}
$$

The result follows. The proof of concavity is left as an exercise.   ∎

We now use some examples to illustrate the theorem. The general strategy is to pick either $W(x, 0)$ or a function bounding it for the weighting function φ. Consider the discounted aggregator $W(x, y) = x^{1-\gamma} + \beta y$ for $0 < \gamma, \beta < 1$. Choose θ such that $\beta\theta^{1-\gamma} < 1$ and take ℓ_θ^∞ as the consumption space. Note that it is possible that $\theta > 1$ so that we allow for consumption growth. Here $W(x, 0) = x^{1-\gamma}$. This may be zero, so we add one and compose with the δ-norm to get a weighting function. That is, $\varphi(c) = 1 + |c|_\theta^{1-\gamma}$. Then $W(c_0, 0) = c_0^{1-\gamma} < |c|_\theta^{1-\gamma} < \varphi(c)$. Thus $W(c_0, 0)$ is bounded under the φ-weighted norm. Also

$$
\begin{aligned}
\beta\varphi(_1c) &= \beta + \beta|_1c|_\theta^{1-\gamma} = \beta + \beta\left(\sup_{t \ge 0} \frac{c_{t+1}}{\theta^t}\right)^{1-\gamma} \\
&< 1 + \beta\theta^{1-\gamma}\left(\sup_{t \ge 0} \frac{c_{t+1}}{\theta^{t+1}}\right)^{1-\gamma} < 1 + (|c|_\theta)^{1-\gamma} = \varphi(c),
\end{aligned}
$$

which implies that

$$\beta \sup_{c \in \ell_\theta^\infty} \frac{\varphi(_1c)}{\varphi(c)} < 1.$$

One limitation of the weighted contraction mapping approach is that it cannot handle the case of aggregators that are unbounded below. Boyd (1990) shows that the partial sum approach can deal with this case.

20.2 Stochastic Case

We now introduce uncertainty in a dynamic setting. We will combine preferences under uncertainty with preferences over time. This task is not trivial because one has to ensure dynamic consistency. As discussed earlier, the most commonly used time-additive expected utility model has several limitations. Since the seminal contribution by Kreps and Porteus (1978), researchers have developed many dynamic utility models that depart from the time-additive expected utility framework. We will start with the Epstein and Zin (1989) model.

20.2.1 Epstein–Zin Preferences

Epstein and Zin (1989) propose a recursive utility framework that can incorporate static utility models under uncertainty in a dynamic setting. This framework ensures dynamic consistency and is tractable to apply in applications because the dynamic programming technique can be used. Additionally it is extremely flexible and can permit a separation between intertemporal substitution and risk aversion. It can also permit a preference for early or late resolution of uncertainty. In this subsection we introduce this framework. We will not discuss its axiomatic foundation.

Consider an infinite-horizon setup and time is indexed by $t = 0, 1, 2 \ldots$. Fix a probability space $(\Omega, \mathcal{F}, P)$ with filtration $\{\mathcal{F}_t\}$ and $\mathcal{F}_0 = \{\Omega, \varnothing\}$. This space may be generated by a Markov process with a finite state space S and a transition matrix $\pi(s'|s)$, $s, s' \in S$. Let $\mathcal{L}$ denote the set of all adapted real-valued processes. A decision maker ranks adapted consumption plans $c = (c_t)_{t \geq 0}$ with $c_t \in \mathbb{R}_+$. Let $\mathcal{C}$ denote the space of consumption plans.

Definition 20.2.1 *A **dynamic utility** on the consumption space $\mathcal{C}$ is a mapping of the form $U : \mathcal{C} \to \mathcal{L}$ such that the **continuation utility** at time t, $U_t(c)$, is independent of past or unrealized consumption; that is, for any $c, c' \in C$,*

$$c_s = c'_s \quad \text{for} \quad s \geq t \Longrightarrow U_t(c) = U_t(c').$$

Given a dynamic utility U, we call $U(c)$ the **utility process** of the consumption plan c. We will focus on dynamically consistent utility.

Definition 20.2.2 *The dynamic utility $U : C \to \mathcal{L}$ is **dynamically consistent** if for any c, c' with $c_s = c'_s$, $0 \leq s < t$, for any t, we have that $U_0(c) > U_0(c')$ if $U_t(c) \geq U_t(c')$ and $U_t(c) > U_t(c')$ with positive probability.*

Epstein and Zin (1989) generalize Koopmans deterministic recursive utility to a stochastic setting. They define a recursive utility function under uncertainty by two primitives: a time aggregator W and a conditional certainty equivalent $\mathcal{M}$.

Definition 20.2.3 *A conditional certainty equivalent (conditional CE) is a mapping $\mathcal{M}$ that assigns to every time t a continuous function $\mathcal{M}_t$ that maps an $\mathcal{F}_{t+1}$-measurable random variable to an $\mathcal{F}_t$-measurable random variable such that $\mathcal{M}_t(\alpha) = \alpha$ for any constant $\alpha \in \mathbb{R}_+$.*

We are ready to define recursive utility. **Recursive utility** under uncertainty is any dynamic utility $U : \mathcal{C} \to \mathcal{L}$ for which there exist a time aggregator $W : \mathbb{R}_+ \times \mathbb{R} \to \mathbb{R}$ and a conditional CE $\mathcal{M}$ such that U satisfies

$$U_t(c) = W(c_t, \mathcal{M}_t(U_{t+1}(c))). \tag{20.2}$$

The time aggregator W captures intertemporal substitution and the conditional certainty equivalent $\mathcal{M}$ captures the attitude toward uncertainty. In applications one only needs to specify these two primitives. Alternatively, one can define recursive utility under uncertainty using a time aggregator W and an **uncertainty aggregator** $\mathcal{R}$. The latter is defined in definition 20.2.3 except that the requirement $\mathcal{R}_t(\alpha) = \alpha$ is removed. This construction gives more flexibility in defining utility. We now give some examples.

Time-Additive Expected Utility Let $W(x, y) = u^{-1}(u(x) + \beta u(y))$ and $\mathcal{M}_t(x_{t+1}) = u^{-1}E_t[u(x_{t+1})]$. The recursive utility satisfies

$$U_t(c) = u^{-1}(u(c_t) + \beta E_t[u(U_{t+1}(c))]),$$

where E_t denotes the conditional expectation operator given information $\mathcal{F}_t$. Let $V_t(c) = u(U_t(c))$. We then obtain

$$V_t(c) = u(c_t) + \beta E_t[V_{t+1}(c)] = E_t\left[\sum_{s=t}^{\infty} \beta^{s-t} u(c_s)\right].$$

Alternatively, we can set $W(x, y) = u(x) + \beta y$ and $\mathcal{R}_t(x_{t+1}) = E_t[x_{t+1}]$. The recursive utility satisfies

$$U_t(c) = u(c_t) + \beta E_t[U_{t+1}(c)]$$

so that

$$U_t(c) = E_t\left[\sum_{s=t}^{\infty} \beta^{s-t} u(c_s)\right].$$

Kreps–Porteus Utility Kreps and Porteus (1978) propose a finite-horizon recursive utility with an expected utility conditional certainty equivalent. Epstein and Zin (1989) and Weil (1990) generalize the Kreps and Porteus model to an infinite horizon. They propose the following specific functional form:

$$W(x,y) = \left((1 - \beta) x^{1-\rho} + \beta y^{1-\rho}\right)^{1/(1-\rho)}$$

and

$$M_t(x_{t+1}) = \left(E_t\left[x_{t+1}^{1-\gamma}\right]\right)^{1/(1-\gamma)},$$

where $\gamma > 0, \neq 1$ and $\rho > 0$. Then the recursive utility satisfies

$$U_t(c) = \left[(1 - \beta) c_t^{1-\rho} + \beta \left(E_t\left[U_{t+1}(c)^{1-\gamma}\right]\right)^{(1-\rho)/(1-\gamma)}\right]^{1/(1-\rho)}. \tag{20.3}$$

This utility is often called the Kreps–Porteus utility, the Epstein–Zin utility, or the Epstein–Zin–Weil utility in the literature. An important feature of the Epstein–Zin utility is that the relative risk aversion parameter is given by γ and the EIS is equal to $1/\rho$, and hence intertemporal substitution and risk aversion are separated, except for the special case in which $\gamma = \rho$. This special case corresponds to the standard time-additive expected power utility. Another feature of this utility is that it is scale-invariant in the sense that it is homothetic. This feature is useful to reduce the number of state variables by one for problems with a homogeneity property.

Weil (1993) considers the exponential certainty equivalent

$$M_t(x_{t+1}) = -\frac{1}{\gamma} \ln E_t \exp(-\gamma x_{t+1})$$

and the CES time aggregator to obtain recursive utility

$$U_t(c) = \left[(1 - \beta) c_t^{1-\rho} + \beta \left(-\frac{1}{\gamma} \ln E_t \exp(-\gamma U_{t+1}(c))\right)^{1-\rho}\right]^{1/(1-\rho)}. \tag{20.4}$$

This utility has a feature of translation invariance. It is convenient for problems with additive risk, such as labor income risk.

It is interesting to consider the limiting case where $\rho \to 1$. We can then show that $V_t(c) \equiv \ln U_t(c)$ satisfies

$$V_t(c) = (1 - \beta) \ln c_t + \frac{\beta}{1 - \gamma} \ln E_t \exp((1 - \gamma) V_{t+1}(c)). \tag{20.5}$$

The log-exponential form in the two equations above has a connection to the robust control and risk sensitive control studied in section 9.6. One can interpret $1/\gamma$ in (20.4) or $1/(\gamma - 1)$ for $\gamma > 1$ in (20.5) as the robustness parameter. A larger degree of risk aversion is identical to a larger degree of concerns for robustness.

The Epstein and Zin utility permits a preference for early or late resolution of uncertainty. We will turn to this issue later.

Chew–Dekel Risk Aggregator   The most restrictive assumption of expected utility is the independence axiom. In the objective risk case it says that if a lottery P is
preferred to another lottery P^*, then any mixture with a common lottery Q will not
change the ordering. Formally,

$$P \succeq P^* \Rightarrow \alpha P + (1 - \alpha) Q \succeq \alpha P^* + (1 - \alpha) Q,$$

where $\alpha \in (0, 1)$ and $\succeq$ is the preference relation. One of the earliest and best-
known examples of systematic violation of the independence axiom is the well-
known **Allais paradox** (Allais 1953, 1979). It is illustrated by the following choices:

$$a_1 : (\$1M, 1) \text{ versus } a_2 : (\$5M, 0.10; \$1M, 0.89; \$0, 0.01)$$

and

$$a_3 : (\$1M, 0.11; \$0, 0.89) \text{ versus } a_4 : (\$5M, 0.10; \$0, 0.90),$$

where M denotes million. Here we used $(x_1, p_1; x_2, p_2)$ to denote a lottery with the
outcome x_1 with probability p_1 and the outcome x_2 with probability p_2. A similar notation applies to other lotteries. Expected utility implies that $a_1 \succeq a_2$ if and
only if $a_3 \succeq a_4$. For example, suppose that the vNM index is given by u with
$u(0) = 0$. Then

$$u(1M) \geq 0.1u(5M) + 0.89u(1M) \Longleftrightarrow 0.11u(1M) \geq 0.1u(5M).$$

However, in most experiments, we have $a_1 \succ a_2$ but $a_4 \succ a_3$.

Most early literature of decision theory under risk has tried to develop new utility models that can resolve the Allais paradox. One prominent class of such models
was developed by Chew (1983, 1989) and Dekel (1986). These models lead to first-
order conditions that are linear in probabilities, hence tractable and amenable to
econometric analysis. To introduce the Chew–Dekel class of utility, we consider a
static setting.

Fix a finite state space S. We consider the case of objective risk with a known
probability measure p on S. We will consider unknown probabilities later. A consumption choice $c : S \to \mathbb{R}_+$ is a random variable on S. The set of all consumption
is denoted by $\mathcal{C}$. Preferences over $\mathcal{C}$ are represented by a utility function:

$$U(c) = U(c(1), ..., c(s)).$$

Instead of working with U, we consider an equivalent representation in terms of
certainty equivalent. We define the certainty equivalent of a consumption choice
c as a certain consequence μ that gives the same level of utility:

$$U(\mu, ..., \mu) = U(c(1), ..., c(s)).$$

If U is strictly increasing, then there is a unique μ. We then obtain a function $\mu : \mathcal{C} \to \mathbb{R}_+$. Using μ to represent preferences has several attractive features. First, it expresses utility in payoff ("consumption") units. Second, it summarizes behavior toward risk directly: since the certainty equivalent of a sure thing is itself, the impact of risk is simply the difference between the certainty equivalent and expected consumption.

The Chew–Dekel certainty equivalent function μ for a consumption choice c is defined implicitly by a risk aggregator $M : \mathbb{R}_+^2 \to \mathbb{R}_+$ satisfying

$$\mu = \sum_s p(s) M(c(s), \mu). \tag{20.6}$$

Such preferences satisfy a weaker condition than the independence axiom that underlies expected utility. We assume M has the following properties: (1) $M(m, m) = m$ (sure things are their own certainty equivalents), (2) M is increasing in its first argument (first-order stochastic dominance), (3) M is concave in its first argument (risk aversion), and (4) $M(kc, m) = kM(c, m)$ for $k > 0$ (linear homogeneity). Most of the analytical convenience of the Chew–Dekel class follows from the linearity of equation (20.6) in probabilities.

We now consider some tractable members of the Chew–Dekel class:

- *Expected utility*   A version with constant relative risk aversion is implied by

$$M(c, m) = c^{1-\gamma} \frac{m^{1-\gamma}}{1-\gamma} + m \left(1 - \frac{1}{1-\gamma} \right).$$

If $\gamma > 0$, then M satisfies the conditions outlined above. Applying (20.6), we find that

$$\mu(c) = \left(\sum_s p(s) c(s)^{1-\gamma} \right)^{1/(1-\gamma)}.$$

This is the usual expected utility with a power utility function.

- *Weighted utility*   Chew (1983) proposes to weight probabilities by a function of outcomes. A constant-elasticity version follows from

$$M(c, m) = \left(\frac{c}{m} \right)^{\eta} \frac{c^{1-\gamma} m^{\gamma}}{1-\gamma} + m \left(1 - \frac{(c/m)^{\eta}}{1-\gamma} \right).$$

For M to be increasing and concave in c in a neighborhood of m, the parameters must satisfy either (1) $0 < \eta < 1$ and $1 - \gamma + \eta < 0$ or (2) $\eta < 0$ and $0 < 1 - \gamma + \eta < 1$. Note that condition 1 implies $\gamma > 1$, condition 2 implies $\gamma < 1$, and both imply $2\eta < \gamma$. The associated certainty equivalent function is given by

$$\mu(c) = \left(\frac{\sum_s p(s) c(s)^{\eta+1-\gamma}}{\sum_s p(s) c(s)^{\eta}} \right)^{1/(1-\gamma)} = \left(\sum_s \hat{p}(s) c(s)^{1-\gamma} \right)^{1/(1-\gamma)},$$

where

$$\hat{p}(s) = \frac{p(s) c(s)^{\eta}}{\sum_s p(s) c(s)^{\eta}}.$$

This version highlights the impact of bad outcomes: they get greater weight than with expected utility if $\eta < 0$, and less weight otherwise. Embedding this risk aggregator in a dynamic setup, we can define recursive weighted utility as

$$U_t(c) = \left[(1-\beta) c_t^{1-\rho} + \beta \left(\mathcal{M}_t \left[U_{t+1}(c)^{1-\gamma} \right] \right)^{(1-\rho)/(1-\gamma)} \right]^{1/(1-\rho)},$$

where the conditional CE is defined as

$$\mathcal{M}_t(x_{t+1}) = \sum_{s_{t+1}} \left(\frac{\pi(s_{t+1}|s_t) U_{t+1}(c)^{\eta}}{\sum_{s_{t+1}} \pi(s_{t+1}|s_t) U_{t+1}(c)^{\eta}} \right) x_{t+1}.$$

Here we assume that the exogenous shock $\{s_t\}$ is Markovian and $\pi(s_{t+1}|s_t)$ denotes the transition probability.

- *Disappointment aversion*   Gul (1991) proposes a model that increases sensitivity to bad events ("disappointments"). Preferences are defined by the risk aggregator

$$M(c,m) = \begin{cases} \frac{c^{1-\gamma}m^{\gamma}}{1-\gamma} + m\left(1 - \frac{1}{1-\gamma}\right) & \text{for } c \geq m, \\ \frac{c^{1-\gamma}m^{\gamma}}{1-\gamma} + m\left(1 - \frac{1}{1-\gamma}\right) + \eta\frac{(c^{1-\gamma}m^{\gamma}-m)}{1-\gamma} & \text{for } c < m, \end{cases}$$

where $\eta \geq 0$ and $1 \neq \gamma > 0$. When $\eta = 0$, it reduces to expected utility. Otherwise, disappointment aversion places additional weight on outcomes worse than the certainty equivalent. The certainty equivalent function satisfies

$$\mu^{1-\gamma} = \sum_s p(s) c(s)^{1-\gamma} - \eta \sum_s p(s) \mathbf{1}_{\{c(s)<\mu\}} \left(\mu^{1-\gamma} - c(s)^{1-\gamma} \right)$$

$$= \sum_s \hat{p}(s) c(s)^{1-\gamma},$$

where $\mathbf{1}_{\{x\}}$ is an indicator function that equals 1 if x is true and zero otherwise, and

$$\hat{p}(s) = p(s) \left(\frac{1 + \eta \mathbf{1}_{\{c(s)<\mu\}}}{1 + \eta \sum_s p(s) \mathbf{1}_{\{c(s)<\mu\}}} \right).$$

This utility differs from weighted utility by scaling up the probabilities of all bad events by the same factor, and scaling down the probabilities of good events by a complementary factor, with good and bad defined as better and worse than the certainty equivalent, respectively.

Using the Gul risk aggregator, we can define recursive disappointment-aversion utility as

$$U_t(c) = \left[(1-\beta) c_t^{1-\rho} + \beta \mathcal{M}_t \left(U_{t+1}(c) \right)^{1-\rho} \right]^{1/(1-\rho)},$$

where $\mathcal{M}_t \left(U_{t+1}(c) \right)$ is the Gul conditional CE defined as the solution for μ_t in the following equation:

$$\mu_t^{1-\gamma} = \sum_{s_{t+1}} \pi(s_{t+1}|s_t) U_{t+1}(c)^{1-\gamma}$$

$$- \eta \sum_{s_{t+1} \in \Delta_{t+1}} \pi(s_{t+1}|s_t) \left(\mu_t^{1-\gamma} - U_{t+1}(c)^{1-\gamma} \right),$$

where

$$\Delta_{t+1} = \{ s_{t+1} \in S : \mu_t > U_{t+1}(c) \}.$$

20.2.2 Ambiguity Aversion

So far we have focused on the case of objective risk in which the probability measure is exogenously given. In the case of subjective uncertainty, the measure is subjective and derived from preferences over choices. There are theories of subjective expected utility and subjective Epstein–Zin utility in the literature. However, there is ample experimental evidence indicating the failure of subjective expected utility. A prominent experiment—the **Ellsberg paradox** (Ellsberg 1961)—has drawn wide attention and active research. A version of the Ellsberg paradox can be described as follows. Suppose that there are two urns, both of which contain 100 black and white balls. You are told that there are 50 black and 50 white balls in the first urn. But you have no information about the composition in the second urn. You are offered to bet on the black ball in the two urns. If you pick a black urn, you obtain $100; otherwise, you obtain nothing. From which urn do you prefer to pick? You might prefer to pick from urn 1 because you are not sure about the composition of ball colors in urn 2 and you are averse to it. But if you are offered to bet on the white ball with the same prize, you might still prefer to pick from urn 1 by the same reasoning. This implies that the total odds of picking a black ball or a white ball from urn 1 are larger than those from urn 2, which is a paradox.

The Ellsberg paradox contradicts expected utility. It shows that people evaluate situations in which probabilities are known differently from situations with unknown probabilities. The former situations are often called risk and the latter are called **ambiguity** or **Knightian uncertainty** (Knight 1921). There are quite a few models in decision theory to resolve the Ellsberg paradox. Here we will focus on three models.

Maxmin Expected Utility   Gilboa and Schmeidler (1989) introduce the following **maxmin expected utility** model:[1]

$$U(c) = \min_{q \in \Delta(S)} \int u(c(s)) \, dq(s),$$

where $\Delta(S)$ is some set of probability measures on S. The decision maker computes expected utility using any measure in $\Delta(S)$ and chooses the worst-case scenario. Epstein and Wang (1994) generalize this model in a dynamic setup and define recursive multiple-priors utility as follows:

$$U_t(c) = u(c_t) + \beta \mathcal{R}_t(U_{t+1}(c)), \tag{20.7}$$

$$\mathcal{R}_t(U_{t+1}(c)) = \min_{\pi \in \mathcal{P}(\cdot|s_t)} \int U_{t+1}(c) \, d\pi(s_{t+1}|s_t),$$

where $\mathcal{P}(\cdot|s_t)$ is a probability kernel correspondence that maps s_t to a set of probability measures on S. Epstein and Schneider (2003) provide an axiomatic foundation for this utility model and show that if we define utility as

$$U_0(c) = \min_{P \in \mathcal{P}} E^P \left[\sum_{t=0}^{\infty} \beta^t u(c_t) \right],$$

where $\mathcal{P}$ is a set of probability measure on the full state space $\Omega = S^{\infty}$, then dynamic consistency may be violated. To ensure dynamic consistency, the set $\mathcal{P}$ must satisfy the "rectangularity" condition so that the utility process satisfies the recursive equation above.

   Hayashi (2005) axiomatizes a model of the following form:

$$U_t(c) = W(c_t, \mathcal{R}_t(U_{t+1}(c))),$$

$$\mathcal{R}_t(U_{t+1}(c)) = \min_{\pi \in \mathcal{P}(\cdot|s_t)} \int U_{t+1}(c) \, d\pi(s_{t+1}|s_t),$$

where W is a time aggregator.

---

1. An important subclass of this model is Choquet expected utility (Schmeidler 1989) defined as

$$U(c) = \int u(c(s)) \, dp(s),$$

where p is a convex capacity or non-additive probability measure.

Variational Utility Maccheroni, Marinacci, and Rustichini (2006a, b) propose the following **variational utility**:

$$U(c) = \min_{q \in \Delta(S)} \int u(c(s)) \, dq(s) + c(q),$$

where $c(q)$ is a convex cost function. The interpretation is the following. The decision maker is unsure about the true distribution underlying the data-generating process. He could use a distorted belief from a set of distributions $\Delta(S)$. But he would be penalized by the cost function $c(q)$. The decision maker attempts at robust decision making by considering the worst-case scenario. This utility model includes the maxmin expected utility as a special case when $c(q) = 0$. It also includes the following **divergence utility** as a special case:

$$U(c) = \min_{q \in \Delta(S)} \int u(c(s)) \, dq(s) + \theta D_\phi^w(q\|p),$$

where $D_\phi^w(q\|p)$ is the w-weighted ϕ divergence of q with respect to p defined as

$$D_\phi^w(q\|p) \equiv \int w(s) \phi\left(\frac{dq}{dp}(s)\right) dp(s).$$

Here $\phi : \mathbb{R}_+ \to \mathbb{R}_+$ is a convex and continuous function satisfying $\phi(1) = 0$ and $\lim_{t \to \infty} \phi(t)/t = \infty$, $w : S \to \mathbb{R}_{++}$ satisfying $\int w(s) \, dp(s) = 1$, and dq/dp is the Radon–Nikodym derivative. Here ϕ represents a **divergence index** that measures the discrepancy between measures q and p. The interpretation of this model follows from Hansen and Sargent (2001, 2008). The decision maker thinks his model p may not be the true one due to model misspecifications or model uncertainty. He thinks that p is only an approximation and takes into account other possible nearby models q. All these models are in the set $\Delta(S)$. Concern about model misspecification induces the decision maker to want robust decision rules that work over that set of nearby models. The relative likelihood of the alternative models is measured by the divergence $D_\phi^w(q\|p)$, while the positive parameter $\theta > 0$ reflects the weight that the decision maker is giving to the possibility that p might not be the true model. As the parameter becomes larger, the agent focuses more on p as the true model, giving less importance to possible alternative models q. When θ goes to infinity, the model reduces to expected utility. A smaller θ means a larger degree of concern for robustness or a larger degree of ambiguity aversion as interpreted by Maccheroni, Marinacci, and Rustichini (2006a).

Maccheroni, Marinacci, and Rustichini (2006a) show that the divergence preferences are **probabilistically sophisticated** if $w = 1$. **Probabilistic sophistication** means that the decision maker bases his choices on probabilistic beliefs. Probabilistic sophisticated preferences include expected utility, as well as many nonexpected utility models that can explain the Allais paradox and related violation of linearity in probabilities. However, these preferences cannot explain the Ellsberg paradox. Maccheroni, Marinacci, and Rustichini (2006a) show that small deviations from the specification $w = 1$ will lead to models that can explain the Ellsberg paradox. They also consider the following two interesting specifications of divergence with $w = 1$:

- Relative entropy (or **Kullback–Leibler divergence**),

  $$\phi(x) = x \ln x - x + 1.$$

  This case corresponds to the **multiplier utility** introduced by Hansen and Sargent (2001, 2008):

  $$U(c) = \min_{q \in \Delta(S)} \int u(c(s)) \, dq(s) + \theta \int \ln\left(\frac{dq}{dp}\right) dq.$$

  Solving the minimization problem yields the risk-sensitive utility model:

  $$U(c) = -\theta \ln \int \exp\left(\frac{-u(c(s))}{\theta}\right) dp(s).$$

  Thus concern for robustness enhances risk aversion by $1/\theta$.

- **Relative Gini concentration index** (or χ^2 divergence),

  $$\phi(x) = \frac{1}{2}(x - 1)^2.$$

  Maccheroni, Marinacci, and Rustichini (2006a) show that this case corresponds to the **monotone mean variance utility**:

  $$U(c) = E[c] - \frac{1}{2\theta} \text{Var}(c),$$

  on the domain $\{c : c - Ec \le \theta\}$, the mean and variance are computed using p.

To construct dynamic models of ambiguity, we can still fix a probability space $(\Omega, \mathcal{F}, P)$ with filtration $\{\mathcal{F}_t\}$ and $\mathcal{F}_0 = \{\Omega, \varnothing\}$. This space is generated by a Markov process with a finite state space S and a transition matrix $\pi(s'|s)$, $s, s' \in S$. Let E_t denote conditional expectation operator under P given $\mathcal{F}_t$. The measure P represents an approximating model used by the decision maker or econometrician. The decision maker's doubts about P are represented by a set of distorted beliefs.

To construct these beliefs, we define a one-step-ahead density as

$$m_{t+1} = \frac{\hat{\pi}(s_{t+1}|s_t)}{\pi(s_{t+1}|s_t)},$$

where $\hat{\pi}(s_{t+1}|s_t)$ is a distorted transition probability. We then define a martingale $\{M_t\}$ recursively as

$$M_{t+1} = m_{t+1}M_t, \quad M_0 = 1, \tag{20.8}$$

where M_t is the ratio of joint densities conditional on date t information. It represents belief distortions. We then define the recursive divergence utility function as

$$U_t(c) = u(c_t) + \beta\mathcal{R}_t(U_{t+1}(c)),$$
$$\mathcal{R}_t(U_{t+1}(c)) = \min_{m_{t+1}} E_t[m_{t+1}U_{t+1}(c) + \theta w_{t+1}\phi(m_{t+1})],$$

subject to $E_t[m_{t+1}] = 1$, where $w_{t+1} > 0$ is a weight satisfying $E_t[w_{t+1}] = 1$. This utility function is dynamically consistent and the time zero utility satisfies

$$U_0(c) = \min_{\{m_{t+1}\}} E\sum_{t=0}^{\infty}\beta^t M_t\{u(c_t) + \beta\theta E_t[w_{t+1}\phi(m_{t+1})]\}$$

subject to (20.8) and $E_t[m_{t+1}] = 1$. Here the discounted divergence over infinite horizon is given by

$$\beta\sum_{t=0}^{\infty}\beta^t E[M_t w_{t+1}\phi(m_{t+1})].$$

Smooth Ambiguity Utility   Klibanoff, Marinacci, and Mukerji (2005) propose the following **smooth ambiguity utility** model:

$$U(c) = v^{-1}\left(\int_\Delta v\left(\int u(c(s))\,dq(s)\right)d\mu(q)\right), \tag{20.9}$$

where Δ is a set of probability measures on S and μ is a prior on this set. The interpretation is the following. The decision maker is not sure about the true measure and is averse to model uncertainty. He puts a prior μ over the set of possible models Δ. For each model q he computes expected utility using u. He ranks consumption according to another expected utility with v and μ over utility values associated with all possible models. Here u represents attitudes toward risk and v represents attitudes toward model uncertainty. This model permits a separation between risk aversion and **ambiguity aversion**.

Klibanoff, Marinacci, and Mukerji (2005), Hayashi and Miao (2011), and Ju and Miao (2012) embed the static model above in a dynamic setting. Time is denoted by $t = 0, 1, 2, ...$ The state space in each period is denoted by S. At time t, the decision maker's information consists of history $s^t = \{s_0, s_1, s_2, ..., s_t\}$ with $s_0 \in S$ given and $s_t \in S$. The decision maker ranks adapted consumption plans $c = (c_t)_{t\geq 0}$. That is, c_t

is a measurable function of s^t. The decision maker is ambiguous about the probability distribution on the full state space S^∞. This uncertainty is described by an unobservable random state z in the space Z. The hidden state z can be interpreted in several different ways. It could be an unknown model parameter, a discrete indicator of alternative models (Chen, Ju, and Miao 2012), or a hidden Markov state that evolves over time in a regime-switching process (Hamilton 1989). The decision maker has a prior μ_0 over the hidden state z. Each value of z gives a probability distribution π_z over the full state space. The posterior μ_t and the conditional likelihood $\pi_{z,t}$ can be obtained by Bayes's rule.

Inspired by Kreps and Porteus (1978) and Epstein and Zin (1989), Hayashi and Miao (2011), and Ju and Miao (2012) propose the following **generalized recursive smooth ambiguity utility** model:

$$U_t\left(c\right) = W\left(c_t, \mathcal{M}_t\left(U_{t+1}\left(c\right)\right)\right), \tag{20.10}$$
$$\mathcal{M}_t\left(x_{t+1}\right) = v^{-1}\left(E_{\mu_t}\left\{v \circ u^{-1} E_{\pi_{z,t}}\left[u\left(x_{t+1}\right)\right]\right\}\right),$$

where u and v admit the same interpretation as in the static setting. When $v \circ u^{-1}$ is linear, (20.10) reduces to the recursive utility model of Epstein and Zin (1989) with hidden states. In this model the posterior μ_t and the likelihood $\pi_{z,t}$ can be reduced to a *predictive distribution*, which is the key idea underlying the Bayesian analysis. When $v \circ u^{-1}$ is nonlinear, μ_t and $\pi_{z,t}$ cannot be reduced to a single distribution for decision making in (20.10), leading to ambiguity-sensitive behavior as in the static model (20.9).

The generalized recursive smooth ambiguity model in (20.10) permits a three-way separation among risk aversion, ambiguity aversion, and intertemporal substitution. In application it proves tractable to consider the following homothetic specification:

$$W\left(c,y\right) = \left[\left(1-\beta\right)c^{1-\rho} + \beta y^{1-\rho}\right]^{1/(1-\rho)}, \quad \rho > 0, \neq 1, \tag{20.11}$$

and u and v are given by

$$u\left(x\right) = \frac{x^{1-\gamma}}{1-\gamma}, \quad \gamma > 0, \neq 1, \tag{20.12}$$

$$v\left(x\right) = \frac{x^{1-\eta}}{1-\eta}, \quad \eta > 0, \neq 1, \tag{20.13}$$

where $\beta \in (0,1)$ is the subjective discount factor, $1/\rho$ represents EIS, γ is the risk aversion parameter, and η is the ambiguity aversion parameter. We then have

$$U_t(C) = \left[(1-\beta)\,C_t^{1-\rho} + \beta\,\{\mathcal{M}_t(U_{t+1}(c))\}^{1-\rho}\right]^{1/(1-\rho)}, \tag{20.14}$$

$$\mathcal{M}_t(x_{t+1}) = \left\{E_{\mu_t}\left(E_{\pi_{z,t}}\left[x_{t+1}^{1-\gamma}\right]\right)^{(1-\eta)/(1-\gamma)}\right\}^{1/(1-\rho)}. \tag{20.15}$$

If $\eta = \gamma$, the decision maker is ambiguity neutral, and (20.14) reduces to the recursive utility model of Epstein and Zin (1989) and Weil (1989). The decision maker displays ambiguity aversion if and only if $\eta > \gamma$. By the property of certainty equivalent, a more ambiguity-averse agent with a higher value of η has a lower utility level.

In the limiting case with $\rho = 1$, (20.14) reduces to

$$V_t = (1-\beta)\ln c_t \tag{20.16}$$
$$+ \frac{\beta}{1-\eta}\ln\left\{E_{\mu_t}\exp\left(\frac{1-\eta}{1-\gamma}\ln\left(E_{\pi_{z,t}}\exp\left((1-\gamma)\,V_{t+1}\right)\right)\right)\right\},$$

where $V_t = \ln U_t$. This specification reduces to the multiplier model with hidden states studied by Hansen (2007) and Hansen and Sargent (2010). In particular, there are two risk-sensitivity adjustments in (20.16). The first risk-sensitivity adjustment for the distribution $\pi_{z,t}$ reflects the agent's concerns about the misspecification in the underlying Markov law given a hidden state z. The second risk-sensitivity adjustment for the distribution μ_t reflects the agent's concerns about the misspecification of the probabilities assigned to the hidden states. More generally, our model in (20.10) nests a version of the recursive multiplier model with hidden states in Hansen and Sargent (2007) as a special case[2] where we set $W(c,y) = h(c) + \beta y$, $u(x) = -\exp(-x/\theta_1)$, and $v(x) = -\exp(-x/\theta_2)$ for $\theta_1, \theta_2 > 0$.

If we further take the limit in (20.16) when $\gamma \to 1$, equation (20.16) becomes

$$V_t(c) = (1-\beta)\ln c_t + \frac{\beta}{1-\eta}\ln\left\{E_{\mu_t}\exp\left((1-\eta)\,E_{\pi_{z,t}}[V_{t+1}(c)]\right)\right\}. \tag{20.17}$$

This is the log-exponential specification studied by Ju and Miao (2007). In this case there is only one risk-sensitive adjustment for the state beliefs μ_t. Following Klibanoff et al. (2005), we can show that when $\eta \to \infty$, (20.17) becomes

$$V_t(c) = (1-\beta)\ln c_t + \beta \min_z E_{\pi_{z,t}}[V_{t+1}(c)]. \tag{20.18}$$

---

2. This model intersects the Kreps–Porteus–Epstein–Zin recursive expected utility model only when $\theta_1 = \theta_2$. By contrast, the multiplier preference model with full information (e.g., Anderson, Hansen, and Sargent 2003; Barillas, Hansen, and Sargent 2009; Hansen and Sargent 2001) is a special case of the Kreps–Porteus–Epstein–Zin model.

This utility function belongs to the class of recursive multiple-priors utility of Epstein and Wang (1994) and Epstein and Schneider (2003). The agent is extremely ambiguity averse by choosing the worst continuation value each period.

The model in (20.10) nests the following Klibanoff, Marinacci, and Mukerji (2009) model as a special case:

$$V_t(c) = u(c_t) + \beta \phi^{-1} \left(\mathbb{E}_{\mu_t} \phi \left(\mathbb{E}_{\pi_{z,t}} [V_{t+1}(c)] \right) \right). \tag{20.19}$$

In this model, risk aversion and intertemporal substitution are confounded. Also Ju and Miao (2007) find that when u is defined as in (20.12) and $\phi(x) = x^{1-\alpha}/(1-\alpha)$ for $x > 0$ and $1 \neq \alpha > 0$, the model (20.19) is not well-defined for $\gamma > 1$. Thus they consider (20.14) and (20.15) with $\gamma = \rho$ and $\alpha \equiv 1 - (1-\eta)/(1-\gamma)$, which is ordinally equivalent to (20.19) when $\gamma \in (0,1)$. The utility function in (20.19) is always well defined for the specification $\phi(x) = -\exp(-x/\theta)$, $\theta > 0$. The nice feature of this specification is that it has a connection with risk-sensitive control and robustness, as studied by Hansen (2007) and Hansen and Sargent (2001). A disadvantage of this specification is that the utility function generally does not have a homogeneity property. Thus the curse of dimensionality makes numerical analysis of the decision maker's dynamic programming problem complicated, except for the special case where $u(c) = \ln(c)$ as in (20.17) (see Ju and Miao 2012; Collard et al. 2009).

20.2.3   Temporal Resolution of Uncertainty

Consider the following four choices in a two-period environment:

1. At the beginning of period 0, flip a fair coin. If it comes up heads, the decision maker receives certain consumption c in period 0 and a lottery m in period 1. Otherwise, he receives certain consumption c in period 0 and a lottery m' in period 1.

2. In period 0, the decision maker receives certain consumption c. At the beginning of period 1, he flips a fair coin. If it comes up heads, the decision maker receives a lottery m in period 1. Otherwise, he receives a lottery m' in period 1.

3. At the beginning of periods 0 and 1, flip a fair coin independently. If it comes up heads, the decision maker receives certain consumption c; otherwise, he receives certain consumption c'.

4. At the beginning of period 0, flip a fair coin. If it comes up heads, the decision maker receives certain consumption c in both periods 0 and 1. Otherwise, he receives certain consumption c' in both periods.

A decision maker with time-additive expected utility is indifferent between choices 1 and 2 and between choices 3 and 4 as well. This implies that such a decision maker is insensitive to the timing of resolution of uncertainty and to long-run risk. Kreps and Porteus (1978) first formalize the notion of preference for the timing of resolution of uncertainty under objective risk. Their analysis has been extended by Chew and Epstein (1989) and Grant, Kajii, and Polak (1998, 2000). Duffie and Epstein (1992) observe that recursive utility typically exhibit sensitivity to long-run risk. This feature is important for asset pricing (e.g., see Bansal and Yaron 2004; Hansen, Heaton, and Li 2008). Recently Strzalecki (2013) formalizes these notions under subjective uncertainty.

Now we introduce Kreps and Porteus's analysis of the preference for the timing of resolution of uncertainty in a two-period setting. Consumption c_t in either period, $t = 0, 1$, is constrained to lie in X, a bounded interval in the nonnegative real line. The space of Borel probability measures on X is denoted $M(X)$. Let $D = M(X \times M(X))$, the space of Borel probability measures on $X \times M(X)$. Elements of D are intertemporal consumption lotteries (or programs). They can be represented by probability trees as in figure 20.1. Note that for $i = a, b$, $\delta \left[c_0^i, m^i \right]$ denotes the measure that assigns all mass to $\{ c_0^i, m^i \}$. In figure 20.1, think of α and $1 - \alpha$ as describing the probability distribution of a random variable that is correlated with consumption levels in both periods and whose realization is observed at the start of period 0. The $t = 0$ consumption level is also observed at the start of period 0, after which the remaining future is described by a probability measure $m^i \in M(X)$ for second period consumption.

Definition 20.2.4   *The decision maker with preference ordering $\succeq$ prefers earlier (later) resolution of uncertainty if*

$$\alpha \delta \left[c_0, m \right] + (1 - \alpha) \delta \left[c_0, m' \right] \succeq (\preceq) \delta \left[c_0, \alpha m + (1 - \alpha) m' \right].$$

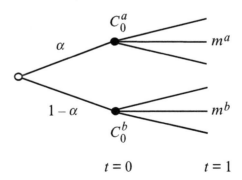

Figure 20.1
Consumption lottery. The consumption lottery takes the form $\alpha \delta \left[c_0^a, m^a \right] + (1 - \alpha) \delta \left[c_0^b, m^b \right]$.

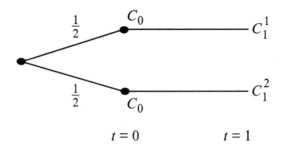

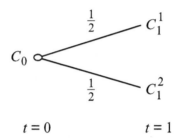

Figure 20.2
Temporal resolution of uncertainty. The consumption lottery at the top panel exhibits earlier resolution of uncertainty than that at the bottom panel.

The consumption lottery on the top panel of figure 20.2 exhibits earlier resolution of uncertainty than that on the bottom panel. If the decision maker prefers earlier resolution of uncertainty, then he must prefer the consumption lottery on the top panel.

Suppose that the decision maker's preferences are represented by recursive utility $U_0 : D \to \mathbb{R}$ and $U_1 : M(X) \to \mathbb{R}$ such that

$$U_0(d) = E_d[W(c_0, E_m U_1(c_1))], \quad d \in D.$$

Kreps and Porteus (1978) establish the following:

Theorem 20.2.1 *The decision maker with the recursive utility above prefers earlier (later) resolution of uncertainty if and only if $W(x, y)$ is convex (concave) in y.*

Proof By definition,

$$\alpha \delta[c_0, m] + (1 - \alpha) \delta[c_0, m'] \succeq \delta[c_0, \alpha m + (1 - \alpha) m']$$

if and only if

$$\alpha W (c_0, E_m U_1 (c_1)) + (1 - \alpha) W (c_0, E_{m'} U_1 (c_1))$$
$$\geq W (c_0, \alpha E_m U_1 (c_1) + (1 - \alpha) E_{m'} U_1 (c_1)).$$

This is equivalent to the property that $W (x, y)$ is convex in y.   ∎

In applying this theorem, one could easily show that an agent with the Epstein–Zin utility in (20.3) has a preference for earlier resolution of uncertainty if and only if $\gamma > \rho$.

20.3   Properties of Recursive Utility

A dynamic utility $U : \mathcal{C} \rightarrow \mathcal{L}$ is defined by a time aggregator W and a conditional CE $\mathcal{M}$ (or uncertainty aggregator $\mathcal{R}$) as in (20.2). The aggregator W captures intertemporal substitution and the operator $\mathcal{M}$ or $\mathcal{R}$ captures risk aversion or ambiguity aversion. This section establishes some important properties of recursive utility that are useful in applications.

20.3.1   Concavity

Concavity is important for the sufficiency of optimality. Strict concavity ensures uniqueness. Here we will focus on the case of strict concavity. The case of weak concavity can be similarly analyzed. Say dynamic utility U is strictly concave if $U_t (c)$ is a strictly concave function for every t. It is natural to expect that if the time aggregator W is strictly increasing and concave and the conditional CE $\mathcal{M}_t$ (or uncertainty aggregator $\mathcal{R}_t$) is strictly concave for all t, then U is strictly concave. This assertion is true for the finite-horizon case by backward induction. It is also true under infinite horizon if the contraction mapping theorem can be applied.

For example, consider the Epstein–Zin utility defined in (20.3) with a finite horizon. Let $U_T (c) = c_T$. Claim that U_t is strictly concave for $t = 0, 1, ..., T - 1$ if $\rho > 0$ and $\gamma > 0$. The following lemma taken from Skiadas (2009) is useful to prove this claim.

Lemma 20.3.1   *Suppose that the function $f : \mathbb{R}^l_{++} \rightarrow \mathbb{R}$ is homogeneous of degree one. Then the following conditions are equivalent:*

a. f is concave.

b. For every $x, y \in \mathbb{R}^l_{++}$ and $\lambda \in (0, 1)$,

$$f (x) = f (y), \quad x \neq y \Longrightarrow f (\lambda x + (1 - \lambda)) \geq f (x).$$

c. For every $x, y \in \mathbb{R}^l_{++}$,

$$f (x + y) \geq f (x) + f (y).$$

20.3.2   Risk Aversion

We first define comparative risk aversion and then define absolute risk aversion. Consider two dynamic utilities, U^1 and U^2, on a common consumption set $\mathcal{C}$, that are ordinally equivalent over deterministic plans. We say that U^1 is **more risk averse** than U^2 if for every $b, c \in \mathcal{C}$ such that b is deterministic,

$$U_t^2(b) > U_t^2(c) \Longrightarrow U_t^1(b) > U_t^1(c), \quad \text{all } t.$$

The interpretation is that if U^1 is more risk averse than U^2, then U^1 prefers a deterministic plan to a risk plan whenever U^2 does. Say that U^1 is risk averse if for every $b, c \in \mathcal{C}$ such that b is deterministic,

$$U_t^2(b) = U_t^2(c) \Longrightarrow U_t^1(b) > U_t^1(c), \quad \text{all } t \text{ and all } U^2.$$

This implies that U^1 is risk averse if it is more risk averse than a risk neutral U^2.

Proposition 20.3.1 *Consider two recursive utility functions U^1 and U^2 with a common increasing time aggregator W and conditional CE $\mathcal{M}^1$ and $\mathcal{M}^2$, respectively. Then U^1 is more risk averse than U^2 if and only if $\mathcal{M}_t^1 \leq \mathcal{M}_t^2$ for all t. Suppose further that each U^i is Epstein–Zin utility, with conditional CE, $(u^i)^{-1} E_t u^i$. Then U^1 is more risk averse than U^2 if and only if there exists an increasing and concave function ϕ such that $u^1 = \phi \circ u^2$.*

Proof   Because U^1 and U^2 agree on the deterministic plans, $U_t^2(b) = U_t^1(b)$. Thus we must have $U_t^1(c) \leq U_t^2(c)$. Fixing identical c_t, we then have $\mathcal{M}_t^1 \leq \mathcal{M}_t^2$. The last claim follows from the standard risk theory.   ∎

Ambiguity aversion can be similarly defined by starting with a comparative notion. Then one needs to define an ambiguity neutrality benchmark. A comparative notion needs to consider comparison of ambiguous acts and unambiguous acts. A natural choice of unambiguous acts is lotteries. A natural choice of an ambiguity neutrality benchmark is expected utility preferences. This is the approach adopted by Ghirardato and Marinacci (2002). Epstein (1999) adopts a different approach and uses probabilistically sophisticated preferences as the benchmark. Here we will not discuss these notions and refer the reader to these papers for details.

20.3.3   Utility Gradients and Pricing Kernels

Utility gradients are useful for characterizing optimality and equilibrium. Duffie and Skiadas (1994) and Skiadas (2009) provide an extensive discussion on this concept and its applications.

Definition 20.3.1   *A gradient density of the time zero utility $U_0 : \mathcal{C} \to \mathbb{R}$ at $c \in \mathcal{C}$ is an adapted process π satisfying*

$$\lim_{\alpha \downarrow 0} \frac{U_0(c + \alpha x) - U_0(c)}{\alpha} = E\left[\sum_{t=0}^{\infty} \pi_t x_t\right]$$

for all $x \in \mathcal{L}$ such that $c + \alpha x \in \mathcal{C}$.

To compute utility gradients for recursive utility, we define the derivative of the conditional CE as follows:

Definition 20.3.2   *The derivative of the conditional CE $\mathcal{M}$ is a mapping κ that assigns to each t a $\mathcal{F}_t$-measurable random random variable z to another $\mathcal{F}_t$-measurable random variable $\kappa_t(z)$ with the property that given any $\varepsilon > 0$, there exists some $\delta > 0$ such that for every $\mathcal{F}_t$-measurable random variable h,*

$$E_{t-1}\left[h^2\right] < \delta \implies \left|\mathcal{M}_{t-1}(z + h) - \mathcal{M}_{t-1}(z) - E_{t-1}\left[\kappa_t(z) h\right]\right| < \varepsilon.$$

The derivative of $\mathcal{M}_t(x_{t+1})$ at x_{t+1} is denoted

$$\frac{\partial \mathcal{M}_t(x_{t+1})}{\partial x_{t+1}} = E_t \kappa_{t+1}(x_{t+1}).$$

We can define the derivative of the uncertainty aggregator $\mathcal{R}$ in a similar way. Informally, this derivative is taken with respect to a random variable state by state. To illustrate the definition above, suppose that the conditional CE takes the form $\mathcal{M}_t(x) = u^{-1}E_t u(x)$ for some continuously differentiable function u. Then the derivative of v exists and is given by

$$\frac{\partial \mathcal{M}_t(x_{t+1})}{\partial x_{t+1}} = E_t \kappa_{t+1}(x_{t+1}) = \frac{E_t u'(x_{t+1})}{u'(\mathcal{M}_t(x_{t+1}))}.$$

The following proposition shows how to compute the gradient density of a recursive utility, where W_1 and W_2 denote the partial derivatives of the aggregator W with respect to its consumption and conditional CE arguments, respectively.

Proposition 20.3.2   *Suppose that $U : \mathcal{C} \to \mathcal{L}$ is a recursive utility with aggregator $W : \mathbb{R}_+ \times \mathbb{R} \to \mathbb{R}$ and conditional CE $\mathcal{M}$. Suppose also that W is differentiable and $\mathcal{M}$ has derivative κ. Given any plan $c \in \mathcal{C}$, let the processes λ and $\mathcal{E}$ be defined by*

$$\lambda_t = W_1\left(c_t, \mathcal{M}_t\left(U_{t+1}(c)\right)\right),$$

$$\mathcal{E}_t = \prod_{s=1}^{t} W_2\left(c_{s-1}, \mathcal{M}_{s-1}\left(U_s(c)\right)\right) \kappa_s\left(U_s(c)\right), \quad \mathcal{E}_0 = 1.$$

Then the process $\pi = \mathcal{E}\lambda$ is the utility gradient of U_0 at c if $\lim_{t \to \infty} E\left[\pi_t x_t\right] = 0$ for any $\{x_t\} \in \mathcal{L}$.

Proof Define

$$\varphi_t(\alpha) = U_t(c + \alpha x)$$

for all $\alpha \in \mathbb{R}, x \in \mathcal{L}$ such that $c + \alpha x \in \mathcal{C}$. We want to compute $\varphi_t'(0)$ recursively using the simple notation:

$$W_1(t) = W_1(c_t, \mathcal{M}_t(U_{t+1}(c))), W_2(t) = W(c_t, \mathcal{M}_t(U_{t+1}(c))).$$

Using the utility recursion,

$$\varphi_t(\alpha) = W(c_t + \alpha x_t, \mathcal{M}_t(\varphi_{t+1}(\alpha))).$$

Differentiation yields

$$\varphi_t'(0) = W_1(t) x_t + W_2(t) E_t\left[\kappa_{t+1}(\varphi_{t+1}(0)) \varphi_{t+1}'(0)\right].$$

Repeated substitution yields $\varphi_0'(0)$ and hence the utility gradient in the proposition. ∎

Here λ_t can be interpreted as the marginal value of wealth at time t. To see this, consider the problem

$$J(w_0) = \max_c U_0(c) \text{ subject to } E\left[\sum_{t=0}^{\infty} p_t c_t\right] \leq w_0,$$

where $\{p_t\}$ is the state price density with $p_0 = 1$ and w_0 is initial wealth. By the envelope condition, $J'(w_0) = \mu$, where μ is the Lagrange multiplier. By the first-order condition, we obtain $W_1(c_0, \mathcal{M}_0(U_1(c))) = \mu$. Thus $\lambda_0 = J'(w_0)$. A similar argument applies to any time t so that $\lambda_t = J'(w_t)$, where w_t is time t wealth.

The **pricing kernel** (or the **intertemporal marginal rate of substitution**) is defined as $M_{t+1} = \pi_{t+1}/\pi_t$, where $\{\pi_t\}$ is the utility gradient density. By proposition 20.3.2,

$$M_{t+1} = \frac{\lambda_{t+1}}{\lambda_t} W_2(c_t, \mathcal{M}_t(U_{t+1}(c))) \kappa_{t+1}(U_{t+1}(c)).$$

The pricing kernel is important for asset pricing as will be shown in the next section.

A utility gradient may not exist due to the lack of differentiability. However, when U_0 is concave, we define **utility supergradient** at $c \in \mathcal{C}$ as an adapted process π such that

$$U_0(c') \leq U_0(c) + E\left[\sum_{t=0}^{\infty} \pi_t(c_t' - c_t)\right], \quad \text{all } c' \in \mathcal{C}.$$

Utility supergradient may not be unique. Let $\partial U_0(c)$ denote the set of all supergradients at c.

Example 20.3.1 *Consider the Epstein–Zin utility defined in (20.3). Its pricing kernel is given by*

$$M_{t+1} = \beta \left(\frac{c_{t+1}}{c_t} \right)^{-\rho} \left[\frac{U_{t+1}(c)}{\mathcal{M}_t(U_{t+1}(c))} \right]^{\rho-\gamma}, \tag{20.20}$$

where

$$\mathcal{M}_t(U_{t+1}(c)) = \left(E_t \left[U_{t+1}^{1-\gamma}(c) \right] \right)^{1/(1-\gamma)}.$$

When the decision maker prefers earlier resolution of uncertainty (i.e. $\gamma > \rho$), the pricing kernel attaches more weight on the low continuation value in bad times. This generates countercyclical pricing kernel, which helps explain the equity premium puzzle.

Example 20.3.2 *Consider the generalized smooth ambiguity utility defined in (20.14) and (20.15). The pricing kernel is given by*

$$M_{z,t+1} = \beta \left(\frac{c_{t+1}}{c_t} \right)^{-\rho} \left(\frac{U_{t+1}(c)}{\mathcal{M}_t(U_{t+1}(c))} \right)^{\rho-\gamma} \left(\frac{\left(\mathbb{E}_{z,t} \left[U_{t+1}^{1-\gamma}(c) \right] \right)^{1/(1-\gamma)}}{\mathcal{M}_t(U_{t+1}(c))} \right)^{-(\eta-\gamma)},$$

where

$$\mathcal{M}_t(x_{t+1}) = \left\{ E_{\mu_t} \left(E_{\pi_{z,t}} \left[x_{t+1}^{1-\gamma} \right] \right)^{(1-\eta)/(1-\gamma)} \right\}^{1/(1-\eta)}.$$

When the decision maker is ambiguity averse (i.e., $\eta > \gamma$), the pricing kernel attaches more weight on the low continuation value in bad times. This helps generate countercyclical pricing kernel. Ju and Miao (2012) show that this feature is important for addressing many asset-pricing puzzles.

Example 20.3.3 *Consider the recursive multiple-priors utility defined in (20.7). This utility is generally not smooth. Epstein and Wang (1994) show that the set of utility supergradients is given by*

$$\partial U(c) = \{ \pi \in \mathcal{L} : \pi_t = u'(c_t) \, m_t^*, m_t^* \in Q_t \},$$

where

$$Q_t = \left\{ m_t = \frac{dq_t}{dp_t} : \int U_{t+1}(c) \, m_t dp_t = \min_{q_t \in \mathcal{P}_t} \int U_{t+1}(c) \, dq_t \right\}.$$

Here p_t is the reference one-step-ahead distribution (or transition probability) and $\mathcal{P}_t$ is the set of one-step-ahead distributions that the decision maker thinks possible.

20.4   Portfolio Choice and Asset Pricing

This section studies an application of the Epstein–Zin utility to the portfolio and asset-pricing problem. Consider an economy with a representative agent having the Epstein–Zin utility given in (20.3). He can trade N assets with returns from periods t to $t+1$, $R_{i,t+1}$, $i=1,...,N$. One asset is riskless, and the risk-free rate is denoted $R_{f,t+1}$. His budget constraint is given by

$$X_{t+1} = R_{w,t+1}(X_t - C_t),$$ (20.21)

where X_t is wealth at time t and

$$R_{w,t+1} = \sum_{i=1}^{N} \psi_{i,t+1} R_{i,t+1}$$

is the portfolio return. This portfolio return is also often called the wealth return or the market return. Here $\psi_{i,t+1}$ denotes the portfolio weight on asset i and satisfies $\sum_i \psi_{i,t+1} = 1$. The agent's problem is to choose portfolio and consumption processes so as to maximize utility. We use dynamic programming to solve this problem.

20.4.1   Optimality and Equilibrium

Let $J_t(X_t)$ denote the value function where we have suppressed other state variables. It satisfies the Bellman equation:

$$J_t(X_t) = \max_{C_t, \psi_{it}} \left[(1-\beta) C_t^{1-\rho} + \beta \left(E_t \left[J_{t+1}(X_{t+1})^{1-\gamma} \right] \right)^{(1-\rho)/(1-\gamma)} \right]^{1/(1-\rho)}.$$

Conjecture that

$$J_t(X_t) = A_t X_t, \quad C_t = a_t X_t,$$

where A_t and a_t are to be determined. Substituting (20.21) and the conjecture into the Bellman equation yields

$$A_t = \max_{a_t, \{\psi_{i,t+1}\}} \left[(1-\beta) a_t^{1-\rho} + (1-a_t)^{1-\rho} \beta \left(E_t \left[(A_{t+1} R_{w,t+1})^{1-\gamma} \right] \right)^{(1-\rho)/(1-\gamma)} \right]^{1/(1-\rho)}.$$

The first-order condition with respect to a_t is given by

$$\left(\frac{a_t}{1-a_t} \right)^{-\rho} = \frac{\beta}{1-\beta} \left(E_t \left[(A_{t+1} R_{w,t+1})^{1-\gamma} \right] \right)^{(1-\rho)(1-\gamma)}.$$ (20.22)

Eliminating the expectation terms in the above two equations, we obtain

$$A_t = (1 - \beta)^{1/(1-\rho)} a_t^{-\rho/(1-\rho)} = (1 - \beta)^{1/(1-\rho)} \left(\frac{C_t}{X_t}\right)^{-\rho/(1-\rho)}. \tag{20.23}$$

Substitute (20.23) into (20.22) to obtain

$$\left(\frac{a_t}{1 - a_t}\right)^{-\rho} = \beta \left(E_t \left[\left(\frac{C_{t+1}}{X_{t+1}}\right)^{-\rho(1-\gamma)/(1-\rho)} R_{w,t+1}^{1-\gamma}\right]\right)^{(1-\rho)/(1-\gamma)}. \tag{20.24}$$

Using the budget constraint and the conjecture $X_t = C_t/a_t$, we obtain

$$X_{t+1} = (X_t - C_t) R_{w,t+1} = R_{w,t+1} C_t \frac{1 - a_t}{a_t}. \tag{20.25}$$

Substitute equation (20.25) into (20.24) and simplify to obtain

$$\beta^{(1-\gamma)/(1-\rho)} E_t \left[\left(\frac{C_{t+1}}{C_t}\right)^{-\rho(1-\gamma)/(1-\rho)} (R_{w,t+1})^{(1-\gamma)/(1-\rho)}\right] = 1. \tag{20.26}$$

Next the portfolio choice is determined by maximizing the certainty equivalent:

$$\max_{\{\psi_{i,t+1}\}} \left(E_t \left[(A_{t+1} R_{w,t+1})^{1-\gamma}\right]\right)^{1/(1-\gamma)}.$$

We derive the first-order condition for any asset i as

$$E_t \left[A_{t+1}^{1-\gamma} R_{w,t+1}^{-\gamma} (R_{i,t+1} - R_{f,t+1})\right] = 0.$$

Substituting (20.23) into the above equation yields:

$$0 = E_t \left[\left(\frac{C_{t+1}}{X_{t+1}}\right)^{-\rho(1-\gamma)/(1-\rho)} R_{w,t+1}^{-\gamma} (R_{i,t+1} - R_{f,t+1})\right].$$

Substituting (20.25) into it yields

$$0 = E_t \left[\left(\frac{C_{t+1}}{C_t}\right)^{-\rho(1-\gamma)/(1-\rho)} R_{w,t+1}^{[(1-\gamma)/(1-\rho)]-1} (R_{i,t+1} - R_{f,t+1})\right]. \tag{20.27}$$

Multiply by $\psi_{i,t+1}$ and sum over to obtain

$$E_t \left[\left(\frac{C_{t+1}}{C_t}\right)^{-\rho(1-\gamma)/(1-\rho)} R_{w,t+1}^{[(1-\gamma)/(1-\rho)]-1} R_{f,t+1}\right]$$

$$= E_t \left[\left(\frac{C_{t+1}}{C_t}\right)^{-\rho(1-\gamma)/(1-\rho)} R_{w,t+1}^{[(1-\gamma)/(1-\rho)]-1}\right].$$

Using (20.26) to substitute the expression on the right-hand side of the equation above, we can derive

$$
E_t \left[\left(\beta \left(\frac{C_{t+1}}{C_t} \right)^{-\rho} \right)^{(1-\gamma)/(1-\rho)} R_{w,t+1}^{[(1-\gamma)/(1-\rho)]-1} R_{f,t+1} \right] = 1. \tag{20.28}
$$

Substitute this equation into (20.27) to obtain the Euler equation:

$$
E_t \left[\bar{M}_{t+1} R_{i,t+1} \right] = 1 \tag{20.29}
$$

for any asset i, where

$$
\bar{M}_{t+1} \equiv \left(\beta \left(\frac{C_{t+1}}{C_t} \right)^{-\rho} \right)^{(1-\gamma)/(1-\rho)} R_{w,t+1}^{(\rho-\gamma)/(1-\rho)}. \tag{20.30}
$$

This suggests that $\bar{M}_{t+1}$ should be a pricing kernel.

What is the relation between $\bar{M}_{t+1}$ and M_{t+1} defined in (20.20)? We want to show that they are identical. Substituting (20.23) into the conjectured value function yields

$$
\frac{X_t}{C_t} = \frac{1}{1-\beta} \left(\frac{U_t}{C_t} \right)^{1-\rho}, \tag{20.31}
$$

where $U_t = J_t(X_t)$ denotes the utility value at the optimal consumption process. This equation links the unobservable utility value to the observable consumption and wealth. We use this equation to eliminate U_t in (20.20):

$$
M_{t+1} = \beta \left(\frac{C_{t+1}}{C_t} \right)^{-\rho} \left[\frac{U_{t+1}}{\mathcal{M}_t(U_{t+1})} \right]^{\rho-\gamma}
$$

$$
= \beta \left(\frac{C_{t+1}}{C_t} \right)^{-\rho} \left[\frac{\left[X_{t+1}(1-\beta) C_{t+1}^{-\rho} \right]^{1/(1-\rho)}}{E_t \left[(A_t X_{t+1})^{1-\gamma} \right]^{1/(1-\gamma)}} \right]^{\rho-\gamma}.
$$

Substituting (20.25) into the equation above yields

$$
M_{t+1} = \beta \left(\frac{C_{t+1}}{C_t} \right)^{-\rho} \left[\frac{\left[R_{w,t+1} C_t \frac{1-a_t}{a_t} (1-\beta) C_{t+1}^{-\rho} \right]^{1/(1-\rho)}}{C_t \frac{1-a_t}{a_t} E_t \left[(A_t R_{w,t+1})^{1-\gamma} \right]^{1/(1-\gamma)}} \right]^{\rho-\gamma}.
$$

Using (20.22) to eliminate $E_t\left[(A_t R_{w,t+1})^{1-\gamma}\right]^{1/(1-\gamma)}$ yields

$$M_{t+1} = \beta\left(\frac{C_{t+1}}{C_t}\right)^{-\rho}\left[\frac{\left[R_{w,t+1}C_t\frac{1-a_t}{a_t}(1-\beta)C_{t+1}^{-\rho}\right]^{1/(1-\rho)}}{C_t\frac{1-a_t}{a_t}\left(\frac{a_t}{1-a_t}\right)^{-\frac{\rho}{(1-\rho)}}\left(\frac{1-\beta}{\beta}\right)^{1/(1-\rho)}}\right]^{\rho-\gamma}.$$

Simplifying yields $M_{t+1} = \bar{M}_{t+1}$.

Epstein and Zin (1991) use (20.30) to test (20.29) by the GMM method. They use proxies for X_t and C_t in the data. Though utility value is unobservable, the formula in (20.20) is more convenient for numerical solutions.

Note that (20.29) holds for the risk-free rate so that

$$R_{f,t+1} = \frac{1}{E_t\left[M_{t+1}\right]}.$$

We can then use (20.29) to derive the conditional equity premium:

$$E_t\left[R_{e,t+1}\right] - R_{f,t+1} = -\frac{Cov_t\left(R_{e,t+1}, M_{t+1}\right)}{E_t\left[M_{t+1}\right]},$$

where $R_{e,t+1}$ denote the equity return. This equation shows that the equity premium is determined by the negative of the covariance between the equity return and the pricing kernel. What is the intuition? The pricing kernel measures the marginal utility of consumption. The agent does not like the stock when it pays off badly during bad times when his marginal utility is high. That is, his demand for the stock is low when the stock return and the pricing kernel are negatively correlated. This causes the stock price to fall and hence the equity premium to rise.

From the equation above, in order to raise the equity premium, one has to raise the covariance between the stock return and the pricing kernel. A simple solution is to raise the countercyclicality of the pricing kernel. Some utility models discussed earlier can generate this feature and hence help resolve the equity premium puzzle.

20.4.2 Log-Linear Approximation

Campbell (1996, 1999) develop an analytically tractable framework to analyze asset-pricing formulas under the assumption that the joint distribution of consumption and asset returns are conditionally lognormal and homoskedastic. His approach exploits the following formula:

$$\ln E_t X = E_t \ln X + \frac{1}{2}\text{Var}_t \ln X,$$

where

$$\text{Var}_t \ln X = E_t\left(\ln X - E_t \ln X\right)^2 = \text{Var}\left(\ln X - E_t \ln X\right).$$

We also use a lower case letter x to the log value of X for any variable. Define

$$\sigma_c = \text{Var}\,(c_{t+1} - E_t c_{t+1}),$$
$$\sigma_w = \text{Var}\,(r_{w,t+1} - E_t r_{w,t+1}),$$
$$\sigma_{ic} = \text{Cov}\,(r_{i,t+1} - E_t r_{i,t+1}, c_{t+1} - E_t c_{t+1}),$$
$$\sigma_{iw} = \text{Cov}\,(r_{i,t+1} - E_t r_{i,t+1}, r_{w,t+1} - E_t r_{w,t+1}).$$

Use (20.26) to derive

$$0 = \frac{(1-\gamma)}{(1-\rho)}\ln\beta - \frac{\rho(1-\gamma)}{1-\rho}E_t\Delta c_{t+1} + \frac{1-\gamma}{1-\rho}E_t r_{w,t+1}$$
$$+ \frac{1}{2}\left[\frac{\rho(1-\gamma)}{1-\rho}\right]^2 \sigma_c^2 - \frac{\rho(1-\gamma)}{1-\rho}\frac{1-\gamma}{1-\rho}\sigma_{cw} + \frac{1}{2}\frac{1-\gamma}{1-\rho}\sigma_w^2.$$

By (20.28),

$$0 = r_{f,t+1} + \frac{(1-\gamma)}{(1-\rho)}\ln\beta - \frac{\rho(1-\gamma)}{1-\rho}E_t\Delta c_{t+1} + \frac{\rho-\gamma}{1-\rho}E_t r_{w,t+1}$$
$$+ \frac{1}{2}\left[\frac{\rho(1-\gamma)}{1-\rho}\right]^2 \sigma_c^2 - \frac{\rho(1-\gamma)}{1-\rho}\frac{\rho-\gamma}{1-\rho}\sigma_{cw} + \frac{1}{2}\left(\frac{\rho-\gamma}{1-\rho}\right)\sigma_w^2. \tag{20.32}$$

Eliminating σ_{cw} from the two equations above yields

$$r_{f,t+1} = -\ln\beta + \rho E_t\Delta c_{t+1} - \frac{1}{2}\frac{\gamma-\rho}{1-\rho}\sigma_w^2 - \frac{\rho^2(1-\gamma)}{2(1-\rho)}\sigma_c^2. \tag{20.33}$$

This equation shows the following: The risk-free rate is lower when the agent is more patient since he saves more. It increases with the consumption growth, since a high interest rate is needed to prevent the agent from borrowing from the future. The sensitivity is equal to ρ the inverse of EIS. When ρ is large, the EIS is small and the impact of consumption growth on the risk free is small. The last two terms reflect precautionary saving. To the extent that these two quadratic terms are small, a high EIS helps reduce the risk-free rate. The Epstein–Zin utility is flexible since changing EIS (or $1/\rho$) is independent of the risk aversion parameter γ.

By (20.29), we obtain

$$0 = E_t r_{i,t+1} + \frac{1-\gamma}{1-\rho}\ln\beta - \frac{\rho(1-\gamma)}{1-\rho}E_t\Delta c_{t+1} + \frac{\rho-\gamma}{1-\rho}E_t r_{w,t+1}$$
$$+ \frac{1}{2}\left[\frac{\rho(1-\gamma)}{1-\rho}\right]^2 \sigma_c^2 - \frac{\rho(1-\gamma)}{1-\rho}\frac{\rho-\gamma}{1-\rho}\sigma_{cw} + \frac{1}{2}\left(\frac{\rho-\gamma}{1-\rho}\right)^2 \sigma_w$$
$$+ \frac{1}{2}\sigma_i^2 - \frac{\rho(1-\gamma)}{1-\rho}\sigma_{ic} + \frac{\rho-\gamma}{1-\rho}\sigma_{iw}. \tag{20.34}$$

Combining (20.32) and (20.34) yields the risk premium for asset i:

$$E_t r_{i,t+1} - r_{f,t+1} + \frac{1}{2}\sigma_i^2 = \frac{\rho(1-\gamma)}{1-\rho}\sigma_{ic} + \frac{\gamma-\rho}{1-\rho}\sigma_{iw}. \tag{20.35}$$

This equation reveals that the risk premium on asset i is a weighted combination of asset i's covariance with consumption growth (multiplied by the inverse of EIS, ρ) and asset i's covariance with wealth returns. The weights are $(1-\gamma)/(1-\rho)$ and $(\gamma-\rho)/(1-\rho)$. Since we typically assume that $\gamma > 1$, the signs of the two weights are determined by whether $\rho > 1$ and whether $\gamma > \rho$. In particular, when $\rho < 1$ (i.e., EIS > 1) and $\gamma > \rho$ (i.e., the agent prefers earlier resolution of uncertainty), the first term on the right-hand side of (20.35) is negative while the second term is positive.

Campbell–Shiller Approximation Campbell and Shiller (1988) derive a log-linear approximation to the price-dividend ratio, which is useful for empirical analysis. By definition,

$$R_{i,t+1} = \frac{P_{i,t+1} + D_{i,t+1}}{P_{it}},$$

where P_{it} and D_{it} denote asset i's price and dividends. Taking logs and Taylor expansion about the mean of the log dividend–price ratio, $\overline{d_{it} - p_{it}}$, we obtain

$$r_{i,t+1} = \kappa + \varrho p_{i,t+1} + (1-\varrho) d_{i,t+1} - p_{it}, \tag{20.36}$$

where

$$\varrho \equiv \frac{1}{1 + \exp\left(\overline{d_{it} - p_{it}}\right)},$$

$$\kappa \equiv -\log(\varrho) - (1-\varrho)\log\left(\frac{1}{\varrho-1}\right).$$

Solving forward and imposing the terminal condition $\lim_{i\to\infty} \varrho^i p_{j,t+i} = 0$, we derive

$$p_{it} - d_{it} = \frac{\kappa}{1-\varrho} + E_t \sum_{k=0}^{\infty} \varrho^k [\Delta d_{i,t+1+k} - r_{i,t+1+k}]. \tag{20.37}$$

Rewrite equation (20.36) as

$$r_{i,t+1} = \kappa + \varrho(p_{i,t+1} - d_{i,t+1}) + \Delta d_{i,t+1} + (d_{i,t} - p_{it}). \tag{20.38}$$

Substituting (20.37) into this equation yields

$$r_{i,t+1} - E_t r_{i,t+1} = (E_{t+1} - E_t) \sum_{k=0}^{\infty} \varrho^k \Delta d_{i,t+1+k}$$

$$- (E_{t+1} - E_t) \sum_{k=1}^{\infty} \varrho^k r_{i,t+1+k}. \tag{20.39}$$

This equation says that unexpected returns on asset i must be associated with changes in expectations of future dividends and changes in expectations of future returns.

Equity Volatility Puzzle   We now use the accounting framework given above to illustrate the stock market volatility puzzle. The intertemporal budget constraint for a representative agent implies that aggregate consumption is the dividend on the portfolio of all invested wealth, denoted by subscript w:

$$d_{wt} = c_t.$$

Many authors, including Grossman and Shiller (1981), Lucas (1978), and Mehra and Prescott (1985), have assumed that the aggregate stock market, denoted by subscript e for equity, is equivalent to the wealth portfolio and thus pays consumption as its dividend. Here we adopt the more realistic assumption that aggregate dividends on the stock market are not equal to aggregate consumption. Following Campbell (1986) and Abel (1999), we assume that they are related by

$$d_{et} = \lambda c_t,$$

where λ can be interpreted as a measure of leverage as in Abel (1999). When $\lambda > 1$, dividends and stock returns are more volatile than the returns on the aggregate wealth portfolio. This framework has the additional advantage that a riskless real bond with infinite maturity—an inflation-indexed consol, denoted by subscript b—can be priced merely by setting $\lambda = 0$.

Equations (20.33) and (20.35) imply that

$$E_t r_{et+1} = \mu_e + \rho E_t [\Delta c_{t+1}],$$

where μ_e an asset-specific constant term. The expected log return on equity, like the expected log return on any other asset, is just a constant plus expected consumption growth divided by the elasticity of intertemporal substitution.

Substitute the preceding two equations into (20.37) through (20.39) to obtain

$$p_{et} - d_{et} = \frac{k_e}{1 - \varrho} + (\lambda - \rho) E_t \sum_{i=0}^{\infty} \varrho^i \Delta c_{t+1+i} \tag{20.40}$$

and

$$r_{e,t+1} - E_t r_{e,t+1} = \lambda (\Delta c_{t+1} - E_t \Delta c_{t+1}) + (\lambda - \rho)(E_{t+1} - E_t) \sum_{i=1}^{\infty} \varrho^i \Delta c_{t+1+i}. \tag{20.41}$$

Expected future consumption growth has offsetting effects on the log price–dividend ratio. It has a direct positive wealth effect by increasing expected future dividends λ-for-one, but it has an indirect negative substitution effect by increasing expected future real interest rates ρ-for-one. The unexpected log return on the stock market is λ times contemporaneous unexpected consumption growth (since contemporaneous consumption growth increases the contemporaneous dividend λ-for-one), plus $(\lambda - \rho)$ times the discounted sum of revisions in expected future consumption growth.

Consider a simple version of the **long-run risk model** of Bansal and Yaron (2004):

$$\Delta c_{t+1} = z_t + \varepsilon_{c,t+1},$$
$$z_{t+1} = (1 - \phi)g + \phi z_t + \varepsilon_{z,t+1},$$

which is a linear version of Cecchetti, Lam, and Mark (1990, 1993) and Kandel and Stambaugh (1991). In the next subsection we will consider more general cases. Substituting these equations into equations (20.40) and (20.41), we have

$$p_{et} - d_{et} = \frac{k_e}{1 - \varrho} + (\lambda - \rho)\left[\frac{g}{1 - \varrho} + \frac{z_t - g}{1 - \varrho\phi}\right], \tag{20.42}$$

$$r_{e,t+1} - E_t r_{e,t+1} = \lambda\varepsilon_{c,t+1} + (\lambda - \rho)\left(\frac{\varrho}{1 - \varrho\phi}\right)\varepsilon_{z,t+1} \tag{20.43}$$

Equation (20.42) shows that the price-dividend ratio is procyclical if $\lambda > \rho$, namely EIS is greater than $\lambda \geq 1$. In this case the wealth effect dominates the substitution effect. Equation (20.43) shows that when λ is large and $\lambda > \rho$, both the innovation to the contemporaneous consumption growth and the innovation to the expected consumption growth help raise equity volatility.

What is the model's prediction of the volatility of the risk-free rate? By setting $\lambda = 1$ in equations (20.42) and (20.43), the log yield and unexpected return on a real consol bond, denoted by a subscript b, are, respectively,

$$y_{bt} = d_{bt} - p_{bt} = -\frac{k_b}{1 - \varrho} + \rho\left[\frac{g}{1 - \varrho} + \frac{z_t - g}{1 - \varrho\phi}\right],$$

$$r_{b,t+1} - E_t r_{b,t+1} = -\rho\left(\frac{\varrho}{1 - \varrho\phi}\right)\varepsilon_{z,t+1}.$$

The equations above reveal that the risk-free rate is countercyclical. Moreover a high EIS (or low ρ) generates a smooth risk-free rate and a smooth bound yield.

The preceding discussion implies that an EIS greater than 1 is needed to explain high equity volatility and low risk-free rate volatility. The empirical literature on the estimate of EIS is highly debated.

Equity Premium Puzzle   We now compute the equity premium using the long-run risk consumption process. We will use (20.35) and compute explicitly the expressions for σ_{ic} and σ_{iw}. First, compute σ_{iw}. Equation (20.35) holds for wealth portfolio $\lambda = 1$,

$$r_{w,t+1} - E_t r_{w,t+1} = (\Delta c_{t+1} - E_t \Delta c_{t+1}) + (1 - \rho)(E_{t+1} - E_t) \sum_{j=0}^{\infty} \varrho^j \Delta c_{t+1+j}.$$

Thus, for any asset i,

$$\sigma_{iw} = \sigma_{ic} + (1 - \rho)\sigma_{ig},$$

where σ_{ig} denotes the covariance of asset return i with revisions in expectations of future consumption growth:

$$\sigma_{ig} = \mathrm{Cov}\left(r_{it+1} - E_t r_{it+1}, (E_{t+1} - E_t) \sum_{i=0}^{\infty} \rho^i \Delta c_{t+1+i}\right).$$

Substitute out σ_{iw} in the pricing equation (20.35) to derive

$$E_t r_{it+1} - r_{ft+1} + \frac{1}{2}\sigma_i^2 = \gamma \sigma_{ic} + (\gamma - \rho)\sigma_{ig}.$$

Given the long-run risk model of consumption, we derive

$$(E_{t+1} - E_t) \sum_{j=1}^{\infty} \varrho^j \Delta c_{t+1+j} = \frac{\varrho}{1 - \varrho\phi} \epsilon_{z,t+1}.$$

Using this equation and equation (20.43) yields

$$E_t r_{et+1} - r_{ft+1} + \frac{\sigma_e^2}{2} = \gamma \left[\lambda \sigma_c^2 + (\lambda - \rho)\frac{\varrho}{1 - \varrho\phi}\sigma_{cz}\right]$$

$$+ (\gamma - \rho)\left[\frac{\lambda \varrho}{1 - \varrho\phi}\sigma_{cz} + (\lambda - \rho)\left(\frac{\varrho}{1 - \varrho\phi}\right)^2 \sigma_z^2\right].$$

This expression nests many of the leading cases explored in the literature on the equity premium puzzle. To understand it, it is helpful to break the equity premium into two components: the premium on real consol bonds ($\lambda = 0$) over the riskless interest rate, and the premium on equities over real consol bonds,

$$E_t r_{bt+1} - r_{ft+1} + \frac{\sigma_b^2}{2} = -\rho\gamma\frac{\varrho}{1 - \varrho\phi}\sigma_{cz} - (\gamma - \rho)\rho\left(\frac{\varrho}{1 - \varrho\phi}\right)^2 \sigma_z^2 \qquad (20.44)$$

and

$$E_t\left[r_{et+1} - r_{bt+1}\right] + \frac{\sigma_e^2}{2} - \frac{\sigma_b^2}{2} \qquad (20.45)$$

$$= \gamma\lambda\left[\sigma_c^2 + \frac{\varrho}{1 - \varrho\phi}\sigma_{cz}\right] + (\gamma - \rho)\lambda\left[\frac{\varrho}{1 - \varrho\phi}\sigma_{cz} + \left(\frac{\varrho}{1 - \varrho\phi}\right)^2 \sigma_z^2\right].$$

The first term in each of these expressions represents the premium under power utility, while the second term represents the effect on the premium of moving to Epstein–Zin utility and allowing the coefficient of risk aversion to differ from the reciprocal of the intertemporal elasticity of substitution.

Under power utility the real bond premium in equation (20.44) is determined by the covariance σ_{cz} of realized consumption growth and innovations to expected future consumption growth. If this covariance is positive, then an increase in consumption is associated with higher expected future consumption growth, higher real interest rates, and lower bond prices. Real bonds accordingly have hedge value, and the real bond premium is negative. If σ_{cz} is negative, then the real bond premium is positive. When the agent prefers earlier resolution of uncertainty (i.e., $\gamma > \rho$), the second term in (20.44) is negative. Thus Epstein–Zin utility generates a negative term premium.

The premium on equities over real bonds is proportional to the coefficient λ that governs the volatility of dividend growth. Under power utility the equity-bond premium is just the risk aversion γ times λ times terms in σ_c^2 and σ_{cz}. Since both σ_c^2 and σ_{cz} must be small to match the observed moments of consumption growth, it is hard to rationalize the large equity-bond premium in the data. But Epstein–Zin utility with $\gamma > \rho$ adds a second positive term in σ_c^2 and σ_{cz}, which helps raise the equity-bond premium.

In conclusion, the consumption-based model with Epstein–Zin utility in the case of a preference for earlier resolution of uncertainty ($\gamma > \rho$) helps generate a large equity premium, but this model generates a negative term premium. This model also needs $\lambda > \rho$ to generate a procyclical price–dividend ratio. Given that $\lambda \geq 1$, this necessarily needs EIS to be greater than 1.

20.4.3   Long-Run Risk

Bansal and Yaron (2004) propose the following long-run risk model of consumption and dividend growth. In this model a persistent component drives the expected consumption and dividend growth. Also the volatility of consumption and dividend growth is time-varying. Formally, let

$$g_{t+1} = \mu + x_t + \sigma_t \eta_{t+1},$$
$$g_{dt+1} = \mu_d + \phi x_t + \varphi_d \sigma_t u_{t+1},$$
$$x_{t+1} = \rho_x x_t + \varphi_e \sigma_t e_{t+1},$$
$$\sigma_{t+1}^2 = \sigma^2 + v_1 \left(\sigma_t^2 - \sigma^2 \right) + \sigma_w w_{t+1},$$

where $g_{t+1} = \Delta \ln c_{t+1}$, $g_{dt+1} = \Delta \ln d_{t+1}$, and η_t, u_t, e_t, and w_t are IID $N(0,1)$.

Bansal and Yaron (2004) use the log-linear approximation method to derive closed-form solutions for asset pricing formulas. To derive these formulas, we first derive the Campbell–Shiller approximation for the return on the aggregate consumption claims. From the definition $R_{w,t+1} = (P_{t+1} + C_{t+1})/P_t$, we can derive

$$r_{w,t+1} = \ln \frac{P_{t+1}}{C_{t+1}} + 1 - \ln\left(\frac{P_t}{C_t}\right) + \ln\left(\frac{C_{t+1}}{C_t}\right)$$

$$= \kappa_0 + \kappa_1 z_{t+1} - z_t + g_{t+1}, \tag{20.46}$$

where $z_t = \ln(P_t/C_t)$, $\bar{z}$ is the long-run mean value of z_t, and

$$\kappa_0 = \ln(e^{\bar{z}} + 1) - \frac{e^{\bar{z}}\bar{z}}{e^{\bar{z}} + 1}, \qquad \kappa_1 = \frac{e^{\bar{z}}}{e^{\bar{z}} + 1} < 1.$$

Note that $\bar{z}$ is endogenous and that we need to solve for it after we derive the equilibrium log price–dividend ratio z_t. That is, it is a fixed point, $\bar{z} = E[z_t]$.

By (20.30), we can write the log pricing kernel as

$$\ln M_{t+1} = \frac{1-\gamma}{1-\rho} \ln \beta - \frac{(1-\gamma)\rho}{1-\rho} g_{t+1} + \frac{\rho-\gamma}{1-\rho} r_{w,t+1}. \tag{20.47}$$

By the Euler equation $E_t[M_{t+1}R_{i,t+1}] = 1$,

$$E_t\left[\exp\left(\frac{1-\gamma}{1-\rho}\ln\beta - \frac{(1-\gamma)\rho}{1-\rho} g_{t+1} + \frac{\rho-\gamma}{1-\rho} r_{w,t+1} + r_{i,t+1}\right)\right] = 1. \tag{20.48}$$

Price–Consumption Ratio   Equation (20.48) holds for the wealth return so that

$$E_t\left[\exp\left(\frac{1-\gamma}{1-\rho}\ln\beta - \frac{(1-\gamma)\rho}{1-\rho} g_{t+1} + \frac{1-\gamma}{1-\rho} r_{w,t+1}\right)\right] = 1. \tag{20.49}$$

Conjecture

$$z_t = A_0 + A_1 x_t + A_2 \sigma_t^2,$$

where A_0, A_1, A_2 are constants to be determined. Substituting this conjecture into (20.46) and (20.49) and matching coefficients for x_t, we obtain

$$-\frac{(1-\gamma)\rho}{1-\rho} + \frac{1-\gamma}{1-\rho}[\kappa_1 A_1 \rho_x - A_1 + 1] = 0.$$

Solving yields

$$A_1 = \frac{1-\rho}{1-\kappa_1 \rho_x}.$$

It is positive if EIS is greater than 1 (or $\rho < 1$). In this case the intertemporal substitution effect dominates the wealth effect. In response to higher expected consumption growth rates, the agent buys more stocks and hence the price–consumption ratio rises. In the standard CRRA utility, the need for a high risk aversion parameter $\gamma > 1$ also implies $\rho = \gamma > 1$, which implies that the price–consumption ratio is countercyclical.

Matching coefficients for σ_t^2 yields

$$
0 = \frac{1 - \gamma}{1 - \rho} \left[\kappa_1 v_1 A_2 - A_2 \right]
$$
$$
+ \frac{1}{2} \left[(1 - \gamma)^2 + \left(\frac{1 - \gamma}{1 - \rho} A_1 \kappa_1 \varphi_e \right)^2 \right].
$$

Solving yields

$$
A_2 = \frac{0.5 \left[(1 - \gamma)^2 + \left(\frac{1-\gamma}{1-\rho} A_1 \kappa_1 \varphi_e \right)^2 \right]}{\frac{1-\gamma}{1-\rho} \left[1 - \kappa_1 v_1 \right]}.
$$

Thus, if $\gamma > 1$ and $\rho < 1$, then $A_2 < 0$, and a rise in volatility lowers the price–consumption ratio. Moreover an increase in v_1 raises A_2 and magnifies the impact of economic uncertainty on the price–consumption ratio.

By (20.46),

$$
r_{w,t+1} - E_t r_{w,t+1} = \kappa_1 \left(z_{t+1} - E_t z_{t+1} \right) + g_{t+1} - E_t g_{t+1}
$$
$$
= \sigma_t \eta_{t+1} + B \sigma_t e_{t+1} + A_2 \kappa_1 \sigma_w w_{t+1}, \tag{20.50}
$$

where $B \equiv \kappa_1 A_1 \varphi_e$. We then obtain

$$
\mathrm{Var}_t \left(r_{w,t+1} \right) = \left(1 + B^2 \right) \sigma_t^2 + \left(A_2 \kappa_1 \right)^2 \sigma_w^2.
$$

Pricing Kernel   By (20.47), we write the pricing kernel in terms of state variables:

$$
m_{t+1} = \ln M_{t+1} = \frac{1 - \gamma}{1 - \rho} \ln \beta - \frac{(1 - \gamma) \rho}{1 - \rho} g_{t+1} + \frac{\rho - \gamma}{1 - \rho} r_{w,t+1},
$$

$$
E_t m_{t+1} = m_0 - \rho x_t + A_2 \left(\kappa_1 v_1 - 1 \right) \frac{\rho - \gamma}{1 - \rho} \sigma_t^2,
$$

$$
m_{t+1} - E_t m_{t+1} = \left(-\frac{(1 - \gamma) \rho}{1 - \rho} + \frac{\rho - \gamma}{1 - \rho} \right) \sigma_t \eta_{t+1} \tag{20.51}
$$
$$
+ \frac{\rho - \gamma}{1 - \rho} \left(A_1 \kappa_1 \varphi_e \right) \sigma_t e_{t+1} + \frac{\rho - \gamma}{1 - \rho} A_2 \kappa_1 \sigma_w w_{t+1}
$$
$$
= -\lambda_{m,\eta} \sigma_t \eta_{t+1} - \lambda_{m,e} \sigma_t e_{t+1} - \lambda_{m,w} \sigma_w w_{t+1},
$$

where

$$\lambda_{m,\eta} \equiv \gamma > 0, \ \lambda_{m,e} \equiv \frac{\gamma - \rho}{1 - \rho}(A_1 \kappa_1 \varphi_e) > 0,$$

$$\lambda_{m,w} \equiv \frac{\gamma - \rho}{1 - \rho}A_2 \kappa_1 > 0,$$

represent the market price of risk for each source of risk, η_{t+1}, e_{t+1}, and w_{t+1}, respectively. The last two terms are positive if the agent prefers early resolution of uncertainty (i.e., $\gamma > \rho$) and EIS is greater than 1 (or $\rho < 1$). Note that $\lambda_{m,e} = \lambda_{m,w} = 0$ for time-additive power utility. For this utility, long-run risk and consumption volatility do not affect pricing kernel innovations.

We can also compute

$$\text{Var}_t(m_{t+1}) = \left(\lambda_{m,\eta}^2 + \lambda_{m,e}^2\right)\sigma_t^2 + \lambda_{m,w}^2\sigma_w^2. \tag{20.52}$$

Risk Premium on Wealth Portfolio   By the Euler equation,

$$E_t\left[M_{t+1}\left(R_{w,t+1} - R_{f,t+1}\right)\right] = 0$$

so that

$$E_t\left(r_{w,t+1} - r_{f,t+1}\right)$$

$$= -\text{Cov}_t\left[m_{t+1} - E_t m_{t+1}, r_{w,t+1} - E_t r_{w,t+1}\right] - \frac{1}{2}\text{Var}_t(r_{w,t+1}).$$

Using (20.50) and (20.51), we derive

$$E_t\left(r_{w,t+1} - r_{f,t+1}\right)$$

$$= \lambda_{m,\eta}\sigma_t^2 + \lambda_{m,e}B\sigma_t^2 + \kappa_1 A_2 \lambda_{m,w}\sigma_w^2 - \frac{1}{2}\text{Var}_t(r_{w,t+1}). \tag{20.53}$$

Equity   Premium   and   Equity   Volatility   Using   the   Euler   equation $E_t\left[M_{t+1}\left(R_{e,t+1} - R_{f,t+1}\right)\right] = 0$ yields

$$E_t\left(r_{e,t+1} - r_{f,t+1}\right) + \frac{1}{2}\text{Var}_t(r_{e,t+1})$$

$$= -\text{Cov}_t\left[m_{t+1} - E_t m_{t+1}, r_{e,t+1} - E_t r_{e,t+1}\right]. \tag{20.54}$$

Conjecture that the price–dividend ratio is given by

$$z_{e,t} = A_{0e} + A_{1e}x_t + A_{2e}\sigma_t^2,$$

where A_{0e}, A_{1e}, and A_{2e} are constants to be determined. We then use the Campbell–Shiller approximation to compute

$$
\begin{aligned}
r_{e,t+1} &= \ln\left(\frac{P_{e,t+1} + D_{t+1}}{P_{e,t}}\right) = \ln\left(\frac{P_{e,t+1} + D_{t+1}}{D_{t+1}} \frac{D_{t+1}}{D_t} \frac{D_t}{P_{e,t}}\right) \\
&= \ln\left(1 + \frac{P_{e,t+1}}{D_{t+1}}\right) + g_{dt+1} - z_{e,t} \\
&= g_{dt+1} + \kappa_1 A_{1e} x_{t+1} - A_{1e} x_t \\
&\quad + \kappa_1 A_{2e}\sigma_{t+1}^2 - A_{2e}\sigma_t^2 + \text{constant.}
\end{aligned}
\tag{20.55}
$$

Thus

$$
\begin{aligned}
r_{e,t+1} - E_t r_{e,t+1} &= \varphi_d \sigma_t u_{t+1} + \kappa_1 A_{1e}\varphi_e \sigma_t e_{t+1} + \kappa_1 A_{2e}\sigma_w w_{t+1} \\
&\equiv \varphi_d \sigma_t u_{t+1} + \beta_{e,e}\sigma_t e_{t+1} + \beta_{e,w}\sigma_w w_{t+1},
\end{aligned}
$$

where

$$
\beta_{e,e} \equiv \kappa_1 A_{1e}\varphi_e > 0, \quad \beta_{e,w} \equiv \kappa_1 A_{2e}.
$$

Moreover

$$
\text{Var}_t\left(r_{e,t+1}\right) = \left(\varphi_d^2 + \beta_{e,e}^2\right)\sigma_t^2 + \beta_{e,w}^2 \sigma_w^2.
$$

We can now use (20.54) to derive the conditional expected equity premium:

$$
E_t\left(r_{e,t+1} - r_{f,t+1}\right) = \beta_{e,e}\lambda_{e,e}\sigma_t^2 + \beta_{e,w}\lambda_{e,w}\sigma_w^2 - \frac{1}{2}\text{Var}_t\left(r_{e,t+1}\right),
\tag{20.56}
$$

and unconditional expected equity premium. Two sources of systemic risk affect the equity premium. The first is related to fluctuations in expected consumption growth, x_t, and the second to fluctuations in consumption volatility.

We can compute A_{1e} and A_{2e} using the Euler equation (20.48):

$$
E_t\left[\exp\left(\frac{1-\gamma}{1-\rho}\ln\beta - \frac{(1-\gamma)\rho}{1-\rho}g_{t+1} + \frac{\rho-\gamma}{1-\rho}r_{w,t+1} + r_{e,t+1}\right)\right] = 1.
\tag{20.57}
$$

Substituting (20.46) and (20.55) into this equation and matching coefficients of x_t, we have

$$
-\rho + \kappa_{1e}A_{1e}\rho_x - A_{1e} + \phi = 0.
$$

Solving yields

$$
A_{1e} = \frac{\phi - \rho}{1 - \kappa_{1e}\rho_x}.
$$

Thus the price–dividend ratio is procyclical when EIS is greater than 1 (since $\phi > \rho$).

Matching coefficients of σ_t^2 yields

$$\frac{\rho - \gamma}{1 - \rho}A_2\left(\kappa_1 v_1 - 1\right) + A_{2e}\left(\kappa_{1e}v_1 - 1\right) + \frac{H_e}{2} = 0,$$

where

$$H_e = \lambda_{m,\eta}^2 + \left(-\lambda_{m,e} + \beta_{e,e}\right)^2 + \varphi_d^2.$$

Thus

$$A_{2e} = \frac{\frac{\gamma - \rho}{1 - \rho}A_2\left(1 - \kappa_1 v_1\right) + 0.5 H_e}{1 - \kappa_{1e}v_1}.$$

Now we compute the unconditional equity volatility:

$$r_{e,t+1} - Er_{e,t+1} = -\rho x_t + \beta_{e,e}\sigma_t e_{t+1} + \varphi_d \sigma_t u_{t+1}$$
$$+ A_{2e}\left(v_1 \kappa_1 - 1\right)\left[\sigma_t^2 - E\sigma_t^2\right] + \beta_{e,w}\sigma_w w_{t+1}.$$

The unconditional equity volatility and the price–dividend ratio volatility are given by

$$\mathrm{Var}\left(r_{e,t+1}\right) = \rho^2 \mathrm{Var}\left(x_t\right) + \left(\beta_{e,e}^2 + \varphi_d^2\right)\sigma^2$$
$$+ \left[A_{2e}\left(v_1 \kappa_1 - 1\right)\right]^2 \mathrm{Var}\left(\sigma_t^2\right) + \beta_{e,w}^2 \sigma_w^2,$$
$$\mathrm{Var}\left(z_{e,t}\right) = A_{1e}^2 \mathrm{Var}\left(x_t\right) + A_{2e}^2 \mathrm{Var}\left(\sigma_t^2\right).$$

Risk-Free Rate   Use the Euler equation $E_t\left[M_{t+1}R_{f,t+1}\right] = 1$ to derive

$$r_{f,t+1} = -\frac{(1 - \gamma)}{(1 - \rho)}\ln\beta + \frac{(1 - \gamma)\rho}{1 - \rho}E_t g_{t+1} + \frac{\rho - \gamma}{1 - \rho}E_t r_{w,t+1} - \frac{1}{2}\mathrm{Var}_t\left(m_{t+1}\right).$$

Subtract $\frac{\rho - \gamma}{1 - \rho}r_{f,t+1}$ from both sides to derive

$$r_{f,t+1} = -\ln\beta + \rho E_t g_{t+1} + \frac{\gamma - \rho}{1 - \gamma}E_t\left[r_{w,t+1} - r_{f,t+1}\right] - \frac{1 - \rho}{2\left(1 - \gamma\right)}\mathrm{Var}_t\left(m_{t+1}\right).$$

We can now compute the mean risk-free rate using the mean risk premium for consumption claims (20.53) and $\mathrm{Var}_t\left(m_{t+1}\right)$ in (20.52).

Finally, risk-free rate volatility is given by

$$\mathrm{Var}\left(r_{f,t+1}\right) = \rho^2 \mathrm{Var}\left(x_t\right) + \left\{\frac{\gamma - \rho}{1 - \gamma}Q_1 - \frac{Q_2\left(1 - \rho\right)}{2\left(1 - \gamma\right)}\right\}^2 \mathrm{Var}\left(\sigma_t^2\right),$$

where

$$Q_1 = -\lambda_{e,\eta} + \frac{\rho - \gamma}{1 - \rho}B^2 - \frac{1}{2}\left(1 + B^2\right),$$
$$Q_2 = \lambda_{e,\eta}^2 + \lambda_{e,e}^2.$$

Note that Q_1 determines the time-varying portion of the risk premium on the wealth portfolio. For reasonable calibration, the time variation of $r_{f,t+1}$ is largely determined by the first term.

20.5   Pareto Optimality

This section studies efficient allocation in a pure-exchange economy with finitely many agents who have recursive utility. There are n agents, and agent i has recursive utility satisfying

$$U_t^i(c) = W^i\left(c_t, \mathcal{R}_t\left(U_{t+1}^i(c)\right)\right),$$

where $\mathcal{R}$ is the uncertainty aggregator. Each agent i has an endowment process $\{e_t^i\}$. Let the aggregate endowment be $e = \sum_{i=1}^n e^i$. The feasible consumption set is given by

$$\mathcal{C}(e) = \left\{ (c^1, ..., c^n) \in \mathcal{C}^n : \sum_{i=1}^n c^i \le e \right\}.$$

The feasible utility set is given by

$$\mathcal{U}_0(e) = \left\{ \left(U_0^1(c^1), ..., U_0^n(c^n)\right) : c \in \mathcal{C}(e) \right\}.$$

Similarly we can define the feasibility set at time t as

$$\mathcal{U}_t(e) = \left\{ \left(U_t^1(c^1), ..., U_t^n(c^n)\right) : {}_t c \in \mathcal{C}({}_t e) \right\}.$$

Lemma 20.5.1 $\mathcal{U}_0(e)$ is convex, closed, and satisfies free disposal in the sense that $u \le u' \in \mathcal{U}_0(e) \Longrightarrow u \in \mathcal{U}_0(e)$.

Definition 20.5.1   A *Pareto optimal allocation* given e is a consumption process $c \in \mathcal{C}(e)$ such that there is no other feasible allocation $(\hat{c}^1, ..., \hat{c}^n) \in \mathcal{C}(e)$ such that $U_0^i(\hat{c}^i) \ge U_0^i(c^i)$ for all i and $U_0^j(\hat{c}^j) > U_0^j(c^j)$ for some j.

Our goal is to characterize a Pareto optimal allocation. The usual approach, following Negishi (1960), is to solve the problem:

$$\sup_{(c^1, ..., c^n) \in \mathcal{C}^n} \sum_{i=1}^n \theta^i U_0^i(c^i) \tag{20.58}$$

subject to

$$\sum_{i=1}^n c^i \le e, \tag{20.59}$$

where $\theta^i \in \mathbb{R}_+$ represents the Pareto weight satisfying $\sum_i \theta^i = 1$. Let $\Delta^n \equiv \{\theta \in \mathbb{R}_+^n : \sum_{i=1}^n \theta^i = 1\}$. Using this approach, one can easily characterize a Pareto optimal allocation for time-additive expected utility as shown in section 13.2. This approach, however, is not computationally efficient for recursive utility. We now introduce two other approaches.

20.5.1   Lucas–Stokey Approach

Lucas and Stokey (1984) propose a recursive formulation of the preceding problem in a deterministic growth model. We can apply their approach to the stochastic endowment economy.[3] Suppose that the aggregate endowment e follows a Markov process. Then a Pareto optimal allocation solves the following Bellman equation:

$$V(e_t, \theta_t) = \max_{c_t, v_{t+1}} \sum_{i=1}^n \theta_t^i W^i \left(c_t^i, \mathcal{R}_t \left(v_{t+1}^i \right) \right) \tag{20.60}$$

subject to (20.59) and for all e_{t+1},

$$\min_{\theta_{t+1} \in \Delta^n} V(e_{t+1}, \theta_{t+1}) - \sum_{i=1}^n \theta_{t+1}^i v_{t+1}^i \geq 0, \tag{20.61}$$

where we use the notation $c_t = \left(c_t^1, ..., c_t^n \right)$, and similar notations apply to θ_t and v_{t+1}. The idea of this dynamic programming problem is to view the problem of choosing an optimal allocation for given endowment e_t and vector of weights θ_t, as one of choosing a feasible current period allocation c_t of consumption, and a vector v_{t+1} of utilities-from-tomorrow-on, subject to the constraint that these utilities be attainable given the next period endowment e_{t+1}, i.e., that v_{t+1} satisfies (20.61). The weights θ_{t+1} that attain the minimum in (20.61) will then be the new weights used in selecting tomorrow's allocation, and so on, ad infinitum.

To see the intuition of the above Bellman equation, let $\hat{V}(e_0, \theta)$ be the value function of problem (20.58). The following lemma is key.

Lemma 20.5.2 $v \in \mathcal{U}_0(e)$ *if and only if*

$$\min_{\theta \in \Delta^n} \hat{V}(e_0, \theta) - \sum_{i=1}^n \theta^i v^i \geq 0. \tag{20.62}$$

Proof   The "only if" part follows from the definition in (20.58). We prove the "if" part.

Suppose, for the converse, that (20.62) holds, but $v \notin \mathcal{U}_0(e)$. Since $\mathcal{U}_0(e)$ is convex, it follows from the separation theorem for convex sets that for some $w \in \mathbb{R}^n$,

---

3. See Anderson (2005) for an application.

$w \neq 0, w \cdot v \geq w \cdot z$ for all $z \in \mathcal{U}_0(e)$. Since $\mathcal{U}_0(e)$ exhibits free disposal, it follows that $w \geq 0$, and we may choose $w \in \Delta^n$. Since $\mathcal{U}_0(e)$ is closed, the inequality is strict: $w \cdot u > w \cdot z$. Now since $\hat{V}(e_0, \theta) \geq \sum_{i=1}^{n} \theta^i v^i$ for all $\theta \in \Delta^n$, $\hat{V}(e_0, w) \geq w \cdot v > w \cdot z$ for all $z \in \mathcal{U}_0(e)$, contradicting the fact that

$$\hat{V}(e_0, w) = \max_{z \in \mathcal{U}_0(e)} w \cdot z.$$

This completes the proof.   ∎

Now we can show the following:

Proposition 20.5.1 $\hat{V}(e_0, \theta)$ *satisfies the Bellman equation (20.60).*

Proof By definition, we have

$$\hat{V}(e_0, \theta) = \max_{c \in \mathcal{C}(e)^n} \sum_{i=1}^{n} \theta^i U_0^i(c)$$

$$= \max_{c \in \mathcal{C}(e)^n} W^i\left(c_0^i, \mathcal{R}_0\left(U_1^i\left(c^i\right)\right)\right)$$

$$= \max_{c_0, v_1 \in \mathcal{U}_1(e)} W^i\left(c_0^i, \mathcal{R}_0\left(v_1^i\right)\right)$$

$$= \max_{c_0, v_1} W^i\left(c_0^i, \mathcal{R}_0\left(v_1^i\right)\right)$$

subject to $\sum_{i=1}^{n} c_0^i \leq e_0$ and

$$\min_{\theta_1 \in \Delta^n} \hat{V}(e_1, \theta_1) - \sum_{i=1}^{n} \theta_1^i v_1^i \geq 0,$$

where the third equality follows from the fact that if an allocation is Pareto optimal at date zero, then the continuation allocation is also Pareto optimal in the economy from any date $t > 0$ on, and the last equality follows from lemma 20.5.2.   ∎

The converse is also true. Let $G(e_t, \theta_t)$ be the optimal policy correspondence derived from the dynamic programming problem (20.60). Given any aggregate endowment e_t and a vector of Pareto weights θ_t, the maximization problem gives a solution for (c_t, v_{t+1}), and the minimization problem gives a solution for θ_{t+1} for each possible realization of e_{t+1} at date $t+1$. Denote the solution for (c_t, v_{t+1}) as a correspondence $G^1(e_t, \theta_t)$ and the solution for θ_{t+1} as a correspondence $G^1(e_t, \theta_t, e_{t+1})$. This correspondence generates a Pareto optimal allocation (c_t) and a process of Pareto weights (θ_t) as follows:

$$(c_t, v_{t+1}) \in G^1(e_t, \theta_t), \quad t = 0, 1, 2, ..., \tag{20.63}$$

$$\theta_{t+1} \in G^2(e_t, \theta_t, e_{t+1}), \quad t = 0, 1, 2, ... \tag{20.64}$$

Proposition 20.5.2 *Any allocation generated from the dynamic programming problem (20.60) is Pareto optimal.*

Proof   Let (20.63) and (20.64) hold. Suppose that (c_t) does not attain $\hat{V}(e_0, \theta_0)$. Then some other allocation $(\tilde{c}_t)$ does. Let $\tilde{v}_{t+1}$ be the utility path associated with (c'_t). Then

$$\hat{V}(e_0, \theta_0) = \sum_i \theta_0^i W^i(\tilde{c}_0, \mathcal{R}_0(\tilde{v}_1)) > \sum_i \theta_0^i W^i(c_0, \mathcal{R}_0(v_1)). \tag{20.65}$$

Since $(\tilde{c}_t)$ is feasible and $\tilde{v}_1 \in \mathcal{U}_1(e)$, lemma 20.5.2 implies that $\hat{V}(e_1, \theta_1) \geq \sum_{i=1}^n \theta_1^i \tilde{v}_1^i$ for all $\theta_1 \in \Delta^n$. But this implies that (20.65) contradicts (20.58) since $\hat{V}$.   ∎

The dynamic programming problem in (20.60) is useful for numerical computation. Below is an algorithm:

Step 1. Start with a guess of the value function $V^0(e, \theta)$ that is continuous and convex in θ.

Step 2. Solve the problem

$$V^1(e_t, \theta_t) = \max_{c_t, v_{t+1}} \sum_{i=1}^n \theta_t^i W^i\left(c_t^i, \mathcal{R}_t\left(v_{t+1}^i\right)\right)$$

subject to (20.59) and for all e_{t+1},

$$\min_{\theta_{t+1} \in \Delta^n} V^0(e_{t+1}, \theta_{t+1}) - \sum_{i=1}^n \theta_{t+1}^i v_{t+1}^i \geq 0.$$

Step 3. If V^1 is sufficiently close to V^0, then stop. Otherwise, update V^0 by V^1 and keep iterating until convergence.

20.5.2   Dumas–Wang–Uppal Approach

Dumas, Wang, and Uppal (2000) propose a different approach to solving a Pareto optimal allocation. Their approach builds on the idea of Geoffard (1996) that a recursive utility can be expressed as a variational utility by duality. To explain this idea, consider the Kreps and Porteus utility

$$U_t(c) = W(c_t, E_t U_{t+1}(c)).$$

Define a function by

$$F(c, \nu) = \max_u \; W(c, u) - (1 - \nu)u.$$

By duality,

$$W(c, u) = \min_\nu \; F(c, \nu) + (1 - \nu)u.$$

We can then rewrite the utility function as

$$U_t(c) = \min_{\nu_t} F(c_t, \nu_t) + (1 - \nu_t) E_t U_{t+1}(c).$$

This utility is called variational utility by Geoffard (1996). It looks like similar to the time-additive utility, allowing for a simple recursive formulation of the Pareto optimality problem:

$$J(e_t, \lambda_t) = \max_{(c_t^i)} \min_{(\nu_t^i)} \lambda_t^i F^i(c_t^i, \nu_t^i) + E_t J(e_{t+1}, \lambda_{t+1})$$

subject to (20.59) and

$$\lambda_{t+1}^i = (1 - \nu_t^i) \lambda_t^i, \quad i = 1, 2, ..., n.$$

This problem seems easier to solve than (20.60) since the value function does not enter the constraint (20.61).

20.6   Exercises

1. Consider the Epstein–Zin utility defined in (20.3) with a finite horizon. Let $U_T(c) = c_T$. Prove that U_t is strictly concave for $t = 0, 1, ..., T - 1$ if $\rho > 0$ and $\gamma > 0$.

2. Derive the pricing kernels for the Epstein–Zin utility, divergence utility, and generalized smooth ambiguity utility.

3. Prove that an agent with Epstein–Zin utility (20.3) prefers earlier resolution of uncertainty if and only if $\gamma > \rho$.

4. Use the parameter values in Bansal and Yaron (2004) to write Matlab codes to replicate the results in their paper as much as you can.

5. (Weil 1993) Suppose that an agent has the utility function given by (20.4). This agent solves a consumption–saving problem with the budget constraint

$$a_{t+1} = R(a_t - c_t) + y_{t+1},$$

where $R > 1$ and a_t and y_t represent cash on hand and labor income, respectively. Let $\{y_t\}$ follow the process

$$y_t = \rho_y y_{t-1} + (1 - \rho_y) \bar{y} + \sigma_y \varepsilon_t,$$

where ε_t is IID standard normal. Derive the optimal consumption and saving rules. Analyze the effects of EIS and risk aversion on these rules.

6. Formulate the Pareto optimality problem in a production economy. Specifically, suppose that the resource constraint is given by

$$\sum_{i=1}^{n} c_t^i + k_{t+1} = z_t F(k_t),$$

where k_t is the capital stock in period t, F is a production function, and $\{z_t\}$ follows a Markov process. Assuming some sufficient smoothness properties, derive the first-order conditions for the Pareto optimal allocation. You could consider the Epstein–Zin utility first.

7. Consider the Pareto optimality problem in the pure-exchange economy. Let the aggregate endowment follow the process

$$\ln e_t = \rho_e \ln e_{t-1} + \sigma_e \varepsilon_t,$$

where ε_t is IID standard normal. Let the two agents utility be given by

$$U_t^i(c^i) = u^i(c_t^i) - \beta \theta^i \ln E_t \exp\left(\frac{-U_{t+1}^i(c^i)}{\theta^i}\right), \quad \theta^i > 0.$$

a. Derive the first-order conditions for a Pareto optimal allocation.

b. Suppose that $u^1(c) = u^2(c) = \ln c$. Pick some parameter values, say $\beta = 0.95$, $\theta^1 = 0.01$, $\theta^2 = 0.1$ or ∞, $\rho_e = 0.9$, $\sigma_e = 0.1$. Write Matlab codes to solve the Pareto optimal allocation.

21 Dynamic Games

Dynamic game theory is used to study strategic interactions among players in a dynamic environment. It has been applied in many fields of economics such as industrial organization, public finance, international economics, development economics, and macroeconomics. A game involves at least two players. A player can be any decision maker, such as a government, a political party, a firm, a regulatory agency, or a household. A **dynamic game** extends over a finite or infinite horizon and typically displays the following properties:

- The players can receive payoffs in every period.
- The payoff that a player receives in a period may depend on both the actions taken in that period and the state of the system in that period, as represented by one or several state variables.
- The overall payoff for a player is the sum of its discounted payoffs over the time horizon, possibly plus some terminal payoff.
- The state of the system changes over time, and its evolution can be represented by a state transition equation, which depends on the players' actions.

When there is no state variable involved and a static game is repeatedly played, we call this dynamic game a **repeated game.**

Three basic solution concepts are used in game theory. The first is the **Nash equilibrium**, in which each player solves his optimization problem taking the other players' strategies as given. This is analogous to the competitive equilibrium in a market economy. The second is the **Stackelberg equilibrium**, in which one player is the dominant player (or a leader) and the other players are followers. The leader plays first. Given his strategy, the followers optimize. The leader will take the followers' reactions into account in choosing his strategy. The final solution concept is the **cooperative solution**, in which a planner maximizes the weighted average of all players' payoffs.

In a dynamic setup these three solutions may not be time consistent or robust to deviations. Kydland and Prescott (1977) open the modern literature on time consistency in government policy and have profound impact on the applications of game theory to policy analysis. An important solution concept for studying time consistency is subgame perfect (Nash) equilibrium, which is a refinement of Nash equilibrium. A **subgame perfect equilibrium** (SPE) is a profile of strategies that induces a Nash equilibrium on every subgame. One special type of subgame perfect equilibrium in dynamic games is a **Markov perfect equilibrium** (MPE). This is a subgame perfect Nash equilibrium in which players condition their own strategies only on the payoff-relevant states in each period. Thus a Markov perfect equilibrium is derived as the solution to a set of dynamic programming problems that each individual player solves. Equilibrium strategies are generated by each player's policy function. The concept of Markov perfect equilibrium was first introduced by Maskin and Tirole (1987, 1988).

In this chapter we will apply the method introduced by Abreu, Pearce, and Stacchetti (henceforth, APS) (1986, 1990) to analyze dynamic games.[1] The idea of this method is to study recursive equations for sets instead of functions and represent the equilibrium payoff set as a fixed point of a set-valued operator. We will use models like those of Chari, Kehoe, and Prescott (1989) and Stokey (1989, 1991) to study what Chari and Kehoe (1990) call sustainable government policies and what Stokey calls credible public policies. We will adapt ideas developed for dynamic games to the contexts in which a single agent (a government) behaves strategically and in which the remaining agents' behavior can be summarized as a competitive equilibrium that responds nonstrategically to the government's choices. Useful references for the material in this chapter are Fudenberg and Tirole (1991), Ljungqvist and Sargent (2004, ch. 22), and Mailath and Samuelson (2006).

21.1   Repeated Games

We first study the case with perfect monitoring and introduce the key idea of the APS method. We then study the case with imperfect monitoring.

21.1.1   Perfect Monitoring
The construction of the repeated game begins with a stage game. A stage game is a standard strategic (normal) form game $G = \{N, A, u\}$, where $N = \{1, 2, ..., n\}$ is the set of players, $A = \times_{i=1}^{n} A_i$ is the product of all players' action sets A_i, and $u = (u_1, u_2, ..., u_n)$ with each $u_i : A \to \mathbb{R}$ being player i's payoff function.

---

1. Feng et al. (2012) apply the APS method to solve for competitive equilibria for nonoptimal economies.

Assumption 21.1.1 A_i *is finite or compact, and* u_i *is bounded and continuous for all* i.

The feasible payoff set $\mathcal{W}$ is the convex hull of the set $\{u(a) \in \mathbb{R}^n : a \in A\}$. Players play the stage game repeatedly over time. Time is discrete and denoted by $t = 1, 2, \ldots$. At the end of each period all players observe the action profile chosen. In other words, the actions of every player are perfectly monitored by all other players.

A history $h^t \in H^t$ is a list of past actions $\{a_1, a_2, \ldots, a_{t-1}\}$. The set of period t histories is given by $H^t = A^{t-1}$ where we define the initial history to be the null $H^1 = \varnothing$. Player i's (pure) strategy σ_i is a sequence of mappings $\{\sigma_{it}\}_{t=1}^{\infty}$ defined as follows:

$$\sigma_{i1}(\varnothing) = \sigma_{i1} \in A_i, \quad \sigma_{it} : A^{t-1} \rightarrow A_i, \quad t \geq 2, \, i \in N.$$

Let Σ_i be the set of player i's strategies. Take any strategy profile $\sigma = (\sigma_1, \ldots, \sigma_n)$, which generates a sequence of action profiles (or a path) $\{a_t(\sigma)\}_{t=1}^{\infty}$ with $a_t(\sigma) = (a_{1t}(\sigma), \ldots, a_{nt}(\sigma))$ as follows:

$$a_{i1}(\sigma) = \sigma_{i1}, \quad a_{it}(\sigma) = \sigma_{it}(h^t), \quad t \geq 2, \, i \in N,$$
$$h^t = \{a_1(\sigma), a_2(\sigma), \ldots, a_{t-1}(\sigma)\}.$$

Then player i's expected discounted average payoff from the strategy profile σ is given by

$$U_i(\sigma) = (1 - \delta) \sum_{t=1}^{\infty} \delta^{t-1} u_i(a_t(\sigma)),$$

where δ is a common discount factor. Let $U = (U_1, \ldots, U_n)$.

We focus on subgame perfect equilibria for repeated games with perfect monitoring. For each history h^t, let $\sigma|_{h^t} = \{\sigma|_{h^t}(\tau)\}_{\tau=0}^{\infty}$ be a profile of continuation strategies for the subgame following h^t defined as

$$\sigma|_{h^t}(\tau)(h^\tau) = \sigma_{t+\tau}(h^{t+\tau}),$$

where $h^{t+\tau} = (h^t, h^\tau)$, $\tau = 0, 1, \ldots$, $h^0 = \varnothing$. The payoff for the subgame is

$$U_i(\sigma|_{h^t}) = (1 - \delta) \sum_{s=t}^{\infty} \delta^{s-t} u_i(a_s(\sigma)),$$

where $\{a_t(\sigma), a_{t+1}(\sigma), \ldots, \}$ is a sequence of action profiles generated by $\sigma|_{h^t}$.

Definition 21.1.1 *The strategy σ^* is a **subgame perfect equilibrium** (SPE) if, for any history $h^t \in H$, $\sigma|_{h^t}$ is a Nash equilibrium of the subgame starting at h^t; that is*

$$U_i\left(\sigma^*|_{h^t}\right) \geq U_i\left(\left(\sigma_i, \sigma^*_{-i}\right)|_{h^t}\right)$$

for all $\sigma_i \in \Sigma_i$ and all i.

Note that the set of continuation strategies is identical to the original strategy set. Indeed every subgame is completely identical to the original game. We exploit this recursive nature of repeated games to characterize the whole set of equilibrium payoffs later.

The preceding definition is not so useful because there are uncountable number of inequalities, making the check of equilibrium difficult. We next show that one only needs to check a particular type of deviation.

Definition 21.1.2 *The strategy σ'_i is a **one-shot deviation** from σ_i if $\sigma'_{it}\left(\bar{h}^t\right) \neq \sigma_{it}\left(\bar{h}^t\right)$ for some $\bar{h}^t \in H_i$ and $\sigma'_{is}\left(h^s\right) = \sigma_{is}\left(h^s\right)$ for all $h^s \in H_i \backslash \left\{\bar{h}^t\right\}$. Denote this one-shot deviation by $\sigma_i^{\bar{h}^t}$. We say $\sigma_i^{\bar{h}^t}$ is a profitable one-shot deviation for player i if*

$$U_i\left(\sigma_i^{\bar{h}^t}|_{\bar{h}^t}, \sigma_{-i}|_{\bar{h}^t}\right) > U_i\left(\sigma|_{\bar{h}^t}\right).$$

Proposition 21.1.1 *(One-shot deviation principle) σ is a subgame-perfect equilibrium if and only if there is no profitable one-shot deviation from a strategy profile σ.*

Proof (Sketch) The "only if" part follows from the definition of SPE. So we just need to prove the "if" part. First, if there is no profitable one-shot deviation, then there is no profitable finite-period deviation. This follows from a simple induction argument. Second, if there is profitable deviation that is different from σ^i for infinite number of periods, then a finite truncation of such deviation must be still profitable if one takes the finite horizon large enough. This is a contradiction, so there should be no profitable infinite-periods deviation either.   ∎

21.1.2 Equilibrium Payoff Set

Note that for a repeated game, any subgame is identical to the original game. Hence any continuation strategy profile of an SPE is an equilibrium profile of the original game. Let V denote the set of SPE payoffs of a repeated game. Then, for any SPE σ^*, $U\left(\sigma^*|_{h^t}\right) \in V$ holds for any history h^t. This fact motivates us to define the following one-shot game. Fix an SPE σ^* and let w be a function from A to $W \subset \mathbb{R}^n$ defined by $w(a) = U\left(\sigma^*|_a\right)$ and $u_w(a) = (1-\delta) u(a) + \delta w(a)$. This defines a strategic form game $\{N, A, u_w\}$. Let a_1^* be the equilibrium action profile in the first period of σ^*. Then clearly a_1^* should also be a Nash equilibrium of $\{N, A, u_w\}$.

Now we explore this observation more formally.

Definition 21.1.3 *For any $W \subset \mathbb{R}^n$, a pair $(a, w(\cdot))$ is admissible with respect to $W \subset \mathbb{R}^n$ if (i) w is a function $w\colon A \to W$, and (ii) a is a Nash equilibrium of the strategic form game $\{N, A, u_w\}$; that is,*

$$(1 - \delta) u_i(a) + \delta w_i(a) \geq (1 - \delta) u_i(a_i', a_{-i}) + \delta w_i(a_i', a_{-i})$$

for all $a_i' \in A_i$ and all i.

Definition 21.1.4 *For any $W \subset \mathbb{R}^n$, $B(W)$ is the set of all $v \in \mathbb{R}^n$ such that there exists a pair $(a, w(\cdot))$ admissible with respect to $W \subset \mathbb{R}^n$ and*

$$v = (1 - \delta) u(a) + \delta w(a).$$

Our observation can be stated more formally using these definitions.

Lemma 21.1.1 $V \subset B(V)$.

We want to show that the opposite inclusion is also true. Say that W is **self-generating** if $W \subset B(W)$.

Lemma 21.1.2 (Self-generation) *If $W \subset \mathbb{R}^n$ is bounded and $W \subset B(W)$, then $B(W) \subset V$.*

Proof   Take any point $v \in B(W)$. By definition, there is an admissible pair $a_1 \in A$ and $w_1 : A \to W$ such that

$$v = (1 - \delta) u(a_1) + \delta w_1(a_1) \quad \text{for } t = 1.$$

Since $W \subset B(W)$, for every $w_1(a_1)$, $a_1 \in A$, there exists an admissible pair $(a_2(a_1), w_2(\cdot|a_1))$ such that

$$w_1(a_1) = (1 - \delta) u(a_2(a_1)) + \delta w_2(a_2(a_1)|a_1) \quad \text{for } t = 2.$$

Continuing in this way, we can find an admissible pair $(a_t(h^t), w_t(\cdot|h^t))$ such that

$$w_{t-1}(h^t) = (1 - \delta) u(a_t(h^t)) + \delta w_t(a_t(h^t)|h^t)$$

for each history $h^t = (h^{t-1}, a_{t-1}) = (a_1, a_2, ..., a_{t-1})$.

Define a strategy profile σ by $\sigma_t(h^t) = a_t(h^t)$ for all h^t. Then $v = U(\sigma)$ and $w_{t-1}(h^t) = U(\sigma(h^t))$ for all h^t because W is bounded. There is no profitable one-shot deviation from σ by construction. Hence σ is a subgame perfect equilibrium by the one-shot deviation principle. ∎

Example 21.1.1 *Consider the prisoner's dilemma game with perfect monitoring. The payoff matrix is given by*

	C	D
C	1, 1	−1, 2
D	2, −1	0, 0

Claim that if $\delta \geq 0.5$, then $W = \{(1,1),(0,0)\}$ is self-generating, and hence $W \subset V$. To prove this, consider $(0,0)$ first. It is easy to see that the strategy profile (D,D) and payoff profile $(0,0)$ are enforced by any δ and the function $w(y) = (0,0)$ for all y, since

$$0 = (1 - \delta) u_i (D,D) + \delta w_i (D,D),$$

and for all $a_i \in \{C,D\}$,

$$0 \geq (1 - \delta) u_i (a_i, D) + \delta w_i (a_i, D).$$

Turn to $(1,1)$. We show that the strategy profile (C,C) and payoff profile $(1,1)$ are enforced by $\delta \geq 1/2$ and W. Let $w(C,C) = (1,1)$ and $w(y) = (0,0)$ for all $y \neq (C,C)$. Then

$$1 = (1 - \delta) u_i (C,C) + \delta w_i (C,C),$$

and for all $a_i \in \{C,D\}$,

$$1 \geq (1 - \delta) u_i (a_i, C) + \delta w_i (a_i, C).$$

So $W \subset B(W)$ for $\delta \geq 0.5$, meaning that W is self-generating.

From the preceding two lemmas, we obtain the following theorem.

Theorem 21.1.1 (Factorization) $V = B(V)$.

Theorem 21.1.1 means that V is a fixed point of the set-valued operator B. By this theorem and lemma 21.1.2, any SPE payoff can be supported by a recursive strategy in the sense that there exist functions g and $\mathcal{V}$ such that

$$a_t = g(v_t) \quad \text{and} \quad v_{t+1} = \mathcal{V}(v_t, a_t), \quad v_1 \in V,$$

where v_t is a state variable used to summarize the history of outcomes before t.

Theorem 21.1.2 *V is the maximal fixed point in the feasible payoff set.*

Proof All the subsets of the feasible payoff set form a lattice with respect to $\cap$ and $\cup$ and a partial order induced by inclusion. Since B is a monotone operator on this lattice as claimed below, Tarski's fixed-point theorem (appendix C) implies that there exists a maximal fixed point and a minimal fixed point, and that all fixed points form a complete lattice. The maximal fixed point is given by $\cup_{\{W\subset V:W\subset B(W)\}}W$ (union of all self-generating sets). Since $V\subset\cup_{\{W\subset V:W\subset B(W)\}}W$ by theorem 21.1.1 and $\cup_{\{W\subset V:W\subset B(W)\}}W\subset V$ by lemma 21.1.2, V is the maximal fixed point of B.   ∎

Proposition 21.1.2   *V is compact.*

Proof   Assume that A is finite. The proof for compact A is left as an exercise. Since V is bounded, we just need to show that it is closed. We sketch two proofs. First proof: Pick $v_k\in V$ and v^* such that $\lim_{k\to\infty}v_k=v^*$. Let $\sigma_k\in\Sigma$ be a subgame perfect equilibrium to support v_k. Then we can find a subsequence of $\{\sigma_{k_n}\}$ that converges to some $\sigma^*\in\Sigma$ at every history. In the limit, σ^* achieves v^* and every one-shot deviation constraint is satisfied for σ^*. Thus σ^* is a subgame perfect equilibrium by one-shot deviation principle, hence $v^*\in V$.

Second Proof   We show that $\bar{V}\subset B\left(\bar{V}\right)$, which implies that $\bar{V}\subset V$ by lemma 21.1.2. Again, pick $v_k\in V$ and v^* such that $\lim_{k\to\infty}v_k=v^*$. Let (a_k,w_k) be an admissible pair with respect to V to achieve v_k. Since A is a finite set and $\bar{V}$ is compact, $\{(a_k,w_k)\}$ has a subsequence that converges to (a^*,w^*), which is admissible with respect to $\bar{V}$ and achieves v^*. Therefore $v^*\in B\left(\bar{V}\right)$.   ∎

21.1.3   Computation
Here we assume that A is finite. We need two useful lemmas about operator B.

Lemma 21.1.3   (Monotonicity) *If $W\subset W'$, then $B\left(W\right)\subset B\left(W'\right)$.*

Lemma 21.1.4   (Compactness) *$B\left(W\right)$ is compact if W is compact.*

The proofs of these lemmas are left as an exercise. They can be used to derive a useful algorithm to obtain the fixed point V.

Theorem 21.1.3   *Let $W_0\supset V$ be compact and $B\left(W_0\right)\subset W_0$. Then $V=\lim_{t\to\infty}B^t\left(W_0\right)$.*

Proof   By assumption, $V\subset W_0$. Applying B to both sides, we obtain $V\subset B\left(W_0\right)\equiv W_1\subset W_0$ by lemma 21.1.3 and theorem 21.1.1. Then, by induction, $W_t=B^t\left(W_0\right)$, $t=1,2,...$, satisfies

$$V\subset...\subset W_t\subset...\subset W_2\subset W_1\subset W_0.$$

Since all W_t are compact sets by lemma 21.1.4, $\cap_t W_t=\lim_t W_t$ is compact and nonempty because V is nonempty. On the one hand, $V\subset\cap_t W_t$. On the other hand, for any $v\in\cap_t W_t$, there exist admissible pairs (a_t,w_t), $t=1,2,...$ such that $w_t:A\to W_t$ and $v=(1-\delta)u\left(a_t\right)+\delta w_t\left(a_t\right)$. Since each W_t is compact, we can take a converging subsequence of $(a_t, w_t) \to (a^*, w^*)$ such that (a^*, w^*) is admissible with respect to each W_t, and hence also admissible with respect $\cap_t W_t$, and $v = (1 - \delta) u (a^*) + \delta w^* (a^*)$. Thus we obtain $\cap_t W_t \subset B (\cap_t W_t)$, which implies that $\cap_t W_t \subset V$ by lemma 21.1.2.   ∎

Since V is an nonempty intersection of compact sets, compactness of V follows from this theorem, too. This theorem still does not offer an explicit method to compute V. Cronshaw and Luenberger (1994) adapt the APS method to the repeated games with perfect monitoring. Judd, Yeltekin, and Conklin (2003) propose an algorithm by introducing public randomization based on APS and Cronshaw and Luenberger (1994).

Define the maximal payoff set as

$$\mathcal{W} = \times_{i=1}^{n} [u_{i \min}, u_{i \max}],$$

where

$$u_{i \min} = \min_{a \in A} u_i (a), \quad u_{i \max} = \max_{a \in A} u_i (a).$$

Define the operator B as

$$B (W) = \cup_{(a,w) \in A \times W} \{(1 - \delta) u (a) + \delta w : IC_i \text{ for all } i\},$$

where $W \in \mathbb{R}^n$ is a compact set and IC_i is the incentive constraint for player i :

$$(1 - \delta) u_i (a) + \delta w_i \geq (1 - \delta) \max_{a_i' \in A_i} u_i (a_i', a_{-i}) + \delta \underline{w}_i$$

and

$$\underline{w}_i = \inf_{w \in W} w_i.$$

Cronshaw and Luenberger (1990) show that V is the largest fixed point of B in the set $\mathcal{W}$ (see theorem 21.1.2).

Let the convex hull of W be denoted by $co (W)$. Judd, Yeltekin, and Conklin (2003) define an operator B^* as

$$B^* (co (W)) = co (B (co (W))).$$

Then B^* is monotone and preserves compactness. They compute the equilibrium value set V^* of the supergame with public randomization by inner and outer approximations using the operator B^*.

21.1.4   Simple Strategies

The set V of pure strategy subgame perfect equilibria can be very complex. Abreu (1988) shows that every pure strategy SPE path is the outcome of some **simple strategy profile**. A simple strategy profile is defined by $n + 1$ paths $(Q^0, Q^1, ..., Q^n)$ as follows:

Definition 21.1.5   *The simple strategy* $\sigma(Q^0, Q^1, ..., Q^n)$ *specifies: (a) Play Q^0 until a player deviates unilaterally from Q^0. (b) If player j deviates unilaterally from Q^i, $i = 0, 1, ..., n$, in which Q^i is an ongoing previously specified path, play Q^j, but continue with Q^i if no player deviates or if there are simultaneous deviations by more than one player.*

Let $Q^i = \{a^i_t\}^{\infty}_{t=1}$. Define

$$U_j(Q^i; t+1) = (1 - \delta) \sum_{s=1}^{\infty} \delta^{s-1} u_j(a^i(t+s))$$

for any $i = 0, 1, ..., n$ and $j = 1, 2, ..., n$. The following proposition offers a simple way to check whether a simple strategy profile is subgame perfect. Its proof follows from the one-shot deviation principle.

Proposition 21.1.3   *The simple strategy profile* $\sigma(Q^0, Q^1, ..., Q^n)$ *is an SPE if and only if*

$$(1 - \delta) u_j(a^i) + \delta U_j(Q^i; t+1) \geq (1 - \delta) u_j(a'_j, a^i_{-j}) + \delta U_j(Q^j; t+1)$$

for all $a'_j \in A_j$, $j \in N$, $i = 0, 1, ..., n$ and $t = 1, 2, ...$

We now construct a simple strategy profile to support all subgame perfect equilibria for a repeated game. Since the equilibrium payoff set V is compact, for each player i there exists an SPE payoff $\underline{w}_i$ which minimizes player i's payoff among V. Let Q^i be the equilibrium path to generate $\underline{w}_i$. Take any equilibrium strategy σ^*, and let Q^0 be the equilibrium path of the equilibrium σ^*. Now the simple strategy $\sigma(Q^0, Q^1, ..., Q^n)$ generates the same payoff as σ^* and is still a subgame perfect equilibrium by the proposition above because all the punishments in σ^* are replaced by the harshest punishments $\underline{w}_i$, $i = 1, 2, ..., n$. This means that every equilibrium payoff can be supported by simple strategies, so we can restrict our attention to $\underline{w}_i$, $i = 1, ..., n$ as punishment without loss of generality.

21.1.5   Imperfect Public Monitoring

In games with perfect monitoring, deviations from the equilibrium path of play can be detected and punished. In this subsection we study games with imperfect monitoring: games in which players have only noisy information about past play. In this case deviations cannot be unambiguously detected. We will focus on the case where the noisy information is observed by all players. This case is referred to as imperfect public monitoring. The commonly observed signals allow players to coordinate their actions in a way that is not possible if the signals observed by some players are not observed by others. The latter case, referred to as private monitoring, will not be treated in this book.

Consider the repeated game introduced in subsection 21.1.1. Instead of observing past actions, at the end of the stage game, players observe a public signal y, independently and identically drawn from a signal space Y. The signal space Y is finite. The probability that the signal y is realized, given the action profile $a \in A$, is denoted by $f(y|a)$. The function $f : Y \times A \to [0,1]$ is continuous (so that ex ante payoffs are continuous functions of actions). Assume that Y is the support of f for all $a \in A$ (full-support assumption).

The players receive no information about opponents' play beyond the signal y. If players receive payoffs at the end of each period, player i's payoff after the realization (y, a) is given by

$$u_i(a) = \sum_{y \in Y} f(y|a) \, r_i(a_i, y)$$

for some function r_i.

Player i's history consists of her own actions and a realization of the public signal in the past. Call a sequence of her own past actions player i's private history and denote it by $h_i^{t\prime} = (a_{i1}, a_{i2}, \dots a_{it-1}) \in A_i^{t-1}$, $t \geq 2$, and $h_i^{1\prime} = \varnothing$. A sequence of the realization of the public signal is called public history and denoted simply by $h^t = (y_1, y_2, \dots, y_{t-1}) \in Y^{t-1}$, $t \geq 2$, and $h^1 = \varnothing$. Hence player i's t period history is $h_i^t = (h^t, h_i^{t\prime})$. Let $H_i = \cup_{t=1}^{\infty} (Y \times A_i)^{t-1}$, with $(Y \times A_i)^0 = \varnothing$. Player i's (pure) strategy σ_i is a mapping from H_i to A_i. A strategy is called a **public strategy** if it only depends on a public history h^t. Using the stage payoff above, we can then define the expected discounted average payoff from a strategy σ.

Let σ^* be a profile of public strategies. We define a class of perfect Bayesian equilibrium based on public strategies.

Definition 21.1.6 *The strategy σ^* is a **perfect public equilibrium** (PPE) if, for any public history $h^t \in Y^{t-1}$, $\sigma^*|_{h^t}$ forms a Nash equilibrium from that period on, that is,*

$$U_i(\sigma^*|_{h^t}) \geq U_i(\sigma_i, \sigma_{-i}^*|_{h^t}), \quad \text{all } \sigma_i \text{ and } i.$$

Although public strategy and PPE are somewhat restrictive, they can support many payoffs. First, it is known that for any pure-strategy sequential equilibrium (hence any pure-strategy Nash equilibrium), there exists a PPE that generates the same equilibrium outcome (distribution). So it is without loss of generality to restrict attention to public strategies and PPE if we are only interested in pure-strategy equilibria. Second, we can prove the Folk Theorem in PPE; under a certain assumption on information structure ($f(y|a)$), any feasible and individually rational (interior) payoff can be supported in PPE as long as players are patient enough.

In repeated games with imperfect public monitoring, we can still find a recursive structure similar to what we find in repeated games with perfect monitoring. Since players use public strategies, the continuation strategy after any realization of public signal is still a PPE of the original game.

As in the case of perfect monitoring, we introduce two definitions:

Definition 21.1.7   *For any $W \subset \mathbb{R}^n$, a pair $(a, w(\cdot))$ is admissible with respect to W if $w(y) \in W$ for all $y \in Y$ and*

$$(1 - \delta) u_i(a) + \delta \sum_y f(y|a) w_i(y) \geq (1 - \delta) u_i(a_i', a_{-i}) + \delta \sum_y f(y|a_i', a_{-i}) w_i(y)$$

for all $a_i' \in A_i$ and all i.

Definition 21.1.8   *For any $W \subset \mathbb{R}^n$, $B(W)$ is the set of all $v \in \mathbb{R}^n$ such that there exists a pair $(a, w(\cdot))$ admissible with respect to $W \subset \mathbb{R}^n$ and*

$$v = (1 - \delta) u(a) + \delta \sum_y f(y|a) w(y).$$

One can show that almost all the results for the case of perfect monitoring carry over to the case of imperfect public monitoring. But different assumptions may be needed.

Example 21.1.2   (Noisy prisoner's dilemma.) *Suppose that the observed outcomes are in $Y = \{G, B\}$ (good and bad) where*

$$f(G|a) = \Pr(G|a) = \begin{cases} p & \text{if } a = (C, C), \\ q & \text{if } a = (C, D) \text{ or } (D, C), \\ r & \text{if } a = (D, D), \end{cases}$$

with $p > q > r$. We assume that $p - q > q - r$. Payoffs are given by

$$r_i(a_i, y) = \begin{cases} 1 + \frac{2 - 2p}{p - q} & \text{if } (a_i, y) = (C, G), \\ 1 - \frac{2p}{p - q} & \text{if } (a_i, y) = (C, B), \\ \frac{2 - 2r}{q - r} & \text{if } (a_i, y) = (D, G), \\ \frac{-2r}{q - r} & \text{if } (a_i, y) = (D, B), \end{cases}$$

which means that expected payoffs $u_i(a)$ are given by the standard prisoners' dilemma matrix in the previous example.

Claim *If $\frac{1}{2p-q-r} \leq \delta \leq \frac{1}{p+q-2r}$, then the set*

$$W = \left\{ \frac{\delta r}{1 - \delta(p-r)}, \frac{1-\delta+\delta r}{1-\delta(p-r)} \right\}^3$$

is self-generating.

Proof Recall that to enforce a payoff v, we need a profile a and a map $w: Y \to W$ from outcomes to continuation payoffs such that

$$v = (1-\delta)\, u_i(a) + \delta \sum_y f(y|a)\, w_i(y),$$

and for all $a_i' \neq a_i$,

$$v \geq (1-\delta)\, u_i(a_i', a_{-i}) + \delta \sum_y f(y|a_i', a_{-i})\, w_i(y).$$

By symmetry, we ignore subscript i. Now let $v = \frac{\delta r}{1-\delta(p-r)}$ and $v' = \frac{1-\delta+\delta r}{1-\delta(p-r)}$ (the bad and good continuation payoffs, respectively). To enforce v, use the profile (D, D) and

$$w(y) = \begin{cases} v' & \text{if } y = G, \\ v & \text{if } y = B. \end{cases}$$

We need to check that

$$v = (1-\delta)(0) + \delta(1-r)v + \delta r v',$$

$$v \geq (1-\delta)(-1) + \delta(1-q)v + \delta q v'.$$

The first equality holds true and the second inequality holds if and only if $\frac{1}{p-r+q-r} \geq \delta$.

To enforce v', use the profile (C, C) and the same $w: Y \to W$. We need to check that

$$v' = (1-\delta)(1) + \delta(1-p)v + \delta p v',$$

$$v' \geq (1-\delta)(2) + \delta(1-q)v + \delta q v'.$$

The first condition is trivially true, while the second holds so long as $\delta \geq \frac{1}{p-q+p-r}$. ∎

21.2 Dynamic Stochastic Games

Stochastic games were introduced by Lloyd Shapley (1953). Repeated games are the special case of this model. An n-player **stochastic game** can be summarized by a tuple $\{S, A, p, \delta, u\}$ where

- S is the state space in some Euclidean space;
- $A = \times_{i=1}^{n} A_i$, with each A_i as the space of player i's actions;
- $p: S \times A \to [0, 1]$ is the transition probability function;
- $u = (u_1, ..., u_n)$, with each $u_i: S \times A \to R$ as player i's payoff function; and
- $\delta = (\delta_1, ..., \delta_n)$, with each $\delta_i \in (0, 1)$ as player i's discount factor.

A general pure strategy for player i is a sequence $\sigma_i = \{\sigma_{it}\}_{t=1}^{\infty}$, where σ_{it} specifies a (pure) action to be taken at date t as a (Borel-measurable) function of the history of all states and actions up to date t. If this history up to date t is limited to the current state, $s_t \in S$, then the strategy is said to be Markov. If a Markov strategy is time invariant such that σ_{it} is independent of t, then the strategy is said to be stationary Markov. For infinite-horizon games, we will focus on stationary Markov strategies. Let $\sigma = (\sigma_1, ..., \sigma_n)$ denote a Markov strategy profile where each σ_{it}: $S \to A_i$, $t = 1, 2, ...$

The game is played as follows. At time 1, the initial state $s_1 \in S$ is given. After observing the initial state, players choose their actions $\sigma_{t=1}(s_1) \in A$ simultaneously and independently from each other. Player i receives a payoff $u_i(s_1, \sigma_{t=1}(s_1))$, and the dynamic system transits from state s_1 to state s_2 according to the (cumulative) probability distribution $p(s_2|s_1, \sigma_{t=1}(s_1))$. In the next round at time $t = 2$, after observing the current state s_2, players choose their actions $\sigma_{t=2}(s_2) \in A$. Then players receive period payoffs $u(s_2, \sigma_{t=2}(s_2))$, and the state of the dynamic system changes again. The game continues in this way.

The expected discounted average payoff from a stationary Markov strategy profile σ is given by

$$U_i(s_1; \sigma) = (1 - \delta_i) E\left[\sum_{t=1}^{\infty} \delta_i^{t-1} u_i(s_t, \sigma_t(s_t)) | s_1\right], \quad i = 1, ..., n,$$

where the expectation is induced by the actions and transition probability function p. Given a Markov strategy σ and a history of observed states s^t up to date t, we define the continuation Markov strategy $\sigma|_{s^t}$ as $\sigma|_{s^t}(\tau): S \to A$ with $\sigma|_{s^t}(\tau)(s_\tau) = \sigma_{t+\tau}(s_{t+\tau})$, $\tau = 0, 1, ...$ Given a state s_t and the continuation strategy $\sigma|_{s^t}$, we can define the continuation value $U_i(s_t; \sigma^*|_{s^t})$ in a standard way.

Definition 21.2.1 *A Markov strategy* $\sigma^* = \{\sigma_t^*\}_{t=1}^{\infty}$ *is a* **Markov perfect equilibrium** *(MPE) if at any state s_t and any history s^t,*

$$U_i(s_t; \sigma^* |_{s^t}) \geq U_i\left(s_t; (\sigma_i, \sigma_{-i}^*) |_{s^t}\right), \quad all \ \sigma_i \ and \ i.$$

It is a stationary MPE if σ_t^* is independent of t.

In applications, state transition is typically specified by a function

$$s_{t+1} = f(s_t, a_t) + \varepsilon_{t+1},$$

where ε_{t+1} is an IID random variable. When ε_{t+1} vanishes, we obtain a deterministic dynamic game.

The APS approach can be applied to find the equilibrium payoff set for stochastic games. We use the deterministic case as an example. Define the Markov perfect equilibrium payoff correspondence as $V^* \equiv \{V_s^* : s \in S\}$. For repeated games, the APS approach uses operators on sets. Here we will index sets by states. Let $\mathcal{P}$ be the set of all correspondences $W : S \to \mathbb{R}^n$ such that the graphs are compact. Define the operator $B : \mathcal{P} \to \mathcal{P}$ as

$$B(W)_s = \cup_{(a,w)} \{(1 - \delta) u_i(s, a) + \delta w\}$$

subject to $w \in W_{f(s,a)}$ and

$$(1 - \delta) u_i(s, a) + \delta w \geq (1 - \delta) u_i(s, a_i', a_{-i}) + \delta \mu_{i, f(s, a_i', a_{-i})},$$

where

$$\mu_{i,s} = \min\{w_i : w \in W_s\}.$$

A correspondence W is self-generating if $W \subset B(W)$. Adapting the arguments used before, we can show that B is monotone and preserves compactness. Additionally V^* is the maximal fixed point of the operator B and V^* can be obtained by repeatedly applying B to any set that contains the graph of V^*.

21.3   Application: The Great Fish War

We consider the Great Fish War model analyzed by Levhari and Mirman (1980). Let x_t be the quantity of fish at time t. Its evolution is given by

$$x_{t+1} = (x_t - c_{1t} - c_{2t})^{\alpha}, \quad \alpha \in (0, 1), \tag{21.1}$$

where c_{it} is the consumption of fish at time t for country i. Suppose that two countries fish the waters. Each country has a utility for the fish it catches in each period and thus has an interest in the long-run effect of its present catch. Moreover each country must take the catch of the other country into consideration when deciding on its own catch. Country i's utility function is given by

$$\sum_{t=0}^{\infty} \beta_i^t \ln c_{it}.$$

We first solve for a stationary MPE in which $c_{it} = f_i(x_t)$ for some function f_i. First, we solve country 1's problem by dynamic programming given country 2's strategy $c_{2t} = f_2(x_t)$:

$$V_1(x_t) = \max_{c_{1t}} \ln c_{1t} + \beta_1 V_1(x_{t+1})$$

subject to (21.1). Conjecture that

$$V_1(x) = \kappa_1 \ln x + \nu_1,$$

where κ_1 and ν_1 are to be determined. We can then derive the first-order condition:

$$\frac{1}{c_1} = \frac{\alpha \beta_1 \kappa_1}{x - c_1 - c_2}.$$

Similarly we conjecture that country 2's value function takes the form

$$V_2(x) = \kappa_2 \ln x + \nu_2,$$

where κ_2 and ν_2 are to be determined. We can also derive the first-order condition:

$$\frac{1}{c_2} = \frac{\alpha \beta_2 \kappa_2}{x - c_1 - c_2}. \tag{21.2}$$

Using the two equations above, we can solve

$$c_1 = \frac{\beta_2 \kappa_2 x}{(1 + \alpha \beta_1 \kappa_1) \beta_2 \kappa_2 + \beta_1 \kappa_1},$$

$$c_2 = \frac{\beta_1 \kappa_1 x}{(1 + \alpha \beta_2 \kappa_2) \beta_1 \kappa_1 + \beta_2 \kappa_2}.$$

Substituting these decision rules back into the value functions, we can solve

$$\kappa_i = \frac{1}{1 - \alpha \beta_i},$$

Thus we obtain the MPE:

$$c_1 = \frac{\alpha\beta_2 \left(1 - \alpha\beta_1\right) x}{1 - \left(1 - \alpha\beta_1\right)\left(1 - \alpha\beta_2\right)},$$

$$c_2 = \frac{\alpha\beta_1 \left(1 - \alpha\beta_2\right) x}{1 - \left(1 - \alpha\beta_1\right)\left(1 - \alpha\beta_2\right)},$$

Substituting this MPE into (21.1) yields

$$x_{t+1} = \left[\frac{\alpha\beta_1\beta_2 x_t}{\beta_1 + \beta_2 - \alpha\beta_1\beta_2}\right]^\alpha.$$

In the steady state

$$\lim_{t\to\infty} x_t = \bar{x} = \left[\frac{\alpha\beta_1\beta_2}{\beta_1 + \beta_2 - \alpha\beta_1\beta_2}\right]^{\alpha/(1-\alpha)}.$$

Next we turn to a Stackelberg solution in which each period country 1 is the leader and country 2 is the follower. Conjecture that the value functions still take the preceding form but with different values of coefficients. Country 2 derives the decision rule given by (21.2) taking country 1's strategy as given. We obtain

$$c_2 = \frac{1}{1 + \alpha\beta_2\kappa_2} \left(x - c_1\right).$$

Substituting this rule into country 1's value function yields

$$\kappa_1 \ln\left(x\right) + \nu_1 = \max_{c_1} \; \ln c_1 + \alpha\beta_1\kappa_1 \ln\left(x - c_1 - \frac{1}{1 + \alpha\beta_2\kappa_2}\left(x - c_1\right)\right) + \beta_1\nu_1.$$

The first-order condition for c_1 is given by

$$\frac{1}{c_1} = \frac{\alpha\beta_1\kappa_1}{x - c_1}.$$

Thus

$$c_1 = \frac{x}{1 + \alpha\beta_1\kappa_1}.$$

Substituting this rule back into the preceding Bellman equation yields $k_1 = 1/(1 - \alpha\beta_1)$ and hence

$$c_1 = (1 - \alpha\beta_1) x.$$

The solution for country 2's consumption is left as an exercise.

21.4   Credible Government Policies

In this section we apply the APS method to study government policies. We borrow heavily from Stokey (1991) and Ljungqvist and Sargent (2004, ch. 22). We will focus on the case without state variables. Chang (1998) and Phelan and Stacchetti (2001) have extended the APS method to settings in which private agents have natural state variables like capital stock so that their best responses to government policies require that intertemporal Euler equations be satisfied. In this case the method in section 21.2 is useful. A thorough analysis is beyond the scope of this book.

21.4.1   One-Period Economy

There is a continuum of identical households, each of which chooses an action $a \in X$. A government chooses an action $y \in Y$. The average level of a across households is denoted by $x \in X$. The utility of a representative household is $u(a, x, y)$ when it chooses a, when the average household's choice is x, and when the government chooses y. The function u is strictly concave and continuously differentiable in a. The sets X and Y are compact.

Given x and y, the representative household solves the problem

$$\max_{a \in X} u(a, x, y).$$

Let the solution be a function $a = f(x, y)$. In a competitive equilibrium $x = a$ since all households are identical. In this case $x = f(x, y)$ and $u(x, x, y) = \max_{a \in X} u(a, x, y)$. For each $y \in Y$, let $x = h(y)$ denote the corresponding competitive equilibrium. Let $C = \{(x, y) : x = h(y)\}$ denote the set of competitive equilibria.

The government is benevolent, so its preferences coincide with those of households: $r(x, y) = u(x, x, y)$, all $(x, y) \in X \times Y$. The following timing of actions underlies a **Ramsey plan**. First, the government selects a $y \in Y$. Then, knowing the setting for y, the private sector responds with a competitive equilibrium. In making its choice of y, the government correctly forecasts that the economy will respond to y with a competitive equilibrium, $x = h(y)$. Formally, the Ramsey problem is $\max_{y \in Y} u(h(y), h(y), y) = \max_{(x,y) \in C} u(x, x, y)$. The policy that attains the maximum for the **Ramsey problem** is denoted y^R. Let $x^R = h(y^R)$. Then (y^R, x^R) is called a **Ramsey plan**.

The timing of actions is important. The Ramsey problem assumes that the government has a technology that permits it to choose first and not to reconsider its action, meaning the government must commit itself. If the government were allowed to reconsider after households had chosen x^R, it would, in general, want to deviate from y^R because there may exist an $\alpha \neq y^R$ for which $u(x^R, x^R, \alpha) > u(x^R, x^R, y^R)$. This is the time-inconsistency problem identified by Kydland and Prescott (1977).

Consider an alternative timing protocol that makes households and the government choose simultaneously or the households choose first. There is no commitment. The solution concept is the Nash equilibrium, which describes the government's discretionary behavior. A **Nash equilibrium** (x^N, y^N) satisfies (1) $(x^N, y^N) \in C$, and (2) given x^N, $u(x^N, x^N, y^N) = \max_{y' \in Y} u(x^N, x^N, y')$. For each x let the solution for $\max_{y' \in Y} u(x, x, y')$ be $y = H(x)$, which is called the reaction function or the best-response function of the government.

Let $v^N = u(x^N, x^N, y^N)$ and $v^R = u(x^R, x^R, y^R)$. Clearly, $v^N \leq v^R$ because

$$v^N \leq \max_{\{(x,y) \in C: y = H(x)\}} u(x, x, y) \leq \max_{(x,y) \in C} u(x, x, y) = v^R.$$

Example 21.4.1 *Consider the one-period economy of Barro and Gordon (1983a, b). The government chooses the inflation rate π to maximize the objective function*

$$\lambda (y - y_n) - \frac{1}{2}\pi^2,$$

subject to the Phillips curve relation

$$y = y_n + a(\pi - \pi^e),$$

where y is the actual output level, y_n is the natural rate of output, π^e is the private sector's average forecast of inflation, and $\lambda, a > 0$ are parameters. Each household chooses its inflation forecast ξ to $\min (\pi - \xi)^2$ so that $\xi = \pi$. In a rational expectations equilibrium, $\xi = \pi^e$. To solve for a Ramsey plan, we first solve for the private agent's forecast $\xi = \pi^e = \pi$ given policy π. Given this forecast, the government chooses π to solve the problem above, yielding $\pi = \pi^e = 0$ and $y = y_n$. To solve for a Nash equilibrium, the government takes π^e as given and solves the problem. The solution is $\pi = a\lambda > 0$ and $y = y_n$. Hence $\pi^e = \pi = a\lambda$. The Ramsey outcome is not time consistent. The reason is that the private agent's forecast of the policy $\pi = 0$ is $\pi^e = 0$. After seeing this forecast, the government will set $\pi = a\lambda > 0$.

Example 21.4.2 *Consider a discrete-choice example of monetary policy taken from Stokey (1991). The government can choose $y_H = 100$ precent, $y_M = 10$ precent, and $y_L = 9$ precent as growth rates of money supply. Households can take actions x_H, x_M, and x_L, which are competitive equilibrium outcomes for high, median, and low money growth rates. The utility values $r(x_i, y_j) = u(x_i, x_i, y_j)$ are given by the following table. Competitive equilibria are marked by asterisks.*

	x_H	x_M	x_L
y_H	0*	−1	1
y_M	7	8*	30
y_L	−1	−1	9.7*

The table shows that (x_L, y_L) is the Ramsey outcome because given the three competitive equilibria, the government's best choice is y_L. Here (x_M, y_M) is the Nash outcome or the no-commitment outcome because given x_M, the government's best response is y_M. The last column shows that the Ramsey outcome is not time consistent. Given the private sector's response x_L to y_L, the government has an incentive to deviate to y_M, yielding 30.

21.4.2 Infinitely Repeated Economy

Consider an economy that repeats the previous one-period economy forever. At each date $t \geq 1$, each household chooses $a_t \in X$, with the average $x_t \in X$, and the government chooses $y_t \in Y$. A history at date $t \geq 2$ is a sequence of past actions, $(x^{t-1}, y^{t-1}) \in X^{t-1} \times Y^{t-1}$ with $x^{t-1} = (x_1, ..., x_{t-1})$ and $y^{t-1} = (y_1, ..., y_{t-1})$. At $t = 1$, let $X^0 = Y^0 = \varnothing$. A **pure strategy** for the household $\sigma^h = \{\sigma_t^h\}_{t=1}^{\infty}$ is a sequence of functions defined as

$$\sigma_1^h \in X, \quad \sigma_t^h : X^{t-1} \times Y^{t-1} \to X, \quad t \geq 2.$$

Similarly a pure strategy for the government $\sigma^g = \{\sigma_t^g\}_{t=1}^{\infty}$ is a sequence of functions defined as

$$\sigma_1^g \in Y, \quad \sigma_t^g : X^{t-1} \times Y^{t-1} \to Y, \quad t \geq 2.$$

We call $\sigma = (\sigma^h, \sigma^g)$ a strategy profile. A strategy profile induces a path $\{x_t(\sigma), y_t(\sigma)\}_{t=1}^{\infty}$:

$$(x_1(\sigma), y_1(\sigma)) = (\sigma_1^h, \sigma_1^g), \quad (x_t(\sigma), y_t(\sigma)) = \sigma_t\left(x(\sigma)^{t-1}, y(\sigma)^{t-1}\right),$$

where

$$x(\sigma)^{t-1} = (x_1(\sigma), ..., x_{t-1}(\sigma)), \quad y(\sigma)^{t-1} = (y_1(\sigma), ..., y_{t-1}(\sigma)).$$

A strategy profile generates a pair of values for the government and the household:

$$U^h(\sigma) = (1 - \delta) \sum_{t=1}^{\infty} \delta^{t-1} u(x_t(\sigma), x_t(\sigma), y_t(\sigma)),$$

$$U^g(\sigma) = (1 - \delta) \sum_{t=1}^{\infty} \delta^{t-1} r(x_t(\sigma), y_t(\sigma)).$$

A strategy profile σ induces a continuation strategy. Let $\sigma|_{(x^t, y^t)}$ denote the strategy profile for a continuation economy whose first period is $t + 1$ and that is initiated after history (x^t, y^t) has been observed. Here $\sigma|_{(x^t, y^t)}(s)$ is the sth component of $\sigma|_{(x^t,y^t)}$, which for $s \geq 2$ is a function that maps $X^{s-1} \times Y^{s-1}$ into $X \times Y$, and for $s = 1$ is a point in $X \times Y$. Formally,

$$\sigma|_{(x^t,y^t)}(1) = \sigma_{t+1}\left(x^t, y^t\right),$$

$$\sigma|_{(x^t,y^t)}(s+1)\left(\xi^s, \eta^s\right) = \sigma_{t+s+1}\left(x^t, \xi^s; y^t, \eta^s\right), \ s \geq 1, \left(\xi^s, \eta^s\right) \in X^s \times Y^s.$$

Definition 21.4.1 *A strategy profile $\sigma = \left(\sigma^h, \sigma^g\right)$ is a **subgame perfect equilibrium** (SPE) of the infinitely repeated economy if for each $t \geq 1$ and each history $\left(x^{t-1}, y^{t-1}\right) \in X^{t-1} \times Y^{t-1}$:*

   a. The private sector outcome $x_t = \sigma_t^h\left(x^{t-1}, y^{t-1}\right)$ is consistent with competitive equilibrium when $y_t = \sigma_t^g\left(x^{t-1}, y^{t-1}\right)$.

   b. For any $\hat{\sigma}^g$,

$$U^g\left(\sigma|_{(x^{t-1},y^{t-1})}\right) \geq U^g\left(\left(\sigma^h, \hat{\sigma}^g\right)|_{(x^{t-1},y^{t-1})}\right).$$

The following lemma relates to the APS method. Its proof follows from the definition and is omitted.

Lemma 21.4.1 *Consider a strategy profile σ, and let the associated first-period outcome be given by $x = \sigma_1^h, y = \sigma_1^g$. The profile σ is an SPE if and only if*
   a. for each $(\xi, \eta) \in X \times Y$, $\sigma|_{(\xi,\eta)}$ is an SPE;
   b. (x, y) is a competitive equilibrium;
   c. for any $\eta \in Y$,

$$(1-\delta)\, r\,(x,y) + \delta U^g\left(\sigma|_{(x,y)}\right) \geq (1-\delta)\, r\,(x,\eta) + \delta U^g\left(\sigma|_{(x,\eta)}\right).$$

This lemma characterizes SPEs in terms of a first-period competitive equilibrium outcome pair (x, y) and a pair of continuation values: a value $U^g\left(\sigma|_{(x,y)}\right)$ to be awarded to the government next period if it adheres to the policy y, and a value $U^g\left(\sigma|_{(x,\eta)}\right), \eta \neq y$, to be awarded to the government if it deviates from y. Each of these values must be supported by some SPE strategy.

Example 21.4.3 *It is trivial to verify that infinite repetition of the one-period Nash equilibrium is an SPE. Using a trigger strategy, we can support a SPE with a better outcome. We use the Barro and Gordon (1983a, b) model analyzed earlier to illustrate this point. Suppose that one-period economy in example 21.4.1 is repeated forever. The government's objective function is given by*

$$(1-\delta)\sum_{t=1}^{\infty}\delta^{t-1}\left[\lambda\left(y_t - y_n\right) - \frac{1}{2}\pi_t^2\right].$$

The Phillips curve relation is

$$y_t = y_n + a\left(\pi_t - \pi_t^e\right).$$

Consider what range of inflation rates π that can be supported by the following trigger strategy: the government chooses π each period until it deviates. If it deviates the private sector's forecast of inflation is equal to λa forever. Clearly, $\pi_t = \pi_t^e = \lambda a$ for all t is a Nash equilibrium and hence is an SPE. For the preceding trigger strategy to be an SPE, the following inequality must hold:

$$-\frac{1}{2}\pi^2 \geq (1-\delta)\left[\lambda a\,(\varepsilon - \pi) - \frac{1}{2}\varepsilon^2\right] + \delta\left(-\frac{1}{2}(\lambda a)^2\right), \quad all\ \varepsilon,$$

where the left-hand side gives the payoff if the government choose π forever, and the right-hand side gives the payoff if it deviates for one period by choosing $\varepsilon \neq \pi$. Clearly, the most profitable deviation is $\varepsilon = \lambda a$. We can then show that

$$(1-2\delta)\lambda a \leq \pi \leq \lambda a \quad for\ 0 < \delta < 0.5.$$

Thus, any inflation rate in the range above can be supported as an SPE by a trigger strategy. The range is larger for a larger δ.

21.4.3   Equilibrium Value Set

In order to support a better outcome, reverting to a Nash equilibrium may not be bad enough. In this case we may be interested in finding a punishment worse than the Nash equilibrium. Consequently we want to find the whole set of equilibrium values. Let

$$V = \{U^g(\sigma) : \sigma \text{ is an SPE}\}.$$

We now use the APS method and define the following concepts.

Definition 21.4.2   Let $W \subset \mathbb{R}$. A tuple $(x, y, w\,(\cdot))$ is admissible with respect to W if (a) $(x, y) \in C$, (b) $w : X \times Y \to W$, and (c)

$$(1-\delta)\,r\,(x, y) + \delta w\,(x, y) \geq (1-\delta)\,r\,(x, y') + \delta w\,(x, y'), \quad y' \in Y.$$

Definition 21.4.3   For $W \subset \mathbb{R}$, let $B\,(W)$ be the set of possible values $v = (1-\delta)\,r\,(x, y) + \delta w\,(x, y)$ associated with admissible tuples (x, y, w).

Definition 21.4.4   The set W is **self-generating** if $W \subset B\,(W)$.

We then have the following results:

Lemma 21.4.2   The operator W is monotone and preserves compactness.

Lemma 21.4.3   (Self-generation) If $W \subset \mathbb{R}$ is bounded and self-generating, then $B\,(W) \subset V$.

Proof   We mimic the proof of lemma 21.1.2. Pick $v \in B(W)$. There exists an admissible tuple (x_1, y_1, w_1) such that $(x_1, y_1) \in C$, $w_1 : X \times Y \to W$,

$$v = (1 - \delta) r(x_1, y_1) + \delta w_1(x_1, y_1) \geq (1 - \delta) r(x_1, y') + \delta w_1(x_1, y'), \quad y' \in Y.$$

Set $\sigma_1 = (x_1, y_1)$. Since $W \subset B(W)$, for every $(x_1, y_1) \in C$, $w_1(x_1, y_1) \in B(W)$ and there exists an admissible tuple $(x_2(x_1, y_1), y_2(x_1, y_1), w_2(\cdot | x_1, y_1))$ such that

$$w_1(x_1, y_1) = (1 - \delta) r(x_2(x_1, y_1), y_2(x_1, y_1))$$
$$+ \delta w_2(x_2(x_1, y_1), y_2(x_1, y_1) | x_1, y_1),$$

for $t = 2$. Continuing in this way, we can construct a strategy profile $\sigma = \{\sigma_t\}_{t=1}^{\infty}$ such that $\sigma_t^h(x^{t-1}, y^{t-1}) = x_t(x^{t-1}, y^{t-1})$, $\sigma_t^g(x^{t-1}, y^{t-1}) = y_t(x^{t-1}, y^{t-1})$ for any history $(x^{t-1}, y^{t-1}) \in X^{t-1} \times Y^{t-1}$. We claim that $U^g(\sigma) = V$ and σ is an SPE.   ∎

By lemma 21.4.1, $V \subset B(W)$. Combining it with the lemma above, we conclude that:

Theorem 21.4.1 $V = B(V)$ *and* V *is the largest fixed point of* B.

Using the preceding results, we can design the following algorithm to find the set V.

Step 1. Start with a large set $W_0 = [w_{\min}^0, w_{\max}^0] \supset V$ and such that $B(W_0) \subset W_0$. For example, take

$$w_{\min}^0 = \min_{(x,y) \in C} r(x, y), \quad w_{\max}^0 = \max_{(x,y) \in C} r(x, y).$$

Step 2. Compute the boundaries of the set $B(W_0) = [w_{\min}^1, w_{\max}^1]$. The value $w_{\max}^1$ solves the problem

$$w_{\max}^1 = \max_{(x,y) \in C} (1 - \delta) r(x, y) + \delta w_{\max}^1$$

subject to

$$(1 - \delta) r(x, y) + \delta w_{\max}^1 \geq (1 - \delta) r(x, y') + \delta w_{\min}^1, \quad \text{all } y' \in Y.$$

The value $w_{\min}^1$ solves the problem

$$w_{\min}^1 = \min_{(x,y) \in C, (w_1, w_2) \in [w_{\min}^0, w_{\max}^0]^2} (1 - \delta) r(x, y) + \delta w_1$$

subject to

$$(1 - \delta) r(x, y) + \delta w_1 \geq (1 - \delta) r(x, y') + \delta w_2, \quad \text{all } y' \in Y.$$

Step 3. Having constructed $W_1 = B(W_0) \subset W_0$, continue to iterate, generating a decreasing sequence of compact sets $W_{j+1} = B(W_j) \subset W_j$. Iterate until the sets converge.

In the next subsection we will present an algorithm without iteration due to Stokey (1991) and Ljungqvist and Sargent (2004).

21.4.4   Best and Worst SPE Values

Adapting Abreu (1988), Stokey (1991) provides a characterization of all SPE paths. Let $(\mathbf{x}, \mathbf{y})$ be an outcome path, where $\mathbf{x} = (x_1, x_2, \dots)$ and $\mathbf{y} = (y_1, y_2, \dots)$. Given this path, define the government's payoff from period t on as

$$U_t^g(\mathbf{x}, \mathbf{y}) = (1 - \delta) \sum_{s=t} \delta^{s-t} r(x_{t+s}, y_{t+s}).$$

Proposition 21.4.1 *Let $v_{\min}$ be the smallest equilibrium payoff in V, and suppose that there exists an SPE strategy to support this payoff. The path $(\mathbf{x}, \mathbf{y})$ is an SPE path if and only if for all $t \geq 1$,*

$$U_t^g(\mathbf{x}, \mathbf{y}) \geq (1 - \delta) r(x_t, y_t') + \delta v_{\min}, \quad y_t' \in Y.$$

The proof is left as an exercise. If $v_{\min}$ can be calculated, then the proposition above can be used to construct the entire set of SPE outcome paths and payoffs. The next task is to find a method for constructing an SPE that has an equilibrium outcome path that attains $v_{\min}$. It has the remarkable property that it is **self-enforcing**.

Let $(\mathbf{x}, \mathbf{y})$ be an outcome path, and let $(\sigma^h(\mathbf{x}, \mathbf{y}), \sigma^g(\mathbf{x}, \mathbf{y}))$ be the strategy that specifies the following:

- Start by playing $\{x_t, y_t\}$.
- If the government deviates from an ongoing path, restart the paths $\{x_t, y_t\}$.

Call $(\mathbf{x}, \mathbf{y})$ a **self-enforcing SPE path** if $(\sigma^h(\mathbf{x}, \mathbf{y}), \sigma^g(\mathbf{x}, \mathbf{y}))$ is an SPE. The following result characterizes self-enforcing paths.

Proposition 21.4.2 *The path $(\mathbf{x}, \mathbf{y})$ is a self-enforcing SPE path if and only if*

$$U_t^g(\mathbf{x}, \mathbf{y}) \geq (1 - \delta) r(x_t, y_t') + \delta U_1^g(\mathbf{x}, \mathbf{y}), \quad y_t' \in Y.$$

An immediate corollary is that:

Proposition 21.4.3 *Let $(\underline{\mathbf{x}}, \underline{\mathbf{y}})$ be the path associated with the SPE strategy that supports the worst equilibrium payoff $v_{\min}$. Then $(\underline{\mathbf{x}}, \underline{\mathbf{y}})$ is self-enforcing.*

By the preceding results, we can compute the worst SPE value as follows:

$$v_{\min} = \min_{y \in Y, v_1 \in V} \ (1 - \delta)\, r\,(h\,(y)\,, y) + \delta v_1$$

subject to

$$(1 - \delta)\, r\,(h\,(y)\,, y) + \delta v_1 \geq (1 - \delta)\, r\,(h\,(y)\,, H\,(h(y))) + \delta v_{\min},$$

where we have used the worst SPE as the continuation value in the event of a deviation. The constraint must bind so that we can compute

$$v_{\min} = \min_{y \in Y} \ r\,(h\,(y)\,, H\,(h\,(y))).$$

But we have to check the solution $v_1 \in V$. To check this condition, we need to know $v_{\max}$.

The computation of $v_{\max}$ uses the fact that it is self-rewarding: the best SPE has continuation value $v_{\max}$ when the government follows the prescribed equilibrium strategy. Thus $v_{\max}$ solves the following problem:

$$v_{\max} = \max_{y \in Y} \ r\,(h\,(y)\,, y)$$

subject to

$$r\,(h\,(y)\,, y) \geq (1 - \delta)\, r\,(h\,(y)\,, H\,(h\,(y))) + \delta v_{\min}.$$

Finally, we have to check v_1 for supporting the worst value is within the equilibrium set $[v_{\min}, v_{\max}]$. If v_1 is not in the set $[v_{\min}, v_{\max}]$ computed above, we have to adjust the set. To see how this case can happen, we compute

$$v_{\min} = r\,(h\,(y_{\min})\,, H\,(h\,(y_{\min}))),$$

for some $y_{\min}$ and that for $y_{\min}$ the continuation value $v_{\min}$ satisfies

$$(1 - \delta)\, r\,(h\,(y_{\min})\,, y_{\min}) + \delta v_1 = (1 - \delta)\, r\,(h\,(y_{\min})\,, H\,(h\,(y_{\min}))) + \delta v_{\min}.$$

Solving for v_1 gives

$$v_1 = \frac{1 - \delta}{\delta}\, [r\,(h\,(y_{\min})\,, H\,(h\,(y_{\min}))) - r\,(h\,(y_{\min})\,, y_{\min})] + v_{\min}.$$

For a small discount factor, v_1 may exceed $v_{\max}$.

To deal with this issue, we reward adherence to the worst with $v_{\max}$. Setting $v_1 = v_{\max}$, we use the following four equations to solve for $v_{\max}, v_{\min}, y_{\max}$ and $y_{\min}$:

$$v_{\min} = r\,(h\,(y_{\min})\,, H\,(h\,(y_{\min}))),$$

$$v_{\max} = \frac{1-\delta}{\delta} \left[r\left(h\left(y_{\min} \right), H\left(h\left(y_{\min} \right) \right) \right) - r\left(h\left(y_{\min} \right), y_{\min} \right) \right] + v_{\min},$$

$$v_{\max} = r\left(h\left(y_{\max} \right), y_{\max} \right),$$

$$r\left(h\left(y_{\max} \right), y_{\max} \right) = (1-\delta) r\left(h\left(y_{\max} \right), H\left(h\left(y_{\max} \right) \right) \right) + \delta v_{\min}.$$

Example 21.4.4 *Consider the infinitely repeated economy in example 21.4.2. Assume that the discount factor $\delta = 0.9$. Can we find a strategy to support the Ramsey outcome (x_L, y_L) in an SPE? Consider the path $(\mathbf{x}, \mathbf{y})$ with $\mathbf{x} = (x_H, x_M, x_M, ...)$ and $\mathbf{y} = (y_H, y_M, y_M, ...)$. This strategy is a self-enforcing SPE strategy, since returning to itself is sufficient to punish the government for deviation. The payoff from this strategy is $0 + 0.9 * 8 / (1 - 0.9) = 72$. By deviating to y_M in the first period and returning to this strategy thereafter, the payoff is $7 + 0.9 * 72 = 71.8$, which is a worse outcome. Use this path to support the Ramsey outcome by defining the following strategy:*

a. *Start by playing the Ramsey outcome (x_L, y_L) in the first period.*

b. *If the government deviates from this path or any ongoing path, start the path $(\mathbf{x}, \mathbf{y})$ defined above.*

By deviating one period and return to $(\mathbf{x}, \mathbf{y})$, the government's payoff is $30 + 0.9 * 72 = 94.8$. Because this is smaller than 97, the payoff from the Ramsey outcome, the Ramsey outcome is an SPE outcome supported by this strategy.

21.4.5 Recursive Strategies

This subsection describes recursive strategies using the continuation value as a state variable.

Definition 21.4.5 *Households and the government follow recursive strategies if there is a tuple of functions $\phi = \left(z^h, z^g, \mathcal{V} \right)$ and an initial condition v with the following structure:*

$$x_t = z^h \left(v_t \right), \quad y_t = z^g \left(v_t \right), \quad v_{t+1} = \mathcal{V} \left(v_t, x_t, y_t \right),$$

and $v_1 = v \in \mathbb{R}$ is given.

A recursive strategy (ϕ, v) is a SPE if and only if $v \in V$ and (a) $\left(z^h \left(v \right), z^g \left(v \right) \right) \in C$, (b) for all $y \in Y$, $\mathcal{V} \left(v, z^h \left(v \right), y \right) \in V$, and (c) for each $y \in Y$,

$$v = (1-\delta) r \left(z^h \left(v \right), z^g \left(v \right) \right) + \delta \mathcal{V} \left(v, z^h \left(v \right), z^g \left(v \right) \right)$$

$$\geq (1-\delta) r \left(z^h \left(v \right), y \right) + \delta \mathcal{V} \left(v, z^h \left(v \right), y \right).$$

We now study two examples of recursive strategies.

Example 21.4.5 (Trigger strategy to support a better-than-Nash outcome) *Let* $v^b = r\left(x^b, y^b\right)$ *be the payoff from infinite repetition of* $\left(x^b, y^b\right)$. *Suppose that* $(v^b > v^N = r\left(x^N, y^N\right)$. *As in example 21.4.1, we can construct the following SPE to support* v^b:

$$v^1 = v^b,$$

$$z^h(v) = \begin{cases} x^b & \text{if } v = v^b, \\ x^N & \text{otherwise;} \end{cases}$$

$$z^g(v) = \begin{cases} y^b & \text{if } v = v^b, \\ y^N & \text{otherwise;} \end{cases}$$

$$\mathcal{V}(v, x, y) = \begin{cases} v^b & \text{if } (v, x, y) = \left(v^b, x^b, y^b\right), \\ v^N & \text{otherwise.} \end{cases}$$

Example 21.4.6 (Stick-and-carrot strategy to support a worse-than-Nash outcome; Abreu 1988) *The "stick" part is an outcome* $(x^*, y^*) \in C$, *which is worse than* $\left(x^N, y^N\right)$. *The "carrot" part is the Ramsey outcome* $\left(x^R, y^R\right)$, *which the government attains forever after it has accepted the stick in the first period of its punishment.*

Abreu proposes to set the continuation value as $\tilde{v}$ *for deviating in order to support the first-period outcome* (x^*, y^*) *and attain the value*

$$\tilde{v} = (1 - \delta) r\left(x^*, y^*\right) + \delta v^R \geq (1 - \delta) r\left(x^*, H\left(x^*\right)\right) + \delta \tilde{v}.$$

The associated SPE strategy is given by

$$v_1 = \tilde{v},$$

$$z^h(v) = \begin{cases} x^R & \text{if } v = v^R, \\ x^* & \text{otherwise;} \end{cases}$$

$$z^g(v) = \begin{cases} y^R & \text{if } v = v^R, \\ y^* & \text{otherwise;} \end{cases}$$

$$\mathcal{V}(v, x, y) = \begin{cases} v^R & \text{if } (x, y) = \left(z^h(v), z^g(v)\right), \\ \tilde{v} & \text{otherwise.} \end{cases}$$

If the stick part is severe enough, this strategy attains a value worse than repetition of Nash. If the government deviates from the bad prescribed first-period policy y^*, *the punishment is to restart the equilibrium. This equilibrium is self-enforcing.*

21.5   Exercises

1. Prove proposition 21.1.2 given the assumption that A is compact.

2. Prove lemma 21.1.4.

3. Consider the Great Fish War model. Solve for country 2's equilibrium consumption in a linear Stackleberg equilibrium.

4. Prove the three propositions in subsection 21.4.4.

5. Consider example 21.4.2. Let $\delta = 0.88$. Show that the path $(\mathbf{x}, \mathbf{y})$ is still self-enforcing, but it can no longer support the Ramsey path as an equilibrium path.

6. Let $X = \{x_L, x_H\}$ and $Y = \{y_L, y_H\}$. For the one-period economy, when $a_i = x_i$, the payoffs to the government are given by the values of $u(x_i, x_i, y_j)$ entered in the following table:

	x_L	x_H
y_L	0*	15
y_H	1	10*

The competitive equilibria are denoted by an asterisk.

   a. Find the Ramsey plan.
   b. Show that there is no pure strategy Nash equilibrium for the one-period economy.
   c. Consider the infinitely repeated version of this economy. Find the value to the government associated with the worst SPE. Find the corresponding outcome path.
   d. Assume that the discount factor is $\delta = 0.9$. Determine whether infinite repetition of the Ramsey outcome is sustainable as a subgame perfect equilibrium. If it is, display the associated subgame perfect equilibrium.
   e. Find the value to the government associated with the best subgame perfect equilibrium.
   f. Find the lowest value for the discount factor for which repetition of the Ramsey outcome is a subgame perfect equilibrium.

22 Recursive Contracts

Incentive problems often arise in contracting relationships due to information asymmetries or **limited commitment**. For example, after an owner of a firm hires a manager, the owner may not be able to observe the manager's effort level. The manager may shirk at the expense of the owner. This case is called **hidden action**. In another example, the manager has better information about the investment opportunities than the owner. The manager may hide this information for his private benefits. This case is called **hidden information**. Even though there are no information asymmetries, in the presence of imperfect enforcement of contracts, contracting parties may renege on a contract due to limited commitment. This case can also lead to an efficiency loss.

Anticipating the problems above, the contracting parties could seek to design a contract that mitigates these problems. We call the contract design problem the **principal–agent problem**. The goal of this chapter is to study such a problem in a dynamic setup. The technical difficulty of this problem is how histories can be encoded recursively and how incentive problems can be managed with contracts that retain memory and make promises. Histories are highly dimensional and are not directly manageable as a state variable. Spear and Srivastava (1987), Thomas and Worrall (1988, 1990), and Abreu, Pearce, and Stacchetti (1990) find that for some problems, histories can be summarized by one-dimensional state variables—continuation values or promised values. Working with such state variables permits us to formulate the dynamic contract design problem recursively.

The reader is referred to part V of Ljungqvist and Sargent (2004) for treatments of recursive contracts closely related to those of this chapter and to Laffont and Martimort (2002) and Bolton and Dewatripont (2005) for more comprehensive treatments of contract theory.

22.1   Limited Commitment

We start with a contracting problem with full information. Due to imperfect enforcement of contracts, both contracting parties or one of them may walk away and take an outside option. For simplicity, we focus on the case of "one-sided limited commitment" in the sense that only the agent can walk away at any time, but the principal has full commitment.[1] An optimal contract is self-enforcing because the agent prefers to conform to it and never walks away in equilibrium.

We will present a model that follows closely the one in chapter 19 of Ljungqvist and Sargent (2004) and in Zhang (2012).[2] Thus we will consider a risk-sharing problem between a risk-neutral principal and a risk-averse agent. The agent receives a stochastic endowment stream $\{y_t\}_{t=0}^{\infty}$. Each y_t takes values in the set $\{\theta_1, \theta_2, ..., \theta_n\}$. Suppose that $\{y_t\}$ follows a Markov process with the transition probability $\pi(y'|y)$ for any $y, y' \in \{\theta_1, \theta_2, ..., \theta_n\}$. The agent cannot borrow or save and can only trade with the principal. The principal has access to a risk-free loan market with the gross interest rate $R = 1/\beta$. In the absence of incentive problems, the risk-neutral principal should fully insure the risk-averse agent so that the agent receives constant consumption over time. However, the presence of limited commitment prevents this first-best contracting solution.

Suppose that the agent can walk away from the contract and take an outside value $U_d(y_t)$ at each time t after observing the realization of endowments, $y_0, y_1, ..., y_t$. One commonly used assumption is that the outside value is equal to the autarky value:

$$U_d(y_t) = E_t \left[\sum_{s=t}^{\infty} \beta^{s-t} u(y_s) \right],$$

where u is the agent's period utility and β is the common discount factor for both the agent and the principal. Assume that u is twice continuously differentiable, strictly concave, and satisfies the usual Inada conditions.

Now formulate the optimal contracting problem as follows:

$$\max_{\{c_t\}_{t \geq 0}} E \sum_{t=0}^{\infty} \beta^t (y_t - c_t)$$

---

1. See Thomas and Worrall (1988), Kocherlakota (1996), and Ljunqvist and Sargent (2004) for models with two-sided limited commitment.
2. Ljungqvist and Sargent (2004) focus on the IID case. Here we consider the general Markov case.

subject to

$$E \sum_{j=0}^{\infty} \beta^j u \left(c_{t+j} \right) \geq U_d \left(y_t \right),$$ (22.1)

$$E \sum_{t=0}^{\infty} \beta^t u \left(c_t \right) \geq v_0,$$ (22.2)

where $v_0 \geq U_d \left(y_0 \right)$ is the initial outside option value to the agent. Equations (22.1) and (22.2) give the incentive and participation constraints, respectively. The incentive constraint ensures that the agent will never walk away in an optimal contract.

We present two methods to solve this problem. We also present a characterization of the optimal contract.

22.1.1   A Dynamic Programming Method

The first method is to write the contracting problem above recursively and then use the dynamic programming theory. The key is to choose the promised value (or continuation value) of the agent as a state variable. The Bellman equation is

$$P \left(\theta_i, v \right) = \max_{c, \{ w_j \}_{j=1}^n} \theta_i - c + \beta \sum_{j=1}^{n} \pi \left(\theta_j | \theta_i \right) P \left(\theta_j, w_j \right)$$

subject to

$$w_j \geq U_d \left(\theta_j \right), \quad j = 1, ..., n,$$ (22.3)

$$u \left(c \right) + \beta \sum_{j=1}^{n} \pi \left(\theta_j | \theta_i \right) w_j \geq v.$$ (22.4)

Here P is the value function for the principal, v is the current promised value to the agent, and w_j is the promised value in the next period in state j. Equations (22.3) and (22.4) give the incentive and participation constraints, respectively. The latter constraint is also often called the **promise-keeping constraint**.

We can show that the constraint set is convex and the value function P is concave in v. Form the Lagrangian

$$L = \theta_i - c + \beta \sum_{j=1}^{n} \pi \left(\theta_j | \theta_i \right) P \left(\theta_j, w_j \right) + \sum_{j=1}^{n} \lambda_j \left(w_j - U_d \left(\theta_j \right) \right)$$

$$+ \mu \left[u \left(c \right) + \beta \sum_{j=1}^{n} \pi \left(\theta_j | \theta_i \right) w_j - v \right].$$

The first-order conditions are given by

$$c : u'(c) = \frac{1}{\mu},$$

(22.5)

$$w_j : \beta\pi\left(\theta_j|\theta_i\right) P_2\left(\theta_j, w_j\right) + \lambda_j + \mu\beta\pi\left(\theta_j|\theta_i\right) = 0.$$

(22.6)

Since $u' > 0$, $\mu > 0$ and so the promise-keeping constraint always binds. The envelope condition is given by

$$P_v\left(\theta_i, v\right) = -\mu.$$

(22.7)

We then obtain

$$u'(c) = -\frac{1}{P_v\left(\theta_i, v\right)}.$$

(22.8)

It follows from (22.6) and (22.7) that

$$P_v\left(\theta_j, w_j\right) = P_v\left(\theta_i, v\right) - \frac{\lambda_j}{\beta\pi\left(\theta_j|\theta_i\right)}.$$

(22.9)

States where $\lambda_i > 0$ In this case the incentive constraint in state i binds, so the promised value in the next period is given by $w_i = U_d\left(\theta_i\right)$. By (22.8), consumption in the next period in state i, satisfies

$$u'(c_i) = -\frac{1}{P_v\left(\theta_i, w_i\right)}.$$

Thus both c_i and w_i will depend on θ_i only and are independent of the history. This property is what Kocherlakota (1996) calls amnesia. We can write the solution as

$$c_i = f_1\left(\theta_i\right), \ w_i = U_d\left(\theta_i\right) > v,$$

for some function f_1.

States where $\lambda_i = 0$ In this case the incentive constraint in state i does not bind. Equation (22.9) implies that $w_i = v$. Thus consumption in the next period c_i also satisfies (22.8) and is equal to the current consumption c. We write the solution to this equation as

$$c_i = f_2\left(\theta_i, v\right) = c$$

for some function f_2.

The Optimal Contract   Combining the preceding two cases, we obtain the optimal policy functions for the next period consumption and continuation value:

$$c = \max \{f_1(y), f_2(y, v)\}, \quad w = \max \{U_d(y), v\}.$$

Once we obtain w_j for each j, we can use (22.4) to solve for the initial consumption. From the equation above, we can see that there is a boundary $y^d(v)$ such that $U_d(y^d(v)) = v$ and that for $y > y^d(v)$, the incentive constraint binds. We can now describe the optimal contract as follows: At any time t, given $v_t \geq U_d(y_t)$ (i.e., $y_t \leq y^d(v_t)$) and the endowment realization y_t, the principal offers the agent $c_t = f_2(y_t, v_t)$. If $y_{t+1} \leq y^d(v_t)$, the principal offers the agent $c_{t+1} = f_2(y_{t+1}, v_t)$ and leaves the promised value unaltered, $v_{t+1} = v_t$. The principal is thus insuring the agent against the states $y_{t+1} \leq y^d(v_t)$. If $y_{t+1} > y^d(v_t)$, the incentive constraint binds at y_{t+1}, so the principal is compelled to induce the agent to surrender some of its current-period endowment in exchange for a raised promised utility $v_{t+1} = U_d(y_{t+1}) > v_t$. The principal offers the agent $c_{t+1} = f_1(y_{t+1}) > f_2(y_{t+1}, v_t) > c_t$. Promised values never decrease. They stay constant for low endowment states and increase in high endowment states that threaten to violate the incentive constraint. Consumption stays constant during periods when the incentive constraint does not bind and increases during periods when it binds. A numerical method is often needed to solve for an optimal contract because one needs to know the value function P in order to derive the optimal consumption policy.

22.1.2   A Lagrangian Method

Marcet and Marimon (1992, 2011) propose a Lagrangian method that uses the Lagrange multipliers on incentive constraints to keep track of promises. Their approach extends the early work of Kydland and Prescott (1980) and has been recently generalized by Messner, Pavoni, and Sleet (2011, 2012).

We now use Marcet and Marimon method to solve the previous contracting problem. Form the Lagrangian as follows:

$$L = E \sum_{t=0}^{\infty} \beta^t (y_t - c_t) + E \sum_{t=0}^{\infty} \beta^t \alpha_t \left(E_t \left[\sum_{s=t}^{\infty} \beta^{s-t} u(c_s) \right] - U_d(y_t) \right)$$
$$+ \phi \left(E \left[\sum_{t=0}^{\infty} \beta^t u(c_t) \right] - v_0 \right),$$

where $\beta^t \alpha_t$ is the Lagrange multiplier associated with date t incentive constraint and ϕ is the Lagrange multiplier associated with the initial participation constraint. Define a sequence $\{\mu_t\}$ recursively as

$$\mu_t = \mu_{t-1} + \alpha_t, \quad \mu_{-1} = 0. \tag{22.10}$$

Then rewrite the Lagrangian above as

$$L = E \sum_{t=0}^{\infty} \beta^t \left[(y_t - c_t) + (\mu_t + \phi) u(c_t) - (\mu_t - \mu_{t-1}) U_d(y_t) \right] - \phi v.$$

For a given value v, we seek a saddle point: a maximum with respect to $\{c_t\}$ and a minimum with respect to $\{\mu_t\}$ and ϕ. The first-order condition with respect to c_t is

$$u'(c_t) = \frac{1}{\mu_t + \phi},$$

which is a version of equation (22.8). Thus $-(\mu_t + \phi)$ is equal to $P_v(y_t, v_t)$, so the multipliers encode the information contained in the partial derivative of the principal's value function. We also have the complementary slackness conditions

$$E_t \left[\sum_{s=t}^{\infty} \beta^{s-t} u(c_s) \right] - U_d(y_t) \geq 0, \quad = 0 \text{ if } \alpha_t > 0;$$

$$E \left[\sum_{t=0}^{\infty} \beta^t u(c_t) \right] = v_0.$$

The preceding three equations together with the law of motion (22.10) characterize the solution for the optimal contract.

The numerical solution to the above equations is complicated by the fact that the complementary slackness conditions involve conditional expectations of future endogenous variables $\{c_{t+j}\}$. Marcet and Marimon (1992) handle this issue using the parameterized expectation method; that is, they replace the conditional expectation by a paramterized function of the state variables. Kehoe and Perri (2002) apply this method in an international trade model with limited commitment.

22.1.3   An Alternative Characterization

Zhang (2012) develops an alternative characterization of the optimal contract for the previous contracting problem based on a stopping-time approach. His approach relies on the observation that the optimal consumption takes the following recursive form:

$$c_t = \max \{c_{t-1}, h(y_t)\}, \quad t \geq 1, \tag{22.11}$$

for some function h. By our previous analysis, consumption increases $c_t > c_{t-1}$ if and only if the incentive constraint in period t binds. If it binds, the continuation value at date t is equal to $U_d(y_t)$ and $c_t = h(y_t)$. The goal is to characterize the function h, which is called the minimum consumption function by Zhang (2012).

For a stopping time $\tau \geq 1$, let $d_i(\tau)$ be the consumption level satisfying the equation

$$E\left[\sum_{t=0}^{\tau-1} \beta^t u(d_i(\tau)) | y_0 = \theta_i\right] = U_d(\theta_i) - E[\beta^\tau U_d(y_\tau) | y_0 = \theta_i].$$

This equation says that at time τ and time 0, the incentive constraints bind, but the consumption from time 0 to time $\tau - 1$ is equal to the constant $d_i(\tau)$. The minimum consumption function is defined as

$$h(\theta_i) = \inf_{\tau \geq 1} d_i(\tau).$$

The intuition for this construction is the following: If $h(\theta_i)$ is not at the minimum, then the principal can move some consumption from periods 0 to $\tau - 1$ in order to relax the incentive constraint in period τ. By choosing a τ that minimizes the average consumption from periods 0 to $\tau - 1$, the principal can achieve the most consumption smoothing that is feasible. Substituting $\{c_t\}_{t \geq 1}$ in (22.11) into the initial binding participation constraint (22.2), we can solve for a unique solution for c_0, denoted by $c_0(v_0, y_0)$.

Zhang (2012) shows that $c_0(U_d(\theta_i), \theta_i) = h(\theta_i)$. Thus $c_0(v_0, \theta_i) > h(\theta_i)$ when $v_0 > U_d(\theta_i)$. He also shows that if $y_0 = \theta_i$, $v_0 \geq U_d(\theta_i)$, and $c_0 = g(v_0, \theta_i)$, then $\{c_t\}_{t \geq 1}$ defined in (22.11) together with c_0 gives the process of optimal consumption. Based on this characterization, Zhang (2012) develops a numerical method that is more efficient than the numerical methods based on either the value function iteration or the Lagrange formulation.

22.2 Hidden Action

In the previous section, we assumed that there is no information asymmetry. Incentive problems arise due to limited commitment. In the following two sections, we assume that there is information asymmetry, but there is full commitment. We start with the case of hidden action by presenting an infinitely repeated version of the standard agency model (e.g., see Holmstrom 1979). Dynamic agency models are difficult to analyze because the history dependence of contracts makes a recursive formulation nontrivial. Spear and Srivastava (1987) make an important breakthrough for this type of model. We present their model below.

A principal owns a production technology and contracts with an agent to operate this technology. At time $t \geq 0$ the agent chooses effort $a_t \in A = [a_{\min}, a_{\max}]$. Then output y_t is drawn from a fixed distribution with pdf $f(y|a_t)$. For any fixed action, output is independently and identically distributed over time. The principal pays the agent compensation c_t at time t. His period utility at time t is $v(y_t - c_t)$, and the agent's period utility at time t is $u(c_t, a_t)$. To incorporate moral hazard, we assume that the principal only observes the past and current output and he does not observe the agent's effort. Let $y^t = \{y_0, y_1, ..., y_t\}$ denote a history of realized output. Contracted compensation at time t depends on y^t only and is given by $c_t = c(y^t)$ for some function c. The agent's effort choice a_t depends on y^{t-1} and is given by $a_t = a(y^{t-1})$ for some function a. Let $a(y^{-1}) = a_0$.

Given $(c, a) = \{(c(y^t), a(y^{t-1})) : \text{all } y^t\}$, we can construct a sequence of probability distributions $\{\pi(y^t; a)\}$ recursively for each history y^t as follows:

$$d\pi(y^0; a) = f(y_0|a_0)\, dy_0,$$

$$d\pi(y^{t+1}; a) = f(y_{t+1}|a(y^t))\, d\pi(y^t; a)\, dy_{t+1}, \quad t \geq 0.$$

Assume that the principal and the agent have an identical subjective discount factor β.

We formulate the dynamic contracting problem as follows:

$$\max_{(c,a)} \sum_{t=0}^{\infty} \beta^t \int v(y_t - c(y^t))\, d\pi(y^t; a)$$

subject to

$$\sum_{t=0}^{\infty} \beta^t \int u(c(y^t), a(y^{t-1}))\, d\pi(y^t; a) \tag{22.12}$$

$$\geq \sum_{t=0}^{\infty} \beta^t \int u(c(y^t), \hat{a}(y^{t-1}))\, d\pi(y^t; \hat{a}), \quad \forall \hat{a},$$

$$\sum_{t=0}^{\infty} \beta^t \int u(c(y^t), a(y^{t-1}))\, d\pi(y^t; a) \geq u_0, \tag{22.13}$$

where u_0 is the outside utility level.

Inequalities (22.12) and (22.13) are incentive and participation constraints, respectively. For simplicity, we assume that the principal is risk neutral and that $u(c, a) = \phi(c) - \psi(a)$, where $\phi' > 0$, $\phi'' < 0$, $\psi' > 0$, and $\psi'' > 0$. Also assume that $f(y|a)$ is twice continuously differentiable in a and that $f_a(y|a)/f(y|a)$ is an increasing function of y. The latter assumption is often called the **monotone likelihood ratio condition** (MLRC). Because the incentive constraint (22.12) is complex, we use the **first-order approach** to simplify it, namely we replace it with the first-order condition with respect to the principal recommended action. As is well known, this approach may not be sufficient for incentive compatibility (e.g., Mirrlees 1975).

Rogerson (1985b) shows that if MLRC and a convexity condition on the conditional probability distribution function hold, then the first-order approach is valid. Instead of stating such sufficient conditions in terms of primitives, we simply assume that this approach is valid for our dynamic problem.

Following Spear and Srivastava (1987), we solve the contracting problem above using dynamic programming:

$$P(v) = \max_{a(v),c(v,y),w(v,y)} \int [(y - c(v,y)) + \beta P(w(v,y))] f(y|a(v)) \, dy$$

subject to

$$\int [\phi(c(v,y)) + \beta w(v,y)] f(y|a(v)) \, dy - \psi(a(v)) \tag{22.14}$$

$$\geq \int [\phi(c(v,y)) + \beta w(v,y)] f(y|\tilde{a}) \, dy - \psi(\tilde{a}), \quad \text{all } \tilde{a} \in A,$$

$$\int [\phi(c(v,y)) + \beta w(v,y)] f(y|a(v)) \, dy - \psi(a(v)) \geq v, \tag{22.15}$$

where P is the value function for the principal, v represents the promised value (continuation value) to the agent, and $w(v,y)$ is the promised value in the next period. The action $a(v)$ is a function of v, but consumption $c(v,y)$ and continuation value in the next period $w(v,y)$ are functions of v and y. This reflects the information structure assumed earlier. The promised value v is a state variable and encodes the history. The interpretation of this recursive contracting problem is as follows: Suppose at beginning of date t before observing the output y, the principal offers the agent the payment schedule $c(v,\cdot)$ and the promised utility function $w(v,\cdot)$ for tomorrow. The agent will follow the principal recommended effort $a(v)$ and obtains the promised value v at date t. At the end of period t, output level y is realized, the agent obtains $c(v,y)$ and $w(v,y)$. At the beginning of date $t+1$, before observing output y', the principal offers contract schedule $c(w(v,y),\cdot)$ and $w(w(v,y),\cdot)$. The agent will follow the principal recommended effort $a(w(v,y))$ and obtains the promised value $w(v,y)$ at date $t+1$. The contract then moves on to date $t+2$, and so on.

Equation (22.14) is the recursive incentive constraint and equation (22.15) is the promise-keeping constraint. We replace the recursive incentive constraint with the first-order condition

$$\int [\phi(c(v,y)) + \beta w(v,y)] f_a(y|a(v)) \, dy - \psi'(a(v)) = 0. \tag{22.16}$$

Spear and Srivastava (1987) show that P is concave and decreasing. Assuming that it is globally differentiable, they show that P is strictly concave. Form the Lagrangian expression

$$L = \int [(y - c(v,y)) + \beta P(w(v,y))] f(y|a(v)) \, dy$$

$$+ \mu(v) \left\{ \int [\phi(c(v,y)) + \beta w(v,y)] f_a(y|a(v)) \, dy - \psi'(a(v)) \right\}$$

$$+ \lambda(v) \left[\int [\phi(c(v,y)) + \beta w(v,y)] f(y|a(v)) \, dy - \psi(a(v)) - v \right],$$

where $\mu(v)$ and $\lambda(v)$ are the Lagrange multipliers associated with (22.16) and (22.15), respectively. The first-order conditions are given by

$$c : \frac{1}{\phi'(c(v,y))} = \lambda(v) + \mu(v) \frac{f_a(y|a)}{f(y|a)}, \tag{22.17}$$

$$a : 0 = \int [y - c(v,y) + \beta P(w(v,y))] f_a(y|a) \, dy \tag{22.18}$$

$$+ \mu(v) \left[\int [\phi(c(v,y)) + \beta w(v,y)] f_{aa}(y|a) \, dy - \psi''(a) \right],$$

$$w : \beta P'(w(v,y)) f(y|a) + \mu \beta f_a(y|a) + \lambda \beta f(y|a) = 0. \tag{22.19}$$

Equations (22.17) and (22.19) imply that

$$P'(w(v,y)) = -\frac{1}{\phi'(c(v,y))}. \tag{22.20}$$

How does the optimal contract evolve over time? Suppose that at the beginning of date t, the contract schedules $c(v,\cdot)$ and $w(v,\cdot)$ are offered. We study how the time $t+1$ contract responds to the observation of y in the end of period t.

Proposition 22.2.1 *For every v there exists an output level $\hat{y}(v)$ such that $v = w(v, \hat{y}(v))$.*

Proof   By the envelope condition,

$$P'(v) = -\lambda(v).$$

Integrating (22.17) with respect to $f(y|a(v))$ and substituting for $\lambda(v)$ yield

$$P'(v) = -\int \frac{1}{\phi'(c(v,y))} f(y|a(v)) \, dy, \tag{22.21}$$

where we have used the fact that $\int f_a(y|a)\,dy = 0$. Since $\phi' > 0$, we can apply the Mean Value Theorem for integration to obtain $\hat{y}$ such that

$$P'(v) = -\frac{1}{\phi'(c(v,\hat{y}(v)))}.\tag{22.22}$$

Combining (22.20) and (22.22) yields

$$P'(v) = P'(w(v,\hat{y}(v))).$$

Thus $v = w(v,\hat{y}(v))$ for all v.   ∎

This proposition implies that if the contract $c(v,\cdot)$ and $w(v,\cdot)$ are offered at time t and the time t output is $\hat{y}(v)$, then the time $t+1$ contract is exactly the same as the time t contract since $v = w(v,\hat{y}(v))$. To understand the dynamics of the contract, we have to understand how the contract changes when $y \neq \hat{y}(v)$ and how the cutoff $\hat{y}(v)$ changes over time.

Proposition 22.2.2 *Suppose that c and w are differentiable with respect to y. Then $\mu(v) > 0$, $c_y > 0$ and $w_y > 0$.*

Proof   By (22.20),

$$P''(w(v,y))\,w_y(v,y) = \frac{\phi''(c(v,y))}{[\phi'(c(v,y))]^2}c_y(v,y).$$

Since P and ϕ are strictly concave, c_y and w_y have the same sign. Suppose that $\mu(v) \leq 0$. By (22.17) and concavity of ϕ, $c_y \leq 0$. So $w_y \leq 0$. It follows that $y - c(v,y) + \beta P(w(v,y))$ is increasing in y since P is decreasing in v. In equation (22.18) the bracketed expression in the second term is the agent's second-order condition and hence is negative. So $\mu(v) \leq 0$ implies that the second term is nonnegative, and it must be that the first term is nonpositive. We can write this term as

$$\int [y - c(v,y) + \beta P(w(v,y))]f_a(y|a)\,dy$$

$$= E\left\{[y - c(v,y) + \beta P(w(v,y))]\frac{f_a(y|a)}{f(y)}\right\}$$

$$= Cov\left([y - c(v,y) + \beta P(w(v,y))],\frac{f_a(y|a)}{f(y)}\right)$$

$$+ E[y - c(v,y) + \beta P(w(v,y))]\,E\left[\frac{f_a(y|a)}{f(y)}\right].$$

Note that $E\left[f_a(y|a)/f(y)\right] = \int f_a(y|a)\,dy = 0$. By MLRC and monotonicity of $[y - c(v,y) + \beta P(w(v,y))]$, the covariance term above is nonnegative, and hence the first term in equation (22.18) is nonnegative and strictly positive if $\mu(v) < 0$. So we must have $\mu(v) = 0$. This makes $c(v,y)$ and $w(v,y)$ independent of y by (22.17) and (22.20). Equation (22.18) then implies that $\int y f_a(y|a)\,dy = 0$. Thus $E\left[y f_a(y|a)/f(y)\right] = 0$, contradicting MLRC.   ∎

To interpret the previous two propositions, we think of $c(v,\hat{y}(v))$ as the "first-best" income level associated with the multiplier $\lambda(v)$. If $c(v,y)$ and $w(v,y)$ are offered at time t and $\hat{y}(v)$ is observed, the agent gets paid this "first-best" income level, and exactly the same contract is offered at $t+1$. If $y > \hat{y}(v)$, the agent is paid more than this "first-best" income and is promised $w(v,y) > y$ at time $t+1$. Thus a relatively high observation of output leads to the agent being rewarded at both t and $t+1$.

We finally present an inverse Euler equation derived first by Rogerson (1985a) in a two-period model.

Proposition 22.2.3   (Inverse Euler equation)

$$\frac{1}{\phi'(c(v,y))} = \int \frac{1}{\phi'(c(w(v,y),y'))} f(y'|a(v))\,dy'.$$

Proof   Substituting $w(v,y)$ into (22.21) yields

$$P'(w(v,y)) = -\int \frac{1}{\phi'(c(w(v,y),y'))} f(y'|a(v))\,dy'.$$

Combining this with (22.20) yields the inverse Euler equation.   ∎

By this proposition,

$$\phi'(c(v,y)) = \left[\int \frac{1}{\phi'(c(w(v,y),y'))} f(y'|a(v))\,dy'\right]^{-1}.$$

It follows from Jensen's inequality that

$$\phi'(c(v,y)) < E\left[\phi'(c(w(v,y),y'))\right].$$

This implies that the agent would not wish to borrow money at the gross interest rate $1/\beta$ but that the agent would wish to save money. This result is first pointed out by Rogerson (1985a).

In addition to the difficulty of replacing the incentive constraint with the first-order condition, the constraint set often fails to be convex in applications. This difficulty was overcome by Phelan and Townsend (1991) by convexifying the constraint set through randomization. They extend the principal's choice to the space of lotteries over actions and outcomes. Phelan and Townsend (1991) also develop a computation procedure that solves for an optimal contract numerically.

22.3 Hidden Information

In this section we study a model of Thomas and Worrall (1990) with hidden information. Suppose that the agent receives stochastic incomes y_t that take values in $\Theta = \{\theta_1, \theta_2, ..., \theta_n\}$, where $\theta_i > \theta_j$ for all $i > j$. Assume that $\{y_t\}$ is IID and that $\Pr(y_t = \theta_i) = \pi_i$. Incentive problems arise because $\{y_t\}$ is the agent's private information. The agent cannot save or borrow but can trade with the principal to smooth consumption. The agent is risk averse and has a period utility function $u : (a, \infty) \to \mathbb{R}$ satisfying:

Assumption 22.3.1 $u' > 0, u'' < 0, \sup u(c) < \infty, \inf u(c) = -\infty, \lim_{c \to a} u'(c) = \infty,$ and $-u''/u'$ is decreasing.

We call the last assumption decreasing absolute risk aversion (DARA). It is critical to establish concavity of the value function.

Both the principal and the agent have a common discount factor $\beta \in (0, 1)$. The principal is risk neutral and cannot observe the agent's actual income. Thus, if he were to offer the agent perfect insurance, the borrower would always underreport income. By the Revelation Principle, for any contract with given reported incomes, there is an equivalent incentive compatible contract such that the agent reports his true income. We thus focus on contracts contingent on true income streams. We formulate the contracting problem by dynamic programming:

$$P(v) = \max_{\{c_i, w_i\}_{i=1}^{n}} \sum_{i=1}^{n} \pi_i \left[-c_i + \beta P(w_i) \right] \tag{22.23}$$

subject to

$$C_{i,j} \equiv u(\theta_i + c_i) + \beta w_i - \left[u(\theta_i + c_j) + \beta w_j \right] \geq 0, \tag{22.24}$$

$$\sum_{i=1}^{n} \pi_i \left[u(\theta_i + c_i) + \beta w_i \right] = v, \tag{22.25}$$

$$c_i \in [a - \theta_i, \infty],$$

$$w_i \in [-\infty, v_{\max}],$$

where $v_{\max} = \sup u(c) / (1 - \beta)$ for all $i, j = 1, 2, ..., n$. Here P is the principal's value function and v is the promised value to the agent from the last period. We use

c_i and w_i to denote the compensation to the agent and the continuation value delivered to the agent if he reports income θ_i. Equation (22.25) is the promise-keeping constraint. The set of constraints (22.24) ensures that the agent has no incentive to lie about his income realization in each state i. These constraints represent incentive compatibility constraints.

We first derive bounds on the value function P. Consider a contract that pays a constant amount $b(v)$ in all periods, where $b(v)$ satisfies

$$\sum_{i=1}^{n} \frac{\pi_i u (\theta_i + b)}{1 - \beta} = v.$$

The contract is incentive compatible and delivers the promised utility v. Thus the discounted value $-b/(1-\beta)$ provides a lower bound on $P(v)$. Additionally $P(v)$ cannot exceed the value of the unconstrained first-best contract that pays $c^*(v) - \theta_i$ in state i in all periods, where $c^*(v)$ satisfies $\sum_{i=1}^{n} \pi_i u (c^*) / (1 - \beta) = v$. In summary, the value function satisfies

$$\frac{-b(v)}{1-\beta} \leq P(v) \leq \sum_{i=1}^{n} \frac{\pi_s [\theta_i - c^*(v)]}{1 - \beta}. \tag{22.26}$$

Figure 22.1 illustrates the value function $P(v)$ and its bounds.

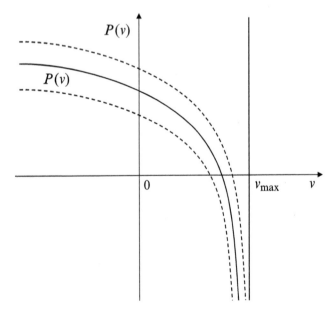

Figure 22.1
Value function and its bounds. The vertical solid line is $v_{\max} = \sup u (c) / (1 - \beta)$.

22.3.1   Characterizations

The following two lemmas are useful.

Lemma 22.3.1   *Incentive constraints imply that $c_{i-1} \geq c_i$ and $w_{i-1} \leq w_i$ for all i.*

Proof   Adding the downward constraint $C_{i,i-1} \geq 0$ and the upward constraint $C_{i-1,i}$ yields

$$u\left(\theta_i + c_i\right) - u\left(\theta_{i-1} + c_i\right) \geq u\left(\theta_i + c_{i-1}\right) - u\left(\theta_{i-1} + c_{i-1}\right).$$

This inequality and the concavity of u imply that $c_{i-1} \geq c_i$. It follows from $C_{i,i-1}$ that $w_{i-1} \leq w_i$.   ∎

This lemma shows that for any v, an agent reporting a lower income receives a higher transfer from the principal in exchange for a lower future utility. The following lemma simplifies the set of incentive constraints.

Lemma 22.3.2   *If the local downward constraints $C_{i,i-1}$ and upward constraints $C_{i,i+1}$ hold for each i, then the global constraints $C_{i,j}$ hold for all i, j.*

Proof   Suppose that the downward constraint $C_{i,k} \geq 0$ holds for some $i > k$,

$$u\left(\theta_i + c_i\right) + \beta w_i \geq u\left(\theta_i + c_k\right) + \beta w_k.$$

From the previous lemma, $c_i \leq c_k$, so the concavity of u implies

$$u\left(\theta_{i+1} + c_i\right) - u\left(\theta_i + c_i\right) \geq u\left(\theta_{i+1} + c_k\right) - u\left(\theta_i + c_k\right).$$

By adding the two inequalities above and using the local downward constraint $C_{i+1,i} \geq 0$, we obtain

$$u\left(\theta_{i+1} + c_{i+1}\right) + \beta w_{i+1} \geq u\left(\theta_{i+1} + c_k\right) + \beta w_k.$$

This means that the downward constraint $C_{i+1,k} \geq 0$ holds. Continuing this argument recursively, we can show that all global downward constraints are satisfied if the local downward constraints hold. A symmetric argument applies to the upward constraints.   ∎

The following proposition establishes properties of the solution to the Bellman equation (22.23). It is not obvious that the value function is concave because the constraint set is not convex. However, the DARA assumption will ensure that there exists a unique solution $(c_i, w_i)_{i=1}^{n}$ and the value function is concave. The idea of the proof is to use an induction argument by successive iteration starting from a one-period problem. Thomas and Worrall (1990) also use a clever idea to get around the nonconvexity of the constraint set.

Proposition 22.3.1   *There are unique P and $\{c_i, w_i\}_{i=1}^n$ that solve the dynamic programming problem (22.23). The value function $P(v)$ is decreasing, concave, and continuously differentiable on $(-\infty, v_{\max})$.*

Proof   Let $\mathbb{F}$ be the space of continuous functions on $(-\infty, v_{\max})$ lying between the bounds in (22.26). Since the gap between these bounds is bounded, $\mathbb{F}$ is a complete metric space in the supremum metric. Let Tf be the operator associated with the right side of equation (22.23) for any function $f \in \mathbb{F}$. By the Blackwell sufficiency condition, T is a contraction mapping. By the Contraction Mapping Theorem, T has a unique fixed point, which is the value function of the Bellman equation. It is also straightforward to show that T maps a decreasing function to a decreasing function. Thus the fixed point of T is also decreasing.

We now show that T maps a strictly concave function P to a strictly concave function TP. Consider any v^0 and v^1 associated with contracts $(c_i^0, w_i^0)_{i=1}^n$ and $(c_i^1, w_i^1)_{i=1}^n$, respectively. Let $w_i^* = \delta w_i^0 + (1-\delta) w_i^1$ and define c_i^* by $u(\theta_i + c_i^*) = \delta u(\theta_i + c_i^0) + (1-\delta)u(\theta_i + c_i^1)$, where $\delta \in (0,1)$. The concavity of u implies that $c_i^* \leq \delta c_i^0 + (1-\delta)c_i^1$. It follows that (c_i^*, w_i^*) gives the agent promised utility $\delta v^0 + (1-\delta)v^1$ and the principal has no less than average utility $\delta TP(v^0) + (1-\delta)TP(v^1)$. If this contract is incentive compatible, then we obtain concavity of $T(P)$. Unfortunately, it may violate incentive constraints. We first check the downward constraints. We can compute

$$C_{i,i-1}^* = \delta C_{i,i-1}^0 + (1-\delta)C_{i,i-1}^1 \\ + [\delta u(\theta_i + c_{i-1}^0) + (1-\delta)u(\theta_i + c_{i-1}^1) - u(\theta_i + c_{i-1}^*)].$$

Since the downward constraints are satisfied for (c_i^0, w_i^0) and (c_i^1, w_i^1), we know that $C_{i,i-1}^0 \geq 0$ and $C_{i,i-1}^1 \geq 0$. By the DARA assumption, the risk premium is a decreasing function of income. It follows that the term on the second line of the equation above is nonnegative. Thus the downward incentive constraints $C_{i,i-1}^*$ are satisfied. However, $(c_i^*, w_i^*)_{i=1}^n$ may violate the upward incentive constraints. In this case we can construct a new contract from $(c_i^*, w_i^*)_{i=1}^n$ that is incentive compatible and that offers both the principal and the agent no less utility. In particular, this new contract delivers the principal utility no less than $\delta TP(v^0) + (1-\delta)TP(v^1)$, and hence

$$TP(\delta v^0 + (1-\delta)v^1) \geq \delta TP(v^0) + (1-\delta)TP(v^1).$$

The construction is as follows: Keep w_1^* fixed and reduce w_2^* until $C_{2,1} = 0$ or $w_2^* = w_1^*$. Reduce w_3^* in the same way, and so on. Add the constant necessarily to leave $\sum_i \pi_i w_i^*$ constant. This step will not make the principal worse off since TP is concave. That is, we have engineered a mean-preserving decrease in the spread of the continuation values w. Now if $w_2^* = w_1^*$, which implies $c_2^* > c_1^*$, reduce c_2^* until $C_{2,1}$ binds. Proceed in the same way for c_3^*, and so on. Since $c_i^* + \theta_i \geq c_{i-1}^* + \theta_{i-1}$, adding a constant to each c_i^* leaves $\sum_i \pi_i c_i^*$ unchanged. In this new contract, $C_{i,i-1} = 0$ and $c_{i-1} \geq c_i$. Thus the upward constraints also hold.

Strict concavity of TP follows from the strict concavity of P because it is not possible to have both $c_i^0 = c_i^1$ and $w_i^0 = w_i^1$ for all i and $v^0 \neq v^1$, so the new contract constructed above yields the principal strictly more than $\delta TP(v^0) + (1 - \delta) TP(v^1)$.

Starting at $P_0(v) = 0$, it is trivial to show that $P_1(v) = TP_0(v)$ is strictly concave. By induction, all $P_k(v) = T^k P_{k-1}(v)$ are strictly concave. Therefore $P(v) = \lim_{k \to \infty} P_k(v)$ is concave.

To prove the uniqueness of the optimal contract $(c_i, w_i)_{i=1}^n$, we observe that it is impossible to have both $c_i = c_i'$ and $w_i \neq w_i'$ for all i for the same v. So nonuniqueness implies that $c_i \neq c_i'$ for some i. Using the preceding construction, we can obtain a strictly high value to the principal, a contradiction.

Finally, to prove continuous differentiability, consider a neighborhood of value of v around any v', and construct an incentive compatible contract for each v by taking the optimal contract at v' and keeping the future utilities constant, but varying the c_i's so as to maintain incentive compatibility and give v (there is a unique way of doing this). The principal's utility is then a concave function v by a similar argument to that given above, and this function is differentiable and equal to P_k at v'. The result follows from applying the Benveniste and Scheinkman theorem. ∎

To simplify the exposition, we make the following stronger assumption, which is not needed for some results derived in Thomas and Worrall (1990).

Assumption 22.3.2 $P(v)$ *is strictly concave.*

Proposition 22.3.2 *In an optimal contract the local upward incentive constraints never bind and the local downward incentive constraints always do.*

Proof The proof use the idea in the previous proposition. Suppose, to the contrary, that $C_{k,k-1} > 0$ for some k. Since $c_k \leq c_{k-1}$, it must be the case that $w_k > w_{k-1}$. Consider changing $(c_i, w_i)_{i=1}^n$ as follows. Keep w_1 fixed, and if necessary, reduce w_2 until $C_{2,1} = 0$. Next reduce w_3 until $C_{3,2} = 0$, and so on, that is, until $C_{k,k-1} = 0$. Add the necessary constant to each w_i to leave the overall expected future promised values $\sum_i \pi_i w_i$ unchanged. The new contract offers the agent the same utility and is incentive compatible since $c_i \leq c_{i-1}$ and $c_{i,i-1} = 0$ together imply that the local upward constraint $C_{i-1,i} \geq 0$ must hold. At the same time, since the mean of promised values is unchanged and the differences $(w_i - w_{i-1})$ have either been left unchanged or reduced, the strict concavity of the value function $P(v)$ implies that the principal's value has increased. That is, we have engineered a mean-preserving decrease in the spread in the continuation values w. Because $P(v)$ is strictly concave, $\sum_i \pi_i P(w_i)$ rises, and hence by the Bellman equation $P(v)$ rises too. Thus the original contract with a nonbinding local downward constraint could not have been an optimal solution.   ∎

The following proposition shows that the optimal contract features co-insurance in the sense that both the agent's utility and the principal's value increase with a higher income realization.

Proposition 22.3.3   *In an optimal contract,*

$$u(\theta_i + c_i) + \beta w_i > u(\theta_{i-1} + c_{i-1}) + \beta w_{i-1},$$
$$-c_i + \beta P(w_i) \geq -c_{i-1} + \beta P(w_{i-1}).$$

Proof   Since the local downward constraints always bind, $C_{i,i-1} = 0$. Thus

$$u(\theta_i + c_i) + \beta w_i = u(\theta_i + c_{i-1}) + \beta w_{i-1}$$
$$> u(\theta_{i-1} + c_{i-1}) + \beta w_{i-1}.$$

Now suppose that $-c_i + \beta P(w_i) < -c_{i-1} + \beta P(w_{i-1})$. Then replacing (c_i, w_i) in the contract with (c_{i-1}, w_{i-1}) raises the principal's value but leaves the agent's utility unchanged since $C_{i,i-1} = 0$. This change is also incentive compatible. This is a contradiction.   ∎

We now derive necessary conditions for optimality. Let λ and μ_i, $i = 2, ..., n$, be the multipliers associated with the constraints (22.25) and (22.24), $i = 2, ..., n$. The first-order conditions with respect to c_i and w_i are

$$\pi_i [1 - \lambda u'(\theta_i + c_i)] = \mu_i u'(\theta_i + c_i) - \mu_{i+1} u'(\theta_{i+1} + c_i), \tag{22.27}$$
$$\pi_i [P'(w_i) + \lambda] = \mu_{i+1} - \mu_i, \tag{22.28}$$

for $i = 1, ..., n$, where $\mu_1 = \mu_{n+1} = 0$. By the envelope condition,

$$P'(v) = -\lambda. \tag{22.29}$$

Summing equation (22.28) over i, we can derive

$$\sum_{i=1}^{n} \pi_i P'(w_i) = P'(v). \tag{22.30}$$

Thus $P'(v)$ is a martingale.

The intuition of this result is as follows. Consider increasing the agent's utility at any date by one unit. One way of doing this is to increase every w_i by a factor of $1/\beta$ while keeping every c_i constant. Such a change preserves incentive compatibility at a cost to the principal of $\sum_{i=1}^{n} \pi_i P'(w_i)$. By the envelope theorem, this is locally as good a way to increase v as any other and so is equal to $P'(v)$.

22.3.2 Long-Run Poverty

In this subsection we consider the long-run properties of the optimal contract.

Lemma 22.3.3 $w_1 < v < w_n$.

Proof To show that $w_n > v$, suppose, to the contrary, that $w_n \leq v$. Since $w_n \geq w_i$ for all i and $P(v)$ is strictly concave, equation (22.30) implies that $w_i = v$ for all i. Substituting (22.30) into (22.28) yields a zero on the left side. Moreover the right side of this equation is equal to μ_2 when $i = 1$ and to $-\mu_n$ when $i = n$. So we can show that all $\mu_i = 0$. It follows from (22.27) that the marginal utility of consumption is equalized across income realizations, $u'(\theta_i + c_i) = 1/\lambda$ for all i. Such consumption smoothing requires $c_{i-1} > c_i$, but from incentive compatibility, $w_{i-1} = w_i$ implies $c_{i-1} = c_i$, a contradiction. We conclude that $w_n > v$. A symmetric argument shows that $w_1 < v$.   ∎

This lemma says that the principal wants to spread out promises to future utility at each date. Otherwise, it would be impossible to provide any insurance in the form of contingent payments today.

Proposition 22.3.4 *The promised value to the agent v_t converges to $-\infty$ almost surely.*

Proof $P'(v_t)$ is a nonpositive martingale. By the Martingale Convergence Theorem (appendix D), $P'(v_t)$ converges to some random variable. Recall that $\lim_{v \to -\infty} P'(v) = 0$ and $\lim_{v \to v_{\max}} P'(v) = -\infty$. If $P'(v_t)$ converges to a finite negative number, then it contradicts the preceding lemma. Thus $P'(v_t)$ converges to zero, and hence v_t converges to $-\infty$.   ∎

This result implies that the agent is impoverished in the long run. The intuition is as follows: Without information asymmetry, the principal should offer a contract such that the agent's consumption is constant over time. But the presence of asymmetric information makes it necessary for the principal to vary future promised values to induce truth telling, which is costly due to the concavity of $P(v)$. For example, if $n = 2$, the cost of spreading w_1 and w_2 an equally small amount ε on either side of their average value $\bar{w}$ is approximately $-0.5\varepsilon^2 P''(\bar{w})$. It follows from the properties of $P(v)$ at its endpoints that $\lim_{v \to -\infty} P''(v) = 0$, and $\lim_{v \to v_{\max}} P''(v) = -\infty$. Thus the cost of spreading promised values goes to zero at one endpoint and to positive infinity at the other endpoint. The concavity of $P(v)$ and incentive compatibility considerations generate a downward drift in future utilities and, consequently, in consumption. A contract in which future promised values fall over time can induce the agent to tell the truth by using large variability in future utility and at the same time smoothing consumption in the initial periods.

22.4   Exercises

1. (Zhang 2012) Consider the deterministic model in section 22.1. Suppose that the outside option is autarky. The problem is as follows:

$$\max_{\{c_t\}_{t\geq 0}} \sum_{t=0}^{\infty} \beta^t (y_t - c_t)$$

subject to

$$\sum_{j=0}^{\infty} \beta^j u (c_{t+j}) \geq U_d (y_t) \equiv \sum_{j=0}^{\infty} \beta^j u (y_{t+j}), \quad t \geq 1,$$

$$\sum_{j=0}^{\infty} \beta^j u (c_j) = U_d (y_0).$$

Prove the following statements:

a. If $\{y_t\}$ is strictly decreasing over time, then the optimal contract is such that $u (c_t) = (1 - \beta) U_d (y_0)$.
b. If $\{y_t\}$ is strictly increasing over time, then the optimal contract is autarky.
c. In general,

$$c_t = \max \{c_{t-1}, \bar{c}_t (y_t)\}, \ t \geq 1, \ c_0 = \bar{c}_0 (y_0),$$

where

$$\bar{c}_t (y_t) = u^{-1} \left(\min_\tau \frac{\sum_{s=0}^{\tau-1} \beta^s u(y_{t+s})}{\sum_{s=0}^{\tau-1} \beta^s} \right).$$

2. Consider the model in section 22.1. Let $\beta = 0.98$. The income process (y_t) satisfies

$$\ln y_t = \rho \ln y_{t-1} + \sigma \varepsilon_t,$$

where $\rho = 0.95$ and $\sigma = 0.10$. The outside option value is autarky.

a. Write down the Bellman equation.
b. Write a Matlab code to solve for the optimal contract for any given initial promised value v. Plot the value function $P (v, y)$.
c. Compute v for $P (v, 1) = 0$.

3. Consider the model in section 22.3. Prove that for any given v, as $\beta \to 1$, the value function $P (v)$ converges to the first-best without information asymmetry.

4. Consider the model in section 22.3. Suppose that $u(c) = -\exp(-\gamma c)$. Prove that the optimal contract takes the following form:

$$c_i = -\frac{1}{\gamma}\ln(-v) + a_i,$$

$$w_i = -vd_i,$$

$$P(v) = \frac{\ln(-v)}{\gamma(1-\beta)} + K,$$

where a_i, $d_i < 0$, and K are some constants to be determined that are independent of v.

Mathematical Appendixes

These appendixes review some basic concepts and results in mathematics used in this book. The reader is referred to the following textbooks for more details: Luenberger (1969), Royden (1988), Billingsley (1995), Rudin (1991), Strang (2006), and Shiryaev (1996).

A Linear Algebra

A (real) **vector space (or linear space)** X is a set of elements (vectors) together with two operations, addition and scalar multiplication. For any two vectors $x, y \in X$, addition gives a vector $x + y \in X$, and for any vector $x \in X$ and any real number $\alpha \in \mathbb{R}$, scalar multiplication gives a vector $\alpha x \in X$. These operations obey the usual algebraic laws; that is, for all $x, y, z \in X$, and $\alpha, \beta \in \mathbb{R}$: (1) $x + y = y + x$, $(x + y) + z = x + (y + z)$; (2) $\alpha (x + y) = \alpha x + \alpha y$, $(\alpha + \beta) x = \alpha x + \beta x$, $(\alpha \beta) x = \alpha(\beta x)$. Moreover there is a zero vector $\theta \in X$ that has the following properties: (3) $x + \theta = x$, $0x = \theta$. Finally, (4) $1x = x$.

An example of linear space is the Euclidean space. The set of all integers is not a vector space. A subset L of the linear space X is a **linear** (or **vector**) **subspace** if it is a linear space itself. The linear subspace generated or spanned by a set of vectors S, denoted as span(S), is the intersection of all linear subspaces that include S. In particular, for a finite set of vectors $S = \{x_1, ..., x_n\}$, the set span(S), also denoted as span($x_1, ..., x_n$), consists of all linear combinations of the form $\lambda_1 x_1 + ... + \lambda_n x_n$, where $\lambda_1, ..., \lambda_n \in \mathbb{R}$.

The vectors $x_1, ..., x_n$ are **linearly independent** if $c_1 x_1 + ... + c_n x_n = 0$ only happens when $c_1 = ... = c_n = 0$. Otherwise, they are **linearly dependent**. A **basis** of a linear space X is a linearly independent set of vectors S that generates X, meaning span(S) = X. A linear space is **finite dimensional** if it has a finite basis and is **infinite dimensional** otherwise. Every basis of a finite-dimensional linear space has the same number of elements, called the space's **dimension**, denoted dim(V) for the space V. A linear space has infinitely many different bases. Whenever an $n \times n$ square matrix is invertible, its columns are independent, and they are a basis for $\mathbb{R}^n$. The **standard basis** (also called **natural basis** or **canonical basis**) for $\mathbb{R}^n$ consists of n **unit vectors**, $e_1, e_2, ..., e_n$, where e_i has 1 in its ith coordinate and zeros elsewhere.

A **linear transformation** T maps a linear space to another linear space, satisfying $T(\alpha x + \beta y) = \alpha T(x) + \beta T(y)$ for any $\alpha, \beta \in \mathbb{R}$. Let A be an $m \times n$ matrix. The rows of A span a subspace of $\mathbb{R}^n$, called the **row space** of A and the columns of A span a subspace of $\mathbb{R}^m$, called the **column space** (**range** or **image**) of $\mathbb{R}^m$. The dimensions of these spaces are called the **row rank** and **column rank**, respectively. The column rank is always equal to the row rank, and this common number is called the **rank** of A. The **nullspace** (**or kernel**) of a matrix A consists of all vectors x such that $Ax = 0$. The **left nullspace** of A is the nullspace of A^T.

Vectors $x, y \in \mathbb{R}^n$ are **orthogonal** if $x \cdot y = \sum_{i=1}^{n} x_i y_i = 0$. The last operation is called the **inner product** of x and y. The vector $x \in \mathbb{R}^n$ is a **unit vector** if $\|x\| = 1$. An **orthonormal basis** of X is a set of mutually orthogonal unit vectors that span X. Two subspaces V and W of the same space $\mathbb{R}^n$ are orthogonal if every vector x in V is orthogonal to every vector y in W. Given a subspace V of $\mathbb{R}^n$, the space of all vectors orthogonal to V is called the **orthogonal complement** of V, denoted by $V^\perp$. An **orthogonal matrix** is a square matrix with orthonormal columns. For square orthogonal matrices, the transpose is the inverse.

Fundamental Theorem of Linear Algebra   (1) For any $m \times n$ matrix A, the nullspace is the orthogonal complement of the row space in $\mathbb{R}^n$ and the left nullspace is the orthogonal complement of the column space in $\mathbb{R}^m$. (2) dim(row space) + dim(nullspace) = number of columns, dim(column space) + dim(left nullspace) = number of rows.

This theorem shows that the row space contains everything orthogonal to the nullspace. The column space contains everything orthogonal to the left nullspace. This determines which equation can be solved. In particular, $Ax = b$ requires b to be in the column space, or requires b to be perpendicular to the left nullspace. Thus $Ax = b$ is solvable if and only if $y^\mathsf{T} b = 0$ whenever $y^\mathsf{T} A = 0$. Intuitively, $Ax = b$ implies that b must be a combination of the columns. Thus b must be orthogonal to every vector that is orthogonal to the columns.

Fundamental Theorem of the System of Linear Equations   Let A be an $m \times n$ matrix. (Existence) $Ax = b$ has at least one solution $x \in \mathbb{R}^n$ for any $b \in \mathbb{R}^m$ if and only if the columns of A span $\mathbb{R}^m$. That is, A has full row rank. (Uniqueness) $Ax = b$ has at most one solution if and only if the columns are linearly independent. That is, A has full column rank.

For any vector $b \in \mathbb{R}^n$, we try to find a **projection** of b on the column space of A. That is, find a point $A\hat{x}$ such that it is the closest to b. Formally, we solve the following least squares problem $\min_x \|Ax - b\|$. The solution must be such that the error $e = Ax - b$ is orthogonal to the column space. The solution is $p = A (A^\mathsf{T} A)^{-1} A^\mathsf{T} b$. The matrix $P = A (A^\mathsf{T} A)^{-1} A^\mathsf{T}$ is a **projection matrix**, which is defined as any symmetric matrix P satisfying $P^2 = P$.

Orthogonal Projection Theorem   Let M be a linear subspace of $\mathbb{R}^n$. For each $x \in \mathbb{R}^n$ we can write x in a unique way as $x = x_M + x_\perp$, where $x_M \in M$ and $x_\perp \in M^\perp$. In addition $\dim M + \dim M^\perp = n$.

Consider the **eigenvalue equation** $Ax = \lambda x$, where A is a square matrix. The number λ is an **eigenvalue** of the matrix A, and the nonzero vector x is the associated **eigenvector**. λ is an eigenvalue of A if and only if $\det(A - \lambda I) = 0$, where det denotes determinant. This equation is called the **characteristic equation** for λ. If eigenvectors $x_1, ..., x_k$ correspond to distinct eigenvalues $\lambda_1, ..., \lambda_k$, then those eigenvectors are linearly independent. The eigenvalues of a projection matrix are 1 or 0. The eigenvalues of a triangular matrix are on the main diagonal. The **trace** of A is equal to the sum of its diagonal elements, which is equal to the sum of all eigenvalues of A. The product of all the eigenvalues equals the determinant of the matrix. The eigenvalues of a matrix are equal to those of its transpose.

Eigendecomposition Theorem   Suppose that the $n \times n$ matrix A has n linearly independent eigenvectors (or n distinct eigenvalues). Then A has the **eigendecomposition** (or **spectral decomposition**) $A = SDS^{-1}$ where D is a diagonal matrix formed from the eigenvalues of A.

The (**complex**) **conjugate** of $a + bi$ is the number $\overline{a + bi} = a - bi$, where $i = \sqrt{-1}$. The **modulus** (or absolute value) of a complex number $a + bi$ is $r = |a + bi| = \sqrt{a^2 + b^2}$. The **polar form** of $a + bi$ is $re^{i\theta} = r(\cos\theta + i\sin\theta)$. The **complex linear space** $\mathbb{C}^n$ contains all vectors with n complex components. The appropriate transpose of a complex vector x (matrix A) is the **conjugate transpose** $x^H = \overline{x}^\mathsf{T}$ ($A^H = \overline{A}^\mathsf{T}$). Sometimes it is also denoted x^*. The inner product of $x, y \in \mathbb{C}^n$ is defined as $x \cdot y = x^H y$. A **Hermitian matrix** is a matrix that is equal to its conjugate transpose. All eigenvalues of a Hermitian matrix are real. Two eigenvectors of a real symmetric matrix or a Hermitian matrix, if they come from different eigenvalues, are orthogonal to one another. A complex matrix with orthonormal columns is called a **unitary matrix**. A unitary matrix U satisfies the property $U^H U = U U^H = I$.

The square matrices A and $M^{-1}AM$ are **similar**. Going from one to the other is a **similarity transformation**. Similar matrices share the same eigenvalues.

Schur's Lemma   There is a unitary matrix U such that $U^{-1}AU = T$ is triangular. The eigenvalues of A appear along the diagonal of this similar matrix T.

Spectral Theorem   Every real symmetric matrix A can be diagonalized by an orthogonal matrix Q. Every Hermitian matrix can be diagonalized by a unitary matrix U such that (real) $Q^{-1}AQ = \Lambda$ and (complex) $U^{-1}AU = \Lambda$. The columns of Q (or U) contain orthonormal eigenvectors of A.

This theorem can be generalized to a larger class of matrices. The matrix N is **normal** if it commutes with $N^H : N^H N = N N^H$.

Spectral Theorem   A square matrix N is normal if and only it is unitarily similar to a diagonal matrix, $U^{-1} N U = \Lambda$. Normal matrices are exactly those that have a complete set of orthonormal eigenvectors.

The spectral theorem for normal matrices can be seen as a special case of Schur's Lemma. In fact, let A be a square matrix. Then, by Schur's Lemma it is unitarily similar to an upper-triangular matrix, say, B. If A is normal, so is B. But then B must be diagonal since a normal upper-triangular matrix is diagonal.

Jordan Decomposition Theorem   Any square real or complex matrix A has the following **Jordan decomposition**: There exists an invertible matrix P such that $J = P^{-1} A P$, where

$$
J = \begin{bmatrix} J_1 & & & \\ & J_2 & & \\ & & \ddots & \\ & & & J_k \end{bmatrix}, \quad
J_i = \begin{bmatrix} \lambda_i & 1 & & \\ & \lambda_i & \cdots & \\ & & \cdots & 1 \\ & & & \lambda_i \end{bmatrix},
$$

and where k is the number of independent eigenvectors of A. Each J_i is called a **Jordan block** whose diagonal elements correspond to one eigenvalue of A.

The matrix J is unique up to permutation, but P is not unique. We emphasize that more than one Jordan block may correspond to the same eigenvalue. The sum of the sizes of all Jordan blocks corresponding to an eigenvalue λ_i is its **algebraic multiplicity,** which is its multiplicity as a root of the characteristic equation. Its **geometric multiplicity** is the number of linearly independent eigenvectors corresponding to λ_i. If the geometric multiplicity is less than the algebraic multiplicity, then the matrix is **defective**.

Suppose that A has l distinct eigenvalues $\lambda_1, \lambda_2, ..., \lambda_l$. Let each λ_i have algebraic multiplicity m_i and geometric multiplicity k_i. Then (1) $k = k_1 + k_2 + \cdots + k_l$, (2) the number of Jordan blocks in J with eigenvalue λ_i is equal to k_i, and (3) λ_i appears on the diagonal of J exactly m_i times.

Below is an example of a Jordan matrix.

$$
J = \begin{bmatrix} \begin{bmatrix} 2 & 1 \\ & 2 \end{bmatrix} & & \\ & \begin{bmatrix} 0 & 1 \\ & 0 \end{bmatrix} & \\ & & [0] \end{bmatrix} = \begin{bmatrix} J_1 & & \\ & J_2 & \\ & & J_3 \end{bmatrix}.
$$

The double eigenvalue $\lambda_1 = 2$ has only a single eigenvector, in the first coordinate direction $e_1 = (1,0,0,0,0)$; as a result $\lambda_1 = 2$ appears only in a single block J_1. The triple eigenvalue $\lambda_2 = 0$ has two eigenvectors, e_3 and e_5, which correspond to the two Jordan blocks, J_2 and J_3. If A had 5 eigenvectors, all blocks would be 1 by 1 and J would be diagonal. An example is the identity matrix.

Each of the following conditions is an equivalent definition for the real symmetric matrix A to be **positive definite**: (1) $x^\mathsf{T} A x > 0$ for all nonzero real vectors x. (2) All the eigenvalues of A are positive. (3) All the upper left submatrices have positive determinants. (4) There is a matrix R with independent columns such that $A = R^\mathsf{T} R$.

More generally, a complex Hermitian matrix A is **positive definite** if $x^H A x$ is real and positive for all nonzero complex vectors x. The **negative definite, positive semidefinite**, and **negative semidefinite** matrices are defined in the same way, except that the formula $x^\mathsf{T} A x$ or $x^H A x$ is required to be always negative, nonnegative, and nonpositive, respectively.

Let A be a square matrix. An ***LU* decomposition** (or ***LU* factorization**) of A is $A = LU$, where L is lower triangular and U is upper triangular matrix.

***LUP* Decomposition Theorem**   Any square matrix A admits an ***LUP* decomposition** $A = LUP$, where P is a **permutation matrix**.

A **permutation matrix** is a square binary matrix that has exactly one entry 1 in each row and each column and 0s elsewhere. Each such matrix represents a specific permutation of m elements and, when used to multiply another matrix, can produce that permutation in the rows or columns of the other matrix. A permutation matrix is an orthogonal matrix.

Not every matrix admits an LU decomposition. When P is an identity matrix, the LUP decomposition reduces to the LU decomposition. The LUP and LU decompositions are useful in solving an n by n system of linear equations $Ax = b$. These decompositions summarize the process of Gaussian elimination in matrix form. Matrix P represents any row interchanges carried out in the process of Gaussian elimination. If Gaussian elimination produces the **row echelon form** without requiring any row interchanges, then $P = I$, so an LU decomposition exists.

A matrix is in **row echelon form** if the following conditions are present:

- All nonzero rows (rows with at least one nonzero element) are above any rows of all zeros (all zero rows, if any, belong at the bottom of the matrix).

- The leading coefficient (the first nonzero number from the left, also called the **pivot**) of a nonzero row is always strictly to the right of the leading coefficient of the row above it.

- All entries in a column below a leading entry are zeros (implied by the first two criteria).

Cholesky Decomposition Theorem   If matrix A is Hermitian positive semidefinite, then A has the **Cholesky decomposition** $A = TT^H$, where T is a lower triangular matrix with nonnegative diagonal entries.

When A is real, T has real entries as well. The Cholesky decomposition is unique when A is positive definite. However, the decomposition need not be unique when A is positive semidefinite.

QR Decomposition Theorem   Any m by n matrix A has the **QR decomposition** $A = QR$, where Q is an orthogonal matrix of size m by m, and R is an upper triangular matrix of size m by n.

The QR decomposition can be computed by the **Gram–Schmidt process**. The QR decomposition provides an alternative way of solving the system of equations $Ax = b$ without inverting the matrix A. The system $Ax = b$ is equivalent to $Rx = Q^\mathsf{T}$, which is easier to solve since R is triangular.

Singular Value Decomposition Theorem   Any m by n real or complex matrix A has the **singular value decomposition** (SVD) $A = UDV^H$, where U is an m by m real or complex unitary matrix, D is an m by n rectangular diagonal matrix with nonnegative real numbers on the diagonal, and V is an n by n real or complex unitary matrix.

The diagonal entries d_i of D are called the **singular values** of A. The m columns of U and the n columns of V are called the **left-singular vectors** and **right-singular vectors** of A, respectively. The left-singular vectors of A are eigenvectors of AA^H. The right-singular vectors of A are eigenvectors of A^HA. The nonzero-singular values of A (found on the diagonal entries of D) are the square roots of the nonzero eigenvalues of both A^HA and AA^H.

Applications of the SVD include computing the pseudoinverse, solving systems of linear equations, least squares fitting of data, matrix approximation, and determining the rank, range and nullspace of a matrix.

The **pseudoinverse** of the matrix A with singular value decomposition $A = UDV^H$ is $A^+ = VD^+U^H$, where D^+ is the pseudoinverse of D, which is formed by replacing every nonzero diagonal entry by its reciprocal and transposing the resulting matrix. The pseudoinverse is one way to solve linear least squares problems.

The **condition number** of a square matrix A is $\|A\| \cdot \|A^{-1}\|$, where $\|A\| = \max_{x \neq 0} \frac{\|Ax\|}{\|x\|}$ is the norm of A.

B Real and Functional Analysis

A **normed vector space** is a vector space S, together with a norm $\|\cdot\|: S \to \mathbb{R}$ such that for all $x, y \in S$ and $\alpha \in \mathbb{R}$, (1) $\|x\| \geq 0$, with equality if and only if $x = \theta$; (2) $\|\alpha x\| = |\alpha| \cdot \|x\|$; (3) $\|x + y\| \leq \|x\| + \|y\|$. A **metric space** is a set S and a function (called) **distance** or **metric**) $d : S \times S \to \mathbb{R}$ such that for all $x, y, z \in S$, (1) $d(x, y) \geq 0$, and $d(x, y) = 0$ if $x = y$; (2) $d(x, y) = d(y, x)$; and (3) $d(x, z) \leq d(x, y) + d(y, z)$. A normed vector space can be viewed as a metric space in which the metric is defined by $d(x, y) = \|x - y\|$.

A sequence $\{x_n\}_{n=0}^{\infty}$ in (S, d) is said to converge to some point $x \in S$ if $d(x, x_n) \to 0$. A sequence $\{x_n\}_{n=0}^{\infty}$ in (S, d) is a **Cauchy sequence** (satisfies the Cauchy criterion) if for each $\varepsilon > 0$, there exists N_ε such that

$$d(x_n, x_m) < \varepsilon, \quad \text{all } n, m \geq N_\varepsilon.$$

A metric space (S, d) is **complete** if every Cauchy sequence in S converges to an element in S. A complete normed vector space is called a **Banach space**.

Many of the best-known function spaces are Banach spaces.

- The space of bounded continuous functions $C(X)$ on a compact space X endowed with the supremum norm:

$$\|f\| = \sup_{x \in X} f(x).$$

- The space $L^p(S, \Sigma, \mu)$ of all real-valued measurable functions that are bounded in the norm:

$$\|f_p\| = \left(\int_S |f|^p \, d\mu \right)^{1/p},$$

where $1 \leq p < \infty$ and (S, Σ, μ) is a measure space. Two functions in this space are identified if they are equal almost surely.

- The space $L^\infty(S, \Sigma, \mu)$ of all real-valued measurable functions that are **essentially bounded** (i.e., bounded up to a set of measure zero), endowed with the **essential supremum norm**:

$$\|f\|_\infty = \inf \{M \geq 0 : |f(x)| < M \text{ almost surely}\}.$$

- The space ℓ^p of sequences $(x_0, x_1, x_2, \ldots)$ that are bounded in the norm:

$$\|x\|_p = \left(\sum_{n=1}^\infty |x_n|^p \right)^{1/p},$$

where $1 \leq p < \infty$.

- The space ℓ^∞ of bounded sequences endowed with the norm:

$$\|x\|_\infty = \sup_n |x_n|.$$

- All Hilbert spaces—the closest relatives of Euclidean spaces.

Let (S, d) be a metric space. The operator $T : S \to S$ is a **contraction mapping** with modulus β if for some $\beta \in (0, 1)$, $d(Tx, Ty) \leq \beta d(x, y)$ for all $x, y \in S$. A point x such that $Tx = x$ is called a **fixed point** of T.

Contraction Mapping Theorem   If (S, d) is a complete metric space and $T : S \to S$ is a contraction mapping with modulus β, then (1) T has a unique fixed point v in S and (2) for any $v_0 \in S, d(T^n v_0, v) \leq \beta^n d(v_0, v)$.

This theorem is very useful to establish the existence of a solution to the Bellman equation. The next theorem is useful to establish properties of a fixed point. For example, we can use it to establish monotonicity and concavity of the value function.

Closed Subset Theorem   (1) Let (S, d) be a complete metric space and S' be a closed subset of S. Then S' is a complete metric space.

(2) Let (S, d) be a complete metric space and $T : S \to S$ be a contraction mapping with fixed point $v \in S$. If S' is a closed subset of S and $T(S') \subset S'$, then $v \in S'$. If in addition $T(S') \subset S'' \subset S'$, then $v \in S''$.

The following theorem provide simple sufficient conditions to check whether an operator is a contraction mapping.

Blackwell Theorem   Let $X \subset \mathbb{R}^l$, and let $B(X)$ be a space of bounded functions $f : X \to \mathbb{R}$, with the sup norm. Let $T : B(X) \to B(X)$ be an operator satisfying

(1) (monotonicity) $f, g \in B(X)$ and $f(x) \leq g(x)$, for all $x \in X$, implies that $Tf(x) \leq Tg(x)$, for all $x \in X$; (2) (discounting) there exists some $\beta \in (0,1)$ such that

$$T(f + a)(x) \leq Tf(x) + \beta a, \quad \text{all} f \in B(X), a \geq 0, x \in X.$$

Then T is a contraction with modulus β.

Let (S, d) be a metric space. The set $B_r(x) = \{y \in S : d(x, y) < r\}$ is called an **open ball** around x with radius $r > 0$. A point x of some set U is called an **interior point** of U if U contains some ball around x. If x is an interior point of U, then U is also called a **neighborhood** of x. A point x is called a **limit point** of U (also **accumulation** or **cluster point**) if $(B_r(x) \setminus \{x\}) \cap U \neq \varnothing$ for every ball around x. Note that a limit point x need not lie in U but U must contain points arbitrarily close to x. A point x is called an **isolated point** of U if there exists a neighborhood of x not containing any other points of U. A set that consists only of isolated points is called a **discrete set**.

The complement of an open ball is called a **closed set**. The **closure** $\overline{A}$ of A is the intersection of all closed sets that contain A. A set D is called **dense** if its closure is all of S, that is, if $\overline{D} = S$. A metric space is **separable** if it contains a countable dense set.

A function f that maps from the metric space (X, d_X) to another metric space (Y, d_Y) is **continuous** at $x \in X$ if for any $\varepsilon > 0$ there exists a $\delta > 0$ such that if $d_X(x, y) < \delta$, then $d_Y(f(x), f(y)) < \varepsilon$. A function $f : X \to Y$ is called **injective** if for each $y \in Y$ there is at most one $x \in X$ such that $f(x) = y$ and **surjective** or **onto** if the range of f is Y. A bijection f is called a **homeomorphism** if both f and its inverse f^{-1} are continuous.

One question of interest in analysis is under what conditions a sequence of functions has a subsequence that is convergent in some sense. The following notion plays a central role in such questions: A family $\mathfrak{F}$ of functions from a metric space X to a metric space (Y, d_Y) is called **equicontinuous at the point** $x \in X$ if, given $\varepsilon > 0$, there is an open set O containing x such that $d_Y(f(x), f(y)) < \varepsilon$ for all y in O all $f \in \mathfrak{F}$. The family is equicontinuous on X if it is equicontinuous at each point $x \in X$.

Ascoli–Arzelá Theorem   Let $\mathfrak{F}$ be an equicontinuous family of functions from a separable space X to a metric space Y. Let $\{f_n\}$ be a sequence in $\mathfrak{F}$ such that for each x in X the closure of the set $\{f_n(x) : n \geq 0\}$ is compact. Then there is a subsequence $\{f_{n_k}\}$ that converges pointwise to a continuous function f, and the convergence is uniform on each compact subset of X.

In general, a space S together with a family of sets $\mathcal{O}$ is called a **topological space** if the sets in $\mathcal{O}$ satisfy the properties: (1) $\varnothing, S \in \mathcal{O}$; (2) $O_1, O_2 \in \mathcal{O}$ implies that $O_1 \cap O_2 \in \mathcal{O}$; (3) $\{O_\alpha\} \subset \mathcal{O}$ implies that $\cup O_\alpha \in \mathcal{O}$. That is, $\mathcal{O}$ is closed under finite intersections and arbitrary unions. Such a family of sets $\mathcal{O}$ is called a **topology** of S. Any set in $\mathcal{O}$ is called an **open set**. The notions of closed set, interior point, limit point, and neighborhood carry over to topological spaces if we replace open ball by open set.

The same set S can have different topologies. Two examples are the **trivial topology** $\mathcal{O} = \{\varnothing, S\}$ and the **discrete topology** in which $\mathcal{O}$ is the collection of all subsets of S. Given two topologies $\mathcal{O}_1$ and $\mathcal{O}_2$ on S, $\mathcal{O}_1$ is called **weaker** (or **coarser**) than $\mathcal{O}_2$ if and only if $\mathcal{O}_1 \subset \mathcal{O}_2$.

Every subspace Y of a topological space X becomes a topological space of its own. We call $O \subset Y$ open if there is some open set $N \subset X$ such that $O = N \cap Y$. This natural topology $O \cap Y$ is known as the **relative topology** (also **subspace** or **induced topology**).

A topological space is called a **Hausdorff space** if for two different points there are always two disjoint neighborhoods. Any metric space is a Hausdorff space. A set $K \subset S$ is **compact** if every open cover of K has a finite subcover. A collection $\mathcal{O}' \subset \mathcal{O}$ is a **base** for $\mathcal{O}$ if every member of $\mathcal{O}$ (i.e., every open set) is a union of members of $\mathcal{O}'$. A set K is said to be **countably compact** if every countable open cover has a finite subcover.

Suppose that X is a topological space, x_0 is a point in X, and $f: X \to \mathbb{R} \cup \{-\infty, +\infty\}$ is an extended real-valued function. We say that f is **upper semi-continuous** at x_0 if for every $\varepsilon > 0$ there exists a neighborhood U of x_0 such that $f(x) \le f(x_0) + \varepsilon$ for all $x \in U$. For the particular case of a metric space, this can be expressed as

$$\limsup_{x \to x_0} f(x) \le f(x_0).$$

The function f is called **upper semi-continuous** if it is upper semi-continuous at every point of its domain. A function is upper semi-continuous if and only if $\{x \in X : f(x) < \alpha\}$ is an open set for every $\alpha \in \mathbb{R}$.

We say that f is **lower semi-continuous** at x_0 if for every $\varepsilon > 0$ there exists a neighborhood U of x_0 such that $f(x) \ge f(x_0) - \varepsilon$ for all $x \in U$. Equivalently this can be expressed as

$$\liminf_{x \to x_0} f(x) \ge f(x_0).$$

The function f is called **lower semi-continuous** if it is lower semi-continuous at every point of its domain. The definition of f to be lower semi-continuous can be equivalently stated as $-f$ is upper semi-continuous or $\{x \in X : f(x) > \alpha\}$ is an open set for every $\alpha \in \mathbb{R}$. A function is **continuous** if and only if it is upper and lower semi-continuous. The pointwise supremum of a sequence of continuous functions is lower semi-continuous. The indicator function of any open set is lower semi-continuous. The indicator function of a closed set is upper semi-continuous.

Extreme Value Theorem I   Let f be an upper semi-continuous real-valued function on a countably compact space X. Then f is bounded from above and assumes its maximum.

Given the (possibly infinite) **Cartesian product** of the topological spaces X_i, indexed by $i \in I$,

$$X \equiv \prod_{i \in I} X_i,$$

and the **canonical projections** $p_i : X \to X_i$, the **product topology** on X is defined to be the coarsest topology (i.e., the topology with the fewest open sets) for which all the projections p_i are continuous. The product topology is sometimes called the **Tychonoff topology**.

Suppose that $\mathcal{O}$ is a topology on a vector space S such that (1) every point of S is a closed set, and (2) the vector space operations are continuous with respect to $\mathcal{O}$. Under these conditions, $\mathcal{O}$ is said to be a **vector topology** on S, and S is a **topological vector space**. The elements of topological vector spaces are typically functions or linear operators acting on topological vector spaces, and the topology is often defined so as to capture a particular notion of convergence of sequences of functions. All normed vector spaces, and hence all Hilbert spaces and Banach spaces, are well-known examples. However, there are topological vector spaces whose topology is not induced by a norm, but they are still of interest in analysis.

A **local base** of a topological vector space S is a collection $\mathfrak{B}$ of neighborhoods of 0 such that every neighborhood of 0 contains a member of $\mathfrak{B}$. The topological space S is **locally convex** if there is a local base $\mathfrak{B}$ whose members are convex. A subset A of a topological vector space is said to be **bounded** if to every neighborhood U of 0 in S corresponds a number $s > 0$ such that $A \subset tU$ for every $t > s$.

A **linear functional** on a normed vector space $(S, \|\cdot\|_S)$ is a function $\phi : S \to \mathbb{R}$ satisfying

$$\phi(\alpha x + \beta y) = \alpha \phi(x) + \beta \phi(y), \quad \text{all } x, y \in S, \text{ all } \alpha, \beta \in \mathbb{R}.$$

The linear functional is **continuous** if $\|x_n - x\|_S \to 0$ implies that $|\phi(x_n) - \phi(x)| \to 0$. It is **bounded** if there exists a constant $M > 0$ such that $|\phi(x)| \le M \|x\|_S$ for all $x \in X$. The norm of a bounded linear functional ϕ is then defined to be

$$\|\phi\|_d = \sup_{\|x\|_S \le 1} |\phi(x)|.$$

If ϕ is continuous at any point in S, it is continuous at all of S, and ϕ is continuous if and only if it is bounded.

For any normed vector space S, the space S^* of all continuous linear functionals on S is called the **dual** of S. S^* is a vector space, and $(S^*, \|\cdot\|_d)$ is a normed vector space. Every dual space is a Banach space. A Banach space is **reflexive** if it coincides with the dual of its dual space. For example, $L^p(S, \Sigma, \mu)$ is reflexive for $1 < p < \infty$, but $L^1(S, \Sigma, \mu)$ is not.

- The dual of $C(X)$ is $rca(X)$, where $rca(X)$ is the Banach space of all countably additive regular Borel measures on X.

- The dual of $L^p(S, \Sigma, \mu)$ is $L^q(S, \Sigma, \mu)$, where $1 < p, q < \infty$ and $1/p + 1/q = 1$.

- The dual of $L^1(S, \Sigma, \mu)$ is $L^\infty(S, \Sigma, \mu)$. But the dual of $L^\infty(S, \Sigma, \mu)$ is $ba(\Sigma, \mu)$, which contains $L^1(S, \Sigma, \mu)$. The space $ba(\Sigma, \mu)$ is the Banach space consisting of all bounded and finitely additive signed measures on Σ that are absolutely continuous with respect to μ.

- The dual of ℓ^p is ℓ^q, where $1 < p, q < \infty$ and $1/p + 1/q = 1$.

- The dual of ℓ^1 is ℓ^∞. But the dual of ℓ^∞ is ba (containing ℓ^1), which is the set of all bounded finitely additive measures on the power set of the natural numbers.

Suppose that S is a normed vector space. The **weak topology** generated by the dual S^* is the weakest topology on S such that $\phi \in S^*$ is continuous. The weak topology is characterized by the following condition: a net (x_α) in X converges in the weak topology to the element $x \in X$ if and only if $\phi(x_\alpha)$ converges to $\phi(x)$ for all $\phi \in X^*$. We usually call the topology generated by the norm the **strong topology**. The **weak* topology** on S^* is the weakest topology such that the linear functional $T_x : S^* \to \mathbb{R}$ defined by $T_x(\phi) = \phi(x)$ remains continuous for all $x \in S$. A net $\{\phi_\alpha\}$ in S^* is convergent to ϕ in the weak* topology if it converges pointwise.

Consider, for example, the difference between strong and weak convergence of functions in the Hilbert space $L^2(S, \Sigma, \mu)$. Strong convergence of a sequence $\{f_n\}$ to f in $L^2(S, \Sigma, \mu)$ means that $\int |f_n - f|^2 d\mu \to 0$. By contrast, weak convergence means that $\int f_n g d\mu \to \int f g d\mu$ for all functions $g \in L^2(S, \Sigma, \mu)$.

Banach–Alaoglu Theorem   If S is a normed vector space, then the closed unit ball in S^* is weak*-compact.

Kakutani Theorem   Let X be a Banach space. The following statements are equivalent:

1. X is reflexive.

2. The closed unit ball of X is compact in the weak topology.

3. Every bounded sequence in X has a weakly convergent subsequence.

Say that a real-valued function f on a Banach space is **coercive** if $f(x) \to +\infty$ as $\|x\| \to \infty$.

Extreme Value Theorem II   Let f be a weakly lower semi-continuous real-valued coercive function on a reflexive Banach space X. Then f is bounded from below and assumes its minimum.

Compared to the Extreme Value Theorem I, this version of the theorem assumes weakly semicontinuity but requires the function to be coercive and defined on a reflexive Banach space.

The Hahn–Banach theorem is a central tool in functional analysis. It allows the extension of bounded linear functionals defined on a subspace of some vector space to the whole space, and it also shows that there are enough continuous linear functionals defined on every normed vector space to make the study of the dual space interesting. Another version of Hahn–Banach theorem is known as the Hahn–Banach separation theorem or the Separating Hyperplane Theorem. We will present this version here.

Hahn–Banach Separation Theorem   Let S be a topological vector space. Suppose that A, B are convex, nonempty disjoint subsets of S:

1. If A is open, then there exists a continuous linear functional ϕ on S and $\alpha \in \mathbb{R}$ such that $\phi(x) < \alpha \leq \phi(y)$ for all $x \in A$ and $y \in B$.
2. If S is locally convex, A is compact, and B is closed, then there exists a continuous linear functional ϕ on S and α, γ such that $\phi(x) < \alpha < \gamma < \phi(y)$ for all $x \in A$ and $y \in B$.

Another form of this theorem is the following:

Hahn–Banach Separation Theorem   Let S be a normed vector space, and let A, B be convex nonempty subsets of S. Assume that either B has an interior point and A contains no interior point of B or S is finite-dimensional and $A \cap B = \varnothing$. Then there exists a continuous linear functional ϕ on S and $\alpha \in \mathbb{R}$ such that $\phi(x) \leq \alpha \leq \phi(y)$ for all $x \in A$ and $y \in B$.

The **convex hull** of a set A is the intersection of all convex sets containing A.

Krein–Milman Theorem   Let K be a compact convex set in a locally convex topological vector space S. Then K is the closed convex hull of its extreme points.

An **inner product** on a linear space S is a bilinear functional $\langle x, y \rangle$ on $S \times S$ to $\mathbb{R}$ such that[1] (1) $\langle \alpha_1 x_1 + \alpha_2 x_2, y \rangle = \alpha_1 \langle x_1, y \rangle + \alpha_2 \langle x_2, y \rangle$, $\alpha_1, \alpha_2 \in \mathbb{R}$; (2) $\langle x, y \rangle = \langle y, x \rangle$;

---

1. Here we focus on the real space. The theory of Hilbert spaces can be developed for the complex space.

(3) $\langle x, x \rangle \geq 0$ with equality if and only if $x = 0$. An **inner product space** (or **pre-Hilbert space**) is a normed vector space with the norm defined by $\|x\| = \sqrt{\langle x, x \rangle}$. A complete inner product space is called a **Hilbert space**. By definition, a Hilbert space is a Banach space. $L^2(S, \Sigma, \mu)$ and ℓ^2 are Hilbert spaces. Geometrically, an inner product in $\mathbb{R}^2$ is related to the cosine of the angle: $\langle x, y \rangle / \|x\| \|y\| = \cos \theta$.

Two vectors are said to be **orthogonal** if $\langle x, y \rangle = 0$, denoted by $x \perp y$. A set is said to be an **orthogonal set** if any two elements in the set are orthogonal. The set is **orthonormal** if moreover each vector in the set has a norm equal to unity. The **orthogonal complement** of M in an inner product space V is the set $\{x \in V : x \perp y, \ y \in M\}$, denoted by $M^\perp$. It is easy to show that $M \cap M^\perp = \{0\}$. An orthonormal sequence $\{e_i\}$ in a Hilbert space H is said to be **complete** if the closed subspace generated by $\{e_i\}$ is H.

Orthogonal Projection Theorem   Let M be a linear subspace of the finite-dimensional real inner product space V. For each $x \in V$, we can write x in a unique way as $x = x_M + x_\perp$, where $x_M \in M$ and $x_\perp \in M^\perp$. Moreover $\dim M + \dim M^\perp = \dim V$.

The following theorem is fundamental for optimization theory and generalizes the above result to infinite dimensional spaces.

Classical Projection Theorem   Let H be a Hilbert space and M a closed subspace of H. For any $x \in H$ there is a unique $m_0 \in M$ that solves the following problem:

$$\min_{m \in M} \ \|x - m\|.$$

A necessary and sufficient condition that $m_0 \in M$ be the unique minimizing vector is that $(x - m_0)$ be orthogonal to M.

Gram–Schmidt Theorem   Let $\{x_i\}$ be a countable or finite sequence of linearly independent vectors in a pre-Hilbert space H. Then there is an orthonormal sequence $\{e_i\}$ such that for each n the space generated by the first n e_i's is the same as the space generated by the first n x_i's.

The proof is constructive. Let $e_1 = x_1 / \|x_1\|$. Let $z_2 = x_2 - \langle x_2, e_1 \rangle e_1$ and $e_2 = z_2 / \|z_2\|$. Then $e_1 \perp e_2$ and e_1 and e_2 span the same space as x_1 and x_2. Continue this process by induction:

$$z_n = x_n - \sum_{i=1}^{n-1} \langle x_n, e_i \rangle e_i \quad \text{and} \quad e_n = \frac{z_n}{\|z_n\|}.$$

Let $\{e_i\}$ be a complete orthonormal sequence. Then any vector x in a Hilbert space can be written as

$$x = \sum_{i=1}^{\infty} \langle x, e_i \rangle e_i,$$

where $\langle x, e_i \rangle$ are the **Fourier coefficients** of x with respect to e_i.

Let H be a Hilbert space, and let H^* denote its dual. If $y \in H$, then the function φ_y defined by

$$\varphi_y(x) = \langle y, x \rangle, \quad \text{any } x \in H,$$

is an element of H^*. The following theorem states that every element of H^* can be written uniquely in this form.

Riesz Representation Theorem   For every continuous linear functional f on a Hilbert space H, there is a unique $y \in H$ such that $f(x) = \langle x, y \rangle$ for all $x \in H$.

For example, if $g : L^2(S, \Sigma, \mu) \to R$ is continuous and linear, then there exists a unique $h \in L^2(S, \Sigma, \mu)$ such that

$$g(f) = \int fh \, d\mu.$$

C Convex Analysis

The conventions for inequalities on $\mathbb{R}^n$ are the following: For $i = 1, 2, ..., n$, $x \geq y \Longleftrightarrow x_i \geq y_i$, $x > y \Longleftrightarrow x_i \geq y_i$, and $x \neq y$; $x >> y \Longleftrightarrow x_i > y_i$. A set C in a linear space is said to be **convex** if, given $x_1, x_2 \in C$, $\alpha x_1 + (1 - \alpha) x_2 \in C$ for all $\alpha \in [0, 1]$. A subset K is called a **cone** if it is closed under positive scalar multiplication. A **polyhedral cone** is a set $C = \{x \in \mathbb{R}^n : Ax \geq 0\}$ for some matrix A. A polyhedral cone is convex and is the convex hull of a finite set of half hyperplanes. The **recession cone** of a set A in a linear space X is given by

$$\{y \in X : x + \lambda y \in A, \text{ all } x \in A, \lambda \in \mathbb{R}_+\}.$$

Farkas's Lemma Let A be an m by n matrix and b an m-dimensional vector. Then exactly one of the following two statements is true:

1. There exists an $x \in \mathbb{R}^n$ such that $Ax = b$ and $x \geq 0$.
2. There exists a $y \in \mathbb{R}^m$ such that $A^\mathsf{T} y \geq 0$ and $b^\mathsf{T} y < 0$.

This lemma states that a vector is either in a given convex cone, or that there exists a hyperplane separating the vector from the cone and there are no other possibilities. Common applications of Farkas's lemma include proving the strong and weak duality theorem associated with linear programming, game theory at a basic level, and the Kuhn–Tucker constraints.

Stiemke's Lemma Let A be an m by n matrix. Then exactly one of the following two statements is true:

1. There exists $x \in \mathbb{R}^n_{++}$ such that $Ax = 0$.
2. There exists $y \in \mathbb{R}^m$ such that $A^\mathsf{T} y > 0$.

These two lemmas are examples of the Theorem of the Alternative. They are useful in arbitrage pricing theory.

A real-valued function f defined on a convex subset C of a linear space is said to be **convex** if

$$f\left(\alpha x_1 + (1-\alpha)x_2\right) \leq \alpha f(x_1) + (1-\alpha)f(x_2)$$

for all $x_1, x_2 \in C$ and all $\alpha \in (0,1)$. If strict inequality holds whenever $x_1 \neq x_2$, then f is said to be **strictly convex**. A function g is **(strictly) concave** if $-g$ is (strictly) convex.

A real-valued function f defined on a convex subset C of a linear space is said to be **quasi-convex** if

$$f\left(\alpha x_1 + (1-\alpha)x_2\right) \leq \min\left\{f(x_1), f(x_2)\right\}$$

for all $x_1, x_2 \in C$ and all $\alpha \in (0,1)$. It is **strictly quasi-convex** if the inequality is strict when $x_1 \neq x_2$. A function f is (strictly) quasi-concave if $-f$ is (strictly) quasi-concave.

Let C be an open and convex set in $\mathbb{R}^n$, and let $f : C \to \mathbb{R}$ be concave. Then f is differentiable everywhere on C, except possibly at a set of points of Lebesgue measure zero. Moreover the derivative $Df = (\partial f / \partial x_1, ..., \partial f / \partial x_n)$ of f is continuous at all points where it exists. For $f : \mathbb{R}^n \to \mathbb{R}^m$, the derivative of f at x is denoted $Df(x) = \left(\partial f_i / \partial x_j(x)\right)_{m \times n}$.

Let C be an open and convex set in $\mathbb{R}^n$, and let $f : C \to \mathbb{R}$ be differentiable on C. Then f is concave on C if and only if

$$Df(x)(y-x) \geq f(y) - f(x) \quad \text{for all } x, y \in C.$$

If $f : C \to \mathbb{R}$ is twice differentiable on an open and convex set C, then f is concave (convex) if and only if $D^2 f(x)$ is a negative (positive) semidefinite matrix for all $x \in C$. If $D^2 f(x)$ is negative (positive) definite for all $x \in C$, then f is strictly concave (convex). The converse of the last result is not true, as shown by $f(x) = -x^4$.

Let X be a real normed vector space, and let X^* be the dual space of X. Denote the **dual pairing** (a bilinear function) by $\langle \cdot, \cdot \rangle : X^* \times X \to \mathbb{R}$. For a functional $f : X \to \mathbb{R} \cup \{+\infty\}$, taking values on the extended real number line, the **convex conjugate** $f^* : X^* \to \mathbb{R} \cup \{+\infty\}$ is defined in terms of the supremum by

$$f^*(x^*) = \sup_{x \in X} \langle x^*, x \rangle - f(x),$$

or, equivalently, in terms of the infimum by

$$f^*(x^*) = -\inf_{x \in X} f(x) - \langle x^*, x \rangle.$$

For example, the convex conjugate of an affine function

$$f(x) = a^{\mathsf{T}}x - b, \ x \in \mathbb{R}^n$$

is

$$f^*(x^*) = \sup_{x \in \mathbb{R}^n} (x^*)^{\mathsf{T}} x - a^{\mathsf{T}}x + b = \begin{cases} b & \text{if } x^* = a, \\ +\infty & \text{if } x^* \neq a. \end{cases}$$

The **indicator function for a set** M on X, denoted by δ_M, is defined as

$$\delta_M(x) = \begin{cases} 0 & \text{if } x \in M, \\ +\infty & \text{if } x \notin M. \end{cases}$$

This function is useful to transform a constrained optimization problem into an unconstraint problem:

$$\inf_{x \in M} f(x) \iff \inf_{x \in X} f(x) + \delta_M(x).$$

Let $f : A \to \mathbb{R} \cup \{\pm\infty\}$. The **effective domain** of f is defined as $\mathrm{dom}(f) = \{x \in A : f(x) < +\infty\}$. It is a **proper function** if $\mathrm{dom}(f) \neq \varnothing$ and $f(x) > -\infty$ for all $x \in A$.

Minmax Theorem Let X and Y be convex subsets of topological vector spaces, with X compact, and let $f : X \times Y \to R$ satisfy (1) for each $x \in X$, the function $f(x, y)$ is upper semicontinuous and quasi-concave on Y, and (2) for each $y \in Y$, the function $f(x, y)$ is lower semicontinuous and quasi-convex on X. Then

$$\sup_{y \in Y} \min_{x \in X} f(x, y) = \min_{x \in X} \sup_{y \in Y} f(x, y).$$

Nonlinear Optimization Problem Consider the following problem:

$$\inf_{x \in \mathbb{R}^n} f(x) \tag{C.1}$$

subject to

$$g_i(x) \leq 0, \quad i = 1, \dots, m, \tag{C.2}$$
$$h_j(x) = 0, \quad j = 1, \dots, p. \tag{C.3}$$

Define the **Lagrangian** as

$$L(x, \lambda, \mu) = f(x) + \lambda \cdot g + \mu \cdot h,$$

where $\lambda = (\lambda_1, ..., \lambda_m)$ and $\mu = (\mu_1, ..., \mu_p)$ are the **Lagrange multipliers** associated with the constraints (C.2) and (C.3), respectively. Define the **dual function** as

$$\phi(\lambda, \mu) = \inf_{x \in \mathbb{R}^n} L(x, \lambda, \mu).$$

Then

$$\phi(\lambda, \mu) \le p^*,$$

where p^* is the solution to the **primal problem** (C.1). Define the **dual problem** as

$$\sup_{(\lambda, \mu) \in \mathbb{R}^m \times \mathbb{R}^p} \phi(\lambda, \mu)$$

subject to $\lambda \ge 0$. Let the solution to the dual problem be d^*. We then have $d^* \le p^*$, which is called **weak duality**. The difference $d^* - p^*$ is called the duality gap. If $d^* = p^*$ holds, we say **strong duality** holds. Under some **constraint qualification conditions**, strong duality holds. One simple condition is **Slater's condition** for convex optimization: The functions f, g_1, ..., and g_m are convex, and there exists a point x such that

$$g_i(x) < 0 \quad \text{and} \quad h_j(x) = 0 \quad \text{all } i, j.$$

If f, g_i, and h_j are all differentiable, then the first-order necessary conditions for optimality (**Kuhn–Tucker conditions**) are given by

$$Df(x) + \lambda \cdot Dg(x) + \mu \cdot Dh(x) = 0,$$
$$\lambda_i \ge 0, \quad \lambda_i g_i(x) = 0, \ i = 1, ..., m,$$
$$g_i(x) \le 0, \quad i = 1, .., m,$$
$$h_j(x) = 0, \quad j = 1, ..., p.$$

For a minimizer x^* to satisfy the Kuhn–Tucker conditions above, we need a constraint qualification condition. One such condition is the Slater condition given above. Another one is that the gradients of the active inequality constraints and the gradients of the equality constraints are linearly independent at x^*. This result also applies to the case where there is no inequality constraint.

If f and all g_i are convex and all h_j are affine, then the preceding Kuhn–Tucker conditions are also sufficient for optimality. In the case without inequality constraints, we have the following sufficient conditions:

Theorem (Sufficient conditions for the Lagrange method)   Suppose that there exist x^* and μ^* such that the gradients of h_j at x^* are linearly independent and

$$Df(x^*) + \mu^* \cdot h(x^*) = 0.$$

Define

$$Z(x^*) = \{z \in \mathbb{R}^n : Dh(x^*) \cdot z = 0\},$$

and let D^2L^* denote the n by n matrix

$$D^2L(x^*, \mu^*) = D^2f(x^*) + \sum_{j=1}^{p} \mu_j^* D^2 h_j(x^*).$$

If $z'D^2L^*z < (>)0$ for all $z \in Z(x^*)$ with $z \neq 0$, then x^* is a local maximizer (minimizer) for f.

Let $X \subset \mathbb{R}^l$, $Y \subset \mathbb{R}^m$. A **correspondence** $\Gamma : X \to Y$ assigns a set $\Gamma(x) \subset Y$ to each $x \in X$. A correspondence $\Gamma : X \to Y$ is **lower hemi-continuous** (l.h.c.) at x if $\Gamma(x)$ is nonempty and if, for every $y \in \Gamma(x)$ and every sequence $x_n \to x$, there exists $N \geq 1$ and a sequence $\{y_n\}_{n=N}^{\infty}$ such that $y_n \to y$ and $y_n \in \Gamma(x_n)$, all $n \geq N$. A compact-valued correspondence $\Gamma : X \to Y$ is **upper hemi-continuous** (u.h.c.) at x if $\Gamma(x)$ is nonempty and if, for every sequence $x_n \to x$ and every sequence $\{y_n\}$ such that $y_n \in \Gamma(x_n)$, all n, there exists a convergent subsequence of $\{y_{n_k}\}$ whose limit point y is in $\Gamma(x)$.

A correspondence $\Gamma : X \to Y$ is **continuous** at x if it is both l.h.c. and u.h.c. at x. If Γ is single valued and u.h.c. (l.h.c.), then it is continuous. Let $f : \mathbb{R}_+^l \to \mathbb{R}_+$ be a continuous function, and define the correspondence $\Gamma : \mathbb{R}_+^l \to \mathbb{R}_+$ by $\Gamma(x) = [0, f(x)]$. Then Γ is continuous.

(Composite rule) If $\phi : X \to Y$ and $\psi : Y \to Z$ are compact valued and u.h.c. (l.h.c.), then the correspondence $\psi \circ \phi = \Gamma : X \to Z$ defined by

$$\Gamma(x) = \{z \in Z : z \in \psi(y) \quad \text{for some } y \in \phi(x)\}$$

is also compact valued and u.h.c. (l.h.c.)

(Product rule) Let $\Gamma_i : X \to Y_i$, $i = 1, ..., k$, be compact valued and u.h.c. (l.h.c.). Then $\Gamma : X \to Y = Y_1 \times \cdots \times Y_k$ defined by

$$\Gamma(x) = \{y \in Y : y = (y_1, ..., y_k), \text{ where } y_i \in \Gamma_i(x), i = 1, ..., k\},$$

is also compact valued and u.h.c. (l.h.c.).

The **graph** of a correspondence $\Gamma : X \to Y$ is the set

$$A = \{(x, y) \in X \times Y : y \in \Gamma(x)\}.$$

Closed Graph Theorem   Let $\Gamma : X \to Y$ be a nonempty-valued correspondence, and let A be the graph of Γ. Suppose that A is closed, and that for any bounded set $\widehat{X} \subset X$, the set $\Gamma(\widehat{X})$ is bounded. Then Γ is compact valued and u.h.c.

Theorem of the Maximum   Let $f : X \times Y \to \mathbb{R}$ be a continuous function, and let $\Gamma : X \to Y$ be a compact-valued and continuous correspondence. Then the function $h : X \to \mathbb{R}$, defined by

$$h(x) = \sup_{y \in \Gamma(x)} f(x,y),$$

is continuous, and the correspondence $G : X \to Y$, defined by

$$G(x) = \{y \in \Gamma(x) : h(x) = f(x,y)\},$$

is nonempty, compact valued, and u.h.c.

We give two examples to illustrate the theorem: (1) Let $X = \mathbb{R}$, $\Gamma(x) = Y = [-1,1]$, $f(x,y) = xy^2$. Then G is u.h.c, but not l.h.c. at $x = 0$. (2) Let $X = \mathbb{R}_+$, $\Gamma(x) = \{y \in \mathbb{R} : -x \le y \le x\}$, and $f(x,y) = \cos(y)$. Then G is u.h.c, but not l.h.c.

The following theorem is a form of the envelope condition.

Benveniste–Scheinkman Theorem   Let $X \subset R^l$ be a convex set, let $V : X \to \mathbb{R}$ be concave, let $x_0 \in \text{int}(X)$, and let D be a neighborhood of x_0. If there is a concave, differentiable function $W : D \to \mathbb{R}$, with $W(x_0) = V(x_0)$ and with $W(x) \le V(x)$ for all $x \in D$, then V is differentiable at x_0, and $V_i(x_0) = W_i(x_0)$, $i = 1, 2, ..., l$.

Theorem (Convergence)   Let $\Gamma : X \to Y$ be a convex- and compact valued, and continuous correspondence. Let $\{f_n\}$ be a sequence of continuous functions on A. Assume that for each n and each x, $f_n(x, \cdot)$ is strictly concave. Assume that f has the same properties and that $f_n \to f$ uniformly. Define

$$g_n(x) = \arg \max_{y \in \Gamma(x)} f_n(x,y),$$

$$g(x) = \arg \max_{y \in \Gamma(x)} f(x,y).$$

Then $g_n \to g$ pointwise. If X is compact, then the convergence is uniform.

A **partially ordered set** is a set X on which there is a binary relation $\preceq$ that satisfies the following properties:

1. (reflexivity) $x \preceq x$ for all $x \in X$.
2. (antisymmetry) If $x \preceq x'$ and $x' \preceq x$, then $x = x'$ for all $x, x' \in X$.
3. (transitivity) If $x \preceq x'$ and $x' \preceq x''$, then $x \preceq x''$ for all $x, x', x'' \in X$.

Let X' be a subset of a partially ordered set X. Say that x' is an **upper (lower) bound** for X' if $x' \in X$ and $x \preceq x' (x' \preceq x)$ for all $x \in X'$. If $x' \in X'$ is an upper (lower) bound for X', then x' is the **greatest (least) element** of X'. The **supremum (infimum)** of X' is the least upper bound (greatest lower bound) of X' and is denoted by $\sup_X(X')(\inf_X(X'))$. The underlying set X is important. For example, suppose that $X = \mathbb{R}, Y = [0,1) \cup \{3\}$, and $X' = [0,1)$. Then $\sup_X(X') = 1 \neq 3 = \sup_Y(X')$.

The **join (meet)** of elements $x, x' \in X$ is the least upper bound (greatest lower bound) of x and x'. They are denoted by $x \vee x'$ and $x \wedge x'$, respectively. A partially ordered set that contains the join and the meet of each pair of its elements is a **lattice**. A lattice in which each nonempty subset has a supremum and an infimum is **complete**. The Euclidean space $\mathbb{R}^n$ endowed with the partial order $\geq$ introduced earlier is a complete lattice. A function $f : X \to X$ is increasing if $f(x) \preceq f(y)$ for any $x \preceq y$.

Tarski's Fixed-Point Theorem   Suppose that X is a nonempty complete lattice and $f(x)$ is an increasing function from X into itself.

1. The set of fixed points of $f(x)$ in X is nonempty, $\sup_X(\{x \in X : x \preceq f(x)\})$ is the greatest fixed point, and $\inf_X(\{x \in X : f(x) \preceq x\})$ is the least fixed point.

2. The set of fixed points of $f(x)$ in X is a nonempty complete lattice.

An important feature of this theorem is that we do not need the function f to be continuous. The theorem fails if f is strictly decreasing, but it can be generalized to increasing correspondences. See Topkis (1998) for a discussion and an introduction to the lattice theory.

D   Measure and Probability Theory

Let S be a set, and let $\mathcal{S}$ be a family of its subsets. Then $\mathcal{S}$ is called an **algebra** if (1) $\varnothing, S \in \mathcal{S}$; (2) $A \in \mathcal{S}$ implies that $A^c = S \backslash A \in \mathcal{S}$; and (3) $A_1, ..., A_n \in \mathcal{S}$ implies that $\cup_{i=1}^n A_i \in \mathcal{S}$. If property (3) is replaced with (3)$'$, $A_n \in \mathcal{S}$, $n = 1, 2, ...$, implies that $\cup_{n=1}^\infty A_n \in \mathcal{S}$, then $\mathcal{S}$ is called a σ-**algebra**. In this case the pair $(S, \mathcal{S})$ is called a **measurable space**. Any set $A \in \mathcal{S}$ is called a **measurable set**.

A trivial σ-algebra is $\{\varnothing, S\}$. If S is finite or countable, then the collection of all subsets of S is a σ-algebra. Given a metric space (S, d), the **Borel algebra** $\mathcal{B}(S)$ is the smallest σ-algebra containing the open balls $A = \{s \in S : d(s, s_0) < \delta\}$, where $s_0 \in S$ and $\delta > 0$. An element of $\mathcal{B}(S)$ is called a **Borel set**.

Let $(S, \mathcal{S})$ be a measurable space. A **measure** is a real-valued function $\mu : \mathcal{S} \to \mathbb{R}$ such that (1) $\mu(\emptyset) = 0$; (2) $\mu(A) \geq 0$, all $A \in \mathcal{S}$; (3) if $\{A_n\}_{n=1}^\infty$ is a countable, disjoint sequence of subsets in $\mathcal{S}$, then $\mu(\cup_{n=1}^\infty A_n) = \sum_{n=1}^\infty \mu(A_n)$. $(S, \mathcal{S}, \mu)$ is called a **measure space**. If $\mu(S) = 1$, then it is called a **probability measure** and $(S, \mathcal{S}, \mu)$ is called a **probability space**. If we remove property 2, then μ is called a **signed measure**.

If the sequence in property 3 is finite, then μ is called a finitely additive measure or a **charge**. A finitely additive measure $v : \mathcal{S} \to \mathbb{R}_+$ is called **purely finitely additive** if whenever $\mu : \mathcal{S} \to \mathbb{R}_+$ is a countably additive measure and $\mu \leq v$ on $\mathcal{S}$, then $\mu = 0$.

Yosida–Hewitt Theorem   If $v : \mathcal{S} \to \mathbb{R}_+$ is a finitely additive measure, then there exists a unique decomposition $v = v_c + v_f$, where $v_c : \mathcal{S} \to \mathbb{R}_+$ is a countably additive measure and $v_f : \mathcal{S} \to \mathbb{R}_+$ is a purely finitely additive measure.

Hahn Decomposition Theorem   Given a measurable space $(S, \mathcal{S})$ and a signed measure μ on it, there exist two measurable sets P and N such that $P \cup N = S$ and $P \cap N = \varnothing$; $\mu(E) \geq 0$ for each $E \in \mathcal{S}$ such that $E \subset P$, meaning, P is a **positive set**; $\mu(E) \leq 0$ for each $E \in \mathcal{S}$ such that $E \subset N$, meaning, N is a **negative set**. Moreover this decomposition is unique up to adding to/subtracting μ-null sets from P and N.

Consider then two nonnegative measures μ^+ and μ^- defined by

$$\mu^+(E) = \mu(P \cap E) \quad \text{and} \quad \mu^-(E) = \mu(N \cap E)$$

for all measurable sets E. One can check that both μ^+ and μ^- are nonnegative measures, with one taking only finite values, and are called the **positive part** and **negative part of** μ, respectively, so that $\mu = \mu^+ - \mu^-$. The measure $|\mu| = \mu^+ + \mu^-$ is called the **variation of** μ, and its maximum possible value, $\|\mu\| = |\mu|(S)$, is called the **total variation of** μ. The set of signed measures is a linear space and the total variation is a norm, which can be equivalently defined as

$$\|\mu\| = \sup_{\{A_i\}} \sum_{i=1}^{k} |\mu(A_i)|,$$

where the supremum is over all finite partitions of S into disjoint measurable subsets.

The sum of two finite signed measures is a finite signed measure, as is the product of a finite signed measure by a real number: they are closed under linear combination. It follows that the set of finite signed measures on a measurable space $(S, \mathcal{S})$ is a real vector space; this is in contrast to positive measures, which form a convex cone but not a vector space. Furthermore the total variation defines a norm in respect to which the space of finite measurable space signed measures becomes a Banach space. If S is a compact separable metric space, then the space of finite signed Borel measures is the dual of the real Banach space of all continuous real-valued functions on S, by the Riesz Representation Theorem. This result can be generalized by removing the restriction of metric spaces.

It is easier to construct a measure on a small collection of sets, algebra, and then extend it to the larger collection, a σ-algebra. The definition of measure on an algebra $\mathcal{A}$ is the same as before, except that property (3) is replaced with (3)': if $\{A_n\}_{n=1}^{\infty}$ is a countable, disjoint sequence of subsets in $\mathcal{A}$ with $\cup_{n=1}^{\infty} A_n \in \mathcal{A}$, then $\mu(\cup_{n=1}^{\infty} A_n) = \sum_{n=1}^{\infty} \mu(A_n)$.

Caratheodory Extension Theorem   Let S be a set, $\mathcal{A}$ an algebra of its subsets, and μ a measure on $\mathcal{A}$. Let $\mathcal{S}$ be the smallest σ-algebra containing $\mathcal{A}$. Then there exits a measure μ^* on $\mathcal{S}$ such that $\mu^*(A) = \mu(A)$ for all $A \in \mathcal{A}$.

This theorem does not state uniqueness. We then introduce the following concept: if there is a sequence of sets $\{A_i\}_{i=1}^{n}$ in $\mathcal{A}$ with $\mu(A_i) < \infty$, all i, and $S = \cup_{i=1}^{\infty} A_i$, then μ is σ-**finite**. Clearly, any probability measure is σ-finite. The next theorem shows that the extension of a σ-finite measure is unique.

Hahn Extension Theorem   If μ is σ-finite, then the extension μ^* to $\mathcal{S}$ is unique.

Given a measure space $(S, \mathcal{S}, \mu)$, one would think that if $A \in \mathcal{S}$ has measure zero, then $C \subset A$ would too. But C may not be in $\mathcal{S}$, and hence $\mu(C)$ may be undefined. This gap is filled by the idea of the completion of a measure space.

Define

$$\mathcal{C} = \{C \subset S : C \subset A \text{ for some } A \in \mathcal{S} \text{ with } \mu(A) = 0\}.$$

Now consider starting with any set $B \in \mathcal{S}$, and then adding and subtracting from sets in $\mathcal{C}$. The **completion** of $\mathcal{S}$ is the family $\mathcal{S}'$ of sets constructed in this way. That is,

$$\mathcal{S}' = \{B' \subset S : B' = (B \cup C_1) \setminus C_2, \ B \in \mathcal{S}, C_1, C_2 \in \mathcal{C}\}.$$

This means that $\mathcal{S}'$ and $\mathcal{S}$ differ in subsets of sets of measure zero. The completion of a σ-algebra is a σ-algebra. The collection of **Lebesgue measurable sets** is the completion of Borel sets. The extension of a measure on the Borel sets to the Lebesgue measurable sets is called the **Lebesgue measure** or simply the **Borel measure**. Note that the Caratheodory Extension Theorem can be applied to the completion of measures.

Given a measurable space $(S, \mathcal{S})$, a real-valued function $f : S \to \mathbb{R}$ is **measurable with respect to $\mathcal{S}$ or ($\mathcal{S}$-measurable)** if

$$\{s \in S : f(s) \leq a\} \in \mathcal{S}, \quad \text{all } a \in \mathbb{R}.$$

If the space is a probability space, the f is called a **random variable**. Note that one can equivalently use "$\leq$", "$\geq$", "$<$", and "$>$." For example, for $S = \{x, y\}$, $\mathcal{S} = \{\varnothing, S, \{x\}, \{y\}\}$ and $\hat{\mathcal{S}} = \{\varnothing, S\}$ are both σ-algebras. All functions on S are $\mathcal{S}$-measurable, but only the constant functions are $\hat{\mathcal{S}}$-measurable. Any monotone or continuous function is measurable. Pointwise convergence preserves measuability. If f and g are $\mathcal{S}$-measuable, then $f + g, fg, |f|$, and cf are $\mathcal{S}$-measurable. The composition of Borel measurable functions are Borel measurable, but this is not true for Lebesgue measurable functions.

We can extend the definition of measurability to functions from any measurable space into any other measurable space. Let $(S, \mathcal{S})$ and $(T, \mathcal{T})$ be measurable spaces. Then the function $f : S \to T$ is **measurable** if the inverse image of every measurable set is measurable. Let Γ be a correspondence of S into T. Then the function $h : S \to T$ is a measurable selection from Γ if h is measurable and $h(s) \in \Gamma(s)$ for all $s \in S$.

Measurable Selection Theorem   Let $\Gamma : S \to T$ be a nonempty compact-valued and upper hemi-continuous correspondence. Then there exists a measurable selection from Γ.

We can establish measurability of a function by showing that it is the limit of a sequence of simpler functions. A function $f : S \to \mathbb{R}$ is called a **simple function** if $f(s) = \sum_{i=1}^{n} a_i \mathbf{1}_{A_i}(s)$, where the sets $\{A_i\}$ form a partition of S and $\mathbf{1}_{A_i}$ is an indicator function. Any measurable function can be approximated by simple functions.

We now define integration. The idea is to start with nonnegative measurable simple functions, and then to extend to nonnegative measurable functions. We finally define integration for arbitrary measurable functions. Let $(S, \mathcal{S}, \mu)$ be a measure space. Let $M(S, \mathcal{S})$ be the space of measurable, extended real-valued functions on S, and let $M^+(S, \mathcal{S})$ be the subset consisting of nonnegative functions.

For any $f \in M^+(S, \mathcal{S})$, the **integral** of f with respect to μ is

$$\int f(s) \mu(ds) = \sup_{\phi \in \wp} \int \phi(s) \mu(ds),$$

where $\wp$ is the set of all simple functions ϕ such that $0 \le \phi \le f$. If $A \in \mathcal{S}$, then the integral of f over A with respect to μ is

$$\int_A f(s) \mu(ds) = \int f(s) \mathbf{1}_A(s) \mu(ds).$$

Note that integrals may be infinity.

For any $f \in M(S, \mathcal{S})$, the **integral** of f with respect to μ is

$$\int f(s) \mu(ds) = \int f^+ d\mu - \int f^- d\mu$$

if both f^+ and f^- have finite integrals. In this case f is **integrable**. Similarly

$$\int_A f(s) \mu(ds) = \int_A f^+ d\mu - \int_A f^- d\mu.$$

A class $\mathcal{C}$ of random variables is called **uniformly integrable** if, given any $\varepsilon > 0$, there exists $K \ge 0$ such that $E\left[|X| \mathbf{1}_{|X| \ge K}\right] \le \varepsilon$ for all $X \in \mathcal{C}$.

The following theorem shows that the definition of integrals does not depend on a particular sequence of simple functions.

Monotone Convergence Theorem   If $\{f_n\}$ is a monotone increasing sequence of functions in $M^+(S, \mathcal{S})$ converging pointwise to f, then $\int f d\mu = \lim_{n \to \infty} \int f_n d\mu$.

The following lemma is useful in proving convergence of a sequence of integrals.

Fatou's Lemma   If $\{f_n\}$ is a sequence of functions in $M^+(S, \mathcal{S})$, then $\int \liminf f_n d\mu \le \liminf \int f_n d\mu$.

Dominated Convergence Theorem   Let $(S, \mathcal{S}, \mu)$ be a measurable space, and let $\{f_n\}$ be a sequence of integrable functions that converges almost surely to a measurable function f. If there exists an integrable function g such that $|f_n| \leq g$ all n, then f is integrable and $\int f d\mu = \lim_{n \to \infty} \int f_n d\mu$.

Let λ and μ be finite measures on $(S, \mathcal{S})$. λ is **absolutely continuous** with respect to μ ($\lambda << \mu$) if $\lambda(A) > 0$ implies that $\mu(A) > 0$ for all $A \in \mathcal{S}$. If there are disjoint measurable sets A, B such that $\lambda(C) = \lambda(A \cap C)$ and $\mu(D) = \lambda(B \cap D)$ for any measurable sets C and D, then λ and μ are **mutually singular**, denoted $\lambda \perp \mu$.

Radon–Nikodym Theorem   Let λ and μ be σ-finite positive measures on (S, S), with $\lambda << \mu$. Then there is an integrable function h such that

$$\lambda(A) = \int_A h(s) \mu(ds), \quad \text{all } A.$$

The function is almost surely unique.

The function h is called the **Radon–Nikodym derivative** of λ with respect to μ, denoted by $d\lambda/d\mu$. If $\lambda << \mu$ and $\mu << \lambda$, then λ and μ are **mutually absolutely continuous** or **equivalent**. In this case $d\lambda/d\mu = (d\mu/d\lambda)^{-1}$.

The probability density function of a random variable is the Radon–Nikodym derivative of the induced measure with respect to some base measure (usually the Lebesgue measure for continuous random variables). The Radon–Nikodym theorem is important in finance and is used for converting a physical measure into a risk-neutral measure.

Using this theorem, we can show that any two measures can be uniquely represented as the sums of "common" and mutually singular parts. Formally, let λ_1 and λ_2 be finite measures on $(S, \mathcal{S})$. Then there is a triple of measures ν, α_1, and α_2 such that $\lambda_i = \nu + \alpha_i$, $i = 1, 2$, and $\alpha_1 \perp \alpha_2$.

The Radon–Nikodym theorem can be used to prove the existence of conditional expectation for probability measures. Let $(\Omega, \mathcal{F}, \mu)$ be a probability space, let $\mathcal{A} \subset \mathcal{F}$ be a σ-algebra, and let $f : \Omega \to \mathbb{R}$ be integrable. Then the **conditional expectation of f relative to $\mathcal{A}$** is an $\mathcal{A}$-measurable function $E[f|\mathcal{A}] : \Omega \to \mathbb{R}$ such that

$$\int_C E[f|\mathcal{A}](\omega) \mu(d\omega) = \int_C f(\omega) \mu(d\omega), \quad \text{all } C \in \mathcal{A}.$$

Let f and g be two random variables, let $\mathcal{G}$ be the σ-algebra generated by g, namely by the sets of the form $\{\omega \in \Omega : g(\omega) \leq a\}$, $a \in \mathbb{R}$. Then $\mathcal{G} \subset \mathcal{F}$, and we write $E[f|\mathcal{G}]$ as $E[f|g]$.

Let P and Q be two probability measures on $(\Omega, \mathcal{F})$ such that $Q << P$. If $E^Q[|f|] < \infty$, then

$$E^Q[f|\mathcal{G}] = \frac{E^P\left[\frac{dQ}{dP}f|\mathcal{G}\right]}{E^P\left[\frac{dQ}{dP}|\mathcal{G}\right]}$$

for any $\mathcal{G} \subset \mathcal{F}$, where E^Q denotes the expectation operator with respect to the measure Q.

Let $(X, \mathcal{X})$ and $(Y, \mathcal{Y})$ be measurable spaces, and let $Z = X \times Y$. A set $C = A \times B \subset Z$ is a **measurable rectangle** if $A \subset \mathcal{X}$ and $B \subset \mathcal{Y}$. Let $\mathcal{C}$ be the set of all measurable rectangles, and $\mathcal{A}$ the set of all finite unions of measurable rectangles. Then $\mathcal{A}$ is an algebra. Let $\mathcal{Z} = \mathcal{X} \otimes \mathcal{Y}$ denote the σ-algebra generated by the algebra $\mathcal{A}$. The measurable space $(Z, \mathcal{Z})$ or $(X \times Y, \mathcal{X} \otimes \mathcal{Y})$ is called the **product space**.

To define a measure on the product space, we use the following result:

Theorem Let $\mu : \mathcal{C} \to \mathbb{R}_+$ have the following properties: (a) $\mu(\varnothing) = 0$, and (b) if $\{C_i\} = \{A_i \times B_i\}_{i=1}^{\infty}$ is a sequence of disjoint sets in $\mathcal{C}$ and $\cup_{i=1}^{\infty} C_i$ is in $\mathcal{C}$, then $\mu(\cup_{i=1}^{\infty} C_i) = \sum_{i=1}^{\infty} \mu(C_i)$. Then there is a measure on the algebra generated by $\mathcal{C}$ that coincides with μ on $\mathcal{C}$.

Using this theorem and the Caratheodory and Hahn Extension Theorems, we deduce that to define a measure on a product space, it is sufficient to find a function μ on the measurable rectangles that satisfies parts a and b of the theorem above. The theorem above can be extended to any space that is the product of a finite number of measurable spaces.

Let $(\Omega_1, \mathcal{F}_1, \mu_1)$ and $(\Omega_2, \mathcal{F}_2, \mu_2)$ be two σ-finite measure spaces. For any measurable rectangle $A_1 \times A_2$, we define

$$\mu(A_1 \times A_2) = \mu_1(A_1)\mu_2(A_2).$$

Then μ can be extended to $\mathcal{F}_1 \otimes \mathcal{F}_2$ such that for all $A \in \mathcal{F}_1 \otimes \mathcal{F}_1$,

$$\mu(A) = \int_{\Omega_1}\left(\int_{\Omega_2} \mathbf{1}_A(x, y)\, d\mu_2(y)\right) d\mu_1(x).$$

We call μ the **product measure** and denote it by $\mu_1 \otimes \mu_2$.

To study properties of product measures, we introduce the following concept and a useful lemma. A **monotone class** is a nonempty collection $\mathfrak{M}$ of sets such that $\mathfrak{M}$ contains (1) the union of every nested increasing sequence of sets $A_1 \subset A_2 \subset \ldots$ of sets in $\mathfrak{M}$ and (2) the intersection of every nested decreasing sequence $A_1 \supset A_2 \supset \ldots$ of sets in $\mathfrak{M}$. Every σ-algebra is a monotone class. If a monotone class is an algebra, then it is a σ-algebra.

Monotone Class Lemma   Let S be a set, and let $\mathcal{A}$ be an algebra of subsets of S. Then the monotone class $\mathfrak{M}$ generated by $\mathcal{A}$ is the same as the σ-algebra $\mathcal{S}$ generated by $\mathcal{A}$.

A very useful argument follows immediately from this lemma. Let P be some property of sets. Then to establish that P holds for all sets in S, it suffices to show that:

1. P holds for all sets in the algebra $\mathcal{A}$; and

2. the family of sets for which P holds is a monotone class.

It is usually easier to prove that the family of sets for which a property holds is a monotone class than it is to prove that the family is a σ-algebra. We will use this argument to show that a property P holds for all sets in a product σ-algebra by focusing on the algebra generated by the measurable rectangles.

Let $(X, \mathcal{X})$ and $(Y, \mathcal{Y})$ be measurable spaces and $(X \times Y, \mathcal{X} \otimes \mathcal{Y})$ be the product space. Let $B \subset X \times Y$ and $x \in X$. Then the x-**section of** B is the set in Y, $B_x = \{y \in Y : (x,y) \in B\}$. The y-section of B denoted B_y is defined similarly. Let $f : X \times Y \to \mathbb{R}$, and let $x \in X$. Then the x-**section of** f is the function $f_x : Y \to \mathbb{R}$ defined by $f_x(y) = f(x,y)$. The y-section of f, $f_y : X \to \mathbb{R}$ is defined similarly. Using the Monotone Class Lemma, we can show that every section of a measurable set is measurable, as is every section of a measurable function.

Fubini Theorem   Let $(\Omega_1, \mathcal{F}_1, \mu_1)$ and $(\Omega_2, \mathcal{F}_2, \mu_2)$ be two σ-finite measure spaces. Let $f : \Omega_1 \times \Omega_2 \to R$ be an integrable measurable function, that is,

$$\int_{\Omega_1 \times \Omega_2} |f| \, d\mu_1 \otimes \mu_2 < \infty.$$

Then

$$\int_{\Omega_1 \times \Omega_2} f d\mu_1 \otimes \mu_2 = \int_{\Omega_1} \left(\int_{\Omega_2} f d\mu_2 \right) d\mu_1 = \int_{\Omega_2} \left(\int_{\Omega_1} f d\mu_1 \right) d\mu_2.$$

Modes of Convergence   We fix a probability space $(\Omega, \mathcal{F}, P)$. Say that a sequence $\{X_t\}$ of random variables **converges in distribution** to a random variable X, written $X_t \xrightarrow{d} X$, if, for any bounded continuous function $f : \mathbb{R} \to \mathbb{R}$, we have $E[f(X_t)] \to E[f(x)]$. If $\{X_t\}$ is real valued, the definition is equivalent to $\lim_{t \to \infty} F_t(x) = F(x)$ for every x at which F is continuous, where F_t and F are cumulative distributions functions of X_t and X, respectively. The process $\{X_t\}$ **converges in probability** to X, written $X_t \xrightarrow{p} X$, if for all $\varepsilon > 0$,

$$P(\omega \in \Omega : |X_t(\omega) - X(\omega)| \geq \varepsilon) \to 0.$$

The process $\{X_t\}$ **converges almost surely** to X, written $X_t \xrightarrow{a.s.} X$, if

$$P(\omega \in \Omega : X_t(\omega) \to X(\omega)) = 1.$$

The process $\{X_t\}$ **converges in** L^p to X, written $X_t \xrightarrow{L^p} X$, if

$$\lim_{t \to \infty} E\left[|X_t - X|^p\right] = 0, \ 0 < p < \infty.$$

Convergence almost surely implies convergence in probability, which in turn implies convergence in distribution. Convergence in L^p implies convergence in probability, which in turn implies convergence almost surely along a subsequence.

Let $(\mathbb{X}, \mathcal{X})$ be a measurable space and let $\{\lambda_n\}$ and λ be measures on it. Then (1) $\{\lambda_n\}$ is defined to **converge weakly** to λ if

$$\lim_{n \to \infty} \int f d\lambda_n = \int f d\lambda$$

for any bounded continuous function $f : \mathbb{X} \to \mathbb{R}$; (2) $\{\lambda_n\}$ is defined to **converge strongly** to λ if

$$\lim_{n \to \infty} \int f d\lambda_n = \int f d\lambda$$

for any bounded measurable function $f : \mathbb{X} \to \mathbb{R}$ and if the rate of convergence is uniform for all f such that $\|f\| = \sup_{x \in \mathbb{X}} |f(x)| \leq 1$.

The sequence of measures $\{\lambda_n\}$ converges strongly to λ if and only if one the following two equivalent conditions holds:

$$\lim_{n \to \infty} \|\lambda_n - \lambda\|_{TV} = 0$$

or

$$\lim_{n \to \infty} |\lambda_n(A) - \lambda(A)| = 0, \quad A \in \mathcal{X},$$

and the latter convergence is uniform in A.

A sequence $\{X_n\}$ of random variables on a given probability space is **independently distributed** if, for any finite subset $\{X_1, ..., X_k\}$ and any bounded measurable functions $f_i : \mathbb{R} \to \mathbb{R}$, $1 \leq i \leq k$, we have

$$E[f_1(X_1)f_2(X_2) ... f_k(X_k)] = E[f_1(X_1)]E[f_2(X_2)] ... E[f_k(X_k)].$$

A **stochastic process** on $(\Omega, \mathcal{F}, P)$ is an increasing sequence of σ-algebras $\mathcal{F}_1 \subset \mathcal{F}_2 \cdots \subset \mathcal{F}$, a measurable space $(Z, \mathcal{Z})$, and a sequence of functions $X_t : \Omega \to Z$ such that each X_t is $\mathcal{F}_t$-measurable. The sequence $\{\mathcal{F}_t\}$ is called a **filtration**. We simply denote this stochastic process by (X_t) or $\{X_t\}$ and say that it is **adapted to** $\{\mathcal{F}_t\}$. A **finite-dimensional probability measure** for a stochastic process (X_t) is

$$P_{t+1,...,t+n}(C) = P(\{\omega \in \Omega : (X_{t+1}(\omega), ..., X_{t+n}(\omega)) \in C\}).$$

This process is **stationary** if $P_{t+1,\ldots,t+n}(C)$ is independent of t for all n and C. A **stopping time** is a random variable $\tau : \Omega \to \{0,1,\ldots+\infty\}$ such that for each time t the event $\{\omega \in \Omega : \tau(\omega) \geq t\}$ is in $\mathcal{F}_t$.

A process (X_t) is a **supermartingale (submartingale)** if X_t is integrable for each t and $E[X_t|\mathcal{F}_s] \leq (\geq) X_s$ for all $t \geq s$. It is a **martingale** if it is both a supermartingale and a submartingale. A martingale can also be equivalently defined as an adapted integrable process such that for any bounded stopping time τ, we have $E[X_\tau] = E[X_0]$.

Define the **conditional density process** of Q with respect to P:

$$\xi_t = E_t\left[\frac{dQ}{dP}\right], \quad t = 0,1,2,\ldots.$$

The process (ξ_t) is a martingale such that $E[\xi_t] = 1$. For any adapted process (x_t),

$$E_t^Q[x_{t+1}] = E_t^P\left[\frac{\xi_{t+1}}{\xi_t}x_t\right].$$

Martingale Convergence Theorem   Let (X_t) be a submartingale such that $\sup_t E[|X_t|] < \infty$. Then $\lim_{t\to\infty} X_t$ exists and is finite almost surely.

The condition of the theorem is satisfied for any nonpositive submartingale, any nonnegative supermatingale, or any martingale that is uniformly bounded from above or from below. For example, if (X_t) is a nonnegative supermartingale, then $E[|X_t|] = E[X_t] \leq E[X_0] < \infty$ for all t.

References

Abel, Andrew B. 1980. Empirical investment equations: An integrated framework. *Journal of Monetary Economics* 12 (6, suppl.): 39–91.

Abel, Andrew B. 1982. Dynamic effects of permanent and temporary tax policies in a Q model of investment. *Journal of Monetary Economics* 9 (3): 353–73.

Abel, Andrew B. 1999. Risk premia and term premia in general equilibrium. *Journal of Monetary Economics* 43 (1): 3–33.

Abel, Andrew B. 2002. An exploration of the effects of pessimism and doubt on asset returns. *Journal of Economic Dynamics and Control* 26 (7–8): 1075–92.

Abel, Andrew B., and Janice C. Eberly. 1994. A unified model of investment under uncertainty. *American Economic Review* 84 (5): 1369–84.

Abreu, Dilip 1988. On the theory of infinitely repeated games with discounting. *Econometrica* 56 (2): 383–96.

Abreu, Dilip, David Pearce, and Ennio Stacchetti. 1986. Optimal cartel equilibria with imperfect monitoring. *Journal of Economic Theory* 39 (1): 251–69.

Abreu, Dilip, David Pearce, and Ennio Stacchetti. 1990. Toward a theory of discounted repeated games with imperfect monitoring. *Econometrica* 58 (5): 1041–63.

Acemoglu, Daron. 2008. *Introduction to Modern Economic Growth*. Princeton: Princeton University Press.

Acemoglu, Daron, and Martin K. Jensen. 2012. Robust comparative statics in large dynamic economies. Working paper. MIT.

Adda, Jerome, and Russell W. Cooper. 2003. *Dynamic Economics: Quantitative Methods and Applications*. Cambridge: MIT Press.

Adjemian Stéphane, Houtan Bastani, Michel Juillard, Frédéric Karamé, Ferhat Mihoubi, George Perendia, Johannes Pfeifer, Marco Ratto, and Sébastien Villemot. 2011. *Dynare: Reference Manual, Version 4*. Dynare working papers, 1. CEPREMAP.

Aiyagari, S. Rao. 1994. Uninsured idiosyncratic risk and aggregate saving. *Quarterly Journal of Economics* 109 (3): 659–84.

Allais, Maurice F. C. 1953. Le comportement de l'homme rationnel devant le risque: Critique des postulats et axiomes de l'école Américaine. *Econometrica* 21 (4): 503–46.

Allais, Maurice F. C. 1979. The so-called Allais paradox and rational decisions under uncertainty. In Maurice F. C. Allais and Ole Hagen, eds., *Expected Utility Hypotheses and the Allais Paradox*. Berlin: Springer, 437–681.

Altug, Sumru. 1989. Time-to-build and aggregate fluctuations: Some new evidence. *International Economic Review* 30 (4): 889–920.

Alvarez, Fernando, and Nancy L. Stokey. 1998. Dynamic programming with homogeneous functions. *Journal of Economic Theory* 82 (1): 167–89.

Amemiya, Takeshi. 1985. The nonlinear two-stage least-squares estimator. *Journal of Econometrics* 2 (2): 105–10.

An, Sungbae, and Frank Schorfheide. 2007. Bayesian analysis of DSGE models. *Econometric Reviews* 26 (2–4): 113–72.

Anderson, Evan W. 2005. The dynamics of risk-sensitive allocations. *Journal of Economic Theory* 125 (2): 93–150.

Anderson, Evan W., Lars Peter Hansen, Ellen R. McGrattan, and Thomas J. Sargent. 1996. Mechanics of forming and estimating dynamic linear economies. In Hans M. Amman, David A. Kendrick, and John Rust, eds., *Handbook of Computational Economics*, vol. 1. Amsterdam: Elsevier, 171–252.

Anderson, Evan W., Lars Peter Hansen, and Thomas J. Sargent. 2003. A quartet of semigroups for model specification, robustness, prices of risk, and model detection. *Journal of the European Economic Association* 1 (1): 68–123.

Andolfatto. David. 1996. Business cycles and labor-market search. *American Economic Review* 86 (1): 112–32.

Andrews, Donald W. K. 1991. Heteroskedasticity and autocorrelation consistent covariance matrix estimation. *Econometrica* 59 (3): 817–58.

Arellano, Manuel. 2003. *Panel Data Econometrics*. New York: Oxford University Press.

Aruoba, S. Borağan, Jesús Fernández-Villaverde, and Juan F. Rubio-Ramírez. 2006. Comparing solution methods for dynamic equilibrium economies. *Journal of Economic Dynamics and Control* 30 (12): 2477–2508.

Auerbach, Alan J. 1979. Wealth maximization and the cost of capital. *Quarterly Journal of Economics* 99 (1): 433–46.

Azariadis. Costas. 1993. *Intertemporal Macroeconomics*. Oxford, UK: Blackwell.

Backus, David, and John Driffill. 1986. The consistency of optimal policy in stochastic rational expectations models. Discussion paper 124. Centre for Economic Policy Research, London.

Backus, David, Bryan Routledge, and Stanley E. Zin. 2004. Exotic preferences for macroeconomists. In Mark Gertler and Kenneth Rogoff, eds., *NBER Macroeconomics Annual 2004*. Cambridge: MIT Press, 319–90.

Balasko, Yves, and Karl Shell. 1980. The overlapping-generations model I: The case of pure exchange without money. *Journal of Economic Theory* 23 (3): 281–306.

Bansal, Ravi, and Amir Yaron. 2004. Risks for the long run: A potential resolution of asset pricing puzzles. *Journal of Finance*, 59 (4): 1481–1509.

Barillas, Francisco, Lars Peter Hansen, and Thomas, J. Sargent. 2009. Doubts or variability? *Journal of Economic Theory* 144 (6): 2388–2418.

Barro, Robert J., and David B. Gordon. 1983a. A positive theory of monetary policy in a natural rate model. *Journal of Political Economy* 91 (4): 589–610.

Barro, Robert J., and David B. Gordon. 1986. Rules, discretion and reputation in a model of monetary policy. *Journal of Monetary Economics* 12 (1): 101–21.

Baumol, William J. 1952. The transaction demand for cash: An inventory theoretic approach. *Quarterly Journal of Economics* 66 (4): 545–56.

Becker, Robert A. 1980. On the long-run steady State in a simple dynamic model of equilibrium with heterogeneous households. *Quarterly Journal of Economics* 95 (2): 375–82.

Bellman, Richard E. 1957. *Dynamic Programming*. Princeton: Princeton University Press.

Benigno, Pierpaolo, and Michael Woodford. 2005. Inflation stabilization and welfare: The case of a distorted steady state. *Journal of the European Economic Association* 3 (6): 1185–1236.

Bernanke, Ben S., and Alan S. Blinder. 1992. The federal funds rate and the channels of monetary transmission. *American Economic Review* 82 (4): 901–21.

Bernanke, Ben S., and Ilian Mihov. 1997. What does the Bundesbank target? *European Economic Review* 41 (6): 1025–53.

Bernanke, Ben S., Mark Gertler, and Simon Gilchrist. 1999. The financial accelerator in a quantitative business cycle framework. In John B. Taylor and Michael Woodford, eds., *Handbook of Macroeconomics*, Vol. 1. Amsterdam: Elsevier, 1341–93.

Berry, Donald A., and Bert Fristedt. 1985. Bandit problems: Sequential allocation of experiments. *Monographs on Statistics and Applied Probability*. London: Chapman and Hall.

Bertsekas, Dimitri P. 1987. *Dynamic Programming: Deterministic and Stochastic Models*. Englewood Cliffs, NJ: Prentice-Hall.

Bertsekas, Dimitri P., and Steven E. Shreve. 1978. *Stochastic Optimal Control: The Discrete Time Case*. New York: Academic Press.

Bewley, Truman F. 1980. The optimum quantity of money. In John H. Kareken and Neil Wallace, eds., *Models of Monetary Economies*. Minneapolis: Federal Reserve Bank of Minneapolis, 169–210.

Bewley, Truman F. 1986. Stationary monetary equilibrium with a continuum of independently fluctuating consumers. In Werner Hildenbrand and Andreu Mas-Colell, eds., *Contributions to Mathematical Economics in Honor of Gerard Debreu*. Amsterdam: North Holland, 79–102

Billingsley, Patrick. 1961. Statistical methods in Markov chains. *Annals of Mathematical Statistics* 32 (1): 12–40.

Billingsley, Patrick. 1995. *Probability and Measure*. New York: Wiley.

Billingsley Patrick. 1999. *Convergence of Probability Measures*, 2nd ed. New York: Wiley.

Blackwell, David. 1965. Discounted dynamic programming. *Annals of Mathematical Statistics* 36 (1): 226–35.

Blanchard, Olivier J., and Stanley Fischer. 1989. *Lectures on Macroeconomics*. Cambridge: MIT Press.

Blanchard, Olivier J., and Charles M. Kahn. 1980. The solution of linear difference models under rational expectations. *Econometrica* 48 (5): 1305–11

Blanchard, Olivier J., and Mark. W. Watson. 1982. Bubbles, rational expectations and speculative markets. In Paul Wachtel, ed., *Crisis in Economic and Financial Structure: Bubbles, Bursts, and Shocks.* Lexington, MA: Lexington Books.

Bolton, Patrick, and Mathias Dewatripont. 2005. *Contract Theory.* Cambridge: MIT Press.

de Boor, Carl. 1978. *A Practical Guide to Splines.* Berlin: Springer.

Boyd III. John H. 1990. Recursive utility and the Ramsey problem. *Journal of Economic Theory* 50 (2): 326–45.

Bradford, David F. 1981. The incidence and allocation effects of a tax on corporate distributions. *Journal of Public Economics* 15 (1): 1–22.

Breeden, Douglas T. 1979. An intertemporal asset pricing model with stochastic consumption and investment opportunities. *Journal of Financial Economics* 7 (3): 265–96.

Brock, William A. 1974. Money and growth: The case of long run perfect foresight. *International Economic Review* 15 (3): 750–77.

Brock, William A., and Leonard Mirman. 1972. Optimal economic growth and uncertainty: The discounted case. *Journal of Economic Theory* 4 (3): 479–513.

Bruno, Michael, and Stanley Fischer. 1986. The inflationary process: Shocks and accommodation. In Yoram Ben Porath, ed., *The Israeli Economy: Maturing through Crises.* Cambridge: Harvard University Press, 347–71.

Bullard, James, and Kaushik Mitra. 2002. Learning about monetary policy rules. *Journal of Monetary Economics* 49 (6): 1105–29.

Cagan, Phillip. 1956. The monetary dynamics of hyperinflation. In Milton Friedman, ed., *Studies in the Quantity Theory of Money.* Chicago: University of Chicago Press.

Calvo, Guillermo A. 1983. Staggered prices in a utility-maximizing framework. *Journal of Monetary Economics* 12 (3): 383–98.

Campanale, Claudio, Rui Castro, and Gian Luca Clementi. 2010. Asset pricing in a production economy with Chew–Dekel preferences. *Review of Economic Dynamics* 13 (2): 379–402.

Campbell, John Y. 1986. Bond and stock returns in a simple exchange model. *Quarterly Jounal of Economics* 101 (4): 785–804.

Campbell, John Y. 1996. Understanding risk and return. *Journal of Political Economy* 104 (2): 298–345.

Campbell, John Y. 1999. Asset prices, consumption, and the business cycle. In John B. Taylor and Michael Woodford, eds., *Handbook of Macroeconomics*, vol. 1. Amsterdam: Elsevier, 1231–1303.

Campbell, John Y., Andrew W. Lo, and A. Craig MacKinglay. 1997. *The Econometrics of Financial Markets.* Princeton: Princeton University Press.

Campbell, John Y., and Robert J. Shiller. 1988. Stock price, earnings, and expected dividends. *Journal of Finance* 43 (3): 661–76.

Carlstrom, Charles T., and Timothy S. Fuerst. 2001. Real indeterminacy in monetary models with nominal interest rate distortions. *Review of Economic Dynamics* 4 (4): 767–89.

Cass, David. 1965. Optimum growth in an aggregative model of capital accumulation. *Review of Economic Studies* 32 (3): 233–40.

Cass, David. 1972. On capital overaccumulation in the aggregate neoclassical model of economic growth: A complete characterization. *Journal of Economic Theory* 4 (2): 200–23.

Cayley, Arthur. 1875. Mathematical questions with their solutions. *The Educational Times* 23: 18–19. See *The Collected Mathematical Papers of Arthur Cayley*, vol. 10. Cambridge: Cambridge University Press, 587–88.

Cecchetti, Stephen G., Pok-sang Lam, and Nelson C., Mark. 1990. Mean reversion in equilibrium asset prices. *American Economic Review* 80 (3): 398–418.

Cecchetti, Stephen G., Pok-sang Lam, and Nelson C., Mark. 1993. The equity premium and the risk-free rate: Matching the moments. *Journal of Monetary Economics* 31 (1): 21–45.

Chamberlain, Gary, and Charles Wilson. 2000. Optimal intertemporal consumption under uncertainty. *Review of Economic Dynamics* 3 (3): 365–95.

Chang, Roberto. 1998. Credible monetary policy in an infinite horizon model: Recursive approach. *Journal of Economic Theory* 81 (2): 431–61.

Chari, V. V., and Patrick J. Kehoe. 1990. Sustainable plans. *Journal of Political Economy* 98 (4): 783–802.

Chari, V. V., Patrick J. Kehoe, and Ellen R. McGrattan. 2007. Business cycle accounting. *Econometrica* 75 (3): 781–836.

Chari, V. V., Patrick J., Kehoe, and Edward C., Prescott. 1989. Time consistency and policy. In Robert Barro, ed., *Modern Business Cycle Theory.* Cambridge: Harvard University Press, 265–305.

Chen, Hui, Nengjiu Ju, and Jianjun Miao. 2012. Dynamic asset allocation with ambiguous return predictability. Working paper 15. Boston University. Department of Economics.

Chew, Soo Hong. 1983. A generalization of the quasilinear mean with application to the measurement of income inequality and decision theory resolving the allais paradox. *Econometrica* 51 (4): 1065–92.

Chew, Soo Hong, and Larry G. Epstein. 1989. The structure of preference and attitudes towards the timing of the resolution of uncertainty. *International Economic Review* 30 (1): 103–17.

Chow, Chee-Seng, and John N. Tsitsiklis. 1991. An optimal multigrid algorithm for continuous state discrete time stochastic control. *IEEE Transactions on Automatic Control* 36 (8): 898–914.

Chow, Gregory. 1997. *Dynamic Economics: Optimization by the Lagrange Method.* New York: Oxford University Press.

Christiano, Lawrence J., and Martin Eichenbaum. 1992. Current real business cycle theories and aggregate labor-market fluctuations. *American Economic Review* 82 (3): 430–50.

Christiano, Lawrence J., and Martin Eichenbaum. 1996. Sticky price and limited participation models of money: A comparison. Working paper 5804 NBER.

Christiano, Lawrence J., and Martin Eichenbaum. 1998. Modeling money. Working paper 6371. NBER.

Christiano, Lawrence J., and Jonas D. M. Fisher. 2000. Algorithms for solving dynamic models with occasionally binding constraints, *Journal of Economic Dynamics and Control* 24 (8): 1179–1232.

Christiano, Lawrence J., Martin Eichenbaum, and Charles Evans. 2005. Nominal rigidities and the dynamic effects of a shock to monetary policy. *Journal of Political Economy* 113 (1): 1–45.

Clarida, Richard H. 1987. Consumption, liquidity constraints and asset accumulation in the presence of random income fluctuations. *International Economic Review* 28 (2): 339–51.

Clower, Robert W. 1967. A reconsideration of the microfoundations of monetary theory. *Western Economic Journal* 6 (1): 1–8.

Cochrane, John H. 2001. *Asset Pricing*. Princeton: Princeton University Press.

Cochrane, John H. 2005. Financial markets and the real economy, Working paper 11193. NBER.

Cogan, John F., Tobias Cwik, John B., Taylor, and Volker Wieland. 2010. New Keynesian versus old Keynesian government spending multipliers. *Journal of Economic Dynamics and Control* 34 (3): 281–95.

Cogley, Timothy, and James M. Nason. 1995. Output dynamics in real-business-cycle models. *American Economic Review* 85 (3): 492–511.

Collard, Fabrice, Sujoy Mukerji, Kevin Sheppard, and Jean-Marc Tallon. 2009. Ambiguiy and the historical equity premium. Working paper. Oxford University.

Cooley, Thomas F. 1995. *Frontier of Business Cycle Research*, Princeton: Princeton University Press.

Cooper, Russell W., and John C., Haltiwanger. 2006. On the nature of capital adjustment costs. *Review of Economic Studies* 73 (3): 611–33.

Cronshaw, Mark B., and David G. Luenberger. 1994. Subgame perfert equilibria in infinitely repeated games with perfect monitoring and discounting. *Games and Economic Behavior* 6 (2): 220–37.

Currie, David, and Paul Levine. 1985. Macroeconomic policy design in an interdependent world. In Willem H. Buiter and Richard C. Marston, eds., *International Economic Policy Coordination*. Cambridge, UK: Cambridge University Press, 228–68.

Currie, David, and Paul Levine. 1993. *Rules, Reputation and Macroeconomic Policy Coordination*. Cambridge, UK: Cambridge University Press.

DeJong, David N., and Chetan Dave. 2007. *Structural Macroeconometrics*. Princeton: Princeton University Press.

Dekel, Eddie. 1986. An axiomatic characterization of preferences under uncertainty: Weakening the independence axiom. *Journal of Economic Theory* 40 (2): 304–18.

Den Haan, Wouter J., Kenneth L. Judd, and Michel Juillard. 2009. Computational suite of models with heterogeneous agents: Incomplete markets and aggregate uncertainty. *Journal of Economic Dynamic and Control* 34 (1): 1–3.

Den Haan, Wouter J., and Albert Marcet. 1990. Solving the stochastic growth model by parameterizing expectations. *Journal of Business Economics and Statistics* 8 (1): 31–34.

Den Haan, Wouter J., Gary Ramey, and Joel Watson. 2000. Job destruction and Propagation of shocks. *American Economic Review* 90 (3): 482–98.

Dennis, Richard. 2010. When in discretion superior to timeless perspective policymaking? *Journal of Monetary Economics* 57 (3): 266–77.

Diamond, Peter A. 1965. National debt in a neoclassical growth model. *American Economic Review* 55 (5): 1126–150.

Diamond, Peter A. 1982. Aggregate demand management in search equilibrium. *Journal of Political Economy* 90 (5): 881–94.

Díaz-Giménez, Javier, Edward C., Prescott, Terry Fitzgerald, and Fernando Alvarez. 1992. Banking in computable general equilibrium economies. *Journal of Economic Dynamics and Control* 16 (3–4): 533–60.

Dixit, Avinash K., and Robert S. Pindyck. 1994. *Investment under Uncertainty*, Princeton: Princeton University Press.

Dornbusch, Rudiger. 1976. Expectations and exchange rate dynamics. *Journal of Political Economy* 84 (6): 1161–76.

Dotsey, Michael, and Robert G. King. 2001. Pricing, production and persistence. Working paper 12076. NBER.

Duffie, Darrell, and Larry G. Epstein. 1992. Stochastic differential utility. *Econometrica* 60 (2): 353–94.

Duffie, Darrell, John Geanakopolos, Andreu Mas-Colell, and Andrew McLennan. 1994. Stationary Markov equilibria. *Econometrica* 62 (4): 745–81.

Duffie, Darrell, and Kenneth J. Singleton. 1993. Simulated moments estimation of markov models of asset prices. *Econometrica* 61 (4): 929–52.

Duffie, Darrell, Mark Schroder, and Costis Skiadas. 1996. Recursive valuation of defaultable securities and the timing of resolution of uncertainty. *Annals of Applied Probability* 6 (4): 1075–90.

Duffie, Darrell, and Costis Skiadas. 1994. Continuous-time security pricing: A utility gradient approach. *Journal of Mathematical Economics* 23 (2): 107–31.

Dumas, Bernard, Raman Uppal, and Tan Wang. 2000. Efficient intertemporal allocations with recursive utility. *Journal of Economic Theory* 93 (2): 240–59.

Durán, Jorge. 2000. On dynamic programming with unbounded returns. *Economic Theory* 15 (2): 339–52.

Durán, Jorge. 2003. Discounting long-run average growth in stochastic dynamic programs. *Economic Theory* 22 (2): 395–413.

Eberly, Janice C., Sergio Rebelo, and Nicolas Vincent. 2011. What explains the lagged investment effect. NBER Working paper 16889.

Edge, Rochelle M., Thomas Laubach, and John C. Williams. 2007. Learning and shifts in long-run productivity growth. *Journal of Monetary Economics* 54 (8): 2421–38.

Eggertsson, Gauti B. 2009. What fiscal policy is effective at zero interest rates? In Daron Acemoglu and Michael Woodford, eds., *NBER Macroeconomics Annual 2010* 25: 59–112.

Ekeland, Ivar, and José A. Scheinkman. 1986. Transversality conditions for some infinite horizon discrete time optimization problems. *Mathematics of Operations Research* 11 (2): 216–29.

Ellsberg, Daniel. 1961. Risk, ambiguity, and the savage axioms. *Quarterly Journal of Economics* 75 (4): 643–69.

Epstein, Larry G. 1992. Behavior under risk: Recent developments in theory and applications. In Jean-Jacques Laffont, ed., *Advances in Economic Theory*, vol. 2. Cambridge, UK: Cambridge University Press, 1–63.

Epstein, Larry G. 1999. A definition of uncertainty aversion. *Review of Economic studies* 16 (3): 579–608.

Epstein, Larry G., Emmanuel Farhi, and Tomasz Strzalecki. 2012. How much would you pay to resolve long-run risk? Working paper. Boston University.

Epstein, Larry G., and Allan J. Hynes. 1983. The rate of time preference and dynamic economic analysis. *Journal of Political Economy* 91 (4): 611–35.

Epstein, Larry G., and Jianjun Miao. 2003. A two-person dynamic Equilibrium under ambiguity. *Journal of Economics Dynamics and Control* 27: 1253–88.

Epstein, Larry G., and Martin Schneider. 2003. Recursive multiple-priors. *Journal of Economic Theory* 113 (1): 1–31.

Epstein, Larry G., and Tan Wang. 1994. Intertemporal asset pricing under Knightian uncertainty. *Econometrica* 62 (2): 283–322.

Epstein, Larry G., and Stanley E. Zin. 1989. Substitution, risk aversion, and the temporal behavior of consumption and asset returns: A theoretical framework. *Econometrica* 57 (4): 937–69.

Epstein, Larry G., and Stanley E. Zin. 1991. Substitution, risk aversion, and the temporal behavior of consumption and asset returns: An empirical analysis. *Journal of Political Economy* 99 (2): 263–86.

Farmer, Roger E. A. 1993. *Macroeconomics of Self-fulfilling Prophecies*. Cambridge: MIT Press.

Feng, Zhigang, Jianjun Miao, Adrian Peralta-Alva, and Manual Santos. 2012. Numerical simulation of nonoptimal dynamic equilibrium models. *International Economic Review*, forthcoming.

Fernández-Villaverde, Jesús. 2010. The econometrics of DSGE models. *Journal of the Spanish Economic Association* 1: 3–49.

Fernández-Villaverde, Jesús, and Juan F. Rubio-Ramírez. 2005. Estimating dynamic equilibrium economies: Linear versus nonlinear likelihood. *Journal of Applied Econometrics* 20: 891–910.

Fernández-Villaverde, Jesús, and Juan F. Rubio-Ramírez. 2007. Estimating macroeconomic models: A likelihood approach. *Review of Economic Studies* 74 (4): 1059–87.

Fernández-Villaverde, Jesús, Pablo Guerrón-Quintana, and Juan F. Rubio-Ramírez. 2010. The new macroeconometries: A Bayesian approach. In Anthony O'Hagan and Mike West, eds., *Handbook of Applied Bayesian Analysis*. Oxford: Oxford University Press.

Fisher, Jonas D. M. 2006. The dynamic effects of neutral and investment-specific technology shocks. *Journal of Political Economy* 114 (3): 413–51.

Fisher, Irving. 1906. *The Nature of Capital and Income*. Norwood, MA: Norwood Press.

Fudenberg, Drew, and Jean Tirole. 1991. *Game Theory*. Cambridge: MIT Press.

Gali, Jordi. 1992. How well does the IS-LM model fit postwar U.S. data? *Quarterly Journal of Economics* 107 (2): 709–38.

Gali, Jordi. 2008. *Monetary Policy, Inflation, and the Business Cycle: An Introduction to the New Keynesian Framework*. Princeton: Princeton University Press.

Gallager, Robert G. 1996. *Discrete Stochastic Processes*. Boston: Kluwer.

Gallant, A. Ronald. 1987. *Nonlinear Statistical Models*. New York: Wiley.

Gallant, A. Ronald, and George Tauchen. 1996. Which moments to match? *Econometric Theory* 12 (4): 657–81.

Garsia, A. M. 1965. A simple proof of E. Hopf's maximal ergodic thoerem. *Journal of Mathematics and Mechanics* 14: 381–82.

Geoffard, Pierre-Yves. 1996. Discounting and optimizing: Capital accumulation problems as variational minmax problem. *Journal of Economic Theory* 69 (1): 53–70.

Ghirardato, Paolo, and Massimo Marinacci. 2002. Ambiguity made precise: A comparative foundation. *Journal of Economic Theory* 102 (2): 251–89.

Gilboa, Itzhak, and David Schmeidler. 1989. Maxmin expected utility with non-unique prior. *Journal of Mathematical Economics* 18 (2): 262–67.

Gilchrist, Simon, and Masashi Saito. 2008. Expectations, asset prices, and monetary policy: The role of learning. In John Y. Campbell, ed., *Asset Prices and Monetary Policy*. Chicago: University of Chicago Press.

Gittins, John, Kevin Glazebrook, and Richard Weber. 2011. *Multi-armed Bandit Allocation Indices*, 2nd ed. New York: Wiley.

Golub, Gene H., and Charles F. van Loan. 1996. *Matrix Computations*. Baltimore: Johns Hopkins University Press.

Goodfriend, Marvin, and Robert G. King. 1997. The new neoclassical synthesis and the role of monetary policy. In Ben S. Bernanke and Julio Rotemberg, eds., *NBER Macroeconomics Annual 1997* 12: 231–96.

Gordin, M. I. 1969. The Central Limit Theorem for stationary process (in Russian). *Dokl. Akad. Nauk. SSSR* 188: 739–41.

Gould, John P. 1968. Adjustment costs in the theory of investment of the firm. *Review of Economic Studies* 35 (1): 47–55.

Gouriéroux, Christian, and Alain Monfort. 1996. *Simulated-based Econometric Methods*. Oxford, UK: Oxford University Press.

Gouriéroux, Christian, and Alain Monfort, and Eric Renault. 1993. Indirect inference. *Journal of Applied Econometrics* 8: S85–118.

Gourio, François, and Jianjun Miao. 2010. Firm heterogeneity and the long-run effects of dividend tax reform. *American Economic Journal: Macroeconomics* 2 (1): 131–68.

Gourio, François, and Jianjun Miao. 2011. Transitional dynamics of dividend and capital gains tax cuts. *Review of Economic Dynamics* 14 (2): 368–83.

Grant, Simon, Atsushi Kajii, and Ben Polak. 1998. Instrinsic preference for information. *Journal of Economic Theory* 83 (2): 233–59.

Grant, Simon, Atsushi Kajii, and Ben Polak. 2000. Temporal resolution of uncertainty and recursive non-expected utility models. *Econometrica* 68 (2): 425–34.

Greene, William H. 2011. *Econometric Analysis*, 7th ed. Upper Saddle River, NJ: Prentice-Hall.

Greenwood, Jeremy, Zvi Hercowitz, and Gregory W. Huffman. 1988. Investment, capacity utilization, and the real business cycle. *American Economic Review* 78 (3): 402–17.

Greenwood, Jeremy, Zvi Hercowitz, and Per Krusell. 1997. Long-run implications of investment-specific technological change. *American Economic Review* 87 (3): 342–62.

Grossman, Sanford J., and Robert J. Shiller. 1981. The determinants of the variability of stock market prices. *American Economic Review* 71 (2): 222–27.

Gul, Faruk. 1991. A theory of disappointment aversion. *Econometrica* 59 (3): 667–86.

Guvenen, Fatih. 2007. Learning your earning: Are labor income shocks really very persistent? *American Economic Review* 97 (3): 687–712.

Hall, Alasdair R. 2005. *Generalized Methods of Moments*. New York: Oxford University Press.

Hall, Robert E. 1978. Stochastic implications of the life cycle-permanent income hypothesis: Theory and evidence. *Journal of Political Economy* 86 (6): 971–87.

Hall, Robert E. 1997. Macroeconomic fluctuations and the allocation of time. *Journal of Labor Economics* 15 (1): 223–50.

Hall, Robert E. 2005. Employment fluctuations with equilibrium wage stickiness. *American Economic Review* 95 (1): 50–65.

Hamilton, James D. 1994. *Time Series Analysis*. Princeton: Princeton University Press.

Hansen, Gary, D. 1985. Indivisible labor and the business cycle. *Journal of Monetary Economics* 16 (3): 309–27.

Hansen, Lars P. 1982. Large sample properties of generalized method of moments estimators. *Econometrica* 50 (4): 1029–54.

Hansen, Lars P. 2007. Beliefs, doubts and learning: Valuing macroeconomic risk. Richard T. Ely Lecture. *American Economic Review* 97 (2): 1–30.

Hansen, Lars P. 2008. Generalized method of moments estimation. In Steven N. Durlauf and Lawrence E. Blume, eds., *The New Palgrave Dictionary of Economics*, 2nd ed. Palgrave Macmillan.

Hansen, Lars P., John C. Heaton, and Nan Li. 2008. Consumption strikes back? Measuring long-run risk. *Journal of Political Economy* 116 (2): 260–302.

Hansen, Lars P., and James J. Heckman. 1996. The empirical foundations of calibration. *Journal of Economic Perspectives* 10 (1): 87–104.

Hansen, Lars P., and Thomas J. Sargent. 1995. Discounted linear exponential quadratic Gaussian control. *IEEE Transactions on Automatic Control* 40: 968–71.

Hansen, Lar P., and Thomas J. Sargent. 2001. Robust control and model uncertainty. *American Economic Review* 91 (2): 60–66.

Hansen, Lars P., and Thomas J. Sargent. 2005. Robust estimation and control under commitment. *Journal of Economic Theory* 124 (2): 258–301.

Hansen, Lars P., and Thomas J. Sargent. 2007. Recursive robust estimation and control without commitment. *Journal of Economic Theory* 136 (1): 1–27.

Hansen, Lars P., and Thomas J. Sargent. 2008. *Robustness*. Princeton: Princeton University Press.

Hansen, Lars P., and Thomas J. Sargent. 2010. Fragile beliefs and the price of uncertainty. *Quantitative Economics* 1 (1): 129–62.

Hansen, Lars P., and Kenneth J. Singleton. 1982. Generalized instrumental variables of nonlinear rational expectations models. *Econometrica* 50 (5): 1269–86.

Hayashi, Fumio. 1982. Tobin's marginal Q and average Q: A neoclassical interpretation. *Econometrica* 50 (1): 213–24.

Hayashi, Fumio, and Christopher A. Sims. 1983. Nearly efficient estimation of time series models with predetermined, but not exogenous, instruments. *Econometrica* 51 (3): 783–98.

Hayashi, Takashi. 2005. Intertemporal substitution, risk aversion and ambiguity aversion. *Economic Theory* 25 (4): 933–56.

Hayashi, Takashi, and Jianjun Miao. 2011. Intertemporal substitution and recursive smooth ambiguity preferences. *Theoretical Economics* 6 (3): 423–72.

Heyde, C. C. 1974. On the Central Limit Theorem for stationary processes. *Z. Wahrschein-lichkeitsth* 30 (4): 315–20.

Holmstrom, Bengt. 1979. Moral hazard and observability. *Bell Journal of Economics* 10 (1): 74–91.

Hopenhayn, Hugo A. 1992. Entry, exit, and firm dynamics in long run equilibrium. *Econometrica* 60 (5): 1127–50.

Huang, Kevin X. D. 2002. Valuation in infinite-horizon sequential markets with portfolio constraints. *Economic Theory* 20 (1): 189–98.

Huggett, Mark. 1993. The risk-free rate in heterogeneous-agent incomplete-insurance economies. *Journal of Economic Dynamics and Control* 17 (5–6): 953–69.

Iglehart, Donald L. 1963. Optimality of (s, S) policies in the infinite horizon dynamic Inventory problem. *Management Science* 9 (2): 259–67.

Imrohoroglu, Ayse. 1992. The welfare cost of inflation under imperfect insurance, *Journal of Economic Dynamics and Control* 16 (1): 79–91.

Ireland, Peter N. 2001. Endogenous money or sticky prices. *Journal of Monetary Economics* 50 (8): 1623–648.

Ireland Peter N. 2004. A method for taking models to the data. *Journal of Economic Dynamics and Control* 28 (6): 1205–26.

Jensen, Michael C., and William H. Meckling. 1976. Theory of the firm: Managerial behavior, agency costs and ownership structure. *Journal of Financial Economics* 3 (4): 305–60.

Ju, Nengjiu, and Jianjun Miao. 2007. Ambiguity, learning, and asset returns. Working paper. Boston University.

Ju, Nengjiu, and Jianjun Miao. 2012. Ambiguity, learning, and asset returns. *Econometrica* 80 (2): 559–91.

Judd, Kenneth L. 1992. Projection methods for solving aggregate growth models. *Journal of Economic Theory* 58 (2): 410–52.

Judd, Kenneth L. 1998. *Numerical Methods in Economics*. Cambridge: MIT Press.

Judd, Kenneth L., Sevin Yeltekin, and James Conklin. 2003. Computing supergame equilibria. *Econometrica* 71 (4): 1239–54.

Kamihigashi, Takashi. 2000. A simple proof of Ekeland and Scheinkman's result on the necessity of a transversality condition. *Economic Theory* 15 (2): 463–68.

Kandel, Shmuel, and Robert F. Stambaugh. 1991. Asset returns and intertemporal preferences. *Journal of Monetary Economics* 27 (1): 39–71.

Karlin, Samuel, and Howard M. Taylor. 1975. *A First Course in Stochastic Processes*, 2nd ed. New York: Academic Press.

Kehoe, Patrick J., and Fabrizio Perri. 2002. International business cycles with endogenous incomplete markets. *Econometrica* 70 (3): 907–28.

Kim, Chang-Jin, and Charles R. Nelson. 1999. *State Space Models with Regime Switching*. Cambridge: MIT Press.

Kim, Jinill. 2000. Constructing and estimating a realistic optimizing model of monetary policy. *Journal of Monetary Economics* 45 (2): 329–59.

Kim, Jinill, Sunghyun Kim, Ernst Schaumburg, and Christopher A. Sims. 2008. Calculating and using second-order accurate solutions of discrete time dynamic equilibrium models. *Journal of Economic Dynamics and Control* 32 (11): 3397–3414.

King, Mervyn A. 1977. *Public Policy and the Corporation*. London: Chapman and Hall.

King, Robert G., Charles I. Plosser, and Sergio T. Rebelo. 1988. Production, growth and business cycles: I. The basic neoclassical model. *Journal of Monetary Economics* 21 (2–3): 195–232.

King, Robert G., Charles I. Plosser, James H. Stock, and Mark W. Watson. 1991. Stochastic trends and economic fluctuations. *American Economic Review* 81 (4): 819–40.

King, Robert G., and Sergio T. Rebelo. 1999. Resuscitating real business cycles. In John B. Taylor and Michael Woodford, eds., *Handbook of Macroeconomics*, vol. 1. Amsterdam: Elsevier, 927–1007.

King, Robert G., and Mark W. Watson. 1998. The solution of singular linear difference systems under rational expectations. *International Economic Review* 39 (4): 1015–26.

King, Robert G., and Mark W. Watson. 2002. System reduction and solution algorithms for singular linear difference systems under rational Expectations. *Computational Economics* 20 (1–2): 57–86.

Kiyotaki, Nobuhiro, and Randall Wright. 1989. On money as a medium of exchange. *Journal of Political Economy* 97 (4): 927–54.

Klein, Paul. 2000. Using the generalized Schur form to solve a multivariate linear rational expectations model. *Journal of Economic Dynamics and Control* 24 (10): 1405–23.

Klibanoff, Peter, Massimo Marinacci, and Sujoy Mukerji. 2005. A smooth model of decision making under ambiguity. *Econometrica* 73 (6): 1849–92.

Klibanoff, Peter, Massimo Marinacci, and Sujoy Mukerji. 2009. Recursive smooth ambiguity preferences. *Journal of Economic Theory* 144 (3): 930–76.

Knight, Frank H. 1921. *Risk, Uncertainty, and Profit*. Boston: Houghton Mifflin.

Kocherlakota, Narayana R. 1992. Bubbles and constraints on debt accumulation. *Journal of Economic Theory* 57 (1): 245–56.

Kocherlakota, Narayana R. 1996. The equity premium: It's still a puzzle. *Journal of Economic Literature* 34 (1): 43–71.

Kocherlakota, Narayana R. 2008. Injecting rational bubbles. *Journal of Economic Theory* 142 (1): 218–32.

Kocherlakota, Narayana R. 2009. Bursting bubbles: Consequences and cures. Working paper. University of Minnesota.

Koopmans, Tjalling C. 1960. Stationary ordinal utility and impatience. *Econometrica* 28 (2): 287–309.

Koopmans, Tjalling C. 1965. On the concept of optimal economic growth. In *The Econometric Approach to Development Planning*. Amsterdam: North Holland.

Koopmans, Tjalling C. 1972a. Representations of preference orderings with independent components of consumption. In C. B. McGuire and Roy Radner, eds., *Decision and Organization*. Amsterdam: North-Holland, 57–78.

Koopmans, Tjalling C. 1972b. Representations of preference orderings over time. In C. B. McGuire and Roy Radner, eds., *Decision and Organization*. Amsterdam: North-Holland, 79–100.

Koopmans, Tjalling C., Peter A. Diamond, and Richard E. Williamson. 1964. Stationary utility and time perspective. *Econometrica* 32 (1–2): 82–100.

Kreps, David M., and Evan L. Porteus. 1978. Temporal resolution of uncertainty and dynamic choice theory. *Econometrica* 46 (1): 185–200.

Krusell, Per, and Anthony A. Smith. Jr. 1998. Income and wealth heterogeneity in the macroeconomy. *Journal of Political Economy* 106 (5): 867–96.

Kubler, Felix, and Karl Schmedders. 2002. Recursive equilibria in economies with incomplete markets. *Macroeconomic Dynamics* 6 (2): 284–306.

Kydland, Finn E., and Edward C. Prescott. 1977. Rules rather than discretion: The inconsistency of optimal plans. *Journal of Political Economy* 85 (3): 473–92.

Kydland, Finn E., and Edward C. Prescott. 1980. Dynamic optimal taxation, rational expectations and optimal control. *Journal of Economic Dynamics and Control* 2 (1): 79–91.

Kydland, Finn E., and Edward C. Prescott. 1982. Time to build and aggregate fluctuations. *Econometrica* 50 (6): 1345–71.

Kydland, Finn E., and Edward C. Prescott. 1996. The computational experiment: An econometric tool. *Journal of Economic Perspectives* 10 (1): 69–85.

Laffont, Jean-Jacques, and David Martimort. 2001. *The Theory of Incentives: The Principal-Agent Model.* Princeton: Princeton University Press.

Laxton, Douglas, and Michel Juillard. 1996. A robust and efficient method for solving nonlinear rational expectations models. Working paper 96/106. IMF.

Le Van, Cuong, and Lisa Morhaim. 2002. Optimal growth models with bounded or unbounded returns: A unifying approach. *Journal of Economic Theory* 105 (1): 158–87.

Le Van, Cuong, and Yiannis Vailakis. 2005. Recurisve utility and optimal growth with bounded or unbounded returns. *Journal of Economic Theory.* 123 (2): 187–209.

Lee, Bong-Soo, and Beth Fisher Ingram. 1991. Simulated estimation of time-series models. *Journal of Econometrics* 47 (2–3): 197–205.

Leeper, Eric M., and Christopher Sims. 1994. Toward a modern macroeconomic model usable for policy analysis, In Stanley Fischer and Julio Rotemberg, eds., *NBER Macroeconomics Annual 1994.* Cambridge: MIT Press, 81–140.

Leeper, Eric M., Christopher A. Sims, and Tao Zha. 1996. What does monetary policy do? *Brookings Papers on Economic Activity* 27 (2): 1–78.

Levhari, David, and Leonard J. Mirman. 1980. The great fish war: An example using a dynamic Cournot-Nash solution. *Bell Journal of Economics* 11 (1): 322–34.

Levhari, David, Leonard J. Mirman, and Itzhak Zilcha. 1980. Capital accumulation under uncertainty. *International Economic Review* 21 (3): 661–71.

Levhari, David, and T. N. Srinivasan. 1969. Optimal savings under uncertainty. *Review of Economic Studies* 36 (2): 153–63.

Lintner, John. 1965. The valuation of risk assets and the selection of risky investments in stock portfolios and capital budgets. *Review of Economics and Statistics* 47 (1): 13–37.

Ljungqvist, Lars, and Thomas J. Sargent. 2004. *Recursive Macroeconomic Theory,* 2nd ed. Cambridge: MIT Press.

Ljungqvist, Lars, and Thomas J. Sargent. 2012. *Recursive Macroeconomic Theory,* 3rd ed. Cambridge: MIT Press.

Long Jr., John B., and Charles I. Plosser. 1983. Real business cycles. *Journal of Political Economy* 91 (1): 39–69.

Lubik, Thomas A., and Frank Schorfheide. 2003. Computing sunspots equilibria in linear rational expectations models. *Journal of Economic Dynamics and Control* 28 (2): 273–85.

Lucas, Robert E., Jr. 1967. Adjustment costs and the theory of supply. *Journal of Political Economy* 75 (4): 321–34.

Lucas, Robert E., Jr. 1978. Asset prices in an exchange economy. *Econometrica* 46 (6): 1429–45.

Lucas, Robert E., Jr., and Nancy L. Stokey. 1984. Optimal growth with many consumers. *Journal of Economic Theory* 32 (1): 139–71.

Luenberger, David G. 1969. *Optimization by Vector Space Methods*. New York: Wiley.

Maccheroni, Fabio, Massimo Marinacci, and Aldo Rustichini. 2006a. Ambiguity aversion, robustness, and the variational representation of preferences. *Econometrica* 74 (6): 1447–98.

Maccheroni, Fabio, Massimo Marinacci, and Aldo Rustichini. 2006b. Dynamic variational preferences. *Journal of Economic Theory* 128 (1): 4–44.

Magill, Michael, and Martine Quinzii. 1994. Infinite horizon incomplete markets. *Econometrica* 62 (4): 853–80.

Magill, Michael, and Martine Quinzii. 1996. Incomplete market over an infinite horizon: Long-lived securities and speculative bubbles. *Journal of Mathematical Economics* 26 (1): 133–70.

Mailath, George J., and Larry Samuelson. 2006. *Repeated Games and Reputations: Long-Run Relationships*. Oxford, UK: Oxford University Press.

Mancini-Griffoli, T. 2010. *An Introduction to the Solution and Estimation of DSGE Models: Dynare v4 User Guide*. Public Beta Version edition.

Mankiw, N. Gregory, and David Romer, eds. 1991. *New Keynesian Economics*. Vol. 1: *Imperfect Competition and Sticky Prices*, and Vol. 2: *Coordination Failures and Real Rigidities*. Cambridge: MIT Press.

Marcet, Albert. 1988. Solving nonlinear stochastic models by parametrizing expectations. Working paper. Carnegie Mellon University.

Marcet, Albert, and Ramon Marimon. 1992. Communication, commitment, and growth. *Journal of Economic Theory* 58 (2): 219–49.

Marcet, Albert, and Ramon Marimon. 2011. Recursive contracts. Economics working paper ECO2011/15. European University Institute, Florence.

Marcet, Albert, and Thomas J. Sargent. 1989. Least squares learning and the dynamics of hyperinflation. In William Barnett, John Geweke, and Karl Shell, eds., *Economic Complexity: Chaos, Sunspots, and Nonlinearity*. New York: Cambridge University Press.

Martins-da-Rocha, Victor F., and Yiannis Vailakis. 2010. Existence and uniqueness of a fixed point for local contractions. *Econometrica* 78 (3): 1127–41.

Mas-Colell, Andrew, Michael D. Whinston, and Jerry R. Green. 1995. *Microeconomic Theory*. New York: Oxford University Press.

Maskin, Eric, and Jean Tirole. 1987. A theory of dynamic oligopoly. III: Cournot competition. *European Economic Review* 31 (4): 947–68.

Maskin, Eric, and Jean Tirole. 1988. A theory of dynamic oligopoly. I: Overview and quantity competition with large fixed costs. *Econometrica* 56 (3): 549–69.

Matkowski, Janusz, and Andrzej S. Nowak. 2011. On discounted dynamic programming with unbounded returns. *Economic Theory* 46 (3): 455–74.

McCall, John J. 1970. Economics of information and job search. *Quarterly Journal of Economics* 84 (1): 113–26.

McCallum, Bennett T., and Marvin S. Goodfriend. 1988. Theoretical analysis of the demand of money. *Federal Reserve Bank of Richmond: Economic Review* 74 (1): 16–24.

McCallum, Bennett T., and Edward Nelson. 1999. An optimizing IS-LM specification for monetary policy and business cycle analysis. *Journal of Money, Credit and Banking* 31 (3): 296–316.

McFadden, Daniel. 1989. A method of simulated moments for estimation of discrete response models without numerical integration. *Econometrica* 57 (5): 995–1026.

McGrattan, Ellen R. 1994. The macroeconomic effects of distortionary taxation. *Journal of Monetary Economics* 33 (3): 573–601.

McGrattan, Ellen R. 1996. Solving the stochastic growth model with a finite element method. *Journal of Economic Dynamics and Control* 20 (1–3): 19–42.

McGrattan, Ellen. R., and Edward C. Prescott. 2005. Taxes, regulations, and the value of U.S. and U.K. corporations. *Review of Economic Studies* 72 (3): 767–96.

Mehra, Rajnish, and Edward C. Prescott. 1985. The equity premium: A puzzle. *Journal of Monetary Economics* 15 (2): 145–61.

Merz, Monika. 1995. Search in the labor market and the real business cycle. *Journal of Monetary Economics* 36 (2): 269–300.

Messner, Matthias, Nicola Pavoni, and Christopher Sleet. 2011. On the dual approach to recursive optimization. Working papers 423. IGIER, Bocconi University.

Messner, Matthias, Nicola Pavoni, and Christopher Sleet. 2012. Recursive methods for incentive problems. *Review of Economic Dynamics* 15 (4): 501–25.

Meyn, S. P., and R. L. Tweedie. 1993. *Markov Chains and Stochastic Stability* Berlin: Springer.

Miao, Jianjun. 2006. Competitive equilibria of economies with a continuum of consumers and aggregate shocks. *Journal of Economic Theory* 128 (1): 274–98.

Miao, Jianjun, and Neng Wang. 2011. Risk, uncertainty and option exercise. *Journal of Economic Dynamics and Control* 35 (4): 442–61.

Miao, Jianjun, and Pengfei Wang. 2009. Lumpy investment and corporate tax policy. Working paper. Boston University.

Miao, Jianjun, and Pengfei Wang. 2011a. A Q-theory model with lumpy investment. Working paper. Boston University.

Miao, Jianjun, and Pengfei Wang, 2011b, Bubbles and credit constraints, Working paper WP2011-030. Boston University.

Miao, Jianjun, and Pengfei Wang. 2011c. Sectoral bubbles and endogenous growth. Working paper WP2011-032. Boston University.

Miao, Jianjun, and Pengfei Wang. 2012a. Bubbles and total factor productivity. *American Economic Review* 102 (3): 82–87.

Miao, Jianjun, and Pengfei Wang. 2012b. Banking bubbles and financial crisis. Working paper WP2012-010. Boston University.

Miao, Jianjun, Pengfei Wang, and Zhiwei Xu. 2013. A Bayesian DSGE model of stock market bubbles and business cycles. Working paper. Boston University.

Miao, Jianjun, Pengfei Wang, and Lifang Xu. 2013. Stock market bubbles and unemployment. Working paper. Boston University.

Miranda, Mario J., and Paul L. Fackler. 2002. *Applied Computational Economics and Finance*. Cambridge: MIT Press.

Mirrlees, James A. 1975. The theory of moral hazard and unobservable behavior: Part I. Mimeo. Nuffield College, Oxford.

Mortensen, Dale T. 1982. The mating process as a noncooperative bargaining game. In John J. McCall, ed., *The Economics of Information and Uncertainty*. Chicago: University of Chicago Press, 233–58.

Mortensen, Dale T., and Christopher A. Pissarides. 1994. Job creation and job destruction in the theory un employment. *Review of Economic Studies* 61 (3): 397–415.

Muth, John F. 1960. Optimal properties of exponentially weighted forecasts. *Journal of the American Statistical Association* 55: 299–306.

Negishi, Mario T. 1960. Welfare economics and existence of an equilibrium for a competitive economy. *Metroeconomica* 12: 92–97.

Newey, Whitney K., and Kenneth D. West. 1987. A simple, positive semi-definite, heteroskedasticity and autocorrelation consistent covariance matrix. *Econometrica* 55 (3): 703–08.

Onicescu, Octav. 1969. *The Principles of Probability Theory*. Bucharest: Publishing House of the Romanian Academy.

Oudiz, G., and Jeffrey D. Sachs. 1985. International policy coordination in dynamic macroeconomic models. In Willem H. Buiter and Richard C. Marston, eds., *International Economic Policy Coordination*. Cambridge, UK: Cambridge University, 275–319.

Pearlman, Joseph, David Currie, and Paul Levine. 1986. Rational expectations models with partial information. *Economic Modelling* 3 (2): 90–105.

Phelan, Christopher, and Ennio Stacchetti. 2001. Sequential equilibria in a Ramsey tax model. *Econometrica* 69 (6): 1491–1518.

Phelan, Christopher, and Robert M. Townsend. 1991. Computing multi-period, information-constrained optima. *Review of Economic Studies* 58 (5): 853–81.

Phelps, Edmund S. 1962. The accumulation of risky capital: A sequential utility analysis. *Econometrica* 30 (4): 729–43.

Pissarides, Christopher A. 1985. Short-run equilibrium dynamics of unemployment, vacancies, and real wages. *American Economic Review* 75 (4): 676–90.

Pissarides, Christopher A. 2000. *Equilibrium Unemployment Theory*, 2nd ed. Cambridge: MIT Press.

Pontryagin, L. S., V. G. Boltyanskii, R.V. Gamkrelidze, and E. F. Mishchenko. 1962. *The Mathematical Theory of Optimal Processes*, transl. from the Russian by K. N. Trirogoff, ed. by L. W. Neustadt. New York: Wiley.

Porteus, Evan L. 1980. Improved iterative computation of the expected discounted return in Markov and semi-Markov chains. *Mathematical Methods of Operations Research* 24 (5): 155–70.

Poterba, James M., and Lawrence H. Summers. 1985. The economic effects of dividend taxation. In Edward Altman and Marti Subrahmanyam, eds., *Recent Advances in Corporate Finance*. Scar borough, ON: Irwin Professional Publishing.

Prescott, Edward C., and Rajnish Mehra. 1980. Recursive competitive equilibrium: The case of homogeneous households. *Econometrica* 48 (6): 1365–79.

Puterman, Martin L., and Shelby L. Brumelle. 1979. On the convergence of policy iteration in stationary dynamic programming. *Mathematics of Operations Research* 4 (1): 60–69.

Puterman, Martin L. 1990. Markov decision processes. In D. P. Heyman and M. J. Sobel, eds., *Handbooks in Operations Research and Management Science*, vol. 2. Amsterdam: Elsevier, 331–434.

Puterman, Martin L. 1994. *Markov Decision Processes: Discrete Stochastic Dynamic Programming*. New York: Wiley.

Qu, Zhongjun, and Denis Tkachenko. 2012. Identification and frequency domain quasi-maximum likelihood estimation of linearized dynamic stochastic general equilibrium models. *Quantitative Economics* 3 (1): 95–132.

Ramsey, Frank P. 1928. A Mathematical theory of saving. *Economic Journal* 38 (152): 543–59.

Rincón-Zapatero, Juan. P., and C. Rodríguez-Palmero. 2003. Existence and uniqueness of solutions to the Bellman equation in the unbounded case. *Econometrica* 71 (5): 1519–55.

Rivlin, Theodore J. 1990. *Chebyshev Polynomials*. New York: Wiley.

Rogerson, Richard. 1988. Indivisible labor, lotteries, and equilibrium, *Journal of Monetary Economics* 21 (1): 3–16.

Rogerson, William P. 1985a. Repeated moral hazard. *Econometrica* 53 (1): 69–76.

Rogerson, William P. 1985b. The first-Order approach to principal–agent problems. *Econometrica* 53 (6): 1357–68.

Romer, Christina D., and David H. Romer. 1989. Does monetary policy matter? A new test in the spirit of Friedman and Schwartz. In Olivier Jean Blanchard and Stanley Fischer, eds., *NBER Macroeconomics Annual 1989* 4: 121–84.

Romer, David H. 2012, *Advanced Macroeconomics*, 4th ed. New York: McGraw-Hill.

Ross, Stephen. 1976. The arbitrage theory of capital asset pricing. *Journal of Economic Theory* 13 (3): 341–60.

Rotemberg, Julio J., and Michael Woodford. 1991. Markups and the business cycle. In Oliver J. Blanchard and Stanley Fischer, eds., *NBER Macroeconomics Annual 1991*, 6: 63–128.

Rotemberg, Julio J., and Michael Woodford. 1997. An optimization based econometric framework for the evaluation of monetary policy. In Oliver J. Blanchard and Stanley Fischer, eds., *NBER Macroeconomic Annual 1997*12: 297–346.

Rotemberg, Julio J., and Michael Woodford. 1999. The cyclical behavior of prices and costs. In John B. Taylor and Michael Woodford, eds., *Handbook of Macroeconomics*, vol. 1B. Amsterdam: Elsevier, 1051–1131.

Rothschild, Michael, and Joseph Stiglitz. 1970. Increasing risk. I: A definition. *Journal of Economic Theory* 2 (3): 225–43.

Royden, Halsey L. 1988. *Real Analysis*. London: Pearson.

Rudin, Walter. 1991. *Functional Analysis*, 2nd ed. New york: McGraw-Hill.

Rust, John. 1985. Stationary equilibrium in a market for durable assets. *Econometrica* 53 (4): 783–805.

Rust, John. 1986. When is it optimal to kill off the market for used durable goods? *Econometrica* 54 (1): 65–86.

Rust, John. 1994. Structural estimation of Markov decision processes. In Robert F. Engle and Daniel L. McFadden, eds., *Handbook of Econometrics*, vol. 4. Amsterdam: Elsevier, 3081–3143.

Rust, John. 1996. Numerical dynamic programming in economics. In H. Amman, D. Kendrick, and J. Rust, eds., *Handbook of Computational Economics*. Amsterdam: Elsevier, 620–729.

Samuelson, Paul A. 1958. An exact consumption-loan model of interest with or without the social contrivance of money. *Journal of Political Economy* 66 (6): 467–82.

Santos, Manuel S., and Michael Woodford. 1997. Rational asset pricing bubbles. *Econometrica* 65 (1): 19–57.

Sargan, John D. 1958. The estimation of economic relationships using instrumental variables. *Econometrica* 26 (3): 393–415.

Sargan, John D. 1959. The estimation of relationships with autocorrelated residuals by the use of instrumental variables. *Journal of the Royal Statistical Society* 21 (1): 91–105.

Sargent, Thomas J. 1987. *Dynamic Macroeconomic Theory*. Cambridge: Harvard University Press.

Scarf, Herbert E. 1959. The optimality of (S, s) Policies in the dynamic inventory problem. In K. J. Arrow, S. Karlin, and P. Suppes, eds., *Mathematical Methods in the Social Sciences*, Stanford: Stanford University Press, 196–202.

Schechtman, Jack, and Vera L. S. Escudero. 1977. Some results on "An Income Fluctuation Problem." *Journal of Economic Theory* 16 (2): 151–166.

Schmeidler, David. 1989. Subjective probability and expected utility without additivity. *Econometrica* 57 (3): 571–87.

Schmitt-Grohé, Stephanie, and Martin Uribe. 2004. Solving dynamic general equilibrium models using a second-order approximation to the policy function. *Journal of Economic Dynamics and Control* 28 (4): 755–75.

Schumaker, Larry L. 1983. On shape preserving quadratic spline interpolation. *SIAM Journal on Numerical Analysis* 20 (4): 854–64.

Shapley, Lloyd Stowell. 1953. Stochastic games. *Proceedings of National Academy of Science* 39: 1095–1100.

Sharpe, William F. 1964. Capital asset prices: A theory of market equilibrium under conditions of risk. *Journal of Finance* 19 (3): 425–42.

Shimer, Robert. 2005. The cyclical behavior of equilibrium unemployment and vacancies. *American Economic Review* 95 (1): 25–49.

Shimer, Robert. 2010. *Labor Markets and Business Cycles*. Princeton: Princeton University Press.

Shiryaev, Albert N. 1996. *Probability*, 2nd Ed. New York: Springer.

Sidrauski, Miguel. 1967. Rational choices and patterns of growth in a monetary economy. *American Economic Review* 57 (2): 534–44.

Sims, Christopher A. 1989. Solving nonlinear stochastic optimization and equilibrium problems backwards. Mimeo 15. Institute for Empirical Macroeconomics, Federal Reserve Bank of Minneapolis.

Sims, Christopher A. 1996, Macroeconomics and methodology. *Journal of Economic Perspectives* 10 (1): 105–20.

Sims, Christopher A. 2000. Solving linear rational expectations models. Working paper. Department of Economics, Princeton University.

Singleton, Kenneth J. 2006. *Empirical Dynamic Asset Pricing: Model Specification and Econometric Assessment*. Princeton: Princeton University Press.

Skiadas, Costis. 2009. *Asset Pricing Theory*. Princeton: Princeton University Press.

Smets, Frank, and Rafael Wouters. 2007. Shocks and frictions in US business cycles: A Bayesian DSGE approach. *American Economic Review* 97 (3): 586–606.

Söderlind, Paul. 1999. Solution and estimation of RE macromodels with optimal policy. *European Economic Review* 43 (4–6): 813–823.

Solow, Robert M. 1956. A contribution to the theory of economic growth. *Quarterly Journal of Economics* 70 (1): 65–94.

Sotomayor, Marlida A. de Oliveira. 1984. On income fluctuations and capital gains. *Journal of Economic Theory* 32 (1): 14–35.

Spear, Stephen E., and Sanjay Srivastava. 1987. On repeated moral hazard with discounting. *Review of Economic Studies* 54 (4): 599–617.

Stokey, Nancy L. 1989. Reputation and time consistency *American Economic Review* 79: 134–39.

Stokey, Nancy L. 1991. Credible public policy. *Journal of Economic Dynamics and Control* 15 (4): 627–56.

Stokey, Nancy, Robert Lucas, and Edward C. Prescott. 1989. *Recursive Methods in Economic Dynamics*. Cambridge: Harvard University Press.

Strang, Gilbert. 2006. *Linear Algebra and Its Applications*, 4th ed. Stamford, CT: Brooks Cole.

Streufert, Peter A. 1990, Stationary recursive utility and dynamic programming under the assumption of biconvergence. *Review of Economic Studies* 57 (1): 79–97.

Strzalecki, Tomasz. 2013. Temporal resolution of uncertainty and recursive models of ambiguity aversion. *Econometrica* 81 (3): 1039–74.

Summers, Lawrence H. 1981. Taxation and corporate investment—A Q-theory approach. *Brookings Papers on Economic Activity* 12 (1): 67–140.

Swan, Trevor W. 1956. Economic growth and capital accumulation. *Economic Record* 32 (2): 334–61.

Tauchen, George. 1986. Finite state Markov chain approximations to univariate and vector autoregressions. *Economic Letters* 20 (2): 177–81.

Tauchen, George, and Robert Hussey. 1991. Quadrature-based methods for obtaining approximate solutions to nonlinear asset pricing models. *Econometrica* 59 (2): 371–96.

Taylor, John B. 1993. Discretion versus policy rules in practice. *Carnegie-Rochester Confernce Series on Public Policy* 39 (1): 195–214.

Thomas, Jonathan, and Tim Worrall. 1988. Self-enforcing wage contracts. *Review of Economic Studies* 55 (4): 541–54.

Thomas, Jonathan, and Tim Worrall. 1990. Income fluctuation and asymmetric information: An example of repeated principal–agent problem, *Journal of Economic Theory* 51 (2): 367–90.

Tirole, Jean. 1985. Asset bubbles and overlapping generations. *Econometrica* 53 (6): 1499–1528.

Tobin, James. 1956. The interest elasticity of the transactions demand for cash. *Review of Economics and Statistics* 38 (3): 241–47.

Tobin, James. 1969. A general equilibrium approach to monetary theory. *Journal of Money, Credit and Banking* 1 (1): 15–29.

Topkis, Donald M. 1998. *Supermodularity and Complementarity*. Princeton: Princeton University Press.

Treadway, A. B. 1969. On rational entrepreneurial behavior and the demand for investment. *Review of Economic Studies* 36 (2): 227–39.

Uhlig, Harald. 1999. A toolkit for analysing nonlinear dynamic stochastic models easily. In Ramon Marimon and Andrew Scott, eds., *Computational Methods for the Study of Dynamic Economies*. Oxford: Oxford University Press, 30–61.

Uzawa, Hirofumi. 1968. Time preference, the consumption function, and optimal asset holdings. In J. N. Wolfe, ed., *Capital and Growth: Papers in Honour of Sir John Hicks*. Chicago: Aldine, 485–504.

Uzawa, Hirofumi. 1969. Time preference and the Penrose effect in a two-class model of economic growth. *Journal of Political Economy* 77 (4): 628–52.

Wallace, Neil. 1980. The overlapping generations model of fiat money. In John Kareken and Neil Wallace, eds., *Models of Monetary Economies*. Minneapolis: Federal Reserve Bank of Minneapolis.

Walsh, Carl. 1998. The new output–inflation trade-off. *Economic Letter*, Federal Reserve Bank of San Francisco, issue Sep 10.

Walsh, Carl. 2010. *Monetary Theory and Policy*, 3rd ed. Cambridge: MIT Press.

Weil, Philippe. 1987. Confidence and the real value of money in an overlapping generations economy. *Quarterly Journal of Economics* 102 (1): 1–22.

Weil, Philippe. 1989. The equity premium puzzle and the risk-free rate puzzle. *Journal of Monetary Economics* 24 (3): 401–421.

Weil, Philippe. 1990. Nonexpected utility in macroeconomics. *Quarterly Journal of Economics* 105 (1): 29–42.

Weil, Philippe. 1993. Precautionary savings and the permanent income hypothesis. *Review of Economic Studies* 60 (2): 367–83.

Weitzman, Martin L. 1973. Duality theory for infinite horizon convex models. *Management Science* 19 (7): 783–89.

Weitzman, Martin L. 1979. Optimal search for the best alternative. *Econometrica* 47 (3): 641–54.

Werner, Jan. 2012. Rational asset pricing bubbles and debt constraints. Working paper. University of Minnesota.

Wessels, J. 1977. Markov programming by successive approximations with respect to weighted supremum norms. *Journal of Mathematical Analysis and Applications* 58 (2): 326–35.

Whittle, Peter. 1982. *Optimization over Time*. New York: Wiley.

Woodford, Michael. 1999. Optimal monetary policy inertia. Working paper 7201. NBER.

Woodford, Michael. 2001. Inflation stabilization and welfare. Working paper 8673. NBER.

Woodford, Michael. 2003. *Interest and Prices: Foundations of a Theory of Monetary Policy*. Princeton: Princeton University Press.

Woodford, Michael. 2011. Simple analytics of the government expenditure multiplier. *American Economic Journal: Macroeconomics* 3 (1): 1–35.

Yun, Tack. 2005. Optimal monetary policy with relative price distortions. *American Economic Review* 95 (1): 89–109.

Zhang, Yuzhe. 2012. Characterization of a risk sharing contract with one-sided commitment. *Journal of Economic Dynamics and Control* 37 (4): 794–809.

Zhou, Kemin, John C. Doyle, and Keith Glover. 1996. *Robust and Optimal Control*. Englewood Cliffs, NJ: Prentice-Hall.

Matlab Index

Name Index

Abel, Andrew B., 209–10, 560
Abreu, Dilip, 576, 583, 597, 600, 603
Acemoglu, Daron, 442n
Adda, Jerome, 267, 297, 308
Adjemian, Stéphane, 24n, 25
Aiyagari, S. Rao, 179, 191, 193–94, 439, 442, 443, 445, 454, 457, 458
Allais, Maurice F. C., 536
Altug, Sumru, 397
Alvarez, Fernando, 160–61, 451n
Amemiya, Takeshi, 298
An, Sungbae, 397
Anderson, Evan W., 43, 230, 545n, 570n
Andolfatto, David, 475
Arellano, Manuel, 298
Aruoba, S. Boragan, 368
Auerbach, Alan J., 362
Azariadis, Costas, 23n

Backus, David, 234n, 238, 528
Balasko, Yves, 424–25, 431
Bansal, Ravi, 528, 547, 561, 563, 573
Barillas, Francisco, 545n
Barro, Robert J., 592, 594
Baumol, William J., 482
Becker, Robert A., 527
Bellman, Richard E., 119
Benigno, Pierpaolo, 493, 494
Bernanke, Ben S., 481n, 493
Berry, Donald A., 111n
Bertsekas, Dimitri P., 106, 120–21, 290
Bewley, Truman F., 193, 447, 449
Billingsley, Patrick, 63, 72, 74, 81, 95, 625
Blackwell, David, 121
Blanchard, Olivier J., 12, 14, 36, 38, 41–43, 48
Blinder, Alan S., 481n

Bolton, Patrick, 603
Boyd, John H., III, 158, 531, 532
Bradford, David F., 362
Breeden, Douglas T., 346
Brock, William A., 353, 482
Brumelle, Shelby L., 292
Bruno, Michael, 453
Bullard, James, 524

Cagan, Phillip, 17, 30, 62
Calvo, Guillermo A., 485, 504, 519
Campbell, John Y., 345n, 557, 559, 560
Carlstrom, Charles T., 483n
Cass, David, 353, 431
Cayley, Arthur, 110
Cecchetti, Stephen G., 561
Chamberlain, Gary, 185, 193–94
Chang, Roberto, 591
Chari, V. V., 459, 576
Chen, Hui, 544
Chew, Soo Hong, 536, 537, 547
Chow, Chee-Seng, 293
Chow, Gregory, 163n
Christiano, Lawrence J., 294–95, 299, 388, 397, 481n, 492, 508n, 518
Clarida, Richard H., 191
Clower, Robert W., 482
Cochrane, John H., 298, 299, 345n
Cogan, John F., 513
Cogley, Timothy, 377
Collard, Fabrice, 546
Conklin, James, 582
Cooper, Russell W., 210, 267, 297, 308
Cronshaw, Mark B., 582
Currie, David, 58, 234n
Cwik, Tobias, 513

Subject Index